Why Do You Need This New Edition?

If you are wondering why you should buy this new edition of *Efficient and Flexible Reading*, here are seven good reasons!

1. **A new Chapter 9 containing detailed information on how to read and interpret a wide range of visuals** provides you with strategies for how to interpret and evaluate graphs, tables, charts, infographics, and photographs. Critical thinking is not limited to text materials. In a world that relies increasingly on the use of visuals to convey information, you need to think critically in order to accurately read and assess visuals.

2. **Chapter 6 has been expanded to provide coverage of crucial textbook reading skills** and now includes a new section that shows you how to use textbooks as learning tools to further your educational goals. It explains how you can use various textbook features to study and learn chapter content and also provides pointers on how to read, understand, and remember scientific and technical material.

3. **Critical thinking is crucial to college success**, so, in addition to the critical thinking chapters in Part 4, eleven of the chapters now contain a section that teaches you how to think critically about the skills and topics presented in the chapter.

4. **New Efficiency and Flexibility Tips** throughout the text provide practical suggestions for how you can apply what you are learning in each chapter to your reading so that you can be more efficient in handling reading assignments and choose the best strategies for reading different types of college materials.

5. **"Planning Your Reading Strategy,"** a new feature that precedes each of the end-of-chapter selections, helps you to preview each selection so that you can choose the best strategies for reading it. A post-selection box titled "Assessing Your Reading Strategy" allows ~~~~ the strategies you chose and to consider future adaptations when rea~~~~

6. **New reading selections have been chosen from a wide range ~~~~ periodicals, newspapers, Web sites, and blogs**—allowing you a~~~~ your reading strategies to suit the wide range of materials you will be ex~~~~ s.

7. **Twelve new readings on current topics will educate about issues in the news and provide additional practice with the skills you learn in the text.** New readings address topics such as Latino heritage, the sociology of sports, green computing, digital dating, interpersonal attraction, sound as energy, the globalization of fast food restaurants, enhancing body image, experiencing music, the Native American Holocaust, improving sleep, and strategies for making a difference in the world.

Efficient and Flexible Reading

Tenth Edition

Kathleen T. McWhorter

Niagara County Community College

PEARSON

Boston Columbus Indianapolis New York San Francisco Upper Saddle River
Amsterdam Cape Town Dubai London Madrid Milan Munich Paris Montreal Toronto
Delhi Mexico City Sao Paulo Sydney Hong Kong Seoul Singapore Taipei Tokyo

In memory of Harry Thompson,
a gentle and loving father

Senior Acquisitions Editor: Nancy Blaine
Senior Development Editor: Gillian Cook
Director of Development: Mary Ellen Curley
Senior Supplements Editor: Donna Campion
Editorial Assistant: Jamie Fortner
Senior Media Producer: Stefanie Snajder
Marketing Manager: Thomas DeMarco
Production Manager: Denise Phillip
**Project Coordination, Text Design, and
  Electronic Page Makeup:** PreMediaGlobal

Cover Design Manager/Cover Designer:
  John Callahan
Cover Images: Gornjak/Shutterstock
Photo Researcher: Jonathan Yonan/Integra
Senior Manufacturing Buyer: Dennis J. Para
Printer and Binder: R. R. Donnelley/
  Crawfordsville
Cover Printer: Lehigh-Phoenix Color/
  Hagerstown

This book was typeset in 9.75/12, ITC Stone Serif Std.

Library of Congress Cataloging-in-Publication Data
McWhorter, Kathleen T.
  Efficient and flexible reading / Kathleen T. McWhorter, Niagara County
Community College. — 10th ed.
      p. cm.
ISBN-13: 978-0-205-90359-7
  1. Developmental reading—Handbooks, manuals, etc.   2. Reading
(Higher education)—Handbooks, manuals, etc.   I. Title.
  LB1050.53.M38 2012
  428'.43—dc23

                                                     2012041695

For permission to use copyrighted material, grateful acknowledgment is made to the copyright holders
on pp. 581–582, which are hereby made part of this copyright page.

2 3 4 5 6 7 8 9 10—DOC—16 15 14 13

Student Edition ISBN-13: 978-0-205-90359-7
Student Edition ISBN-10:   0-205-90359-2

Brief Contents

Detailed Contents

Part 3   Reading and Learning From College Texts 304

Part 4   Reading Critically 413

Preface

To succeed in college, students must learn to understand a wide variety of reading material. Textbooks—the student's primary reading material—represent unique academic disciplines, each with its own style, content, and conceptual complexity. Many students are also required to read literature, supplementary assignments, reference materials, online source periodicals, manuals, handbooks, and study guides.

Each of these materials offers unique reading challenges, and even more important, the student's purpose for reading each is different. A student may read to prepare for a class lecture, make notes for a discussion, review for an exam, or locate information for a paper. To handle these diverse reading situations effectively, a student must develop reading flexibility, adjusting strategies and techniques to suit each reading situation.

College students face rigorous course requirements and must cope with time restraints created by jobs, family, and social activities. Reading and study must be accomplished within a realistic time frame and result in effective learning. Reading efficiency, then, is also vitally important. *Efficient and Flexible Reading* is designed to enable students to become efficient and flexible readers capable of meeting the challenging demands of college.

■ Goals and Themes

The primary goal of this text is to teach students how to accomplish reading tasks within an efficient and realistic framework. It guides students in developing reading flexibility—adjusting both comprehension and rate to suit the purpose, type, and complexity of the material, as well as degree of familiarity with the content. A second, more specific, goal of the text is to encourage students to develop successful active academic reading strategies. To enable students to learn more efficiently from both print and electronic texts, this text focuses on the development of vocabulary, comprehension, study-reading, and critical analysis techniques. A third goal of the text is to encourage students to approach reading as a thinking process. Metacomprehension—the student's awareness of and control over the reading and learning process and its attendant thought processes—is a theme emphasized throughout.

■ Changes to the Tenth Edition

The changes to the tenth edition achieve two goals: (1) to strengthen the emphasis on efficiency and flexibility by guiding students in adapting reading skills to suit their purpose and the nature of the material and (2) to build students' critical thinking skills, including the ability to interpret and analyze visuals.

Specific changes include the following:

- **NEW Chapter on Reading and Evaluating Visuals.** Critical thinking is not limited to text materials. Chapter 9 recognizes that students need to think critically about a wide range of graphics and visuals; it guides students in interpreting and evaluating graphs, tables, charts, infographics, and photographs.

- **NEW Integration of Critical Thinking Topics.** In addition to the critical thinking chapters in Part 4, many chapters now contain a section that leads students to think critically about skills and topics presented in the chapter. For example, the chapter on main ideas (Chapter 4) discusses how to think critically about topic sentences and how to evaluate whether they express facts or opinions.

- **NEW Coverage of Textbook Reading Skills.** Chapter 6 has been expanded to include a section that features textbooks as learning tools. It shows students how to use parts and features of textbooks to learn and study chapter content. The chapter also contains coverage of reading scientific and technical material.

- **NEW Efficiency and Flexibility Tips.** To further the emphasis on efficiency and flexibility, Chapters 1–11 offer practical tips for flexibly and/ or efficiently applying chapter content. For example, in Chapter 2, in relation to the topic of previewing, the efficiency tip advises students to preview textbook assignments and assess their difficulty in order to plan sufficient time to complete them.

- **NEW Metacognitive Boxes to Accompany Full-Length Readings.** Each reading selection contains a pre- and post-metacognitive box. The pre-metacognitive box titled "Planning Your Reading Strategy" leads students to assess the reading based on previewing it and selecting the most appropriate strategies for reading it. The post-metacognitive box titled "Assessing Your Reading Strategy" encourages students to assess the effectiveness of their chosen strategies and consider future adaptations when reading similar material.

- **NEW Diverse Sources for Reading Selections.** Because students need to adapt their reading skills to suit the nature of the material, the new reading selections were chosen to be representative of a wide range of sources. The sources include textbooks, periodicals, newspapers, Web sites, and blogs.

- **NEW Twelve Reading Selections.** Twelve readings have been replaced with fresh, high-interest readings. Topics include the Latino heritage, the sociology of sports, green computing, digital dating, interpersonal attraction, sound as energy, the globalization of fast food restaurants, enhancing body image, experiencing music, the Native American Holocaust, improving sleep, and strategies for making a difference in the world.

■ Content Overview

Efficient and Flexible Reading, Tenth Edition, offers a blend of reading comprehension, retention, vocabulary development, critical reading, visual literacy strategies, and rate building techniques that have proven essential for college students.

Part 1 Developing a Basis for Reading and Learning. This part presents the organization and framework for the text, developing and explaining the concepts and principles of efficiency and flexibility and emphasizing reading as a thinking process. Strategies for active reading are presented, concentration and retention techniques are described, and basic vocabulary-building techniques are explained.

Part 2 Improving Your Comprehension. Methods for improving comprehension skills through knowledge and use of text structure is the focus of Part 2. The location of main ideas, the structure of paragraphs, types of transitions, and the organization of ideas into thought patterns are described. Strategies for reading textbooks, articles, essays, scholarly journal articles, and scientific/technical material are presented.

Part 3 Reading and Learning from College Texts. Part 3 is concerned with reading and learning from college textbooks. Techniques for learning and retaining course material, including specialized and technical vocabulary, are emphasized. Other topics include SQ3R, highlighting, annotating, paraphrasing, outlining, mapping, and summarizing. Graphic and visual literacy skills are presented.

Part 4 Reading Critically. Critical reading skills are the focus of Part 4. Skills for making inferences, distinguishing between fact and opinion, recognizing generalizations, understanding tone, identifying the author's purpose, recognizing bias, and reading and evaluating online sources are included. Students learn to locate reliable Web sites and to evaluate their content, accuracy, timeliness, purpose, and structure. Techniques for evaluating arguments and persuasive writing are emphasized, including recognizing types of evidence and identifying logical fallacies.

Part 5 Increasing Your Rate and Flexibility. Part 5 details specific techniques for improving reading rate and flexibility, including skimming, scanning, and techniques for reading faster. Some instructors may choose to teach this material earlier in the course.

Part 6 Application of Textbook Reading Skills. Chapter 14 offers an excerpt from a sociology chapter. It is preceded by a discussion of the learning aids used in the chapter; exercises follow the chapter to guide students in applying and integrating the skills taught in each of the previous parts of *Efficient and Flexible Reading.*

■ Features

The following features enhance the text's effectiveness for both instructor and student:

Focus on Academic Reading Skills. The text provides the necessary instruction in literal and critical reading, vocabulary development, and study-reading skills to meet the demands of academic reading assignments.

Emphasis on Active Reading. The text encourages students to become active readers by enabling them to interact with the text by predicting, questioning, and evaluating ideas (Chapter 2).

Emphasis on Critical Thinking Skills. Throughout the text, critical thinking is highlighted as being crucial to effective, efficient, and flexible reading. Part 4 focuses on critical analysis, evaluating online sources, and evaluating arguments. Chapter 9 discusses critical thinking in the context of visual literacy, and eleven chapters end with a section on critical thinking in relation to the chapter content.

Emphasis on Visual Literacy Skills. Students live in a world in which reading has expanded to include interpreting and evaluating a wide range of visuals. The new Chapter 9 acknowledges this trend and provides students with techniques for understanding and thinking critically about the graphics they will encounter in a wide variety of texts.

Focus on Evaluation of Online Sources. Because college students are increasingly required to use the Internet, evaluating online sources is a continuing emphasis in the text. Chapter 10 discusses how to locate and evaluate Internet sources and examines the new ways of reading and thinking required by online text.

Integration of Metacognition. Metacognition is the reader's awareness of his or her own comprehension processes. Mature and proficient readers exert a great deal of cognitive control over their reading; they analyze reading tasks, select appropriate reading strategies, and evaluate the effectiveness of those strategies. The text guides students in developing these metacognitive strategies and includes a Learning Style Questionnaire that enables students to assess how they learn and process information (Chapter 1), and pre- and post-metacognitive boxes that encourage students to choose and evaluate reading strategies for different types of material accompany each full-length reading selection.

Discussion of Academic Thought Patterns. The text describes six primary thought patterns—chronological order/process, definition, classification, comparison-contrast, cause-effect, and enumeration—that are used in various academic disciplines to organize and structure ideas. Five additional patterns are also briefly discussed: statement and clarification, summary, generalization and example, addition, and spatial order/location. These patterns, presented as organizing schemata, are used to improve comprehension and recall of textbook material (Chapter 5).

High-Interest and Relevant Reading Selections. Chapters conclude with reading selections representative of the types of reading expected of college students. Included are numerous textbook excerpts, as well as articles and essays. The questions that follow each reading have been grouped into four categories: "Checking Your Vocabulary," emphasizing context clues and word parts; "Checking Your Comprehension," measuring literal and critical comprehension; "Thinking Critically," requiring interpretive reading skills; and "Questions for Discussion." For Chapters 1–11, odd-numbered readings use a multiple-choice format. Open-ended questions for each of these readings are available in the Instructor's Manual. Even-numbered readings feature both multiple-choice and open-ended questions for writing or group activities.

■ Text-Specific Supplements

Annotated Instructor's Edition. This is an exact replica of the student text, with answers provided on the write-on lines in the text. (0-321-82931-X)

Instructor's Manual and Test Bank. The instructor's manual portion offers teaching tips, sample syllabi, and other teaching resources; and the test bank portion offers a series of skill and reading quizzes for each chapter, formatted for ease of copying and distribution. (0-321-82932-8)

Vocabulary Supplement. Instructors may choose to shrink-wrap *Efficient and Flexible Reading* with a copy of *Expanding Your Vocabulary*. Written by Kathleen T. McWhorter, this book works well as a supplemental text, providing additional instruction and practice in vocabulary. Students can work through the text independently, or units may be incorporated into weekly lesson plans. Topics covered include methods of vocabulary learning, contextual aids, word parts, connotative meanings, idioms, euphemisms, and many more interesting and fun topics. The book concludes with vocabulary lists and exercises representative of ten academic disciplines. To preview this book, contact your Pearson representative for an examination copy.

■ Acknowledgments

I wish to acknowledge the contributions of my colleagues and reviewers who provided valuable advice and suggestions, both for this edition and for previous editions.

The editorial staff of Pearson Education deserve special recognition and thanks for the guidance, support, and direction they have provided. In particular I wish to thank Gillian Cook, my development editor, for her valuable advice and assistance, and Nancy Blaine, acquisitions editor, for her enthusiastic support of the revision.

KATHLEEN T. MCWHORTER

Your Guide to ACADEMIC SUCCESS

3 SIMPLE TRUTHS

1 College is all about reading and studying. Attending lectures is not enough.

2 To do well in your courses, you must be able to adapt your reading and study skills to different disciplines.

3 There is no substitute for reading. It is at the center of your college education.

Efficient and Flexible Reading is designed to help you achieve success in college by helping you become an active reader and learner. In the pages that follow, you'll learn how to make the most of this course, this textbook, and your college experience. Here are nine tips to help you take charge of your learning:

Tips

TIP 1 Connect College Reading to Your Life

FACE THE CHALLENGE

Obtaining a Degree

Obtaining a degree means taking a wide range of courses. Some will be highly interesting to you; others may seem boring, even unnecessary. You will enjoy and benefit more from all of your courses if you actively seek ways to make them relevant to your life, your interests, and your career aspirations.

LEARN THE SKILLS

Information Is Power

The more information you have about the courses you'll be taking, the better prepared you will be to do well and get the most out of them. As you plan your course of study, do the following:

- *Meet with your advisor.* He or she will be able to describe each of the required courses you need to take, as well as advise you on which electives best match your interests.
- *Consult the course catalog.* Every college provides a catalog that describes each course in detail. Read these course descriptions so you know exactly what you'll be learning about.
- *Network with other students.* Ask for their opinions about who are the best instructors and how to be successful in specific courses.
- *Pay close attention to real-world examples presented in lectures and textbooks.* As you read or listen, ask yourself: How does this apply to me? What can I do with this information? How can this information benefit my life or career? It's especially important to ask these questions when the material you're reading does *not* seem relevant to your life or goals (see below).
- *Read your course syllabus.* It will tell you what topics will be covered, how they will be taught (lecture, discussion group, field study, etc.), and what your instructor considers most important, as well as due dates for required assignments, quizzes, and exams.

TAKE ACTION

Connect Your College Reading to Your Life

To practice connecting your college courses and related reading to your life, read the sample situation below and complete the following activity.

The situation: Maria is a freshman who would like to become an elementary school teacher. She has one young child of her own. She discovers that she needs to take several required courses before she can take any education courses. To keep herself motivated, she sits down with her schedule and figures out how each course could be relevant to the career she wants to pursue.

Required Course	Maria's Thoughts and Ideas
English 101: College Writing	*Writing is a valuable skill. I'm not really that good with grammar, but if I'm going to be teaching children, I really should know the basics. This class will really help me when I have to write my résumé and cover letters when I am applying for jobs. And my advisor told me that I'm going to have to write a lot of papers in my education courses, so doing well in this class will help me do better in my other courses, too.*
History 101: American History	*This has always been the subject that bores me the most! But a lot has happened in America lately . . . we have a presidential election coming up, and the economy has gone through some tough times. Maybe this course will help me understand how we got to where we are today. It would be great to know more about the early 1900s when my great-great-grandparents came over from Ireland!*
Math 099: Algebra and Precalculus	*I hate math, and I've never been good at it. But having a better foundation in math will help me manage my money better and achieve my financial goals, such as buying a house someday. And if I'm going to teach children, I have to be able to do the math problems before I can show them how to do them!*

Activity: Relating Your Courses to Your Life

Complete the following grid by listing the three courses you expect to be most difficult this term. For each, explain how you will make the course relevant to you.

Your major (or career goal, or key area of interest): _____

Course Title	Making It Relevant

USE THIS TEXTBOOK

Efficient and Flexible Reading contains hundreds of textbook excerpts from a wide range of college courses. As you read them, think about how they apply to your life, and what you already know about them, so you will make connections and look for answers even before you read.

TIP 2 Understand the Basics of College Success

FACE THE CHALLENGE

Being Successful in College

It is easy to feel overwhelmed by the many different courses and assignments that compete for your attention. There are three things you must do to be successful in college: (1) You must attend classes regularly and complete your assignments on time. (2) You must do well on quizzes and examinations. (3) You must establish and maintain academic integrity.

LEARN THE SKILLS

Complete Assignments, Do Well on Tests, and Maintain Academic Integrity

Here are some specific suggestions to help you establish a baseline for college success.

1. **Attend classes and complete your assignments on time.**
   - *Schedule your classes at times that will maximize your attendance.* Try not to schedule early morning classes if you are not a morning person.
   - *Arrive for class on time and do not leave early.* Turn off your cell phone.
   - *Participate in class.* Most instructors want students' active participation in discussions. Some even make participation part of the final grade. Do not be reluctant to ask questions in class; your instructor's job is to answer those questions. Do not talk with friends or send text messages during class.
   - *Keep and refer to the course syllabus.* Mark all key dates with a highlighter and transfer them to a master calendar to help you plan your workload. Do not wait until the last minute to start an assignment.
   - *Read your textbook.* You will get much more out of the lecture if you have read the textbook assignment prior to class. Learning occurs, and memorization is easier, when you are exposed to the material multiple times and in different ways.
   - *Talk to your professor if you need help.* All instructors have office hours during which they are available to help students.

2. Do well on quizzes and examinations.

- *Keep up with your reading assignments.* These are often the materials on which quizzes are based.

- *Start a study group.* Many students find that a small study group can help them review material and prepare for exams. Be sure to use your group time for studying, not for socializing.

- *Attend review sessions.* Some professors offer optional "review sessions" before exams. These are extremely valuable and greatly improve your chances of getting a good grade on the test, because the instructor is likely to go over the specific materials that will be tested. If necessary, rearrange your schedule so that you can attend review sessions.

- *Do not wait until the night before a test to start studying.* "Cramming" is not effective. It is better to have briefer, focused review sessions each day for a week before the exam.

- *Find ways to test yourself.* Make flash cards of key terms. Ask classmates what questions they think will be on the test, then make sure you know the answers. Write out questions and answers to help solidify the information in your head.

- *Get enough sleep the night before an exam.* Being exhausted lowers your chances of doing well on the test.

- *Do not miss the exam or ask for a make-up test.* Many instructors have a zero-tolerance policy for missed exams and will make an exception only in the case of a true medical emergency.

- *Read the instructions on the test before you begin answering the questions.*

- *Understand time constraints.* Quickly look over the test when you get it. Multiple-choice questions can take more time than you expect; so can essay questions. Plan how much time you can spend on each part of the exam, and wear a watch so that you can pace yourself.

3. Establish and maintain academic integrity.

Colleges and universities expect students to maintain the highest levels of honest and ethical behavior. In college, as in life, your reputation is essential to success. Getting caught in unethical behavior will usually cause you to fail the course. In some cases, the college may ask you to leave and not return.

- *Do not cheat.* "Cheating" is a catch-all term that encompasses many types of dishonest behavior, from looking at someone else's answers on an exam, to copying someone's homework, to falsifying your results in a lab report. If you think you might be cheating, you probably are.

- *Do not plagiarize.* Plagiarism means using someone's ideas or exact words without giving them credit. If you take information on the work of Leonardo da Vinci from a reference book and do not indicate where you found it, you have plagiarized. Many students do not realize that it is perfectly acceptable (and even encouraged in some courses) to report or summarize other people's words or ideas as long as they credit the original sources.

TAKE ACTION

Practice Problem Solving

Practice the basics of college success by completing the following activities.

Activity 1: Brainstorming Solutions

Alone or with other students, think about the best ways to respond to the following challenges.

1. You are not a morning person, but a course that is required for your major (that is, a course you *must* take to earn your degree) is scheduled only at 8:00 A.M.

2. Due to a conflict with your job, you have to miss two classes the week before an exam.

3. The parking situation at your campus is terrible. Every morning you drive around for 20 minutes looking for an open parking spot, which makes you 15 minutes late for your 9:00 A.M. class.

4. You see that a paper is due the week you are scheduled to go on vacation with your family.

5. You read the textbook chapter twice, and you listened closely to the lecture, but you just don't understand what is going on. And the test is next week.

Activity 2: Thinking About Academic Integrity

Place a check mark next to the situations that you think would violate your academic integrity.

_____ Getting the answers to the textbook exercises from the fraternity house

_____ Meeting with fellow students to talk about the upcoming test and what types of questions you think the instructor will ask

_____ Purchasing a term paper from someone selling papers on the Internet

_____ Hiring an "A" student to take an exam for you

_____ Asking students who had your instructor last semester about the best way to study for a test in that course

_____ Flirting with the instructor to try to get a better grade

_____ E-mailing your instructor for clarification about a topic you do not understand

_____ Changing answers after you receive your exam back and then asking for a better grade

_____ Asking your instructor for a better grade on an exam because you believe your answer deserves more credit than the instructor has given

_____ Being tutored by a graduate student who knows the subject very well

USE THIS TEXTBOOK

Efficient and Flexible Reading offers further tips for college success in Chapter 1, "Developing Your Efficiency and Flexibility." In that chapter, you will learn how to manage your time better, get organized, analyze your learning style, and develop an action plan for learning.

TIP **3**   Balance School, Family, and Work

FACE THE CHALLENGE

Balancing School, Family, and Work

College is never easy, and it is even more challenging when you have to juggle your schoolwork with family, parenting, and/or work responsibilities.

LEARN THE SKILLS

Manage Your Time, Involve Your Family, and Take Care of Yourself!

Here are some suggestions for finding a healthy balance among the various components of your life.

- *Understand how much you can handle.* It is good to be ambitious, but don't take on too much. For example, you may feel much less stress if you think about taking an extra year to complete your degree. You will have more time for work and family.

- *Have a family conversation.* Your family benefits from your college degree. Discuss all family members' responsibilities and the roles they play in your college success. It is important for everyone to understand that some sacrifices must be made for the family's benefit.

- *Take study breaks at your job.* At most jobs, employees have coffee breaks and lunch breaks. Find a quiet place to read or review your notes while you eat a light lunch or dinner. You will have less to do at home.

- *Schedule your classes close together on selected days.* This will minimize the time you spend traveling to and from campus. If you have time between classes, find a quiet place in the library to study.

- *Increase your efficiency by doing things at off-peak times.* Don't go to the grocery store on a busy Saturday morning. Instead, go late at night when the store is empty and you won't have to wait in long lines.
- *Use weekends wisely.* Some students think of weekdays as the time to concentrate on school and work, and weekends as the time to have fun. This approach can lead to very stressful weeks. Make your weekdays less stressful by scheduling study or reading time each weekend.
- *Take advantage of campus services.* Many campuses now offer free or inexpensive child care for parents, as well as evening, weekend, and Internet classes.

And most important:

- *Take care of yourself.* Eat a healthy diet, get some exercise, and take some time for yourself occasionally. "Reward" yourself with small things when you accomplish important tasks—for example, a new song for your iPod when you have finished writing your paper, or a cup of coffee at the local coffeehouse after you have taken your exam.

TAKE ACTION

Practice Setting Priorities

Practice balancing school, work, and family by completing the following activity.

Activity: Setting Priorities

On Sunday evening, you sit down and make a list of everything you need or want to get done during the coming week. In the space provided, indicate:

1: for top priority—you must get this done early in the week

2: for medium priority—you need this done by the end of the week

3: for low priority—this can be put off until next week if necessary

_____ See that new movie that is a sequel to one of my favorite films.

_____ Turn in psychology assignment/worksheet to my professor on Tuesday, when it's due—I haven't even started it yet!

_____ Write the note of permission allowing my daughter to go on her field trip. Her teacher said she needs it by Friday.

_____ Prepare for the presentation I need to give at work on Tuesday.

_____ Meet up with my three old high school friends at a local diner.

_____ Study for my sociology exam, which will be given on Thursday.

_____ Start the research for my English paper, which is due a month from tomorrow.

_____ Take Mom to her doctor's appointment on Monday.

_____ Read that new vampire novel that I have been looking forward to.

_____ Make child care arrangements so that I can attend the biology exam review session on Thursday.

USE THIS TEXTBOOK

As you balance the elements of your life and set priorities, you will undoubtedly encounter some stress. Having a good set of strategies to help you cope with stress can help your situation tremendously. The reading and learning strategies included in this book will give you confidence in your ability to handle the challenges your courses offer and, thereby, help eliminate or reduce stress.

TIP 4 Develop Communication Skills

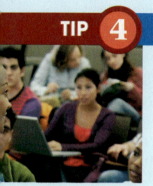

FACE THE CHALLENGE

Developing Communication Skills

College is all about learning new ideas, about the conversation between instructors and students. It's also about working with and learning from other students through group projects and discussions. Therefore, developing your communication skills is essential to college success.

LEARN THE SKILLS

Listen, Speak, and Write Effectively

Communication skills include listening actively, speaking effectively, taking notes, and writing clearly. Learning these skills will help you not only in college but also in your chosen career.

Do's and Don'ts for Active Listening

(During lectures, presentations, labs, group work, and personal conversations)

Do

- *Stay focused.* Look at the speaker/teacher. Don't get so wrapped up in taking notes that you stop listening to what's being said.
- *Keep an open mind.* Your college courses will ask you to consider issues in ways that may be different from your personal opinions about them. Be open to new ways of thinking.

- *Show that you're listening.* In a one-on-one conversation, nod your head or say "OK" to indicate that you are paying close attention.
- *Ask questions if you don't understand.* You can only benefit from asking your instructor to clarify a concept, example, or word you don't understand.
- *Be mindful of details.* This is especially important when your instructor is teaching you a process (for example, how to conduct a lab experiment). Sometimes the details are just as important as, or more important than, the big picture.

Don't

- *Talk.* You can't listen when you are speaking or having a side conversation.
- *Tune out when you're not interested.* When you're not interested, you should pay *more* attention, not less.
- *Text during class.* Cell phones, text messages, and BlackBerry devices interfere with your ability to concentrate. Turn them off when you're in class, lab, or the library, and keep them off when you are studying.

Tips for Speaking Effectively

(In class, when talking to your instructors, when working with other students, in personal conversations)

- *Remember: timing is everything.* Choose a time and place to speak when others will best be able to listen. Don't interrupt professors in the middle of a sentence. Jot down your question and ask it during a lull in the lecture. Also, remember that most instructors will stop the lecture occasionally to ask, "Any questions?"
- *Be as concise as possible.* When speaking to a group, use as few words as possible to get your point across.
- *Do not interrupt.* During group study sessions and projects, it's important for all members of the team to be heard. Don't interrupt others while they are speaking, even if you disagree with them.
- *Speak at the appropriate volume.* In a large lecture hall, you may need to raise your voice to be heard. In a one-on-one conversation, speaking too loudly can seem aggressive or be annoying.

Polish Your Writing Skills

In college, writing is one of your primary means of communication. The stronger your writing skills, the better you will do on class assignments, essay exams, and research papers. Regardless of whether it is required, take a writing class. There is always room for improvement, and you will reap the benefits in higher grades.

TAKE ACTION

Consider Ways to Use Technology to Communicate

Brainstorm the pros and cons of different communication methods by completing the following activity.

Activity: Assessing Electronic Communication Options

Below is a list of options for communicating electronically with classmates and instructors. Make a list of the possible benefits and drawbacks of each method for both groups. When would it be effective to use each option? In what circumstances should you *not* use each option? When is it best to have a face-to-face meeting or conversation?

> ### Electronic Means of Communicating with Classmates and Instructors
>
> E-mail
>
> Phone
>
> Text messages
>
> Instant messages (IMs)
>
> Social networks (e.g., Facebook, Twitter)
>
> Message board in online course (e.g., WebCT or Blackboard)

USE THIS TEXTBOOK

Listening and speaking occur when you are with others. But in college, you will often be working by yourself, reading, studying, and preparing for exams. Chapter 2 of *Efficient and Flexible Reading* teaches the active reading and learning strategies you need to be successful on your own.

TIP 5   Take Notes and Write to Learn

FACE THE CHALLENGE

Taking Notes and Learning by Writing

Many studies have shown that students learn material better and faster when they write about it. This is the purpose of taking notes when your instructor lectures and when you read your textbook. Writing what you are learning helps you to memorize and retain the material.

LEARN THE SKILLS

Take Effective Lecture Notes

Here are some tips for taking effective lecture notes and writing textbook notes.

- *Read the textbook material on which the lecture will be based before attending the lecture.*
- *Listen carefully to the lecturer's opening comments.* They often reveal the purpose, focus, or organization of the lecture.
- *Focus on big ideas, not on recording everything the instructor says.* Remember that your textbook serves as a useful reference for any material you may miss in lecture.
- *Follow the thought pattern(s) on which the lecture is based and use it to organize your notes.* Use an indentation system to show the relative importance of ideas.
- *Record the main ideas and enough details and examples so that your notes make sense to you later.*
- *After class, review your notes and compare them with a classmate's to see if you missed any important points.* It can also be helpful to review lecture notes with a group of classmates prior to an exam.
- *Leave plenty of blank space as you take notes.* You may want to fill in missed or additional information later.
- *Use abbreviations.* To save time, abbreviate commonly used words (psy = psychology, w/ = with, and so on).

Tips for Writing in Your Textbook

Think of your textbook as a second notebook. It is an active learning tool that provides you with an additional opportunity to take notes and engage with the material. Here are some tips for annotating your textbook as you read:

- *Use a highlighter to highlight main ideas or key points.* Be sure to use a color that is easy to read through.
- *Use different colored highlighters for different purposes.* For example, you might use yellow to highlight summary statements and pink to highlight key vocabulary words.
- *Do not over highlight (or underline).* The goal of highlighting is to help you find key information quickly. If you highlight or underline too much, you will not be able to distinguish main points from less important ones.
- *Use the margins.* Most textbooks have blank margins that allow you to write notes, ask yourself or the author questions, or work out problems.

TAKE ACTION

Practice Note Taking and Annotation

Practice your note-taking and annotation skills by completing the following activities.

> ### Activity 1: Taking Notes on Lectures
> Use the suggestions above to take notes for your next lecture in this class. At the end of the class, compare your notes with those of a classmate and brainstorm ways you can improve your note-taking skills.

> ### Activity 2: Writing in Your Textbook
> Use the suggestions above to mark and make notes in a chapter of one of your other textbooks.

USE THIS TEXTBOOK

Chapter 4 of *Efficient and Flexible Reading*, "Main Ideas and Paragraph Structure," will help you to identify main ideas in your lectures, while Chapter 5, "Patterns: Relationships Among Ideas," will teach you about thought patterns in lectures. Additional coverage of, and practice with, textbook highlighting and annotating appears in Chapter 7, "Techniques for Learning Textbook Material."

TIP 6 · Think Critically

Fancy a breath of fresh air?

Fancy a breath of fresh air?

FACE THE CHALLENGE

Thinking Critically

Much of elementary and high school education focuses on memorization. The focus is on facts. In college, you are expected not only to learn and memorize new information, but also to *analyze* what you are learning, to formulate your own opinions and to conduct your own research. In other words, your college instructors expect you to *think critically*—to interpret and evaluate what you read and hear.

LEARN THE SKILLS

Develop a Critical Thinking Mind-Set

Developing your critical thinking skills should be one of your key goals as you further your education. Thinking critically not only provides you with valuable insights, it also makes you a much more savvy consumer. People who read and think critically are not easily cheated, taken advantage of, or misled.

At the heart of critical thinking is the development of a questioning mind-set, an approach to thinking in which you evaluate what you read as you read it. Critical thinking involves skills such as the following.

Critical Thinking Skills: Evaluate Ideas, Consider Sources, and Weigh the Evidence

- Thinking about what the author *means*, not just what he or she *says*
- Evaluating whether or not the author presents information fairly
- Considering the sources of information and whether or not they can be trusted
- Seeing how people, organizations, or writers appeal to your emotions, not your intellect, to get your support or money
- Differentiating between an informed opinion based on learning and/or experience, and an uninformed opinion based on prejudice, bias, or incomplete or incorrect information

As you proceed through college, you will encounter new ways of thinking and new ideas. As your knowledge base grows, you will become more and more skilled at evaluating what you read.

TAKE ACTION

Practice Thinking Critically

Start developing your critical thinking skills by completing the following activity.

Activity: Looking More Closely

Think carefully about the following questions. Compare your answers with those of your classmates.

1. Every day you see advertisements—on billboards, in magazines, on the Internet, even on park benches. What is the one thing that *all* advertising seeks to accomplish?

2. You receive a credit card offer that promises you instant credit. All you have to do is sign the application and return it. In return for giving you "easy credit," what does the credit card company receive?

3. On the first day of a history class, your professor announces, "Throughout this course, I will take a feminist perspective on the historical events we discuss." What exactly does she mean by this statement? What can you assume about her political opinions? If the instructor's political beliefs are different from yours, does this mean you should withdraw from the class?

4. You purchase a required novel for your English class. The back cover is filled with quotations from people saying how superb the book is. Does the fact that publications like *The New York Times* and *Library Journal* reviewed the novel well mean that you will enjoy it too? What motives do publishers have for listing excerpts from book reviews on book jackets?

5. You are considering going to see a new movie. There's an ad for the movie in your campus newspaper. At the top of the ad is a quotation from *The Washington Post* that reads ". . . quite a movie! The actors are . . . quite good, and the storytelling is . . . top-notch." Does this excerpt imply that the critic at *The Washington Post* completely loved the movie? What other sources might you check to see what other critics had to say about the film? (Also think about why the people who review books and movies are called "critics.")

USE THIS TEXTBOOK

To help you develop your critical reading skills, *Efficient and Flexible Reading* contains two full chapters on critical reading: Chapter 10, "Critical Analysis and Evaluating Online Services," and Chapter 11, "Evaluating Arguments and Persuasive Writing."

TIP 7 — Use Visual Tools

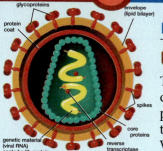

glycoproteins
envelope (lipid bilayer)
protein coat
spikes
core proteins
genetic material (viral RNA) coated with protein
reverse transcriptase

FACE THE CHALLENGE

Using Visual Tools

The world is an increasingly visual place, a fact that benefits the many students who are visual learners. Textbooks from three decades ago were composed mostly of words. Today, images are extremely common not only in textbooks but also in other reading materials, from magazines to utility bills. Visuals are not just "window dressing." They are created by skilled artists and photographers to help readers better understand written material. You will be more successful in your college courses if you understand how to use the visual tools textbooks offer.

LEARN THE SKILLS

Study Visuals, Note Titles and Captions, and Use and Create Visuals as Study Aids

To make visual tools work for you, keep the following in mind:

• *Don't skip over them.* Photographs, charts, and diagrams are included in a text for a reason. They are not "optional"—they are an important part of the book. Read them as carefully as you read the written material.

- *Read the title and caption.* These are essential. Sometimes they summarize the text, but often they provide new and important information.
- *Study photographs—don't just glance at them.* Take the time to really look at each photo closely and ask yourself how it relates to what you are reading. What is its purpose—to explain, to illustrate, to entertain, or make a point?
- *Keep track of visuals.* Textbook publishers always try to place visuals near the text they explain or illustrate. Sometimes, however, it's not possible to put the discussion and the visual right next to each other. In these cases, you may need to flip a page or two forward or backward. Be patient and take the time to do this.
- *Use visuals as study and review tools.* Mark key diagrams and use them to study for exams. Some textbooks even label certain diagrams or graphs (for example, "Key Diagrams") to let you know which are the most important.
- *Create your own visuals to help you study.* Draw your own diagrams or charts to help you learn and retain what you are studying.

TAKE ACTION

Practice Previewing Visuals

An old saying states that a picture is worth a thousand words. While visuals are best used together with the reading assignment they illustrate, they can also be valuable on their own, and you can use them to preview a chapter (or other assignment) before beginning it. To get a sense of how much information you can get by previewing visuals, try the following activity.

Activity: Previewing Visuals

Preview the visual materials for each question that follows, then think about and answer the questions.

1. Flip quickly through Chapter 4 of this text, "Main Ideas and Paragraph Structure." Which visuals do you think summarize key material and will serve as useful study tools?

2. Look at Figure A on p. 80 in Reading Selection 3. Is this a topic you have ever thought much about? Does it fit with what you have observed in the sport? Do you think stacking occurs in other sports as well?

3. View the photograph and caption on p. 236 in Reading Selection 9. What issues does it introduce? What questions does it raise in your mind?

4. Look quickly at the photo on page 13 for Academic Success Tip #6. What point do you think the author is trying to make with this photograph?

USE THIS TEXTBOOK

Efficient and Flexible Reading contains a complete chapter dedicated to helping you further develop your visual skills. Chapter 9, "Reading and Evaluating Visuals," provides not only specific tips for reading different types of visuals, but also tips for how to think critically about them.

TIP 8 Make Technology Work for You

OWL at Purdue, http://owl.english .purdue.edu/owl. Reprinted by permission of Purdue University.

FACE THE CHALLENGE

Making Technology Work for You

We are surrounded by technology, from the simple digital clocks to the massive networks that allow people around the globe to send literally billions of e-mails and text messages each day. In the past, the college classroom was composed of an instructor, students, a blackboard, and textbooks. Today, instructors use all types of technology, from video clips that illustrate key points to practice quizzes on the Web. Technology is extremely powerful, and you need to make it work for you.

LEARN THE SKILLS

Know Your Computer, Use Electronic Study Aids, and Understand Electronic Course Expectations

Harnessing the benefits of technology is all about understanding what it can do and what it cannot do. Technology *can* help you study and save time. It *cannot* get you an automatic "A" or serve as a substitute for attending class or reading your assignments. Here are some other tips on how to make technology work for you:

- *Be computer literate.* Having a basic understanding of computer hardware and software is essential to all students. (This is a valuable career skill as well.) You should have a basic familiarity with common software programs (such as Microsoft Word) as well as know how the tools built into the software can help you work better. (For example, Word contains spell-check and grammar-check programs that can be useful when you are writing term papers.)

- *Separate work and fun.* Because so much technology is used for entertainment, it's important to understand when it is being used educationally and to adjust your expectations accordingly. Keep separate e-mail accounts—one for friends and family, one for school and work. When working on the Internet in class, do not visit irrelevant Web sites. Stay focused.

- *Use electronic study tools.* Most textbooks now come with Web sites or online labs that offer a wealth of study resources, such as chapter quizzes, electronic vocabulary flash cards, and demonstrations. Use these tools to help you study and review before the exam.

- *Understand your instructors' use of technology.* Many instructors now post their syllabi online and encourage students to participate in electronic message boards. Some instructors even keep their gradebooks electronically, which means you must submit your assignments electronically in order to get credit for them.

- *Don't assume that technology assignments are "easier."* They are just as serious as textbook reading assignments and often take just as long to read and understand.

- *Remember your academic integrity.* The Internet has made cheating and other unethical forms of behavior easy. Resist the temptation to get the answers from someone who has already done the assignment. And never trust Wikipedia, which is not a scholarly resource and is never acceptable as a citation in research papers.

TAKE ACTION

Practice Using Online Study Aids

In addition to textbook-specific Web sites, many online study aids are available. To explore some of these possibilities, complete the following activity.

Activity: Making the Most of Online Resources

Choose two academic disciplines and do an Internet search to locate useful study aids. Review several sites you locate. Do you find the sites helpful? Do they offer valuable materials? (*Note:* Once you have visited these sites, you can bookmark them to find them easily in the future.)

USE THIS TEXTBOOK

Efficient and Flexible Reading contains several features to help you make the most of technology. Chapter 10, "Critical Analysis and Evaluating Online Sources" will help you think critically about the information you find on the Internet. Throughout the text, "Tech Support" boxes in each chapter provide additional tips for using technology to work more effectively.

TIP **9** Adapt Your Reading Skills to Each of Your Courses

FACE THE CHALLENGE

Reading Across the Disciplines

An essential part of the college experience is taking courses in areas you may be unfamiliar with. For example, students who want to major in psychology often do not realize they will also have to take courses in statistics and biology. There are also subfields and specialty areas within psychology, such as developmental psychology and social psychology. At first these new fields of study may seem unfamiliar, foreign, or intimidating. Each field has its own specialized language, requires new types of learning and thinking, and uses unique approaches and methods. To be successful in college, you must be able to adapt your reading skills to each course, subject, and instructor.

LEARN THE SKILLS

Customize Your Reading Skills

The good news is that customizing your reading skills to each of your courses is not difficult. All it takes is some patience and practice. Use the following suggestions when approaching a new field of study:

- *Establish an overview of the field.* Spend time studying your textbook's table of contents; it provides an outline of the course. Look for patterns, progression of ideas, and recurring themes or approaches.

- *Understand the need for prerequisites.* Most academic fields begin with foundation courses that teach you the basics of the discipline, including its specialized vocabulary. These are followed by more specialized courses that focus on subareas of the subject. Take courses in the order recommended by your advisor. Don't attempt an upper-level class without taking the "101" course first.

- *Look for similarities between new subject matter and other areas that are already familiar to you.* For example, most of the physical sciences (chemistry, physics, engineering) require a foundation in math. The reading and study skills you learn in your math courses can help you in your chemistry courses.

- *Obtain discipline-specific reference materials.* Some college texts delve into a subject immediately, providing only a brief introduction before getting into the heavy-duty materials. Many reference works are available in your college library (and online) to help you. These include research guides, encyclopedias, and dictionaries. These publications can provide you with key concepts, names, dates, statistics, and events. Use this basic knowledge as a framework on which to build deeper learning. Remember: you can't understand more difficult material without knowing the basics first.

- *Overlearn until you discover what is expected.* Until you discover what is most important in a course and figure out the best way to learn it, learn more information than you may need; learn too much rather than too little.

- *Focus on key terms.* You cannot fully understand a course until you understand its specific terminology. Most textbook chapters contain a list of key terms. When you have finished reading a chapter, you should be able to define all those terms. An important part of understanding key terms is knowing their abbreviations and notations, and how these may vary from discipline to discipline. For example, the Greek letter pi (π) means "3.1416" to mathematicians but "inflation" to economists.

- *Think in new ways.* Many college courses ask you to change your fundamental way of thinking. For example, many economics professors say they want their students to "think like an economist," which means understanding the trade-offs involved in all choices. Geography professors ask students to "think geographically," which means looking at how human beings interact with their locations, and vice versa. To do well in a course, you must be able to adjust your thinking and your ways of approaching the material.

- *Study the examples.* Many students find that examples are the single best way of understanding a concept. If your textbook or instructor does not provide an example, ask for one.

- *Master the patterns of organization.* Different disciplines tend to focus on different patterns of thought. For example, history often focuses on chronology, literature emphasizes comparison-contrast, and biology focuses on process or cause-effect. Being able to recognize these patterns will help you greatly in every course you take. Refer to Chapter 5 for coverage of these patterns.

TAKE ACTION

Practice Customizing Your Reading Skills

Practice adapting your reading and thinking skills by completing the following activity.

Activity: Developing New Perspectives

Each of the following questions asks you to look at common ideas from a new perspective.

1. Sociologists often discuss two different perspectives on society. The *functionalist perspective* maintains that social institutions (such as the education system and the family) work for society's good and have many benefits. The *conflict perspective* maintains that the same institutions set up a system in which certain people benefit at the expense of others. Question: Think about the idea of arranged marriages, in which the parents arrange their children's marriages to suitable partners. What would sociologists with a functionalist perspective say about arranged marriages? What would sociologists with a conflict perspective say about the same topic?

2. For many years, art historians focused on the history of great works (painting, sculpture, architecture) by well-known artists such as Michelangelo and Leonardo da Vinci. In recent years, however, more art historians have begun studying the craft arts, such as basket weaving and quilt making. What do you think might be driving this trend? (*Hint:* Think about the social class and status of those who can afford to purchase classic works of art.)

USE THIS TEXTBOOK

The key goal of *Efficient and Flexible Reading* is to teach you the college reading skills you need as the foundation for success. Chapter 1, "Developing Your Efficiency and Flexibility," teaches you how to adjust your reading process based on the material you are studying. Chapter 3, "Strengthening Your Word Power," helps you learn key terms, and Chapter 5, "Patterns: Relationships Among Ideas" provides an overview of the academic thought patterns. In addition, textbook excerpts and readings from many college disciplines are provided throughout the text as examples and for practice with skills.

CHAPTER

1

Developing Your Efficiency and Flexibility

think VISUALLY...

This vehicle is marketed as a fuel-efficient car. But what exactly does the term *fuel efficient* mean? A fuel-efficient car is one that uses less fuel and conserves energy. The term *efficiency*, then, refers to the ability to perform with the minimum amount of effort, expense, or waste.

Efficiency involves the effective use of time or resources to accomplish a specific task. As you think more about the concept of efficiency, you may begin to realize that it is a major objective in our work- and time-oriented society. For example, a mechanic who takes an hour to change a tire, a short-order cook who takes 25 minutes to prepare a cheeseburger, or a sales clerk who takes five minutes to package a purchase is not efficient.

Learning GOALS

In this chapter, you will learn how to . . .

Goal 1 Analyze your reading efficiency

Goal 2 Understand principles that govern efficiency and flexibility

Goal 3 Analyze your learning style

Goal 4 Improve your reading efficiency

Goal 5 Read more flexibly

Goal 6 Develop critical thinking skills

■ Understanding Reading Efficiency

Goal 1

Analyze your reading efficiency

When you are a college student, many heavy demands are placed on your time. One of the best ways to handle the demands and pressures of college life is to become more efficient—to get more done in less time.

> Reading efficiency is the successful completion of a task (reading, writing, or studying) within a realistic time frame in keeping with your goals.

Many students think that the only way to become more efficient is to read faster. They believe that slow reading is poor reading. This is not true. *How* you read is more important than *how fast* you read. If you read a 12-page assignment in one hour but remember only 60 percent of what you read, you are not reading efficiently. Efficient reading involves adequate comprehension and recall within a reasonable time frame.

The Efficiency Questionnaire below will help you assess whether you are an efficient reader. Answer *yes* or *no* to each question. Be honest with yourself!

Efficiency Questionnaire

	Yes	No
1. Do you set goals and time limits for yourself at the beginning of each reading study session?	❏	❏
2. Do you have particular questions in mind as you begin to read an assignment?	❏	❏
3. Do you spend a few minutes looking over an assignment before you begin reading it?	❏	❏
4. When reading, do you try to predict or anticipate what the writer will say next?	❏	❏
5. When you finish reading an assignment, do you take a few minutes to review what you have read?	❏	❏
6. Are you on the alert for words and phrases that signal change or continuation in thought?	❏	❏
7. Do you sort out more and less important details as you read?	❏	❏
8. When you read a word you do not know, do you try to determine its meaning from the way it is used in the sentence?	❏	❏
9. Do you regularly use highlighting, summary notes, and marginal annotations to identify important information?	❏	❏
10. When reading nontextbook material, do you try to determine the author's purpose for writing?	❏	❏

If you answered *yes* to all or most of these questions, you are well on your way to becoming an efficient reader. If you answered *no* to some or many of the questions, you need to improve your efficiency. You will learn more specific approaches as you proceed through the rest of the text.

■ Principles of Efficiency and Flexibility

Goal 2
Understand principles that govern efficiency and flexibility

Each of the following statements expresses one of the major principles on which the techniques presented in this book are built. Are you surprised by any of them? Do any of the statements seem to contradict what you have been taught previously?

1. **You do not always have to read everything the same way.** In this text you will see that, depending on your purpose for reading, it may be perfectly acceptable and even advisable to skim portions of sentences, paragraphs, and articles or to scan for particular information.

2. **Not everything on a page is of equal importance.** Sentences, paragraphs, and longer selections each contain a mixture of important and less important information. You will learn to identify what is important and to see how the remaining parts of the sentence, paragraph, or article relate to it.

3. **Shortcuts can save valuable time and make reading or studying easier.** Reading is not simply a matter of opening a book and jumping in. There are specific techniques you can use before you begin reading, while you are reading, and after you have finished reading that will greatly increase your efficiency.

4. **Not everything that appears in print is true.** An active reader must question and evaluate the source, authority, and evidence offered in support of statements that are not verifiable.

5. **You can increase your reading rate without losing comprehension.** Most students can increase their rate by applying techniques for improving their comprehension and retention. Of course, you cannot expect to double or triple your rate while maintaining a high level of comprehension, but you can make a significant improvement.

Throughout the rest of this book, each of these principles will be demonstrated and applied to a variety of reading situations. For additional strategies you can use to increase your efficiency and flexibility, look for the Efficiency Tips and Flexibility Tips in the margins.

■ Analyzing Your Learning Style

Goal 3
Analyze your learning style

Have you noticed that some types of tasks are easier than others? Have you also discovered that some study methods work better than others? Have you ever found that a study method that works well for a classmate does not work as well for you? These differences can be explained by what is known as *learning style.* Just as you have a unique personality, you also have a unique learning style. People differ in how they learn and in the methods and strategies they use to learn. Your learning style can, in part, explain why some courses are easier than others and why you learn better from one instructor than from another. Learning style can also explain why certain assignments are difficult and other learning tasks are easy. The following brief Learning Style Questionnaire will help you discover the features of your learning style.

Learning Style Questionnaire

Directions: *Each item presents two choices. Select the alternative that best describes you. In cases in which neither choice suits you, select the one that is closest to your preference. Write the letter of your choice on the line to the left of each item.*

Part One

_b_ 1. I would prefer to follow a set of
   a. oral directions.
   b. printed directions.

_a_ 2. I would prefer to
   a. attend a lecture given by a famous psychologist.
   b. read an online article written by the psychologist.

_b_ 3. When I am introduced to someone, it is easier for me to remember the person's
   a. name.
   b. face.

_b_ 4. I find it easier to learn new information by using
   a. language (words).
   b. images (pictures).

_a_ 5. I prefer classes in which the instructor
   a. lectures and answers questions.
   b. uses PowerPoint illustrations and videos.

_a_ 6. To follow current events, I prefer to
   a. listen to the news on the radio.
   b. read the newspaper.

_b_ 7. To learn how to operate a difficult-to-operate machine, I would prefer to
   a. listen to a friend's explanation.
   b. watch a demonstration.

Part Two

_a_ 8. I prefer to
   a. work with facts and details.
   b. construct theories and ideas.

_A_ 9. I would prefer a job involving
   a. following specific instructions.
   b. reading, writing, and analyzing.

_B_ 10. I prefer to
   a. solve math problems using a formula.
   b. discover why the formula works.

_b_ 11. I would prefer to write a term paper explaining
   a. how a process works.
   b. a theory.

_____ 12. I prefer tasks that require me to
   a. follow careful, detailed instructions.
   b. use reasoning and critical analysis.

_____ 13. For a criminal justice course, I would prefer to
   a. discover how and when a law can be used.
   b. learn how and why it became law.

_____ 14. To learn more about the operation of a robot, I would prefer to
   a. work with several types of robots.
   b. understand the principles on which they operate.

Part Three

_____ 15. To solve a math problem, I would prefer to
   a. draw or visualize the problem.
   b. study a sample problem and use it as a model.

_____ 16. To best remember something, I
   a. create a mental picture.
   b. write it down.

_____ 17. Assembling a bicycle from a diagram would be
   a. easy.
   b. challenging.

_____ 18. I prefer classes in which I
   a. handle equipment or work with models.
   b. participate in a class discussion.

_____ 19. To understand and remember how a machine works, I would
   a. draw a diagram.
   b. write notes.

_____ 20. I enjoy
   a. drawing or working with my hands.
   b. speaking, writing, and listening.

_____ 21. If I were trying to locate an office on an unfamiliar campus, I would prefer
   a. a map.
   b. printed directions.

Part Four

_____ 22. For a grade in biology lab, I would prefer to
   a. work with a lab partner.
   b. work alone.

_____ 23. When faced with a difficult personal problem I prefer to
   a. discuss it with others.
   b. resolve it myself.

_a_ 24. Many instructors could improve their classes by
    a. including more discussion and group activities.
    b. allowing students to work on their own more frequently.

_b_ 25. When listening to a lecture by a speaker, I respond more to the
    a. person presenting the ideas.
    b. ideas themselves.

_b_ 26. When on a team project, I prefer to
    a. work with several team members.
    b. divide the tasks and complete those assigned to me.

_b_ 27. I prefer to shop and do errands
    a. with friends.
    b. by myself.

_b_ 28. A job in a busy office is
    a. more appealing than working alone.
    b. less appealing than working alone.

Part Five

_a_ 29. To make decisions, I rely on
    a. my experiences and gut feelings.
    b. facts and objective data.

_a_ 30. To complete a task, I
    a. can use whatever is available to get the job done.
    b. must have everything I need at hand.

_b_ 31. I prefer to express my ideas and feelings through
    a. music, song, or poetry.
    b. direct, concise language.

_b_ 32. I prefer instructors who
    a. allow students to be guided by their own interests.
    b. make their own expectations clear and explicit.

_b_ 33. I tend to
    a. challenge and question what I hear and read.
    b. accept what I hear and read.

_b_ 34. I prefer
    a. essay exams.
    b. objective exams.

_b_ 35. In completing an assignment, I prefer to
    a. figure out my own approach.
    b. be told exactly what to do.

    To score your questionnaire, record the total number of _a_'s you selected and the total number of _b_'s for each part of the questionnaire. Record your totals in the scoring grid provided (see p. 28).

```
┌─────────────────────────────────────────────────────────────────────────┐
│ ┌───────────────┐                                                          │
│ │ Scoring Grid  │                                                          │
│ └───────────────┘                                                          │
│                                                                            │
│   Parts            Total # of Choice A        Total # of Choice B          │
│                                                                            │
│   Part One            ____3____                   ____4____                │
│                        Auditory                     Visual                 │
│   Part Two            ____5____                   ____2____                │
│                        Applied                    Conceptual               │
│   Part Three          ____1____                   ____6____                │
│                        Spatial                      Verbal                 │
│   Part Four           ____2____                   ____5____                │
│                        Social                     Independent              │
│   Part Five           ____2____                   ____5____                │
│                        Creative                    Pragmatic               │
│                                                                            │
└─────────────────────────────────────────────────────────────────────────┘
```

Now, circle your higher score for each part of the questionnaire. The word below the score you circled indicates a strength of your learning style. The next section explains how to interpret your scores.

Interpreting Your Scores

Each of the five parts of the questionnaire identifies one aspect of your learning style. These five aspects are explained here.

Part One: Auditory or Visual Learners

This score indicates whether you learn more effectively by listening (auditory) or by seeing (visual). If you have a higher score on auditory than visual, you tend to be an auditory learner. That is, you tend to learn more easily by hearing than by reading. A higher score on visual suggests strengths with visual modes of learning—reading, studying pictures, reading diagrams, and so forth.

Part Two: Applied or Conceptual Learners

This score describes the types of learning tasks and learning situations you prefer and find easiest to handle. If you are an applied learner, you prefer tasks that involve real objects and situations. Practical, real-life examples are ideal for you. If you are a conceptual learner, you prefer to work with language and ideas; you do not need practical applications for understanding.

Part Three: Spatial or Verbal Learners

This score reveals your ability to work with spatial relationships. Spatial learners are able to visualize or mentally see how things work or how they are positioned in space. Their strengths may include drawing, assembling, or repairing things. Verbal learners lack skills in positioning things in space. Instead they rely on verbal or language skills.

Part Four: Social or Independent Learners

This score reveals whether you like to work alone or with others. If you are a social learner, you prefer to work with others—both classmates and instructors—closely and directly. You tend to be people oriented and enjoy personal interaction. If you are an independent learner, you prefer to work alone and study alone. You tend to be self-directed or self-motivated and often goal-oriented.

Part Five: Creative or Pragmatic Learners

This score describes the approach you prefer to take toward learning tasks. Creative learners are imaginative and innovative. They prefer to learn through discovery or experimentation. They are comfortable taking risks and following hunches. Pragmatic learners are practical, logical, and systematic. They seek order and are comfortable following rules.

If you disagree with any part of the Learning Style Questionnaire, go with your own instincts rather than the questionnaire results. The questionnaire is just a quick assessment; trust your knowledge of yourself in areas of dispute.

Developing a Learning Action Plan

Now that you know how *you* learn, you are ready to develop an action plan for learning what you read. Suppose you discovered that you are an auditory learner. You still have to read your assignments, which is a visual task. However, to learn the assignment you should translate the material into an auditory form. For example, you could repeat aloud, using your own words, information that you want to remember, or you could record key information and play it back. If you are also a social learner, you could work with a classmate, testing each other out loud.

Table 1.1 on page 30 lists each aspect of learning style and offers suggestions for how to learn from a reading assignment. To use the table:

1. **Circle the five aspects of your learning style in which you received the highest scores.** Disregard the others.
2. **Read through the suggestions that apply to you.**
3. **Place a check mark in front of suggestions that you think will work for you.** Choose at least one from each category.
4. **List the suggestions that you chose in the "Action Plan for Learning" box below.**
5. **Experiment with these techniques, one at a time.** Continue using the techniques that you find work. Revise or modify those that do not. Do not hesitate to experiment with other techniques listed in the table as well.

Action Plan for Learning

Learning Strategy 1: _____

_____

Learning Strategy 2: _____

_____

Learning Strategy 3: _____

_____

Learning Strategy 4: _____

_____

Learning Strategy 5: _____

_____

Learning Strategy 6: _____

_____

EXERCISE 1–1

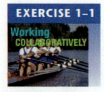

CONSIDERING LEARNING STYLE

Directions: *The class should form two groups: applied learners and conceptual learners. Each group should discuss effective learning strategies that take into account this type of learning style.*

TABLE 1.1 Learning Styles and Reading/Learning Strategies

If Your Learning Style Is . . .	Then the Reading/Learning Strategies to Use Are . . .
Auditory	Discuss/study with friends. Talk aloud when studying. Record self-testing questions and answers.
Visual	Draw diagrams, charts, and/or tables. Try to visualize events. Use videos when available. Use software when available.
Applied	Think of practical situations to which learning applies. Associate ideas with their application. Use case studies, examples, and applications to cue your learning.
Conceptual	Organize materials that lack order. Use outlining. Focus on organizational patterns.

If Your Learning Style Is . . .	Then the Reading/Learning Strategies to Use Are . . .
Spatial	Use mapping. Use outlining. Draw diagrams; make charts and sketches. Use visualization.
Verbal	Translate diagrams and drawings into language. Record steps, processes, and procedures in words. Write summaries. Write your interpretation next to textbook drawings, maps, and graphics.
Social	Form study groups. Find a study partner. Interact with the instructor. Work with a tutor.
Independent	Use computer-assisted instruction when available. Purchase review workbooks or study guides when available.
Creative	Ask and answer questions. Record your own ideas in the margins of textbooks.
Pragmatic	Study in an organized environment. Write lists of steps, procedures, and processes. Paraphrase difficult materials.

EXERCISE 1–2   ANALYZING LEARNING STYLE

Directions: *Write a brief description of yourself as a learner based on the results of the Learning Style Questionnaire. Describe your strengths and weaknesses. Include examples from your own experience as a student.*   ■

■ Improving Your Reading Efficiency

Goal 4
Improve your
reading efficiency

There are many easy and simple things you can do to read more efficiently. If you use the following suggestions, you will find yourself learning and remembering more of what you read and accomplishing more in a set period of time.

Getting Organized and Managing Your Time Efficiently

Reading at the wrong time or in an unsuitable environment will detract from your efficiency. Use the following suggestions:

1. **Organize a place to study.** Select a quiet, comfortable location and study in the same place each day. Be sure to have all your materials (paper, pens, etc.) at hand. Use a table or desk where you can spread out your books and papers. Avoid that comfortable chair near the TV.

2. **Use a pocket or online calendar and a small notebook.** Record exams and due dates for papers on the calendar; record daily assignments in the notebook.

3. **Develop a weekly study plan.** Allocate time for reading, reviewing, doing homework, and studying for exams. Select several specific times each

week for working on each of your courses. As a rule of thumb, reserve two study hours for each hour you spend in class. Do not schedule anything else during those times. If you are a parent, make sure you have reliable child care arranged for your study times.

4. **Establish goals and time limits for assignments.** Deadlines will keep you motivated, and you will be less likely to daydream.

5. **Study difficult subjects first.** While it is tempting to get easy tasks out of the way first, resist that temptation. When you start studying your mind is fresh and alert. This is the time you are best equipped to handle difficult subjects.

TECH SUPPORT **Using Electronic Calendars**

Many Internet service providers, such as Google and Yahoo, offer Web-based electronic calendars. These calendars provide daily, weekly, or monthly scheduling options into which you can enter your academic, work, and social activities. You can share calendars and coordinate activities via e-mail with your friends and classmates; set repeating obligations (such as classes that meet on a regular basis) by typing them in once; have meeting or appointment reminders sent to you via e-mail or cell phone; and even link activities to other Web sites or online documents.

Improving Your Concentration

Maintaining a high level of concentration can improve your efficiency. Time is wasted if you are daydreaming or not devoting full attention to the page in front of you. Take the concentration quiz, and then use the following suggestions to improve your concentration level.

Concentration Quiz

	Yes	No
1. Are you sitting on a comfortable chair or lying on a comfortable bed?	❑	❑
2. Is a television on nearby?	❑	❑
3. Are friends or family who are not studying in the room with you?	❑	❑
4. Do you wish you didn't have to read this chapter?	❑	❑
5. Are you reading this chapter only because it was assigned by your instructor?	❑	❑
6. Are you worried about anything or trying to make an important decision?	❑	❑
7. Are you tired, either physically or mentally?	❑	❑
8. Are you thinking about other things you have to do while you are reading?	❑	❑

If your answer is *yes* to any of the questions, reading and studying this chapter will probably take you more time than it should. A *yes* answer indicates that you are not operating at your peak level of concentration.

Controlling External Distractions

1. **Shut off your cell phone.** Calls and text message are a major distraction.

2. **Choose a place to study that is relatively free of interruptions.** You may need to figure out what types of interruptions occur most frequently and then choose a place where you will be free of them. For instance, if your home, apartment, or dorm has many interruptions such as friends stopping by or family members talking or watching TV, it may be necessary to find a different place to study. The campus or neighborhood library is often quiet and free of interruptions.

3. **Choose a place free of distractions.** Although your living room, for example, may be quiet and free of interruptions, you may not be able to concentrate there. You may be distracted by noises from the street, the view from a window, the presence of a TV, or a project you are working on.

4. **Study in the same place.** Once you have located a good place to study, try to study in this place regularly. You will become familiar with the surroundings and begin to form associations between the place and the activity you perform there. Eventually, as soon as you enter the room or sit down at the desk, you will begin to feel as though you should study.

5. **Choose a time of day when you are mentally alert.** Give yourself the advantage of reading or studying when your mind is sharp and ready to pick up new information. Avoid studying when you are hungry or tired because it is most difficult to concentrate at these times. Study at the same time every day, as it will help you develop regular study habits.

6. **Keep a distractions list.** As you are reading, often you will think of something you should remember to do. You might remember that you need to call your sister or buy a Mother's Day card. Write these items on a "To Do" list. Writing the item on paper will keep it from continuing to flash through your mind.

7. **Vary your reading.** It is easy to tire of reading about a particular subject if you spend too long on it. To overcome this problem, work on several assignments in an evening rather than finishing one assignment completely.

8. **Combine physical and mental activities.** Reading is primarily a mental activity. Because the rest of your body is not involved in the reading process, it is easy to become restless or feel a need to *do* something. Activities such as highlighting, underlining, making marginal notes, or writing summary outlines provide an outlet for physical energy.

EXERCISE 1–3 **ANALYZING YOUR CONCENTRATION**

Directions: *Now that you are aware of the factors that influence your concentration, answer the following questions about where and how you are reading this chapter. Your answers will give you an idea of how well you are controlling the factors that influence concentration.*

1. Are you reading in a place relatively free of distractions and interruptions?

   _____

2. Are you reading in the same place in which you usually read and study?

   _____

3. Notice what time of day it is. Is this a high or low concentration period? Is it the same time that you usually study?

   _____

4. What is your purpose for reading this chapter?

   _____

5. How long do you expect to spend reading this chapter?

   _____

Considering Your Background Knowledge

EFFICIENCY TIP
In general, the more background knowledge you have about a topic, the more quickly you can read materials related to that topic.

The amount of knowledge you have about a topic influences how easily and quickly you will be able to read about it. Suppose you were asked to read an excerpt from an organic chemistry text. If you had completed several chemistry courses, the excerpt would be fairly easy to understand. If you had never taken a chemistry course, even in high school, the excerpt would be extremely difficult to read, and you would probably understand very little.

Building Your Interest Level

Most people have little difficulty understanding and remembering material if the subject is highly interesting. Interest can improve comprehension and rate; a lack of interest or motivation can have a negative effect.

LEARNING STYLE TIPS

If you tend to be a ...	Then build interest in what you read by . . .
Creative learner	1. Assuming you will interview the author. What questions will you ask?
	2. Imagining or recreating a scene involving the subject you are reading about.
Pragmatic learner	1. Identifying why the material is important; focusing on its value.

■ Developing Your Reading Flexibility

Goal 5
Read more flexibly

Do you read the newspaper in the same way and at the same speed that you read a chemistry textbook? Do you read poetry in the same way and at the same speed that you read an article in *Time* magazine? Surprisingly, for many adults the answer to these questions is *yes*. Many adults, including college graduates, read everything in nearly the same way at the same rate.

Efficient and flexible readers, however, read the newspaper both *faster* and *differently* than they read a chemistry book because the newspaper is usually easier to read and because they have a different purpose for reading each. Flexible readers read poetry more slowly and in a different way than they read magazine articles.

> Reading flexibility involves adjusting your reading strategies, reading rate, and level of comprehension to suit the task, the material, and your background knowledge.

To become a flexible reader, you make decisions about how you will read a given piece of material. *How* you read depends on *why* you are reading and *how much* you intend to remember. Rate and comprehension are the two most important factors. Think of them as weights on a balancing scale: as one increases, the other decreases. Your goal is to achieve a balance that suits the nature of the material and your purpose for reading. This chapter discusses how to achieve this balance.

Assessing Difficulty

The first step in determining how to read a given piece of writing is to assess its difficulty. Many features of the reading material itself influence how easily and how quickly you can read it. Figure 1.1 lists important characteristics to consider.

FIGURE 1.1 Checklist To Evaluate Difficulty

Format
- ❑ helpful
- ❑ difficult to follow

Graphic/Visual Aids
- ❑ yes
- ❑ no

Typographical Aids
- ❑ yes
- ❑ no

Language Features
- ❑ short sentences and paragraphs
- ❑ long sentences and paragraphs

Vocabulary Level
- ❑ difficult vocabulary
- ❑ understandable vocabulary

Subject Matter
- ❑ complex
- ❑ understandable
- ❑ familiar

Length
- ❑ short
- ❑ moderate
- ❑ long

Organization
- ❑ strong
- ❑ moderate
- ❑ weak

Your Background Knowledge
- ❑ strong
- ❑ moderate
- ❑ weak

Your Physical/Mental State
- ❑ alert
- ❑ moderately alert
- ❑ distractible

Your Interest Level
- ❑ high
- ❑ moderate
- ❑ low

The easiest way to assess the difficulty of a selection is to preview it. Previewing (see Chapter 2) reveals how well the material is organized and gives you a feeling for its difficulty. Once you have made a quick estimate of the material's difficulty, you can adjust your reading strategies accordingly.

EXERCISE 1–4   **ASSESSING DIFFICULTY**

Directions: *Use the characteristics listed in Figure 1.1 to assess the difficulty of each reading selection that appears at the end of this chapter (pages 41–43 and 46–48). Then answer the following questions.*

1. Which selection appears to be more difficult? List the features that make it appear difficult.

   _____

   _____

2. What features make the other selection seem easier to read?

   _____

   _____

EXERCISE 1–5   **ASSESSING DIFFICULTY**

Academic
APPLICATION

Directions: *Use the characteristics listed in Figure 1.1 to assess the difficulty of each textbook you have been assigned this semester. Also consider your interest, skills, and background knowledge for each discipline. Rank your texts from most to least difficult.*

FLEXIBILITY TIP

When you read to entertain yourself, you usually can read more quickly than you would read your college textbooks.

Defining Your Purpose

Your purpose for reading a particular piece should influence *how* you read it. Different situations require different levels of comprehension and recall. For example, you may not need to recall every fact when leisurely reading an article in the newspaper, but you *do* need a high level of comprehension when reading a contract that you plan to sign. When reading course assignments, your purpose may also vary. You might read a psychology assignment very closely in preparation for an objective exam. You might read or reread a portion of a chemistry text only to learn how to solve a particular problem. Your reading can range from paying careful, close attention to a very brief, quick reading for only main ideas. Then, as your comprehension varies, so does your reading rate. If close, careful comprehension is not required, you can read faster. You will generally find that as your comprehension decreases, your reading rate increases. The Need to Know box "The Relationship Among Purpose, Rate, and Comprehension" illustrates this relationship.

EXERCISE 1–6   **DEFINING YOUR PURPOSE**

Working
COLLABORATIVELY

Directions: *Each day you read a wide variety of materials, and your purpose is slightly different for each. Make a list of materials you have read this week, and describe your purpose for reading each. (Don't forget such everyday items* *as labels, instructions, menus, etc.) Compare your list with that of a classmate.*

_____

_____

_____

_____

NEED TO KNOW The Relationship Among Purpose, Rate, and Comprehension

Type of Material	Purpose in Reading	Desired Level of Comprehension	Approximate Range of Reading Rate
Poetry, legal documents, argumentative writing	Analyze, criticize, evaluate	Complete (100%)	Under 200 wpm
Textbooks, manuals, research documents	High comprehension recall for exams, writing research reports, following directions	High (90–100%)	200–300 wpm
Novels, paperbacks, newspapers, magazines, blogs, social networking sites	Entertainment, enjoyment, general information	Moderate (60–90%)	300–500 wpm
Reference materials, catalogs, magazines, nonfiction, Web sites	Overview of material, locating specific facts, review of previously read material	Low (60% or below)	600–800 wpm or above

EXERCISE 1-7   **CHOOSING A LEVEL OF COMPREHENSION**

Directions: *For each of the following situations, define your purpose for reading and indicate the level of comprehension that seems appropriate. Refer to the Need to Know box "The Relationship Among Purpose, Rate, and Comprehension" if necessary.*

1. You are reading a case study at the end of a chapter in your criminology textbook in preparation for an essay exam.

   Purpose: _____

   Level of Comprehension: _____

2. You are reading sample problems in a chapter in your mathematics text that you feel confident you know how to solve.

Purpose: _____

Level of Comprehension: _____

3. You are reading the end-of-chapter review questions in your economics text in preparation for an exam that is likely to contain similar questions.

Purpose: _____

Level of Comprehension: _____

4. You are reading a section of a chapter in your economics textbook that refers to a series of graphs and illustrations in the chapter; you can understand the information in the graphs easily.

Purpose: _____

Level of Comprehension: _____

5. You are reading a critical essay that discusses an e. e. cummings poem you are studying in a literature class in preparation for writing a paper on that poem.

Purpose: _____

Level of Comprehension: _____ ■

EXERCISE 1–8

CHOOSING A LEVEL OF COMPREHENSION

Directions: *For each of the following situations, identify the appropriate level of comprehension (low to high).*

1. You are reading the classified ads to find an apartment to rent.

   _____

2. You are reading a friend's English composition to help him or her revise it.

   _____

3. You are reviewing an essay that you read last evening for a literature course.

   _____

4. You are reading your lab manual in preparation for a biology lab.

   _____

5. You are reading an article in *Newsweek* about trends in violent crime in America for a sociology class discussion.

   _____ ■

EXERCISE 1–9

Academic
APPLICATION

ANALYZING ASSIGNMENTS

Directions: *Make a list of reading assignments your instructors expect you to complete in the next two weeks. Indicate the level of comprehension that you should achieve for each assignment.* ■

■ Developing Critical Thinking Skills

Goal 6

Develop critical thinking skills

An efficient and flexible reader is also a critical reader. Your college instructors expect you not only to understand and recall what you read, but also to interpret and evaluate it. They expect you to read and think critically. The word *critical,* when used in this context, does not mean being negative or finding fault. Instead, it means having a curious, questioning, and open mind. To get a better sense of what critical thinking involves, and to assess your current level of critical reading and thinking skills, complete the following mini-questionnaire.

When You Read, Do You	Always	Sometimes	Never
1. Question the author's motives?	❏	❏	❏
2. Think about what the author *means* as well as what he or she *says*?	❏	❏	❏
3. Ask questions such as Why? or How? as you read?	❏	❏	❏
4. Pay attention to the author's choice of words and notice their impact on you?	❏	❏	❏
5. Evaluate the evidence or reasons an author provides to support an idea?	❏	❏	❏

If you answered *always* or *sometimes* to at least one of these questions, you are on your way to becoming a critical reader. If you answered *never* to some of the questions, you will learn more about these skills and develop your critical thinking abilities in each chapter of this book. In addition, Chapter 10, "Critical Analysis and Evaluating Online Sources," provides detailed information on the critical thinking skills you will need for your college reading assignments.

EXERCISE 1–10   **THINKING CRITICALLY ABOUT A READING**

Directions: *Use Reading Selection 2, "Talking a Stranger Through the Night" (pp. 46–48), to answer the following questions.*

1. Read paragraph 1. Based on this paragraph, what do you believe the author's motive is for writing the piece?

_____

_____

_____

2. Read paragraph 13. Which words or phrases have the strongest emotional impact?

_____

3. Based on your reading of just the first and last paragraphs of the reading, what do you expect from the reading? _____

_____

SELF-TEST SUMMARY

Goal 1	1. What is meant by reading efficiency?	Reading efficiency is a vital concept for college readers. Efficiency refers to the ability to accomplish tasks effectively within a reasonable period of time.
Goal 2	2. What are the five major principles behind the techniques presented in this book?	• You do not always have to read everything the same way. • Not everything on a page is of equal importance. • Shortcuts can save valuable time and make reading or studying easier. • Not everything that appears in print is true. • You can increase your reading rate without losing comprehension.
Goal 3	3. What is learning style?	Learning style refers to each person's unique strengths and weaknesses as a learner.
Goal 4	4. How can you improve your reading efficiency?	• Get organized and manage your time. • Improve your concentration. • Control external distractions. • Consider your background knowledge. • Build your interest level.
Goal 5	5. How can you improve your reading flexibility?	• Assess the material's difficulty. • Define your purpose.
Goal 6	6. What is critical thinking?	Critical thinking means having a curious, questioning, and open mind.

READING SELECTION 1   **SOCIOLOGY/HISTORY**

Latino Heritage Month: Who We Are… and Why We Celebrate

Luis J. Rodriguez

About the Reading

ONLINE ARTICLE

This opinion piece was originally published online in The Huffington Post, *which bills itself as "the Internet newspaper." Like printed newspapers,* The Huffington Post *covers business, world news, entertainment, politics, and the media. It can be found online at http://www.huffingtonpost.com.*

Planning Your Reading Strategy*

Directions: *Previewing is a way to take a quick look at the reading to find out what it is about and how difficult it will be. Read the Need to Know box in Chapter 2 on page 64 to find out exactly how to do this. Then preview the article before you read it and answer the following questions.*

1. After previewing, write a few sentences explaining what you learned about the article's topic, organization, or content.

   _____

   _____

   _____

2. Based on your preview of the reading, how quickly do you think you should read the selection? (Circle one.) Explain your answer.

   Very slowly   Slowly   At a moderate pace   Quickly   Very quickly

   _____

   _____

3. How do you define your own racial and ethnic background? Do you think your definition is widely shared among the people of your racial or ethnic heritage? How do you think perceptions of race and ethnicity have changed in the United States, if at all, over the last two generations?

1   I recently visited Orlando, Florida, home to more Puerto Ricans on the mainland than New York City. I was there to spend time with my grandson Ricardo, who earlier this year graduated from high school with honors and is now into his first year of college. Ricardo is part of the Puerto Rican side of my family, wonderful law-abiding Christians, who worked hard and provided a loving home for my grandson when the world around him seemed bleak.

* The Scorecard on p. 45 enables you to compute your reading rate. In order to do so, be sure to record your starting time in the Scorecard box before you begin reading.

2   For fifteen years, I lived in a mostly Puerto Rican community of Chicago, where Ricardo's mother grew up. Although I am Chicano, born on the Mexico-U.S, border, I've also lived among Mexican migrants, Central Americans, African Americans, Asians, Cuban Americans, and European Americans in Los Angeles, the San Francisco Bay Area, Miami, San Bernardino, and San Fernando. For years, I've spoken at and participated in ceremonies in Native American reservations (a Navajo medicine man and his wife around ten years ago adopted my present wife). My other grandchildren are half German, half Scottish-Irish, and half Hungarian.

3   My former wives and live-in girlfriends include a barrio-raised Chicana, an undocumented Mexican, a Mexican/Colombian, a poor white mother of two, and an African American. My own roots are with the indigenous Tarahumara (who call themselves Raramuri) of Chihuahua on my mother's side. My father—and you could see this on his face and in his hair—was native, Spanish, and African from the Mexican state of Guerrero.

4   In fact, Ricardo's girlfriend is from Guyana, and her family was originally from India.

5   To say the least, my extended family is complex and vibrant, made up of all skin colors, ethnicities, and languages . . . and as "American" as apple pie (or burritos, for that matter, since these were created on the U.S. side of that border).

6   Purportedly I'm a Latino, although I rarely call myself this. I mean the original Latinos are Italians, right? Yet Italian Americans are not considered Latinos in this country. And so-called Latinos have origins in Native America, Africa, Europe, Asian, and a vast array of mixtures thereof. We are known as the largest "minority" group in the United States, yet we do not constitute one ethnic group or culture. Let me put it this way: Despite the umbrella of "Latino" above our heads, Puerto Ricans are not the same as Dominicans. And many Salvadorans

I know don't want to be confused with being Mexican.

7   Still, today we officially launch Latino Heritage Month, configured to run from September 15 to October 15, largely to coincide with the Independence Days of countries like Mexico, El Salvador, and others. Unofficially, of course, people who claim roots in Latino countries celebrate every day—they're also into the Fourth of July, Christmas, Martin Luther King Jr. Day, Hanukkah, and Native American Sun Dance ceremonies. Regardless of their country of origin, these people are central to the American soul and deeply intertwined with the social fabric. Despite this Latinos seem to be a rumor in the country, a "middle people," neither black nor white, hardly in the popular culture, mostly shadows and shouts in the distance.

8   Maybe what we celebrate is the complexities, the richness, the expansiveness of who we are. Maybe we celebrate that Latinos have bled and sweated for this country. Hundreds from the Dominican Republic, Colombia, Mexico, Ecuador, Argentina, and other Latin American countries died during the 9/11 attacks. People with Spanish or Portuguese surnames garnered more medals of honor during World War II and had a disproportionate number of casualties during the Vietnam War. The first known U.S. death from the Iraq War was a young man originally from Guatemala.

9   Perhaps we celebrate that Latinos have worked in the auto plants of Detroit, steel mills of Chicago, cotton fields of Texas, textile centers of Massachusetts, and crop fields of California. That they are among the best in professional sports, and I'm not limiting this to soccer—they have been some of the world's best boxers, baseball players, footballs players, golfers, and tennis players.

10   Let's celebrate that Latinos have been in the forefront of the organized labor movement and fought alongside African Americans against slavery and for Civil Rights, that

they are among the oldest residents of the continent as indigenous peoples from places like Mexico, Central America or Peru. And they are the majority of this country's most recent arrivals.

11   Let's recognize that U.S. Latinos can be found among scientists, professors, doctors, politicians, and judges. That renowned actors, musicians, and writers include Carlos Santana, Ricky Martin, Jennifer Lopez, George Lopez, Danny Trejo, Celia Cruz, Oscar Hijuelos, Sandra Cisneros, Junot Diaz, Salma Hayek, Antonio Banderas, Los Lobos, Cheech Marin, Shakira, Javier Bardem, Penelope Cruz, Eva Mendes, and Bruno Mars.

Jennifer Lopez

12   Our ancestors were former slaves and former slaveholders, peons and nobles, poets and conquistadors, African miners and native rebels. They included practitioners of the Flamenco and canto hondo with ties to the Roma people (so-called Gypsies) and the Arab/Muslim world, which once ruled Spain for close to 800 years. And so-called Latinos still use words, herbs, dance, and clothing from the wondrous civilizations of the Olmeca, Mexica (so-called Aztec), Maya, and Inca.

13   The fact is Latino heritage is U.S. heritage. You wouldn't have such "American" phenomena as cowboys, guitars, rubber balls, gold mining, horses, corn, and even Jazz, Rock-and-Roll, and Hip Hop, without the contribution of Latinos. And besides the hundreds of Spanish words that now grace the English language (lariat, rodeo,

Ricky Martin

buckaroo, adios, cafeteria, hasta la vista, baby), there are also indigenous words that English can't do without . . . chocolate, ocelot, coyote, tomato, avocado, maize, and barbecue, among others.

14   Unfortunately, as we contemplate what Latino Heritage means, we have to be reminded that Latinos have been among the most scapegoated during the current financial crisis. States have established more laws against brown-skinned undocumented migrants while Arizona is trying to outlaw teachings on Mexican/Ethnic history and culture. They are also among the poorest, least healthy, and most neglected Americans. Spanish-surnamed people are now the majority in the federal prison system and the largest single group in the state penitentiaries of California, New Mexico, and Texas. They are also concentrated among this country's homeless and drug-addicted populations.

15   So while all Americans have much to celebrate in Latino heritage, like most Americans we also have a long way to go.

16   Whatever one thinks of Latinos, one thing is for sure: They have given much to this country and have much more to give. I'm convinced any revolutionary changes in the economy, politics, technology, cultural life, social equity and justice must have Latinos (regardless of race, background, religion, social class, or political strain) at the heart of them. They are integral to the past, present, and future of this country.

17   And this is a beautiful thing, baby.

Examining Reading Selection 1*

Checking Your Vocabulary

Directions: *Use context, word parts, or a dictionary, if necessary, to determine the meaning of each word as it is used in the reading.*

____ 1. bleak (paragraph 1)
   a. calm
   b. dismal
   c. proper
   d. bright

____ 2. indigenous (paragraph 3)
   a. individual
   b. unrelated
   c. native
   d. ordinary

____ 3. constitute (paragraph 6)
   a. disagree
   b. allow
   c. replace
   d. make up

____ 4. garnered (paragraph 8)
   a. earned
   b. warned
   c. gave away
   d. removed

____ 5. integral (paragraph 16)
   a. profitable
   b. essential
   c. separated
   d. trivial

Checking Your Comprehension

Directions: *Select the best answer.*

____ 6. This essay is mostly about
   a. Latino families.
   b. Latino heritage.
   c. Latino holidays.
   d. famous Latino Americans.

____ 7. The author wrote this essay in order to
   a. describe the diversity and influence of Latinos in America.
   b. criticize how the *Latino* label is applied in America.
   c. describe the history of Latin American countries.
   d. expose discrimination against Latino Americans.

____ 8. Latino Heritage Month was organized to coincide with the celebration of
   a. Christmas.
   b. the Fourth of July.
   c. Native American Sun Dance ceremonies.
   d. the Independence Days of Latino countries.

____ 9. According to the author, the reasons Latinos celebrate include
   a. their important contributions to American life.
   b. the richness and complexities of the Latino culture.
   c. the sacrifices they have made on behalf of their country.
   d. all of the above.

____ 10. The statement that best expresses the central thought of this essay is
   a. "To say the least, my extended family is complex and vibrant, made up of all skin colors, ethnicities, and languages."
   b. "People who claim roots in Latino countries celebrate every day."
   c. "Regardless of their country of origin, these people are central to the American soul and deeply intertwined with the social fabric."
   d. "Maybe we celebrate that Latinos have bled and sweated for this country."

---

*Writing About the Reading questions appear in the Instructor's Manual.

Thinking Critically

___11. By describing the people in his extended family, the author illustrates their
a. closeness.
b. diversity.
c. simplicity.
d. similarity.

___12. Based on the essay, one conclusion that the author would agree with is:
a. The term *Latino* should apply only to people from Mexico.
b. Arizona should outlaw teachings on Mexican/Ethnic history.
c. Poverty, drugs, and health care are not issues for the Latino population.
d. While Latinos have much to be proud of, they also have serious problems to address.

___13. When the author says Latinos have been *scapegoated* during the current financial crisis, he means that they have been
a. neglected.
b. given credit.
c. excluded from responsibility.
d. treated with hostility or blamed.

___14. The author's attitude toward the subject can best be described as
a. critical.
b. indifferent.
c. proud.
d. objective.

___15. The author probably chose to include the photos with this reading for all of the following reasons, except:
a. to provide examples of famous Latinos.
b. to illustrate that Latinos are America's most successful ethnic group.
c. to emphasize Latinos' contributions to culture in the United States.
d. to demonstrate that Latinos have achieved success in a variety of endeavors.

Questions for Discussion

1. Describe your own ethnic heritage or "roots." Do you celebrate holidays associated with your heritage? Why or why not?

2. What does the author mean when he says, "Latinos seem to be a rumor in the country . . . mostly shadows and shouts in the distance" (paragraph 7)? Do you agree or disagree?

3. Why does the author say he rarely calls himself Latino? How would you describe him, based on what he says in his essay?

4. Discuss the author's list of renowned U.S. Latinos. Whom do you recognize and for what are they well-known?

Scorecard

Selection 1:   1,166 words

Finishing Time: _____ _____ _____
                    HR.   MIN.   SEC.

Starting Time: _____ _____ _____
                    HR.   MIN.   SEC.

Reading Time: _____ _____
                           MIN.   SEC.

Words Per Minute
(WPM) Score: _____

Comprehension Score: for Items 6–15
Number Right: _____ × 10 = _____%

Assessing Your Reading Strategy

1. How would you rate your comprehension of the reading (Circle one.)?
Excellent   Good   Fair   Poor

2. Was reading strategy effective?
Yes   No

3. Suppose you were given an assignment to read a similar article (a personal essay about one person's ethnic background) from the same online source. Based on your experience with this selection, how would you adjust your reading strategy (if at all)?

_____

READING SELECTION 2   SOCIOLOGY

Talking a Stranger Through the Night

Sherry Amatenstein
From *Newsweek* magazine

About the Reading

This article was originally published in Newsweek, *a popular weekly news magazine. In addition to news,* Newsweek *also features guest columnists who write about social and personal issues.*

MyReadingLab™ *The exercises following this selection can be completed online at myreadinglab.com*

Planning Your Reading Strategy*

Directions: *Previewing is a way to take a quick look at the reading to find out what it is about and how difficult it will be. Read the Need to Know box in Chapter 2 on page 64 to find out exactly how to do this. Then preview the article before you read it and answer the following questions.*

_____ 1. To what type of information in the reading should you pay the most attention?
    a. the examples of crank callers
    b. the author's experience with Sandy
    c. the New York City location
    d. the history of the Holocaust

    2. Based on your preview of the reading, how quickly do you think you should read the selection? (Circle one.)

    Very slowly   Slowly   At a moderate pace   Quickly   Very quickly

_____ 3. Which of the following is the best clue regarding the rate at which you should read the selection?
    a. the fact that it comes from a popular magazine, *Newsweek*
    b. the inclusion of conversations between the author and the hotline callers
    c. the author's family history, as summarized in the first paragraph
    d. the inclusion of a photo of a call center

1   The call came 60 minutes into my third shift as a volunteer at the crisis hotline. As the child of Holocaust survivors, I grew up wanting to ease other people's pain. But it wasn't until after September 11 that I contacted Help Line, the nonprofit telephone service headquartered in New York. The instructor of the nine-week training course taught us how to handle a variety of callers, from depressed seniors to "repeats" (those who checked in numerous times a day).

2   We spent two sessions on suicide calls, but I prayed I wouldn't get one until I felt

*The Scorecard on p. 49 enables you to compute your reading rate. In order to do so, be sure to record your starting time in the Scorecard box before you begin reading.

A suicide hotline worker helps a caller.

comfortable on the line. Drummed over and over into the 30 trainees' heads was that our role wasn't to give advice. Rather, we were to act as empathetic sounding boards and encourage callers to figure out how to take action.

3   My idealism about the hotline's value faded that first night, as in quick succession I heard from men who wanted to masturbate while I listened, repeats who told me again and again about their horrific childhoods, know-nothing shrinks and luckless lives, and three separate callers who railed about the low intellect of everyone living in Queens (my borough!). Sprinkled into the mix were people who turned abusive when I refused to tell them how to solve their problems.

4   I tried to remain sympathetic. If I, who had it together (an exciting career, great friends and family), found New York isolating, I could imagine how frightening it was for people so untethered they needed a hotline for company. That rationale didn't help. After only 10 hours, I no longer cringed each time the phone rang, terrified it signified a problem I wasn't equipped to handle. Instead I wondered what fresh torture this caller had up his unstable sleeve.

5   Then Sandy's (not her real name) quavering voice nipped into my ear: "I want to kill myself." I snapped to attention, remembering my training. Did she have an imminent plan to do herself in? Luckily, no. Sandy knew a man who'd attempted suicide via pills, threw them up and lived. She was afraid of botching a similar attempt. Since she was handicapped, she couldn't even walk to her window to jump out.

6   Sandy's life was certainly Help Line material. Her parents had disowned her 40 years before. She'd worked as a secretary until a bone-crushing fall put her out of commission. Years later she was working again and had a boyfriend who stuck with her even after a cab struck Sandy and put her back on the disabled list. They became engaged, and then, soap-opera like, tragedy struck again. Sandy's boyfriend was diagnosed with cancer and passed away last year. Now she was in constant pain, confined to a dark apartment, her only companion a nurse's aide. "There's nothing left," she cried. "Give me a reason to live."

7   Her plea drove home the wisdom of the "no advice" dictum. How could I summon the words to give someone else's life meaning? The best I could do was to help Sandy fan the spark that had led her to reach out. I tossed life-affirming statements at her like paint on a canvas, hoping some would stick. I ended with "Sandy, I won't whitewash your problems. You've had more than your share of sorrow. But surely there are some things that have given you pleasure."

8   She thought hard and remembered an interest in books on spirituality. The downside followed immediately. Sandy's limited eyesight made it difficult for her to read. She rasped, "My throat hurts from crying, but I'm afraid if I get off the phone I'll want to kill myself again."

9   I said, "I'm here as long as you need me."

10   We spoke another two hours. She recalled long-ago incidents—most depressing, a few semi-joyful. There were some things she still enjoyed: peanuts, "Oprah," the smell of autumn. I again broached the topic of spirituality. My supervisor, whom I'd long ago motioned to listen

in on another phone, handed me a prayer book. I read, and Sandy listened. After "amen," she said, "I think I'll be all right for the night."

11   Naturally, she couldn't promise to feel better tomorrow. For all of us, life is one day, sometimes even one minute, at a time. She asked, "When are you on again?"

12   I said, "My schedule is irregular, but we're all here for you, any time you want. Thanks so much for calling."

13   As I hung up, I realized the call had meant as much to me as to Sandy, if not more. Despite having people in my life, lately I'd felt achingly lonely. I hadn't called a hotline, but I'd manned one, and this night had been my best in a long time. Instead of having dinner at an overpriced restaurant or watching HBO, I'd connected with another troubled soul in New York City.

Examining Reading Selection 2

Complete this Exercise at myreadinglab.com

Checking Your Vocabulary

Directions: *Use context, word parts, or a dictionary, if necessary, to determine the meaning of each word as it is used in the reading.*

____ 1. succession (paragraph 3)
   a. challenge
   b. extent
   c. confusion
   d. sequence

____ 2. railed (paragraph 3)
   a. condemned at length
   b. argued about
   c. made fun of
   d. blamed

____ 3. imminent (paragraph 5)
   a. frightening
   b. dangerous
   c. about to happen
   d. complicated

____ 4. out of commission (paragraph 6)
   a. not in working order
   b. inhumane
   c. not available
   d. incomprehensible

____ 5. dictum (paragraph 7)
   a. cue
   b. rule
   c. message
   d. opportunity

Checking Your Comprehension

Directions: *Select the best answer.*

____ 6. This article is primarily about
   a. how to work a crisis line.
   b. the way the author helped someone and was helped in return.
   c. why hotline volunteers need training.
   d. the downside to working with the public.

____ 7. Why was Sandy so upset?
   a. She had a life full of tragedy and pain.
   b. She lacks religious faith.
   c. Her family did not trust her.
   d. Someone she knew had committed suicide.

____ 8. The author was trained to
   a. say whatever the caller wants to hear.
   b. recommend a good psychiatrist, if necessary.
   c. trace phone calls.
   d. listen sympathetically but not to give advice.

____ 9. How did the author help Sandy?
   a. She stayed on the phone for two hours.
   b. She agreed that she had numerous problems.

c. She consulted her supervisor.

d. She encouraged her to remember pleasant things about life.

Thinking Critically

___ 10. How did the author feel after Sandy's call?

a. pleased that Sandy wanted to talk to her again

b. satisfied that she had helped someone

c. relieved that Sandy decided to refocus her life and make new friends

d. happy to get off the phone

___ 11. The author wrote the article to

a. emphasize the value of helping others.

b. demonstrate the need for more help lines.

c. express the joy of life.

d. reveal the tragedy of suicide.

___ 12. The author supports her ideas on volunteering by

a. providing statistics.

b. describing personal experience.

c. citing research studies.

d. interviewing Help Line supervisors.

___ 13. From the reading, you can infer that the author

a. lives alone.

b. has never experienced the death of a loved one.

c. leads a very busy and thrilling life.

d. is a well-to-do New York City resident with a rewarding career.

___ 14. This reading is organized

a. chronologically, in the order in which events occurred.

b. using cause-effect relationships.

c. from most to least important ideas.

d. spatially, according to where events occurred.

___ 15. Which part of the photo on page 47 provides the strongest clue that the women work on a crisis hotline?

a. the telephones

b. the filing cabinets

c. the form being filled out by the woman in the red T-shirt

d. the "Contra Costa" sign hanging in the background

Scorecard

Selection 2:   889 words

Finishing Time: ___ ___ ___
                HR. MIN. SEC.

Starting Time: ___ ___ ___
               HR. MIN. SEC.

Reading Time: ___ ___
              MIN. SEC.

WPM Score: ___

Comprehension Score: for Items 6–15

Number Right: ___ × 10 = ___ %

Assessing Your Reading Strategy

1. How would you rate your comprehension of the reading? (Circle one.)
Excellent   Good   Fair   Poor

2. Did you find your reading strategy effective?   Yes   No

3. Suppose you were given an assignment to read a similar article (about one person's experience) from the same source. Based on your experience with this selection, how would you adjust your reading strategy (if at all)?

_____

_____

Writing About Reading Selection 2

Checking Your Vocabulary

Directions: *Complete each of the following items; refer to a dictionary if necessary.*

1. Discuss the connotative meanings of the word *suicide*.

2. Define the word *empathetic* (paragraph 2) and underline the word or phrase that provides a context clue for its meaning.

   _____

   _____

   _____

3. Define the word *botching* (paragraph 5) and underline the word or phrase that provides a context clue for its meaning.

   _____

   _____

   _____

4. Determine the meanings of the following words by using word parts:
   a. *nonprofit* (paragraph 1)

   _____

   b. *untethered* (paragraph 4)

   _____

   c. *unstable* (paragraph 4)

   _____

   d. *spirituality* (paragraph 8)

   _____

   e. *irregular* (paragraph 12)

   _____

Checking Your Comprehension

5. What main point does the author make?

   _____

   _____

6. Describe Sandy's life.

   _____

   _____

   _____

7. Describe the training the author received.

   _____

   _____

8. How and when was the author's idealism about the hotline shattered?

   _____

   _____

   _____

   _____

Thinking Critically

9. How did Sandy's call change the author's attitude toward the hotline?

   _____

   _____

   _____

10. Describe the organization of this selection. What organizational pattern predominates?

   _____

   _____

11. Cite several examples that suggest that the author was helpful to Sandy.

   _____

   _____

   _____

   _____

12. What is the author's purpose?

   _____

   _____

_____

_____

13. What can you infer about the author's lifestyle from information contained in the reading?

_____

_____

_____

Questions for Discussion

1. Discuss why it is the hotline's policy not to offer advice.

2. Evaluate the level of training and supervision the hotline offered its volunteers.

3. Discuss situations in which you did something to help another person and it resulted in making you feel better about yourself.

4. Brainstorm a list of volunteer options on campus or in your community. Discuss potential rewards; try to anticipate potential problems.

Active Reading and Learning

think VISUALLY...

This photograph shows people attending a sporting event.

This photograph demonstrates active involvement. The fans in the photograph are responding and reacting to the event on the field. They direct plays, criticize the calls, encourage the players, and reprimand the coaches. In a similar way, active readers get involved with the material they are reading. They think, question, challenge, and criticize the author's ideas. They try to make the material *their* material. This chapter will give you some strategies for becoming an active, successful reader. You will learn to preview and predict, form guide questions, and monitor your comprehension.

Learning GOALS

In this chapter, you will learn how to . . .

Goal 1 Read actively

Goal 2 Develop critical thinking skills

Goal 3 Monitor your comprehension

Goal 4 Preview and predict before reading

Goal 5 Develop guide questions

Goal 6 Develop a questioning mind-set

■ Reading Actively

Goal 1
Read actively

Reading at first may appear to be a routine activity in which individual words are combined to produce meaning. Consequently, many college students approach reading as a single-step process. They open the book, read, and close the book. Research shows that active reading is not a single-step process but a complex set of skills involving activities before, during, and after reading. Here is a partial list of those skills:

Before Reading

- Determine the subject of the material.
- Determine how the material is organized.
- Decide what you need to remember from the material.
- Define your purpose for reading.

During Reading

- Identify what is important.
- Determine how key ideas are supported.
- Identify patterns of thought.
- Draw connections between ideas.
- Anticipate what is to come next.
- Relate ideas to what you already know.

During and After Reading

- Identify the author's purpose for writing.
- Analyze the writer's technique and language.
- Evaluate the writer's competence or authority.
- Ask critical questions.
- Evaluate the nature and type of supporting evidence.

Table 2.1 (p. 54) lists additional examples of successful active reading strategies and contrasts them with passive (unsuccessful) approaches. Throughout this chapter and the remainder of the text, you will learn numerous techniques and strategies for becoming a more active reader.

EXERCISE 2–1

ANALYZING ASSIGNMENTS

Directions: *Using Table 2.1 (p. 54), analyze how you read. Place check marks beside items that describe you. Are you an active or a passive reader?* ■

TABLE 2.1 Active Versus Passive Reading

Active Readers . . .	Passive Readers . . .
Read each assignment differently	Read all assignments the same way
Analyze the purpose of an assignment	Read an assignment because it was assigned
Adjust their speed to suit their purpose	Read everything at the same speed
Question ideas	Accept whatever is in print as true
Compare and connect textbook readings with lecture content	Study each separately
Find out what an assignment is about before reading it	Check the length of an assignment before reading it
Keep track of their level of comprehension and concentration	Read until the assignment is completed
Read with pencil in hand, highlighting, jotting notes, and marking key vocabulary	Read

EXERCISE 2–2

Working
COLLABORATIVELY

ANALYZING ASSIGNMENTS

Directions: *Consider each of the following reading assignments. Discuss ways to get actively involved in each assignment.*

1. Reading two poems by Walt Whitman for an American literature class

   _____

   _____

2. Reading the procedures for your next biology lab

   _____

   _____

3. Reading an article in *Time* magazine assigned by your political science instructor in preparation for a class discussion

   _____

   _____

EXERCISE 2–3

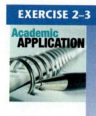

Academic
APPLICATION

READING ACTIVELY

Directions: *Compile a list of active reading strategies you already use. Discuss new strategies that could be used with your instructor or classmates. Add these to your list.*

_____

_____

_____

_____ ■

■ Thinking Critically

Goal 2
Develop critical thinking skills

Active reading requires critical thinking. To be an active reader, you must think beyond a factual, literal level. Instructors expect you to understand ideas, but they also expect you to apply, analyze, and evaluate information and to create new ideas. The Need to Know box "Levels of Thinking" describes a progression of academic thinking skills ranging from basic to more complex. Because critical thinking is an essential part of most college courses, each chapter in this book features a section to help you build your critical thinking skills.

FLEXIBILITY TIP
Critical thinking does not necessarily require you to read more slowly. However, it does require you to stop and think more deeply about what you are reading. As you read more critically, your total time spent on a task may increase.

NEED TO KNOW Levels of Thinking

Level	Examples
Remembering: Recalling information; repeating information with no changes	Recalling definitions; memorizing dates
Understanding: Understanding ideas; using rules and following directions	Explaining a theory; recognizing what is important
Applying: Applying knowledge to a new situation	Using knowledge of formulas to solve a new physics problem
Analyzing: Seeing relationships; breaking information into parts; analyzing how things work	Comparing two essays by the same author
Evaluating: Making judgments; assessing value or worth of information	Evaluating the effectiveness of an argument opposing the death penalty
Creating: Putting ideas and information together in a unique way; creating something new	Designing a new computer program

Sources: Bloom, B., et al., eds., *Taxonomy of Educational Objectives.* New York: McKay, 1956, and Anderson, Lorin, et al., *Taxonomy for Learning, Teaching and Assessing: A Revision of Bloom's Taxonomy of Educational Objectives.* Boston: Allyn and Bacon, 2000.

When instructors assign papers, write exam questions, or conduct class discussions, they often ask you to do more than just remember and understand. Table 2.2 gives a few sample exam questions from a course in interpersonal communication.

TABLE 2.2	Test Items and Levels of Thinking	
Test Item		**Level of Thinking Required**
Define nonverbal communication.		Remembering
Explain how nonverbal communication works.		Understanding
Describe three instances in which you have observed nonverbal communication.		Applying
Study the two video segments and analyze the motives of each person.		Analyzing
Evaluate an essay whose major premise is "Nonverbal communication skills should be taught formally as part of the educational process."		Evaluating
Read the short story and then create an alternative ending.		Creating

The following passage is taken from a human biology textbook. Read the passage and study the list of questions that follow.

COMMUNICATION AND THE SKIN

We generally think of communication as a matter of voice and gesture, but the skin is an important communicative organ. Animals communicate their moods and sometimes make threats by fluffing their fur or causing it to rise on the backs of their neck and shoulders; humans cannot do that. However, the patterns of human hair distribution and color do signal sex and age. Fair-complexioned people can also—involuntarily—change blood flow to the skin and blush to indicate embarrassment, turn red with rage, and go pale with shock. In addition, we have considerable voluntary control over subcutaneous muscles in the face and neck, many of which attach to the skin to produce the stretchings and wrinklings of facial expressions.

An additional communicative role is served by the skin's apocrine sweat glands, particularly in adults. The substances they secrete have strong odors, especially after they have been worked on by the bacteria that dwell on the skin, and these glands are found in areas, such as the armpits, groin, and anal region, that have wicklike tufts of hair that can spread the odor into the air. Emotionally charged situations are likely to stimulate apocrine secretions, which may signal that a certain level of sexual readiness or fear or anxiety (emotional intensity) has been attained.

—Rischer and Easton, *Focus on Human Biology,* 2e, HarperCollins Publishers.

Remembering	What happens when fair-complexioned people blush?
Understanding	Why is the skin an important vehicle for communication?
Applying	Study two facial portraits and discuss how the people are using their skin to communicate.
Analyzing	How does stretching of the skin produce communication?
Evaluating	Why is it important to know that skin can communicate?
Creating	Write a set of guidelines for determining what messages can be sent by skin movement.

EXERCISE 2–4   **IDENTIFYING LEVELS OF THINKING**

Directions: *For each of the following activities or situations, identify which levels of thinking are primarily involved.*

1. You are reading and comparing research from several sources to write a term paper for sociology.

   _____

2. You received a "C" grade on an essay you wrote for your freshman composition course. Your instructor will allow you to revise it to improve your grade.

   _____

3. You are translating an essay from Spanish to English.

   _____

4. You are dissecting a frog in your biology class.

   _____

5. You are bathing a patient as part of your clinical experience course in nursing.

   _____

EXERCISE 2–5   **IDENTIFYING LEVELS OF THINKING**

Directions: *Read the following excerpt from a history textbook. Then read the questions that follow and identify the level of thinking that each requires.*

AFRICAN-AMERICAN WOMEN AS WRITERS

Phillis Wheatley was a young, African-American slave who belonged to land-owner John Wheatley in Colonial America. She was also a poet and the first African-American ever to publish a book. Her *Poems on Various Subjects, Religious and Moral* was printed in Boston in 1773, three years before the penning of the Declaration of Independence.

Early slaves were generally denied education (it was deemed dangerous), but Wheatley was allowed by her owner to study poetry, Latin, and the Bible, and by the time she reached her late teens she had written enough poetry to put together a slender book of verse. Even so, publication was difficult. Proper Bostonians, fearful of a hoax, forced her to submit to a scholarly examination by a board of educated men, including the colonial governor and the same John Hancock who later copied out the Declaration of Independence and signed it with a flourish. The board of judges questioned Wheatley extensively and ruled that she was literate enough to have written the book. Only then was publication permitted.

Wheatley may have been the first, but she was not the only slave to write a book during the growing days of the republic. Unfortunately, most of the early popular African-American writers have been all but forgotten in modern times. Until now. A Cornell professor, Henry Louis Gates, recently started a research project, looking into 19th-century African-American fiction and poetry. In the process, he uncovered numerous lost works, almost half of which were written by African-American women. In varied literary styles, the newly resurfaced manuscripts offered a rich repository of African-American culture, recreating, among other things, the early days of slavery and the importance of religion to people under subjugation.

The literary finds were important. So important, in fact, that 30 of the lost books were republished in the late 1980s by Oxford University Press. The newly reclaimed writers range from poet Wheatley to novelist Frances Harper, essayist Ann Plato, and outspoken feminist Anna Julia Cooper. Perhaps this time they won't be lost.

—Merrill, Lee and Friedlander, *Modern Mass Media,* 2e, HarperCollins Publishers.

1. Who was the first African-American to publish a book?

   _____

2. Explain why Phillis Wheatley was forced to submit to a scholarly examination.

   _____

3. Name two writers who have been recently rediscovered.

   _____

4. Read two poems by Phillis Wheatley and compare them.

_____

5. Why does the writer of this article hope the newly reclaimed work won't be lost?

_____

6. Read a poem by Phillis Wheatley and explain what meaning it has to your life.

_____

7. Critique one of Wheatley's poems; discuss its strengths and weaknesses.

_____

8. Discuss the possible reasons Wheatley's owner allowed her to study.

_____

9. Read five essays by Ann Plato, and develop a list of issues with which she is concerned.

_____

10. Decide whether it was fair to ask Wheatley to submit to a scholarly examination.

_____

■ Monitoring Your Comprehension

Goal 3

Monitor your comprehension

Have you ever read an assignment only to realize later, perhaps much later during an exam, that you did not really understand it? Or have you ever spent your time supposedly reading several pages or more, only to discover later that you really understood very little? If so, you can develop a very important and useful skill to overcome these problems. It is known as *metacognition* and it means keeping track or being aware of what is happening mentally as you read. In metacognitive monitoring you stay aware of your level of understanding by picking up clues or signals that indicate whether you are understanding what you are reading.

Think for a moment about what occurs when you read material you can understand easily. Then compare this feeling with what happens when you read complicated material that is difficult for you to understand. When you read certain material, does it seem that everything "clicks"? Do ideas seem to fit together and make sense? At other times is that "click" noticeably absent?

Read each of the following paragraphs. As you read, be alert to your level of understanding of each.

PARAGRAPH 1

Probably the major error beginning speakers make is to try to cover a huge topic in too short a time. The inevitable result is that nothing specific is covered; everything is touched on, but only superficially. No depth is achieved with a broad topic, so all you can succeed in doing is telling the audience what it already knows. To be suitable for a public speech, a topic must be limited in scope; it must be narrowed down to fit the same constraints and to permit some depth of coverage.

—Joseph A. DeVito, *The Elements of Public Speaking,* Seventh Edition, p. 109. New York: Longman, 2000.

PARAGRAPH 2

Large-quantity waste generators and SQGs must comply with the RCRA regulations, including obtaining an EPA identification (EPA ID) number, proper handling of the waste before transport, manifesting the waste (discussed in the next section), and proper record keeping and reporting. Conditionally exempt SQGs do not require EPA ID numbers. Appropriate pre-transport handling requires suitable packaging to prevent leakage and labeling of the packaged waste to identify its characteristics and dangers.

—Jerry A. Nathanson, *Basic Environmental Technology: Water Supply, Waste Management, and Pollution Control,* Third Edition, p. 351. Upper Saddle River, NJ: Prentice-Hall, 2000.

Most likely, as you read Paragraph 1, everything seemed to fit together and make sense. Ideas led from one to another; you could easily follow the author's train of thought. While reading Paragraph 2, you may have experienced difficulty and confusion. You realized that ideas weren't making sense. Unfamiliar terms were used and unfamiliar concepts were discussed; consequently, you could not see the flow of ideas.

Recognizing Comprehension Signals

The two examples were quite clear-cut: In one case understanding was easy; in the other it was difficult. In many situations, however, the distinction between understanding and the lack of it is not as clear. As you learned in Chapter 1, your comprehension depends on numerous factors; it may vary from high to low even within a single piece of material. In those cases, you have to pick up on more subtle clues or signals. The Need to Know box "Comprehension Signals" lists and compares some common signals that may assist you in monitoring your comprehension. Not all signals must appear at the same time, and not all signals work for everyone.

NEED TO KNOW   Comprehension Signals

Positive Signals	Negative Signals
Everything seems to fit and make sense; ideas flow logically from one to another.	Some pieces do not seem to belong; the material seems disjointed.
You are able to see where the author is leading.	You feel as if you are struggling to stay with the author and are unable to think ahead.
You are able to make connections and see patterns of thought developing.	You are unable to detect relationships; the organization is not apparent.
You read at a regular, comfortable pace without slowing down or rereading.	You need to slow down or reread frequently and you make frequent regressions.
You understand why the material was assigned.	You do not know why the material was assigned and cannot explain why it is important.
You feel comfortable and have some knowledge about the topic.	The topic is unfamiliar, yet the author assumes you understand it.
You recognize most words or can figure them out from context.	Many words are unfamiliar.
You can express the main ideas in your own words.	You must reread and use the author's language to explain an idea.
You understand what is important.	Nothing or everything seems important.

EXERCISE 2–6   **MONITORING YOUR COMPREHENSION**

Directions: *Select a two- to three-page section from one of your textbooks or choose one of the readings at the end of the chapter. As you read it, monitor your level of understanding. After reading the material, answer the following questions.*

1. In what sections was your comprehension strongest?

   _____

2. Did you feel at any time that you had lost, or were about to lose, comprehension? If so, go back to that section now. What made the section difficult to read?

   _____

3. Analyze any sections where you slowed down or reread. Why was this necessary?

_____

4. How did you connect the content with your background knowledge and experience?

_____

Correcting Incomplete Comprehension

Once you recognize clues that signal your level of understanding, you will find situations in which you are not comprehending as well as you should. When this happens, try the following:

1. **Analyze the time and place in which you are reading.** If you've been reading or studying for several hours, mental fatigue may be the source of the problem. If you are reading in a place with numerous distractions or interruptions, lack of concentration may contribute to comprehension loss.

2. **Rephrase each paragraph in your own words.** You might approach extremely complicated material sentence-by-sentence, expressing each in your own words.

3. **Read aloud sentences or sections that are particularly difficult.** Oral reading often provides auditory feedback signals that aid comprehension.

4. **Write a brief outline of the major points of the article.** This will help you to see the overall organization and progression of ideas in the material. (Chapter 7 discusses outlining and summary notes in greater detail.)

5. **Do not hesitate to reread difficult or complicated sections.** In fact, at times several rereadings are appropriate and necessary.

6. **Highlight important ideas.** After you've read a section, go back and think about and highlight what is important. Highlighting forces you to sort out what is important, and this sorting process facilitates overall comprehension and recall. (See Chapter 7 for suggestions about how to highlight effectively.)

7. **Slow down your reading rate if you feel you're beginning to lose comprehension.** On occasion simply reading more slowly will provide the needed boost in comprehension.

8. **Summarize.** Test your recall by summarizing each section after you have read it.

If none of these suggestions is effective, you may be lacking the necessary background knowledge that a particular writer assumes the reader has.

If you feel you are lacking background knowledge in a particular discipline or about a particular topic, take immediate steps to correct the problem. You might:

1. **Do an Internet search.** Google the topic to get an overview of what it involves.

2. **Review several encyclopedia entries and other reference or online sources** to obtain an overview of the subject.

3. **Ask your instructor to suggest reference sources, Web sites, guidebooks, or review books that will be helpful.**

✔ LEARNING STYLE TIPS

If you tend to be a(n) . . .	Then improve your comprehension by . . .
Applied learner	Thinking of real-life situations that illustrate ideas in the material
Conceptual learner	Asking questions

■ Previewing and Predicting

Goal 4
Preview and predict before reading

Before reading an assignment, it is useful to discover what it is about—preview—and to anticipate what the material will cover—predict. Previewing is an active way to approach any reading assignment.

EFFICIENCY TIP
Many students complain that they "ran out of time" and were not able to complete their reading assignment. Prevent this from happening by previewing the reading selection as soon as it's assigned. Assessing the reading's difficulty level will help you schedule the appropriate amount of time for reading it.

Previewing

What is the first thing you do as you begin reading a text assignment? If you are like many students, you check to see how long it is and then begin to read. Many students do not realize that they should preview before reading. **Previewing** is a way to familiarize yourself quickly with the organization and content of the material. It is easy to use, and it makes a dramatic difference in your reading efficiency. Previewing involves getting a quick impression of what you are going to read before you read it. As a result, you will be able to read faster and follow the author's train of thought more easily. Previewing is similar to looking at a road map before you start out on a drive to an unfamiliar place. The road map, like previewing, gives you an idea of what lies ahead and how it is arranged.

How to Preview

When you preview a textbook chapter, you look only at those parts of the material that tell you what it is about or how it is organized. Use the steps listed in the box on the next page to preview effectively.

NEED TO KNOW **Previewing Steps**

1. **Read the title.** Often the title functions as a label and tells you what the material is about. It identifies the overall topic or subject.

2. **Read the introduction or opening paragraphs.** The first few paragraphs of a piece of writing are usually introductory. The author may explain the subject, outline his or her ideas, or give some clues about his or her direction of thought. If the introduction is long, read only the first two or three paragraphs.

3. **Read each boldfaced heading.** Headings, like titles, serve as labels and identify the content of the material they head. Together, the headings form a mini-outline of the important ideas.

4. **Read the first sentence under each heading.** Although the heading often announces the topic that will be discussed, the first sentence following the heading frequently explains the heading and states the central thought of the passage.

5. **If there are no or few headings, read the first sentence of a few paragraphs per page.** These sentences are often topic sentences and express key points.

6. **Notice any typographical aids.** The typographical aids include all features of the page that make facts or ideas outstanding or more understandable. These include *italics* (slanted print), **boldfaced type**, marginal notes, colored ink, CAPITALIZATION, underlining, and enumeration (listing).

7. **Notice any graphs or visuals, and read their captions.** Graphs, charts, and pictures are used for two purposes. First, they emphasize important ideas. Second, they clarify or simplify information and relationships. Therefore, they are always important to notice when you are previewing.

8. **Read the last paragraph or summary.** The last paragraph of a chapter often serves as a conclusion or summary. In some chapters, more than one paragraph may be used for this purpose. In some textbooks, these last few paragraphs may be labeled "Summary" or "Conclusion." By reading the summary before reading the chapter you will learn the general focus and content of the material.

Now preview the textbook excerpt titled "Types of Nonverbal Cues." To illustrate how previewing is done, these pages have been specially marked. Everything that you should read has been shaded. After you have previewed the selection, complete the quiz in Exercise 2–7.

TYPES OF NONVERBAL CUES

Let's look more closely at these cues that tell others about us or that tell us about them. Our own self-awareness and empathic skills will increase as we become more sensitive to different kinds of nonverbal cues. The broader our base of understanding, the more likely we are to be able to interpret the cues we perceive. But we know that nonverbal communication can be ambiguous, and we must be careful not to overgeneralize from the behavior we observe. We may feel hurt by the listless "Hi" we receive from a good friend unless we remember that the listlessness could have been brought on by a headache, lack of sleep, preoccupation, or some other factor we don't know about. We would be unwise to assume we are being personally rejected if this friend doesn't smile and stop to talk with us every single morning.

We should always be alert to *all* cues and try to get as much information as possible on which to base our conclusions. One way to organize our thinking about nonverbal communication is to think in terms of spatial cues, visual cues, and vocal cues. In considering each of these, we should not overlook the fact that any communication occurs in a specific environmental setting. This setting influences much of the nonverbal interaction that takes place. The weather can affect how we behave just as much as the actual setting—cafeteria, classroom, car, park bench, or wherever.

SPATIAL CUES

Spatial cues are the distances we choose to stand or sit from others. Each of us carries with us something called "informal space." We might think of this as a bubble; we occupy the center of the bubble. This bubble expands or contracts depending on varying conditions and circumstances such as the

Age and sex of those involved
Cultural and ethnic background of the participants
Topic or subject matter
Setting for the interaction
Physical characteristics of the participants (size or shape)
Attitudinal and emotional orientation of partners
Characteristics of the interpersonal relationship (like friendship)
Personality characteristics of those involved

In his book *The Silent Language*, Edward T. Hall, a cultural anthropologist, identifies the distances that we assume when we talk with others. He calls these distances intimate, personal, social, and public. In many cases, the adjustments that occur in these distances result from some of the factors listed above.

Intimate Distance

At an *intimate distance* (0 to 18 inches), we often use a soft or barely audible whisper to share intimate or confidential information. Physical contact becomes easy at this distance. This is the distance we use for physical comforting, love-making, and physical fighting, among other things.

Personal Distance

Hall identified the range of 18 inches to 4 feet as *personal distance*. When we disclose ourselves to someone, we are likely to do it within this distance. The topics we discuss at this range may be somewhat confidential, and usually are personal and mutually involving. At personal distance we are still able to touch each other if we want to. This is likely to be the distance between people conversing at a party, between classmates in a casual conversation, or within many work relationships. This distance assumes a well-established acquaintanceship. This is probably the most comfortable distance for free exchange of feedback.

Social Distance

When we are talking at a normal level with another person, sharing concerns that are not of a personal nature, we usually use the *social distance* (4 to 12 feet). Many of our on-the-job conversations take place at this distance. Seating arrangements in living rooms may be based on "conversation groups" of chairs placed at a distance of 4 to 7 feet from each other. Hall calls 4 to 7 feet the close phase of social distance; from 7 to 12 feet is the far phase of social distance.

The greater the distance, the more formal the business or social discourse conducted is likely to be. Often, the desks of important people are broad enough to hold visitors at a distance of 7 to 12 feet. Eye contact at this distance becomes more important to the flow of communication; without visual contact one party is likely to feel shut out and the conversation may come to a halt.

Public Distance

Public distance (12 feet and farther) is well outside the range for close involvement with another person. It is impractical for interpersonal communication. We are limited to what we can see and hear at that distance; topics for conversation are relatively impersonal and formal; and most of the communication that occurs is in the public-speaking style, with subjects planned in advance and limited opportunities for feedback. . . .

VISUAL CUES

Greater visibility increases our potential for communicating because the more we see and the more we can be seen, the more information we can send and receive. Mehrabian found that the more we direct our face toward the person we're talking to, the more we convey a positive feeling to this person. Another researcher has confirmed something most of us discovered long ago, that looking directly at a person, smiling, and leaning toward him or her conveys a feeling of warmth.

Facial Expression

The face is probably the most expressive part of the human body. It can reveal complex and often confusing kinds of information. It commands attention because it is visible and omnipresent. It can move from signs of ecstasy to signs of despair in less than a second. Research results suggest that there are ten basic classes of meaning that can be communicated facially: happiness, surprise, fear, anger, sadness, disgust, contempt, interest, bewilderment, and determination. Research has also shown that the face may communicate information other than the emotional state of the person—it may reveal the thought processes as well. In addition, it has been shown that we are capable of facially conveying not just a single emotional state but multiple emotions at the same time. . . .

Eye Contact

A great deal can be conveyed through the eyes. If we seek feedback from another person, we usually maintain strong eye contact. We can open and close communication channels with our eyes as well. Think of a conversation involving more than two people . . .

The Body

The body reinforces facial communication. But gestures, postures, and other body movements can also communicate attitudes. They can reveal differences in status, and they can also indicate the presence of deception. With respect to attitudes, as noted previously, body movements also reveal feelings of liking between people.

According to some investigators, a person who wants to be perceived as warm should shift his or her posture toward the other person, smile, maintain direct eye contact, and keep the hands still. People who are cold tend to look around, slump, drum their fingers, and, generally, refrain from smiling. . . .

Personal Appearance

Even if we believe the cliché that beauty is only skin-deep, we must recognize that not only does our personal appearance have a profound effect on our self-image, but it also affects our behavior and the behavior of people around us. Our physical appearance provides a basis for first and sometimes long-lasting impressions. . . .

—Weaver, Richard, *Understanding Interpersonal Communication,* 5th Ed., © 1990. Reprinted and electronically reproduced by permission of Pearson Education, Inc., Upper Saddle River, NJ.

EXERCISE 2–7

CHECKING YOUR RECALL

Directions: *Complete this exercise after you have previewed the selection titled "Types of Nonverbal Cues." For each item, indicate whether the statement is true or false by marking T or F in the space provided.*

_____ 1. Spatial cues refer to the manner and posture in which we sit or stand.

_____ 2. Nonverbal communication is sometimes ambiguous or unclear.

_____ 3. The social distance is used for nonpersonal conversations.

_____ 4. Voices are slightly louder and higher pitched in the intimate distance.

_____ 5. The distance in which people are farthest apart is the social distance.

_____ 6. Hands are the most expressive part of the body.

_____ 7. The author discusses four types of distance.

_____ 8. Personal distance can affect the behavior of other people.

_____ 9. Visual cues are provided by facial expression, eye contact, personal appearance, and body movement.

_____10. Gesture and posture provide important nonverbal cues.   ■

Did you score 80 percent or higher on the exercise? You may have noticed that the exercise did not test you on specific facts and details. Rather, the questions provided a fairly accurate measure of your recall of the *main ideas* of the selection. If you scored 80 percent or above, your previewing was successful because it acquainted you with most of the major ideas contained in the selection.

This exercise suggests that previewing provides you with a great deal of information about the overall content of the article before you read it. It allows you to become familiar with the main ideas and acquaints you with the basic structure of the material.

TECH SUPPORT **Previewing Online Sources**

Previewing online sources is different from previewing written sources, and is even more important to do, since online sources vary widely in content, format, and reliability (see Chapter 10). Use the following tips:

- Get a sense of the layout of the page.
- Take note of advertisements and delete them, if possible.
- Locate the search box.
- Discover how to navigate the site. Look for tabs, buttons, or links.
- Check to see whether the site has "Contact" and "About Us" tabs.

Adapting Previewing to Various Types of Materials

If the key to becoming a flexible reader lies in adapting techniques to fit the material and your learning style, the key to successful previewing is the same. You must adjust the way you preview to the type of material you are working with. A few suggestions to help you make these adjustments are summarized in the Need to Know box "How to Adjust Previewing to the Material."

NEED TO KNOW How to Adjust Previewing to the Material

Type of Material	Special Features to Consider
Textbook chapters	Summary
	Vocabulary list
	Review and discussion questions
Articles and essays	Title
	Introductory paragraphs
	Concluding paragraphs
Articles without headings	First sentences of paragraphs
Tests and exams	Instructions and directions
	Number of items
	Types of questions
	Point distribution
Web sites	Functions (search box, etc.)
	Navigation
	Source, About/Contact Information
	Advertisements (or lack thereof)

LEARNING STYLE TIPS

If you tend to be a(n) . . .	Then strengthen your previewing skills by . . .
Auditory learner	Asking and answering guide questions aloud
Visual learner	Writing guide questions and their answers

Why Previewing Is Effective

Previewing is effective because it

- Helps you become interested and involved with what you will read.
- Gives you basic information about the organization and content of the article.
- Focuses your attention on the content of the article.
- Allows you to read somewhat faster because the material is familiar.
- Provides you with a mental outline of the material.

EXERCISE 2–8

ADAPTING PREVIEWING

Directions: *Working with another student, choose three of the materials from the following list. Discuss how you would adapt your previewing technique to suit the material.*

1. a front-page newspaper article
2. a poem
3. a short story
4. a mathematics textbook
5. a newspaper editorial or letter to the editor
6. a new edition of your college catalog
7. a sales brochure from a local department store

EXERCISE 2–9

PREVIEWING A TEXTBOOK CHAPTER

Directions: *Select a chapter from one of your textbooks and preview it, using the guidelines included in this chapter. Then answer the following questions.*

Textbook title: _____

Chapter title: _____

1. What general subject does the chapter discuss?

    _____

2. How does the textbook author approach or divide the subject?

    _____

3. What special features does the chapter contain to aid you in learning the content of the chapter?

    _____

4. What are the major topics discussed in this chapter?

    _____

Predicting

Previewing is similar to watching a film preview. When you see a film preview, you think about what the film will be about, how it will achieve its cinematic goals, and whether or not you want to see it. To do this, you anticipate or make predictions based on the preview. For example, you may predict that the film will be violent and frightening or sentimental and romantic. You might also predict how the film will develop or how it will end.

After previewing you should be able to make predictions about the content and organization of the material and make connections with what you already know about the topic.

Making Predictions

Predictions are educated guesses about the material to be read. For example, you might predict an essay's focus, a chapter's method of development, or the key points to be presented within a chapter section. Table 2.3 presents examples of predictions that may be made.

TABLE 2.3 Sample Predictions

Headings	Predictions
Highlights of Marketing Research History	An overview of the history of market research will be presented.
Why Do Hot Dogs Come in Packs of Ten?	Packaging of products and profitability will be discussed.
A Sample Fast-Food Promotional Plan	A fast-food chain will be used as an example to show how fast-food restaurants promote (sell) their products.

Opening Sentences	Predictions
Marketers have been the objects of criticism from several consumer groups as well as from governmental agencies.	The section will discuss consumer groups' objections first, then governmental objections.
The situations and problems consumers face directly influence their purchasing behavior.	The section will give examples of situations and problems and explain why or how purchasing behavior is affected.
The key to determining a product's demand is the estimation of the total market and its anticipated share.	The section will explain this process.

You make predictions based on your experience with written language, your background knowledge, and your familiarity with the subject. As you work through remaining chapters in this text, you will become more familiar with the organization of written materials, and your ability to make predictions will improve.

To get started making predictions, keep the following questions in mind:

- What clues does the author give?
- What will this material be about?
- What logically would follow?
- How could this be organized?

| EXERCISE 2–10 | **MAKING PREDICTIONS** |

Directions: *Predict the content or organization of each of the following sections of a sociology textbook based on these chapter headings.*

1. Inequality in the United States

   _____

   _____

2. Nontraditional Marital and Family Lifestyles

   _____

   _____

3. The Development of Religious Movements

   _____

   _____

4. Education and Change in the 1990s

   _____

   _____

5. The Automobile, the Assembly Line, and Social Change

   _____

   _____

6. Health-Care Systems in Other Countries

   _____

   _____

7. Computers in the Schools

   _____

   _____

8. Sociology and the Other Sciences

   _____

   _____

9. The Consequences of Sexual Inequality

   _____

   _____

10. What Is Religion?

   _____

   _____

Making Connections

Once you have previewed an assignment and predicted its content and organization, an important next step is to call to mind what you already know about the subject. Do this by making connections between the material to be read and your background knowledge and experience.

There are several reasons for making such connections:

1. **Learning occurs more easily if you can relate new information to information already stored.**

2. **Tasks become more interesting and meaningful if you can connect them to your own experience or to a subject you have already learned.**

3. **Material is easier to learn if it is familiar and meaningful.** For example, it is easier to learn a list of real words (sat, can) than a list of nonsense syllables (taf, cag). Similarly, it is easier to learn basic laws of economics if you have examples from your experience with which to associate them.

Search your previous knowledge and experience for ideas or information that you can connect the new material to in an assignment. Think of this process as tying a mental string between already stored information and new information. As you pull out old information you will find that you also recall new information. Here are a few examples of the kinds of connections students have made:

- "This chapter section is titled Stages of Adulthood—it should be interesting to see which one I'm in and which my parents are in."

- "I'll be reading about types of therapy for treating mental problems. I remember hearing about the group therapy sessions my aunt attended after her divorce . . . ."

- "This chapter is titled "Genetics"—I wonder if it will discuss chromosome mapping or genetic testing."

Use the suggestions in the box below to activate your prior knowledge.

NEED TO KNOW Using Prior Knowledge

To draw on your prior knowledge and experience for less familiar subjects, think about the subject using one of the following techniques:

1. Ask as many questions as you can about the topic, and attempt to answer them.

2. Divide the subject into as many features or subtopics as possible.

3. Free-associate or write down anything that comes to mind related to the topic.

Each of these techniques is demonstrated in Figure 2.1 (p. 74). Although the results differ, each technique forces you to think, draw from your experience, and focus your attention.

Which technique you use depends on the subject matter you are working with and on your learning style. Dividing a subject into subtopics may *not* work well for an essay in philosophy but may be effective for reading about television programming. Likewise, free association may work well for a creative learner, while dividing into subtopics may be more effective for a more pragmatic learner.

FIGURE 2.1 Techniques for Activating Your Knowledge

Topic: The Immune System

Technique	*Demonstration*
Asking questions	How does the immune system work?
	What does it do?
	What happens when it does not work?
	Are there other diseases, similar to AIDS, yet undiscovered?
	Does stress affect the immune system?
	Does diet affect the immune system?
Dividing into subtopics	Diseases of immune system
	Operation
	Functions
	Effects
	Limitations
Free association	The immune system protects the body from disease and infection.
	It attacks body invaders and destroys them.
	When illness occurs the immune system has failed. AIDS is a disease affecting the immune system.
	Stress may affect the body's defenses.

EXERCISE 2–11   **MAKING CONNECTIONS**

Directions: *Assume you have previewed a chapter in a sociology text on domestic violence. Discover what you already know about domestic violence by writing a list of questions about the topic.*

■

EXERCISE 2–12   **ACTIVATING YOUR BACKGROUND KNOWLEDGE**

Directions:

Step 1: *Preview one of the readings at the end of the chapter. Activate your previous knowledge and experience by*

1. dividing the subject into subtopics.

2. writing a list of questions about the topic.

3. writing for two minutes about the topic, recording whatever comes to mind.

Step 2: *Evaluate the techniques used in Step 1 by answering the following questions:*

1. Which technique seemed most effective? Why?

2. Might your choice of technique be influenced by the subject matter with which you are working?

3. Did you discover you knew more about the topic than you initially thought?

EXERCISE 2–13

Working
COLLABORATIVELY

ACTIVATING YOUR KNOWLEDGE

Directions: *Connect each of the following headings, taken from a psychology text, with your own knowledge or experience. Discuss or summarize what you already know about each subject.*

1. Pain and Its Control

2. Television and Aggressive Behavior

3. Problems of Aging

4. Sources of Stress

5. Eating Disorders

■ Developing Guide Questions

Goal 5
Develop guide
questions

When you order a hamburger, go to the bank, or send a text message, you have a specific purpose in mind. In fact, most of your daily activities are purposeful; you do things for specific reasons to accomplish some goal.

Reading should also be a purposeful activity. Before you begin reading any article, selection, or chapter, you should know what you want to accomplish by reading it. Your purpose should vary with the situation. You might read a magazine article on child abuse to learn more about the extent of the problem. You may read a sociology text chapter to locate facts and figures about the causes, effects, and extent of child abuse. Your purpose for reading should be as specific as possible. One of the best ways to develop specific purposes is to form guide questions.

How to Develop Guide Questions

Guide questions can be formed by turning the chapter or essay titles and headings into questions that you try to answer as you read. For instance, for a chapter from a sociology text titled "Methods of Studying Society," you could ask, "What are the methods of studying society?" As you read the

> **EFFICIENCY TIP**
> College reading assignments often have two parts: (1) a reading and (2) an activity based on the reading. Previewing the *activity* you will need to complete is often an effective way to determine your reading purpose. For example, if the assignment asks you to list three good examples from the reading, you should watch for and mark good examples as you read.

chapter, look for the answer. Here are a few other titles or headings and questions that you might ask about them:

Title:	Bringing Science Under the Law
Questions:	How can science be brought under the law?
	Why should science be brought under the law?
Heading:	The Life Cycle of Social Problems
Questions:	What are the stages in the life cycle of social problems?
	What social problems have a life cycle?
Heading:	The Development of the Women's Movement
Questions:	How did the women's movement develop?
	Why did it develop?

Asking the Right Guide Questions

To put guide questions to their best use, you must ask the right questions:

- *What, why,* or *how* questions are useful because they usually require you to think or to consolidate information and ideas.
- *Who, when,* or *where* questions are less useful because they can often be answered in a word or two; they often refer to a specific fact or detail rather than to larger ideas or concepts.

EXERCISE 2–14   **WRITING GUIDE QUESTIONS**

Directions: *For each of the following titles or headings, write a guide question that would be useful in guiding your reading of the material.*

1. We Ask the Wrong Questions About Crime Sample Answers

   _____

2. The Constitution: New Challenges

   _____

3. Political Party Functions

   _____

4. Ghana and Zimbabwe—A Study in Contrasts

   _____

5. Comparing X-Rays and Visible Light

   _____

| **EXERCISE 2-15** | **WRITING GUIDE QUESTIONS** |

Directions: *Select a chapter from one of your textbooks that you are about to read. Write a guide question for each title and major heading. After you have used these questions to guide your reading, identify the weak questions and rephrase them in a way that would have been more useful to you.*

■ Thinking Critically: Developing a Questioning Mind-Set

Goal 6
Develop a questioning mind-set

Guide questions help you identify what is important to learn and remember, but they are not the only type of questions you should ask. It is also useful to ask *critical questions*—questions that will help you analyze and interpret what you read. Here are several critical questions that will help you develop a questioning mind-set.

1. What does the writer expect me to understand or believe after reading this?
2. What is the writer leading up to? (What ideas will come next?)
3. How much and what kind of evidence does the writer offer in support of his or her ideas?
4. Does the writer present both sides of the story, or only one side?
5. Is the writer biased in favor of or against the topic?
6. Does the reading come from a reliable source?
7. What are the writer's qualifications?
8. Why are these ideas important?
9. How does this information fit with other things I'm learning?
10. How can I use this information?

EXERCISE 2-16   **ANSWERING QUESTIONS ABOUT READING EXCERPTS**

Directions: *Use the excerpts found in this chapter to answer the following questions.*

1. Reread "Communication and the Skin" (p. 56). What is the single most important point the authors expect you to understand after you have read the selection? How does this new understanding add to your knowledge of or experience with the topic of human communication?

_____

_____

_____

2. Reread "African-American Women as Writers" (p. 58). Underline at least two sentences that reveal the authors' attitude toward the subject.

3. How could you use the information found in "Types of Nonverbal Cues" (pp. 64–67)?

_____

_____

SELF-TEST SUMMARY

Goal 1	1. What does active reading mean?	Active reading is a process of staying focused on the material you are reading before, during, and after reading it. It involves the activities of reading, thinking, predicting, connecting, and assessing your performance. It means participating consciously and directly in the reading process.
Goal 2	2. What academic thinking skills do your instructors expect you to demonstrate?	Your instructors expect you to function at six different levels of thinking. They expect you to work with ideas that involve: • Remembering—recalling information or facts • Understanding—grasping the meaning of facts • Applying—using knowledge in new situations • Analyzing—seeing relationships among ideas and how things work • Evaluating—making judgments about ideas • Creating—putting ideas together to form something new
Goal 3	3. What is the purpose of comprehension monitoring?	Comprehension monitoring helps you keep track of your comprehension while reading. By recognizing positive and negative comprehension signals, you will be aware of your level of comprehension and will be able to correct incomplete comprehension.
Goal 4	4. Why are previewing and predicting useful activities?	Previewing allows you to become familiar with the organization and content of the material before reading it, providing you with a "road map" to guide you through the material. Predicting helps you discover what you already know about a topic and connect this with the material to be read.
Goal 5	5. How are guide questions helpful?	Guide questions enable you to establish purposes for reading. They focus your attention and improve your retention.
Goal 6	6. How can you develop a questioning mind-set?	Ask critical questions that help you analyze and interpret content.

READING SELECTION 3 SOCIOLOGY

The Sociology of Sports

John J. Macionis

About the Reading

TEXTBOOK
EXCERPT

"The Sociology of Sports" is taken from an introductory sociology textbook by John J. Macionis. Much of college reading examines different perspectives on a topic. This reading provides an example of multiple viewpoints on the topic of sports.

Planning Your Reading Strategy*

Directions: *Activate your thinking by previewing the reading (see the Need to Know box on page 64) and answering the following questions.*

_____ 1. Based on your preview of the graphic included with the reading, which topic do you think the reading will discuss?
   a. the differences between baseball and football
   b. racial patterns in professional sports
   c. the difference between baseball's Major Leagues and Minor Leagues
   d. college sports championships, such as the NCAA tournament

_____ 2. Based on your preview of the reading, which of the following is not a function of sports?
   a. They reflect the players' social status.
   b. They help people get into good physical shape.
   c. They provide opportunities for international Olympics competitions.
   d. They provide recreation and the ability to release aggression.

3. Which sport(s) do you play or follow? Do you have a favorite team? Have you ever thought about the pros and cons of professional sports and their effects on society?

■ Apply

1 Who doesn't enjoy sports? Children as young as six or seven take part in organized sports, and many teens become skilled at three or more. Weekend television is filled with sporting events for viewers of all ages, and whole sections of our newspapers are devoted to teams, players, and scores. In the United States, top players such as Alex Rodriguez (baseball), Tiger Woods (golf), and Serena Williams (tennis) are among our most famous celebrities. Sports in the United States are also a multibillion-dollar industry. What can we learn by applying sociology's theoretical approaches to this familiar part of everyday life?

■ The Functions of Sports

2 The functions of sports include providing recreation as well as offering a means of getting in physical shape and a relatively harmless way to let off steam. Sports have important latent functions as well, which include building social relationships and also creating tens of thousands of jobs across the country. Participating in sports encourages competition and the pursuit of success, both of which are

---

* The Scorecard on p. 83 enables you to compute your reading rate. In order to do so, be sure to record your starting time in the Scorecard box before you begin reading.

values that are central to our society's way of life.

3   Sports also have dysfunctional consequences. For example, colleges and universities try to field winning teams to build a school's reputation and also to raise money from alumni and corporate sponsors. In the process, however, these schools sometimes recruit students for their athletic skill rather than their academic ability. This practice not only lowers the academic standards of the college or university but also shortchanges athletes, who spend little time doing the academic work that will prepare them for later careers.

■ Sports and Conflict

4   The games people play reflect their social standing. Some sports—including tennis, swimming, golf, sailing, and skiing—are expensive, so taking part is largely limited to the well-to-do. Football, baseball, and basketball, however, are accessible to people at almost all income levels. Thus the games people play are not simply a matter of individual choice but also a reflection of their social standing.

5   Throughout history, men have dominated the world of sports. For example, the first modern Olympic Games, held in 1896, barred women from competition. Throughout most of the twentieth century, Little League teams barred girls based on the traditional ideas that girls and women lack the strength to play sports and risk losing their femininity if they do. Both the Olympics and the Little League are now open to females as well as males, but even today, our society still encourages men to become athletes while expecting women to be attentive observers and cheerleaders. At the college level, men's athletics attracts a greater amount of attention and resources compared to women's athletics, and men greatly outnumber women as coaches, even in women's sports. At the professional level, women also take a back seat to men, particularly in the sports with the most earning power and social prestige.

6   For decades, big league sports excluded people of color, who were forced to form leagues of their own. Only in 1947 did Major League Baseball admit the first African American player when Jackie Robinson joined the Brooklyn Dodgers. More than fifty years later, professional baseball honored Robinson's amazing career by retiring his number 42 on *all* of the teams in the league. In 2009, African Americans (13 percent of the U.S. population) accounted for 9 percent of Major League Baseball players, 67 percent of National Football League (NFL) players, and 77 percent of National Basketball Association (NBA) players.

7   One reason for the high number of African Americans in many professional sports is

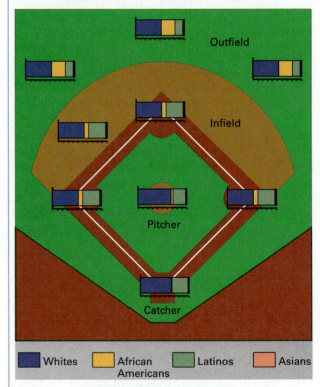

Whites   African Americans   Latinos   Asians

FIGURE A "Stacking" in Professional Baseball

Does race play a part in professional sports? Looking at the various positions in professional baseball, we see that white players are more likely to play the central positions in the infield, while people of color are more likely to play in the outfield. What do you make of this pattern?

Henslin, James M., Sociology. 14th Ed., (c) N/A. Reprinted and electronically reproduced by permission of Pearson Education, Inc., Upper Saddle River, NJ.

that athletic performance—in terms of batting average or number of points scored per game—can be precisely measured and is not influenced by racial prejudice. It is also true that some people of color make a particular effort to excel in athletics, where they see greater opportunity than in other careers. In recent years, in fact, African American athletes have earned higher salaries, on average, than white players.

8   But racial discrimination still exists in professional sports. For one thing, race is linked to the *positions* athletes play on the field, in a pattern called "stacking." Figure A shows the results of a study of race in professional baseball. Notice that white athletes are more concentrated in the central "thinking" positions of pitcher (68 percent) and catcher (64 percent). By contrast, African Americans represent only 4 percent of pitchers and 1

percent of catchers. At the same time, 9 percent of infielders African Americans, as are 28 percent of outfielders, positions characterized as requiring "speed and reactive ability."

9   More broadly, African Americans have a large share of players in only five sports: baseball, basketball, football, boxing, and track. And across all professional sports, the vast majority of managers, head coaches, and team owners are white.

10   Who benefits most from professional sports? Although many individual players get sky-high salaries and millions of fans enjoy following their teams, the vast profits sports generate are controlled by small number of people—predominantly white men. In sum, sports in the United States are bound up with inequalities based on gender, race, and wealth.

Examining Reading Selection 3*

Checking Your Vocabulary

Directions: *Use context, word parts, or a dictionary, if necessary, to determine the meaning of each word as it is used in the reading.*

___ 1. latent (paragraph 2)
   a. misguided
   b. expensive
   c. less apparent
   d. damaging

___ 2. dysfunctional (paragraph 3)
   a. typical
   b. unhealthy
   c. agreeable
   d. essential

___ 3. accessible (paragraph 4)
   a. unnecessary
   b. encouraged
   c. exclusive
   d. available

___ 4. excel (paragraph 7)
   a. do well
   b. attempt
   c. take part
   d. go away

___ 5. predominantly (paragraph 10)
   a. hardly
   b. poorly
   c. mainly
   d. secretly

Checking Your Comprehension

Directions: *Select the best answer.*

___ 6. This reading is primarily concerned with
   a. sociology.
   b. sports.
   c. gender differences.
   d. professional athletes.

*Writing About the Reading questions appear in the Instructor's Manual.

____ 7. The author wrote this selection in order to
   a. explore sports as a part of our society.
   b. encourage greater participation in sports.
   c. discuss discrimination in professional sports.
   d. argue that Americans place too much emphasis on sports.

____ 8. For most of the twentieth century, girls were not allowed to participate in Little League because of the idea that
   a. boys would be distracted by female teammates.
   b. girls were not strong enough to play.
   c. sports would damage girls' social standing.
   d. girls would not be able to learn the rules.

____ 9. The term "stacking" describes a pattern in which race is linked to
   a. the types of sports athletes play.
   b. the number of points scored per game.
   c. the positions athletes play on the field.
   d. coaching and management opportunities.

____ 10. An example of a sport that is limited to those with higher income levels is
   a. football.
   b. baseball.
   c. basketball.
   d. tennis.

Thinking Critically

____ 11. The best guide question based on this reading is
   a. What are the functions of sports?
   b. Which professional sport generates the most profits?
   c. When did sports become a multibillion-dollar industry?
   d. What percentage of NFL players are African American?

____ 12. Based on the reading, all of the following statements are true *except*
   a. Sports can have both positive and negative consequences.
   b. Women have achieved equal status with men in sports.
   c. Sports can be an indicator of social standing or prestige.
   d. In recent years, African American athletes have earned more than white players.

____ 13. The purpose of Figure A ("'Stacking' in Professional Baseball") is to
   a. demonstrate how baseball managers develop winning strategies.
   b. illustrate the skills required at each position in professional baseball.
   c. explain why the majority of major league pitchers are white.
   d. illustrate the concept of race being linked to the positions athletes play.

____ 14. The author's final point is that professional sports in the United States
   a. are a valid way for individual players to become rich.
   b. provide enjoyment for millions of fans.
   c. generate huge profits.
   d. still have inequalities of gender, race, and wealth.

____ 15. The author's attitude toward the subject can best be described as
   a. admiring.
   b. sarcastic.
   c. objective.
   d. informal.

Questions for Discussion

1. Discuss other functions and consequences of sports in addition to the ones described in paragraphs 2 and 3. Do you think the benefits outweigh any of the negative aspects of sports? Why or why not?

2. In what ways does society encourage men to become athletes and women to be observers? Do you think college and/ or professional sports are improving in this regard? Discuss why or why not.

3. Discuss the phenomenon of celebrity-athletes. Why do so many athletes become celebrities? Should professional athletes be viewed as role models?

4. Address the questions posed in the caption of Figure A. In your opinion, does race play a part in professional sports? Can you apply the concept of stacking to other sports?

Scorecard

Selection 3:   938 words

Finishing Time: ____   ____   ____
                HR.   MIN.   SEC.

Starting Time: ____   ____   ____
                HR.   MIN.   SEC.

Reading Time: ____   ____
                       MIN.   SEC.

WPM Score: _____

Comprehension Score: for Items 6–15
Number Right: _____ × 10 = _____%

Assessing Your Reading Strategy

1. How would you rate your comprehension of the reading? (Circle one.)
   Excellent   Good   Fair   Poor

2. Did you find your reading strategy effective?   Yes   No

3. Suppose you were given an assignment to read another article from a sociology textbook. Based on your experience with this selection, how would you adjust your reading strategy (if at all)?

_____

_____

READING SELECTION 4   LITERATURE: ESSAY

Just Walk On By: A Black Man Ponders His Power to Alter Public Space

Brent Staples
From *Harper's* magazine

About the Reading

MAGAZINE
ARTICLE

Brent Staples is a well-known black writer and New York Times *editorial columnist. This reading originally appeared in* Harper's *magazine, which often features lengthy articles examining controversial issues.*

Planning Your Reading Strategy*

Directions: *Activate your thinking by previewing the reading (see the Need to Know box on page 64) and answering the following questions.*

____ 1. To what type of information should you pay the most attention?
  a. the people mugged by the author when he was a young man
  b. the author's experiences and what they reveal about race in America
  c. the behavior of women in urban environments
  d. the author's perceptions of Chicago and New York

____ 2. This reading comes from *Harper's* magazine. Based on your preview, what kind of magazine do you think *Harper's* is?
  a. a celebrity gossip magazine
  b. a magazine geared toward businesspeople
  c. a fashion-oriented magazine with many photographs
  d. an intellectual magazine for educated people

  3. Based on your preview of the reading, how quickly do you think you should read the selection? (Circle one.)

  Very slowly   Slowly   At a moderate pace   Quickly   Very quickly

  4. What stereotypes exist for black males? How does the author encounter these stereotypes?

1 My first victim was a woman—white, well dressed, probably in her early twenties. I came upon her late one evening on a deserted street in Hyde Park, a relatively affluent neighborhood in an otherwise mean, impoverished section of Chicago. As I swung onto the avenue behind her, there seemed to be a discreet, uninflammatory distance between us. Not so. She cast back a worried glance. To her, the youngish black man—a broad six feet two inches with a beard and billowing hair, both hands shoved into the pockets of a bulky military jacket—seemed menacingly close. After a few more quick glimpses, she picked up her pace and was soon running in earnest. Within seconds she disappeared into a cross street.

"Just Walk on By" by Brent Staples in Ms. Magazine.

*The Scorecard on p. 89 enables you to compute your reading rate. In order to do so, be sure to record your starting time in the Scorecard box before you begin reading.

2   That was more than a decade ago. I was twenty-two years old, a graduate student newly arrived at the University of Chicago. It was in the echo of that terrified woman's footfalls that I first began to know the unwieldy inheritance I'd come into—the ability to alter public space in ugly ways. It was clear that she thought herself the quarry of a mugger, a rapist, or worse. Suffering a bout of insomnia, however, I was stalking sleep, not defenseless wayfarers. As a softy who is scarcely able to take a knife to a raw chicken—let alone hold it to a person's throat—I was surprised, embarrassed, and dismayed all at once. Her flight made me feel like an accomplice in tyranny. It also made it clear that I was indistinguishable from the muggers who occasionally seeped into the area from the surrounding ghetto. That first encounter, and those that followed, signified that a vast, unnerving gulf lay between nighttime pedestrians—particularly women—and me. And I soon gathered that being perceived as dangerous is a hazard in itself. I only needed to turn a corner into a dicey situation, or crowd some frightened, armed person in a foyer somewhere, or make an errant move after being pulled over by a policeman. Where fear and weapons meet—and they often do in urban America—there is always the possibility of death.

3   In that first year, my first away from my hometown, I was to become thoroughly familiar with the language of fear. At dark, shadowy intersections in Chicago, I could cross in front of a car stopped at a traffic light and elicit the *thunk, thunk, thunk, thunk* of the driver—black, white, male, or female—hammering down the door locks. On less traveled streets after dark, I grew accustomed to but never comfortable with people who crossed to the other side of the street rather than pass me. Then there were the standard unpleasantries with police, doormen, bouncers, cab drivers, and others whose business it is to screen out troublesome individuals *before* there is any nastiness.

4   I moved to New York nearly two years ago and I have remained an avid night walker.

In central Manhattan, the near-constant crowd cover minimizes tense one-on-one street encounters. Elsewhere—visiting friends in SoHo, where sidewalks are narrow and tightly spaced buildings shut out the sky—things can get very taut indeed.

5   Black men have a firm place in New York mugging literature. Norman Podhoretz in his famed (or infamous) 1963 essay, "My Negro Problem—And Ours," recalls growing up in terror of black males; they "were tougher than we were, more ruthless," he writes—and as an adult on the Upper West Side of Manhattan, he continues, he cannot constrain his nervousness when he meets black men on certain streets. Similarly, a decade later, the essayist and novelist Edward Hoagland extols a New York where once "Negro bitterness bore down mainly on other Negroes." Where some see mere panhandlers, Hoagland sees "a mugger who is clearly screwing up his nerve to do more than just *ask* for money." But Hoagland has "the New Yorker's quick-hunch posture for broken-field maneuvering," and the bad guy swerves away.

6   I often witness that "hunch posture," from women after dark on the warrenlike streets of Brooklyn where I live. They seem to set their faces on neutral and, with their purse straps strung across their chests bandolier style, they forge ahead as though bracing themselves against being tackled. I understand, of course, that the danger they perceive is not a hallucination. Women are particularly vulnerable to street violence, and young black males are drastically overrepresented among the perpetrators of that violence. Yet these truths are no solace against the kind of alienation that

comes of being ever the suspect, against being set apart, a fearsome entity with whom pedestrians avoid making eye contact.

7   It is not altogether clear to me how I reached the ripe old age of twenty-two without being conscious of the lethality nighttime pedestrians attributed to me. Perhaps it was because in Chester, Pennsylvania, the small, angry industrial town where I came of age in the 1960s, I was scarcely noticeable against a backdrop of gang warfare, street knifings, and murders. I grew up one of the good boys, had perhaps a half-dozen fist fights. In retrospect, my shyness of combat has clear sources.

8   Many things go into the making of a young thug. One of those things is the consummation of the male romance with the power to intimidate. An infant discovers that random flailings send the baby bottle flying out of the crib and crashing to the floor. Delighted, the joyful babe repeats those motions again and again, seeking to duplicate the feat. Just so, I recall the points at which some of my boyhood friends were finally seduced by the perception of themselves as tough guys. When a mark cowered and surrendered his money without resistance, myth and reality merged—and paid off. It is, after all, only manly to embrace the power to frighten and intimidate. We, as men, are not supposed to give an inch of our lane on the highway; we are to seize the fighter's edge in work and in play and even in love; we are to be valiant in the face of hostile forces.

9   Unfortunately, poor and powerless young men seem to take all this nonsense literally. As a boy, I saw countless tough guys locked away; I have since buried several, too. They were babies, really—a teenage cousin, a brother of twenty-two, a childhood friend in his mid-twenties—all gone down in episodes of bravado played out in the streets. I came to doubt the virtues of intimidation early on. I chose, perhaps even unconsciously, to remain a shadow—timid, but a survivor.

10   The fearsomeness mistakenly attributed to me in public places often has a perilous flavor. The most frightening of these confusions occurred in the late 1970s and early 1980s when I worked as a journalist in Chicago. One day, rushing into the office of a magazine I was writing for with a deadline story in hand, I was mistaken for a burglar. The office manager called security and, with an ad hoc posse, pursued me through the labyrinthine halls, nearly to my editor's door. I had no way of proving who I was. I could only move briskly toward the company of someone who knew me.

11   Another time I was on assignment for a local paper and killing time before an interview. I entered a jewelry store on the city's affluent Near North Side. The proprietor excused herself and returned with an enormous red Doberman pinscher straining at the end of a leash. She stood, the dog extended toward me, silent to my questions, her eyes bulging nearly out of her head. I took a cursory look around, nodded, and bade her good night. Relatively speaking, however, I never fared as badly as another black male journalist. He went to nearby Waukegan, Illinois, a couple of summers ago to work on a story about a murderer who was born there. Mistaking the reporter for the killer, police hauled him from his car at gunpoint and but for his press credentials would probably have tried to book him. Such episodes are not uncommon. Black men trade tales like this all the time.

12   In "My Negro Problem—And Ours," Podhoretz writes that the hatred he feels for blacks makes itself known to him through a variety of avenues—one being his discomfort with that "special brand of paranoid touchiness" to which he says blacks are prone. No doubt he is speaking here of black men. In time, I learned to smother the rage I felt at so often being taken for a criminal. Not to do so would surely have led to madness—via that special "paranoid touchiness" that so annoyed Podhoretz at the time he wrote the essay.

13   I began to take precautions to make myself less threatening. I move about with care, particularly late in the evening. I give a wide berth to nervous people on subway platforms during the wee hours, particularly when I have exchanged business clothes for jeans. If I happen to be entering a building behind some people who appear skittish, I may walk by, letting them clear the lobby before I return, so as not to seem to be following them. I have been calm and extremely congenial on those rare occasions when I've been pulled over by the police.

14   And on late-evening constitutionals along streets less traveled by, I employ what has proved to be an excellent tension-reducing measure: I whistle melodies from Beethoven and Vivaldi and the more popular classical composers. Even steely New Yorkers hunching toward nighttime destinations seem to relax, and occasionally they even join in the tune. Virtually everybody seems to sense that a mugger wouldn't be warbling bright, sunny selections from Vivaldi's *Four Seasons*. It is my equivalent of the cowbell that hikers wear when they know they are in bear country.

Examining Reading Selection 4

Complete this Exercise at myreadinglab.com

Checking Your Vocabulary

Directions: *Use context, word parts, or a dictionary, if necessary, to determine the meaning of each word as it is used in the reading.*

____ 1. affluent (paragraph 1)
    a. wealthy
    b. distant
    c. important
    d. foreign

____ 2. menacingly (paragraph 1)
    a. strikingly
    b. threateningly
    c. obviously
    d. seriously

____ 3. elicit (paragraph 3)
    a. create
    b. bring out
    c. disturb
    d. draw back

____ 4. avid (paragraph 4)
    a. careful
    b. frightened
    c. fearful
    d. enthusiastic

____ 5. retrospect (paragraph 7)
    a. looking forward in time
    b. looking back in time
    c. regretting an action or event
    d. dwelling on an action or event

Checking Your Comprehension

Directions: *Select the best answer.*

____ 6. Which of the following statements best describes the reading?
    a. It is an essay about why white women fear black men.
    b. It is a description of racial tensions in large cities.
    c. It is an argument for greater racial equality.
    d. It is a personal account of a black man's experiences and feelings about the way he is perceived in public places.

____ 7. The author may have been unaware of public reactions to him before age 22 because
    a. he was a member of a gang.
    b. he lived in a small town in Pennsylvania.

c. he wasn't noticeable among criminals and street gangs.
d. he was shy and withdrawn.

____ 8. The "mugging literature" the author
cites is
a. writings of other authors about
   fear of black males.
b. crime statistics about muggers.
c. writings that present statistics and
   objective facts about muggers.
d. literature describing the role of
   black men in society.

____ 9. The author regards the attitude that
men must be powerful and valiant as
a. a personal expression.
b. nonsense.
c. having historical justification.
d. legitimate.

____ 10. The "hunch posture" as described by
the author, is a(n)
a. protective, defensive posture.
b. disrespectful gesture.
c. aggressive movement.
d. signal that assistance is needed.

Thinking Critically

____ 11. The author's primary purpose in writing the article is to
a. persuade people to alter their public behavior toward blacks.
b. describe his feelings about reactions to him in public space.
c. familiarize the reader with problems of large cities.
d. argue that public space should not
   be altered.

____ 12. The author whistles Vivaldi to
a. state his music preferences.
b. suggest that he is unlike typical
   muggers.
c. indicate his level of musical
   expertise.
d. announce that he is unafraid.

____ 13. Which of the following best describes
the author's attitude about women's
fear of black men?
a. The author thinks their fear is
   unfounded.
b. The author regards their fear as
   exaggerated, as a hallucination.
c. The author finds their fear understandable but still has difficulty
   when it is applied to him.
d. The author is angry and feels he is
   not understood.

____ 14. To communicate his ideas, the author
relies most heavily on
a. logical reasoning.
b. statistics and "mugging
   literature."
c. personal experience.
d. fact.

____ 15. Which of the following would be the
best caption for the photo on page 85?
That is, which one works best with the
content of the article?
a. The author, Brent Staples, has a
   beard and close-cropped hair.
b. Some black men prefer to be
   called African-Americans.
c. Today Brent Staples looks more
   conservative then he did as a
   younger man.
d. Brent Staples.

Scorecard

Selection 4:   1,670 words

Finishing Time: _____ _____ _____
                  HR.   MIN.   SEC.

Starting Time: _____ _____ _____
                 HR.   MIN.   SEC.

Reading Time: _____ _____
                       MIN.   SEC.

WPM Score: _____

Comprehension Score: for Items 6–15
Number Right: _____ × 10 = _____%

Assessing Your Reading Strategy

1. How would you rate your comprehension of the reading? (Circle one.)
   Excellent   Good   Fair   Poor
2. Did you find your reading strategy effective?   Yes   No
3. Suppose you were given an assignment to read another article from *Harper's* magazine. Based on your experience with this selection, how would you adjust your reading strategy (if at all)?

   _____

   _____

Writing About Reading Selection 4

Checking Your Vocabulary

Directions: *Complete each of the following items; refer to a dictionary if necessary.*

1. Discuss the connotative meanings of the word *victim* (paragraph 1).

2. Define the word *quarry* (paragraph 2) and underline the word or phrase that provides a context clue for its meaning.

   _____

   _____

3. Define the word *episodes* (paragraph 11) and underline the word or phrase that provides a context clue for its meaning.

   _____

   _____

4. Determine the meanings of the following words by using word parts.
   a. *uninflammatory* (paragraph 1)

   _____

   _____

b. *unwieldy* (paragraph 2)

   _____

c. *unpleasantries* (paragraph 3)

   _____

d. *overrepresented* (paragraph 6)

   _____

   _____

e. *lethality* (paragraph 7)

   _____

Checking Your Comprehension

5. Summarize the problem the author is describing.

   _____

   _____

   _____

6. Why was Staples unaware of this problem until the age of 22?

   _____

7. In what sense does Staples use the word *victim*? In what sense is Staples himself a "victim"?

8. How has Staples altered his behavior in public?

Thinking Critically

9. Discuss the meaning of the title. How does Staples alter public space? How has it affected his life?

10. Discuss Staples' attitude toward his "victims." Does he perceive them as rational or irrational? Is he sympathetic? angry?

Questions for Discussion

1. In what other situations can an individual alter public space?
2. What is your opinion of the behavior of Staples' "victims"?
3. Do you feel Staples should have altered his behavior in public? Would you do the same?
4. After reading only the first paragraph, what did you think was happening?

think VISUALLY...

A portion of this photograph has been removed. Can you figure out what is missing? There are clues in the photograph to help you, including the placement of the object next to the girl's face and the fact that her mouth is open.

When reading a sentence or paragraph, if you find a word missing from your vocabulary, you can figure it out by studying the words around it that provide clues to meaning just as you studied the details in the photograph to help you figure out what was missing. In this chapter you will learn how to use context clues to figure out words you do not know. You will also learn how to expand your vocabulary, how to use word parts as clues to meaning, how to use word mapping, how to use an index card system for learning meanings, and how to use reference sources to build your vocabulary.

Learning GOALS

In this chapter, you will learn how to . . .

Goal 1 Expand your vocabulary

Goal 2 Determine a word's meaning from its context

Goal 3 Use word parts to figure out meanings of new words

Goal 4 Use the index card system to expand your vocabulary

Goal 5 Select and use the best vocabulary reference sources

Goal 6 Grasp denotative and connotative meanings

■ Expanding Your Vocabulary

Goal 1
Expand your
vocabulary

Your vocabulary can be one of your strongest assets or one of your greatest liabilities. It defines and describes you by revealing a great deal about your level of education and your experience. Your vocabulary contributes significantly to that all-important first impression people form when they meet you.

Are you constantly looking for new words that can expand your vocabulary? To stimulate your "word awareness," try the following quiz. Answer each item as either true or false.

_____ 1. There are 135 different meanings for the word *run*.

_____ 2. If you read an unfamiliar word in a textbook, the first thing you should do is look it up in the dictionary.

_____ 3. If *psycho* means "mind" and *-osis* means "diseased or abnormal condition," then a psychosis is a disease of the mind.

_____ 4. Memorizing a list is the most effective way to learn new vocabulary.

_____ 5. If you were taking a psychology course and were having difficulty distinguishing between the terms *drive* and *motive,* the most detailed reference source to consult would be a collegiate dictionary.

_____ 6. The statement "as the crow flies" means flapping one's wings like a crow.

Now, check your answers on the facing page.

These questions illustrate important topics covered in this chapter and ways you can expand your vocabulary.

A strong vocabulary provides both immediate academic benefits and long-term career effects. This portion of the chapter offers numerous suggestions for directing and developing your vocabulary so that it becomes one of your most valuable assets.

Remembering Words You Encounter

Regardless of how much time you spend recording and looking up words, most likely you will remember only those you use fairly soon after you learn them. Forgetting occurs rapidly after learning unless you take action to use and remember what you have learned.

Using What You Already Know

You recognize and understand certain words as you read, but you never use them in your own writing. Similarly, you understand certain words while listening, but you don't use them as part of your speaking vocabulary. Most likely your listening and reading vocabularies are larger than your speaking and writing vocabularies. In other words, you already know a large number of words that you are not using. Read the following list of words. You may know or have heard each word, but you probably do not use them in your own speech or writing.

conform	cosmic	contrite
congenial	congeal	cosmopolitan
congenital	contour	cosmos

You can begin to strengthen your vocabulary by experimenting with words you already know but do not use. Make a point of using one of these words each day, in both speaking and writing.

Answer Key

1. True. Yes! There are 135 meanings. One way you can expand your vocabulary is to learn additional meanings for already familiar words.
2. False. The first thing you should do is keep reading and try to figure out the word from the way it is used in the sentence (its context), as described in this chapter.
3. True. This item illustrates how knowledge of word parts can help you figure out unfamiliar words. Common word parts are discussed in this chapter.
4. False. List learning is ineffective; this chapter suggests a more effective index card system.
5. False. A more detailed source is a subject-area dictionary (see p. 116).
6. False. The statement is an idiom. It means flying in a straight line.

Learning Multiple Word Meanings

When you took the word awareness quiz, were you surprised to learn that the word *run* has a total of 135 meanings? You probably thought of meanings such as to *run* fast, a home *run*, and a *run* in a stocking, but the word has so many meanings that the entry requires nearly an entire dictionary page. You certainly have heard the word used in the following ways: to *run* the store, *run* upstream, *run* a machine, *run* a fever. On the other hand, you may not have known that *run* is a term used in billiards meaning a series of uninterrupted strokes or that in golf, *run* means to cause the ball to roll.

Most words in the English language have more than one meaning. Just open any standard dictionary to any page and glance down one column of words. You will see that more than one meaning is given for most words. Also, you can see that there is considerable opportunity to expand your vocabulary by becoming aware of additional meanings of words you already know.

✓ LEARNING STYLE TIPS

If you tend to be a . . .	Then strengthen your vocabulary by . . .
Creative learner	Experimenting with new words in both speech and writing
Pragmatic learner	Creating lists or computer files of words you need to learn

EXERCISE 3–1

Working
COLLABORATIVELY

UNDERSTANDING UNCOMMON MEANINGS

Directions: *Each of the following sentences uses a relatively uncommon meaning of the underlined word. After reading each sentence, write a synonym or brief definition of the underlined word. You may need to check a dictionary to locate a precise meaning. Compare your definitions with those of a classmate.*

1. Investors should keep at least a portion of their assets <u>fluid</u>.

   _____

2. The speech therapist noted that the child had difficulty with <u>glides</u>.

   _____

   _____

3. The prisoner held a <u>jaundiced</u> view of life.

   _____

4. The two garden hoses could not be connected without a <u>male</u> fitting.

   _____

5. The outcome of the debate was a <u>moral</u> certainty.

   _____

   _____

■ Using Contextual Aids

Goal 2

Determine a word's meaning from its context

The following tests are intended to demonstrate an important principle of vocabulary development. Before continuing with this section, try these vocabulary tests. Complete *both* tests before checking your answers, which appear in the paragraph following test B. While working on the second test *do not* return to the first test to change any answers.

Test A: Words Without Context

Directions: *For each item, choose the word that is closest in meaning to the first word.*

___ 1. verbatim
   a. word for word
   b. using verbs
   c. idea by idea
   d. using abbreviations

___ 2. sedentary
   a. very routine
   b. dull and boring
   c. exciting
   d. involves sitting

___ 3. thwarted
   a. initiated
   b. blocked
   c. disagreed
   d. imposed

___ 4. renounced
   a. gave up
   b. kept
   c. criticized
   d. applied for

___ 5. audacity
   a. patience
   b. boldness
   c. courtesy
   d. understanding

Number Correct: _____

Test B: Words in Context

Directions: *For each item, choose the word that is closest in meaning to the underlined word.*

___ 1. It is more efficient to take lecture notes in your own words than to try to record the lecture verbatim.
   a. word for word
   b. using verbs
   c. idea by idea
   d. using abbreviations

___ 2. Office work is quite sedentary, while in factory work you are able to move around more.
   a. very routine
   b. dull and boring
   c. exciting
   d. involves sitting

___ 3. Joe's parents thwarted his efforts to get a student loan; they refused to co-sign for him.
   a. initiated
   b. blocked
   c. disagreed
   d. imposed

___ 4. Despite his love of the country, he renounced his citizenship when the war broke out.
   a. gave up
   b. kept
   c. criticized
   d. applied for

___ 5. The woman had the audacity to return the dress to the store after wearing it several times.
   a. patience
   b. boldness
   c. courtesy
   d. understanding

Number Correct: _____

Now score each test. The answers to both tests are the same. They are (1) a, (2) d, (3) b, (4) a, (5) b. You most likely had more items correct on test B than on test A. Why did your scores differ when the words and choices were the same on both tests? The answer is that test B was easier because the words were presented *in context;* the words around the underlined word provide clues to its meaning. Test A, on the other hand, had no sentences in which the words were used, and it provided no meaningful clues at all.

These tests demonstrate that you can often figure out the meaning of an unknown word by looking for clues in the sentence or paragraph in which it appears. In the rest of this section you will learn how to use the four most common clues that context can provide about the meaning of an unknown word.

EFFICIENCY TIP
Examining context clues is often the fastest way to figure out the meaning of an unknown word. Context clues fall into four general categories: *definition clues, example clues, contrast clues,* and *inference clues.*

Definition Clues

There are two common ways writers provide definitions:

- As **formal definitions**, such as those you might find in a dictionary. In these cases the meaning of the word is stated directly.
- As **indirect definitions**, which means the author restates an idea or offers a synonym, a word that means the same thing as the unfamiliar word.

FORMAL DEFINITIONS

Horology is the science of measuring time.

Induction refers to the process of reasoning from the known to the unknown.

Metabolism refers to the rate at which the body's cells manufacture energy from food or produce new cells.

Notice that in each example the boldfaced word is clearly and directly defined (by the highlighted part of the sentence). In fact, each sentence was written for the sole purpose of defining a term.

INDIRECT DEFINITIONS

Hypochondria, excessive worry over one's health, afflicts many Americans over 40.

There was a **consensus,** or agreement, among the faculty to require one term paper for each course.

Referring to the ability to "see" without using the normal sensory organs, **clairvoyance** is being studied at the Psychic Research Center.

Middle age (35 years to 65 years) is a time for strengthening and maintaining life goals.

In each of these examples, a meaning is also provided for the boldfaced term. A complete definition is not given, but sufficient information (highlighted) is included to give you a general idea of the meaning so that you can continue reading without stopping to check a dictionary. These definitions are usually set apart from the main part of a sentence by commas or parentheses, or they are expressed in a phrase or clause that further explains the sentence's core parts.

EXERCISE 3–2   **USING DEFINITION CLUES**

Directions: *In each sentence underline the portion that gives a definition clue for the boldfaced term.*

1. **Chemical reactivity,** the tendency of an element to participate in chemical reactions, is an important concept in combining elements.

2. The **effectiveness adjustment,** the process by which an organism meets the demands of its environment, depends on many factors.

3. **Deductive thinking** involves drawing a conclusion from a set of general principles.

4. **Interrogation,** or questioning, can be psychologically and emotionally draining.

5. The boy was **maimed,** or disfigured, as a result of the accident.   ■

Example Clues

A second way to determine the meaning of an unknown word is to look for examples that explain or clarify it. Suppose you do not know the meaning of the word *trauma*, and you find it used in the following sentence:

> Diane experienced many **traumas** during early childhood, including injury in an auto accident, the death of her grandmother, and the divorce of her parents.

This sentence gives three examples of traumas, and from the examples given you can conclude that *trauma* means a shocking or psychologically damaging experience. Here are a few other examples of sentences that contain example clues:

> **Toxic** materials, such as arsenic, asbestos, pesticides, and lead, can cause permanent bodily damage.
>
> **Unconditioned responses,** including heartbeat, blinking, and breathing, occur naturally in all humans.
>
> Crickets, grasshoppers, and cockroaches, for example, are **Orthopterans** and thrive in damp conditions.

You may have noticed in these sentences that the examples are signaled by certain words or phrases. *Such as, including,* and *for example* are used here. Other common signals are *for instance* and *to illustrate.*

USING EXAMPLE CLUES

> **Directions:** *Read each sentence and write a definition or synonym for each boldfaced word or phrase. Use the example clue to help you determine the meaning of the word or phrase.*

1. Because of their **metallic properties**, such as thermal and electrical conductivity, luster, and ductility (ability to be shaped into thin pieces), copper and lead are used for electrical wiring.

   _____

2. Perceiving, learning, and thinking are examples of **cognitive** processes.

   _____

3. Many **debilities** of old age, including loss of hearing, poor eyesight, and diseases such as arthritis, can be treated medically.

   _____

4. **Phobias** such as fear of heights, fear of water, or fear of crowds can be eliminated through conditioning.

   _____

5. Humans have built-in **coping mechanisms**; we shout when we are angry, cry when we are sad, and tremble when we are nervous.

   _____

Contrast Clues

It is sometimes possible to determine the meaning of an unknown word from a word or phrase in the context that has an opposite meaning. In the following sentence, notice how a word opposite in meaning from the boldfaced word provides a clue to its meaning.

> During the concert the audience was quiet, but afterward the crowd became **boisterous.**

Although you may not know the meaning of *boisterous*, you know that the audience was quiet during the concert and that afterward it acted differently. The word *but* suggests this. You know, then, that the crowd became the opposite of quiet (loud and noisy). Here are a few additional examples of sentences containing contrast clues:

> I **loathe** cats even though most of my friends love them.
>
> Although the cottage appeared **derelict,** we discovered that a family lived there on weekends.
>
> Pete, through long hours of study, successfully passed the exam; on the other hand, Sam's efforts were **futile.**

In these examples, you may have noticed that each contains a word or phrase that indicates that an opposite or contrasting situation exists. The signal words used in the examples were *even though, although,* and *on the other hand.* Other words that also signal a contrasting idea include *however, despite, rather, while, yet,* and *nevertheless.*

EXERCISE 3–4   **USING CONTRAST CLUES**

Directions: *Read each sentence and write a definition or synonym for each boldfaced word. Use the contrast clue to help you determine the meaning of the word.*

1. Al was always talkative, whereas Ed remained **taciturn.**

   _____

2. The microwave oven is becoming **obsolete;** the newer microwave-convection oven offers the user more cooking options.

   _____

3. My brother lives in the **remote** hills of Kentucky, so he seldom has the opportunity to shop in big cities.

   _____

4. One of the shoppers **succumbed** to the temptation of buying a new dress, but the others resisted.

   _____

5. Most members of Western society marry only one person at a time, but in other cultures **polygamy** is common and acceptable.

   _____

Inference Clues

Many times you can determine the meaning of a word you do not know by guessing or figuring it out. This process is called "drawing an inference." From the information that is given in the context you can infer the meaning of a word you are not familiar with. For instance, look at the following sentence:

My father is a **versatile** man; he is a successful businessman, sportsman, author, and sports car mechanic.

You can see that the father is successful at many types of activities, and you could reason that *versatile* means capable of doing many things competently.

Similarly, in the following example the general sense of the context provides clues to the meaning of the word *robust:*

> At the age of 77, Mr. George was still playing a skillful game of tennis. He jogged four miles each day and seldom missed his daily swim. For a man of his age he was extremely **robust.**

From the facts presented about Mr. George, you can infer that *robust* means full of health and vigor.

Sometimes your knowledge and experience can help you figure out the meaning of an unknown word. Consider, for instance, the following sentence:

> After tasting and eating most of seven different desserts, my appetite was completely **satiated.**

Your own experience would suggest that if you ate seven desserts, you would no longer feel like eating. Thus you could reason that *satiated* means full or satisfied.

✓ LEARNING STYLE **TIPS**

If you tend to be a(n) . . .	Then use context by . . .
Auditory learner	Reading the context aloud
Visual learner	Visualizing the context

EXERCISE 3–5   **USING INFERENCE CLUES**

Directions: *Read each sentence and write a definition or synonym for each boldfaced word. Try to figure out the meaning of each word by using information provided in the context.*

1. Although my grandfather is 82, he is far from **infirm;** he is active, ambitious, and healthy.

   _____

2. My **unscrupulous** uncle tried to sell as an antique a rocking chair he bought just last year.

   _____

3. My sister's lifestyle always angered and disappointed my mother; yet she **redeemed** herself by doing special favors for my mother's friends.

   _____

4. The wind howling around the corner of the house, the one rumored to have ghosts, made an **eerie** sound.

_____

5. We burst out laughing at the **ludicrous** sight of the basketball team dressed up as cheerleaders.

_____

EXERCISE 3–6   **USING CONTEXT CLUES**

Directions: _The meaning of the boldfaced word in each of the following sentences can be determined from the context. Underline the part of the sentence that contains the clue to the meaning of that word. Then write a definition or synonym for the boldfaced word._

1. Tremendous **variability** characterized the treatment of the mentally retarded during the Medieval Era, ranging from treatment as innocents to toleration as fools to persecution as witches.

_____

2. A citizen review panel **exonerated** the public official of any possible misconduct or involvement in the acceptance of bribes.

_____

3. The **tenacious** residents living near the polluted landfill held fast in opposition to the court's recommended settlement, while the chemical industry immediately agreed to the court settlement.

_____

4. The economy was in continual **flux**; inflation increased one month and decreased the next.

_____

5. The short story contained a series of **morbid** events: the death of the mother, the suicide of the grandmother, and the murder of a young child.

_____

6. Certain societies practice the custom of **levirate**, the required remarriage of a widow to her deceased husband's brother.

_____

7. Contrasted with a corporation, the risk and liability of a privately owned **proprietorship** are much higher.

_____

8. Many cultural systems are **dynamic**; they change with environment, innovations, and contact with other groups.

_____

9. Personality is the **configuration** of feelings and behaviors created in a person throughout the process of growing up.

_____

10. A **cornucopia** of luxury and leisure-time goods, designed to meet the requirements of the upper-middle-class standard of living, has flooded the economic market.

_____

EXERCISE 3–7

Academic APPLICATION

USING CONTEXT CLUES

Directions: *Select a chapter in one of your textbooks and identify at least five words whose meanings can be understood by using context clues. Write definitions for each of these words and list the types of context clues you used to arrive at their meanings.*

■ Analyzing Word Parts

Goal 3
Use word parts to figure out meanings of new words

Many words in the English language are made up of word parts called **prefixes**, **roots**, and **suffixes**. You might think of these as the beginning, middle, and ending of a word. These word parts have specific meanings and when added together can provide strong clues to the meaning of a particular word.

The prefixes, roots, and suffixes listed in the following tables (see Tables 3.1 to 3.3, pages 103–107) occur in thousands of words. For instance, suppose you do not know the meaning of the word *pseudonym*. If you know that *pseudo* means "false" and *nym* means "name," you can add the two parts together and realize that *pseudonym* means "a false name."

Before you begin to use these tables to figure out new words, you need to know:

1. Words do not always have a prefix or suffix.
2. Roots may vary in spelling when they are combined with certain prefixes.
3. Some roots are commonly found at the beginnings of words, others at the end, and still others can be found in either position.
4. You may recognize a group of letters but find that it does not carry the meaning of a prefix or root. For example, the letters **mis** in the word **missile** are part of the root and are not the prefix **mis-**, which means "wrong, bad."
5. Words can have more than one prefix, root, or suffix.

TABLE 3.1 Common Prefixes

Prefix	Meaning	Sample Word	Meaning of Sample Word
Prefixes referring to amount or number			
mono-/uni-	one	monocle/ unicycle	eyeglass for one eye/one wheel vehicle
bi-/di-/duo-	two	bimonthly/ diandrous/duet	twice a month/flower with two stamens/two singers
tri-	three	triangle	a figure with three sides and three angles
quad-	four	quadrant	any of four parts into which something is divided
quint-/pent-	five	quintet/ pentagon	a group of five/five-sided figure
deci-	ten	decimal	based on the number ten
centi-	hundred	centigrade	divided into 100 degrees, as a thermometer scale
milli-	thousand	milligram	one thousandth of a gram
micro-	small	microscope	an instrument used to see a magnified image of a small object
multi-/poly-	many	multipurpose/ polygon	having several purposes/figure with three or more sides
semi-	half	semicircle	half of a circle
equi-	equal	equidistant	at equal distances
Prefixes meaning "not" (negative)			
a-	not	asymmetrical	not identical on both sides of a central line
anti-	against	antiwar	against war
contra-	against, opposite	contradict	deny by stating the opposite
dis-	apart, away, not	disagree	have a different opinion
in-/il-/ir-/im-	not	incorrect/ illogical/ impossible	wrong/not having sound reasoning/not possible
mis-	wrongly	misunderstand	fail to understand correctly
non-	not	nonfiction	writing that is factual, not fiction
pseudo-	false	pseudoscientific	a system of theories or methods mistakenly regarded as scientific
un-	not	unpopular	not popular

(continued)

| TABLE 3.1 | **Common Prefixes** | (*Continued*) | |

Prefix	Meaning	Sample Word	Meaning of Sample Word
Prefixes giving direction, location, or placement			*not popular*
ab-	away	absent	away or missing from a place
ad-	toward	adhesive	able to stick to a surface
ante-/pre-	before	antecedent/ premarital	something that came before/before marriage
circum-/peri-	around	circumference/ perimeter	the distance around something/ border of an area
com-/col-/ con-	with, together	compile/collide/ convene	put together/come into violent contact/come together
de-	away, from	depart	leave, go away from
dia-	through	diameter	a straight line passing through the center of a circle
ex-/extra-	from, out of, former	ex-wife/ extramarital	former wife/occurring outside marriage
hyper-	over, excessive	hyperactive	unusually or abnormally active
inter-	between	interpersonal	existing or occurring between people
intro-/intra-	within, into, in	introvert/ intramural	turn or direct inwards/involving only students within the same school
post-	after	posttest	a test given after completion of a program or course
re-	back, again	review	go over or inspect again
retro-	backward	retrospect	a survey or review of the past
sub-	under, below	submarine	a ship designed to operate under water
super-	above, extra	supercharge	increase or boost the power of something
tele-	far	telescope	an instrument for making distant objects appear nearer
trans-	across, over	transcontinental	extending across a continent

TABLE 3.2 | Common Roots

Common Root	Meaning	Sample Word	Meaning of Sample Word
aster/astro	star	astronaut	a person trained to travel in space
aud/audit	hear	audible	able to be heard
bene	good, well	benefit	an advantage gained from something
bio	life	biology	the scientific study of living organisms
cap	take, seize	captive	a person who has been taken prisoner
chron/chrono	time	chronology	the order in which events occur
cog	to learn	cognitive	relating to mental processes
corp	body	corpse	dead body
cred	believe	incredible	difficult/impossible to believe
dict/dic	tell, say	predict	declare something will happen in the future
duc/duct	lead	introduce	bring in or present for the first time
fact/fac	make, do	factory	a building where goods are manufactured
geo	earth	geophysics	the physics of the earth
graph	write	telegraph	a system for sending messages to a distant place
log/logo/logy	study, thought	psychology	the scientific study of the human mind
mit/miss	send	permit/dismiss	allow or make possible
mort/mor	die, death	immortal	everlasting, not subject to death
path	feeling	sympathy	sharing the feelings of another
phon	sound, voice	telephone	a device used to transmit voices
photo	light	photosensitive	responding to light
port	carry	transport	carry from one place to another
scop	seeing	microscope	an instrument that magnifies small objects
scrib/script	write	inscription	a written note
sen/sent	feel	insensitive	lacking concern for others' feelings
spec/spic/spect	look, see	retrospect	a survey or review of the past
tend/tens/tent	stretch or strain	tension	mental or emotional strain
terr/terre	land, earth	territory	a geographic area, a tract of land
theo	god	theology	the study of the nature of God and religious belief

(continued)

TABLE 3.2   Common Roots   *(Continued)*

Common Root	Meaning	Sample Word	Meaning of Sample Word
ven/vent	come	convention	a meeting or formal assembly
vert/vers	turn	invert	put upside down or in the opposite position
vis/vid	see	invisible/video	not able to be seen
voc	call	vocation	a person's occupation or calling

TABLE 3.3   Common Suffixes

Suffix	Meaning	Sample Word	Meaning of Sample Word
Suffixes that refer to a state, condition, or quality			
-able	capable of	touchable	capable of being touched
-ance	characterized by	assistance	the action of helping
-ation	action or process	confrontation	an act of confronting or meeting face to face
-ence	state or condition	reference	an act or instance of referring or mentioning
-ible	capable of	tangible	capable of being felt, having substance
-ion	action or process	discussion	
-ity	state or quality	superiority	the quality or condition of being higher in rank or status
-ive	performing action	permissive	characterized by freedom of behavior
-ment	action or process	amazement	a state of overwhelming surprise or astonishment
-ness	state, quality, condition	kindness	the quality of being kind
-ous	possessing, full of	jealous	envious or resentful of another
-ty·	condition, quality characterized by	loyalty	the state of being loyal or faithful
-y		creamy	resembling or containing cream

(continued)

TABLE 3.3	Common Suffixes *(Continued)*		
Suffix	Meaning	Sample Word	Meaning of Sample Word
Suffixes that mean "one who"			
-an		Italian	one who is from Italy
-ant		participant	one who participates
-ee		referee	one who enforces the rules of a game or sport
-eer		engineer	one who is trained in engineering
-ent		resident	one who lives in a place
-er		teacher	one who teaches
-ist		activist	one who takes action to promote or advocate a cause
-or		advisor	one who advises
Suffixes that mean "pertaining to or referring to"			
-al		autumnal	occurring in or pertaining to autumn
-ship		friendship	the state of being friends
-hood		brotherhood	the relationship between brothers
-ward		homeward	leading towards home

✔ LEARNING STYLE TIPS

If you tend to be a(n) . . .	Then learn word parts by . . .
Social learner	Studying with a group of classmates
Independent learner	Making up review tests, or asking a friend to do so, and practicing taking the tests

EXERCISE 3–8 **USING PREFIXES**

Directions: *Use the list of common prefixes (Table 3.1, p. 103) to determine the meaning of each of the following words. Write a brief definition or synonym for each. If you are unfamiliar with the root, you may need to check a dictionary.*

1. misinformed

_____

2. rephrase

_____

3. interoffice

_____

4. circumscribe

_____

5. irreversible

_____

6. substandard

_____

7. supernatural

_____

8. telecommunications

_____

9. unqualified

_____

10. subdivision

_____

11. transcend

_____

12. hypercritical

_____

13. pseudointellectual

_____

14. contraception

_____

15. equivalence

_____

EXERCISE 3–9   **USING WORD PARTS**

Directions: _Use the list of common prefixes (Table 3.1, p. 103), the list of common roots (Table 3.2, p. 105), and the list of common suffixes (Table 3.3, p. 106) to determine the meaning of each of the following words. Write a brief definition or synonym for each, checking a dictionary if necessary._

1. chronology

_____

2. photocomposition

_____

3. introspection

_____

4. biology

_____

5. subterranean

_____

6. captivate

_____

7. conversion

_____

8. teleprompter

_____

9. monotheism

_____

10. exportation

_____ ■

EXERCISE 3–10   **IDENTIFYING WORD PARTS**

Academic APPLICATION

Directions: *From a chapter of one of your textbooks, select at least five new words made up of two or more word parts. For each word, identify those parts, list the meaning of each part, and then write a brief definition of the word.* ■

■ A System for Learning Unfamiliar Words

Goal 4
Use the index card system to expand your vocabulary

You are constantly exposed to new words in the normal course of your day. However, unless you make a deliberate effort to remember and use these words, many of them will fade from your memory. One of the most practical and easy-to-use systems for expanding your vocabulary is the index card system. It works like this:

1. **Whenever you hear or read a new word that you intend to learn, jot it down in the margin of your notes or mark it in some way in the material you are reading.**

2. **Later, write each new word on the front of an index card, then look up the meaning (or meanings) of the word and write it on the back.** You might also record the word's pronunciation or a sample sentence in which the word is used. Your cards should look like the ones shown in Figure 3.1

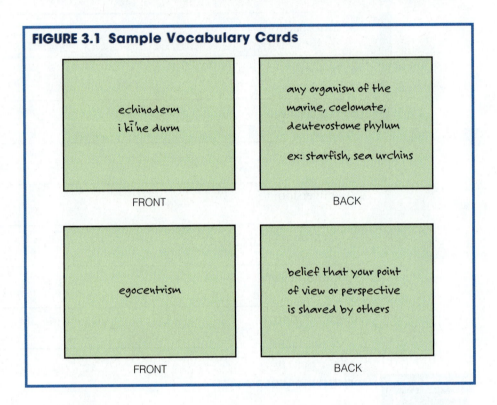

FIGURE 3.1 Sample Vocabulary Cards

echinoderm
i ki'ne durm

FRONT

any organism of the
marine, coelomate,
deuterostome phylum

ex: starfish, sea urchins

BACK

egocentrism

FRONT

belief that your point
of view or perspective
is shared by others

BACK

3. **Whenever you have a few spare minutes, go through your pack of index cards.** For each card, look at the word on the front and try to recall its meaning. Then check the back of the card to see if you were correct. If you were unable to recall the meaning or if you confused it with another word, retest yourself. Shuffle the cards after each use.

4. **After you have gone through your pack of cards several times, sort the cards into two piles;** separate the words you know from those that you have not learned. Then, putting the "known words" aside, concentrate on the words still to be learned. Shuffle the cards to change their order.

5. **Once you have mastered the entire pack of cards, periodically review them to refresh your memory and to keep the words current in your mind.**

6. **If you tend to be a social learner (see Learning Style Questionnaire, page 25 in Chapter 1), arrange to work with a classmate.** Quiz each other and discuss ways to remember difficult or confusing terms.

   This word card system of learning vocabulary is effective for several reasons:

   - It can be used in the spare moments that are often wasted waiting for a return phone call, waiting for a class to begin, or riding a bus.
   - The system enables you to spend time learning what you do *not* know rather than wasting time studying what you already know.
   - It prevents you from learning the material in a fixed order.

EXERCISE 3–11

Academic APPLICATION

PREPARING VOCABULARY CARDS

Directions: *Prepare a set of vocabulary cards for the new terminology in one chapter of one of your textbooks.*

Using Newly Learned Words

You must *use* a word for it to remain a part of your vocabulary. The first time you use a new word you may be unsure if you are using it correctly. Don't let this element of risk discourage you from trying new words. The first place to use the new words is in course-related situations. Try to use new words when studying with a friend or participating in a class discussion.

Be conscious of your word choices as you write. Select words that most clearly and accurately convey the meaning you intend. As a general rule, it is best to record your ideas first without thinking about exact choices of words. Then, as you reread what you have written, try to think of words that express your ideas more accurately or that provide more complete information.

■ Using Vocabulary Reference Sources

Goal 5
Select and use the best vocabulary reference sources

To develop a strong vocabulary you need the basic tools with which to work. Just as an artist cannot begin to paint without having a canvas and brushes, you cannot begin to strengthen your vocabulary without owning the necessary reference sources—a dictionary and a thesaurus—and having access to a subject-area dictionary.

Using a Dictionary

Types of Dictionaries

There are several types of dictionaries, each with its own purpose and use:

- **Online dictionaries** are readily available. Two of the most widely used are Merriam-Webster (http://www.m-w.com) and American Heritage (http://yourdictionary.com/index.shtml). Both of these sites feature an audio component that allows you to hear how a word is pronounced.

FLEXIBILITY TIP

In lighter reading materials (such as novels), you can often skip over unknown words and still achieve good comprehension. In academic materials, however, understanding a key term may be essential to understanding everything that follows it. In this case, it's worth stopping to consult a dictionary (or other reference) to determine the word's exact meaning. This is particularly true when reading math and science textbooks.

- **A pocket or paperback dictionary** is an inexpensive, easy-to-carry, shortened version of a standard desk dictionary. It is small enough to carry to classes and costs around $7.
- **A desk dictionary** is a more complete and extensive dictionary. Although a pocket dictionary is convenient, it is also limited in use. A pocket edition lists about 50,000 to 60,000 words; a standard desk edition lists up to 150,000 words. Also, the desk edition provides much more complete information about each word.

Several standard dictionaries are available in both desk and paperback editions. These include:

The Random House Dictionary of the English Language
Merriam-Webster's Collegiate Dictionary
The American Heritage Dictionary of the English Language

- An **unabridged dictionary** is found in the reference section of the library. The unabridged edition provides the most complete information on each word in the English language.

TECH SUPPORT **Using Online Dictionaries**

Online dictionaries have several important advantages over print dictionaries.

- **Audio component.** Some online dictionaries such as *Merriam-Webster Online* and *The American Heritage Dictionary of the English Language* feature an audio component that allows you to hear how words are pronounced.
- **Multiple dictionary entries.** Some sites, such as Dictionary.com, display entries from several dictionaries for each word you look up.
- **Misspellings.** If you aren't sure of how a word is spelled or mistype it, several possible words and their meanings will be provided.

Types of Information to Find in a Dictionary

A dictionary contains other types of useful information that can significantly expand your vocabulary. Here are some types of information a dictionary provides as shown in the sample online entry from http://www.dictionary.com.

com·ple·ment 🔊 [*n.* **kom**-pl*uh*-m*uh* nt; *v.* **kom**-pl*uh*-ment] —— Word pronunciation

? Origin

Parts of speech

noun

1. something that completes or makes perfect: *A good wine is a complement to a good meal.*

2. the quantity or amount that completes anything: *We now have a full complement of packers.*

3. either of two parts or things needed to complete the whole; counterpart.

4. full quantity or amount; complete allowance.

5. the full number of officers and crew required on a ship.

Meanings

⊕ **EXPAND** —————— Click here for additional, restrictive meanings

6. *Grammar.*
   a. a <u>word</u> or group of words that completes a grammatical construction in the predicate and that describes or is identified with the subject or <u>object</u>, as *small* in *The house is small* or *president* in *They elected her president.* Compare <u>object complement</u>, <u>subject complement</u>.

   b. any word or group of words used to complete a grammatical construction, especially in the predicate, including adverbials, as *on the table* in *He put it on the table,* infinitives, as *to go* in *They are ready to go,* and sometimes objects, as *ball* in *He caught the ball.*

7. *Geometry.* the quantity by <u>which</u> an angle or an arc falls short of 90° or a quarter of a circle. Compare <u>supplement</u> def. 4.

8. Also called **absolute complement**. *Mathematics.* the <u>set</u> of all the elements of a universal set not included in a given set.

9. *Music.* the interval that completes an octave when added to a given interval.

Meanings

verb (used with object)

12. to complete; form a complement to: *This belt complements the dress better than that one.*

13. *Obsolete.* to compliment.

Meanings

verb (used without object)

14. *Obsolete.* to compliment.

Meanings

Origin: ————————————— Word history

1350–1400; Middle English < Latin *complēmentum* something that completes, equivalent to complē (re) to fill up (see complete) + *-mentum* -ment

Related forms

com·ple·ment·er, *noun* ——————————— Alternate form of the word

Can be confused: complement, <u>compliment</u>, <u>supplement</u> (see synonym and usage notes at the current entry). ——————— Possible confusions

Synonyms

12. Complement, Supplement both mean to make additions to something. To complement is to provide something felt to be lacking or needed; it is often applied to putting together two things, each of which supplies what is lacking in the other, to make a complete whole: *Two statements from different points of view may complement each other.* To supplement is merely to add to: *Some additional remarks may supplement his address.*

Usage note

Complement and complement, which are pronounced alike and originally shared some meanings, have become separate words with entirely different meanings. As a noun, complement means "something that completes or makes perfect": *The rare old brandy was a perfect complement to the delicious meal.* As a verb, complement means "to complete": *A bright scarf complements a dark suit.*

Usage

—complement. Dictionary.com. Dictionary.com Unabridged. Random House, Inc. http://dictionary.reference.com/browse/complement. Based on the Random House Dictionary, © Random House, Inc. 2012.

1. **Word pronunciation.** Immediately after the word entry, you will find a pronunciation key that spells the word the way it sounds divided into syllables. The accented syllable of the word is in darker print.

2. **Part(s) of speech.** A word's part of speech is listed (sometimes in abbreviated form) after the word's pronunciation. If a word can function as several different parts of speech, the meanings are often divided according to part of speech.

3. **Variations of the word.** The entry often shows variations of the word and how spellings change when the word becomes plural or when an ending such as -*ing* is added.

4. **Information on word history.** This historical information tells you the language or languages from which the word evolved.

5. **Restrictive meanings.** Restrictive meanings are definitions that apply only when the word is being used in a specific field of study. For example, the sample online entry lists restrictive meanings in grammar, geometry, and music.

6. **Foreign expressions used in English.** Certain expressions from other languages have become widely used in the English language. These phrases often more accurately express an idea or feeling than do the English translations. The French expression *faux pas*, translated to mean a social blunder, is a good example.

7. **Idioms.** An idiom is a phrase that has meaning other than what the common meanings of the words in the phrase mean. For example, the phrase "wipe the slate clean" is not about slates. It means to start over. To find the meaning of an idiom, look under the key words in the phrase. To find the meaning of "eat crow," look under the entry for *crow*. You will discover that it means to admit you have been wrong.

EXERCISE 3–12   **USING A DICTIONARY**

Directions: *Use a dictionary to answer each of the following items. Write your answer in the space provided.*

1. What does the abbreviation *e.g.* stand for?

   _____

2. How is the word *deleterious* pronounced? (Record its phonetic spelling.)

   _____

3. From what languages is the word *delicatessen* taken?

   _____

4. Locate one restricted meaning for the word *configuration*.

   _____

   _____

5. What is the history of the word *mascot*?

_____

_____

_____

_____

6. What is the plural spelling of *addendum*?

_____

7. What type of punctuation is a virgule?

_____

_____

8. List a few words that contain the following sound: ī.

_____

9. Who or what is a Semite?

_____

10. Can the word *phrase* be used other than as a noun? If so, how?

_____

Choosing the Appropriate Meaning

A dictionary lists all the common meanings of a word, but usually you are looking for only one definition. For instance, suppose you were to read the following sentence and could not determine the meaning of *isometrics* from its context.

> The executive found that doing *isometrics* helped him to relax between business meetings.

The dictionary entry (*American Heritage Desk Dictionary*) for *isometrics* is:

> **i•so•met•ric** (īsə-mĕt'rĭk) or **i•so•met•ri[cal]** (-rĭ-kəl) adj. **1.** Of or exhibiting equality in dimensions or measurements. **2.** Of or being a crystal system of three equal axes at right angles to one another. **3.** Of or involving muscle contractions in which the ends of the muscle are held in place so that there is an increase in tension rather than a shortening of the muscle: *isometric exercises.* —n. **1.** A line connecting isometric points. **2. isometrics** *(used with a sing. verb).* Isometric exercise. [From Greek *isometros,* of equal measure : *isos,* equal + *metron,* measure.]

Notice that the meanings are grouped and numbered consecutively according to part of speech. If you are able to identify the part of speech of the word you are looking up, you can skip over all parts of the entry that do not pertain to that part of speech. For example, in the sample sentence, you can tell that *isometrics* is a noun.

If you cannot identify the part of speech of a word you are looking up, begin with the first meaning listed. Generally, the most common meaning appears first, and more specialized meanings appear toward the end of the entry.

When you find a meaning that could fit into the sentence you are working with, replace the word with its definition and then read the entire sentence. If the definition makes sense in the sentence, you can be fairly certain that you have selected the appropriate meaning.

EXERCISE 3–13   **FINDING MEANINGS**

Directions: *Write an appropriate meaning for the underlined word in each of the following sentences. Use the dictionary to help you find the meaning that makes sense in the sentence.*

1. He <u>affected</u> a French accent.

   _____

2. The <u>amphibian</u> took us to our destination in less than an hour.

   _____

3. The plane stalled on the <u>apron</u>.

   _____

4. We <u>circumvented</u> the problem by calculating in metrics.

   _____

5. Many consumers have become <u>embroiled</u> in the debate over the rising inflation rate.

   _____ ■

EXERCISE 3–14   **UNDERSTANDING FOREIGN EXPRESSIONS**

Directions: *Working in pairs, explain the meaning of each of the following foreign expressions (use a dictionary if needed). On a sheet of paper, for each expression, write a sentence that uses it correctly.*

1. *non sequitur*

   _____

   _____

2. *coup d'état*

   _____

   _____

3. *kowtow*

_____

_____

_____

4. *barrio*

_____

_____

_____

5. *Zeitgeist*

_____

_____ ■

Using a Thesaurus

A **thesaurus** is a dictionary of synonyms. Thesauruses are available in hardback and paperback, as well as on CD-ROM. They are written for the specific purpose of grouping words with similar meanings. A thesaurus is particularly useful when you have a word "on the tip of your tongue," so to speak, but cannot think of the exact word. It is also useful for locating a precise, accurate, or descriptive phrase to fit a particular situation.

Online thesauruses, such as http://www.thesaurus.com, can be particularly helpful. On these sites, you simply enter the word you wish to find a synonym for in the search bar. The results will then be divided into various definitions of the words and the different synonyms for that definition. For example, for the word *slow*, there are various definitions. One meaning is "unhurried or lazy" and another meaning is "behind or late." The online thesaurus gives you synonyms for both of these different meanings.

EXERCISE 3–15   **USING A THESAURUS**

Directions: *Using a print or online thesaurus, replace the underlined word or phrase with a more precise or descriptive word. You may rephrase the sentence if necessary.*

1. The instructor <u>talked about</u> several economic theories.

_____

2. My sisters, who had been apart for three years, were <u>happy</u> to be reunited at the wedding.

_____

3. The professor announced a <u>big</u> test for the end of next week.

_____

4. The student <u>watched</u> the elderly professor climb the stairs.

_____

5. Although it was short, the movie was <u>good</u>.

_____

Subject-Area Dictionaries

Many academic disciplines have specialized dictionaries that index important terminology used in that field. They list specialized meanings and
indicate how and when the words are used. For instance, the field of music
has *The New Grove Dictionary of Music and Musicians,* which lists and defines specialized vocabulary used in the field. Other subject-area dictionaries include:

> *Taber's Cyclopedic Medical Dictionary*
>
> *A Dictionary of Anthropology*
>
> *A Dictionary of Economics*

Find out if there is a subject-area dictionary for your major. Most of these
dictionaries are available in hardbound editions and online through your
library.

EXERCISE 3–16

Academic APPLICATION

IDENTIFYING SUBJECT-AREA DICTIONARIES

Directions: *Visit your college library or its Web site and discover and list
which subject-area dictionaries are available for the courses you are taking this
semester.*

■ Thinking Critically: Grasping Denotative and Connotative Meanings

Goal 6
Grasp denotative
and connotative
meanings

Suppose you own a jacket that looks like leather but is not made of real
leather. Would you prefer someone to describe your jacket as *fake, artificial,* or *acrylic*? Most likely, you would prefer *acrylic*. *Fake* suggests that you
are trying to cover up the fact that it is not real leather. *Artificial* suggests,
in a negative way, that something was made to look like something else.
Acrylic, however, refers to a fiber, even if it is a manmade fiber. The word
acrylic at least implies that your coat is somehow "natural." You can see

that, in addition to their dictionary meanings, words may suggest additional meanings.

The meaning of a word as indicated in a dictionary is its **denotation**. The word's **connotation** consists of the additional meanings a word may take on. As an example, think of the word *walk*, which means "to move forward by placing one foot in front of the other." Here are a few words that also mean "to move forward" but have different connotations.

The newlyweds <u>strolled</u> down the streets of Paris.

(*Stroll* suggests a leisurely, carefree walk.)

The wealthy businessman <u>swaggered</u> into the restaurant and demanded a table.

(*Swagger* suggests walking in a bold, arrogant manner.)

The overweight man <u>lumbered</u> along, breathing heavily and occasionally tripping.

(*Lumber* connotes a clumsy, awkward movement.)

Often writers communicate subtle messages or lead you to respond in a certain way toward an object, action, or idea by choosing words with positive or negative connotations. As you read, carefully consider word connotations and the effects they are having on you.

EXERCISE 3–17   **FINDING CONNOTATIVE MEANINGS**

Directions: *For each word listed, write another word that has the same denotation but a different connotation.*

EXAMPLE: to drink   guzzle _____

1. to eat   _____

2. to talk   _____

3. fair   _____

4. famous   _____

5. group   _____

6. to take   _____

7. ability   _____

8. dog   _____

9. fast   _____

10. to fall   _____

EXERCISE 3–18   **WRITING CONNOTATIVE MEANINGS**

Directions: *For each word listed, write a word that has a similar denotation but a negative connotation. Then write a word that has a positive connotation. Consult a dictionary if necessary.*

	Negative	Positive
EXAMPLE		
clean	decontaminate	polish
1. to show	_____	_____
2. to leave	_____	_____
3. to ask	_____	_____
4. task	_____	_____
5. to forget	_____	_____
6. look at	_____	_____
7. unable	_____	_____
8. weak	_____	_____
9. car	_____	_____
10. mistake	_____	_____

EXERCISE 3–19   **IDENTIFYING CONNOTATIVE MEANINGS**

Directions: *Read each of the following statements, paying particular attention to connotations. In each statement, underline at least one word or phrase with a strong connotation. Decide whether it is positive, negative, or neutral and justify your answer. Then suggest a substitute word with a different connotation that changes the statement's meaning.*

1. Educating the electorate about the nature and actual perils of nuclear weapons is a frightening task.

   _____

   _____

2. Recently, the anti-gun forces throughout the nation were trumpeting the fact that violent crimes decreased in cities with strict gun-control laws.

   _____

   _____

3. What I want to get rid of is the human garbage that willfully perpetrates outrages against the rest of humanity and whom we have come to call terrorists. (Rivers)

_____

_____

4. Not unlike drugs or alcohol, the television experience allows the participant to blot out the real world and enter into a pleasurable and passive state. (Winn)

_____

_____

5. I found Simon Wheeler dozing comfortably by the bar-room stove of the dilapidated tavern in the decaying mining camp of Angel's, and I noticed that he was fat and bald-headed, and had an expression of winning gentleness and simplicity upon his tranquil countenance. (Twain)

_____

_____

_____

Vague Versus Clear Meanings

All words have a denotation and many have connotations. But some words are so vague that they have almost no meaning. A word whose meaning is vague or unclear can lead to misinterpretation and confusion. Here are a few sentences whose meaning is unclear because the meaning of the underlined word is not specific.

> The movie was <u>great</u>!
> (What was good about it?)
>
> <u>All</u> drugs should be tightly controlled.
> (Which drugs? All drugs? Aspirin and caffeine too?)
>
> The candidate received a <u>large</u> sum of money.
> (How large is large?)

As a critical thinker, be alert for the use of undefined terms and unclear words. Writers may use them to avoid giving specific information ("substantial losses" instead of exact amounts) or to create a false impression, hide facts, or "spin" information.

SELF-TEST SUMMARY

Goal 1

1. How can you expand your vocabulary?

You can expand your vocabulary and reap immediate benefits as well as long-term career advantages by
- deliberately using newly learned words
- using words you already know
- learning multiple word meanings

Goal 2

2. What are the four types of context clues?

The four types of context clues are:
- **Definition**—a word's meaning is either stated directly or given indirectly.
- **Example**—examples are used to explain or clarify a word's meaning.
- **Contrast**—a word or phrase opposite in meaning provides a clue to meaning.
- **Inference**—a word's meaning can be figured out by reasoning about contextual information.

Goal 3

3. What are the three parts from which many English words are formed?

Why is it useful to learn about word parts?

Many words in our language are made up of:
- **prefixes**—the beginnings of words
- **roots**—the middles of words
- **suffixes**—the endings of words

When their meanings are added together they can provide strong clues to the meaning of a new word and can unlock the meanings of thousands of English words.

Goal 4

4. What is the index card system?

The index card system is a method for learning unfamiliar words. Write each new word on the front of an index card and its meaning on the back. Study by sorting the cards into two piles—known and unknown words. Review periodically to keep them fresh in your mind.

Goal 5

5. What resources are available to build vocabulary and what are their uses?

Resources include:
- **Dictionaries** to locate information on a word's meanings, pronunciation, part of speach, history, synonyms, and usage.
- **Thesauruses** to loacate synonyms and precise meanings.
- **Subject-Area Dictionaries** to locate specialized meanings within a particular field of study.

Goal 6

6. What are denotative and connotative meanings?

A word's denotation is its dictionary meaning. A word's connotations are the additional subjective or emotional meanings it may take on.

READING SELECTION 5   **SOCIOLOGY**

My Black Skin Makes My White Coat Vanish

Mana Lumumba-Kasongo
From *Newsweek*

About the Reading

MAGAZINE
ARTICLE

Dr. Mana Lumumba-Kasongo was born in Africa's Democratic Republic of Congo and is currently an attending physician at a Georgia hospital. This article was originally published in Newsweek, *a popular weekly news magazine.*

Planning Your Reading Strategy*

Directions: *Activate your thinking by previewing the reading (see the Need to Know box on page 64) and answering the following questions.*

____ 1. Which strategy should you use while reading "My Black Skin Makes My White Coat Vanish"?
   a. Read to learn about "a day in the life" of a typical hospital.
   b. Read to examine the differences between the U.S. and African medical systems.
   c. Read to learn about the author's experiences in medical school.
   d. Read to identify the issues encountered by the author and their effects on her.

____ 2. All of the following are clues that you can read this article fairly quickly, *except*
   a. The reading does not contain any complicated scientific diagrams.
   b. The reading does not appear to introduce vocabulary words that are specific to the medical profession.
   c. The article discusses an issue that society has not resolved.
   d. The article was originally published in a general-interest magazine, *Newsweek*.

3. Does racial discrimination exist in many or all professions? What stereotypes might people hold about medical doctors?

Even in one of the world's most diverse cities, I have to convince my patients that I am the doctor.

1   The first time it happened I was a brand-spanking-new M.D., filled with an intern's enthusiasm.

Proudly wearing my pristine white coat and feeling sure that I was going to save the world, I walked into my patient's room.

2   "Hello, I'm Dr. Kasongo. How can I help you?" I asked cheerfully. The patient was a pleasant African-American woman whose chief

*The Scorecard on p. 127 enables you to compute your reading rate. In order to do so, be sure to record your starting time in the Scorecard box before you begin reading.

complaint was abdominal pain. I spent the next 10 minutes taking her history, examining her thoroughly and doing a rectal exam to spot signs of internal bleeding. I explained that I'd treat her pain, check her blood work and urine samples, and go from there. "That's great," she said with a smile, "When is the doctor going to see me?"

3   I frowned. Hadn't she heard me? Hadn't I just administered an invasive exam on her posterior? "I *am* the doctor," I told her, making myself smile again. Did she sense my newness? Was it my lack of confidence that made it hard for her to believe I had a medical degree? I decided that even though I was a 30-year-old intern, it must be the youthful appearance I inherited from my ageless mother that was confusing her.

4   That was four years ago. There have been many such incidents since then, ranging from the irritating to the comical, and I no longer have much doubt that what baffled my patient was the color of my skin. Several months later, I was having dinner at an upscale hotel in Las Vegas with a friend, when she started choking on a piece of food. As she flailed her arms in obvious distress, frantic cries of "Is there a doctor in the room?" rang out from nearby tables. I assured everyone that I was a doctor and administered the Heimlich maneuver successfully. Even as my friend regained her bearings, people at the surrounding tables kept screaming for a physician. Once the "real doctors"—two white males—came to the table and saw that her airway was clear, they told the staff that it appeared that I was in fact a doctor and that my friend was going to be fine. Yet, far from comforting them, this information produced only quizzical looks.

5   Over the years, the inability of patients and others to believe that I am a doctor has left me utterly demoralized. Their incredulity persists even now that I am a senior resident, working in one of the world's busiest hospital emergency rooms. How can it be that with all the years of experience I have, all the procedures I've performed and all the people I've interacted with in emergency situations, I still get what I call "the look"? It's too predictable. I walk in the

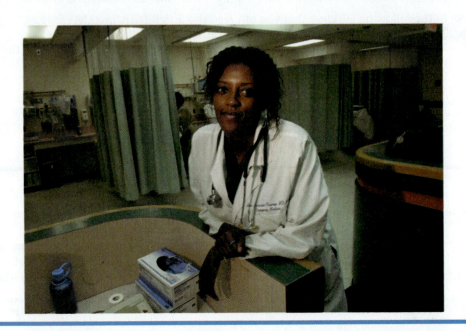

room and introduce myself, then wait for the patient—whether he or she is black, white or Asian—to steal glances at the ID card that is attached to my scrubs or white coat. (I've thought of having it changed to read something like: *It's true. I'm a real doctor, Perhaps you've seen a black one on TV?*)

6   I remember talking to one of the white, male attending physicians in my training program after he witnessed one such encounter. "Listen," he said, trying to comfort me, "I can walk in wearing a T shirt and jeans and I'll always be seen as the doctor, even without an introduction. You will not." My heart sank as I thought of Malcolm X's words, "Do you know what white racists call black Ph.D.'s? N—r!"

7   Only a small portion of the growing number of female doctors—not quite 4 percent—look like me. Perhaps that's why, for most people, "doctor" still doesn't fit the stereotypical image of a black woman in this country. Unfortunately, black children may be even more adversely affected by this than white ones. That point was driven home to me months ago, when

a 6-year-old black girl refused to let me treat her when her mother brought her to the emergency room and left us alone. She insisted on being seen by a white doctor, leaving me feeling both embarrassed and humiliated.

8   Throughout the years, I've spoken to other female doctors about their experiences. While my white, female colleagues sometimes get "the look," it doesn't happen nearly as often as it does for black, female doctors. My African-American peers have their own ways of dealing with it: some even preempt suspicious patients by saying, "Yes, I am a doctor, and you can check online when you get home."

9   I've decided to try not to be bothered by my patients' attitudes. Like all doctors, I've worked hard to get to where I am. And occasionally I see that there is hope for humanity. A few months ago I treated a white, eighty-something man who had pneumonia. As I set up his IV line, I noticed that he was staring at me. Finally he said, "It must have been very hard for you to make it." After a pause, he added, "A woman—and black." We both laughed. Someone understood.

Examining Reading Selection 5*

Checking Your Vocabulary

Directions: *Use context, word parts, or a dictionary, if necessary, to determine the meaning of each word as it is used in the reading.*

____ 1. pristine (paragraph 1)
   a. important and useful
   b. clean and neat
   c. pretty
   d. embroidered

____ 2. quizzical (paragraph 4)
   a. annoying
   b. disturbing
   c. angry
   d. questioning

____ 3. demoralized (paragraph 5)
   a. discouraged
   b. exhausted
   c. fearful
   d. overwhelmed

____ 4. incredulity (paragraph 5)
   a. indignation
   b. disbelief
   c. rejection
   d. hostility

____ 5. preempt (paragraph 8)
   a. to accuse falsely
   b. to insult
   c. to deny
   d. to get ahead of

*Writing About the Reading questions appear in the Instructor's Manual.

Checking Your Comprehension

Directions: *Select the best answer.*

____ 6. The author was first questioned by a patient when she was
   a. about to go into a surgery.
   b. a brand new intern.
   c. in medical school.
   d. assisting another doctor.

____ 7. The restaurant patrons did not believe the author was a doctor and
   a. kept calling for a doctor until white male doctors arrived.
   b. believed she was harming her friend.
   c. tried to stop her from doing the Heimlich.
   d. called her a derogatory name.

____ 8. The author currently
   a. no longer treats patients.
   b. is earning her medical degree.
   c. is a senior resident in an emergency room.
   d. has plans to leave medicine.

____ 9. After introducing herself, the author finds that patients often
   a. look at her ID card.
   b. ask her what country she is from.
   c. refuse to be treated by her.
   d. ask for a second opinion.

____ 10. The number of black female doctors
   a. is decreasing.
   b. makes up 25 percent of all doctors.
   c. makes up 4 percent of female doctors.
   d. is higher in inner city hospitals.

____ 11. The author deals with stereotypes by deciding that
   a. every patient she will have will be prejudiced.
   b. she will try not to be bothered by patients' reactions.
   c. she will form a black female doctors' association.
   d. children are the most nonprejudiced patients.

Thinking Critically

____ 12. Reasons why patients may not believe the author is a doctor include all of the following *except*
   a. they are unused to black women doctors.
   b. they don't believe black women can become doctors.
   c. they have no evidence she is a doctor.
   d. they are prejudiced.

____ 13. Which of the following statements from the reading supports the notion that not everyone holds the same stereotypes and prejudices against female black doctors?
   a. "How can I help you?" (paragraph 2)
   b. "Is there a doctor in the room?" (paragraph 4)
   c. "Do you know what white racists call black Ph.D.'s?" (paragraph 6)
   d. "It must have been very hard for you to make it." (paragraph 9)

____ 14. The author implies that patients
   a. expect to be treated by people of the same race as they are.
   b. have difficulty imagining a black woman in a doctor's role.
   c. prefer female doctors.
   d. have disrespect for the medical profession.

____ 15. This essay was written to
   a. prove black female doctors are excellent doctors.
   b. increase the number of black women who attend medical school.
   c. urge patients to verify their doctor's credentials.
   d. expose the prejudice against black female doctors.

Questions for Discussion

1. Are there other professions in which stereotypes and racial prejudice exist? Give several examples.

2. When people are ill and in a hospital, how do you think their behavior changes? Do they treat people differently and say things they normally might not? Why or why not?

3. What could be done to educate people about the role black women play in medicine? Give several examples.

Scorecard

Selection 5:   926 words

Finishing Time: _____ _____ _____
                HR.   MIN.   SEC.

Starting Time: _____ _____ _____
              HR.   MIN.   SEC.

Reading Time: _____ _____
                   MIN.   SEC.

WPM Score: _____

Comprehension Score: for Items 6–15
Number Right: _____ × 10 = _____%

Assessing Your Reading Strategy

1. How would you rate your comprehension of the reading? (Circle one.)
   Excellent   Good   Fair   Poor

2. Did you find your reading strategy effective?   Yes   No

3. Suppose you were given an assignment to read another article from a popular news magazine. Based on your experience with this selection, how would you adjust your reading strategy (if at all)?

   _____

   _____

   _____

READING SELECTION 6   TECHNOLOGY

Green Computing

George Beekman and Ben Beekman

About the Reading

"Green Computing" is a boxed insert included in an information technology/computer science textbook titled Digital Planet: Tomorrow's Technology and You. *This insert falls under the general heading "Working Wisdom."*

MyReadingLab™ *The exercises following this selection can be completed online at myreadinglab.com*

Planning Your Reading Strategy*

Directions: *Activate your thinking by previewing the reading (see the Need to Know box on page 64) and answering the following questions.*

_____ 1. Based on your preview, what type of information should you look for as you read "Green Computing"?
  a. tips on how to save energy and natural resources
  b. suggestions for making your college or university more environmentally conscious
  c. the history of computer technology
  d. the applications of solar panels to laptop computing

_____ 2. Based on the reading's title ("Working Wisdom"), subtitle ("Green Computing"), and the title of the textbook, you can expect the reading to include all of the following information *except*
  a. practical knowledge that you can put to use in your life.
  b. a discussion of the key role that technologies now play in your life.
  c. a focus on the use of computer technology in the United States only.
  d. an examination of "green," or environmentally conscious, practices.

3. How much thought have you given to the amount of energy used by your computer and other electronic devices (such as your smartphone or MP3 player)? How does saving energy benefit both you and the planet as a whole?

1   When compared with heavy industries, such as automobiles and energy, the computer industry is relatively easy on the environment. But the manufacturing and use of computer, hardware and software does have a significant environmental impact, especially now that so many of us are using the technology. Fortunately, you have some control over the environmental impact of your computing activities. Here are a few tips to help minimize your impact:

2   *Buy green equipment.* Today's computer equipment uses relatively little energy, but as world energy resources dwindle, less is always better. Many modern computers and peripherals are specifically designed to consume less energy. Look for the Environmental Protection

Beekman, George; Beekman, Ben, Digital Planet: Tomorrow's Technology and You, Complete, 10th Ed., © 2012. Reprinted and electronically reproduced by permission of Pearson Education, Inc., Upper Saddle River, NJ.

*The Scorecard on p. 132 enables you to compute your reading rate. In order to do so, be sure to record your starting time in the Scorecard box before you begin reading.

Agency's Energy Star certification on the package.

3 *Use a laptop.* Portable computers use far less energy than desktop computers. They're engineered to preserve precious battery power. But if you use a laptop, keep it plugged in when you have easy access to an electrical outlet. Batteries wear out from repeated usage, and their disposal can cause environmental problems of a different sort. Some batteries last longer if you occasionally drain and recharge them; check online to see what's best for your particular battery. (If you're the kind of person who always needs to have the latest and greatest technology, a notebook isn't the best choice because notebooks are difficult or impossible to upgrade.)

4 *Take advantage of energy-saving features.* Most systems can be set up to go to sleep (a sort of suspended animation state that uses just enough power to preserve RAM) and turn off the monitor or printer when idle for more than an hour or so. If your equipment has automatic energy-saving features, use them. You'll save energy and money.

5 *Turn it off when you're away.* If you're just leaving your computer for an hour or two, you won't save much energy by turning the computer off. But if you're leaving it for more than a few hours and it's not on duty receiving faxes, email, or other messages, you'll do the environment a favor by turning it off or putting it to sleep.

6 *Save energy, not screens.* Your monitor may be the biggest power guzzler in your system, especially if it's not a flat-panel display. (If you don't have a flat-panel monitor, consider upgrading to one. Old-style CRTs aren't ecofriendly.) A screen saver can be fun to watch, but it doesn't save your screen, and it doesn't save energy, either. As long as your monitor is displaying an image, it's consuming power. Use sleep as your screen saver, and you'll save energy, too.

7 *Turn it all the way off.* Many electronic devices consume power even when they're turned off. Some stay in a "ready" state so there's no delay when they're turned on; others just continue to consume power because it was easier or cheaper to design them that way. If you plug your system

components (CPU, monitor, printer, external drives, audio/video gear) into a power strip with a switch, you can use that switch to cut off power completely to all of them, saving yourself time, energy, and money. Similarly, you'll save energy by unplugging your mobile phone charger from the wall when it's not charging your phone.

8 *Avoid moving parts.* In general, things that move consume more energy than things that don't. Disk drives are the movers and shakers of the PC world. If you can store your, Information on a flash drive instead of a hard disk or optical disk, you'll save energy.

9 *Print only once.* Don't print out a rough draft just to proofread; try to get it clean on-screen. (Most people find this one hard to follow 100 percent of

FIGURE A

Laptop computers consume less energy than desktop PCs. This makes it possible to use solar panels to power them in remote locations.

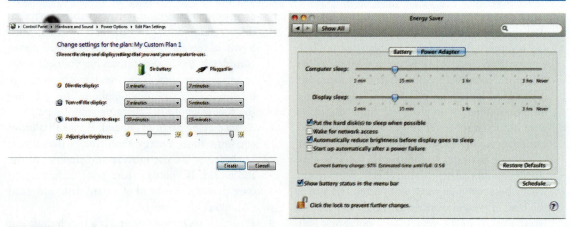

FIGURE B

Windows and Mac OS X systems have advanced energy-saver control panels that can be used to switch the monitor, hard drive, and CPU to lower-power sleep modes automatically after specified periods of inactivity.

the time; some errors just don't seem to show up until you proofread a hard copy.)

10 *Use a green font.* Some fonts use less ink than others. The Internet offers many options for environmentally-friendly fonts that can save ink, save the environment, and save money. The University of Wisconsin, Green Bay, found that it could save thousands of dollars per year when it switched its default font in its email system to Century Gothic, a font with a thin print line.

11 *E-cycle your waste products.* When you reprint that 20-page report because of a missing paragraph on page 1, recycle the flawed printout. When your printer's inkjet or toner cartridge runs dry, ship or deliver it to a company that can refill or recycle it. The company may even pay you a few dollars for the empty cartridge. When a battery in one of your portable electronics dies, follow the manufacturer's instructions for recycling it. If your computer or printer dies, don't bury it in the landfill. Take advantage of the gear-recycling programs offered by many companies and communities. While you're in

recycling mode, don't forget all those computer magazines and catalogs.

12 *Pass it on.* When you outgrow a piece of hardware or software, don't throw it away. Donate it to a school, civic organization, family member, or friend who can put it to good use. Make sure to delete your data first, though, or you might end up the victim of identity theft.

13 *Send bits, not atoms.* It takes far more resources to send a letter by truck, train, or plane than to send an electronic message through the Internet. Whenever possible, use your Internet connection instead of your printer.

14 *Consider hidden environmental costs of your decisions.* The amount you pay for something doesn't always reflect its true cost. Somebody, somewhere, at some time will pay for the environmental damage done by companies that refuse to be good citizens of the planet. You may pay a few dollars less for a gadget produced by such a company, but is it worth it? If you want to do comparative ecoshopping, you can find environmental scorecards for most big companies on the Web.

Examining Reading Selection 6

⚙ ⎡Complete this Exercise at myreadinglab.com

Checking Your Vocabulary

Directions: *Use context, word parts, or a dictionary, if necessary, to determine the meaning of each word as it is used in the reading.*

___ 1. minimize (paragraph 1)
   a. imitate
   b. reduce
   c. maintain
   d. display

___ 2. dwindle (paragraph 2)
   a. allow
   b. share
   c. decline
   d. develop

___ 3. idle (paragraph 4)
   a. permanent
   b. handy
   c. restored
   d. unused

___ 4. flawed (paragraph 11)
   a. imperfect
   b. doubtful
   c. valuable
   d. specific

___ 5. mode (paragraph 11)
   a. monitor
   b. method
   c. equipment
   d. replacement

Checking Your Comprehension

Directions: *Select the best answer.*

___ 6. This reading is primarily concerned with
   a. why recycling is good for the environment.
   b. how to improve the efficiency of computers.
   c. how to reduce the environmental impact of computer use.
   d. how technology companies are causing environmental damage.

___ 7. The authors wrote this selection in order to
   a. criticize the computer industry.
   b. offer advice to computer users.
   c. promote the latest technology.
   d. discuss environmental problems.

___ 8. According to the selection, all of the following are ways to save energy *except*
   a. using a screen saver.
   b. upgrading to a flat-panel monitor.
   c. setting up your system to go to sleep when it is not being used.
   d. storing your information on a flash drive instead of a hard disk or optical disk.

___ 9. The authors recommend that you
   a. always print out rough drafts for proofreading.
   b. switch to a font that uses a thick print line.
   c. recycle printouts, printer cartridges, and batteries.
   d. take old computers or printers to the landfill.

___ 10. When you are shopping for an electronic device, an environmental scorecard can help you compare companies in terms of
   a. the latest and greatest technology.
   b. environmental responsibility.
   c. customer service.
   d. price.

Thinking Critically

___ 11. The authors' attitude toward this subject can best be described as
   a. helpful and informative.
   b. cynical and pessimistic.
   c. disapproving and judgmental.
   d. carefree and lighthearted.

___12. According to Figure A, laptop comput-
ers can be powered by solar panels
because they
  a. are portable enough to be used at
     high altitudes.
  b. have automatic energy-saving
     features.
  c. do not require batteries.
  d. use less energy than desktop PCs.

___13. The authors support their ideas pri-
marily by
  a. describing their personal
     experience.
  b. providing explanations and
     reasons.
  c. citing research studies.
  d. quoting experts.

___14. The purpose of Figure B is to
  a. compare two different types of
     computer systems.
  b. illustrate the energy-saving
     features of Windows and Mac
     systems.
  c. endorse the energy-saving features
     of the Windows system.
  d. show that the Mac is more user-
     friendly than the Windows
     system.

___15. When the authors say "send bits, not
atoms," they mean it is better to
  a. keep letters very short.
  b. send letters by air mail.
  c. send messages electronically.
  d. send handwritten letters.

Scorecard

Selection 6:   1,075 words

Finishing Time: _____ _____ _____
                  HR.   MIN.   SEC.

Starting Time: _____ _____ _____
                  HR.   MIN.   SEC.

Reading Time: _____ _____
                         MIN.   SEC.

WPM Score: _____

Comprehension Score: for Items 6–15
Number Right: _____ × 10 = _____%

Assessing Your Reading Strategy

1. How would you rate your comprehension
   of the reading? (Circle one.)
   Excellent   Good   Fair   Poor

2. Did you find your reading strategy
   effective?   Yes   No

3. Suppose you were given an assignment to
   read another boxed feature from the same
   source (a technology textbook). Based on
   your experience with this selection, how
   would you adjust your reading strategy (if
   at all)?
   _____
   _____

Writing About Reading Selection 6

Complete this Exercise at myreadinglab.com

Checking Your Vocabulary

Directions: *Complete each of the following items; refer to a dictionary if necessary.*

1. Describe the denotative and connotative meanings of the word *green* in the title and in paragraphs 2 and 10.

   _____

   _____

   _____

   _____

2. Define the phrase "suspended animation" (paragraph 4) and underline the word or phrase that provides a clue for its meaning.

   _____

3. Describe the denotative and connotative meanings of the word *guzzler* in paragraph 6.

   _____

   _____

   _____

   _____

4. Define the word *components* (paragraph 7) and underline the words or phrases that provide a clue for its meaning.

   _____

   _____

5. Explain the meaning of the phrase "movers and shakers" and how it is used in paragraph 8.

   _____

   _____

   _____

   _____

   _____

   _____

   _____

6. Determine the meanings of the following words by using word parts:
   a. certification (paragraph 2)

   _____

   _____

   _____

   b. portable (paragraph 3)

   _____

   c. ecofriendly (paragraph 6)

   _____

   d. audio (paragraph 7)

   _____

   e. video (paragraph 7)

   _____

Checking Your Comprehension

7. What heavy industries do the authors compare the computer industry with in the opening paragraph?

   _____

8. What are five ways the authors suggest for saving energy?

   _____

   _____

   _____

   _____

   _____

   _____

   _____

9. What potential danger is associated with donating your computer once you have finished with it and how can you avoid it?

_____

_____

10. Why do the authors say notebooks are not the best choice?

_____

_____

Thinking Critically

11. What do the authors mean when they recommend buying "green" equipment?

_____

_____

_____

_____

12. Why do the authors say that "you'll do the environment a favor" if you turn off your computer or put it to sleep?

_____

_____

_____

13. What would the authors say is more important: to get the best deal possible on an electronic device or to pay more to cover environmental costs?

_____

_____

_____

_____

14. Why is the photo on page 129 appropriate to include with this article?

_____

_____

_____

Questions for Discussion

1. Think about your technology habits, including how you use your computer and how you dispose of electronic waste. How much attention do you typically give to saving energy? Which of the authors' suggestions are you most likely to adopt? Explain why.

2. What does it mean to be "green"? Describe some of the ways you make an effort to be environmentally friendly in your daily life.

3. What responsibility do manufacturers of computers and other electronic devices have to the environment? Discuss the importance of companies being "good citizens of the planet."

4. Does your community offer gear-recycling programs? What other environmentally friendly initiatives are available to you on your campus or in your town?

CHAPTER

4

Main Ideas and Paragraph Structure

think VISUALLY...

What single overall feeling do you get from this photograph? Do you sense the family's joy and elation? Many photographs convey a single impression, as this one does. Details in the photograph support that impression. Paragraphs also convey a single impression— a single important idea— and details support that impression. In this chapter you will learn how sentences in a paragraph are organized and how they work together to express a single idea.

Learning GOALS

In this chapter, you will learn how to . . .

Goal 1 Recognize the organization of a paragraph

Goal 2 Identify the topic of a paragraph

Goal 3 Identify the main idea and topic sentence of a paragraph

Goal 4 Develop expectations about the writer's ideas

Goal 5 Recognize major and minor details and their relationship to the main idea

Goal 6 Recognize different types of details

Goal 7 Use transitions to see the connections between ideas

Goal 8 Understand implied main ideas

Goal 9 Think critically about main ideas and details

135

■ Paragraph Organization

Goal 1
Recognize the organization of a paragraph

The way we organize and present ideas in writing is similar to the way we present them when speaking. When we speak, we speak in groups of sentences. Seldom does our conversation consist of isolated statements or a series of unrelated ideas. For example, you probably would *not* simply say to a friend, "I think you are making a mistake if you move out of the dorm." Instead, you would support your statement by offering reasons or giving an example of someone else who made what you think is a similar mistake. Similarly, in writing, we group ideas into paragraphs.

A **paragraph** is a group of related sentences that develop one main thought or idea about a single topic. A paragraph has the parts shown below.

Topic

Topic Sentence — There is some evidence that colors affect you physiologically. For example, when subjects are exposed to red light respiratory movements increase; exposure to blue decreases respiratory movements. Similarly, eye blinks increase in frequency when eyes are exposed to red light and decrease when exposed to blue. This seems con-
Details — sistent with intuitive feelings about blue being more soothing and red being more arousing. After changing a school's walls from orange and white to blue, the blood pressure of the students decreased while their academic performance improved.

—From Joseph A. DeVito, *The Interpersonal Communication Book,* Ninth Edition, p. 182. New York: Addison Wesley Longman, 2001.

NEED TO KNOW Essential Elements of a Paragraph

A paragraph has the following parts:

- **Topic**—the one thing the entire paragraph is about.
- **Main idea**—the single idea that is the focus of the paragraph. This idea is often expressed in a single sentence called the **topic sentence**.
- **Supporting details**—all the other sentences in the paragraph that explain or support the main idea. These details are often linked together using words and phrases called **transitions**.

■ Identifying the Topic

Goal 2
Identify the topic of a paragraph

A paragraph can be defined as a group of related ideas. The sentences relate to one another in the sense that each is about a common person, place, thing, or idea. This common subject or idea is called the **topic**. The topic is what the entire paragraph is about.

As you read the following paragraph, notice that each sentence describes Costa Rica:

Costa Rica is a country in Central America where Christopher Columbus arrived in 1502. Costa Rica is widely regarded as a leader in eco-tourism, with its natural beauty, rich heritage and culture, and friendly, well-educated people. Costa Rica is slightly smaller than West Virginia with a population of about 4 million and a predominant influence from Spain, which is evident in the official language of Spanish, religion of Roman Catholicism, and the architecture of the buildings. The World Heritage Committee has designated the Cocos Island National Park a World Heritage site; it is located 550 kilometers off the Pacific Coast of Costa Rica and is the only island in the eastern Pacific with a tropical rainforest. With a coastline on both the Atlantic and Pacific Oceans, Costa Rica has many beautiful beaches where surfing is popular in the warm waters and diving is among the best in the world.

—John R. Walker and Josielyn T. Walker, *Tourism: Concepts and Practices,*
Boston: Prentice Hall, © 2001, p. 286.

FLEXIBILITY TIP
Identifying the topic allows you to assess your level of prior knowledge, which in turns helps you identify the rate at which you should read.

To identify the topic of a paragraph, ask yourself this question: "Who or what is the paragraph about?" Your answer to this question will be the topic of the paragraph. Now, try using this question as you read the following paragraph.

The star system has been the backbone of the American film industry since the mid-1910s. Stars are the creation of the public, its reigning favorites. Their influence in the fields of fashion, values, and public behavior has been enormous. "The social history of a nation can be written in terms of its film stars," Raymond Durgnat has observed. Stars confer instant consequence to any film they star in. Their fees have staggered the public. In the 1920s, Mary Pickford and Charles Chaplin were the two highest paid employees in the world. Contemporary stars such as Julia Roberts and Tom Cruise command salaries of many millions per film, so popular are these box-office giants. Some stars had careers that spanned five decades: Bette Davis and John Wayne, to name just two. Stars are the direct or indirect reflection of the needs, drives, and anxieties of their audience: They are the food of dreams, allowing us to live out our deepest fantasies and obsessions. Like the ancient gods and goddesses, stars have been adored, envied, and venerated as mythic icons.

—Louis Gianetti, *Understanding Movies,* 12e, Boston: Allyn & Bacon, © 2011, p. 251.

In this paragraph, the question leads you directly to the topic—movie stars. Each sentence in the paragraph discusses an aspect of Hollywood stardom.

EXERCISE 4–1   **IDENTIFYING THE TOPIC**

Directions: *Read each of the following paragraphs and then select the topic of the paragraph from the choices given.*

____ 1.   An estimated 6 percent of Americans suffer from seasonal affective disorder (SAD), a type of depression, and an additional 14 percent experience a milder form of the disorder known as winter blues. SAD strikes during the winter months and is associated with reduced exposure to sunlight. People with SAD suffer from irritability, apathy, carbohydrate craving and weight gain, increases in sleep time, and general sadness. Researchers believe that SAD is caused by a malfunction in the hypothalamus, the gland responsible for regulating responses to external stimuli. Stress may also play a role in SAD.

—Rebecca J. Donatelle, *Access to Health,* Seventh Edition, p. 73.
San Francisco: Benjamin Cummings, 2002.

a. hypothalamus malfunction

b. winter blues

c. seasonal affective disorder

d. depression

____ 2.   In recent years there have been many media reports about young people mostly in their twenties living with their parents as if they were still adolescents. They are called "twixters." Who exactly are they? They are by definition people who are in transition from adolescence to adulthood, that is, caught betwixt and between these two stages of life. Their age ranges from 18 to 29. They are "fully grown men and women who still live with their parents, who dress and talk and party as they did in their teens, hopping from job to job and date to date, having fun but seemingly going nowhere." Their ranks are relatively enormous, constituting more than half of the adults aged 18 to 24 and about 10 percent of those aged 25 to 34.

—Thio, Alex D., *Sociology: A Brief Introduction,* 7th Ed., © 2009. Reprinted and electronically
reproduced by permission of Pearson Education, Inc., Upper Saddle River, NJ.

a. twixters

b. media reports

c. adolescents

d. adults aged 18 to 24

____ 3.   Today, the formal educational standard for lawyers is 2 to 3 years of graduate study beyond the bachelor's degree. The most common career path for modern lawyers is to complete a bachelor's degree followed by law school. Law schools do not require a specific undergraduate curriculum for admission but recommend a good liberal arts background with emphasis on writing, comprehension, and analytical thinking. In addition to an undergraduate degree, nearly all law schools require the student to take the Law School Aptitude Test (LSAT). The LSAT is a standardized test that measures the student's analytical thinking and writing abilities. The LSAT does not measure the student's knowledge of the law.

—James A. Fagin, *Criminal Justice,* p. 285. Boston: Allyn & Bacon, 2003.

a. completing law school

b. general liberal arts background

c. the LSAT

d. educational preparation for law school

EXERCISE 4–2   **IDENTIFYING THE TOPIC**

Directions: *Read each of the following paragraphs and then select the topic of the paragraph from the choices given.*

____ 1.   Because conflict is inevitable, an essential relationship skill involves fighting fair. Winning at all costs, beating down the other person, getting one's own way, and the like have little use in a primary relationship or family. Instead, cooperation, compromise, and mutual understanding must be substituted. If we enter conflict with a person we love with the idea that we must win and the other must lose, the conflict has to hurt at least one partner, very often both. In these situations the loser gets hurt and frequently retaliates so that no one really wins in any meaningful sense. On the other hand, if we enter a conflict to achieve some kind of mutual understanding, neither party need be hurt. Both parties, in fact, may benefit from the clash of ideas or desires and from the airing of differences.

—Devito, *Messages: Building Interpersonal Communication Skills,* 3rd Ed., © 1996. Reprinted and electronically reproduced by permission of Pearson Education, Inc., Upper Saddle River, NJ.

a. relationships

b. airing differences

c. fighting fair

d. conflicts

____ 2.   Both potential and kinetic energies can take many different forms. For example, a car battery has potential electrical energy. (We might also refer to it as chemical energy.) When the electrical energy is released to turn the starter, it becomes mechanical energy. As the parts of the starter move, friction causes some of the initial energy from the battery to be dissipated as heat energy. Thus, we see that not only can energy exist in different forms, it can also be converted from one form to another.

—Wallace, Robert A., *Biology: The World of Life,* 7th Ed., © 1997. Reprinted and electronically reproduced by permission of Pearson Education, Inc., Upper Saddle River, NJ.

a. forms of energy

b. energy in batteries

c. potential and kinetic energy

d. mechanical energy

____ 3.   Different species forage in different ways. Basically, animals can be described as either generalists or specialists. Generalists are those species with a broad range of acceptable food items. They are often opportunists and will take advantage of whatever is available, with certain preferences, depending on the situation.

Crows are an example of feeding generalists; they will eat anything from corn to carrion. Specialists are those with narrow ranges of acceptable food items. Some species are extremely specialized, such as the Everglade kite, or snail kite, which feeds almost exclusively on freshwater snails. There is a wide range of intermediate types between the two extremes, and in some species an animal will switch from being one type to being another depending on conditions, such as food availability or the demands of offspring.

—Robert J. Ferl, Robert A. Wallace, and Gerald P. Sanders,
Biology: The Realm of Life, Third Edition, p. 790.

a. species of animals

b. generalists

c. demands of offspring

d. types of foragers

____ 4.   Much as we touch and are touched, we also avoid touch from certain people and in certain circumstances. Researchers in nonverbal communication have found some interesting relationships between touch avoidance and other significant communication variables. For example, touch avoidance is positively related to communication apprehension; those who fear oral communication also score high on touch avoidance. Touch avoidance is also high with those who self-disclose little. Both touch and self-disclosure are intimate forms of communication; thus, people who are reluctant to get close to another person by self-disclosing also seem reluctant to get close by touching.

—Devito, *Messages: Building Interpersonal Communication Skills,* 3rd Ed., © 1996. Reprinted and electronically reproduced by permission of Pearson Education, Inc., Upper Saddle River, NJ.

a. nonverbal communication

b. self-disclosure

c. touch avoidance

d. communication apprehension

____ 5.   The current high divorce rate in the United States does not mean, as common sense would suggest, that the institution of marriage is very unpopular. On the contrary, people seem to love marriage too much, as suggested by several pieces of evidence. First, our society has the highest rate of marriage in the industrial world despite having the highest rate of divorce. Second, within the United States, most of the southeastern, southwestern, and western states have higher divorce rates than the national average but also have higher marriage rates. And third, the majority of those who are divorced eventually remarry. Why don't they behave like Mark Twain's cat, who after having been burned by a hot stove would not go near any stove? Apparently, divorce in U.S. society does not represent a rejection of marriage but only a specific partner.

—Thio, *Sociology,* 4e, HarperCollins Publishers.

a. the marriage rate

b. popularity of marriage

c. high divorce rates

d. rejection of marriage

EXERCISE 4–3   **WRITING THE TOPIC**

Directions: *Read each of the following paragraphs and identify the topic.*

1.   We know that changes in sea level have occurred in the past. In some instances, however, these were not related to changes in the volume of water, as was caused by melting or forming of glaciers. Rather, sea level shifted in response to changes in the shape of the ocean basin itself. Reducing the dimensions of the ocean basin (especially depth) by increasing the rates of subduction or seafloor spreading could cause a rise in sea level worldwide. An increase in the size of the ocean basin could cause a drop in sea level.

—Ross, *Introduction to Oceanography,* HarperCollins Publishers.

Topic: _____

2.   Every culture has its theories about dreams. In some cultures, dreams are thought to occur when the spirit leaves the body to wander the world or speak to the gods. In others, dreams are thought to reveal the future. A Chinese Taoist of the third century B.C. pondered the possible reality of the dream world. He told of dreaming that he was a butterfly flitting about. "Suddenly I woke up and I was indeed Chuang Tzu. Did Chuang Tzu dream he was a butterfly, or did the butterfly dream he was Chuang Tzu?"

—Carole Wade and Carol Tavris, *Psychology,* Sixth Edition, p. 153.
Upper Saddle River, NJ: Prentice-Hall, Inc., 2000.

Topic: _____

3.   All surfaces have textures that can be experienced by touching or through visual suggestion. Textures are categorized as either actual or simulated. *Actual* textures are those we can feel by touching, such as polished marble, wood, sand, or swirls of thick paint. *Simulated* (or implied) textures are those created to look like something other than paint on a flat surface. A painter can simulate textures that look like real fur or wood but to the touch would feel like smooth paint. Artists can also invent actual or simulated textures. We can appreciate most textures even when we are not permitted to touch them, because we know, from experience, how they would feel.

—Preble, Duane; Preble, Sarah; Frank, Patrick L., *Artforms,* 6th Ed., © 1999. Reprinted and electronically
reproduced by permission of Pearson Education, Inc., Upper Saddle River, NJ.

Topic: _____

4.   The spread of desert in Saharan Africa is not new. During the last ice age and the early post–ice-age period, the Sahara supported woodlands and grasslands. Rivers flowed northward through this land to the Mediterranean Sea, and the region was home to early agriculturists. Progressive climatic change over the last 6000 years has steadily reduced rainfall in the region, and the desert has spread to cover the cities and once-fertile lands. The climatic cycles of the last several thousand years have minor wetter and drier phases superimposed on a general drying trend. Thus, the spread of the Saharan desert is basically a natural phenomenon. The most recent drought in northern Africa has caused a further expansion of the

desert into the marginal semidesert areas at its edge, and actions of humans trying to survive in these areas have hastened the degradation of the land.

—By permission of Mark Bush, *Ecology of a Changing Planet,* Second Edition, © 1997.

Topic: _____

5.   People in the United States have an abiding faith in the value of education. They see education as necessary for participating in democracy, for righting injustices, and for attaining personal happiness. Belief in education transcends the social divisions of race, class, and gender: Whites and nonwhites, women and men, the poor and the wealthy all believe that education is vital for the survival of a free people and for the individual's social and economic advancement. This belief has led the United States to spend more than $500 billion a year on education and to develop the most comprehensive educational system in the world.

—Curry, Tim; Jiobu, Robert M.; Schwirian, Kent, *Sociology for the Twenty-First Century,* 2nd Ed., © 1999. Reprinted and electronically reproduced by permission of Pearson Education, Inc., Upper Saddle River, NJ.

Topic: _____ ■

■ Finding the Main Idea and Topic Sentence

Goal 3

Identify the main idea and topic sentence of a paragraph

When you make phone calls have you found it helpful to state the general purpose of your call as you begin your conversation? Have you found that in answering a help-wanted ad, it is useful to begin by saying, "I'm calling about your ad in…"? Or, when calling a doctor's office to make an appointment, you might say, "I'm calling to make an appointment to see Dr. —." Beginning with a general statement such as these helps your listener focus his or her attention before you begin to give the details of your situation. The general statement also gives the listener a chance to organize himself or herself or to get ready to receive the information.

Readers, like listeners, sometimes need assistance in focusing and organizing their thoughts and in anticipating the development of the message. Writers, therefore, often provide a general, organizing statement of the main idea of each paragraph. The sentence that most clearly states this main idea is called the **topic sentence**.

This section discusses several of the most common placements of topic sentences and the clues that each offers the reader about paragraph development and organization.

EFFICIENCY TIP
Previewing is effective because the topic sentence is often the first sentence in a paragraph. By previewing, you effectively locate many or most of the reading's main ideas.

Topic Sentence First

The most common location of the topic sentence is the beginning of the paragraph. It may appear as the very first sentence or after an introductory or transitional sentence (one that connects this paragraph to the preceding paragraph). When the topic sentence is first, the author states his or her main idea and then moves on to specifics that explain and develop that idea, as in the following paragraph:

Americans even differ in their preferences for "munchies." The average consumer eats 21 pounds of snack foods in a year (hopefully not all at one sitting), but people in the West Central part of the country consume the most (24 pounds per person) whereas those in the Pacific and Southeast regions eat "only" 19 pounds per person. Pretzels are the most popular snack in the Mid-Atlantic area, pork rinds are most likely to be eaten in the South, and multigrain chips turn up as a favorite in the West. Not surprisingly, the Hispanic influence in the Southwest has influenced snacking preferences—consumers in that part of the United States eat about 50 percent more tortilla chips than do people elsewhere.

—Michael R. Solomon, *Consumer Behavior: Buying, Having, and Being,* Fourth Edition, p. 184. Upper Saddle River, NJ: Prentice-Hall, Inc., 1999.

Notice that the author begins by stating that Americans differ in their preferences for "munchies" or snack foods. Then, throughout the remainder of the paragraph, he explains how they differ in the amounts and types of snacks they eat. When the topic sentence appears first in the paragraph, it announces what the paragraph will be about and what to expect in the remainder of the paragraph.

Topic Sentence Last

The second most likely place for a topic sentence to appear is the end of the paragraph. However, on occasion you may find that it is expressed in the second-to-last sentence, with the last sentence functioning as a restatement or as a transition to connect the paragraph with what follows. When the topic sentence occurs last, you can expect the writer to build a structure of ideas and offer the topic sentence as a concluding statement. This structure is commonly used in argumentative or persuasive writing.

We can measure the radioactivity of plants and animals today and compare this with the radioactivity of ancient organic matter. If we extract a small, but precise, quantity of carbon from an ancient wooden ax handle, for example, and find it has one-half as much radioactivity as an equal quantity of carbon extracted from a living tree, then the old wood must have come from a tree that was cut down or made from a log that died 5730 years ago. In this way, we can probe into the past as much as 50,000 years to find out such things as the age of ancient civilizations or the times of the ice ages that covered the earth.

—Hewitt, Paul G., *Conceptual Physics,* 7th Ed., © 1993. Reprinted and electronically reproduced by permission of Pearson Education, Inc., Upper Saddle River, NJ.

In this paragraph the author begins by explaining that the radioactivity of plants and animals can be measured and compared with older organic matter. Then he uses an example describing how the radioactivity of an ancient ax handle can be measured and how its age can be determined. In the last sentence the author states the main idea, that this procedure can be used to learn about the past.

Topic Sentence in the Middle

If it is neither first nor last, the topic sentence will appear somewhere in the middle of the paragraph. In this case, the topic sentence splits the paragraph into two parts. The sentences that precede the topic sentence often lead up to or introduce the main idea. At other times, the preceding sentences may function as a transition, connecting the ideas to be expressed in the paragraph with ideas in previous paragraphs. The sentences that follow the topic sentence usually explain, describe, or provide further information about the main idea.

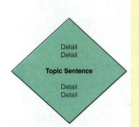

Unlike people in the United States, who believe that different individuals have different abilities, the Japanese believe that all students have much the same innate ability and that differences in academic performance must be due to differences in effort. Therefore, the key to superior performance is hard work, which begins at an early age. Before most Japanese children even enroll in school, their parents—usually their mothers—have taught them numbers, the alphabet, and some art skills. By age four, more than 90 percent of Japanese children are attending preschool in order to receive a head start on their education. The typical Japanese student spends six to seven hours a day in school, five full days a week and a half-day on Saturday.

—Curry, Tim; Jiobu, Robert M.; Schwirian, Kent, *Sociology for the Twenty-First Century,* 2nd Ed., © 1999. Reprinted and electronically reproduced by permission of Pearson Education, Inc., Upper Saddle River, NJ.

The paragraph begins by comparing Japanese and American beliefs about academic performance. In the middle of the paragraph the writer makes a general statement about what the Japanese believe is the key to superior performance. This is the topic sentence of the paragraph. The author then offers additional facts that support the topic sentence.

Topic Sentence First and Last

Occasionally you may find a paragraph in which the main idea is stated at the beginning and again at the end. This structure is often used for emphasis or clarification. In the following paragraph notice that both the first and last sentences state, in different words, the same idea.

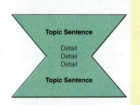

The study of prehistoric humans is, of necessity, the study of their fossil remains. To begin to understand who our ancestors were and what they were like, we must be able to interpret the fragments of them that are coming to the surface in increasing numbers. Given fairly reliable methods to determine their age, we can now turn with more confidence to primate fossils for an answer to the all-important question: How do we tell monkeys, apes, and humans apart? For present-day species this is no problem; all have evolved sufficiently so that they no longer resemble one another. But since they all have a common ancestor, the farther back we go in time, the more similar their fossils begin to look. There finally comes a point when they are indistinguishable. The construction of a primate fossil family tree is essential if we are ever going to discover the line of descent from early hominid to modern human.

—Campbell and Loy, *Humankind Emerging,* 7e, HarperCollins Publishers.

In the preceding paragraph, both the first and last sentences state that the study of fossils enables us to study prehistoric humans. The other sentences explain why fossils are important and how they can be used to distinguish stages in the development of humans.

✔ LEARNING STYLE TIPS

If you tend to be a . . .	Then find the topic sentence by . . .
Creative learner	Looking away from the paragraph and stating its main point in your own words. Find a sentence that matches your statement.
Pragmatic learner	Reading through the paragraph, sentence by sentence, evaluating each sentence.

EXERCISE 4–4   IDENTIFYING TOPIC SENTENCES

Directions: *Read the following paragraphs and underline the topic sentence in each.*

1.   People are affected by various elements of climate. The number of hours of sunshine in a day and the degree of cloudiness are important to anyone who is active out of doors—gardeners, farmers, hunters, builders, vacationers at the beach—and residents of homes heated by solar energy. Amounts of rainfall and snowfall make great differences in how we build our homes and roads from place to place. The windiness of a place is important in designing structures and harnessing wind power. Pollutants in the air can have both short-term and long-term effects on human and animal health. Counts of pollen and mold spores are important to those who suffer allergies.

   —Edward F. Bergman and William H. Renwick, *Introduction to Geography: People, Places, and Environment,* Updated Second Edition, p. 69. Upper Saddle River, NJ: Prentice Hall, 2003.

2.   Manners or etiquette are the rules of a society and different societies have different manners. For example, in Great Britain, parts of Canada, and several European countries, it is customary to hold the knife in the right hand and use it to push food around the plate and onto the fork. This is called the "Continental style" while the "American style" of table manners prohibits pushing food onto the fork with a knife. In general, European-based cultures have similar rules of etiquette. Asian and Arab cultures tend to be very different from Western cultures in their manners.

   —Roy A. Cook, Laura J. Yale, and Joseph J. Marqua, *Tourism: The Business of Travel,* Second Edition, p. 370. Upper Saddle River, NJ: Prentice Hall, 2002.

3.   When you're in debt, you speak of being "in the red"; when you make a profit, you're "in the black." When you're sad, you're "blue"; when you're healthy, you're "in the pink"; when you're jealous, you're "green with envy." To be a coward is to be "yellow" and to be inexperienced is to be "green." When you talk a great deal, you talk "a blue streak"; when you're angry, you "see red." As revealed through these timeworn cliches, language abounds in color symbolism.

—Joseph A. DeVito, *The Interpersonal Communication Book,* Ninth Edition,
p. 219. New York: Addison Wesley Longman, 2001.

4.   Suppose a friend holds up her hand, palm flattened, to signal "stop" to someone standing across the room from her. A basketball coach may motion "time out" with his hands to communicate to a player on the court that the player should signal the referee to stop play so that the team can discuss a new strategy. Both of these situations demonstrate the use of emblems—body motions that take the place of words. In order for emblems to be an effective form of nonverbal communication, both parties must readily understand the motions being used. A spectator unfamiliar with sports might not understand the "time out" motion used by those involved in the game and therefore might question why the referee officially signaled time out. Emblems also can be used effectively when there are obstacles to verbal communication. The example of the basketball game applies here as well; the coach may signal to a player to call for time out because the crowd is generating too much noise for the coach to be heard by the player.

—Joseph A. DeVito, *The Interpersonal Communication Book,* Ninth Edition,
p. 219. New York: Addison Wesley Longman, 2001.

5.   At Steelcase, Inc., the country's largest maker of office furniture, two very talented women in the marketing division both wanted to work only part-time. The solution: They now share a single full-time job. With each working 2.5 days a week, both got their wish and the job gets done—and done well. In another situation, one person might work mornings and the other afternoons. The practice, known as work sharing (or job sharing), has improved job satisfaction among employees.

—Ronald J. Ebert and Ricky W. Griffin, *Business Essentials,* Fourth Edition,
p. 208. Upper Saddle River, NJ: Prentice Hall, 2003.

EXERCISE 4–5

FINDING THE MAIN IDEA

Directions: *Read each of the following paragraphs and then select the main idea of each from the choices given.*

____ 1.   If legislation can compel people to give up discrimination, what about their prejudice? It is true, as many lawmakers believe, that we cannot legislate against prejudice because such legislation is practically unenforceable. That is probably why we do not have any antiprejudice law. But by legislating against discrimination, we can gradually eliminate prejudice. Sample research has long established that people tend to change their attitude if it has been inconsistent for some time with their behavior. This usually involves changing their attitude so that it becomes consistent with their behavior. Thus, people can be expected to gradually change their prejudicial attitude into an unprejudicial one after they have been legally forced to develop the habit of behaving nondiscriminatorily. Indeed, since 1954 a series of civil rights laws and court rulings have caused many whites to stop their discriminatory practices and to reevaluate their attitude toward blacks. Today fewer whites are prejudiced. They do not express their prejudice in the traditional stereo-typical "redneck" way but in a more indirect, subtle manner.

—Thio, *Sociology,* Fourth Edition, pp. 170–171.

a. Prejudice can be defeated by passing laws against discrimination.

b. Civil rights laws have stopped whites from discriminating against blacks.

c. Most white Americans are prejudiced.

d. We cannot legislate against prejudice.

_____ 2.   The major benefit of steroids seems to be to allow muscles to recover more quickly from exercise, so that the athlete can train harder. As athletes were reporting remarkable results with steroids, the medical community began testing the effects of the drugs and the drugs were soon banned. Medical researchers reported a variety of serious side effects of steroid use, including liver cancer, heart disease, and kidney damage. One problem with the drugs is that, along with tissue building, they also "masculinize." The masculinization is particularly acute for women, who may grow facial hair as their voices deepen and their breasts decrease in size. They may, indeed, gain muscle mass, but the masculinizing effects may be impossible to reverse. In adolescents, steroids hasten maturation and may cause growth to stop and the loss of hair in boys. Strangely, in men, the high levels of steroids in the body may cause the body's own production of male hormone to cease, resulting in enlarged breasts and shrunken testes.

—Wallace, Robert A., *Biology: The World of Life,* 7th Ed., © 1997. Reprinted and electronically reproduced by permission of Pearson Education, Inc., Upper Saddle River, NJ.

a. Muscle recovery from exercise is aided by steroids.

b. The medical community recently began testing the results of steroids.

c. There are a number of serious side effects from steroid use.

d. Some women grow facial hair as a result of steroids.

_____ 3.   In addition to expressing their feelings toward others through consumption, people commonly find (or devise) reasons to give themselves something as well. It is common for consumers to purchase **self-gifts** as a way to regulate their behavior. This ritual provides a socially acceptable way of rewarding themselves for good deeds, consoling themselves after negative events, or motivating themselves to accomplish some goal. Indeed, retailers report that it is becoming increasingly common for people to treat themselves while they are ostensibly searching for goodies for others. As one shopper admitted recently, "It's one for them, one for me, one for them."

—Solomon, *Consumer Behavior: Buying, Having, and Being,* Fourth Edition, p. 503.

a. People express feelings toward others through gift giving.

b. Retailers promote self–gift giving.

c. Gift giving is socially acceptable.

d. People use gifts to themselves to regulate their behavior.

_____ 4.   Assertive people are willing to assert their own rights. Unlike their aggressive counterparts, however, they do not hurt others in the process. Assertive people speak their minds and welcome others doing likewise. Robert Alberti and Michael Emmons (1970), in *Your Perfect Right*, the first book on assertiveness training, note that "behavior which enables a person to act in his own best interest, to stand up for himself without undue anxiety, to express his honest feelings comfortably, or to exercise his own rights without denying the rights of others we call assertive behavior." Furthermore, "The assertive individual is fully in charge of himself in interpersonal relationships, feels confident and capable without cockiness or hostility, is basically spontaneous in the expression of feelings and emotions, and is generally looked up to and admired by others." Surely this is the picture of an effective individual.

—Devito, *Messages: Building Interpersonal Communication Skills*,
3rd Ed., © 1996. Reprinted and electronically reproduced
by permission of Pearson Education, Inc., Upper Saddle River, NJ.

a. Assertive people stand up for themselves without hurting others.

b. Aggressive individuals do not care if they hurt other people.

c. Alberti and Emmons wrote the first book on assertiveness training.

d. Effective individuals are the result of assertiveness training.

_____ 5.   Like all the topics covered in this text, power too has an important cultural dimension. In some cultures power is concentrated in the hands of a few and there is a great difference in the power held by these people and by the ordinary citizen: These are called high power distance cultures; examples include Mexico, Brazil, India, and the Philippines. In low power distance cultures, power is more evenly distributed throughout the citizenry; examples include Denmark, New Zealand, Sweden, and to a lesser extent, the United States. These differences impact on communication in a number of ways. For example, in high power distance cultures there is a great power distance between students and teachers; students are expected to be modest, polite, and totally respectful. In the United States, on the other hand, students are expected to demonstrate their knowledge and command of the subject matter, participate in discussions with the teacher, and even challenge the teacher, something many African and Asian students wouldn't even think of doing.

—Devito, *Messages: Building Interpersonal Communication Skills*,
3rd Ed., © 1996. Reprinted and electronically reproduced by
permission of Pearson Education, Inc., Upper Saddle River, NJ.

a. Low power distance cultures distribute power evenly.

b. African and Asian students would never challenge the teacher.

c. How power is distributed in a culture determines people's behaviors.

d. Only a few people possess power in Mexico, Brazil, India, and the Philippines.

| EXERCISE 4–6 | **IDENTIFYING TOPIC SENTENCES** |

Directions: *The following excerpt is taken from a biology textbook chapter titled "Bioethics, Technology, and Environment." Read the excerpt and underline the topic sentence in each paragraph.*

POLLUTION BY PESTICIDES

Pesticides are biologically rather interesting substances. Most have no known counterpart in the natural world, and most didn't even exist fifty years ago. Today, however, a metabolic product of DDT, called DDE, may be the most common synthetic chemical on earth. It has been found in the tissues of living things from polar regions to the remotest parts of the oceans, forests, and mountains. Although the permissible level of DDT in cow's milk, set by the U.S. Food and Drug Administration, is 0.05 parts per million, it often occurs in human milk in concentrations as high as five parts per million and in human fat at levels of more than twelve parts per million.

Pesticides, of course, are products that kill pests. But what is a pest? Biologically, the term has no meaning. The Colorado potato beetle, for example, was never regarded as a pest until it made its way (carried by humans) to Europe, where it began to seriously interfere with potato production. Perhaps this episode best illustrates a definition of a pest: it is something that interferes with humans.

It seems that the greatest pesticidal efforts have been directed at insects and, clearly, much of it has been beneficial. The heavy application of DDT after World War II decreased malaria and yellow fever in certain areas of the world. But DDT and other chlorinated hydrocarbons have continued to be spread indiscriminately any place in which insect pests are found. The result of course, is a kind of (is it artificial or natural?) selection. The problem was that some insects had a bit more resistance to these chemicals than did others. These resistant ones then reproduced and, in turn, the most resistant of their offspring continued the line. The result is that we now have insects that can almost bathe in these chemicals without harm, and malaria is again on the rise.

There are also other risks involved in such wide use of insecticides. For example, most are unselective in their targets; they kill virtually *all* the insect species they contact. Many insects, of course, are beneficial and may form an important part of large ecosystems. Also, some chemical insecticides move easily through the environment and can permeate far larger areas than intended. Another particularly serious problem with pesticides is that many of them persist in the environment for long periods. In other words, some chemicals are very stable and it is difficult for natural processes to break them down to their harmless components. Newer chemical pesticides are deadly in the short run, but quickly break down into harmless by-products.

In the past, the tendency of DDT to be magnified in food chains has been particularly disastrous for predators that fed high on the food pyramid. This is because as one animal eats another in the food chain, the pesticide from each level is added to the next. Thus, species high on the food chain, the predators, tend to accumulate very high levels of these chemicals. In this light, recall that humans are often the top predator in food chains. Before it was banned in the United States, the effects of accumulated DDT on predatory birds was substantial. Reproductive failures in peregrine falcons, the brown pelican, and the Bermuda petrel have been attributed to ingesting high levels of DDT. The problem is that the pesticide interferes with the birds' ability to metabolize calcium. As a result, they were laying eggs with shells too thin to support the weight of a nesting parent. With the decline in the use of the pesticide, many bird populations have recovered.

—Wallace, Robert A., *Biology: The World of Life,* 7th Ed., © 1997. Reprinted and electronically reproduced by permission of Pearson Education, Inc., Upper Saddle River, NJ.

EXERCISE 4–7   WRITING THE MAIN IDEA

Directions: *Read each of the following paragraphs, and then write a statement that expresses the main idea of the paragraph.*

1.   Many flowers pollinated by birds are red or pink, colors to which bird eyes are especially sensitive. The shape of the flower may also be important. Flowers that depend largely on hummingbirds, for example, typically have their nectar located deep in a floral tube, where only the long, thin beak and tongue of the bird are likely to reach. As a hummingbird flies among flowers in search of nectar, its feathers and beak pick up pollen from the anthers of the flowers. It will deposit the pollen in other flowers of the same shape, and so probably of the same species, as it continues to feed.

—Neil Campbell, Lawrence Mitchell, and Jane Reece, *Biology: Concepts & Connections,* Third Edition, p. 358. San Francisco, CA: Benjamin/Cummings, 2000.

Main idea: _____

2.   People migrate for two broad reasons. The first, called *push factors,* are the reasons for leaving a place. Although there may be any number of personal reasons for leaving, the underlying reasons are mostly political and economic. For instance, during the nineteenth century the failure of the potato crop in Ireland "pushed" thousands of Irish to the United States. *Pull factors,* on the other hand, are the forces that attract migrants to a place, such as a congenial government or good weather conditions. Push and pull factors work together. People being pushed from one place will, if they have a choice, go to places that have many pull factors.

—Curry, Tim; Jiobu, Robert M.; Schwirian, Kent, *Sociology for the Twenty-First Century,* 2nd Ed., © 1999. Reprinted and electronically reproduced by permission of Pearson Education, Inc., Upper Saddle River, NJ.

Main idea: _____

3.   A consumer's overall evaluation of a product sometimes accounts for the bulk of his or her attitude. When market researchers want to assess attitudes, it can be sufficient for them to simply ask consumers, "How do you feel about Budweiser?" However, as we saw earlier, attitudes can be composed of many *attributes,* or qualities—some of these may be more important than others to particular people. Another problem is that a person's decision to act on his or

her attitude is affected by other factors, such as whether it is felt that buying a product would be met with approval by friends or family. As a result *attitude models* have been developed that try to specify the different elements that might work together to influence people's evaluations of attitude objects.

—Michael R. Solomon, *Consumer Behavior: Buying, Having, and Being,* Fourth Edition, pp. 218–219.

Main idea: _____

_____

4.   The head muscles are an interesting group. They have many specific functions but are usually grouped into two large categories—facial muscles and chewing muscles. Facial muscles are unique because they are inserted into soft tissues such as other muscles or skin. When they pull on the skin of the face, they permit us to smile faintly, grin widely, frown, pout, deliver a kiss, and so forth. The chewing muscles begin the breakdown of food for the body.

—Elaine N. Marieb, *Essentials of Human Anatomy and Physiology,* Sixth Edition, p. 173. San Francisco: Benjamin/Cummings, 2000.

Main idea: _____

_____

5.   Earth is surrounded by a life-giving gaseous envelope called the **atmosphere**. When we watch a high-flying jet plane cross the sky, it seems that the atmosphere extends upward for a great distance. However, when compared to the thickness (radius) of the solid Earth (about 6400 kilometers or 4000 miles), the atmosphere is a very shallow layer. One-half lies below an altitude of 5.6 kilometers (3.5 miles), and 90 percent occurs within just 16 kilometers (10 miles) of Earth's surface. Despite its modest dimensions, this thin blanket of air is an integral part of the planet. It not only provides the air that we breathe but also acts to protect us from the Sun's intense heat and dangerous ultraviolet radiation. The energy exchanges that continually occur between the atmosphere and the surface and between the atmosphere and space produce the effects we call weather and climate.

—Frederick K. Lutgens and Edward J. Tarbuck, Illustrated by Dennis Tasa, *Essentials of Geology,* Tenth Edition, p. 13 (2009).

Main idea: _____

_____

■ Developing Expectations as You Read

Goal 4

Develop expectations about the writer's ideas

At the beginning of a conversation you can often predict in what direction the conversation is headed. If a friend starts a conversation with "I can't decide whether I can afford to quit my part-time job at Walmart" you can guess what you will hear next. Your friend will discuss the pros and cons of quitting the job as it relates to his financial situation.

Similarly, as you begin to read a paragraph, often you will find sufficient clues to enable you to know what to expect throughout. You may anticipate what ideas are to follow and/or how they will be organized. The topic sentence, especially if it appears first in the paragraph, will often suggest how the paragraph will be developed. Suppose a paragraph were to begin with the following topic sentence:

> The unemployment rate in the past several years has increased due to a variety of economic factors.

What do you expect the rest of the paragraph to include? It will probably be about the various economic factors that cause unemployment. Now, look at this topic sentence:

> Minorities differ in racial or cultural visibility, in the amount of discrimination they suffer, in the character of their adjustment, both as individuals and as groups, and in the length of time they survive as identifiable populations or individuals.

This sentence indicates that the paragraph will contain a discussion of four ways that minority groups differ. This topic sentence also suggests the order in which these differences will be discussed. The factor mentioned first in the sentence (visibility) will be discussed first, the second idea mentioned will appear next, and so forth.

EXERCISE 4–8

ANTICIPATING IDEAS

Directions: *Assume that each of the following statements is the topic sentence of a paragraph. Read each sentence, and then, working in small groups, discuss what you would expect a paragraph to include if it began with that sentence. Summarize your expectations. In some cases, more than one correct set of expectations is possible.*

1. Conventional musical instruments can be grouped into three classes.

   _____

   _____

2. The distinction between storage and retrieval has important implications for memory researchers.

   _____

   _____

3. When Charles Darwin published his theories of evolution, people objected on scientific and religious grounds.

   _____

   _____

4. Narcotics such as opium, morphine, and heroin are derived from different sources and vary in strength and aftereffects.

_____

_____

5. Not all factors that contribute to intelligence are measurable.

_____

■ Major and Minor Supporting Details

Goal 5

Recognize major and minor details and their relationship to the main idea

In conversation, you can explain an idea in a number of ways. If you were trying to explain to someone that dogs make better pets than cats, you could develop your idea by giving examples of the behaviors of particular dogs and cats. You could also give the basic reasons why you hold that opinion, or you could present facts about dogs and cats that support your position. As in conversation, a writer can explain an idea in many ways. In a paragraph a writer includes details that explain, support, or provide further information about the main idea.

All the details in a paragraph support the topic sentence. Not all details are equally important, however. For example, in the following paragraph the highlighted ideas provide very important information about the main idea. As you read the paragraph notice how these ideas directly explain the topic sentence.

> There are potential disadvantages to group therapy. Many psychologists feel that the interactions in group situations are too superficial to be of much benefit. A patient with deep-seated conflicts may be better treated by a psychotherapist in individual therapy; the therapist can exert consistent pressure, refusing to let the patient avoid the crucial issues, and she or he can control the therapeutic environment more effectively. Another criticism of groups is that they are too powerful. If the group starts to focus on one individual's defense mechanisms—which are used for a reason, remember—that individual might break down. If no trained therapist is present—which is often the case in encounter groups—the result can be disastrous.
>
> —James Geiwitz, *Psychology: Looking at Ourselves,* 2e, Little, Brown and Company.

Each of the highlighted details states one of the disadvantages of group therapy. These are called **major details** because they directly explain and support the main idea. Now look back at the details that were not highlighted. Can you see that they are of lesser importance in relation to the main idea? You can think of these as details that further explain details. These details are called **minor details**. They provide information that qualifies, describes, or explains the major details. For example, the third sentence further explains the disadvantage described in the second sentence. Also, the sentences that follow the second highlighted sentence explain what may happen as a result of a group becoming too powerful.

Especially if you are a visual learner, it may be helpful to visualize a paragraph as organized in the following way.

> Main Idea
>   Major Detail
>   minor detail
>   minor detail
>   Major Detail
>   minor detail
>   Major Detail

To find the most important, or major, supporting details, ask yourself this question: "Which statements directly prove or explain the main idea?" Your answer will lead you to the important details in the paragraph. Now apply this question to the following paragraph. As you read it, first identify the main idea, then highlight three major details that *directly* explain this idea.

Today American women and men have similar levels of education. Although this might suggest that full equality has been achieved in education, some notable differences remain. First, the highest levels of education (such as Ph.D.s) are dominated by men. Second, fields of study in higher education are gender labeled, and female and male students are segregated by major. Women cluster in the humanities, health sciences, and education, while men cluster in the physical sciences. Third, the highest levels within a field tend to be male dominated. For instance, while men were awarded 49 percent of the bachelor's degrees in international relations, they received 79 percent of the doctoral degrees in that field. A similar pattern holds for mathematics. The fields of study chosen by women seem to reflect stereotyped ideas about women's and men's interests and abilities; that is, women are nurturant and emotional and more highly skilled in verbal areas, whereas men are rational, and more highly skilled in mathematics. Research shows that such differences are quite small, and not always in the expected direction.

—Constance Shehan, *Marriages and Families,* copyright © 2002 Allyn & Bacon, a division of Pearson Education, Inc.

In this paragraph you should have highlighted the three ways that inequality exists in education between men and women. These are identified using the words *First, Second*, and *Third*. Other sentences in the paragraph further explain each reason and can be considered less important.

| EXERCISE 4–9 | **EVALUATING DETAILS** |

Directions: *Each of the following statements could function as the topic sentence of a paragraph. After each statement are sentences containing details that may be related to the main idea statement. Read each sentence and put a check mark beside those with details that **do not** directly support the main idea statement.*

1. **Topic Sentence:**

From infancy to adulthood, women demonstrate marked superiority in verbal and linguistic abilities.

Details:

_____ a. Girls begin to talk at an earlier age than boys and also learn to speak in sentences earlier.

_____ b. Males excel in the area of arithmetic reasoning as evidenced by their higher test scores.

_____ c. Women learn foreign languages much more rapidly and are more fluent in them than men.

_____ d. The incidence of reading disabilities is much lower for girls than for boys.

2. **Topic Sentence:**

Employment opportunities for college graduates are plentiful in the technical and business fields, but prospects are bleak for the liberal arts areas.

Details:

_____ a. Career counseling is provided too late in their college careers to assist students in making effective career decisions.

_____ b. The competition for jobs in journalism and sociology is highly aggressive and can be characterized as frantic.

_____ c. Over the last year, the demand for accountants and computer programmers and technicians has increased by more than 16 percent.

_____ d. There is only one position available for every ten job applicants in the liberal arts field.

3. **Topic Sentence:**

Quality and content are not the only factors that determine whether a book can achieve best-seller status.

Details:

_____ a. Name recognition of the author exerts a strong influence on sales.

_____ b. The timing of a book's release during the appropriate season or in conjunction with major news events plays a major role.

_____ c. Readers appreciate well-crafted books that are both literate and engaging.

_____ d. The book-buying public clearly responds well to well-conceived advance publicity.

4. **Topic Sentence:**

Showing how a theory can be developed may be the best way to describe one.

Details:

_____ a. Careful testing of a hypothesis leads to more confidence being placed in the idea.

_____ b. After an idea has been carefully described and its premises defined, it becomes a hypothesis.

_____ c. One first comes up with an idea that could explain something that can be observed in nature.

_____ d. A hypothesis is a provisional statement or possible explanation to be tested.

5. **Topic Sentence:**

The vibrations of objects produce longitudinal waves that result in sounds.

Details:

_____ a. Infrasonic and ultrasonic waves cannot be detected by human hearing.

_____ b. Sound travels more slowly in more dense mediums, such as water, than it does in less dense ones like air.

_____ c. Plucking the strings of a guitar or striking a piano's sounding board are good examples.

_____ d. The vibration of the vocal cords is what produces human voice.

EXERCISE 4–10   **IDENTIFYING TOPIC SENTENCES AND DETAILS**

Directions: *Read the following paragraphs and select the answer that best completes each statement.*

The Abkhasians (an agricultural people who live in a mountainous region of Georgia, a republic of the former Soviet Union), may be the longest-lived people on earth. Many claim to live past 100—some beyond 120 and even 130. Although it is difficult to document the accuracy of these claims, government records indicate that an extraordinary number of Abkhasians do live to a very old age. Three main factors appear to account for their long lives. The first is their diet, which consists of little meat, much fresh fruit, vegetables, garlic, goat cheese, cornmeal, buttermilk and wine. The second is their lifelong physical activity. They do slow down after age 80, but even after the age of 100 they still work about four hours a day. The third factor—a highly developed sense of community—goes to the very heart of the Abkhasian culture. From childhood, each individual is integrated into a primary group, and remains so throughout life. There is no such thing as a nursing home, nor do the elderly live alone.

—Henslin, James M., *Sociology: A Down-to-Earth Approach: Core Concepts,* 1st Ed., © 206. Reprinted and electronically reproduced by permission of Pearson Education, Inc., Upper Saddle River, NJ.

___ 1. The sentence that begins "The Abkhasians (an agricultural" is
    a. the topic sentence.
    b. a major detail.
    c. a minor detail.

___ 2. The sentence that begins "The second is their lifelong" is
    a. the topic sentence.
    b. a major detail.
    c. a minor detail.

___ 3. The sentence that begins "They do slow down" is
    a. the topic sentence.
    b. a major detail.
    c. a minor detail.

Small group discussions progress through four phases. The first is orientation, when the members become comfortable with each other. Second is the conflict phase. Disagreements and tensions become evident. The amount of conflict varies with each group. The third phase is known as emergence. The members begin to try to reach a decision. The members who created conflict begin to move towards a middle road. The final phase is the reinforcement phase when the decision is reached. The members of the group offer positive reinforcement towards each other and the decision.

___ 4. The sentence that begins "Small group discussions" is
    a. the topic sentence.
    b. a major detail.
    c. a minor detail.

___ 5. The sentence that begins "The amount of conflict" is
    a. the topic sentence.
    b. a major detail.
    c. a minor detail.

___ 6. The sentence that begins "The third phase" is

    a. the topic sentence.

    b. a major detail.

    c. a minor detail.

A person's personality type can determine how he or she creates and reacts to self-imposed stress. The first kind of personality is known as Type A. Type A personalities work hard, are anxious, competitive, and driven and often create high expectations for themselves. Type A's are more likely to have heart attacks. Type B is the second personality type. Type B's tend to be relaxed, laid back and noncompetitive. A third type of personality type is Type C. Type C's are Type A's who thrive under stress, achieve things and experience little or no stress-related health problems. The more stress Type C's experience, the more productive they become.

___ 7. The sentence that begins "A person's personality type" is

    a. the topic sentence.

    b. a major detail.

    c. a minor detail.

___ 8. The sentence that begins "Type A's are more likely" is

    a. the topic sentence.

    b. a major detail.

    c. a minor detail.

___ 9. The sentence that begins "A third type" is

    a. the topic sentence.

    b. a major detail.

    c. a minor detail.

___10. The sentence that begins "The more stress" is

    a. the topic sentence.

    b. a major detail.

    c. a minor detail.

EXERCISE 4–11   **IDENTIFYING TOPIC SENTENCES AND MAJOR SUPPORTING DETAILS**

Directions: *Highlight the topic sentence in each of the following paragraphs. Then underline the major supporting details in each. Underline only those details that directly explain or support the main idea.*

1. Using money costs money, as anyone who's ever taken out a mortgage or a college loan understands. When a firm borrows money, it must pay interest for every day it has the use of the money. Conversely, if a firm has excess cash, it is able to invest that cash and make money from its money. The bottom line: Having cash is an advantage. For this reason many firms try to entice their customers to pay their bills quickly by offering *cash discounts.* For example, a firm selling to a retailer may state that the terms of the sale are "2 percent 10 days, net 30 days." This means that if the retailer pays the producer for the goods within 10 days, the amount due is cut by 2 percent. The total amount is due within 30 days, and after 30 days, the payment is late.

—Solomon, Michael R.; Stuart, Elnora, *Marketing: Real People, Real Choices,* 2nd Ed., © 2000. Reprinted and electronically reproduced by permission of Pearson Education, Inc., Upper Saddle River, NJ.

2. By regularly rewarding good actions and punishing bad ones, the agents of social control seek to condition us to obey society's norms. If they are successful, obedience becomes habitual and automatic. We obey the norms even when no one is around to reward or punish us, even when we are not thinking of possible rewards and punishments. But human beings are very complicated and not easily conditioned, as animals are, by rewards and punishments alone. Thus, sanctions are not sufficient to produce the widespread, day-to-day conformity to norms that occur in societies all over the world.

—Thio, *Sociology,* Fourth Edition, p. 54., copyright © 1999 Allyn & Bacon, a division of Pearson Education Inc.

3. The skin itself is the largest organ of the body, is composed of epithelial, and connective tissue components, and forms a pliable protective covering over the external body surface. It accounts for about 7 percent of the body weight and receives about 30 percent of the left ventricular output of blood. The term protective, as used here, includes not only resistance to bacterial invasion or attack from the outside, but also protection against large changes in the internal environment. Control of body temperature, prevention of excessive water loss, and prevention of excessive loss of organic and inorganic materials are necessary to the maintenance of internal homeostasis and continued normal activity of individual cells. In addition, the skin acts as an important area of storage, receives a variety of stimuli, and synthesizes several important substances used in the overall body economy.

—Crouch and McClintic, *Human Anatomy and Physiology,* 2e, John Wiley & Sons, Inc.

4. Assume you are an industrial/organizational psychologist hired by a company to help select a manager for one of its retail stores in a local shopping center. You could not begin to tell your employers what sort of person they were looking for until you had a complete description of the job this new manager was to do. You would have to know the duties and responsibilities of a store manager in this company. Then, you could translate that job description into measurable characteristics a successful store manager should have. That is, you would begin with a job analysis, "the systematic study of the tasks, duties, and responsibilities of a job and the knowledge, skills, and abilities needed to perform it."

—Gerow Joshua R., *Psychology: An Introduction,* 5th Ed., © 1997. Reprinted and electronically reproduced by permission of Pearson Education, Inc., Upper Saddle River, NJ.

5.   ==Climate is the most influential control of soil formation.== Just as temperature and precipitation are the climatic elements that influence people the most, so too are they the elements that exert the strongest impact on soil formation. Variations in temperature and precipitation determine whether chemical or mechanical weathering predominates. They also greatly influence the rate and depth of weathering. For instance, a hot, wet climate may produce a thick layer of chemically weathered soil in the same amount of time that a cold, dry climate produces a thin mantle of mechanically weathered debris. Also, the amount of precipitation influences the degree to which various materials are removed (leached) from the soil, thereby affecting soil fertility. Finally, climatic conditions are important factors controlling the type of plant and animal life present.

—Edward Tarbuck and Frederick Lutgens, *Earth Science,* Ninth Edition, p. 70. Upper Saddle River, NJ: Prentice-Hall, Inc., 2000.

EXERCISE 4–12   **IDENTIFYING TOPIC SENTENCES AND DETAILS**

Academic APPLICATION

Directions: *Select a section of five or more paragraphs from one of your textbooks and place brackets around the topic sentence in each paragraph. If there is no topic sentence, write a brief statement of the main idea in the margin. Then underline only the major supporting details in each paragraph.*

TECH SUPPORT **Paragraphs in Online Writing**

Paragraphs, as we have seen, are a way of organizing related thoughts and concepts. A well-organized paragraph helps readers understand a writer's main points. Online writing (such as e-mails, Web pages, e-portfolios, etc.) also requires paragraphs to include a topic, main idea, and details. However, research has shown that very long paragraphs are not as comfortable to read online as briefer paragraphs. When communicating online, be sure that your text is clear and comfortable to read. Don't let paragraphs get too long. Consider changing font sizes or adding an additional line break between paragraphs to assist your reader.

■ Types of Supporting Details

Goal 6
Recognize different types of details

A writer can use many types of details to explain or support a main idea. As you read, notice the type of details a writer uses and be able to identify the details that are most important. As you will see in later chapters on evaluating and interpreting, the manner in which a writer explains and supports an idea may influence how readily you will accept or agree with the idea. Among the most common types of supporting details are illustrations and examples, facts and statistics, reasons, and descriptions. Each is discussed briefly.

Illustrations and Examples

One way you will find ideas explained is through the use of illustrations or examples. Usually a writer uses examples to make a concept, problem, or process understandable by showing its application in a particular situation. In the following paragraph, numerous examples are provided that explain how different languages have different phonemes.

example 1
example 2
example 3

example 4

Every language has its own set of phonemes. English, for example, contains about 21 vowel sounds and 24 consonant sounds; Cantonese, a Chinese dialect, has 8 vowel sounds and 17 consonant sounds; South African Khoisan or "Bushman" has 7 vowel sounds and 41 consonant sounds. Native speakers recognize and produce phonemes from their own language as distinct sounds. For instance, babies in English-speaking communities begin to recognize the sound of the letter *r* as the same sound in *run* and *tear*. Meanwhile, babies in Arabic-speaking communities learn their own set of phonemes, which do not include the same short vowel sounds used in English. Thus, to a native speaker of Arabic, the English words *bet* and *bit* sound the same.

—Laura Uba and Karen Huang, *Psychology,* p. 406, copyright © 1999 Pearson Education, Inc.

As you read illustrations and examples, be sure to grasp the relationship between the illustration or example and the concept or idea it illustrates.

Facts and Statistics

Another way a writer supports an idea is by including facts or statistics that further explain the main idea. Notice how, in the following paragraph, the main idea is explained by the use of statistics.

statistic

statistic

statistic

statistic

To date, scientists have described and formally named about 1.8 million species. Some biologists believe that the total number of species is about 10 million, but others estimate it to be as high as 200 million. Because we do not know the number of species currently in existence, we cannot determine the actual rate of species loss. But by some estimates, the global extinction rate may be as much as 1,000 times higher than at any time in the past 100,000 years. Several researchers estimate that at the current rate of destruction, over half of all currently living plant and animal species will be gone by the end of the 21st century.

—Neil A. Campbell et al., *Biology: Concepts and Connections,* Fifth Edition, p. 766, copyright © 2006 Pearson Education, Inc.

When reading paragraphs developed by the use of facts and statistics, you can expect that these details will answer questions such as what, when, where, or how about the main idea.

Reasons

Certain types of main ideas are most easily explained by giving reasons. Especially in argumentative and persuasive writing, you will find that a writer supports an opinion, belief, or action by discussing *why* the thought or action is appropriate. In the following paragraph the writer provides reasons why so few women become involved in quantitative fields.

reason 1

reason 2

reason 3

What accounts for the scarcity of women in quantitative fields? In early grades, girls show about the same mathematical aptitude as boys, but by high school they score lower than boys on standardized tests. Evidently, mathematical and other quantitative subjects have been labeled "masculine." As a result, girls are not eager to excel in these areas, because such an achievement would make them appear unusual and perhaps unattractive to their peers. Another factor is unconscious bias on the part of teachers and guidance counselors. Despite increased sensitivity to minority and women's issues, counselors still steer women away from college preparatory courses in mathematics and the sciences. Finally, many fields contain so few women that they supply no role models for younger women.

—Curry, Tim; Jiobu, Robert M.; Schwirian, Kent, *Sociology for the Twenty-First Century*, 2nd Ed., © 1999. Reprinted and electronically reproduced by permission of Pearson Education, Inc., Upper Saddle River, NJ.

You can see that the writers offer numerous reasons for the scarcity of women in these professions, including peer influences, bias in the schools, and a lack of role models.

Descriptions

If the purpose of a paragraph is to help the reader understand or visualize the appearance, structure, organization, or composition of an object, then descriptions are often used as a means of paragraph development. Descriptive details are facts that help you visualize the person, object, or event being described. The following paragraph describes the eruption of Mount St. Helens, a volcano in Washington state.

descriptive
details

The slumping north face of the mountain produced the greatest landslide witnessed in recorded history; about 2.75 km³ (0.67 mi³) of rock, ice, and trapped air, all fluidized with steam, surged at speeds approaching 250 kmph (155 mph). Landslide materials traveled for 21 km (13 mi) into the valley, blanketing the forest, covering a lake, filling the rivers below. The eruption continued with intensity for 9 hours, first clearing out old rock from the throat of the volcano and then blasting new material.

—Robert W. Christopherson, *Geosystems: An Introduction to Physical Geography*, Fourth Edition, p. 368, copyright Pearson Education, Inc.

Notice how each detail contributes to the impression of a tremendously forceful landslide. Details such as "rock, ice, and trapped air, all fluidized with steam" help you visually re-create a picture of the eruption. In reading descriptive details, you must pay close attention to each detail as you try to form a visual impression of what is being described.

EXERCISE 4–13

Working
COLLABORATIVELY

IDENTIFYING TYPES OF SUPPORTING DETAILS

Directions: *Working in pairs, read each of the following topic sentences, and discuss what types of supporting details you would expect to be used to develop the paragraph. Be prepared to justify your answers.*

1. It is much easier to sell a product to a buyer who possesses complete purchasing authority than to sell to one who has little authority.

   Type of detail: _____

2. The concept of insurance is an ancient one, beginning with the Babylonians.

   Type of detail: _____

3. It was cold in the fall in Rome, and the evening fell suddenly and with great importance.

   Type of detail: _____

4. Government documents indicate that the total number of Americans living in poverty has decreased, but the definition of the poverty line has also been changed.

   Type of detail: _____

5. A sudden explosion at 200 decibels can cause massive and permanent hearing loss.

   Type of detail: _____

■ Using Transitions

Goal 7
Use transitions to see the connections between ideas

Have you ever tried to find your way to an unfamiliar place without any road signs to guide you? Do you remember your relief when you discovered one sign post and then another and finally realized you were being led in the right direction? Like road signs, transitions in written material can help you find your way to a writer's meaning. **Transitions** are linking words or phrases writers use to lead the reader from one idea to another. If you get in the habit of recognizing transitions, you will see that they often guide you through a paragraph, helping you read it more easily.

In the following paragraph, notice how the highlighted transitions lead you from one important detail to the next.

As a speaker, you should consider the dominant attitudes of your listeners. Audiences may have attitudes toward you, your speech subject, and your speech purpose. Your listeners may think you know a lot about your topic, and they may be interested in learning more. This is an ideal situation. *However,* if they think you're not very credible and they resist learning more, you must deal with their attitudes. *For example,* if a speaker tells you that you can earn extra money in your spare time by selling magazine subscriptions, you may have several reactions. The thought of extra income from a part-time job is enticing. *At the same time,* you suspect that it might be a scam and you feel uncomfortable because you don't know the speaker well. These attitudes toward the speech topic, purpose, and speaker will undoubtedly influence your final decision about selling subscriptions.

—From Bruce E. Gronbeck, Kathleen German, Douglas Ehninger, and Alan H. Monroe, *Principles of Speech Communication,* Twelfth Brief Edition, pp. 57–58. New York: HarperCollins College Publishers, 1995.

Not all paragraphs contain such obvious transitions, and not all transitions serve as such clear markers of major details. Transitions may be used to alert you to what will come next in the paragraph. If you see the phrase *for instance* at the beginning of a sentence, then you know that an example will follow. When you see the phrase *on the other hand,* you can predict that a different, opposing idea will follow. The Need to Know box "Common Transitions" lists some of the most common transitions used within paragraphs and indicates what they tell you. In the next chapter you will see that these transitional words also signal the author's organizational pattern.

NEED TO KNOW **Common Transitions**

Type of Transition	Examples	What They Tell the Reader
Time-Sequence	*first, later, next, finally, then*	The author is arranging ideas in the order in which they happened.
Example	*for example, for instance, to illustrate, such as*	An example will follow.
Enumeration	*first, second, third, last, another, next*	The author is marking or identifying each major point. (Sometimes these may be used to suggest order of importance.)
Continuation	*also, in addition, and, further, another*	The author is continuing with the same idea and is going to provide additional information.

Type of Transition	Examples	What They Tell the Reader
Contrast	*on the other hand, in contrast, however*	The author is switching to an idea that is different from, opposite to, or in contrast to an idea that was previously discussed.
Comparison	*like, likewise, similarly*	The writer is showing how the previous idea is similar to what follows.
Cause-Effect	*because, thus, therefore, since, consequently*	The writer is showing a connection between two or more things, how one thing caused another, or how something happened as a result of something else.
Addition	*furthermore, additionally, also, besides, further, in addition, moreover, again*	The writer indicates that additional information will follow.

EXERCISE 4–14   **SELECTING TRANSITIONS**

Directions: *Select the transitional word or phrase from the box below that best completes each of the following sentences. The transitions in the box may be used more than once or not at all.*

on the other hand	for example	because	in addition
similarly	later	next	however

1. In order to sight-read music, you should begin by scanning it. _____ you should identify the key and tempo.

2. Many fruits are high in calories; vegetables, _____, are usually low in calories.

3. Many rock stars have met with tragic ends. _____, John Lennon was gunned down, Buddy Holly and Ritchie Valens were killed in a plane crash, and Janis Joplin died of a drug overdose.

4. Research has shown that the best ways to lose weight are to diet and to exercise. _____, you should always consult your doctor before beginning any new diet or exercise plan.

5. As a young poet, e. e. cummings was traditional in his use of punctuation and capitalization. _____, he began to create his own grammatical rules.

6. AIDS is often thought of as the biggest killer, but in fact there are many diseases that take a higher toll on human life. _____, cancer and heart disease kill more Americans than does AIDS.

7. _____ there was no centralized government in Europe in the Middle Ages, feudal lords were in charge of creating order within the lands that were under their control.

8. Decisions by the Supreme Court cannot be overruled by any other court. _____, Congress can pass a law changing a law that the Supreme Court has upheld.

9. The roots of mass tourism are clear. Tourism became an important industry during the first half of the twentieth century when paid vacations were created. _____, World War II had made distant places seem closer, and many soldiers and their families made journeys after the war to explore them.

10. Silence permits the speaker time to collect his or her thoughts and prepare for what he or she is going to communicate next. _____, silence allows the listener time to absorb what is being said and prepare for the next phase of the conversation. ■

EXERCISE 4–15   **IDENTIFYING TRANSITIONAL WORDS**

Directions: *Circle the transitional words or phrases used in paragraphs in Exercise 4–2 (pages 139–140).* ■

EXERCISE 4–16   **IDENTIFYING TRANSITIONAL WORDS**

Directions: *Highlight the transitional words or phrases used in each paragraph in Exercise 4–11 (pages 158–160).* ■

■ Implied Main Ideas

Goal 8
Understand implied main ideas

Although most paragraphs have a topic sentence, some do not. Such paragraphs contain only details or specifics that, taken together, point to the main idea. The main idea, then, is implied but not directly stated. When reading such paragraphs, you must infer, or reason out, the main idea. This is a process of adding up the details and deciding what they mean together or what main idea they all support or explain. You can visualize this process as summarized and shown below.

NEED TO KNOW **How to Find Implied Main Ideas**

Use the following steps to grasp implied main ideas:

- Identify the topic by asking yourself: What is the one thing this entire paragraph is about?
- Decide what the writer wants you to know about the topic. Look at each detail and decide what larger idea each explains.
- Express this idea in your own words.

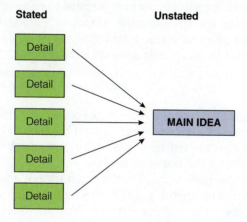

Here is a paragraph that does not contain a topic sentence:

The process of becoming hypnotized begins when the people who will be hypnotized find a comfortable body position and become thoroughly relaxed. Without letting their minds wander to other matters, they focus their attention on a specific object or sound, such as a metronome or the hypnotist's voice. Then, based on both what the hypnotherapist expects to occur and actually sees occurring, she or he tells the clients how they will feel as the hypnotic process continues. For instance, the hypnotist may say, "You are feeling completely relaxed" or "Your eyelids are becoming heavy." When people being hypnotized recognize that their feelings match the hypnotist's comments, they are likely to believe that some change is taking place. That belief seems to increase their openness to other statements made by the hypnotist.

—Uba and Huang, *Psychology,* copyright © 1999 Longman, a division of Pearson Education, Inc.

The topic of this paragraph is hypnosis. The paragraph discusses the steps that occur in the process of hypnosis. The first sentence tells how the process begins (with relaxation and a comfortable body position) and the second presents what happens next (focusing the mind), and so forth. Each sentence is concerned with a different step on the way to being hypnotized. Although this paragraph lacks a topic sentence that explains what the paragraph is about, the main idea is quite clear: "The process of being hypnotized follows several steps."

Here is another example:

> The word *biologist* may cause some to conjure up the image of a little old man with a squeaky right shoe, padding through aisles of dusty books on the trail of some ancient description of an extinct lizard. Others may visualize a butterfly chaser with thick glasses, net poised, leaping gleefully through the bushes. Others may think of a biologist as a bird-watcher in sensible shoes, peering through field glasses in the cold, wet dawn in hope of catching a glimpse of the rare double-breasted sapsucker. Maybe such images do fit some biologists, but there are others who search for the mysteries of life in other places, such as in clean, well-lit laboratories amid sparkling glassware.

—Wallace, Robert A., *Biology: The World of Life,* 7th Ed., © 1997. Reprinted and electronically reproduced by permission of Pearson Education, Inc., Upper Saddle River, NJ.

The paragraph describes various images of what biologists do. Each sentence contributes a different image. Taken together, these descriptions indicate that biologists are engaged in a wide range of activities that include, but also extend beyond the popular images.

Once you have identified the main idea in a paragraph in which it is implied, write it in the margin. Then, when you are reviewing the material, you will not have to reread the entire paragraph.

FLEXIBILITY TIP
Because implied main ideas are not stated overtly, you may need to slow down or stop every so often to ask yourself, "What is the main idea of what I have just read?" If you don't ask yourself this question, you may find yourself remembering only details from the reading, not its key ideas.

EXERCISE 4–17

UNDERSTANDING IMPLIED MAIN IDEAS

Directions: *Each of the following paragraphs lacks a topic sentence. Read each paragraph and select the statement that best expresses the implied main idea of the paragraph.*

_____ 1.　Movies from the United States are seen worldwide. Consumer products made in the United States are sold in most countries throughout the world. Many clothing styles that become popular in foreign countries first begin in the United States. American restaurant chains like McDonald's exist even in Communist countries. U.S. television shows are routinely translated and broadcast in non-English-speaking countries. American music is played by radio stations across the globe and American pop stars enjoy fame on other continents.

    a. American products and trends have a broad impact on the rest of the world.

    b. Foreign countries are not as familiar with American culture.

    c. Communist countries are most resistant to the influence of American culture.

    d. American culture can be used to affect the views and opinions of the people of other countries.

____ **2.**   The benefits of IM [Instant Messaging] include its rapid response to urgent messages, lower cost than both phone calls and e-mail, ability to mimic conversation more closely than e-mail, and availability on a wide range of devices from PCs to mobile phones to PDAs. In addition, because it more closely mimics real conversation, IM doesn't get misused as a broadcast mechanism as often as e-mail does. Of course, wherever technology goes, trouble seems to follow. The potential drawbacks of IM include security problems (both the risks of computer viruses and the worry that sensitive messages might be intercepted by outsiders), the need for *user authentication* (making sure that online correspondents are really who they appear to be), the challenge of logging messages for later review and archiving, and incompatibility between competing IM systems. Fortunately, with the growth of *enterprise instant messaging* (*EIM*), IM systems designed for large-scale corporate use, many of these problems are being overcome.

—Bovee, Courtland L.; Thill, John V., *Business Communication Today,* 9th Ed., © 2008. Reprinted and electronically reproduced by permission of Pearson Education, Inc., Upper Saddle River, NJ.

    a. IM allows rapid response to important messages.

    b. IM resembles real face-to-face conversation.

    c. IM has numerous security problems.

    d. IM has both benefits and risks.

____ **3.**   Facebook is satisfying an unmet desire on the part of students to connect with and stay connected to other students in an electronic, easy-to-use, and fun format. The success also is related to influencers to whom students are exposed when deciding to participate in a social networking Web site. For example, reference groups are huge influencers when it comes to consumers deciding on which movies to see, what jeans to wear, or any number of other consumption decisions. As a result, if someone establishes a profile on Facebook and invites his or her friends to also develop a profile, the desire to be "part of the group" almost guarantees that those friends will use Facebook. In addition, self-concept is a very powerful motivator for some people. Since Facebook is an electronic networking site, it is possible for an individual to develop an online persona that is different from his or her in-person identity. Consequently, student users have the opportunity to develop a profile that transforms their in-person identity into the type of person they wish to portray. In some cases, they even develop more than one persona to appeal to different reference groups.

—Michael R. Solomon, Greg W. Marshall, and Elnora W. Stuart, *Marketing: Real People, Real Choices,* Fifth Edition, p. 170 (2008).

   a. Facebook allows users to develop their own personal identities.

   b. A variety of factors contribute to Facebook's success.

   c. Reference groups are especially important on social network sites.

   d. Social network sites, including Facebook, allow users to stay connected.

___ 4.   As recently as 20 years ago, textbooks on child psychology seldom devoted more than a few paragraphs to the behaviors of the neonate—the newborn through the first 2 weeks of life. It seemed as if the neonate did not do much worth writing about. Today, most child psychology texts devote substantially more space to discussing the abilities of newborns. It is unlikely that over the past 20 years neonates have gotten smarter or more able. Rather, psychologists have. They have devised new and clever ways of measuring the abilities and capacities of neonates.

—Gerow, Joshua R., *Psychology: An Introduction,* 5th Ed., © 1997. Reprinted and electronically reproduced by permission of Pearson Education, Inc., Upper Saddle River, NJ.

   a. Psychologists felt neonates were not worth including in textbooks.

   b. Coverage of neonates in psychology textbooks has increased as psychologists have learned more about them.

   c. Psychologists have become more skilled in measuring the characteristics of neonates.

   d. Current textbooks offer detailed coverage of neonates.

___ 5.   High rollers are gamblers who spend more and play games that require skill. They also are the gamblers with the highest incomes or assets, allowing them to bet more than other gamblers. Day-trippers are mostly retirees who enjoy playing slots. They spend more than most gamblers, but not as much as high rollers. Low stakes gamblers are those who are just beginning to discover gambling close to home and view it as a form of entertainment. Family vacationers make up the other category of gamblers. For these, gambling is a small part of a vacation.

   a. Gambling is done mostly by retirees.

   b. High rollers spend the most and play games of skill.

   c. Gambling is an important part of vacation plans for many people.

   d. There are four main types of gamblers with distinctive characteristics.

EXERCISE 4–18   **IDENTIFYING IMPLIED MAIN IDEAS**

Directions: *Read the following paragraphs, which contain no topic sentences, and then select the implied main idea of each from the choices given.*

___ 1.   Much like others form images of you based on what you do, you also react to your own behavior; you interpret it and evaluate it. For example, let us say you believe that lying is wrong. If you lie, you will evaluate this behavior in terms of your internalized beliefs about lying. You will thus react negatively to your own behavior. You may, for example, experience guilt because your behavior contradicts your beliefs. On the other hand, let's say that you pulled someone out of a burning building at great personal risk. You would probably evaluate this behavior positively; you will feel good about this behavior and, as a result, about yourself.

—Devito, *Messages: Building Interpersonal Communication Skills,* 3rd Ed., © 1996. Reprinted and electronically reproduced by permission of Pearson Education, Inc., Upper Saddle River, NJ.

a. If you feel good about your behavior you will feel good about yourself.

b. How you react to your own behavior helps you to form a self-concept.

c. You feel guilt when your behavior contradicts your beliefs.

d. You need to take risks to feel good about yourself.

___ 2.   If you are using an object, bring it into view as it becomes the "center" of your speech, and then take the time to remove it from view. Otherwise, your audience's attention both before and after the demonstration will be focused on the object rather than the message. If your speech concerns steps in a process, and using objects helps clarify the methods employed, bring samples of finished stages with you. Do not attempt to work through a complex procedure on a single object. If you need to pass the object around the room, realize that as it moves from person to person less attention will be focused on your message. If you have the time and can continue discussing features of the object as it is passed around, you can focus the listeners' attention on your comments. You will find this approach makes it easier to move on to other phases of your message as you retrieve the object and place it out of sight. If this approach is impractical, and you have to leave the object in plain view, you can refocus attention by using other visual aids.

—Benjamin and McKerrow, *Business and Professional Communication,* copyright © 1993 HarperCollins Publishers.

a. When giving a speech about a physical object, pass it around the room.

b. Use objects when giving speeches about steps in a process.

c. Use other visual aids to refocus attention during speeches involving objects.

d. When giving a speech involving an object, plan how you will use it in advance.

___ 3.   People's acceptance of a product is largely determined by its package. The very same coffee taken from a yellow can was described as weak, from a dark brown can too strong, from a red can rich, and from a blue can mild. Even our acceptance of a person may depend on the colors worn. Consider, for example, the comments of one color expert "If you have to pick the wardrobe for your defense lawyer heading into court and choose anything but blue, you deserve to lose the case. . . ." Black is so powerful it could work against the lawyer with the jury. Brown lacks sufficient authority. Green would probably elicit a negative response.

—Devito, *Messages: Building Interpersonal Communication Skills,* 3rd Ed., © 1996. Reprinted and electronically reproduced by permission of Pearson Education, Inc., Upper Saddle River, NJ.

   a. Colors have an influence on how we think and act.

   b. A product's package largely determines how we accept it.

   c. How effective lawyers are depends on their wardrobe colors.

   d. Color experts rank blue as the most influential to be worn.

___ 4.   Bonds hold atoms together, forming molecules. An ionic bond, due to the attractive force between two ions of opposite charge, is formed when electrons are transferred from one atom to another. A covalent bond is formed when atoms share electrons. In some molecules shared electrons are more strongly attracted to one of the atoms, polarizing the molecule. A hydrogen bond is a weak bond formed when the positive end of a hydrogen atom that is covalently bonded to one molecule is attracted to the negative end of another polar molecule. Hydrogen bonding between water molecules gives water some of its unusual characteristics.

—Wallace, Robert A., *Biology: The World of Life,* 7th Ed., © 1997. Reprinted and electronically reproduced by permission of Pearson Education, Inc., Upper Saddle River, NJ.

   a. Ionic bonds involve the transfer of electrons between atoms.

   b. A number of bonds can be involved in molecule formation.

   c. The attraction between electrons and atoms causes bonds.

   d. Covalent bonds are formed when atoms share electrons.

___ 5.   For many smokers, the road to quitting is too rough to travel alone. Some smokers turn to nontobacco products to help them quit; products such as nicotine chewing gum and the nicotine patch replace depleted levels of nicotine in the bloodstream and ease the process of quitting. Aversion therapy techniques attempt to reduce smoking by pairing the act of smoking with some sort of noxious stimulus so that smoking itself is perceived as unpleasant. For example, the technique of rapid smoking instructs patients to smoke rapidly and continuously until they exceed their tolerance for cigarette smoke, producing unpleasant sensations. Proponents of self-control strategies view smoking as a learned habit associated with specific situations. Therapy is aimed at identifying these situations and teaching smokers the skills necessary to resist smoking.

—Rebecca J. Donatelle and Lorraine G. Davis, *Access to Health,* Sixth Edition, pp. 285–286, copyright © 2000 Pearson Education Inc.

a. Quitting smoking is a difficult and challenging task.

b. Aversion therapy pairs smoking with an unpleasant activity.

c. A variety of techniques are available to help smokers quit smoking.

d. Nontobacco products have helped some smokers quit. ■

EXERCISE 4–19   **WRITING IMPLIED MAIN IDEAS**

Directions: *Read each of the following paragraphs, none of which has a topic sentence. For each, write your own statement of the implied main idea of the paragraph.*

1.   Some agricultural and business interests, eager to exploit this supply of cheap labor, have opposed strict enforcement of immigration laws. Others have pointed out that ending illegal immigration could have negative effects: It might lead even more industries to relocate to foreign countries where labor is cheap, cause the rate of inflation to rise, and damage diplomatic relations. Labor unions, on the other hand, fearing a possible loss of jobs for Americans, have favored a crackdown on illegal immigration. And population-minded groups have insisted that the influx of immigrants is canceling out the benefits that have accrued from recent declines in the U.S. birth rate.

—Popenoe, David, Sociology, 11th Ed., © 2000. Reprinted and electronically reproduced
by permission of Pearson Education, Inc., Upper Saddle River, NJ.

Main idea: _____

_____

2.   Imagine that you have filled a glass up to its rim with water. Carefully adding a few more drops of water or dropping in some pennies does not cause the water to overflow. Instead the water seems to adhere to itself, forming a dome that rises slightly above the rim of the glass. This effect is the result of the polarity of water. Throughout the liquid in the glass, water molecules are attracted in all directions by surrounding water molecules. However, the water molecules on the surface are pulled like a skin toward the rest of the water in the glass. As a result, the water molecules on the surface become more tightly packed, a feature called **surface tension.** Because of surface tension, a needle floats on the top of water, certain water bugs can travel across the surface of a pond or lake, and drops of water are spherical.

—Timberlake, Chemistry: An Introduction to General, Organic, and Biological Chemistry,
11th edition, copyright © 2011 Pearson Education Inc.

Main idea: _____

_____

_____

3.   Polls can be found indicating strong support for a woman's right to choose, whereas other polls indicate strong majorities opposing unlimited abortion. Proponents of choice believe that access to abortion is essential if women are to be fully autonomous human beings. Opponents call themselves pro-life because they believe that the fetus is fully human; therefore, an abortion deprives a fetus of the right to life. These positions are irreconcilable, making abortion a politician's nightmare. Wherever a politician stands on this divisive issue, a large number of voters will be enraged.

—*Government In America: People, Politics & Policy,* Pearson Education.

Main idea: _____

4.   Most hospitals, designed to handle injuries and acute illness that are common in the young, do not have the facilities or personnel to treat the chronic degenerative diseases of the elderly. Many doctors are also ill-prepared to deal with such problems. As Fred Cottrell points out, "There is a widespread feeling among the aged that most doctors are not interested in them and are reluctant to treat people who are as little likely to contribute to the future as the aged are reputed to." Even with the help of Medicare, the elderly in the United States often have a difficult time paying for the health care they need.

—Coleman and Cressey, *Social Problems,* HarperCollins Publishers.

Main idea: _____

_____

5.   In 1950, only two cities, London and New York, had populations over 8 million; today there are 20 of these huge cities, 14 of them in developing countries. At present, the total urban population of the developing countries is an estimated 1.3 billion people—more than the total populations of Europe, Japan and North America combined. At a growth rate of 50 million new urbanites every year, due both to natural increases in resident populations and immigration from rural areas, over half the people in the developing world will live in cities by the year 2020.

—Hicks and Gwynne, *Cultural Anthropology,* HarperCollins Publishers.

Main idea: _____

EXERCISE 4–20   **IDENTIFYING TOPIC SENTENCES**

Directions: *From a chapter of one of your textbooks, select a headed section of at least five substantial paragraphs and for each paragraph, identify the topic sentence. If there is no clear topic sentence, write your own statement of the implied main idea of the paragraph.*

■ Thinking Critically: Evaluating Main Ideas and Details

Goal 9

Think critically about main ideas and details

Often, main ideas or topic sentences are simple statements of fact that cannot be disputed. However, not all main ideas and topic sentences are completely factual. Sometimes, a main idea presents an opinion about a topic, and that statement may not offer all sides of the story. Look at the following passage:

> No doubt about it, lobbying is a growth industry. Every state has hundreds of public relations practitioners whose specialty is representing their clients to legislative bodies and government agencies. The number of registered lobbyists in Washington, D.C., exceeds 10,000 today.
>
> In one sense, lobbyists are expediters. They know local traditions and customs, and they know who is in a position to affect policy. Lobbyists advise their clients, which include trade associations, corporations, public interest groups, and regulated utilities and industries, on how to achieve their goals by working with legislators and government regulators. Many lobbyists call themselves "government relations specialists."

—Vivian, *The Media of Mass Communication,* 10e, pp. 278–279, copyright © Allyn & Bacon, a division of Pearson Education, Inc.

The main idea of the first paragraph is a statement of fact. The author can prove without a doubt that "lobbying is a growth industry." The main idea of the second paragraph is: Lobbyists are expediters. That is, lobbyists help their clients influence the government in their favor. But this main idea presents only one side of the topic. What is the other side? Lobbying is a controversial activity, and many people believe that lobbyists spend large amounts of money influencing government employees in unethical or illegal ways. However, that belief is not reflected in the main idea of this passage.

Writers choose their details to support their main idea. However, they rarely have the time, or the space, to list every available supporting detail. Consider the following paragraph:

> Cross-sex friendships [that is, friendships between a man and a woman] have many benefits. Befriending a person of the opposite sex can give one a unique perspective on the other sex, and gender roles become mitigated. Cross-sex friendships are even associated with higher self-esteem and self-confidence.

—Kunz, *THINK Marriages and Family,* p. 83, copyright © 2011 Pearson Education, Inc.

Here, the author provides two details to support the topic sentence "Cross-sex friendships have many benefits." These are: (1) having a friend of the opposite sex can help you better understand the opposite sex, and (2) friends of the opposite sex can make you feel better about yourself. But the author could also have chosen other details. For example, some people believe that men become better listeners when they have female friends. As you read, be aware of the details that the writer has chosen to include. Has the writer omitted any important details to make a stronger case? Has she used any specific words to influence you?

EXERCISE 4–21   **REWRITING TOPIC SENTENCES**

Directions: *For each of the following topic sentences, write another topic sentence that expresses a different opinion or point of view.*

1. It is better to live in a city than in the country because the city offers many more activities and opportunities to its residents.

   _____

   _____

2. Because tobacco products harm people's health, all tobacco products should be banned.

   _____

   _____

3. Social networking sites like Facebook and MySpace create communities of close-knit friends.

   _____

   _____

EXERCISE 4–22   **Directions:** *Use the excerpts found in this chapter to answer the following questions.*

1. Refer to the paragraph about the American star system on page 137. Name at least two other actors/actresses the author could have used as examples of today's box-office giants.

   _____

2. Refer to Exercise 4–1, passage 2 (p. 138). How might the main idea of this paragraph be strengthened?

   _____

   _____

   _____

3. Refer to Exercise 4–7, passage 2 (p. 150). Name at least one other "pull factor" not mentioned by the author.

   _____

   _____

4. Refer to Exercise 4–17, passage 3 (p. 169). What is the author's attitude toward Facebook in this paragraph? What is the other side of the argument?

   _____

   _____

   _____

SELF-TEST SUMMARY

Goal 1	1. What is a paragraph?	A paragraph is a group of related sentences about a single topic. It explains, supports, or gives information about a main idea related to that particular topic. A paragraph has three essential parts: • topic: the subject of the paragraph • main idea: the most important idea expressed about the topic • details: the information that explains or supports the main idea
Goal 2	2. What is the topic of a paragraph and how can you find it?	The topic of a paragraph is the subject the entire paragraph is about. Find it by asking yourself, "Who or what is this paragraph about?"
Goal 3	3. Where is the topic sentence most likely to be found?	The topic sentence expresses the main idea of the paragraph. It may be located anywhere in the paragraph, but the most common positions are first and last.
Goal 4	4. What clues in paragraphs can help you anticipate the writer's ideas?	Clues to a writer's direction are often evident in the topic sentence, which can suggest how the paragraph will be developed.
Goal 5	5. What are major and minor supporting details?	Major details are those that directly support the main idea. Minor details are those that provide information that qualifies, describes, or explains the major details.
Goal 6	6. What are the most common types of details used to explain or support a main idea?	Both major details that directly support the main idea and minor details that provide less essential information are of four types: • illustrations and examples • facts and statistics • reasons • descriptions
Goal 7	7. What are transitions and why are they used?	Transitions are words and phrases that link ideas together. They are used to guide readers from one idea to another.
Goal 8	8. How can you identify implied main ideas that are not stated in a topic sentence?	To find an unstated main idea, ask yourself: What does the writer want me to know about the topic?
Goal 9	9. Why should you think critically about main ideas?	Main ideas may present an opinion about a topic, or may not offer all viewpoints on the topic.

READING SELECTION 7   SOCIOLOGY

Status Update: Broken Heart: How the Digital World is Changing the Rules of Campus Courtship

Jessica Bennett

About the Reading

MAGAZINE ARTICLE

This article was originally published in Newsweek, *a popular weekly news magazine. In addition to news,* Newsweek *also features articles about business, entertainment, and social trends.*

Planning Your Reading Strategy*

Directions: *Activate your thinking by previewing the reading and answering the following questions.*

1. The Need to Know box on page 64 recommends that you preview the first sentence under each heading, along with the title and the first and last paragraphs. Would this type of preview be adequate for this article? Why or why not? If not, how would you adjust your previewing strategy?

    _____

    _____

___ 2. Based on the first and last paragraphs, what might be a good alternative title for the reading?
    a. "The Benefits of Match.com"
    b. "Dating and the Internet: Pro and Con"
    c. "Finding Your Soul Mate Online"
    d. "The Dark Side of Facebook"

3. Based on your preview of the reading, how quickly do you think you should read the selection? (Circle one.) Explain your answer.

    Very slowly   Slowly   At a moderate pace   Quickly   Very quickly

    _____

    _____

1   Katie Vojtko had been dating her boyfriend for eight months. The two had met at a party at the University of Pittsburgh, where both of them were students. The attraction was instant: he asked Vojtko out, the two became a couple, things were good. But then one day Vojtko logged on to Facebook and noticed something funny: her "boyfriend" had changed his relationship status to "single." "I'll never forget it," Vojtko remembers. "I was at one of the libraries

*The Scorecard on p. 182 enables you to compute your reading rate. In order to do so, be sure to record your starting time in the Scorecard box before you begin reading.

on campus with my best friend. I logged on, and on my newsfeed, it said, 'Brad is no longer in a relationship.' I was like, 'What?!'"

2   It took a moment to comprehend, but Vojtko realized she'd just been dumped—on Facebook. She immediately texted Brad: "'Thanks for letting me know you wanted to end this relationship,'" she quipped. She then changed her status message, too—and immediately started receiving notes from friends. "Are you OK?" one asked. "What happened?" questioned another. It was months before she'd talk to Brad again.

3   It wasn't so long ago that the idea of a college romance playing out online—for better or for worse—would have been deemed weird, nerdy, or just plain pathetic. As the thinking went, if you had to go to the Web to find a mate, or break up with one, it must have meant you weren't capable of attracting anyone in the real world. But then MySpace came along, and Facebook took over— and today, college courtship has become a flurry of status messages, e-mail flirtation, and, not so uncommonly, breakups that play out publicly for all 400 of your not-so-closest friends. And while a Facebook split is clearly not the ideal, Katie Vojtko has been on the other side of it, too: she ended a recent romance through an e-mail—to which she never heard back. "It's not something I'm proud of," says the 22-year-old, who graduated in April. "But this is just the way things are today."

4   Gone is the awkward etiquette of the past. Now a relationship may still begin by locking eyes across a crowded bar, but instead of asking for a phone number, the next step almost surely involves a Facebook friendship offer. Then may come an e-mail exchange, a conversation on IM, maybe even a flirtatious text message. But there are at least three methods of communicating that are likely to come before an actual verbal conversation. "These are natural stages of relationship progression that have just become a ubiquitous part of college culture now," says Julie Albright, a sociologist at the University of Southern California, in Los Angeles, who has studied dating online. "And you don't even have to be on the computer to engage in it."

5   That can be a good thing, with the Web serving as a kind of buffer zone for uncomfortable interaction. It's easier to face rejection, there aren't lulls in conversation or geographic boundaries—and social networking is like a window into the lives of potential mates. Say two people meet on Facebook, though a mutual friend. Immediately, they know whether the other person is single— without having to ask. They can see where that person grew up, their political interests, whether they're "looking for a relationship" or only interested in "hooking up." It's all the details a person might encounter on a first or

second date, without ever having to go on one. As David Yarus, a recent graduate of Babson College, outside Boston, puts it: "Facebook has taken the potentially awkward first stages of flirting [and] getting to know someone into the comfort of your own home."

6   That idea, college students agree, has changed the dating scene dramatically. It's made it easier to approach each other, to talk casually, to get to know one another and feel out romantic potential without ever having to truly put themselves out there. It's made the dating process public, so that a breakup like Vojtko's is followed by concern—or even blatant propositions. It can also provide an unforeseen leg up in the dating game. David Heinzinger, a 24-year-old new-media specialist in New York, recently asked a girl he met at a happy hour to dinner. She immediately friended him on Facebook—and he checked out her profile. When it came time for dinner, he took advantage of a detail the girl didn't remember her Facebook profile had divulged: that she

was a vegetarian. "I texted something like 'Not sure if you're into vegetarian food, but there's a new place I've been dying to try,' to which, of course, she responded 'YES!' "says Heinzinger. "I looked like a mind reader, when in fact she provided me with all of the necessary info."

7   It certainly makes things easier. But the more technology at our fingertips, of course, the more novel the idea that a guy—or girl—would be willing to go the extra mile. "My friends and I have found that it's the men who do not use these easy forms of communication that we find most attractive," says Vojtko. And it's the girls the guys find most attractive, says Heinzinger, for whom they'll make that extra effort. "I remember the feeling you get when she gives you her number; the excitement to call her and ask her out; asking her friends what her favorite food is so you can take her somewhere great," he says. "I would still do that the hard way if it was someone I was really into." Of course, he adds, the chances are all that information is online already.

Examining Reading Selection 7*

Checking Your Vocabulary

Directions: *Use context, word parts, or a dictionary, if necessary, to determine the meaning of each word as it is used in the reading.*

___ 1. comprehend (paragraph 2)
    a. offer
    b. deny
    c. understand
    d. overlook

___ 2. deemed (paragraph 3)
    a. considered
    b. listened
    c. compared
    d. pushed

___ 3. ubiquitous (paragraph 4)
    a. remote
    b. common
    c. doubtful
    d. unnecessary

___ 4. blatant (paragraph 6)
    a. normal
    b. cautious
    c. useless
    d. obvious

___ 5. divulged (paragraph 6)
    a. damaged
    b. revealed
    c. watched
    d. studied

*Writing About the Reading questions appear in the Instructor's Manual.

Checking Your Comprehension

Directions: *Select the best answer.*

____ 6. This reading is primarily concerned with the
   a. popularity of social networking.
   b. use of online dating services.
   c. Internet's effect on dating.
   d. benefits of online communication.

____ 7. The author wrote this selection in order to
   a. explain why online relationships are not usually successful.
   b. argue that online dating is the best way to meet a potential mate.
   c. promote the use of social networking sites such as Facebook.
   d. discuss how the process of dating has changed because of the Internet.

____ 8. According to the author, the first step after meeting someone these days almost always consists of
   a. asking for a phone number.
   b. a Facebook friendship offer.
   c. an actual verbal conversation.
   d. a conversation on IM or e-mail.

____ 9. The sociologist who has studied dating online is named
   a. Katie Vojtko.
   b. Julie Albright.
   c. David Yarus.
   d. David Heinzinger.

____ 10. The Web acts as a "buffer zone" by doing all of the following *except*
   a. making it easier to end a relationship.
   b. eliminating awkward conversations and geographic boundaries.
   c. making the dating process more private.
   d. disclosing information about potential mates.

Thinking Critically

____ 11. The author supports her ideas with all of the following types of details *except*
   a. examples.
   b. reasons.
   c. an expert opinion.
   d. her personal experience.

____ 12. The author's attitude toward the subject can best be described as
   a. judgmental.
   b. indifferent.
   c. informative.
   d. mocking.

____ 13. The author chose the photo on page 179 to accompany the reading for all of the following reasons *except*
   a. the people in the photo are about the same age as the students discussed in the reading.
   b. the photo shows how college-age students are tied to their personal technologies.
   c. the body language makes it clear that the two people are dating, and dating is a key topic in the reading.
   d. the author believes that technology is used for dating only by people under the age of 30.

____ 14. Of the following statements based on the selection, the one that best expresses the main idea is
   a. The Internet has changed the dating scene dramatically.
   b. If you have to go on the Web to find a mate, you aren't able to attract one in the real world.
   c. In college culture, relationships progress through several stages of online communication.
   d. The more technology we have, the more unusual it is to try to learn about a person.

____ 15. When the author uses the word
etiquette in paragraph 4, she is referring to
a. good taste.
b. good manners.
c. old-fashioned modesty or
decorum.
d. rules of behavior.

Questions for Discussion

1. Based on your own observations and
experiences, how has the Internet
changed the dating scene for the better?
In what ways has dating been changed
for the worse?

2. What do you consider the "natural
stages of relationship progression" for
you and your friends? Do you think it
is acceptable to break up with someone online? Discuss whether your experiences reflect what is described in
the selection.

3. What types of details do you reveal
about yourself on Facebook or other
social networking sites? What details
do you look for in the profiles of potential dates?

4. Consider the statement that "it's the
men who do not use these easy forms
of communication that we find most
attractive." Do you agree or disagree
that "going the extra mile" makes
someone more attractive?

Scorecard

Selection 7:   991 words

Finishing Time: _____ _____ _____
                    HR.   MIN.   SEC.

Starting Time: _____ _____ _____
                    HR.   MIN.   SEC.

Reading Time: _____ _____
                          MIN.   SEC.

WPM Score: _____

Comprehension Score: for Items 6–15
Number Right: _____ × 10 = _____%

Assessing Your Reading Strategy

1. How would you rate your comprehension of the reading? (Circle one.)
Excellent   Good   Fair   Poor

2. Did you find your reading strategy
effective?   Yes   No

3. Suppose you were given an assignment
to read another selection from the same
source (a popular news magazine). Based
on your experience with this selection,
how would you adjust your reading
strategy (if at all)?

READING SELECTION 8   BUSINESS

Cutting-Edge Word-of-Mouth Advertising Strategies

Michael R. Solomon
From *Consumer Behavior: Buying, Having, and Being*

About the Reading

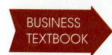

BUSINESS
TEXTBOOK

This selection is taken from a business textbook, Consumer Behavior: Buying, Having, and Being. *Courses in consumer behavior focus on why people choose to buy certain products and what goes into their decision-making process. Textbooks in this area often provide suggestions for effective advertising and marketing techniques.*

MyReadingLab™ *The exercises following this selection can be completed online at myreadinglab.com*

Planning Your Reading Strategy*

Directions: *Activate your thinking by previewing the reading (see the Need to Know box on page 64) and answering the following questions.*

_____ 1. What do the headings found within the reading have in common?
  a. They are all Internet-based strategies.
  b. They are all modern marketing techniques.
  c. They were all developed to sell toys.
  d. They have all been in use for decades.

_____ 2. All of the following clues indicate that you may be able to read the selection somewhat quickly, *except*
  a. You are likely already familiar with some of the concepts you encountered in your preview (such as YouTube).
  b. It will be difficult to find applications of this selection to your life or the world around you.
  c. The author works to ensure that the reading seems "hip," "with it," and modern.
  d. The author has included graphic aids to grab and keep your attention.

  3. What marketing techniques and promotional strategies have you observed (or participated in) in the past year? How has the Internet influenced your buying behavior?

1 In the "old days" (i.e., a few years ago), here's how a toy company would launch a new product: Unveil a hot holiday toy during a spring trade fair, run a November–December saturation television ad campaign during cartoon prime time to sell the toy to kids, then sit back and watch as desperate parents scramble through the aisles at Toys-R-Us and wait for the resulting media coverage to drive still more sales. In today's so-called *New Media/Web2.0 market*, a

* The Scorecard on p. 189 enables you to compute your reading rate. In order to do so, be sure to record your starting time in the Scorecard box before you begin reading.

toy marketer is more likely to encourage buzz from bloggers; instant messaging; subtle product placement in targeted TV shows, movies, and videos "gone viral" on YouTube and hundreds of smaller Web sites dedicated to highly involved hobbyists.

2   As marketers increasingly recognize the power of WOM (word of mouth) to make or break a new product, they are coming up with new ways to get consumers to help them sell. Let's review some successful strategies.

■ Virtual Communities

3   In ancient times (that is, before the Web was widely accessible), most membership reference groups consisted of people who had face-to-face contact. Now, it's possible to share interests with people you've never met—and probably never will. Consider the case of Widespread Panic. The band has never had a music video on MTV or cracked the Billboard Top 200. But it's one of the top 40 touring bands in the United States. How did it get to be so successful? Simple—the group built a virtual community of fans and opened itself up to them. It enlisted listeners to help promote the group in exchange for free tickets and backstage passes. Then, it went virtual: The band lets fans send messages to its recording studio, and hard-core followers can find out vital information such as what band members ate for lunch via regular updates on their Web sites.

4   A **virtual community of consumption** is a collection of people who interact online to share their enthusiasm for and knowledge about a specific consumption activity. These groups form around common love for a product, whether it's Barbie dolls or BlackBerry PDAs. However, members remain anonymous because they only interact with each other in cyberspace. Still, these groups can and do make their voices heard. In one recent effort, nearly 14,000 people banded together on Facebook to beg Cadbury Schweppes to bring back Wispa, a chocolate bar the company discontinued in 2003. Sure enough, Cadbury announced in late 2007 that it is reintroducing the candy bar.

5   How do people get drawn into consumption communities? Internet users tend to progress from asocial information gathering ("lurkers" are surfers who like to watch but don't participate) to increasingly affiliative social activities. At first they will merely browse the site, but later they may well be drawn into active participation.

■ Guerrilla Marketing

6   To promote their hip-hop albums, Def Jam and other labels start building a buzz months before a release, leaking advance copies to deejays who put together "mix tapes" to sell on the street. If the kids seem to like a song, *street teams* then push it to club deejays. As the official release date nears, these groups of fans start slapping up posters around the inner city. They plaster telephone poles, sides of buildings, and car windshields with promotions announcing the release of new albums. These streetwise strategies started in the mid-1970s, when pioneering deejays like Kool DJ Herc and Afrika Bambaataa promoted their parties through graffiti-style flyers. As Ice Cube observed, "Even though I'm an established artist, I still like to leak my music to a kid on the street and let him duplicate it for his homies before it hits radio."

7   This type of grassroots effort epitomizes **guerrilla marketing**: promotional strategies that use unconventional locations and intensive word-of-mouth campaigns to push products. These campaigns often recruit legions of real consumers who agree to engage in some kind of street theater or other activity in order to convince others to use the product or service. Scion for example often reaches out to its young buyers with street teams that distribute merchandise and hang wild posters wherever they can to

encourage twentysomethings to check out the videos and multiplayer games on its Web site.

8   Today, big companies are buying into guerrilla marketing strategies big-time, Here are some guerrilla campaigns that built buzz:

- Procter & Gamble started a unit called Tremor to spread the word about its products among young people. It recruited almost 300,000 kids between the ages of 13 and 19 to deliver endorsements in school cafeterias, at sleepovers, by cell phone, and by e-mail. It taps these Tremorites to talk up just about everything, from movies and music (such as new releases by artists like Lenny Kravitz and Coldplay) to milk and motor oil—and they do it free. Tremor looks for kids with a wide social circle and a gift of gab. To register, kids fill out a questionnaire, which asks them, among other things, to report how many friends, family members, and acquaintances they communicate with every day. P&G rewards the kids for their help by sending them exclusive music mixes and other trinkets, such as shampoo and cheap watches.

- *Brand ambassadors* pop up in eye-catching outfits to announce a new brand or service. AT&T sent its ambassadors to high-traffic areas of California and New Jersey, doing random favors such as handing dog biscuits to people walking their dogs and providing binoculars to concertgoers to promote its

A campaign to create a buzz for the Mini Cooper was disguised as a debate over whether a British engineer built robots out of Mini car parts. It extended across Web sites, postings in chat rooms, and booklets inserted in magazines like Motor Trend *and* Rolling Stone. *The 40-page booklets pretended to be excerpts from a book,* Men of Metal: Eyewitness Accounts of Humanoid Robots, *from a fake London publisher specializing in conspiracy-theory literature covering the likes of Bigfoot, the Loch Ness monster, and UFOs. One goal of the campaign was to appeal to mechanically minded male drivers who may be put off by women's praise of the Mini as "cute."*

new AT&T Local Service. Hyatt Hotels unleashed 100 bellhops in Manhattan, who spent the day opening doors, carrying packages, and handing out pillow mints to thousands of consumers.

■ Viral Marketing

9   Many students are big fans of Hotmail, a free e-mail service. But there's no such thing as a free lunch: Hotmail inserts a small ad on every message sent, making each user a salesperson. The company had 5 million subscribers in its first year and it continues to grow exponentially.

Viral marketing refers to the strategy of getting visitors to a Web site to forward information on the site to their friends in order to make still more consumers aware of the product—usually by creating online content that is entertaining or just plain weird. To promote a use for a razor that it could never discuss on TV, Philips launched a Norelco Web site, shaveeverywhere.com. The ad features a guy in a bathrobe explaining how to use the shaver in places, well, not on your head. The site uses pictures of fruit and vegetables to refer to male body parts.

At threadless.com, users vote on which T-shirt designs the company will print and sell.

Reprinted by permission of Threadless.com

■ Social Networking and Crowd Power

10 Odds are you've already logged in some serious time on Facebook or MySpace before you started reading this paragraph today. **Social networking**, where members post information about themselves and make contact with others who share similar interests and opinions, may well be the biggest development in consumer behavior since the TV dinner! Almost daily we hear about yet another social networking site where users can set up a home page with photos, a profile, and links to others in their social networks. They can browse for friends, dates, partners for activities, or contacts of all kinds and invite them to join the users' personal networks as "friends."

11   Fun aside, social networking has some really serious marketing implications. Indeed, it's fair to say that aspects of this technology revolution are fundamentally changing business models in many industries—especially because they empower end consumers to literally become partners and shape markets. It's hard to overstate the impact this change will have on how we create, distribute, promote, and consume products and services.

12   In a sense a lot of social networking sites let their members dictate purchase decisions. For example, at Threadless.com, customers rank T-shirt designs ahead of time and the company prints the winning ideas. Every week, contestants upload T-shirts designs to the site, where about 700 compete to be among the six that it will print during that time. Threadless visitors score designs on a scale of 0 to 5, and the staff selects winners from the most popular entrants. The six lucky artists each get $2,000 in cash and merchandise. Threadless sells out of every shirt it offers. This business model has made a small fortune for a few designers "the crowd" particularly likes. One pair of Chicago-based artists sold $16 million worth of T-shirts.

Examining Reading Selection 8

🔧 ⌐Complete this Exercise at **myreadinglab.com**

Checking Your Vocabulary

Directions: *Use context, word parts, or a dictionary, if necessary, to determine the meaning of each word as it is used in the reading.*

____ 1. subtle (paragraph 1)
   a. improper
   b. hard to detect
   c. instant
   d. obvious

____ 2. vital (paragraph 3)
   a. careful
   b. essential
   c. extraordinary
   d. professional

____ 3. epitomizes (paragraph 7)
   a. avoids
   b. changes
   c. is typical of
   d. leaves out

____ 4. legions (paragraph 7)
   a. products
   b. multitudes
   c. critics
   d. locations

____ 5. empower (paragraph 11)
   a. give authority
   b. strongly agree
   c. impair or prevent
   d. misdirect or misguide

Checking Your Comprehension

Directions: *Select the best answer.*

____ 6. This selection is primarily concerned with
   a. blogging.
   b. marketing.
   c. online gaming.
   d. social networking.

____ 7. The main point of the selection is that
   a. traditional marketing techniques are outdated and have no place in today's world.
   b. marketers are using online technologies and other unconventional techniques to get consumers to help them sell products.
   c. online social networking communities have an important impact on the way people live, work, and play.
   d. consumers rely on many different factors when they are making a purchase decision.

____ 8. The type of promotional strategy that uses unconventional locations and intensive word-of-mouth campaigns to push products is called
   a. guerrilla marketing.
   b. a virtual consumption community.
   c. a saturation campaign.
   d. product placement.

____ 9. *Viral marketing* refers to the strategy of
   a. wearing attention-getting outfits to announce a new brand or service.
   b. getting visitors to a Web site to forward information on the site to their friends.
   c. sending street teams out to put up posters and flyers around the inner city.
   d. recruiting teenagers to deliver product endorsements at school.

____ 10. The author supports his ideas primarily with
   a. examples.
   b. statistics.
   c. personal experience.
   d. reasons.

Thinking Critically

____ 11. In paragraph 1, the author compares
   a. television and the Internet.
   b. types of social networks.
   c. types of consumer decisions.
   d. old and new ways of marketing products.

____ 12. Based on the selection, all of the following statements about consumption communities are true *except*
   a. Consumption communities typically form around a common love for a product.
   b. Consumption communities are sponsored by a specific company marketing a product.
   c. People who browse a consumption community site without participating are known as "lurkers."
   d. Members of a consumption community remain anonymous because they only interact with each other in cyberspace.

____ 13. The photo from http://www.miniusa.com (p. 185) was included in the selection as an example of
   a. a social networking site for people interested in robots.
   b. an online gaming site for Mini Cooper car hobbyists.
   c. a Web site devoted to debates over conspiracy theories.
   d. a creative marketing campaign created for the Mini Cooper.

___ 14. The tone of this selection is
    a. informative.
    b. critical.
    c. argumentative.
    d. indifferent.

___ 15. The photo of threadless.com's Web
    site on page 186 is an example of
    which strategy?
    a. guerrilla marketing
    b. viral marketing
    c. crowd power
    d. brand ambassadors

Scorecard

Selection 8:   1,569 words

Finishing Time: _____ _____ _____
              HR.   MIN.   SEC.

Starting Time: _____ _____ _____
              HR.   MIN.   SEC.

Reading Time: _____ _____
                  MIN.   SEC.

WPM Score: _____

Comprehension Score: for Items 6–15
Number Right: _____ × 10 = _____%

Assessing Your Reading Strategy

1. How would you rate your comprehension
of the reading? (Circle one.)
Excellent   Good   Fair   Poor

2. Did you find your reading strategy
effective?   Yes   No

3. Suppose you were given an assignment
to read another selection from the same
source (a consumer-behavior textbook).
Based on your experience with this selection, how would you adjust your reading
strategy (if at all)?

Writing About Reading Selection 8

⚙ Complete this Exercise at myreadinglab.com

Checking Your Vocabulary

Directions: *Complete each of the following items; refer to a dictionary if necessary.*

1. Discuss the denotative and connotative
meanings of the word *guerrilla* in paragraph 7.

_____

_____

_____

_____

_____

2. Define the word *affiliative* (paragraph 5)
and underline the word or phrase

that provides a context clue for its
meaning.

_____

_____

3. Define the word *trinkets* (paragraph 8)
and underline the word or phrase that
provides a context clue for its meaning.

_____

_____

4. Determine the meanings of the following words by using word parts:
a. *unveil* (paragraph 1)

_____

b. *hobbyists* (paragraph 1)

_____

c. *discontinued* (paragraph 4)

_____

d. *asocial* (paragraph 5)

_____

e. *multiplayer* (paragraph 7)

_____

_____

Checking Your Comprehension

5. What is a "virtual community of consumption" and how do people get
drawn into one?

_____

_____

_____

_____

_____

_____

6. For each of the following types of marketing strategies, identify at least one
product or service associated with the
strategy in the reading selection.
a. guerrilla marketing:

_____

_____

b. viral marketing:

_____

c. social networking:

_____

7. According to the selection, how did
the band Widespread Panic become so
successful?

_____

_____

_____

8. When and how did street teams get
started as a marketing strategy?

_____

_____

_____

Thinking Critically

9. What does Procter & Gamble look for in
its "Tremorites"?

_____

_____

_____

_____

10. Why does the author say aspects of the
technology revolution are fundamentally changing business models?

_____

_____

_____

_____

11. What does the author mean when he
says "there's no such thing as a free
lunch" (paragraph 9)?

_____

_____

_____

_____

12. What is the purpose of the Mini Cooper
ad on page 185?

_____

_____

1. The selection mentions product placement in TV shows and movies and on the Internet. In your opinion, how effective is product placement as a marketing strategy? Describe instances of product placement that you have observed and discuss how product placement has affected your own consumer behavior.

2. Do you belong to any virtual consumption communities? Describe your experiences in virtual communities and discuss the benefits of being a member.

3. Would you ever consider being a brand ambassador or participating in some other guerrilla marketing campaign? Why or why not? Have you ever participated in a viral marketing campaign? How is that different from other types of guerrilla marketing?

think VISUALLY...

This photograph shows shoes in a store displayed in pairs arranged by size, style, and color. Can you imagine how confusing it would be to shop if all the shoes had been mixed together randomly? Stores and markets group items together for the convenience of their customers. Similarly, writers group their ideas together into organized sequences for the convenience of the reader—to make their ideas clear and easy to understand. This chapter will show you basic patterns writers use to organize their ideas.

Learning GOALS

In this chapter, you will learn how to . . .

Goal 1 Recognize common organizational patterns to improve recall

Goal 2 Use six common organizational patterns to aid in comprehension

Goal 3 Use other patterns to build comprehension

Goal 4 Use transitional words to understand relationships within and among sentences

Goal 5 Think critically about cause-effect relationships

■ How Recognizing a Pattern Improves Recall

Goal 1

Recognize common organizational patterns to improve recall

Which of the following phone numbers would be easier to remember?

> 876–5432
>
> 792–6538

Which of the following sets of directions would be easier to remember?

> After you pass two signals, turn left. Then pass two more signals, and turn right. Next, pass two more signals, and turn left.
>
> After you pass two streets, turn left. Then after you pass three more streets, turn right. Next, pass one more street, and turn right.

Which of the following shopping lists would be easier to remember if you forgot your list?

> paint, brushes, paint remover, drop cloth
>
> milk, deodorant, nails, comb

In each example, you probably selected the first choice as easier to remember. Now, let us consider *why* each is easier to remember than the other choice. The first choices each had a pattern. The items were connected in some way that made it possible to remember them together. The phone number consists of consecutive digits in reverse order; the directions consist of two left, two right, two left; the shopping list contains items related to a particular task—painting. From these examples you can see that items are easier to remember if they are related in some way.

Lists A and B each contain five facts. Which would be easier to learn?

List A

> 1. Cheeseburgers contain more calories than hamburgers.
> 2. Christmas cactus plants bloom once a year.
> 3. Many herbs have medicinal uses.
> 4. Many ethnic groups live in Toronto.
> 5. Fiction books are arranged alphabetically by author.

List B

> 1. Effective advertising has several characteristics.
> 2. An ad must be unique.
> 3. An ad must be believable.
> 4. An ad must make a lasting impression.
> 5. An ad must substantiate a claim.

Most likely, you chose list B. There is no connection between the facts in list A; the facts in list B, however, are related. The first sentence made a general statement, and each remaining sentence gave a particular characteristic of effective advertising. Together they fit into a pattern.

The details of a paragraph, paragraphs within an essay, events within a short story, or sections within a textbook often fit a pattern. If you can recognize the pattern, you will find it easier to remember the content. You will be able to remember a unified whole rather than independent pieces of information.

You will find that patterns are useful in other academic situations in addition to reading textbooks.

- Professors use patterns to organize their lectures. If you can recognize the pattern of a lecture, note taking will become an easier task.
- Patterns will help you write stronger papers and class assignments.
- Essay exams often contain questions that require you to use one or more patterns.
- Patterns will help you organize your speech, both in formal presentations and in classroom discussions.

■ Six Common Organizational Patterns

Goal 2

Use six common organizational patterns to aid in comprehension

The most common organizational patterns are *chronological order, definition, classification, comparison-contrast, cause-effect,* and *enumeration.* To help you visualize these patterns, a diagram called a **map** is presented for each. These maps are useful ways to organize information for study and review, especially if you are a visual learner. If you are an applied learner, you may find that maps make abstract ideas more tangible and concrete. As you will see in the section titled "Mixed Patterns" (on p. 219), patterns sometimes overlap.

TECH SUPPORT Creating Organizational Patterns

Many thought patterns, such as *chronological order, process,* and *cause-effect,* can be visually depicted. Organizing your ideas with a visual diagram is an effective learning strategy; it can also help you with drafting writing assignments. Most word processing programs include tools that can help you visually organize your ideas. On yours, you might find "Diagram," "AutoShapes," or "Organization Charts" on the drop-down "Insert" menus.

Chronological Order/Process

One of the most obvious patterns is time order, also called sequence of events or chronological order/process. In this pattern, ideas are presented in the order in which they occur in time. The event that happened first appears

FLEXIBILITY TIP

It is often helpful to know when the steps in a process must be followed in exact order. For instance, in a recipe it usually doesn't matter if you add water to flour, or the other way around. But if you are an emergency medical technician and need to provide life support, the order of your activities is extremely important. As you read, ask yourself if a process must be completed in a particular order to be effective.

first in the paragraph, the event that occurred next in time appears next, and so on. You can visualize the pattern as follows:

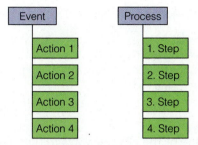

Chronological order is used frequently to report current events. Directions and instructions are often written using this pattern. The following paragraph, taken from an American government text, is organized using chronological order:

Ours is an ethnically, religiously, and racially diverse society. The white European Protestants, black slaves, and Native Americans who made up the bulk of the U.S. population when the first census was taken in 1790 were joined by Catholic immigrants from Ireland and Germany in the 1840s and 1850s. In the 1870s, Chinese migrated to America drawn by jobs in railroad construction. Around the turn of the twentieth century, most immigration was from Eastern, Central, and Southern Europe, with its many ethnic, linguistic, and religious groups. Today, most immigration is from Asia and Latin America.

—Edward Greenberg and Benjamin Page, *The Struggle for Democracy,* Brief Version, Second Edition, p. 71. Copyright © 1999 Longman, a division of Pearson Education, Inc.

This excerpt could be mapped by using a time line:

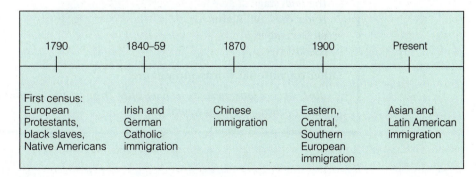

Entire passages and chapters, or even books, may be organized using the chronological order pattern. Here are the section headings from a chapter in an advertising textbook. Notice how the topics proceed in order by time.

THE HISTORY OF ADVERTISING

Early History
How the Advertising Agency Grew Up
Early Twentieth-Century Advertising
Advertising Today

—Dorothy Cohen, *Advertising,* pp. ii–iii. Copyright © 1988
Scott Foresman, a division of Pearson Education, Inc.

One of the clearest ways to describe how to do something is to use steps that follow the order in which they are to be done. This is why chronological order is often used to describe the steps in a process or to outline a method or procedure. The following excerpt from a visual arts text describes the process of etching.

The process of making an *etching* begins with the preparation of a metal plate with a *ground*—a protective coating of acid-resistant material that covers the copper or zinc. The printmaker then draws easily through the ground with a pointed tool, exposing the metal. Finally, the plate is immersed in acid. Acid "bites" into the plate where the drawing has exposed the metal, making a groove that varies in depth according to the strength of the acid and the length of time the plate is in the acid bath.

—Preble, Duane; Preble, Sarah; Frank, Patrick L., *Artforms,* 6th Ed., © 1999. Reprinted
and electronically reproduced by permission of Pearson Education, Inc., Upper Saddle River, NJ.

Materials organized in chronological order use transitional words or phrases to connect the events or steps.

Chronological Order/Process Transitional Words/Phrases

in the Middle Ages . . .
the *final* stage . . .
before the Civil Rights Act . . .
on December 7 . . .
the *last* step . . .

Other transitional words/phrases are:

first, second, later, next, as soon as, after, then, finally, meanwhile, last, during, when, by the time, until

| EXERCISE 5–1 | **USING CHRONOLOGICAL ORDER** |

Directions: *Using chronological order/process, put each of the following groups of sentences in the correct order. For each sentence, write a number from 1 to 4, beginning with the topic sentence.*

A.

____ Finally, the completed Voters Guides were distributed to libraries throughout the region one month prior to election day.

____ Two months before the election, we asked each candidate to submit answers to preselected questions.

____ The document was then sent out to be printed.

____ The answers were edited over the course of the next two weeks and compiled into the Voters Guide.

B.

____ On October 22, this situation was revealed by President Kennedy.

____ In the fall of 1962, the Soviet Union began setting up missile bases in Cuba with weapons that could easily strike the United States.

____ Six days later, after a U.S. Naval barricade was established to prevent more shipments of military equipment, Kennedy and Soviet Premier Kruschev resolved the crisis.

____ On November 2, the president assured Americans that the Cuban missile crisis was over.

C.

____ During the Ming Dynasty (1368–1644), the wall reached completion.

____ In 210 B.C., these parts were unified into the first major section.

____ The very first parts of the Great Wall of China were built in the 4th century B.C.

____ Today, two main visitor centers provide tourists with access to this human-made marvel. ■

| EXERCISE 5–2 | **PREDICTING CHRONOLOGICAL ORDER** |

Directions: *Which of the following topic sentences suggest that their paragraphs will be developed by using chronology? Put check marks beside your answers.*

____ 1. The human brain is divided into two halves, each of which is responsible for separate functions.

____ 2. Advertising has appeared in magazines since the late 1700s.

___ 3. The life cycle of a product is the stages it goes through from when it is first created to when it is no longer produced.

___ 4. There are really only two ways to gather information from human beings about what they are currently thinking or feeling.

___ 5. To determine whether you will vote for a particular presidential candidate, you should first examine his or her philosophy of government. ■

EXERCISE 5–3   **ANALYZING CHRONOLOGICAL ORDER**

Directions: *Read the following excerpt from a political science textbook and answer the questions that follow.*

POLITICAL BACKGROUND OF SEGREGATION

The end of the Civil War and the emancipation of the slaves did not give blacks the full rights of citizenship, nor did the passing of the Thirteenth Amendment in 1865 (which outlawed slavery), or the Fourteenth Amendment in 1868 (which extended "equal protection of the laws" to all citizens), or the Fifteenth Amendment in 1870 (which guaranteed the right to vote to all male citizens regardless of "race, color, or previous condition of servitude"). Between 1866 and 1877 the "radical Republicans" controlled Congress. Although the sometimes corrupt period of *Reconstruction* partly deserves the bad name it has gotten in the South, it was a time when blacks won a number of political rights. In 1875 Congress passed a civil rights act designed to prevent any public form of discrimination—in theaters, restaurants, transportation, and the like—against blacks. Congress's right to forbid a *state* to act contrary to the Constitution was unquestioned. But this law, based on the Fourteenth Amendment, assumed that Congress could also prevent racial discrimination by private individuals.

The Supreme Court disagreed. In 1883 it declared the Civil Rights Act of 1875 unconstitutional. The majority of the Court ruled that Congress could pass legislation only to correct *states'* violations of the Fourteenth Amendment. Congress had no power to enact "primary and direct" legislation on individuals; that was left to the states. This decision meant the federal government could not lawfully protect blacks against most forms of discrimination. In other words, white supremacy was beyond federal control.

—Gary Wasserman, *The Basics of American Politics,* Eighth Edition, pp. 163–164.
Copyright © 1999 Longman, a division of Pearson Education, Inc.

1. Draw a map of the major events discussed in this article in the order in which they occurred.

2. List the transitional words used in this excerpt.

■

Definition

Each academic discipline has its own specialized vocabulary. One of the primary purposes of introductory textbooks is to introduce students to this new language. Consequently, definition is a commonly used pattern throughout most introductory-level texts.

Suppose you were asked to define the word *comedian* for someone unfamiliar with the term. First, you would probably say that a comedian is a person who entertains. Then you might distinguish a comedian from other types of entertainers by saying that a comedian is an entertainer who tells jokes and makes others laugh. Finally, you might mention, by way of example, the names of several well-known comedians who have appeared on television. Although you may have presented it informally, your definition would have followed the standard, classic pattern. The first part of your definition tells what general class or group the term belongs to (entertainers). The second part tells what distinguishes the term from other items in the same class or category. The third part includes further explanation, characteristics, examples, or applications.

Here are two additional examples:

Term	General Class	Distinguishing Features
Stress	Physiological reaction	A response to a perceived threat
Mutant	Organism	Carries a gene that has undergone a change

You can map the definition pattern as follows:

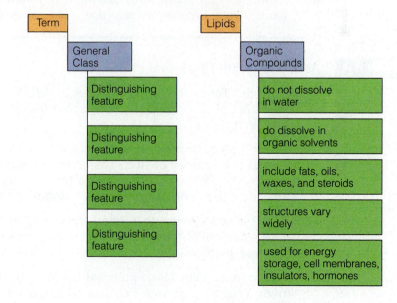

In the following excerpt, the writer defines the term *lipids*:

> The lipids are a diverse group of energy-rich organic compounds whose main common feature is that they do not dissolve in water. They do, however, dissolve in various organic solvents such as ether, chloroform, and benzene. They include the fats, oils, waxes, and steroids. Their structures vary widely, and they are employed as energy storage molecules (especially in animals), components of cell membranes, insulators for the nervous system, and hormones—just to mention a few. We will focus next on two of the major lipid categories.
>
> —Rischer and Easton, *Focus on Human Biology*, 2e, HarperCollins Publishers.

In this paragraph, the general class of lipids is "organic compounds." Their distinguishing feature is that they do not dissolve in water but do dissolve in organic solvents. The remainder of the paragraph gives examples and explains their structure and use.

Definition Pattern Transitional Words/Phrases

nepotism *is . . .*
classical conditioning *refers to . . .*
acceleration *can be defined as . . .*
empathy *means . . .*

Other transitional words/phrases are:

consists of, is a term that, involves, is called, is characterized by, that is, occurs when, exists when, are those that, entails, corresponds to, is literally

EXERCISE 5–4   **ANALYZING DEFINITIONS**

Directions: *For each of the following brief definitions, circle the term being defined. Then place a box around the class to which it belongs and underline the distinguishing features.*

1. Partnership is a form of ownership used by small businesses. A partnership has two or more owners. The partners establish their own rules for the operation of the business and for how money is spent. The partners also divide up responsibilities and decision-making authority.

2. Natural selection refers to a theory developed by Charles Darwin in the 1850s. Also called "survival of the fittest," this theory postulates that over time, living things best suited to their environment tend to survive.

3. A very strong man-made material is concrete. This mixture of sand, stones, cement, and water creates a compact and very hard building material once it is completely set.

4. The troposphere—one of the layers of air that surround our planet—is the lowest and most dense layer and the one in which the most weather occurs.

5. Jainism is thought to be the oldest religion in the world from which many other religions have developed. Jains believe in strict noninterference with other living things and therefore follow a vegetarian diet. ■

EXERCISE 5–5   **PREDICTING THE DEFINITION PATTERN**

Directions: *From the following textbook chapter headings, select those that are most likely to use the definition pattern. Put check marks beside your answers.*

___ 1. The Nature of Culture

___ 2. What Is Conditioning?

___ 3. Stressors: The Roots of Stress

___ 4. The Origin of Life

___ 5. Second Law of Thermodynamics   ■

EXERCISE 5–6   **ANALYZING THE DEFINITION PATTERN**

Directions: *Read the following excerpt from a geography textbook and answer the questions that follow.*

SHIFTING CULTIVATION

The native peoples of remote tropical lowlands and hills in the Americas, Africa, Southeast Asia, and Indonesia practice an agricultural system known as **shifting cultivation.** Essentially, this is a land-rotation system. Using machetes or other bladed instruments, farmers chop away the undergrowth from small patches of land and kill the trees by cutting off a strip of bark completely around the trunk. After the dead vegetation has dried out, the farmers set it on fire to clear the land. These clearing techniques have given shifting cultivation the name of "slash-and-burn" agriculture. Working with digging sticks or hoes, the farmers then plant a variety of crops in the clearings, varying from the corn, beans, bananas, and manioc of American Indians to the yams and nonirrigated rice grown by hill tribes in Southeast Asia. Different crops are typically planted together in the same clearing, a practice called **intertillage.** This allows taller, stronger crops to shelter lower, more fragile ones from the tropical downpours and reveals the rich lore and learning acquired by shifting cultivators over many centuries. Relatively little tending of the plants is necessary until harvest time, and no fertilizer is applied to the fields. Farmers repeat the planting and harvesting cycle in the same clearings for perhaps four or five years, until the soil has lost much of its fertility. Then these areas are abandoned, and the farmers prepare new clearings to replace them. The abandoned fields lie unused and recuperate for 10 to 20 years before farmers clear and cultivate them again. Shifting cultivation is one form of **subsistence agriculture**—that is, involving food production mainly for the family and local community rather than for market.

—Jordan, Domosh, and Rowntree, *The Human Mosaic: A Thematic Introduction to Cultural Geography,* 6e, HarperCollins Publishers.

1. In your own words, write a definition for each of the three terms defined in the paragraph (see **boldfaced print**).

_____

_____

_____

_____

_____

_____

2. For each definition, identify the general class and distinguishing characteristics as given in the passage.

_____

_____

_____

_____

_____

3. Underline any transitional words used in the passage.

Classification

If you were asked to describe types of Web sites, you might mention informational, commercial, personal, and so forth. By dividing a broad topic into its major categories, you are using a pattern known as *classification*.

This pattern is widely used in many academic fields. For example, a psychology text might explain human needs by classifying them into two categories: primary and secondary. In a chemistry textbook, various compounds may be grouped and discussed according to common characteristics such as the presence of hydrogen or oxygen. The classification pattern divides a topic into parts based on common or shared characteristics.

You can visualize the classification pattern as follows:

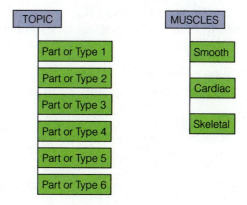

Read the following paragraph to discover how the author classifies muscles:

TYPES OF MUSCLES IN HUMANS

Human muscles can be divided into three groups according to their structure and the nerves that activate them. **Smooth muscle** is found in a number of internal structures, such as the walls of the digestive tract, around some blood vessels, and in certain internal organs. **Cardiac muscle** is found in the walls of the heart. Both of these are involuntary, since they function without conscious control. Thus, you don't have to lie awake nights keeping your heart beating. There is some fascinating evidence that "involuntary" responses can be voluntarily controlled to a degree. . . . **Skeletal muscles** are the voluntary muscles.

—Wallace, Robert, *Biology: World of Life,* 6th Ed., © 1992. Reprinted and electronically reproduced by permission of Pearson Education, Inc., Upper Saddle River, NJ.

This paragraph classifies muscles into three types: smooth, cardiac, and skeletal. The classification is based on their structure and the nerves that activate them.

Classification Pattern Transitional Words/Phrases

There are *several types of* bones . . .
An S-corporation *is composed of* . . .
Another kind of memory is . . .
Societies can be *classified as* . . .

Other transitional words/phrases are:

comprises, one type, a second class of, another group, several varieties of, kinds, divisions, categories

EXERCISE 5–7

USING CLASSIFICATION

Directions: *Each item below consists of a topic and several subtopics into which it can be classified. For each word group, fill in the missing information.*

1. Topic: Literature
   Types of literature: poems, short stories, _____

2. Topic: Taxes
   Types of taxes: sales, property, _____

3. Topic: Natural disasters
   Types of natural disasters: earthquakes, hurricanes, _____

4. Topic: Geography
   Geographic features: mountains, lakes, _____

5. Topic: Medicine
   Medical specialties: pediatrics, orthopedics, _____ ■

EXERCISE 5–8

PREDICTING THE CLASSIFICATION PATTERN

Directions: *Identify and put a check mark next to the topics in the following list that might be developed by using the classification pattern.*

____ 1. Types of utility   ____ 6. The discovery of DNA

____ 2. The staffing process   ____ 7. Formal organizations

____ 3. Growth of plant life   ____ 8. Animal tissues

____ 4. Functions of dating   ____ 9. Effects of negative feelings

____ 5. Theories of evolution   ____ 10. Classifying emotions ■

EXERCISE 5–9

ANALYZING CLASSIFICATION

Directions: *Read the following excerpt from a biology textbook and answer the questions that follow.*

ANGIOSPERMS

All plants that develop a *true flower* are classified as **angiosperms.** The angiosperms vary with respect to their number of floral parts, but all **flowers** are reproductive structures that contain both male and female reproductive parts, and their seeds develop within fruits. More than 300 families of angiosperms are separated into two major classes, monocots and dicots.

Monocots

Monocots develop from germinated seeds that have a single embryonic leaf (called a cotyledon) and grow into plants with parallel leaf venation and floral parts that occur in threes or multiples of three. The vascular tissues in cross sections of monocot stems appear as scattered bundles of cells.

Monocots include most species that are cultivated as food crops by humans. The grass family is by far the largest and most important; it includes rice, wheat, barley, oats, other grains, and the grasses on which most animal *herbivores* feed [. . . .] The largest monocot species belong to the pineapple, banana, and palm families.

Many spring wildflowers are monocots in the lily, iris, and orchid families. The orchid family has the largest number of flowering plants, over 20,000 species, most of which grow in tropical or subtropical regions of the world.

Dicots

Dicots develop from germinated seeds that have two cotyledons, grow into plants with nested leaf venation, and produce flowers with parts in fours or fives or multiples of four or five. The vascular tissue in the dicot stem forms a circular pattern when viewed in cross section.

—Mix, Michael C., *Biology: The Network of Life,* 1st Ed., © 1992. Reprinted and electronically reproduced by permission of Pearson Education Inc., Upper Saddle River, NJ.

1. What is the subject of the classification?

   _____

2. How is it divided?

   _____

3. Circle the words in this excerpt that suggest the organizational pattern being used. ■

EXERCISE 5–10

IDENTIFYING PATTERNS

Directions: *Select a brief section from a textbook chapter you are currently studying that uses either the* chronological, definition, *or* classification *pattern. State which pattern is being used and list the transitional words or phrases that provided you with clues to the type of pattern.* ■

Comparison-Contrast

Often a writer will explain an object or idea, especially if it is unfamiliar to the reader, by showing how it is similar to or different from a familiar object or idea. At other times, it may be the writer's purpose to show how two ideas, places, objects, or people are similar or different. In each of these situations a writer commonly uses a pattern called comparison-contrast. This pattern emphasizes the similarities or differences between two or more items. There are several variations on this pattern: a paragraph

FLEXIBILITY TIP

While the order, definition, and classification patterns are primarily *descriptive*, the comparison-contrast pattern often indicates a reading that is more *analytical* and thus more likely to require close attention and slower reading.

may focus on similarities only, differences only, or both. The comparison pattern can be visualized and mapped as follows:

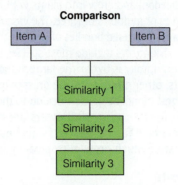

For material that focuses on differences, you might use a map like this:

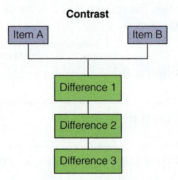

The following passage contrasts two types of advisory groups: councils and committees.

Councils and committees are advisory groups found in many different kinds of societies. We have briefly mentioned **councils** among the Shavante, Tetum, and Qashgai. They meet in public and are usually made up of informally appointed elders. **Committees** differ from councils in that they meet privately. Moreover, whereas councils are typical of simpler political organizations, committees are more characteristic of states. But the two kinds of groups can and often do coexist within the same political organization. When this occurs, councils are superior to committees, whose tasks and powers are delegated to them by councils.

Councils tend to be consensus-seeking bodies, while committees are more likely to achieve agreement by voting (although either kind of body may reach decisions in either way). Consensus seeking is typical of small social groups whose members have frequent personal interaction. Once a council or committee increases to more than about 50 members, decision by consensus is no longer possible. Voting is typical of larger groups whose members do not see much of one another in daily life and who owe their main allegiance not to other group members but to people (perhaps many millions) outside the council or committee. Members may in fact represent these outside people, as is the case with the U.S. Congress.

—Hicks and Gwynne, *Cultural Anthropology*, 2e, HarperCollins Publishers.

A map of the passage could look like this:

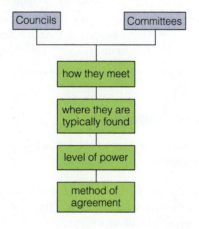

Look for both similarities and differences. First establish what is being compared or contrasted to what. Next determine whether similarities, differences, or both are presented. Often the title, heading, or topic sentence will express the basic relationship between the items or ideas discussed. A topic sentence that states, "It is important to make a distinction between amnesia and forgetting," indicates that the paragraph is primarily concerned with differences. On the other hand, a heading such as "Two Compatible Proposals for Economic Development" emphasizes similarities. Finally, decide whether the comparison or the contrast is the author's central purpose or whether it is used only as a means of support for the main idea.

Comparison–Contrast Transitional Words/Phrases

Comparison	Contrast
both Faulkner and Williams . . .	*unlike* primary groups, secondary groups . . .
values, norms, and ethics *share* . . .	a drive *differs from* a need in that . . .

Other transitional words/phrases are:

Comparison: *likewise, in comparison, to compare, resembles, is similar, in the same way, correspondingly, as well as, like*

Contrast: *in contrast, on the contrary, although, even though, similarly, however, on the other hand, as opposed to, whereas, instead, in spite of*

EXERCISE 5–11   **ANALYZING COMPARISONS**

Directions: *In each of the following sentences, underline the two items that are being compared.*

1. Humans are complex organisms made up of many sophisticated systems. Yet humans share several characteristics with primates such as gorillas and New World Monkeys.

2. Students of education need to learn about human behavior in order to become perceptive teachers. Courses in sociology and psychology will provide a strong foundation since both these subjects deal with how people act under certain circumstances.

3. Face-to-face communication and electronic communication share a common goal—the transmission of information.

4. Microbiology deals with a broad range of scientific subjects. Two of these, immunology and virology, are of particular interest to medical researchers who study infectious diseases.

5. Flame retardant and flame resistant fabrics each provide a degree of protection to the person wearing them.

| EXERCISE 5–12 | **ANALYZING CONTRASTS** |

Directions: *In each of the following sentences, underline the two items that are being contrasted.*

1. Educators differ in their approaches to teaching reading. One method, whole language, applies a holistic model to literacy. The other main approach, seen as old-fashioned by some, is phonics, where children learn to read by "sounding out" letters and letter combinations.

2. Many people misuse the two common terms *sex* and *gender*. Sex refers to the two main categories of male and female into which humans and most living things are divided on the basis of their reproductive functions. Gender is typically used with reference to social and cultural differences rather than biological ones.

3. Mystery novels come in many types. At the most gentle end of the spectrum are cozies, books that are typically set in a country village and contain an appealing cast of quirky characters. At the darkest end of the spectrum is *noir*, which often features psychopaths and people in the criminal underworld.

4. Most scientists believe in a Darwinian view of evolution. However, there are some in the scientific community who sympathize with the Creationist point of view and would like to meld the two theories together.

5. Many actors believe that stage acting requires more overall skill than movie acting. Unlike filmmaking, where actors can make mistake after mistake, knowing that the scene will just be shot again and again until it is right, live theater demands more concentration and preparation since retakes are not possible.   ■

| EXERCISE 5–13 | **PREDICTING THE COMPARISON-CONTRAST PATTERN** |

Directions: *Which of the following topic sentences suggest that their paragraphs will be developed by using comparison-contrast? Put check marks beside your answers.*

_____ 1. Sociology and psychology both focus on human behavior.

_____ 2. The category of mammals contains many different kinds of animals.

_____ 3. Two types of leaders can usually be identified in organizations: informal and formal.

_____ 4. Interpersonal communication is far more complex than intrapersonal communication.

_____ 5. The first step in grasping a novel's theme is to read it closely for literal content, including plot and character development.   ■

ANALYZING COMPARISON-CONTRAST

Directions: *Read the following excerpt and answer the questions that follow.*

Social institutions are often confused with social groups and social organizations, which are described in the next chapter. They are not the same, however. Like institutions, groups and organizations exist to meet some goals, but groups and organizations are deliberately constructed bodies of individuals, whereas institutions are systems of norms. Thus education is an institution; the University of Vermont is an organization. Religion is an institution; the Baptist church is an organization.

The confusion between institutions and organizations stems in part from the fact that the names of institutions can often be used to describe concrete entities as well. In its abstract sense, for example, the word *family* is used to refer to an institution. Using the word in this way, we might say, "During the 1980s, the family in the United States began to undergo important changes." We can also use the word *family* to refer to an actual group of people, however. Using the word in this concrete sense, we might say, "I am going to spend my vacation with my family." The speaker is referring to an existing group of individuals— mother, father, sisters, and brothers. The two meanings of the word are closely related but nevertheless distinct. The word *institution* is an abstraction; the word *organization* refers to an existing group. The distinction should become clearer as we discuss social groups and social organizations in the next chapter and specific institutions in Chapters 12 through 17.

—Eshleman, Cashion, and Basirico, *Sociology: An Introduction,* 4e, HarperCollins Publishers.

1. Identify two topics that are discussed in the excerpt. Does the excerpt compare, contrast, or compare *and* contrast these two topics?

   _____

   _____

2. Draw a map of the similarities or differences between the two topics.

   _____

3. List any transitional words used in the selection.

   _____

Cause-Effect

The cause-effect pattern describes or discusses an event or action that is caused by another event or action. Four possible relationships are described by the cause-effect pattern:

1. **Single Cause–Single Effect.** One cause produces one effect.

   Example: Omitting a key command will cause a computer program to fail.

2. **Single Cause–Multiple Effects.** One event produces several effects.

   Example: The effects of inflation include shrinking real income, increasing prices, and higher interest rates.

   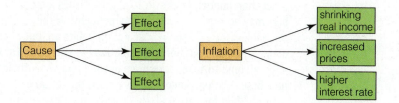

3. **Multiple Causes–Single Effect.** Several events work together to produce a single effect.

   Example: Attending class regularly, reading assignments carefully, and taking good lecture notes produce good exam grades.

   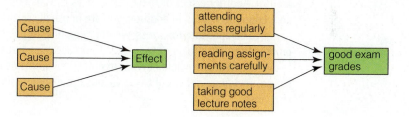

4. **Multiple Causes–Multiple Effects.** Several events work together to produce several effects.

   Example: Because you missed the bus and couldn't get a ride, you missed your first class and did not stop at the library.

   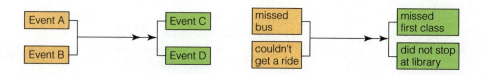

Read the following excerpt and determine what type of cause-effect relationship it illustrates.

External Factors in Obesity

The external cue theory holds that environmental cues prompt us to eat. This means that rather than relying on internal physical hunger cues, we respond to sight, color, and availability of food or to the time of day when we are programmed to eat. This is further complicated by the fact that food is available around the clock—at home, at work, in restaurants and grocery stores (some restaurants even offer home delivery!).

Other factors that may contribute to people's attitudes toward food are the way in which individual families perceive food. Some families are "food centered," which means they tend to overeat at mealtime, eat rapidly, snack excessively, eat for reasons other than hunger, or eat until all their dishes are empty. Unwittingly, family members may become involved as codependents in the exercise of overeating, and serve as enablers for a person whose eating habits are out of control. Overeating by children may be an imitation of overeating by parents. Obese children, over a given time interval, tend to take more bites of food and chew their food less thoroughly than nonobese children. Some parents preach the "clean plate ethic" by which they praise their children for eating all the food on their plates as a token of thanks for having enough food to eat.

Some people eat in response to stress, boredom, insecurity, anxiety, loneliness, or as a reward for being good. Parents who console a child with food may be initiating a life-long behavior pattern. Some people use food as an inappropriate response to psychological stimuli. As you experience pain, anxiety, insecurity, stress, arousal, or excitement, the brain responds by producing substances that soothe pain and lessen arousal. Another effect of these substances is that they enhance appetite for food and reduce activity. If, in addition, you are unusually sensitive to stress, you are likely to eat to compensate for stress, whether negative or positive. Eating may be an appropriate response to all of these stimuli on occasion, but the person who uses them to overeat creates a whole new set of emotional problems relating to his or her overeating. They may get caught in a vicious cycle—depression causing overeating and vice versa.

—Byer and Shainberg, *Living Well: Health in Your Hands,* 2e, Jones and Bartlett Publishers.

The first paragraph discusses environmental cues that may stimulate people to eat. The second paragraph examines how a family's perceptions of food can contribute to overeating. The third paragraph explains how some people eat in response to emotional stimuli. It could be mapped as follows:

External Factors in Obesity

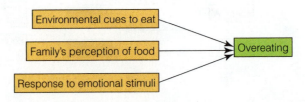

When reading material is organized in the cause-effect pattern, pay close attention to the topic sentence. It usually states the cause-effect relationship that is detailed throughout the paragraph. As you read through the paragraph, read to find specific causes and specific effects. Determine the connection between causes and effects: Why did a particular event or action occur? What happened as a result of it?

Cause–Effect Transitional Words/Phrases

hypertension *causes* . . .
Napoleon was defeated at Waterloo: *consequently* . . .
an interest rate increase *resulted in* . . .
hatred *breeds* . . .

Other transitional words/phrases are:

therefore, hence, for this reason, since, leads to, creates, yields, stems from, produces, for, because, as a result, due to, thus

---

EXERCISE 5–15   **IDENTIFYING CAUSES AND EFFECTS**

Directions: *In each of the following paragraphs, circle the cause(s) and underline the effect(s).*

1. Research has shown that mental illnesses have various causes, but the causes are not fully understood. Some mental disorders are due to physical changes in the brain resulting from illness or injury. Chemical imbalances in the brain may cause other mental illnesses. Still other disorders are mainly due to conditions in the environment that affect a person's mental state. These conditions include unpleasant childhood experiences and severe emotional stress.

2. Many regions are experiencing high levels of unemployment. Unfortunately, widespread job loss affects more than household income levels. Household tensions and even domestic violence rise. Indeed, some communities see an increase in all crimes. Loss of self-esteem and hope are some of the more personal ways unemployment hurts.

3. Government leaders need to look harder at the true reasons our violent crime rates have risen. What they will see are people living in poverty, desperately trying to survive. Add to that rampant drug use and you have the perfect conditions for violent gang activity. Furthermore, budget cuts have lessened the police presence and done away with special police programs that were working to keep neighborhoods safe.

4. The Earth is always moving in one way or another. When there is volcanic activity, an earthquake can occur. Also, shifting plates of the

Earth's crust along faults will make the ground shake beneath us. Most earthquakes cannot be felt but are measured by sensitive equipment at seismic centers around the globe.

5. Low standardized test scores among minorities caused by biased questions leads teachers to "teach to the test." These same students may improve their performance on the next standardized test but do not receive the well-rounded education needed to succeed in school as a whole and ultimately in life. ■

EXERCISE 5–16   **PREDICTING THE CAUSE-EFFECT PATTERN**

Directions: *Put a check mark next to the textbook chapter headings that are most likely to use the cause-effect pattern.*

_____ 1. The Nature of the Judicial System

_____ 2. Why Bureaucracies Exist

_____ 3. Explaining the Increase in Homelessness

_____ 4. How Walt Whitman Uses Imagery

_____ 5. Types of Special Interest Groups ■

EXERCISE 5–17   **ANALYZING THE CAUSE-EFFECT PATTERN**

Directions: *Read the following excerpt and answer the questions that follow.*

One of the most intriguing hormones is melatonin, which is secreted by the pea-sized pineal gland nestled at the base of the brain. We have known for decades about its role in our daily rhythms, such as our sleep-awake cycles. As night draws near and less light reaches the retina, melatonin levels surge in our blood, only to dwindle as dawn brings the first light. In recent years, melatonin has been taken as a safe, effective sleeping aid, but researchers now tell us that perhaps the hormone has other, more far-reaching effects as well. For example, it "sops up" free radicals, those disruptive parts of oxygen molecules that contribute to aging and diseases. Other antioxidants (such as Vitamins C, E, and beta carotene) may only function in certain cells, but melatonin can reach all cells, including those protected areas of the brain. Researchers also suggest that melatonin may boost immune function, retard aging, prevent or retard cancer, prevent pregnancy (in large doses), prevent heart attacks, and extend life. The hormone can also be used to combat jet lag.

—Wallace, Robert A., *Biology: The World of Life,* 7th Ed., © 1997. Reprinted and electronically reproduced by permission of Pearson Education, Inc., Upper Saddle River, NJ.

1. Underline the sentence that states the central cause-effect relationship discussed throughout this excerpt.

2. List, or draw a map of, the various effects of melatonin.

_____

_____

_____

3. List any transitional words used in this excerpt.

_____

Enumeration/Simple Listing

The enumeration pattern is a list of information. The order of named or listed items is not important. For example, a section in an anthropology text may list and describe characteristics of an ancient culture, or a psychology text may present facts about aggressive behavior.

The listing pattern can be visualized and mapped as follows:

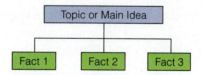

Often the writer chooses to present the items in a way that is easiest to explain or that is easiest for the reader to understand. Even so, there is still no obvious pattern that will help you organize and remember the information. The following excerpt is an example of a paragraph that lists information.

> Social networks perform several important functions. For one, many decisions and preferences are influenced by networks of friends, family, and co-workers. Networks are also a primary source of information and advice, whether for an immigrant searching for a place to live, a student seeking a summer job, or a parent looking for a good day-care center. Networks can also provide individuals with companionship.

—Popenoe, David, *Sociology,* 11th Ed., © 2000. Reprinted and electronically reproduced by permission of Pearson Education, Inc., Upper Saddle River, NJ.

This paragraph on social networks could be mapped like this:

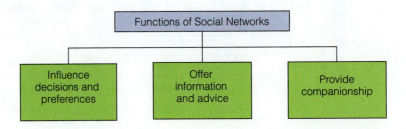

Enumeration Pattern Transitional Words/Phrases

there are *several* characteristics of . . .
one feature of families is . . .
Government serves *the following* functions . . .

Other enumeration pattern transitional words/phrases are:

first, second, third, numerals (1., 2., 3.), letters (a., b., c.), another, also, too, finally

---

EXERCISE 5–18   **IDENTIFYING ENUMERATION**

Directions: *Each of the following paragraphs lists information. Circle the topic, and underline each item in the list.*

1. Audiences favor speakers who communicate in a personal rather than an impersonal style, who speak *with* them rather than *at* them. There are several ways to develop a personal style. First, use personal pronouns, such as *I, me, he, she,* and *you,* which will create bridges to the audience. Using personal pronouns is better than using impersonal expressions such as "One is led to believe. . . ." In addition, try to involve the audience by asking questions. When you direct questions to your listeners, they feel that they are part of the public speaking experience. You should also try to create immediacy—a sense of connectedness—with your audience. You can do this in numerous ways, such as by using personal examples, complimenting the audience, or referring to what you and the audience have in common.

—Joseph A. DeVito, *The Elements of Public Speaking,* Seventh Edition, p. 164.
Copyright © 2000 Longman, a division of Pearson Education, Inc.

2.   In a workplace setting, motivation can be assessed by measuring four indicators. First, engagement reflects the degree of energy, enthusiasm, and effort each employee brings to his or her work. If you're "just not into it," chances are you won't perform your best. Second, satisfaction indicates how happy employees are with the experience of work and the way they are treated. Third, commitment suggests the degree to which employees support the company and its mission. Fourth, intention to quit predicts the likelihood that employees will leave their jobs. A person who is engaged, satisfied, and committed and who has no intention of quitting can be safely said to be *motivated.*

—Courtland L. Bovée and John V. Thill, *Business in Action with Real-Time Updates,* 5e, p. 213.
Copyright © 2011 Prentice Hall, a division of Pearson Education, Inc.

3.   Beginning teachers have a great deal of preparation before that all-important first day of school. Creating a classroom atmosphere conducive to learning is one of the most crucial elements of this preparation. The new teacher should first consult resources about classroom environment, such as books and articles. After all, other teachers have already created wonderful spaces! Then, measure and draw your classroom so you can start to make real plans. Once you have your ideas down on paper, put them into action. Arrange your classroom a few weeks before school starts in case you need to make adjustments. Finally, and most importantly, be open to changes once your students arrive. You may find that your design performs differently when the room is full of people!   ■

EXERCISE 5–19   **PREDICTING THE ENUMERATION PATTERN**

Directions: *Identify and put a check mark next to the topics listed below that might be developed by using the enumeration pattern.*

____ 1. Freud's versus Jung's theories

____ 2. Consumer research technology

____ 3. Varieties of theft

____ 4. Purposes of legal punishment

____ 5. The process of gene splicing

____ 6. Learning theories

____ 7. Hormones and reproduction

____ 8. Why teenagers rebel

____ 9. How acid rain occurs

____ 10. The impact of environment on intelligence   ■

| EXERCISE 5–20 | **ANALYZING THE ENUMERATION PATTERN** |

Directions: *Read the following excerpt and answer the questions that follow.*

THE STIMULUS FOR HEARING: SOUND

The stimulus for vision is light; for hearing, the stimulus is sound. Sound consists of a series of vibrations (carried through air or some other medium, such as water) beating against our ear. We can represent these pressures as sound waves. As a source of sound vibrates, it pushes air against our ears in waves. As was the case for light waves, there are three major physical characteristics of sound waves: amplitude, frequency (the inverse of wavelength), and purity. Each is related to a different psychological experience. We'll briefly consider each in turn.

The amplitude of a sound wave depicts its intensity—the force with which air strikes the ear. The intensity of a sound determines the psychological experience we call loudness. That is, the higher the amplitude, the louder we perceive the sound. Quiet, soft sounds have low amplitudes.

The second physical characteristic of sound to consider is wave frequency, the number of times a wave repeats itself within a given period. For sound, frequency is measured in terms of how many waves of pressure are exerted every second. The unit of sound frequency is the hertz, abbreviated Hz. If a sound wave repeats itself 50 times in one second, it is a 50-Hz sound; 500 repetitions is a 500-Hz sound, and so on.

The psychological experience produced by sound wave frequency is pitch. Pitch is our experience of how high or low a tone is. The musical scale represents differences in pitch. Low frequencies correspond to bass tones, such as those made by foghorns or tubas. High-frequency vibrations give rise to the experience of high-pitched sounds, such as musical tones produced by flutes or the squeals of smoke detectors.

A third characteristic of sound waves is wave purity, or wave complexity. You'll recall that we seldom experience pure, monochromatic lights. Pure sounds are also uncommon in our everyday experience. A pure sound would be one in which all waves from the sound source were vibrating at exactly the same frequency. Such sounds can be produced electronically, and tuning forks produce approximations, but most of the sounds we hear every day are complex sounds consisting of many different sound wave frequencies.

The psychological quality or characteristic of a sound, reflecting its degree of purity, is called timbre. For example, each musical instrument produces a unique variety or mixture of overtones, so each type of musical instrument tends to sound a little different from all others. If a trumpet, a violin, and a piano were to play the same note, we could still tell the instruments apart because of our experience of timbre. In fact, any instrument can display different timbres, depending on how it is constructed and played.

—Gerow, Joshua R., *Psychology: An Introduction,* 5th Ed., © 1997. Reprinted and electronically reproduced by permission of Pearson Education, Inc., Upper Saddle River, NJ.

1. Underline the sentence that states what the entire passage will discuss.

2. Explain in your own words the three major physical characteristics of sound waves and their related psychological experiences.

   _____

   _____

   _____

   _____

3. List the transitional words or phrases used in this excerpt.

   _____ ■

Mixed Patterns

Many texts contain sections and passages that combine one or more organizational patterns. For instance, in listing characteristics of a newly developed computer program, an author may explain it by comparing it with similar existing programs. Or, in describing an event or process, the writer may also include the reasons (causes) an event occurred or explain why the steps in a process must be followed in the prescribed order.

Read the following paragraph about stalking, and determine what two patterns are used.

Stalking is defined differently in different states. A typical definition is "willful, malicious, and repeated following and harassing of another person." However, three states include "lying in wait," and seven include "surveillance." Many states require a pattern of behavior, and some require that victims have a "reasonable" fear for their safety. Texas requires that the victim continue to be stalked *after* law enforcement officials have been notified. A model definition of stalking developed by the National Institute of Justice is as follows: "a course of conduct directed at a specific person that involves repeated visual or physical proximity, nonconsensual communication, or verbal, written or implied threats, or a combination thereof that would cause a reasonable person fear." Applying this definition, a national survey of 8,000 men and 8,000 women estimated that 1 in 12 American women and 1 in 45 American men had been stalked at some time in their lives.

—From Hugh Barlow, *Criminal Justice in America,* p. 19. Copyright © 2000 Pearson Education, Inc.

In this paragraph the textbook author is defining the term *stalking*. He is also, however, as the topic sentence (first sentence) of the paragraph states, considering how "stalking is defined differently in different states." Specifically, the author compares what various states, including Texas, require in the definition and quotes a model definition from the National Institute of Justice. Thus, two patterns, definition and comparison-contrast are used in the paragraph.

When reading mixed patterns, focus on one of the patterns and use it to guide your reading. Whenever possible, choose the predominant or most obvious pattern. However, regardless of which pattern you choose, it will serve to organize the author's thoughts and make them easier to recall.

Because more than one pattern is evident in mixed patterns, you can expect a mix or combination of transitional words as well.

✔ LEARNING STYLE TIPS

If you tend to be a...	Then identify thought patterns by...
Spatial learner	Drawing a diagram of the ideas in the passage
Verbal learner	Outlining the passage

EXERCISE 5–21

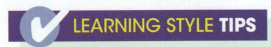

PREDICTING PATTERNS

Directions: *Working in pairs, study the following topic sentences. Anticipate and discuss what pattern that paragraph is likely to exhibit. Write the name of the pattern in the space provided.*

1. _____ Unlike Japan and the Western European countries, Canada has been relatively removed from the balance of terror debate.

2. _____ The sections of a comprehensive medical history are introduction, chief concern, history of present illness, past medical history, family medical history, and review of symptoms.

3. _____ Consumers' buying decisions influence the prices farmers receive for their products.

4. _____ The battle for women's suffrage was carried out in the late 1800s and the early 1900s.

5. _____ The majority of Americans will be better off in the year 2025 than they are today.

6. _____ A mild stimulant, such as caffeine, appears to change a person's ability to maintain attention and concentration.

7. _____ The GNP (gross national product) is an economic measure that considers the total value of goods and services that a country produces during a given year.

8. _____Managers experience a number of different personnel problems that must be solved before a department can work effectively.

9. _____A health maintenance organization is a medical corporation that takes care of the medical needs of its members.

10. _____ Geomorphology, the study of landforms and the events and processes that create them, has three major branches of study. ■

EXERCISE 5–22   **ANALYZING PATTERNS**

Directions: *Read the following excerpt and answer the questions that follow.*

THE CHARACTERISTICS OF RELIGIONS

Let's look carefully at six characteristics that religions tend to share.

All religions have some sort of history, often told as a sacred story or *myth*, that underlies the practices and beliefs of its people. In everyday speech, we tend to use that term to mean a story that is not true. In the study of religion, though, "myth" has no negative connotation—it simply means a story that explains the world. You may be familiar with the creation myths from the Bible or Greek and Roman mythology, which explain how the world came to be. Religions tend to rely on myths to educate and explain the world in a narrative way—a story that shows us where we have been, so that we might guess where we're going.

Religions also tend to develop *doctrine*, a set of principles that often guide people's understanding or actions. In Islam, for example, there is one core doctrine that all Muslims must believe: "There is no other god but God, and Mohammed is the Prophet of God."

A third important aspect of a religion is its distinct *rituals* that help define life within that tradition. While Buddhists might regularly leave fruit in front of a statue of the Buddha, Daoists might burn incense in front of a shrine or practice tai chi to develop their own inner life. Scholars have studied rituals extensively, showing how they bond people together in time and space while also linking them to their spiritual world.

Religions also rely on *shared experiences and emotions* to support believers in good times and bad. They may include rituals to support life's major events—births, weddings, and deaths—but also everyday experiences like eating. In this way, emotion and experience intertwine with religious practice. You can imagine how this happens: having a parent or child die can be an excruciating, debilitating experience. For millennia, religious traditions across the globe have helped people make sense of and cope with forces outside their control.

In addition, religions often set off some places from the rest of the world. In this way, they become sacred. They could be mountains, buildings, or caves. For example, followers of Hinduism may visit temples devoted to one or more gods and goddesses. Likewise, a Native American may find strength in walking the land where his grandfather lived, while a Daoist may remove herself away to a sacred mountain. Spaces can be created or found, modest or grandiose. They share only their power as spots separate from the mundane world.

Not all religions provide ethical or moral codes, but most religious traditions do offer codes of conduct that apply to personal and social situations. Some traditions self-consciously adapt to the changing world, while others seek to slow down the rate of change and retain moral and ethical codes from generation to generation. In many cases, adherents perceive a code of conduct as coming from a sacred or divine source. Others, however, emphasize the human development of ethical codes.

—Robson, Roy R., *Think World Traditions,* 1st Ed., © 2011. Reprinted and electronically reproduced by Pearson Education, Inc., Upper Saddle River, NJ.

1. What patterns are evident in this excerpt? Which do you think is predominant?

_____

_____

2. Underline the transitional words that suggest these patterns.

3. Draw a map of this excerpt.

4. Explain in your own words the six characteristics of a religion.

_____

_____

_____

EXERCISE 5–23   **IDENTIFYING ORGANIZATIONAL PATTERNS**

Directions: *Read each of the following paragraphs and identify the predominant organizational pattern used. Choose from among the following patterns: chronological order, definition, classification, comparison-contrast, cause-effect, and enumeration. Draw a map of each paragraph.*

1.   Erik Erikson (1902–1994) was heavily influenced by Freud. However, because he modified Freud's theories, he is commonly referred to as a "neo-Freudian." Freud emphasized the drives of the id; Erikson's main concern was the more "rational" world of the ego. Erikson saw self-development as proceeding through eight *psychosocial* stages that involve the way we respond to the changing demands made on us as we go through life. Freud focused on childhood; Erikson's stages continue into old age. Thus Erikson believed that the personality is molded throughout life, not just in childhood.

—Popenoe, David, *Sociology,* 11th Ed., © 2000. Reprinted and electronically reproduced by permission of Pearson Education, Inc., Upper Saddle River, NJ.

Pattern: _____

2.   The impact of international migration is even greater than the numbers might suggest. Immigrants are often greeted with apprehension, and immigration has become an explosive political issue in many receiving countries. This is for several reasons. First, official statistics substantially underestimate actual numbers; undocumented migration is rising everywhere. Second, migrants are usually in the peak years of fertility. Therefore, they are playing an increasing role in the total population growth in the rich target countries. Third, migrant settlements are generally concentrated in a few places within a country. This usually adds to the immigrants' visibility and increases the perception of cultural differences.

> —Bergman, Edward F.; Renwick, William H., *Introduction to Geography: People, Places, and Environment,* 1st Ed., © 1999. Reprinted and electronically reproduced by permission of Pearson Education, Inc., Upper Saddle River, NJ.

Pattern: _____

3.   The technologies for both printing and papermaking came to Europe from China. By the ninth century, the Chinese were printing pictures; by the eleventh century, they had invented (but seldom used) movable type. Printmaking was developed in Europe by the fifteenth century—first to meet the demand for inexpensive religious icons and playing cards, then to illustrate books printed with the new European movable type. Since the fifteenth century, the art of printmaking has been closely associated with the illustration of books.

> —Preble, Duane; Preble, Sarah; Frank, Patrick L., *Artforms,* 6th Ed., © 1999. Reprinted and electronically reproduced by permission of Pearson Education, Inc., Upper Saddle River, NJ.

Pattern: _____

4.   The patterns of stars seen in the sky are usually called constellations. In astronomy, however, the term constellation refers to a *region* of the sky. Any place you point in the sky belongs to some constellation; familiar patterns of stars merely help locate particular constellations. For example, the constellation Orion includes all the stars in the familiar pattern of the hunter, *along with* the region of the sky in which these stars are found.

> —Jeffrey Bennett, Megan Donahue, Nicholas Schneider, and Mark Voit, *The Cosmic Perspective,* Brief Edition, p. 28. San Francisco: Addison Wesley Longman, copyright © 2000 Pearson Education, Inc.

Pattern: _____

5.   The suburbs developed in response to several social forces. The multilane freeways that go around the perimeter of the city (the outerbelts) spurred the development of suburban places along the city's rim. Now, rather than going from the suburb to the central city to work, to shop, to see a doctor, or to enjoy the movies, suburbanites can obtain the same services by driving along the outer belt from one suburban community to another. Another factor has been the decentralization of jobs. Faster transportation and communications have encouraged manufacturing plants and distribution centers to relocate from the central city to the outer rings of the city—that is, to the suburbs. Yet another factor has been the aging of the central city. Facilities in many

downtown areas are simply worn out or obsolete. Parking is expensive and inconvenient; buildings are dirty and run-down. In contrast, suburban shopping malls and industrial centers typically have bright new facilities and ample parking.

—Curry, Tim; Jiobu, Robert M.; Schwirian, Kent, *Sociology for the Twenty-First Century*, 2nd Ed., © 1999. Reprinted and electronically reproduced by permission of Pearson Education, Inc., Upper Saddle River, NJ.

Pattern: _____

EXERCISE 5–24   IDENTIFYING PATTERNS AND TRANSITIONS

Directions: *Turn to Reading Selection 9 or 10 at the end of the chapter. Read the selection and answer the questions. Then review the selection and identify the organizational pattern of each paragraph. In the margin next to each paragraph, write the name of the pattern. Underline any transitional words that you find.*

EXERCISE 5–25   IDENTIFYING PATTERNS

Directions: *Suppose your instructor asked you to write a paper on one of the following topics. Identify which organizational pattern(s) might be useful in developing and organizing a paper on each topic.*

1. The reasons behind recent movements to overthrow Middle Eastern governments

_____

2. How a child's brain develops

_____

3. A study of what is "cool"

_____

4. An explanation of extreme sports

_____

5. An explanation of attention deficit disorder

_____

NEED TO KNOW A Review of Patterns and Transitional Words

Pattern	Characteristics	Transitional Words
Chronological order	Describes events, processes, procedures	*first, second, later, before, next, as soon as, after, then, finally, meanwhile, following, last, during, when, until, on (date), in (date)*
Definition	Explains the meaning of a word or phrase	*is, refers to, can be defined as, means, consists of, involves, is a term that, is called, is characterized by, occurs when, are those that, entails, corresponds to, is literally*
Classification	Divides a topic into parts based on shared characteristics	*classified as, comprises, is composed of, several varieties of, one type, a second class of, another group, kinds, divisions, categories*
Comparison-Contrast	Discusses similarities and/or differences among ideas, theories, concepts, objects, or persons	**Similarities:** *both, also, similarly, like, likewise, too, as well as, resembles, correspondingly, in the same way, to compare, in comparison, share* **Differences:** *unlike, differs from, in contrast, on the contrary, on the other hand, instead, despite, nevertheless, however, in spite of, whereas, as opposed to, although, even though*
Cause-Effect	Describes how one or more things cause or are related to another	**Causes:** *because, because of, for, since, stems from, one cause is, one reason is, leads to, causes, creates, yields, produces, due to, breeds, for this reason* **Effects:** *consequently, results in, one result is, therefore, thus, as a result, hence*
Enumeration/Simple listing	Items are named or listed in an order that is not important	*the following, several, one, another, also, too, first, second, numerals (1., 2.), letters (a., b.), finally*

EXERCISE 5-26   **IDENTIFYING PATTERNS**

Directions: *Choose a section from one of your current textbook chapters. Identify the organizational pattern used in each paragraph by writing CO (Chronological Order), CC (Comparison-Contrast), D (Definition), CL (Classification), CE (Cause-Effect), or E (Enumeration) in the margin beside each paragraph. Underline the transitional words in each paragraph.*

■ Other Useful Patterns of Organization

Goal 3

Use other patterns to build comprehension

The patterns presented in the preceding section are the most common. The Need to Know box "A Review of Patterns and Transitional Words," on page 225, presents a brief review of those patterns and their corresponding transitional words. However, writers do not limit themselves to these six patterns. Especially in academic writing, you may find one or more of the patterns listed in the Need to Know box "Additional Patterns and Transitional Words," on this page. Here is a brief review of each of these additional patterns.

NEED TO KNOW Additional Patterns and Transitional Words

Pattern	Characteristics	Transitional Words
Statement and clarification	Indicates that information explaining an idea or concept will follow	*in fact, in other words, clearly, evidently, obviously*
Summary	Indicates that a condensed review of an idea or piece of writing will follow	*in summary, in conclusion, in brief, to summarize, to sum up, in short, on the whole*
Generalization and example	Provides examples that clarify a broad, general statement	*for example, for instance, that is, to illustrate*
Addition	Indicates that additional information will follow	*furthermore, additionally, also, besides, further, in addition, moreover, again*
Spatial order/ Location	Describes physical location or position in space	*above, below, besides, next to, in front of, behind, inside, outside, opposite, within, nearby*

Statement and Clarification

Many writers make a statement of fact and then proceed to clarify or explain that statement. For instance, a writer may open a paragraph by stating that "The best education for you may not be the best education for someone else." The remainder of the paragraph would then discuss that statement and make its meaning clear by explaining how educational needs are individual and based on one's talents, skills, and goals. Transitional words associated with this pattern are listed in the Need to Know box above.

Here is a sample paragraph. Notice that the author makes a statement in the first sentence and then explains it throughout the remainder of the paragraph. Notice, too, the highlighted transitional phrase.

Sex ratios in the poor countries do not show a consistent pattern. In some poor countries men outnumber women, but in others, in tropical Africa, for example, women outnumber men. In fact, variations in sex ratios can be explained only by a combination of national economic and cultural factors. In the countries of North America and Europe and in Japan, women may suffer many kinds of discrimination, but they are not generally discriminated against when it comes to access to medical care.

—Edward F. Bergman and William H. Renwick, *Introduction to Geography: People, Places, and Environment,*
Updated Second Edition, p. 185. Upper Saddle River, NJ: Prentice Hall, copyright © 2003 Pearson Education Inc.

Summary

A **summary** is a condensed statement that provides the key points of a larger idea or piece of writing. The summaries at the end of each chapter of this text provide a quick review of the chapter's contents. Often writers summarize what they have already said or what someone else has said. For example, in a psychology textbook you will find many summaries of research. Instead of asking you to read an entire research study, the textbook author will summarize the study's findings. Other times a writer may repeat in condensed form what he or she has already said as a means of emphasis or clarification. Transitional words associated with this pattern are listed in the Need to Know box "Additional Patterns and Transitional Words."

Here is a sample paragraph in which the author summarizes changes in the magazine industry. Notice that he moves from idea to idea without providing detailed explanation of each idea.

In summary, the magazine industry is adapting to the new world of electronic multimedia information and entertainment, with formats that will be quite different from the familiar ones. Computer-generated publishing has become the norm in the magazine business, expanding beyond its uses in producing newsletters and other specialized publications. Most general circulation magazines already rely heavily on desktop computers, interacting with other electronic equipment to produce high-quality, graphics-filled products.

—Wilson Dizard, Jr., *Old Media, New Media,* Third Edition, p. 169.
New York: Longman, copyright © 2000 Pearson Education, Inc.

Generalization and Example

Examples are one of the best ways to explain something that is unfamiliar or unknown. Examples are specific instances or situations that illustrate a concept or idea. Often writers may give a general statement, or generalization, and then explain it by giving examples to make its meaning clear. In a social problems textbook, you may find the following generalization: Computer theft by employees is on the increase. The section may then go on to offer examples from specific companies in which employees insert fictitious information into the company's computer program and steal company funds. Transitional words associated with this pattern are listed in the Need to Know box "Additional Patterns and Transitional Words (p. 226)."

In the following paragraph about dreams, the writer makes a general statement about dreams and then gives examples to explain his statement.

> Different cultures place varying emphases on dreams and support different beliefs concerning dreams. For example, many people in the United States view dreams as irrelevant fantasy with no connection to everyday life. By contrast, people in other cultures view dreams as key sources of information about the future, the spiritual world, and the dreamer. Such cultural views can influence the probability of dream recall. In many modern Western cultures, people rarely remember their dreams upon awakening. The Parintintin of South America, however, typically remember several dreams every night and the Senoi of Malaysia discuss their dreams with family members in the morning.

—Stephen Davis and Joseph Palladino, *Psychology,* Third Edition, p. 210. Upper Saddle River, NJ: Prentice Hall, copyright © 2000 Pearson Education, Inc.

Addition

Writers often introduce an idea or make a statement and then supply additional information about that idea or statement. For instance, an education textbook may introduce the concept of homeschooling and then provide in-depth information about its benefits. This pattern is often used to expand, elaborate, or discuss an idea in greater detail. Transitional words associated with this pattern are listed in the Need to Know box "Additional Patterns and Transitional Words."

In the following paragraph about pathogens, the writer uses addition.

> Some pathogens [disease-causing organisms] evolve and mutate naturally. Also, patients who fail to complete the full portion of their antibiotic prescriptions allow drug-resistant pathogens to multiply. The use of antibiotics in animal feed and sprayed on fruits and vegetables during food processing increases opportunities for resistant organisms to evolve and thrive. Furthermore, there is evidence that the disruption of Earth's natural habitats can trigger the evolution of new pathogens.

—Edward F. Bergman and William H. Renwick, *Introduction to Geography: People, Places, and Environment,* Updated Second Edition, p. 182. Upper Saddle River, NJ: Prentice Hall, copyright © 2003 Pearson Education, Inc.

Notice that the writer states that some pathogens mutate naturally and then goes on to add that they also mutate as a result of human activities.

Spatial Order/Location

Spatial order is concerned with physical location or position in space. Spatial order is used in disciplines in which physical descriptions are important. A photography textbook may use spatial order to describe the parts of a camera. An automotive technology textbook may use spatial order to describe disk brake operation. Transitional words associated with this pattern are listed in the Need to Know box "Additional Patterns and Transitional Words." Here is a sample paragraph in which the author's description of blood circulation uses spatial order.

> Pulmonary circulation conducts blood between the heart and the lungs. Oxygen-poor, CO_2-laden blood returns through two large veins (venae cavae) from tissues within the body, enters the right atrium, and is then moved into the right ventricle of the heart. From there, it is pumped into the pulmonary artery, which divides into two branches, each leading to one of the lungs. In the lung, the arteries undergo extensive branching, giving rise to vast networks of capillaries where gas exchange takes place, with blood becoming oxygenated while CO_2 is discharged. Oxygen-rich blood then returns to the heart via the pulmonary veins.

—Mix, Farber, and King, *Biology: The Network of Life*, 2e, HarperCollins Publishers.

EXERCISE 5–27   **IDENTIFYING PATTERNS**

Directions: *For each of the following statements, identify the pattern that is evident and write its name in the space provided. Choose from among the following patterns:* statement and clarification, summary, generalization and example, addition, *and* spatial order/location.

1. _____ Short fibers, dendrites, branch out around the cell body and a single long fiber, the axon, extends from the cell body.

2. _____ When faced with a life-threatening illness, people tend to deny its existence. In addition, family members may also participate in the denial.

3. _____ If our criminal justice system works, the recidivism rate—the percentage of people released from prison who return—should decrease. In other words, in a successful system, there should be a decrease in the number of criminals who are released from prison that become repeat offenders.

4. _____ Students who are informed about drugs tend to use them in greater moderation. Furthermore, they tend to help educate others.

5. _____ A successful drug addiction treatment program would offer free or very cheap drugs to addicts. Heroin addicts, for example, could be prescribed heroin when under a physician's care.

6. _____ In conclusion, it is safe to say that women have made many gains in the workplace, but there is still a long way to go before full pay equality is achieved.

7. _____ The pollutants we have just discussed all involve chemicals; we can conclude that they threaten our environment and our well-being.

8. _____ A residual check valve that maintains slight pressure on the hydraulic system is located in the master cylinder at the outlet for the drum brakes.

9. _____ Sociologists study how we are socialized into sex roles, the attitudes expected of males and females. Sex roles, in fact, identify some activities and behaviors as clearly male and others as clearly female.

10. _____ Patients often consult a lay referral network to discuss their medical problems. Cancer patients, for instance, can access Internet discussion groups that provide both information and support.

■ Using Transitional Words to Anticipate Ideas

Goal 4
Use transitional words to understand relationships within and among sentences

Transitional words are also helpful in discovering or clarifying relationships between and among ideas in any piece of writing. Specifically, **transitional words** help you grasp connections between and within sentences. Transitional words can help you predict what is to come next within a paragraph. For instance, if you are reading along and come upon the phrase *in conclusion*, you know that the writer will soon present a summary. If you encounter the word *furthermore*, you know that the writer is about to present additional information about the subject at hand. If you encounter the word *consequently* in the middle of a sentence (The law was repealed; consequently,...), you know that the writer is about to explain what happened as a result of the repeal. The Need to Know boxes on pages 225 and 226 list the transitional words that correspond to the patterns discussed in this chapter.

EXERCISE 5–28   **USING TRANSITIONS**

Directions: *Each of the following beginnings of paragraphs uses a transitional word or phrase to tell the reader what will follow in the paragraph. Read each, paying particular attention to the highlighted transitional word or phrase. Then, working with a classmate, describe as specifically as you can what you would expect to find next in the paragraph.*

1. Many Web sites on the Internet are reliable and trustworthy. However, . . .

   _____

2. One advantage of using a computer to take notes is that you can rearrange information easily. Another . . .

   _____

3. There are a number of ways to avoid catching the cold virus. First of all, . . .

   _____

4. Jupiter is a planet surrounded by several moons. Likewise . . .

   _____

5. When planning a speech, you should choose a topic that is familiar or that you are knowledgeable about. Next, . . .

   _____

6. Following a high-protein diet may be rewarding because it often produces quick weight loss. On the other hand, . . .

   _____

7. The iris is a doughnut-shaped portion of the eyeball. In the center . . .

   _____

8. Price is not the only factor consumers consider when making a major purchase. They also . . .

   _____

9. Asbestos, a common material found in many older buildings in which people have worked for decades, has been shown to cause cancer. Consequently, . . .

   _____

10. Many Web sites provide valuable links to related sites. To illustrate, visit . . .

   _____

■ Thinking Critically: Analyzing Cause-Effect Relationships

Goal 5

Think critically about cause-effect relationships

All of the organizational patterns discussed in this chapter offer opportunities for critical thinking. Cause-effect relationships can be particularly complex and often can be misleading. Consider the following situation:

> Sarah earned her bachelor's degree in three years instead of four by attending summer sessions. Since she graduated, she has never held a job for longer than three weeks. Obviously, condensing her studies was not a good idea.

In this situation, the writer assumes that a cause-effect relationship exists: Sarah cannot hold a job because she condensed her studies into three years. But this assumption may not be correct at all. Sarah may be unable to hold a job because she is frequently late or cannot get along with her co-workers or is competing with many more highly qualified people in a poor job market.

A common error in reasoning is to assume that because two events occurred at around the same time, one event caused the other. This is not necessarily the case. Suppose you leave your house and it starts raining. Did it start raining *because* you left your house? Of course not.

Some advertising encourages people to infer false cause-effect relationships. For example, an ad may show a happy family eating a particular brand of breakfast cereal. The ad implies that you will have a happy family if you buy that particular brand. Always analyze cause-effect relationships; look for evidence that one event or action is in fact the direct cause of another.

EXERCISE 5–29

RECOGNIZING VALID CAUSE-EFFECT RELATIONSHIPS

Directions: *Read each of the following statements, and ask yourself what is the stated cause and what is the stated effect? Put a check mark beside each of the valid cause-effect statements.*

_____ 1. Joanie was so nervous about her first date with Josh that she found herself talking too fast and dropping things.

_____ 2. Smoking cigarettes is a direct cause of lung cancer.

_____ 3. Teenagers become juvenile delinquents because their parents fed them an unhealthy diet when they were babies.

_____ 4. I failed the course because I'm an Aquarius, and the teacher is a Pisces.

_____ 5. Rain occurs when evaporated water in the atmosphere condenses back into liquid form and falls to Earth.

SELF-TEST SUMMARY

Goal 1	1. Why is it helpful to recognize the organizational pattern of a paragraph or passage?	When you recognize the specific pattern of the material you are reading, you will be better able to follow the ideas being presented and to predict what will be presented next. You will find that you have made connections among the important ideas so that recalling one idea will help you to recall the others. As a result, you will find it easier to learn and remember them.
Goal 2	2. What are the six common organizational patterns?	The six common organizational patterns are • **Chronological order/process:** events or procedures are described in the order in which they occur in time. • **Definition:** an object or idea is explained by describing the general class or group to which it belongs and how the item differs from others in the same group (distinguishing features). • **Classification:** an object or idea is explained by dividing it into parts and describing or explaining each. • **Comparison-contrast:** an idea or item is explained by showing how it is similar to or different from another idea or item. • **Cause-effect:** connections between events are explained by showing what caused an event or what happened as a result of a particular event. • **Enumeration:** information is organized into lists on the basis of characteristics, features, or parts, or according to categories.
Goal 3	3. What other patterns do writers use?	Writers also use statement and clarification, summary, generalization and example, addition, and spatial order/location.
Goal 4	4. What are transitional words and how are they useful?	Transitional words or phrases guide you from one important idea in a paragraph or passage to another. These linking words or phrases are signals or clues to the way a piece of writing is organized and allow you to more easily follow a writer's thoughts. They also reveal relationships between and within sentences.
Goal 5	5. How should I analyze cause-effect relationships?	Analyze cause-effect relationships by being sure that two events that occur in the same time frame are actually connected and one caused the other.

New Ways of Administering Justice and Punishment

Jay S. Albanese
From *Criminal Justice*

About the Reading

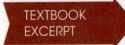

TEXTBOOK EXCERPT

This selection is taken from a criminal justice textbook. Courses in criminal justice study not only criminal behavior but also the court system, how crimes can be prevented, and how prisoners can be rehabilitated.

Planning Your Reading Strategy*

Directions: *Activate your thinking by previewing the reading (see the Need to Know box on page 64) and answering the following questions.*

_____ 1. What do all of the reading's headings have in common?
   a. They all make use of the Global Positioning System.
   b. They are all intended for use with adults.
   c. They focus on technology or preventing children from turning to crime.
   d. They all make use of surgical implants or other on-the-body technologies.

_____ 2. Based on your preview, what key questions should you ask before you begin reading the full selection?
   a. What percentage of crimes in the United States is committed by women? What percentage is committed by men?
   b. How can we stop children from turning to a life of crime? How do we punish parents for their children's behavior?
   c. What are the ethical issues involved in modern prison technologies? Is it fair to send so many young Americans to prison?
   d. How can prisons help prepare prisoners for release? Are there more effective and less expensive alternatives to prison?

3. Based on your preview of the reading, how quickly do you think you should read the selection?

   (Circle one.)

   Very slowly   Slowly   At a moderate pace   Quickly   Very quickly

4. Should all criminals be imprisoned? What are the costs of imprisonment for society and for prisoners?

---

*The Scorecard on p. 240 enables you to compute your reading rate. In order to do so, be sure to record your starting time in the Scorecard box before you begin reading.

New Ways of Administering Justice and Punishment

1   Technological advances, and the realization that virtually all offenders in prison will return to the community one day after serving their sentences, have spurred the creation of new strategies to deal with offenders. The average prison sentence in the United States is approximately five years, and most offenders in prison were sentenced for drug offenses, robbery, burglary, and other crimes for which release from prison is inevitable. Can prisons do more to prepare these offenders for a noncriminal life upon release, and are there more effective and less expensive alternatives to prison for nonviolent offenders?

Technocorrections

2   **Technocorrections** is the use of technology to monitor offenders and prevent future crimes. The most popular form of this technology is electronic "bracelets" placed around the ankles of probationers to monitor their whereabouts. A more advanced form of this technology is "probation kiosks," which have been used in New York City. These kiosks are similar to automatic teller machines and are scattered around the city. They identify probationers using a scan of the geometry of the hand on the device and allow the probationer to respond to questions and to schedule meetings with probation officers. These kiosks are designed as a way to monitor low-risk, nonviolent offenders, thereby

A probation kiosk in New York City which automates the monitoring of offenders serving probation sentences in the community. Why do you believe automated devices like this have become popular? Do you believe they are effective at monitoring offenders?

permitting probation officers to devote closer supervision to higher-risk offenders.

3   Miniaturization of technology will allow for similar experiments with tiny cameras that could be placed in offenders' homes or in high-risk places (such as known drug areas or the residence of a battered spouse). Other technologies are being developed that would be more difficult for offenders to disable and that would permit certain behaviors or movements by offenders to trigger alarms.

4   Risk assessment involves classifying and evaluating offenders based on their characteristics, crimes, and backgrounds to determine the likelihood of reoffending. Classifying and evaluating offenders has become more sophisticated and accurate over the last two decades. Studies have had at least three important findings involving variation, reliability, and statistics. First, there is tremendous variation among offenders and there is no "one size fits all" in trying

to isolate the characteristics of an offender. Offender characteristics such as mental health and substance abuse are important considerations, as are situational characteristics that trigger offender predispositions. Second, offenders change over time, so it is necessary for periodic reevaluations in order for risk assessments to be reliable. Third, "gut feelings" about criminal propensities have given way to statistical assessments, which compare the behaviors of groups of offenders in the past to similar offenders under current evaluation. This form of statistical assessment, or statistical profiling has been shown to be superior to clinical assessments by psychologists.

5   Risk assessments will be become even more important in the future because the threshold for violence may be lower now than in times past. In another road rage case, a middle-aged man in Minnesota noticed a car in front of him moving erratically. As he passed the car, the driver

Will this encounter escalate into violence leading to criminal liability? How could statistical profiling and risk assessment help in preventing crimes such as road rage assaults and killings?

swerved to hit him and made an obscene gesture. He returned the gesture. Later, after he arrived home, there was a knock on the door. The man opened the door, and the other driver threw battery acid on him, causing burns to his face. Although these bizarre incidents appear unique, they are now occurring with increasing frequency, permitting the establishment of statistical profiles that will probably be used in the future at trial and in providing treatment to those offenders whose anger results in criminal violence.

■ Early Life Interventions

6   A fifteen-year-old boy was sentenced to twenty years in prison for participating in a gang rape of a fourteen-year-old girl. It was his first offense. How does someone choose such a serious offense as a first crime? In most cases there is a progression of behaviors from nonserious to serious crime. It is likely that the offender in this case had committed previous, lesser crimes, but had not been caught. Recognition of this progression from nonserious to serious crimes has been the basis for early childhood intervention in preventing later juvenile delinquency.

7   Early life interventions are important because studies have identified childhood risk factors for later delinquency. These include poor language skills, poor attachment to parents and caregivers, poor parenting skills, and multiple stresses on the family. These risk factors lead to failure in school, which is significantly related to delinquency. The Prenatal and Early Childhood Nurse Home Visitation Program is a program that is directed to reduce these identified risk factors that contribute to delinquency. This program builds parenting skills and family unity as it impacts on child rearing. The Boys and Girls Clubs of America is a national network of more than 2,500 clubs that involve more than three million school-age boys and girls in constructive youth development activities, educational support, and adult supervision. A group

of researchers convened by the U.S. Office of Juvenile Justice and Delinquency Prevention agreed that "implementing family, school, and community interventions is the best way to prevent children from developing into serious violent juvenile offenders." Although none of the programs described in this section is primarily a crime prevention program, they all have direct implications for the prevention of crime and the involvement of the criminal justice system in the future.

■ Virtual Prison

8   Despite the best efforts at crime prevention, there always will be offenders who require close supervision. Those who are not dangerous may not require imprisonment but something more than probation supervision or an electronic bracelet may be desired. A potential middle ground for close supervision that is less than prison might be "**virtual prison**." A private company has introduced the Satellite Monitoring and Remote Tracking System (SMART), which is billed as "a virtual prison with an orbiting warden." The offender wears an ankle bracelet and a wireless tracking device that is monitored using Global Positioning Satellites (GPS) and the cellular network. In this way the offender is continuously monitored. The offender can also be signalled instantly when entering a prohibited area, which might be a spouse's neighborhood, school, or drug-trafficking area. Several states are evaluating the system's cost-effectiveness as an alternative to prison.

9   Injected or surgical implants have been proposed as an alternative to electronic bracelets because they cannot be tampered with or defeated effectively. These implants can also be monitored via Global Positioning Satellites. Questions have been raised about the potential for misuse of such Big Brother technology, but it is unlikely that offenders will oppose a technology that offers more freedom than prison.

Examining Reading Selection 9*

Checking Your Vocabulary

Directions: *Use context, word parts, or a dictionary, if necessary, to determine the meaning of each word as it is used in the reading.*

____ 1. propensities (paragraph 4)
- a. offenses
- b. variations
- c. situations
- d. tendencies

____ 2. threshold (paragraph 5)
- a. starting point
- b. importance
- c. behavior
- d. ability

____ 3. convened (paragraph 7)
- a. argued
- b. brought together
- c. attempted
- d. committed

____ 4. implications (paragraph 7)
- a. reasons
- b. consequences
- c. penalties
- d. systems

____ 5. prohibited (paragraph 8)
- a. promoted
- b. alternative
- c. not allowed
- d. defeated

Checking Your Comprehension

Directions: *Select the best answer.*

____ 6. The subject of this selection is
- a. community crime prevention programs.
- b. new ways of dealing with offenders.
- c. support for nonviolent offenders.
- d. problems with electronic monitoring devices.

____ 7. The author wrote this selection in order to
- a. explain why the use of electronic monitoring devices for offenders is too risky.
- b. argue that nonviolent offenders should not be sent to prison.
- c. describe new strategies for administering justice and punishment to offenders.
- d. promote the use of risk assessment and profiling in dealing with offenders.

____ 8. The term *technocorrections* refers to the use of technology to
- a. identify potential offenders.
- b. administer punishment in a prison setting.
- c. monitor high-crime areas within a city.
- d. monitor offenders and prevent future crimes.

____ 9. The main point of paragraph 7 is that
- a. early life interventions are important in preventing juvenile delinquency.
- b. studies have identified certain childhood risk factors that lead to failure in school.
- c. the Boys and Girls Clubs of America is a national network of more than 2,500 clubs involving millions of children.
- d. the Prenatal and Early Childhood Nurse Home Visitation Program teaches parenting skills and family unity.

*Writing About the Reading questions appear in the Instructor's Manual.

_____ 10. According to the reading, virtual prison is most appropriate for offenders who
   a. are considered high-risk or dangerous.
   b. require extremely close supervision.
   c. require more than probation but less than imprisonment.
   d. have repeatedly disabled electronic monitoring devices.

Thinking Critically

_____ 11. The author develops his ideas by
   a. contrasting prison conditions with alternatives to imprisonment.
   b. presenting his own personal experience in the criminal justice system.
   c. providing examples and descriptions and citing research.
   d. describing the process of criminal justice from crime to punishment.

_____ 12. The author's attitude toward his subject can best be described as
   a. angry.
   b. critical.
   c. excited.
   d. objective.

_____ 13. The photograph of the probation kiosk is intended to
   a. create sympathy for offenders who have to use the kiosks.
   b. illustrate what a probation kiosk looks like.
   c. demonstrate the ineffectiveness of probation kiosks.
   d. show that kiosks are superior to other forms of electronic monitoring.

_____ 14. One conclusion that can be made based on information in the reading is that
   a. most offenders would choose technocorrections such as electronic monitoring or surgical implants over prison.
   b. risk assessments tend to be based on stereotypes and involve profiling of offenders by race, age, and sex.
   c. childhood risk factors related to poor parenting have little or no effect on future delinquency.
   d. technology that relies on satellite monitoring and tracking of offenders violates the privacy of such individuals.

_____ 15. This reading includes two photographs. Suppose the author wished to add a third. Based on the content and title of the selection, which of the following would be the _least_ appropriate photo to add?
   a. prison guards mistreating a prisoner.
   b. the exterior of a local Boys and Girls Club of America.
   c. a GPS tracking device.
   d. an ankle bracelet worn by a prisoner.

Questions for Discussion

1. What do you think are the advantages and disadvantages of using probation kiosks and other forms of technocorrections?

2. The author states that the threshold for violence may be lower now than in the past. What evidence do you see to support or refute this assertion?

3. Do you agree that early life interventions are the best way to prevent the development of juvenile delinquency? What responsibility does the community have in supporting such programs?

4. In your opinion, which alternatives to prison (e.g., electronic monitoring, virtual prison, implants) seem to have the best potential for success? Why?

Scorecard

Selection 9:   1,190 words

Finishing Time: _____ _____ _____
                  HR.   MIN.   SEC.

Starting Time: _____ _____ _____
                  HR.   MIN.   SEC.

Reading Time: _____ _____
                         MIN.   SEC.

WPM Score:_____

Comprehension Score: for items 6–15
Number Right: _____ × 10 = _____%

Assessing Your Reading Strategy

1. How would you rate your comprehension of the reading? (Circle one.)

   Excellent   Good   Fair   Poor

2. Did you find your reading strategy effective?   Yes   No

3. Suppose you were given an assignment to read another selection from the same source. Based on your experience with this selection, how would you adjust your reading strategy (if at all)?

   _____

   _____

READING SELECTION 10   EDUCATION

How Students Get Lost in Cyberspace

Steven R. Knowlton
From *The New York Times*

About the Reading

NEWSPAPER ARTICLE

This article is reprinted from a special "Education Life" issue of The New York Times, *one of the world's most respected newspapers. Articles in* The New York Times *are generally considered reliable sources of information.*

MyReadingLab™ *The exercises following this selection can be completed online at myreadinglab.com*

Planning Your Reading Strategy*

Directions: *Activate your thinking by previewing the reading (see the Need to Know box on page 64) and answering the following questions.*

—— 1. To what type of information should you pay the most attention while reading the selection?
   a. each student's individual experience
   b. the minor supporting details in each paragraph
   c. the superiority of the Internet over library research
   d. the best ways to apply the article's advice to your own studies

—— 2. Previewing this article effectively is likely to take some time because
   a. the topic of the article has limited practical value
   b. the article contains many paragraphs and no headings
   c. the article does not provide quotations from any educated people
   d. the photo included with the article is not a good clue to the article's contents

3. Is all the information you find on the Internet reliable and accurate? Have you ever gotten "lost" on the Internet?

1   When Adam Pasick, a political science major at the University of Wisconsin at Madison, started working on his senior honors thesis this fall, he began where the nation's more than 14 million college students increasingly do: not at the campus library, but at his computer terminal.

2   As he roamed the World Wide Web, he found journal articles, abstracts, indexes and other pieces of useful information. But it wasn't until he sought help from his professor, Charles H. Franklin, that he found the mother lode.

3   Dr. Franklin steered Mr. Pasick to thousands of pages of raw data from a long-term study of political attitudes, information crucial to Mr. Pasick's inquiry into how family structure affects political thinking.

4   The Web site containing all this data is no secret to political scientists, Dr. Franklin said, but can be hard for students to find.

5   "It is barely possible that if you did a Web search, you would show it up," he said. "Whether the average undergraduate could is

by Steven R. Knowlton, reprinted from Education Life/The New York Times, November 2, 1997.

*The Scorecard on p. 245 enables you to compute your reading rate. In order to do so, be sure to record your starting time in the Scorecard box before you begin reading.

another question." It would be even harder for the uninitiated to find their way around the site, he said. "One of the things you're missing on the Web is a reference librarian."

6   It is just such difficulties that worry many educators. They are concerned that the Internet makes readily available so much information, much of it unreliable, that students think research is far easier than it really is. As a result, educators say, students are producing superficial research papers, full of data—some of it suspect—and little thought. Many of the best sources on the Web are hard to find with conventional search engines or make their information available only at a steep price, which is usually borne by universities that pay annual fees for access to the data.

7   Mr. Pasick, 21, of Ann Arbor, Mich., whose conversation is filled with computer and Web search terms, admits that he would have never found the site, much less the data, on his own.

8   "All the search engines are so imprecise," Mr. Pasick said. "Whenever I have tried to find something precise that I was reasonably sure is out there, I have had trouble."

9   Dr. David B. Rothenberg, a philosophy professor at the New Jersey Institute of Technology, in Newark, said his students' papers had declined in quality since they began using the Web for research.

10   "There are these strange references that don't quite connect," he said. "There's not much sense of intelligence. We're indexing, but we're not thinking about things."

11   One way to improve the quality of students' research is to insist that students be more thorough, said Elliot King, a professor of mass communication at Loyola College of Maryland and author of "The Online Student," a textbook for on-line searching.

12   "Because information is so accessible, students stop far too quickly," he said. If a research paper should have 15 sources, he

said, the professor should insist students find, say, 50 sources and use the best 15. When Dr. King assigns research papers in his own classes, he insists that students submit all the sources they did not use, along with those they finally selected.

13   The jumble in Web-based student papers mirrors the information jumble that is found on line, said Gerald M. Santoro, the lead research programmer at the Pennsylvania State University's Center for Academic Computing in State College, Pa.

14   The Internet, he said, is commonly thought of as a library, although a poorly catalogued one, given the limitations of the search engines available. But he prefers another analogy.

15   "In fact, it is like a bookstore," Dr. Santoro said, explaining that Web sites exist because someone wants them there, not because any independent judge has determined them worthy of inclusion.

16   Dr. William Miller, dean of libraries at Florida Atlantic University in Boca Raton, and the immediate past president of the Association of College and Research Libraries, cautioned that free Web sites were often constructed "because somebody has an ax to grind or a company wants to crow about its

own products." And he said that the creators of many sites neglect to keep them up to date, so much information on the Web may be obsolete.

17   "For the average person looking for what is the cheapest flight to Chicago this weekend, or what is the weather like in Brazil, the Web is good," Dr. Miller said. But much of its material, he added, is simply not useful to scholars.

18   Yet despite the Web's limitations, educators like Dr. King still see it as a way to "blast your way out of the limitations of your own library."

19   Some of the most valuable information comes from home pages set up by the government and universities. One example, said Dr. King, was research conducted by a student trying to find information on cuts in financing for the Corporation for Public Broadcasting. The relevant books in the college's library were few and outdated, he said, but, with his help, the student found full texts of Congressional hearings about public broadcasting's budget.

20   "Her essay no longer consisted of relying on books or magazines," he said, "but in getting raw data on which the books and magazines are based."

21   On the Web, students can also find electronic versions of the most popular academic journals, the mainstay of research for faculty and advanced students. Most university libraries now have electronic subscriptions to a few hundred journals. Dr. Miller warned, however, that while that may be a tenth of the journals in the library of a small liberal arts college, it is a tiny fraction of the journals subscribed to by a large research university, which may order more

than 100,000. The trend is clearly toward electronic versions of academic journals, he added, but most are still not on-line and the ones that are tend to be expensive. On-line subscriptions, for instance, can often run into thousands of dollars a year.

22   The time will surely come, Dr. Miller said, when most academic journals are on line, "but you'll need either a credit card number or a password" from an institution that has bought an electronic subscription. "And if you don't have one or the other, you won't get in," he said.

23   When Mr. Pasick turned to Dr. Franklin for help, the professor's expertise was only one of the necessary ingredients for success. The other was the University of Wisconsin's access to the Web site, as one of 450 research institutions that pay up to $10,000 a year for the privilege. (The site is operated by the Interuniversity Consortium for Political and Social Research, at http://www.icpsr.umich.edu.)

24   Even at an institution with the resources to take full advantage of cyberspace, there are some forms of assistance that the Web will never provide, some educators say.

25   Dr. Santoro describes academic research as a three-step process: finding the relevant information, assessing the quality of that information and then using that information "either to try to conclude something, to uncover something, to prove something or to argue something." At its best, he explained, the Internet, like a library, provides only data.

26   In the research process, he said, "the Internet mainly is only useful for that first part, and also a little bit for the second. It is not useful at all in the third."

Examining Reading Selection 10

⚙✂ [Complete this Exercise at myreadinglab.com

Checking Your Vocabulary

Directions: *Use context, word parts, or a dictionary, if necessary, to determine the meaning of each word as it is used in the reading.*

____ 1. roamed (paragraph 2)
    a. wandered
    b. studied
    c. critiqued
    d. accessed

____ 2. analogy (paragraph 14)
    a. explanation
    b. version
    c. comparison
    d. analysis

____ 3. obsolete (paragraph 16)
    a. false
    b. inaccurate
    c. opinionated
    d. outdated

____ 4. mainstay (paragraph 21)
    a. principal source
    b. topic of research
    c. best direction
    d. best location

____ 5. expertise (paragraph 23)
    a. patience
    b. success
    c. knowledge
    d. opinion

Checking Your Comprehension

Directions: *Select the best answer.*

____ 6. According to the reading, the World Wide Web is useful for
    a. scholars.
    b. professors.
    c. students at universities.
    d. the average citizen.

____ 7. The Internet is least useful for _____
    a. focusing information to make a point.
    b. finding information related to a topic.
    c. determining the reliability of sources.
    d. overcoming the limitations of your college library.

____ 8. At what point did Adam Pasick find the information that he needed?
    a. when he first searched the Internet
    b. when he was guided by a reference librarian
    c. when he asked his professor for help
    d. when he decided to use paper journals not on the Internet

____ 9. From the point of view of a professor, the problem with doing research on the World Wide Web is
    a. there is so much information available students don't research an issue thoroughly.
    b. students often plagiarize information from the Internet.
    c. students can't tell the reliable information on the Internet from the unreliable.
    d. students will become unaccustomed to using paper sources in the library when they need to.

____ 10. Students can expect to find the least valuable information for research papers at a home page set up by
    a. an academic publication.
    b. an educational institution or foundation.
    c. an agency of the federal government.
    d. an individual with an ax to grind or something to sell.

Thinking Critically

____ 11. When beginning a research project, you should first
   a. select the most efficient search engine.
   b. browse the Web for useful information.
   c. go directly to a home page.
   d. seek the assistance of a reference librarian.

____ 12. The problem with online subscriptions is that they are
   a. wasteful since the journals are available in paper also.
   b. not reliable sources of information.
   c. too difficult to locate on the Web.
   d. too expensive for many colleges.

____ 13. One form of assistance that the Web will probably never provide in the future is
   a. a wide variety of search engines.
   b. screening for the reliability of information.

   c. a wide range of scholarly journals.
   d. an efficient method to search for information.

____ 14. The best reason for including both Internet and paper sources in a major research paper is to
   a. lend it the variety it needs.
   b. save time doing the research.
   c. produce a more thorough paper.
   d. add interest to it.

____ 15. All of the following would be good captions for the photo on page 242, *except*
   a. The Internet is more like a bookstore than a library.
   b. The Internet has greatly improved the quality of students' research papers.
   c. Many useful Web sites for college students do not show up in a Web search.
   d. The most valuable Web sites are often set up by universities or the government.

Scorecard

Selection 10:   1,260 words

Finishing Time: _____   _____   _____
                    HR.   MIN.   SEC.

Starting Time: _____   _____   _____
                    HR.   MIN.   SEC.

Reading Time: _____   _____
                            MIN.   SEC.

WPM Score: _____

Comprehension Score: for Items 6–15
Number Right: _____ × 10 = _____%

Assessing Your Reading Strategy

1. How would you rate your comprehension of the reading? (Circle one.)
   Excellent   Good   Fair   Poor

2. Did you find your reading strategy effective?   Yes   No

3. Suppose you were given an assignment to read another lengthy selection from the same source (*The New York Times*). Based on your experience with this selection, how would you adjust your reading strategy (if at all)?

   _____

   _____

Writing About Reading Selection 10

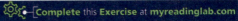 Complete this Exercise at myreadinglab.com

Checking Your Vocabulary

Directions: *Complete each of the following items; refer to a dictionary if necessary.*

1. Discuss the connotative meanings of the word *Internet* (paragraph 6).

2. Define the word *superficial* (paragraph 6) and underline the word or phrase that provides a context clue for its meaning.

3. Define the word *inclusion* (paragraph 15) and underline the word or phrase that provides a context clue for its meaning.

4. Determine the meanings of the following words by using word parts:
   a. *undergraduate* (paragraph 5)

   b. *uninitiated* (paragraph 5)

   c. *unreliable* (paragraph 6)

   d. *imprecise* (paragraph 8)

   e. *Interuniversity* (paragraph 23)

Checking Your Comprehension

5. How did Adam Pasick finally find the information he needed on the Internet?

6. What are the major problems with students doing research on the Internet?

7. One professor complained that because "information is so accessible, students stop far too quickly" when doing research. How did this professor solve this problem?

8. This reading discusses online subscriptions to academic journals. According to the reading, why are most journals not available online at many colleges?

_____

_____

_____

Thinking Critically

9. Should students rely on the Internet exclusively to do academic research? Why or why not?

_____

_____

_____

_____

_____

10. How can a student tell if information on the Internet is reliable?

_____

_____

_____

_____

11. Explain what Dr. Santoro means when he states that the Internet is more "like a bookstore" than a library.

_____

_____

_____

_____

_____

_____

_____

_____

_____

_____

_____

_____

12. What impression does the photograph of people working at computers create?

_____

_____

13. Do you agree with the author's advice about the best place to begin a research project? Why?

_____

_____

_____

_____

Questions for Discussion

1. In the reading, Dr. Santoro states that one of the reasons students do academic research is to "prove something or to argue something," and he goes on to state that the Internet "is not useful at all" to this end. Do you agree or disagree with Dr. Santoro? Justify your answer.

2. The reading suggests that in many ways the Internet is not useful for academic research. Are there better alternatives to the Web? What are they?

3. How would you proceed with a research project on "solutions to homelessness" for a sociology class? Would you use the Internet? How would you begin the project? What search engines might you use to find the information you need? At what point might you use the library and for what specific reason(s)?

CHAPTER 6

Reading Textbooks, Essays, Articles, and Technical Material

think VISUALLY...

The student in the photo faces a wide range of reading materials and wishes she had more time to read about fun topics of interest to her. Like many students, she has a heavy reading load for his college classes—textbooks as well as outside reading assignments.

While textbooks are the primary source of information for college students, they are by no means the only source. Many instructors assign supplemental readings, often in the form of essays and articles.

This chapter discusses how to read textbooks, articles, essays, and technical material. By learning their parts and knowing how they are organized, you will be able to read them more efficiently. You might even have time left over for recreational, fun reading.

Learning GOALS

In this chapter, you will learn how to . . .

Goal 1 Use textbooks as learning tools

Goal 2 Read essays effectively

Goal 3 Read popular press articles effectively

Goal 4 Read scholarly journal articles effectively

Goal 5 Analyze essays and articles

Goal 6 Read scientific material effectively

Goal 7 Think critically about research sources

■ Textbooks as Learning Tools

Goal 1
Use textbooks as
learning tools

While textbooks may seem to be long and impersonal, they are actually carefully crafted teaching and learning systems. They are designed to work with your instructor's lecture to provide you with reliable and accurate information and to help you practice your skills.

Why Buy and Study Textbooks?

Did you know the following facts about textbooks?

- **Nearly all textbook authors are college teachers**. They work with students daily and understand students' needs.
- **Along with your instructor, your textbook is the single best source of information for the subject you are studying**.
- **The average textbook costs only about $7 a week**. For about the price of a movie ticket, you are getting a complete learning system that includes not only a textbook but also a companion Web site and other study materials.
- **Your textbook can be a valuable reference tool in your profession**. For example, many nursing majors keep their textbooks and refer to them often when they begin their career.

Textbooks are an investment in your education and in your future. A textbook is your ally—your partner in learning.

Using Textbook Organization to Your Advantage

Have you ever walked into an unfamiliar supermarket and felt lost? How did you finally find what you needed? Most likely, you looked for the signs hanging over the aisles indicating the types of products shelved in each section. Walking along the aisle, you no doubt found that similar products were grouped together. For example, all the cereal was in one place, all the meat was in another, and so forth.

You can easily feel lost or intimidated when beginning to read a textbook chapter, too. It may seem like a huge collection of unrelated facts, ideas, and numbers that have to be memorized. Actually, a textbook chapter is much like a supermarket. It, too, has signs that identify what is located in each section. These signs are the major **headings** that divide the chapter into topics. Underneath each heading, similar ideas are grouped together, just as similar products are grouped together in a supermarket aisle. In most cases, several paragraphs come under each heading.

Sometimes headings are further divided into **subheadings** (usually set in smaller type than the main heading or indented or set in a different color). Using headings and subheadings, chapters take a major idea, break it into its important parts, and then break those parts into smaller parts, so you can learn it one step a time.

A typical textbook chapter might have an organization that looks like the diagram on the left, following. Notice that this diagram shows a chapter divided into seven major headings, and the first major heading is divided into three subheadings. The number of major headings and subheadings and the number of paragraphs under each will vary from chapter to chapter in a book.

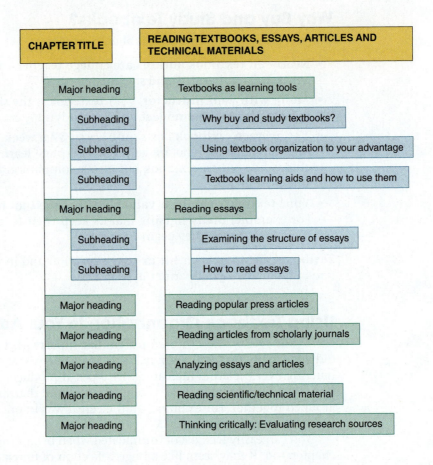

Once you know how a chapter is organized, you can use this knowledge to guide your reading. Once you are familiar with the organization, you will also begin to see how ideas are connected.

Look at the following partial list of headings and subheadings from a chapter of a sociology textbook.

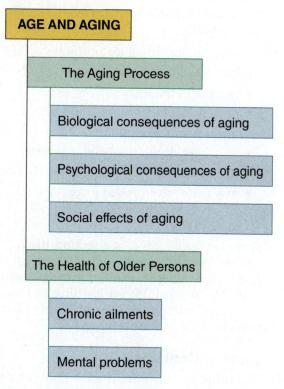

The titles and headings, taken together, form a brief outline of a chapter. In this chapter on age and aging, "The Aging Process" and "The Health of Older Persons" are the first two major topics. The topic "The Aging Process" is broken into three parts: biological consequences, psychological consequences, and social effects. "The Health of Older Persons" is divided into two parts: chronic ailments and mental problems.

Textbook Learning Aids and How to Use Them

Textbooks contain numerous features to help you learn. Features vary from book to book and from discipline to discipline, but most textbooks contain the following:

- preface
- "To the Student"
- table of contents
- opening chapter
- typographical aids
- chapter exercises and questions
- boxes and case studies
- vocabulary lists
- chapter summary
- glossary
- index

Preface

The **preface** is the author's introduction to the text. It presents information you should know before you begin reading Chapter 1. It may contain such information as:

- why and for whom the author wrote the text
- how the text is organized
- purpose of the text
- references and authorities consulted
- major points of emphasis
- learning aids included and how to use them
- special features of the text
- new materials included since the book's last update

To the Student

Some textbooks contain a section titled "To the Student." This section is written specifically for you. It contains practical information about the text. It may, for example, explain textbook features and how to use them, or it may offer suggestions for learning and studying the text. Often, a "To the Instructor" section precedes or follows "To the Student" and contains information useful to your instructor.

Table of Contents

The **table of contents** is an outline of a text found at the beginning of the book. It lists all the important topics and subtopics covered. Glancing through a table of contents will give you an overview of a text and suggest its organization.

Before beginning to read a chapter, refer to the table of contents. Although chapters are intended to be separate parts of a book, it is important to see how they fit together as parts of the whole—the textbook itself.

A table of contents can be a useful study aid when preparing for exams. To review the material on which you will be tested, read through the table of contents listings for chapters covered on the exam. This review will give you a sense of which topics you are already familiar with and which topics you have yet to learn about.

Opening Chapter

The first chapter of a textbook is one of the most important and deserves close attention. Here the author sets the stage for what is to follow. More important, it defines the discipline, explains basic principles, and introduces terminology that will be used throughout the text. Typically, you can expect to find as many as 20 to 50 new words introduced and defined in the first chapter. These words are the language of the course, so to speak. To be successful in any new subject area, you must learn to read and speak its language.

Typographical Aids

Textbooks contain various **typographical aids** (arrangements or types of print) that make it easy to pick out what is important to learn and remember. These include the following:

1. **Different types of font.** Italic type (*slanted print*) and boldfaced type (**dark print**) are often used to call attention to a particular word or phrase. Often new terms are printed in italics or boldface in the sentence in which they are defined.

2. **Enumeration. Enumeration** refers to the numbering or lettering of facts and ideas within a paragraph. It is used to emphasize key ideas and make them easy to locate.

3. **Listing. Bulleted lists** and **numbered lists** provide important information in a list format. (A bullet looks like this: •). These lists are typically indented, which makes them easy to find as you read and review the chapter.

Chapter Exercises and Questions

Exercises and questions fall into several categories.

1. *Review questions* **cover the factual content of the chapter.**
   - Distinguish between a trademark and a brand name.

2. *Discussion questions* **deal with interpretations of content.** These are often meant to be jumping-off points for discussion in the classroom or with other students.
   - What do you think is the future of generic products?

3. *Application questions* **ask you to apply your knowledge to the world around you or to a real-life situation.**
   - How would you go about developing a brand name for a new type of soft drink?

4. *Critical thinking questions* **ask you to think deeply about a topic or issue.** These questions require close attention and are often asked on exams.
   - How is advertising good for society? How is it bad for society?

5. *Problem questions* **are usually mathematical in nature.** Working with problems is one of the most important parts of any math, science, or technical course. Here is a sample problems:
   - If a microwave oven costs the retailer $325 and the markup is 35%, find the selling price of the microwave.

Boxes and Case Studies

Many textbooks include boxed inserts or case studies that are set off from the text. Generally, these "boxes" contain interesting information or extended examples to illustrate text concepts. Boxes are sometimes a key to what the author considers important.

Case studies usually follow the life history of a person, or the business practices of a particular company. These are valuable applications of the textbook concepts to the real world.

Vocabulary Lists

Textbooks usually contain a list of new terms introduced in each chapter. This list may appear at the beginning or end of the chapter.

Chapter Summary

In most textbooks, each chapter ends with a **chapter summary** that reviews all the chapter's key points. While the summary is sometimes in paragraph form, it is more often formatted as a numbered list. If you are having difficulty extracting the main points from the chapter, the summary is an excellent resource.

This text features a "Self-Test Summary" at the end of each chapter. For an example, see page 290. Note how the summary is provided in a question-and-answer format to help you quiz yourself on the concepts.

Glossary

Usually found at the end of the book, a **glossary** is a mini-dictionary that lists alphabetically the important vocabulary used in the book. Because it is built into the textbook, a glossary is faster to use and more convenient than a dictionary. It does not list all the common meanings of a word, as a dictionary does, but instead gives only the meaning used in the text.

Index

The book's **index**, found at the end of the book, is an alphabetical listing of all the topics in the book. It includes not only key terms, but also topics, names of authors, and titles of texts or readings.

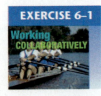

EXERCISE 6–1

EVALUATING TEXTBOOK LEARNING AIDS

Directions: *With a partner or in a small group, choose a textbook from one of your other courses. Each person in the group should take turns answering the following questions and showing examples.*

1. What learning aids does the book contain? Does it contain any special features not listed in this section? If so, what are they and what is their function? Which of these features do you expect to use most often?

   _____

   _____

2. How is the information given in the preface important?

   _____

   _____

3. Look at the opening chapter. What is its function?

   _____

   _____

4. Review the table of contents. What are its major parts?

   _____

   _____

■ Reading Essays

Goal 2
Read essays
effectively

Essays present the personal views of an author on a subject. They tend to be subjective because they frequently emphasize the author's individual feelings. This does not mean that essays are not factual or accurate. Essays simply provide a personal approach to the information presented.

Understanding how essays are organized and recognizing the different types will help you read them more effectively and efficiently.

Examining the Structure of Essays

Essays are short pieces of writing that examine a single topic and focus on a single idea about that topic. They may be encountered in anthologies, newspapers, and magazines of all types. Essays follow a standard organization and have the following parts:

- title
- introduction
- thesis statement
- body, containing supporting information
- summary or conclusion

The structure of an essay is similar to that of a paragraph. Like a paragraph, an essay has a topic. It also explores a single idea about the topic; in an essay this is called the **thesis statement**. Like a paragraph, an essay provides ideas and details that support the thesis statement. However, unlike a paragraph, an essay deals with a broader topic and the idea that it explores is often more complex. You can visualize the structure of an essay as follows:

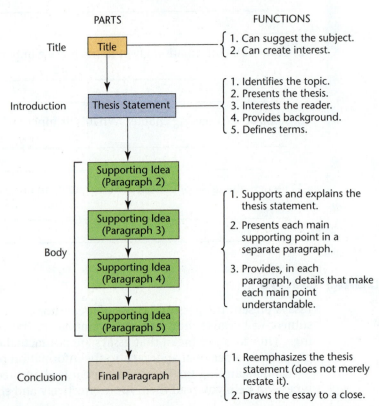

The Structure of an Essay

PARTS   FUNCTIONS

Title

Title
1. Can suggest the subject.
2. Can create interest.

Introduction

Thesis Statement
1. Identifies the topic.
2. Presents the thesis.
3. Interests the reader.
4. Provides background.
5. Defines terms.

Body

Supporting Idea (Paragraph 2)

Supporting Idea (Paragraph 3)

Supporting Idea (Paragraph 4)

Supporting Idea (Paragraph 5)

1. Supports and explains the thesis statement.
2. Presents each main supporting point in a separate paragraph.
3. Provides, in each paragraph, details that make each main point understandable.

Conclusion

Final Paragraph
1. Reemphasizes the thesis statement (does not merely restate it).
2. Draws the essay to a close.

Note: There is no set number of paragraphs that an essay should contain. This model shows six paragraphs, but in actual essays, the number will vary greatly.

Let's examine the function of each of these parts of an essay in greater detail by referring to an essay titled "To Catch a Liar." It was written by Sandra Parshall and first appeared in a blog titled Poe's Deadly Daughters.

Title

To Catch a Liar

Author

by Sandra Parshall

introduction: interest catching question

1   Do you think you're pretty good at spotting when somebody's lying? Sorry, but I'll bet you're not as sharp as you think you are.

background information on success of catching liars

2   Researchers have found that most people have a dismally low success rate, even in a lab setting where they know for certain that some of those they're studying are lying. If we're especially vigilant, we might spot half of all lies—which means we'll miss half. Police officers aren't much better than the rest of us, although they improve with experience. Those super-cops who can always detect a

—From blog entitled "Poe's Deadly Daughters" by Sandra Parshall. Reprinted by permission of the author.

lie, like the fictional Special Agent Gibbs on the TV show *NCIS*, do exist in reality, but they're extremely rare and psychologists have yet to determine how they do it. Since the detective's ability to spot lies is crucial to crime-solving, some scientists are finding ways to teach the skill to cops.

thesis statement

3   *Scientific American Mind* magazine's September/October issue reports on experiments conducted by one of them, social psychologist Aldert Vrij of the University of Portsmouth in England. Vrij's work is based on the human mind's inability to think along multiple tracks simultaneously. Lying is more demanding than simply telling the truth, so if the interrogator gives the suspect's mind too much to process at one time, the person being questioned is likely to slip up if he's trying to sell a phony story.

details about Vrij's research study

4   Here's the premise: The liar has to worry about keeping his story consistent and believable, first of all—which means suppressing all thought of the truth so it doesn't inadvertently slip out—but he also has to "look honest" by controlling his expression and body movements. And he's constantly monitoring the cop's reaction to what he's saying. All that is exhausting, and if the interrogator adds even a little more pressure, that may be enough to trip up a liar.

explanation of why lying is complicated

5   Vrij and his colleagues have found several useful strategies for applying that extra pressure.

strategies for catching liars

body

- First, discount sweating and general nervousness. Even an honest person will be nervous under police scrutiny.

- One way to trip up a liar is to ask the suspect to tell his or her story backward, beginning at the end. Devising a false story and keeping it straight is hard enough without the burden of having to recount phony events in reverse. In lab tests, this greatly increased mistakes and the likelihood of catching a liar.

- Interrogators can also rattle a suspect by insisting that he maintain eye contact. Liars have trouble concentrating on their stories if they're looking directly into the eyes of the people they're lying to.

- Asking suspects to draw pictures of what they're describing can also reveal the liars. Their pictures will show fewer details than those drawn by truth-tellers, and often the pictures won't be consistent with verbal descriptions.

conclusion

6   These easy techniques have proven highly effective in the lab and should help police in the real world do their work more efficiently. Best of all, they're simple enough to be used by fictional cops who aren't endowed with the special mental powers of Special Agent Gibbs.

final comment on the usefulness of the strategies

The Title

The title usually suggests the subject of the essay and is intended to capture the reader's interest. Some titles are highly descriptive and announce exactly what the essay will be about. For example, the title "To Catch a Liar" announces the subject of the essay. Other titles are less directly informative.

Some essays have both a title and a subtitle. In these essays, the subtitle may suggest the subject matter more directly. In an essay titled "Citizenship or Slavery?" the title is mainly intended to capture your interest rather than to directly announce the subject. The subtitle, "How Schools Take the Volunteer Out of Volunteering," focuses you more clearly on what the essay will be about.

EXERCISE 6–2

Working
COLLABORATIVELY

ANALYZING TITLES

Directions: *Working with a classmate, decide what you expect to be discussed in essays with each of the following titles.*

1. Animal Rights: Right or Wrong

   _____

   _____

2. Firearms, Violence, and Public Policy

   _____

   _____

3. The Price of Power: Living in the Nuclear Age

   _____

   _____

4. The Nature and Significance of Play

   _____

5. Uncivil Rights—The Cultural Rules of Anger

   _____

   _____

The Introduction

The introduction, usually one or two paragraphs long, sets the scene for the essay and places the subject within a framework or context. The introduction may

- present the thesis statement of the essay
- offer background information (explain television addiction as an issue, for example)
- define technical or unfamiliar terms (define *addiction*, for example)
- build your interest (give an instance of an extreme case of television addiction)

Notice how in the sample essay "To Catch a Liar" these goals are accomplished in its first two paragraphs.

ANALYZING AN INTRODUCTION

Directions: *Read only the first two paragraphs of the essay "Mind Your Own Browser" by Simson L. Garfinkel below. What types of information do they provide?*

_____

_____

_____

MIND YOUR OWN BROWSER
Averting the watchful eyes of online advertisers

by Simson L. Garfinkel, from *Technology Review*

introduction

1   MOST OF US DEPEND on free web services, from Google to Facebook, but unless you're careful, using them has a price; your privacy. Web advertisers, which keep these sites in business, track what you do online in order to deliver targeted, attention-grabbing ads. Your web browser reveals a surprising amount about you, and advertisers are keen to find out even more.

2   A new draft report from the Federal Trade Commission (FTC) recommends the creation of a "Do Not Track" mechanism that would let Internet users choose, with the click of a button, whether to allow advertisers to track them. While this would offer better privacy controls than exist currently, the FTC's approach falls short, because tracking technology is interwoven into our most popular websites and mobile services. Without tracking, they simply don't work.

body

3   Few people realize that many web ads are tailored using huge amounts of personal data collected, combined, and cross-referenced from multiple sources—an approach known as "behavioral advertising." Advertisers ferret out clues to where you live, where you work, what you buy, and which TV shows you watch, then refine their ads accordingly.

4   Behavioral advertising works. A study conducted by Microsoft Research Asia found that users were up to seven times likelier to click on targeted ads than on nontargeted ones. Targeted ads earn much more for statistics—an average of $4.12 per thousand views versus *statistics* $1.98 per thousand for regular ads, according to a study commissioned by the Network Advertising Initiative, a trade group that promotes self-regulation.

5   While many people are simply opposed on principle to unrestricted tracking, there are real risks involved. Without safeguards, tracking techniques could be exploited to steal identities or to back into computers. And the big databases that advertisers are building could be misused by unscrupulous employers or malicious governments.

6   Over the past 15 years the United States has developed a peculiar approach to protecting consumer privacy. Companies publish detailed

"privacy policies" that are supposed to explain what information they collect and what they plan to do with it. Consumers can then choose whether they want to participate.

7   The FTC report says that this model no longer works (if it ever did). "Many companies are not disclosing their practices," FTC chairman Jon Leibowitz says. "And even if companies do disclose them, they do so in long, incomprehensible privacy policies and user agreements that consumers don't read, let alone understand." *quotation from authority*

8   The FTC is trying to rein this in. It recommends, for example, that companies collect information only when there is a legitimate business need to do so, and asks them to destroy that information when they no longer need it. It also wants companies to do a better job of explaining their policies to consumers.

9   Of course, real choice requires more than clear information—it requires options. At the moment, that means activating the "private browsing" mode built into modern web browsers (which prevents sites from accessing cookies) or using browser plug-ins that automatically block ads and certain tracking technologies. *explanation*

10   But there is no rule prohibiting advertisers from circumventing private-browsing modes, and many are doing so. The FTC's solution to this problem is "Do Not Track," loosely modeled on the agency's popular "Do Not Call" list. Instead of a centralized list of consumers

body

who don't want to be tracked, however, they envision a browser setting that would transmit an anonymity request to web advertisers. If behaviorally targeted ads really are beneficial to consumers, most people will leave the feature switched off. Otherwise, websites better get used to $1.98 per thousand ads viewed.

11   Browser makers have started building tracking controls for their software. Google recently released an add-on for Chrome called Keep My Opt-Outs, and Microsoft has announced a similar feature for Internet Explorer 9 called Tracking Protection. These features tell websites when someone doesn't want to be tracked. But it's still up to companies to honor this request. And, unsurprisingly, the advertising industry fiercely opposes tracking restrictions, especially if they are enabled in browsers by default.

12   The real problem with "Do Not Track" is that it derives from an earlier understanding of web advertising—that ads are distributed to news sites, search engines, and other destinations that don't necessarily need to know who you are. Nowadays many popular websites are unusable unless you let them track you.

13   Take Facebook: The website has seen explosive ad-revenue growth precisely because it tracks users' interests in great detail. There's no way to turn off tracking and still use the site. Thanks to Facebook Connect, which lets you log on to other websites with your Facebook credentials, and the "Like" button, which sends links from external pages back to your profile, Facebook now tracks you across the web. Or, more accurately, you tell Facebook where you are.

14   Smartphones will accelerate this trend. Already, many phones deliver ads based on your GPS-determined position. Future ads might depend on the applications you've installed, whom you've called, even the contents of your address book.

15   There is a way to resolve this conundrum; Create simple and enforceable policies that limit companies' retention and use of consumer data. These could be dictated by the government or, conceivably, built into browsers and customized by users. For example, you could tell Google to archive your searches forever, but make them anonymous after six months. You could tell Facebook to keep your posts indefinitely, but use them for advertising purposes only for a year.

16   Unfortunately, any kind of reform will face stiff opposition from vested interests. But if the government wants to defend us from privacy-trampling advertising, it needs more than "Do Not Track."

The Thesis Statement

The **thesis statement** of an essay is its main point. All other ideas and paragraphs in the essay support this idea. Once you identify an essay's thesis, you have discovered the key to its meaning. The thesis is usually stated in a single sentence and this sentence appears in the introductory paragraphs. It often follows the background information and the attention-getter. In the sample essay "To Catch a Liar" the thesis is stated at the end of the second paragraph (see p. 257). Occasionally, an author will first present evidence in support of the thesis and finally state the thesis at the end of the essay. This organization is most common in argumentative essays (see Chapter 11).

You may also find, on occasion, that an author implies rather than directly states the thesis; the thesis is revealed through the supporting paragraphs. When you cannot find a clear statement of the thesis, ask yourself this question: "What is the one main point the author is making?" Your answer is the implied thesis statement.

Here are a few sample thesis statements.

> Due to its negative health effects, cigarette smoking is once again being regarded as a form of deviant behavior.
>
> Career choice is influenced by numerous factors including skills and abilities, attitudes, and life goals.
>
> Year-round school will provide children with a better education that is more cost-effective.

EXERCISE 6–4

IDENTIFYING A THESIS STATEMENT

Directions: *Read the entire essay "Mind Your Own Browser" (pp. 259–261) and identify its thesis statement.*

_____

_____

The Body

The **body** of the essay contains sentences and paragraphs that explain or support the thesis statement. This support may be in the form of

- examples
- descriptions
- facts
- statistics
- reasons
- anecdotes (stories that illustrate a point)
- personal experiences and observations
- quotations from or references to authorities and experts
- comparisons
- research
- explanations

EFFICIENCY TIP
Support given for a thesis statement falls into two categories: *subjective* support, based on the experience of individuals (anecdotes, personal stories), and *objective* support, based on facts and statistics. If you are tight on time, it is probably better to spend more time reading the scientific/objective evidence, because this is the information on which you are likely to be tested.

Most writers use various types of supporting information. In the sample essay "To Catch a Liar" (pp. 256–257), the author uses several types of information in her supporting paragraphs. Notice how she gives an example of a super-cop in paragraph 2 and offers reasons for why lying is complex in paragraph 4. Paragraph 5 presents facts and descriptions.

EXERCISE 6–5 **ANALYZING SUPPORTING INFORMATION**

Directions: *Review the essay "Mind Your Own Browser" and mark where the body begins and ends. Then identify the type(s) of supporting information the author used.*

_____

_____ ■

FLEXIBILITY TIP
Some articles will explore both sides of a question and ask readers to form their own opinions based on the facts and examples presented. Such articles require careful reading and critical thinking.

The Conclusion

An essay is brought to a close with a brief conclusion, not a summary. (A summary provides a review of the key ideas presented in an article. Think of a summary as an outline in paragraph form. The order in which the information appears in the summary reflects the order in which it appears in the article itself.) A **conclusion** is a final statement about the subject of the essay. A conclusion does not review content as a summary does. Instead, a conclusion often refers back to, but does not repeat, the thesis statement. It may also suggest a direction for further thought or introduce a new way of looking at what has already been said. The sample essay "To Catch a Liar" (pp. 256–257) ends with a conclusion that comments on the usefulness of the strategies presented.

EXERCISE 6–6 **ANALYZING A CONCLUSION**

Directions: *Explain how the conclusion of "Mind Your Own Browser" draws this essay to a close.*

_____

_____ ■

EXERCISE 6–7 **ANALYZING AN ESSAY**

Directions: *"Latino Heritage Month: Who We Are . . . And Why We Celebrate" (pp. 41–43) is an example of an essay. Read or review the essay and answer the following questions.*

1. What is the purpose of the essay?

   _____

   _____

2. What types of supporting evidence does Rodriguez use to support his thesis?

   _____

3. To what extent are the author's experiences, opinions, and beliefs expressed in the essay?

   _____

   _____

4. Why does Rodriguez explain where he has lived and who his former wives and girlfriends are?

_____

_____

How to Read Essays

An **essay** usually presents information on a specific topic from a particular writer's point of view. When reading essays, use the following guidelines.

NEED TO KNOW How to Read Essays

1. **Establish the authority of the author whenever possible.** In order to trust that the author presented accurate, reliable information, make sure he or she is knowledgeable about or experienced with the subject.

2. **Pay attention to background information the author provides.** Especially if the subject is one with which you are unfamiliar, you must fill in gaps in your knowledge. If the background supplied is insufficient, consult other sources to get the information you need.

3. **Identify the author's thesis.** Determine exactly what information the author is presenting about the subject. Test your understanding by expressing it in your own words.

4. **Identify the organizational pattern.** Depending on a writer's purpose, he or she may choose a specific pattern, as shown here.

If a Writer's Purpose Is To	The Pattern Used Is
Trace the history or sequence of events	Chronological order
Explain how something works	Chronological order
Explain a subject by describing types or parts	Classification
Explain why something happened	Cause-Effect
Explain what something is	Definition
Emphasize similarities or differences between two or more things	Comparison-Contrast

5. **Pay attention to new terminology.** Mark or underline new terms as you read them. If some are not defined and you cannot determine their meaning from context, be sure to look them up.

6. **Highlight as you read.** Mark the thesis statement and each major supporting detail.

7. **Outline, map, or summarize the essay.** To ensure recall of the information, as well as to test your understanding of it, use some form of writing. (See Chapter 7.)

■ Reading Popular Press Articles

Goal 3
Read popular press articles effectively

Articles can tell a story, describe, or inform. Articles differ from essays in that they are generally more objective. When writing an article, the author assumes the role of a reporter. He or she avoids expressing personal feelings or viewpoints and concentrates on directly stating the facts.

FLEXIBILITY TIP
In general, articles from the popular press can be read faster than scholarly materials. Popular press articles often contain graphics (such as photos) that make the pages turn more quickly.

Articles that appear primarily in magazines and newspapers assume a different style and format from most essays. While popular press articles examine a topic and focus on an aspect of it, they tend to be more loosely or informally structured than most essays and scholarly journal articles. The title is usually eye-catching and descriptive. The introductory section may be less fully developed, and a formal paragraph conclusion may not be used.

The two most common types of popular press articles found in both newspapers and magazines are hard news articles and feature articles. They have essentially the same form, consisting of a beginning, called the *lead;* the story itself, called the *body* or *development;* and sometimes a formal *conclusion* as an ending.

Hard News Articles

Articles that directly report serious news are known as hard news articles. They are stories about conflict, death, and destruction as well as items of interest and importance in government, politics, science, medicine, business, and the economy. Articles of this type may be organized in one of two ways.

Inverted Structure

The traditional structure used in newspaper articles, either print or online, is known as the *inverted pyramid* because the article moves from general to more specific information. It contains the following parts:

- **Title.** Titles, or headlines, used in hard news stories are brief and directly informative about the article's content. They are usually expressed in active language, somewhat in the form of a telegraph message: "President Threatens Veto over Budget" or "Diet Drug Thought to Be Health Risk." Reading the title is usually sufficient to help you decide whether to read the article.

- **Datelines, Credit Lines, and Bylines.** These follow the title and come just before the summary lead. *Datelines* appear on all but local news stories and generally only give the place where the story came from; occasionally the date will be given. *Credit lines* may also appear before the lead and supplement datelines. They give the name of the wire service or newspaper from which the story was taken, such as "Associated Press" or *Washington Post. Bylines* name the writer of the article and are sometimes also included between the title and the lead.

- **Summary Lead.** This opening paragraph contains a summary of the most essential information in the story. It is similar to the *thesis statement* in an essay and the *abstract* in a scholarly article. Reading this lead alone may provide you with all the information you need from the article and will help you to determine whether you need to read further to get the information you want.

- **Body or Development.** The supporting facts are presented here—arranged in descending order of importance or interest. The most important details are placed first, followed by those second in importance or interest, and so on, until those facts most easily dispensed with are placed at the end of the story. If the lead paragraph doesn't contain the information you need, this type of organization will permit you to locate it easily. Since the *inverted pyramid* structure contains no conclusion there is no need to skip to the end of the article when previewing it.

Look at the following online news article and note where its parts are located.

title or headline ## WOMAN PUNCHES BEAR TO SAVE HER DOG

dateline Posted: August 30, 2011 – 9:01 PM

byline By Jonathan Grass

credit line *Juneau Empire*

summary lead Black bears in residential neighborhoods aren't exactly unheard of in Juneau. While many people stay inside when bears are about, one local woman says she had a different instinct when she saw her dog was in trouble.

body It started out as a typical evening for 22-year-old Brooke Collins. She let her dogs out as usual but this time, she said there was a black bear outside who took hold of her dachshund

Michael Penn/Juneau Empire
Brook Collins holds her dog, Fudge, at home on Tuesday. Collins punched a black bear on the snout after the bear attacked Fudge on Sunday.

Fudge. She said she feared for her pet's life and, in an instant, ran over and punched the bear right in the face to make it let go.

"It was all so fast. All I could think about was my dog was going to die," said Collins.

"It was a stupid thing but I couldn't help it," she said. "I know you're not supposed to do that but I didn't want my dog to be killed."

Collins said she didn't see the bear outside when she let the dogs out around 7:30 P.M. Sunday. She said Fudge just darted out and the barking could be heard almost instantly. She said that barking was "the most horrible sound in the world."

Collins said when she looked outside she saw a bear was crouching down with Fudge in in its paws and was biting the back of the dog's neck.

"That bear was carrying her like a salmon," she said.

She said she almost instinctively went up and did the first thing she thought of. She punched the bear's face and scooped away her dog when it let go.

It all happened too fast to really think about but she had flashes of hearing about how some animals will back off from a punch to the nose, she said.

body

She said her boyfriend Regan O'Toole came out upon hearing the screaming. O'Toole said the bear already looked startled from being punched at that point. He said the animal went down the driveway and into the bushes to the mountain as he ran toward it.

Her dog suffered some claw and bite marks but they weren't deep so she said she decided not to take Fudge to the vet. She said the dog appeared to be more shocked than injured. She's keeping an eye on the marks and will get Fudge checked out if they appear infected.

She said she also got a mark on her thumb from where the bear and Fudge bit her, but it didn't need medical attention, she said.

Collins said she's very close to her dogs, which is why she reacted this way. She said after this experience, however, she'll keep a closer eye on them outside, as she fears an encounter with her other canine, a Pomeranian named Toki.

Collins lives in a neighborhood tucked up against Mount Juneau and uphill from the AWARE shelter. She said black bear sightings are a regular occurrence there. She believes this same one has been around her house many times and is not afraid of people.

She said if this is that bear, it's definitely used to people and keeps coming back and may even know what days the trash will be out. She said she's even followed it to take pictures before.

O'Toole said he's seen five bears in the area this year, including a sow with two cubs.

"We haven't had any attacks over the years and they're around all the time," he said.

Collins said one scary thing in hindsight was the bear's size, which she said was very large even when it was crouching. O'Toole said it was definitely a large one.

Collins said the whole experience of a physical encounter shook her up, calling the whole thing an eye-opener. She said she'll be taking a lot more caution from now on and definitely won't be approaching neighborhood bears.

"It's definitely changed my opinion because I never thought one would attack my dog," she said. "I wasn't in my right mind at the moment but I would never think of doing it again."

Bear sightings should be reported to the Alaska Department of Fish & Game's regional office. Call 465-4267 for biologist Neil Barten or 465-4359 for biologist Ryan Scott.

• Contact reporter Jonathan Grass at 523-2276 or at jonathan.grass@ juneauempire.com.

Action Story

A second common format for hard news articles is the *action story*. It contains all the parts of the inverted pyramid with a few variations. It also begins with a telegraphic title that can be followed by a byline, credit line, and dateline. Its opening paragraph is also in the form of a summary lead. However, its body presents the events in chronological order of their occurrence, rather than in order of importance or interest. Furthermore, this format includes a conclusion that contains additional information that does not fit within the chronology used in the body.

EXERCISE 6–8   **ANALYZING A HARD NEWS ARTICLE**

> **Directions:** *Locate a hard news article in a newspaper or magazine. Determine which format is used, the inverted pyramid or the action story. Then label the article's parts.* ■

Feature Articles

A second type of popular press article is the feature article. Found in both newspapers and magazines, either print or online, the feature article is longer and goes into greater depth than the usual hard news article. It usually deals with larger issues and subjects. Because of its length, this type of article requires a different structure from hard news articles.

It also begins with a *title* that is often in the form of a complete sentence and may contain a byline, credit line, and dateline. Its other parts may differ, though.

- **Feature Lead.** The lead in a feature article does not usually summarize its contents. Instead, it is intended to spark your interest in the topic being presented. It may begin with an interesting anecdote, present some highlight of the article, or offer an example of something you will learn more about later. Since the feature lead is primarily an interest builder, you may be able to skim through it quickly when reading the article.

- **Nut Graph.** The nut graph explains the nature and scope of the article. Depending upon the length of the article it may be one paragraph, or it may run to several paragraphs. When reading feature articles, read this section carefully. It will offer clues to the organization and content of the article and help you to grasp its main points.

- **Body or Development.** This is where the detailed information of the article is presented. Unlike hard new stories, the information can be organized in more than one way. Each paragraph or section may use a different thought pattern to develop its ideas, much like the expository essay. Mark and annotate this section as you read it, sifting through the main and secondary points.

- **Conclusion.** Feature articles often end with a conclusion, which, like the conclusion of a formal essay, makes a final statement about the subject of the article. Rather than summarizing the information presented, it may refer back to the nut graph, introduce a new way of looking at the information, or suggest a direction for further thought.

Refer to the following feature article to see an example of this structure.

title **WINNING HEARTS ON THE FRONT LINES**

Buffalo News July 16, 2012 page B1, B2

byline By Lou Michel

News Staff Reporter

feature lead A victory on the battlefield need not always require firepower.

nut graph Jennifer R. Curtis, who hails from Riverside, proved that last year during her eight months in Afghanistan.

Honored with the Bronze Star, the Air Force captain put her medical skills as a family nurse practitioner to work on the war's front lines, not only treating wounded troops, but winning over the Afghan people in their hardscrabble existence.

body or development Curtis, whose maiden name is Saddleson, was embedded with an Army Special Forces unit, serving as the chief female treatment team leader at a forward operating base along the Afghanistan-Pakistan border until last December.

And not only was there the enemy to contend with, she said, but vast cultural differences. A woman healer seeking to do good in a society where men are dominant and women subservient is, well, a tall order.

"It was challenging because I had to go through men on my team to interact with the village elders. The elders wouldn't talk to me directly because I was a woman," Curtis said. "Often times, the elders wouldn't allow us to talk to their women because they didn't want us to Americanize them."

When alone with Afghan women, Curtis added, she came to realize that the local females were indeed well aware that they were being oppressed.

But Curtis' mission was not to liberate them.

body Local midwives quickly realized the Air Force captain and mother of two young sons, Jacob and Andrew, was out to improve health in the remote region.

Armed with an anatomically correct birthing model that simulated childbirth, Curtis provided instruction on the do's and don'ts of assisting in delivering newborns, according to Army Major Darrell E. Jones, who recommended her for the Bronze Star medal.

"This training increased the ability for the midwives to care for the pregnant women, decreasing the mortality rate of delivering women and newborn children," Jones stated, adding that Curtis' devotion helped foster stability in the villages.

But making her way to those outlying areas was far from safe. Numerous times the convoys she traveled with came under enemy fire and Curtis ended up practicing battlefield medicine, which resulted in saving lives.

The same happened at the base, where the enemy routinely attacked.

"Stressful, that was what it was like taking care of catastrophic injuries with limited medical supplies and staff," Curtis recalled.

In his written recommendation for the Bronze Star, Jones also stated, "She used her primary care and trauma experience to care for more than 50 patients . . . leading to 13 successful medevacs of Coalition and Afghan forces."

Her service, in fact, also earned her the Combat Medic Award, making the Air Force family nurse practitioner among the few to receive this high honor the Army bestows on its own medics.

But it was her peaceful endeavors that really impressed the brass.

"She conducted over 10 engagements at local girls and boys schools teaching hygiene, medical care and disease prevention," the major wrote. "Capt. Curtis' unmatched professional and medical expertise marked the great success of the first female treatment team officer [to be embedded in an Army Special Forces unit.]"

And when she could not get out in the field to work directly with Afghans, Curtis took to the airwaves to promote better health practices among the villagers.

"... to the point that the radio station began to receive more requests for her messages," Jones stated.

Curtis said her mini radio show covered very basic tips on good health practices.

"I'd talk about hand washing, water sanitation, treating simple ailments such as fever and diarrhea, and also sexually transmitted diseases," Curtis said.

Now stationed at Hill Air Force Base in Utah, she officially received the Bronze Star in June, with her sons and husband, Chad Curtis, present for the ceremony.

She said her husband, an occupational therapy aide, made her deployment a lot easier since he stayed at home and took care of their sons.

The captain's recognition has also brought great joy to her mother, Susan Jaworski, who works at Buffalo State College's E.H. Butler Library.

"Jenn is my hero. It's so neat when a girl can do so much great work with so little on the front lines," Jaworski said. "She is amazing."

body

body

conclusion

—"Winning hearts on the front lines," by Lou Michel, from the Buffalo News, July 16, 2012, pp B1–B2.

EXERCISE 6–9   **ANALYZING A FEATURE ARTICLE**

Directions: *Select a feature article from a periodical. Label its parts, then mark and annotate it.*

■ Reading Articles from Scholarly Journals

Goal 4
Read scholarly journal articles effectively

Scholarly journals are publications by professional societies or college and university presses that report developments and research in a particular academic discipline. For example, in the field of psychology, scholarly journals include *American Journal of Psychology, Journal of Abnormal Psychology,* and *Psychological Bulletin.* Articles published in scholarly journals are usually peer reviewed. That is, before an article is published, other professionals in the field read the article and confirm that it is legitimate, accurate, and worthwhile.

You need to read articles from scholarly journals when you research a topic for a paper or write a research paper. Some professors distribute a reading list each semester, of which scholarly articles are a part. Others supplement text assignments by assigning articles and placing copies of them on reserve in the library. Many scholarly articles, especially those that report research conducted by the author, follow a similar format and often include the following parts, although different journals use different headings to organize their articles, or may not label all sections with headings.

EFFICIENCY TIP
The single best place to get summary information about an article in a scholarly journal is the abstract included at the beginning of it. The abstract presents the results of a study in clear, concise language.

- **Abstract.** An abstract is a brief summary of the article and its findings and is sometimes labeled as "Summary." It usually appears at the beginning of the article following the title and author. Read the abstract to get an overview of the article and, when doing research, to determine whether the study or report contains the information you need.

- **Summary of Related Research.** Many research articles begin by summarizing research that has already been done on the topic. Here authors will cite other studies and briefly report their findings. This summary brings you up to date on the most current research and suggests a rationale for why the author's study or research is necessary and appropriate. In some journals, this rationale may appear in a section called "Statement of the Problem."

- **Description of Research.** In this section, which may also be labeled "Method," the author describes his or her research or explains his or her ideas. For experimental research, you can expect the author to present the research design, including the purpose of the research, description of the population involved, sample size, methodology, and statistical tests applied.

- **Results.** Results of the research are presented in this section.

- **Implications, Discussion, and Conclusions.** Here the author explains what the results mean and draws possible implications and conclusions.

- **Further Research.** Based on their findings, some authors end the article by suggesting additional research that is needed to further explain the problem or issue being studied.

Here is a sample scholarly article that was originally published in *Psychological Science.* The article follows many of the conventions of scholarly journals, but it does not include an abstract.

A Picture's Worth
Partner Photographs Reduce Experimentally Induced Pain

Psychological Science

Sarah L. Master, Naomi I. Eisenberger, Shelley E. Taylor, Bruce D. Naliboff, David Shirinyan, and Matthew D. Lieberman

University of California, Los Angeles

summary of related research

Social support is associated with reduced pain experience across several domains (Cogan & Spinnato, 1988; Kulik & Mahler, 1989; Zaza & Baine, 2002); intriguingly, a handful of experimental studies suggest that this connection may reflect a causal relationship. Participants who received interactive support during a cold pressor task reported less pain than participants who completed the task alone or engaged in nonsupportive interactions (Brown, Sheffield, Leary, & Robinson, 2003; Jackson, Iezzi, Chen, Ebnet, & Eglitis, 2005). Moreover, the mere presence of another supportive individual (vs. being alone) reduced pain ratings in a cold pressor task (Brown et al., 2003; but see McClelland & McCubbin, 2008) and reduced pain ratings among fibromyalgia patients following stimulation to a painful body site (Montoya, Larbig, Braun, Preissl, & Birbaumer, 2004).

purpose of the study

Could the same pain-attenuating effects of social support be observed by merely activating the mental representation of a supportive other? Previous work has shown that activating mental representations of important others can produce effects similar to those created by the actual presence of these individuals (Fitzsimons & Bargh, 2003; Mikulincer & Shaver, 2001). Building on this research, the current study examined whether simply viewing a photograph of one's romantic partner could reduce physical-pain experience. We examined how this condition compared with one that is more consistent with previous conceptualizations of social support—one in which the participant held her partner's hand.

purpose of the study

METHOD

sample population and size

Participants were 28 right-handed women in long-term relationships (> 6 months). Three were excluded because of technical failures (final sample: n = 25). Upon arrival, each participant was taken into the testing room; her partner was taken to a separate room to have his photograph taken for later use.

description of how the study was conducted

After the participant provided consent, her pain threshold for thermal stimulation (a rating of 10, corresponding to moderate discomfort, on a scale from 0 to 20) was determined. She then placed her left arm behind an opaque curtain that was suspended from the ceiling. Throughout the study, a male experimenter behind the curtain delivered 6-s thermal stimulations to three alternating locations on

—Master et al., A Picture's Worth: Partner Photographs Reduce Experimentally Induced Pain, *Psychological Science*, SAGE Publications.

description of
how the study
was conducted

the participant's left volar forearm, using a 9-cm² computer-controlled Peltier-type thermode (TSAII, Medoc Inc., Ramat Yishai, Israel).

Each participant received a total of 84 thermal stimulations: Six stimulations (separated by 20-s intervals) were given during each of seven task conditions, and each condition was presented twice. Unbeknownst to the participant, half of the stimulations were at her threshold temperature and half were at her threshold plus 1°C. The seven study conditions (each lasting 3 min 14 s) were as follows: (a) holding the hand of the partner (as he sat behind the curtain), (b) holding the hand of a male stranger (the experimenter behind the curtain),[1] (c) holding an object (a squeeze ball), (d) viewing the partner's photographs (taken upon his arrival) on a computer screen, (e) viewing photographs of a male stranger (ethnicity-matched to the participant's partner), (f) viewing photographs of an object (a chair), and (g) viewing a fixation crosshair (no manipulation). Half of the participants completed the hand- and object-holding conditions first, and half completed the photograph conditions first.[2]

The participant rated each stimulation's "unpleasantness" by pointing to a number on the Gracely Box Scale (Gracely, McGrath, & Dubner, 1978), which is a 21-box numerical descriptor

scale anchored with previously quantified verbal descriptors of pain unpleasantness. A female experimenter (who was on the participant's side of the curtain) recorded the ratings. To address a competing hypothesis that social support reduces pain because it distracts one from pain (Hodes, Howland, Lightfoot, & Cleeland, 1990), we recorded participants' reaction times (i.e., the time it took them to press the space bar on the computer keyboard in front of them) to computer-generated beeps that were infrequently and randomly emitted throughout the study. This allowed us to assess whether participants were more distracted (as demonstrated by longer reaction times to the beeps) in the support conditions (partner hand-holding, partner photographs) than in the other conditions.

description
of how the
study was
conducted

RESULTS AND DISCUSSION

Average reaction times to the computer-generated beeps during the seven conditions were submitted to a one-way repeated measures analysis of variance (ANOVA). The manipulations were not found to be differentially distracting, $F(6, 144) = 0.42$, $p = .87$, $P_{rep} = .21$; thus, it appears that social support was not confounded with distraction. For ease of interpretation, we calculated difference scores, subtracting mean pain ratings in the fixation

data analysis

data analysis
and results

[1] Although participants could not see behind the curtain, the experimenter told them whose hand they were holding—their partner's hand or a stranger's hand—in the respective conditions. All participants reported that they believed the experimenter.

[2] The fixation condition was randomly included with either the hand-holding/object-holding conditions or the photograph conditions, to form a set. The order of presentation was randomized within each set of three or four conditions.

condition from mean pain ratings in each of the other conditions. A one-way ANOVA showed a significant main effect of condition on pain scores, $F(5, 120) = 19.63$, $p_{rep} > .99$. Planned pair-wise comparisons revealed that, as expected, holding the partner's hand led to significantly lower pain ratings ($M = 0.48$, $SD = 1.97$) than holding an object ($M = 0.89$, $SD = 1.41$), $t(24) = 4.73$, $p_{rep} = .99$, $d = 0.80$, or holding a stranger's hand ($M = 1.55$, $SD = 1.47$), $t(24) = 5.33$, $P_{rep} = .99$, $d = 1.17$. Interestingly, the photograph conditions showed similar effects (Fig. A)—viewing a partner's photographs led to significantly lower pain ratings ($M = -1.01$, $SD = 1.56$) than viewing photographs of an object ($M = 0.14$, $SD = 1.62$), $t(24) = 4.37$, $p_{rep} = .99$, $d = 0.72$, or viewing a stranger's photographs ($M = 0.22$, $SD = 0.84$), $t(24) = -5.09$, $p_{rep} = .99$, $d = 0.98$. In addition, pain ratings in the partner-photographs condition were marginally lower than those in the partner-handholding condition, $t(24) = -1.83$, $p = .08$, $P_{rep} = .84$.[3]

These findings confirm the notion that simply viewing a loved one's picture can have pain-attenuating effects, and they fit with social psychological research showing that being primed with a social construct is enough to activate associated mental representations and to bias behavior (Ferguson & Bargh, 2004).

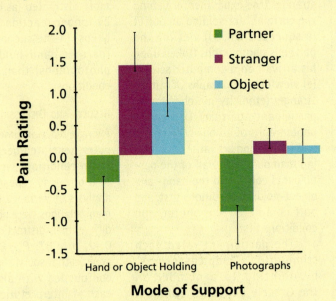

Fig. A.   Mean pain rating as a function of mode and source of support. Pain ratings on the ordinate are difference scores, which were calculated by subtracting mean pain ratings in the fixation condition from the mean pain ratings in each of the other conditions. Thus, negative numbers indicate lower pain ratings during the condition of interest compared with fixation.

[3] *These effects of partner photographs are not likely due to expectancy effects; a separate sample of women who were in relationships (> 6 months; n = 11) and were asked to imagine that they had completed the study predicted that they would have felt significantly less pain (relative to fixation) when holding their partner's hand than when viewing his photograph, t(10) = 3.24, P_{rep} = .95, d = 0.77.*

conclusion

Thus, seeing photographs of loved ones may prime associated mental representations of being loved and supported, which may be sufficient to attenuate pain experience. The findings suggest that bringing loved ones' photographs to painful procedures may be beneficial, particularly if those individuals cannot be there. In fact, because loved ones vary in their ability to provide support, photographs may, in some cases, be more effective than in-person support. In sum, these findings challenge the notion that the beneficial effects of social support come solely from supportive social interactions and suggest that simple reminders of loved ones may be sufficient to engender feelings of support.

REFERENCES

Brown, J.L., Sheffield, D., Leary, M.R., & Robinson, M.E. (2003). Social support and experimental pain. *Psychosomatic Medicine*, 65, 276–283.

Cogan, R., & Spinnato, J.A. (1988). Social support during premature labor: Effects on labor and the newborn. *Journal of Psychosomatic Obstetrics and Gynecology*, 8, 209–216.

sources used

Ferguson, M.J., & Bargh, J.A. (2004). How social perception can automatically influence behavior. *Trends in Cognitive Sciences*, 8, 33–39.

Fitzsimons, G.M., & Bargh, J.A. (2003). Thinking of you: Nonconscious pursuit of interpersonal goals associated with Relationship partners. *Journal of Personality and Social Psychology*, 84, 148–164.

Gracely, R.H., McGrath, F., & Dubner, R. (1978). Ratio scales of sensory and affective verbal pain descriptors. *Pain*, 5, 5–18.

Hodes, R.L., Howland, E.W., Lightfoot, N., & Cleeland, C.S. (1990). The effects of distraction on responses to cold pressor pain. *Pain*, 41, 109–114.

Jackson, T., Iezzi, T., Chen, H., Ebnet, S., & Eglitis, K. (2005). Gender, interpersonal transactions, and the perception of pain: An experimental analysis. *The Journal of Pain*, 6, 228–236.

Kulik, J.A., & Mahler, H.I. (1989). Social support and recovery from surgery. *Health Psychology*, 8, 221–238.

McClelland, L.E., & McCubbin, J.A. (2008). Social influence and pain response in women and men. *Journal of Behavioral Medicine*, 31, 413–420.

sources used

Mikulincer, M., & Shaver, P.R. (2001). Attachment theory and intergroup bias: Evidence that priming the secure base schema attenuates negative reactions to out-groups. *Journal of Personality and Social Psychology*, 81, 97–115.

Montoya, P., Larbig, W., Braun, C., Preissl, H., & Birbaumer, N. (2004). Influence of social support and emotional context on pain processing and magnetic brain responses in fibromyalgia. *Arthritis and Rheumatism*, 50, 4035–4044.

Zaza, C., & Baine, N. (2002). Cancer pain and psychosocial factors: A critical review of the literature. *Journ of Pain and Symptom Management*, 24, 526–542.

When reading scholarly journals, keep the tips in the Need to Know box below in mind.

NEED TO KNOW How to Read Scholarly Journals

1. **Be sure you understand the author's purpose.** Determine why the study was conducted.
2. **Highlight as you read.** You may need to refer back to information presented earlier in the article. Identify each part listed on page 271.
3. **Use index cards.** If you are reading numerous articles, keep a 4×6 index card for each. Write a brief summary of the purpose and findings.
4. **Use quotations.** If you take notes from the article, be sure to place in quotation marks any information you copy directly from the article. If you fail to do so, you may inadvertently plagiarize. Plagiarism, presenting someone else's ideas as your own, carries stiff academic and legal penalties.

■ Analyzing Essays and Articles

Goal 5
Analyze essays and articles

Essays and articles require close analysis and evaluation. While textbooks usually present reliable, unbiased factual information, essays and even some articles often express opinions and represent particular viewpoints; consequently, you must read them critically. Use the following questions to guide your analysis.

NEED TO KNOW How to Analyze Articles and Essays

1. **Who is the author?** Check to see if it is a name you recognize. Try to discover whether or not the author is qualified to write about the subject.
2. **What is the author's purpose?** Is the writer trying to present information, convince you of something, entertain you, or express a viewpoint?
3. **What does the introduction or lead add to the piece of writing?** Does it interest you or supply background information, for example?
4. **What is the author's thesis?** Try to express it in your own words. By doing so, you may find bias or discover a viewpoint you had not previously recognized.
5. **Does the author adequately support the thesis?** Is a variety of supporting information provided? An article that relies entirely upon the author's personal experiences, for example, to support a thesis may be of limited use.
6. **Does the author supply sources, references, or citations for the facts and statistics presented?** You should be able to verify the information presented and turn to those sources should you wish to read more about the subject.

For more information on thinking critically about essays and articles, refer to Chapters 10 and 11 in Part Four, "Reading Critically."

✔ LEARNING STYLE TIPS

If you tend to be a . . .	Then build your evaluation skills by . . .
Creative learner	Asking "What if . . .?" and "So what?" questions to help you free up new ideas and new ways of looking at a subject
Pragmatic learner	Writing marginal notes and recording your thoughts, reactions, and impressions

EXERCISE 6–10

Working COLLABORATIVELY

ANALYZING AN ESSAY

Directions: *Evaluate the essay "Latino Heritage Month: Who We Are . . . and Why We Celebrate" (p.41) by answering each of the questions listed in the Need to Know box "How to Analyze Articles and Essays" on page 276. Compare your answers with those of a classmate, and discuss any that differ.*

1. _____

_____

2. _____

_____

3. _____

_____

4. _____

_____

5. _____

_____

6. _____

_____

■ Reading Scientific/Technical Material

Goal 6
Read scientific
material effectively

If you are taking courses in the sciences, technologies, engineering, data processing, or health-related fields, you are working with a specialized type of textbook. In this section you will see how scientific and technical textbooks differ from those used in other classes. You will also learn several specific approaches to reading technical material. The key to reading technical material efficiently is to recognize how it differs from other types of material. Be sure to adapt your reading and study methods to accommodate these differences.

Each of the following passages describes earthquakes and whether these destructive events can be predicated. Read them and figure out how they differ.

PASSAGE 1

Earthquakes, Human Activity, and Plate Tectonics

Earthquakes induced by human activity have been documented in a few locations in the United States, Japan, and Canada. The cause was injection of fluids into deep wells for waste disposal and secondary recovery of oil and the use of reservoirs for water supplies. Most of these earthquakes were minor. The largest and most widely known resulted from fluid injection at the Rocky Mountain Arsenal near Denver, Colorado. In 1967, an earthquake of magnitude 5.5 followed a series of smaller earthquakes. Injection had been discontinued at the site in the previous year once the link between the fluid injection and the earlier series of earthquakes was established.

Other human activities, even nuclear detonations, have not been linked to earthquake activity. Energy from nuclear blasts dissipates quickly along the Earth's surface. Earthquakes are part of a global tectonic process that generally occurs well beyond the influence or control of humans. The focus (point of origin) of earthquakes is typically tens to hundreds of miles underground. The scale and force necessary to produce earthquakes are well beyond our daily lives. We cannot prevent earthquakes; however, we can significantly mitigate their effects by identifying hazards, building safer structures, and providing education on earthquake safety.

Scientists have never predicted a major earthquake. They do not know how, and they do not expect to know how any time in the foreseeable future. However, based on scientific data, probabilities can be calculated for potential future earthquakes. For example, scientists estimate that over the next 30 years the probability of a major earthquake occurring in the San Francisco Bay area is 67% and 60% in Southern California.

—U.G. Geological Survey at earthquake.usgs.gov

PASSAGE 2

Quake Warnings Before the Shaking Starts

Exciting progress is being made in *real-time earthquake warnings*. It's an old idea, that you could hook up a radio to a seismograph and have it send you a message when it feels a quake. You'd have a useful amount of time to react—even five seconds would be enough for a classroom of kids to get under their desks, or for you to save that file you're working on. And with 30 seconds' warning, you could pull a fire engine out of its garage, start your hospital's emergency power, do quick computer backups and prepare in many other ways.

—© 2012 Andrew L. Alden (http://geology.about.com). Used with permission of About, Inc.

Did you notice that the first passage presents only precise, factual information? The explanation is straightforward and no-nonsense, and it makes use of specific scientific terms like *"global tectonic process."* It also assumes that the reader understands the Richter scale ("magnitude 5.5"), which is the scientific scale for measuring the severity of earthquakes. Because of the language, the passage does not allow for interpretation or expression of opinion. The purpose of the passage is clearly to inform the reader about earthquakes caused by human activity and the possibility of predicting earthquakes through the use of statistics.

The second passage is written quite differently; it presents fewer facts and more examples. Words such as "exciting progress" and "useful" reveal the writer's attitude toward the subject. This passage helps you imagine how advance notice can help people prepare for an earthquake. In contrast, passage 1 is more focused on long-term preparation for earthquakes through safer building techniques and identification of hazards.

Passage 1 is an example of scientific/technical writing. It is very precise, exact, and factual. This section discusses the particular features of scientific/technical material and gives suggestions for reading this type of writing.

Fact Density

Scientific and technical writing is highly factual, dense, and concise. A large amount of information is closely packed together into a relatively small space on the page. Compared to many other forms of writing, technical writing may seem complicated and difficult. Here are a few suggestions for handling densely written material:

1. **Read technical material more slowly and carefully than other textbook content.** Plan to spend more time on a technical reading assignment than on other assignments.

2. **Plan on rereading certain sections several times.** Sometimes it is useful to read a section once rather quickly just to learn what main ideas it contains. Then read it carefully a second time, fitting together all the facts that explain the important ideas.

3. **Keep a notebook of significant information.** Because technical books are so highly factual, highlighting may not be effective. Instead, use a notebook to record information you need to remember. Recording this information in your own words is a useful way of checking whether or not you have really understood it and will increase your retention. Figure 6.1 (p. 280) shows an excerpt from a nursing student's notebook. Notice that this student included definitions and diagrams as well as detail.

FIGURE 6.1 SAMPLE NOTEBOOK PAGE

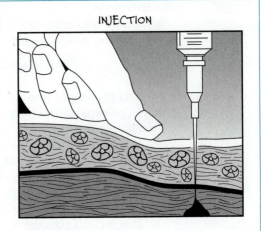

INJECTION

Intradermal Injection
- shallow penetration
- needle 3/8" gauge #25 or #26

Steps
1. change needle after medicine prepared
   in syringe—(remove med. from sides of needle)
2. add 2 minums air
3. use thumb & finger to pull tissue firmly
   to left of injection site
4. hold tissue while needle is inserted &
   med. injected
5. as withdraw needle, release tissue
   (needle track will be broken)

The Vocabulary of Technical Writing

Scientific/technical writing in each subject area is built on a set of very precise, exact word meanings. Each field has its own language, and you must learn the language in order to understand the material. Here are a couple of sentences taken from textbooks in several technical fields. As you read, notice the large number of technical words used in each.

MEDICAL ASSISTING

The inflammatory process produces dilation of blood vessels due to an increased blood flow, production of watery fluids and materials (exudate), and the invasion of monocytes (white blood cells) and neutrophils into the injured tissues to produce phagocytosis.

—Fremgen, Bonnie, *Essentials of Medical Assisting: Administrative and Clinical Competencies,* copyright © 1997 Pearson Education, Inc.

ENVIRONMENTAL TECHNOLOGY

Glucuronosyltransferases represent one of the major enzymes that carry out the reactions of exogenous and endogenous compounds to polar water-soluble compounds.

—Ostler et al., *Health Effects of Hazardous Materials,* copyright © 1996 Pearson Education, Inc.

In these examples, some words are familiar ones with new, unfamiliar meanings (*reactions, polar*). Others are words you've probably never seen (*phagocytosis, endogenous*).

In scientific/technical writing you'll encounter two types of specialized vocabulary. First, everyday words with which you are familiar are given entirely new, technical meanings. Here are a few examples.

- **Institution** (sociology): a cluster of values, norms, statuses, and roles that develop around a basic social goal
- **Pan** (photography): to follow the motion of a moving object with a camera
- **Cabinet** (government): a group of presidential advisers who head executive departments

A second type of specialized vocabulary uses words you may have never heard or seen such as those shown in the sentence on environmental technology.

Abbreviation and Notation Systems

Many scientific/technical fields use a set of abbreviations and notations (signs and symbols) extensively. These are used as shortcuts to writing out complete words or meanings and are used in formulas, charts, and drawings. Here are a few examples:

Field	Symbol	Meaning
Chemistry	C	carbon
	O	oxygen
Biology	♂	crossed with male organism
Astronomy	D	diameter
	Δ	distance

FLEXIBILITY TIP

Note the important difference between abbreviations and symbols in scientific texts and the abbreviations and symbols you use when annotating a textbook. Scientific symbols are an important part of the study of science. You must learn and use these exact symbols. You cannot make up your own symbols and abbreviations, as you do when annotating a reading.

To read scientific/technical material efficiently, learn the abbreviation and notation systems as soon as possible. You will save time and avoid interrupting your reading to look up a particular symbol. Check to see if lists of abbreviations and symbols are included in the appendix (reference section) in the back of your text. Also, make a list in your notebook of those symbols you need to learn. Make a point of using these symbols in your class notes whenever possible; regular use is the key to learning them.

Illustrations

Most scientific/technical books contain numerous drawings, charts, tables, and diagrams. Illustrations give you a visual picture of the idea or process being explained and make understanding it easier. See the Need to Know box on the following page.

NEED TO KNOW **How to Learn from Illustrations**

Here are a few suggestions on how to learn from illustrations:

1. **Go back and forth between the text paragraphs and the illustrations.** Illustrations are intended to be used with the paragraphs that refer to them. You may have to stop several times while reading the text to refer to an illustration. You may also have to reread parts of the explanation several times.

2. **Study each illustration carefully.** Notice its title or caption. This tells you what the illustration is intended to show. Then look at each part and try to see how they connect. Note any abbreviations, symbols, arrows, or labels.

3. **Test your understanding of an illustration by drawing and labeling your own illustration without looking at the one in the text.** Then compare your drawing with the one in the text. If you left anything out, continue drawing and checking until your drawing is complete and correct. Make a final drawing in your notebook and use it for review and study.

Examples and Sample Problems

Technical books include numerous examples and sample problems. Use the following suggestions when working with examples and problems.

1. **Pay more attention to examples than you normally do in other textbooks.** Often, examples or sample problems in technical books help you understand how rules, principles, theories, or formulas are actually used. Creative learners who usually prefer experimentation and avoid rules and examples may find that sample problems simplify an otherwise complex process. Think of examples as connections between ideas on paper and the practical, everyday use of those ideas.

2. **Be sure to work through sample problems.** Make sure that you understand what was done in each step and why it was done. For particularly difficult problems, write a step-by-step list of how to solve that type of problem in your notebook. Refer back to sample problems as guides or models when working problems at the end of the chapter or others assigned by your instructor.

3. **Use the problems at the end of the chapter as a self-test.** As you work through each problem, keep track of rules and formulas that you didn't know and had to look up. Also, notice the types of problems you could not solve without looking back at the sample problems. You'll need further practice with each of these types.

READING SCIENTIFIC MATERIAL

Directions: *Read the following excerpt from* Biology: Science for Life, *an introductory biology textbook by Colleen Belk and Virginia Borden Maier, and answer the questions that follow.*

THE BRAIN

1   The brain is the region of the body where decisions are reached and where bodily activities are directed and coordinated. The human brain is about the size of a small cantaloupe. Brains of the evolutionary ancestors to humans tend to be smaller and less complex *(Figure A)*. The brain is housed inside the skull, where it sits in a liquid bath, called **cerebrospinal fluid,** that protects and cushions it.

2   In addition to housing 100–200 billion neurons, the brain is composed of other cells called **glial cells.** There are 10 times as many glial cells in the brain as there are neurons. In contrast to neurons, glial cells do not carry messages. Instead, they support the neurons by supplying nutrients, helping to repair the brain after injury, and attacking invading bacteria. Structurally, the brain is subdivided into many important anatomical regions, including the cerebrum, thalamus, hypothalamus, cerebellum, and brain stem *(Figure B)*.

Cerebrum

3   The **cerebrum** fills the whole upper part of the skull. This part of the brain controls language, memory, sensations, and decision making. The cerebrum has two hemispheres, each divided into four lobes *(Figure C)*:

1. The **temporal lobe** is involved in processing auditory and olfactory information and is important in memory and emotion.
2. The **occipital lobe** processes visual information from the eyes.

FIGURE A   Evolution of Larger Brains

These skulls of early human ancestors show that the volume of the skull taken up by the brain has increased over the last 3–5 million years from about 400 to 1400 milliliters.

(a)

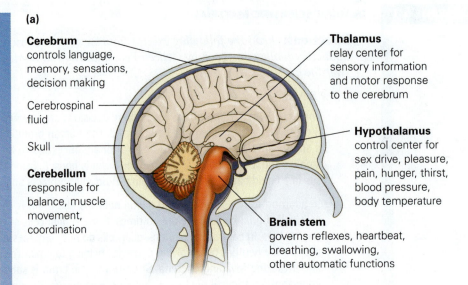

Cerebrum
controls language, memory, sensations, decision making

Cerebrospinal fluid

Skull

Cerebellum
responsible for balance, muscle movement, coordination

Thalamus
relay center for sensory information and motor response to the cerebrum

Hypothalamus
control center for sex drive, pleasure, pain, hunger, thirst, blood pressure, body temperature

Brain stem
governs reflexes, heartbeat, breathing, swallowing, other automatic functions

(b)

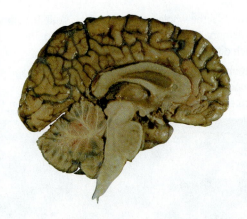

FIGURE B   Anatomy of the Brain

(a) The location and function of the cerebrum, thalamus, hypothalamus, brain stem, and cerebellum are shown. (b) Photo of a human brain.

Visualize This: *Find the location of the cerebrum, thalamus, hypothalamus, brain stem, and cerebellum in the photo.*

3. The **parietal lobe** processes information about touch and is involved in self-awareness.
4. The **frontal lobe** processes voluntary muscle movements and is involved in planning and organizing future expressive behavior.

4 The deeply wrinkled outer surface of the cerebrum is called the **cerebral cortex.** In humans, the cerebral cortex, if unfolded, would be the size of a 16-inch pizza. The folding of the cortex increases the surface area and allows this structure to fit inside the skull. The cortex contains areas for understanding and generating speech, areas that receive input from the eyes, and areas that receive other sensory information from the body. It also contains areas that allow planning.

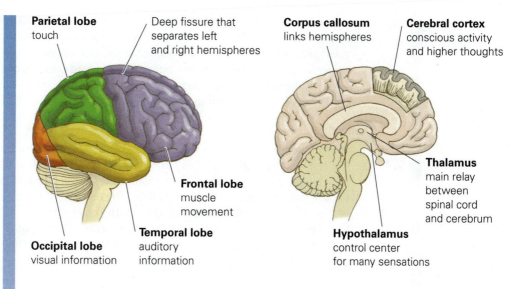

Parietal lobe
touch

Deep fissure that
separates left
and right hemispheres

Corpus callosum
links hemispheres

Cerebral cortex
conscious activity
and higher thoughts

Thalamus
main relay
between
spinal cord
and cerebrum

Frontal lobe
muscle
movement

Temporal lobe
auditory
information

Hypothalamus
control center
for many sensations

Occipital lobe
visual information

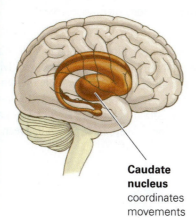

**Caudate
nucleus**
coordinates
movements

FIGURE C   Structure of the Cerebrum

*The highly convoluted cerebral cortex is divided down
the middle into the left and right hemispheres, and each
hemisphere is divided into four lobes: temporal, occipital,
parietal, and frontal. The hemispheres are connected
by the corpus callosum. Deep inside and between the
two cerebral hemispheres are the thalamus and the
hypothalamus. A caudate nucleus is located within each
cerebral hemisphere.*

Visualize This: *Consider the functions of the parts of the
cerebrum as depicted. Structural abnormalities of one of
these structures is correlated with ADD. Which structure
is the most likely candidate?*

5   The cerebrum and its cortex are divided from front to back into two halves—the
right and left cerebral hemispheres—by a deep groove or fissure. At the base of this
fissure lies a thick bundle of nerve fibers, the **corpus callosum,** which functions as
a communication link between the hemispheres. The **caudate nuclei** are paired
structures found deep within each cerebral hemisphere. These structures function
as part of the pathway that coordinates movement.

Thalamus and Hypothalamus

6   Deep inside the brain, lying between the two cerebral hemispheres, are the thalamus and the hypothalamus. The **thalamus** relays information between the spinal
cord and the cerebrum. The thalamus is the first region of the brain to receive
messages signaling such sensations as pain, pressure, and temperature. The thalamus suppresses some signals and enhances others, which are then relayed to the

cerebrum. The cerebrum processes these messages and sends signals to the spinal cord and to neurons in muscles when action is necessary. The **hypothalamus**, located just under the thalamus and about the size of a kidney bean, is the control center for sex drive, pleasure, pain, hunger, thirst, blood pressure, and body temperature. The hypothalamus also releases hormones, including those that regulate the production of sperm and egg cells as well as the menstrual cycle.

Cerebellum

7   The **cerebellum** controls balance, muscle movement, and coordination (cerebellum means "little brain" in Latin). Since this brain region ensures that muscles contract and relax smoothly, damage to the cerebellum can result in rigidity and, in severe cases, jerky motions. The cerebellum looks like a smaller version of the cerebrum. It is tucked beneath the cerebral hemispheres and, like the cerebrum, has two hemispheres connected to each other by a thick band of nerves. Additional nerves connect the cerebellum to the rest of your brain.

Brain Stem

8   The **brain stem** lies below the thalamus and hypothalamus *(Figure D)*. It governs reflexes and some spontaneous functions such as heartbeat, respiration, swallowing, and coughing.

9   The brain stem is composed of the midbrain, pons, and medulla oblongata. Highest on the brain stem is the **midbrain**, which adjusts the sensitivity of your eyes to light and of your ears to sound. Below the midbrain is the **pons** (pons means "bridge"). The pons functions as a bridge, allowing messages to travel between the brain and the spinal cord. The **medulla oblongata** is the lower part of the brain stem. It helps control heart rate and conveys information between the spinal cord and other parts of the brain.

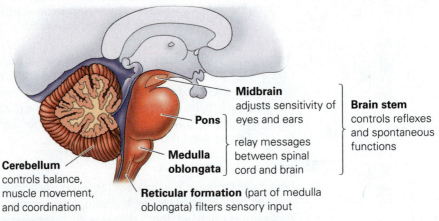

Midbrain
adjusts sensitivity of eyes and ears

Pons

relay messages between spinal cord and brain

Medulla oblongata

Cerebellum
controls balance, muscle movement, and coordination

Reticular formation (part of medulla oblongata) filters sensory input

Brain stem
controls reflexes and spontaneous functions

FIGURE D   The Cerebellum and Brain Stem

The brain stem consists of the middle brain, pons, and medulla oblongata.

10   The functions of the brain are divided between the left and right hemispheres. Because many nerve fibers cross over each other to the opposite side, the brain's left hemisphere controls the right half of the body, and vice versa. The areas that control speech, reading, and the ability to solve mathematical problems are located in the left hemisphere, while areas that govern spatial perceptions (the ability to understand shape and form) and the centers of musical and artistic creation reside in the right hemisphere.

11   The **reticular formation,** found in the medulla oblongata, is an intricate network of neurons that radiates toward the cerebral cortex. The reticular formation functions as a filter for sensory input; it analyzes the constant onslaught of sensory information and filters out stimuli that require no response. This prevents the brain from having to react to repetitive, familiar stimuli such as the sound of automobile traffic outside your dorm room or the sound of your roommate's talking while you are trying to sleep.

1. How would you describe the reading on each of the follow criteria?

a. Fact density _____

b. Number of technical terms _____

_____

c. Number and use of illustrations _____

_____

_____

d. Number of examples _____

_____

_____

_____

2. Underline the terminology you would need to learn to pass an exam based on this reading.

3. Explain the purpose of each of the following figures:

a. Figure A: _____

_____

b. Figure B: _____

c. Figure C: _____

d. Figure D: _____

4. Answer the "Visualize This" questions that appear in the captions for Figures B and C.

Figure B: _____

Figure C: _____ ■

■ Thinking Critically: Evaluating Research Sources

Goal 7

Think critically about research sources

When you conduct research, you will read a variety of articles and essays, as well as other source material. Not all sources you encounter while preparing a research paper are equally worthwhile or appropriate. Therefore, it is essential to critically evaluate all your sources. To evaluate your reference sources, do the following:

1. **Check your source's copyright date.** Make certain you are using a current source. For many assignments, such as those exploring controversial issues or scientific or medical advances, only the most up-to-date sources are useful.

2. **Be sure to use an authoritative source.** The material should be written by a recognized expert or by someone who is working within his or her field.

3. **Choose sources that provide the most complete and concrete (fact-based) information.**

4. **Select first-hand accounts of an event or experience rather than second- or third-hand accounts whenever possible.** In other words, the most reliable information usually comes from the people who are closest to the event or controversy.

5. **Avoid using sources that present biased information, and be wary of those that include personal opinion and reactions.**

6. **Be especially wary of sources you find on the Internet, many of which are speculative, based on opinion or gossip (such as blogs), or just factually incorrect.** For more information on how to evaluate Internet sources, see Chapter 10.

EXERCISE 6–12   **EVALUATING SOURCES**

Directions: *For each question, place a check mark next to the valid research sources for the given project.*

1. Project: a research paper on global warming

___ an environmental science textbook published in 2012

___ a blog sponsored by an environmental awareness group

___ a Facebook page dedicated to cleaning up the Great Lakes

___ an article from the scholarly journal *Environmental Research* outlining the effects of oil drilling on temperatures in affected areas

2. Project: an essay on population change in the United States over the last decade

___ a discussion with a friend who is a recent immigrant to the country

___ *The Statistical Abstract of the United States*, a government publication offering population statistics

___ data prepared by the chairperson of the sociology department at Columbia University, an Ivy League university located in New York City

___ a report published by a group that is advocating for English as the national language of the United States

 ## TECH SUPPORT Reading Articles and Essays Online

When you are reading articles online, many of the articles are from a database. Most likely you are reading a PDF file, which is a scan of the article as it originally appeared in print.

If you are reading articles on a newspaper or magazine Web site, try to stay focused on the article and ignore the ads or other distractions. Also, be aware of sidebars or boxes that include supplementary material to click on. For example, in a news story about an earthquake, there might be a small map you can click on or a photo gallery. However, the more interactivity a site offers, the greater the opportunity to get off track and lose your focus.

EXERCISE 6–13

Academic
APPLICATION

ANALYZING AN ELECTRONIC MAGAZINE ARTICLE

Directions: *Use an Internet source to locate an article or essay. Try to locate one from an electronic magazine, rather than from an electronic version of a print magazine. Then answer the following questions.*

1. Answer questions 1–6 in the Need to Know box "How to Analyze Articles and Essays" (p. 276) for analyzing essays and articles.

2. In what ways is the article similar to print magazine articles, and in what ways is it different?

3. What are the advantages of electronic magazines over print magazines?

SELF-TEST SUMMARY

Goal 1

1. How are textbook chapters organized, and what parts of the textbook are useful for learning and study?

Textbook chapters are organized using headings and subheadings, which break ideas down into smaller and smaller parts. Textbook learning aids include the preface, to the student, table of contents, opening chapter, typographical aids, chapter exercises and questions, boxes and case studies, vocabulary lists, summaries, glossary and index.

Goal 2

2. What are the parts of an essay and how can you read essays effectively?

Essays have five essential parts with different functions:
- **title**—suggests the subject and attracts the reader
- **introduction**—offers background, builds interest, defines terms, and states the thesis
- **thesis statement**—clearly expresses the main point of the essay.
- **body**—presents, in a number of paragraphs, information that supports or explains the thesis
- **conclusion**—brings the essay to a close by making a final statement on the subject

When reading essays you should
- check that the author can be trusted to present the facts fairly and accurately
- be sure the background information given is complete
- get the writer's thesis clearly in mind
- identify the organizational pattern used
- focus on new terminology used
- mark and highlight the thesis statement and important terms
- make an outline, map, or summary to ensure your recall

Goal 3

3. How are popular press articles organized?

Articles found in magazines and newspapers have a different style and format from essays. Hard news stories, action stories, and feature articles have some differences in format but can contain the following parts:
- **title**—often eye-catching and descriptive
- **dateline**—the location and date of the story
- **credit line**—the wire service or newspaper the story came from
- **byline**—the name of the writer
- **lead**—an opening paragraph that either summarizes major information (news stories) or sparks interest in the topic (feature stories)
- **nut graph**—one or more paragraphs that define a feature article's nature and scope
- **body or development**—the section that presents the supporting facts
- **conclusion**—the final statement about the subject of the article

Goal 4	4. What are the parts of most scholarly journal articles?	Professional societies publish journals that report research and developments in their fields. They often contain the following six parts, which may or may not be labeled: • **Abstract or Summary**—follows the title and author and summarizes the article's content • **Summary of Related Research**—reviews current research on the topic • **Description of Research**—also called "Method," tells how the research was carried out or explains the author's ideas, including the purpose of the study • **Results**—states the outcomes of the study • **Implications, Discussion, and Conclusions**—explains the meaning and implications of the study's results • **Further Research**—suggests additional studies needed
Goal 5	5. How can you read essays and articles critically?	To closely analyze and evaluate essays and articles, ask these questions: • Who is the author? • What is his or her purpose? • What does the introduction or lead add to the piece of writing? • What is the thesis? • Is the thesis adequately supported? • Are sources, references, or citations given for the facts and statistics used?
Goal 6	6. How does writing in the scientific/technical fields differ from that in other areas of study?	Textbooks in scientific/technical fields are highly specialized and differ from other texts in that technical material • is factually dense • uses technical vocabulary • uses abbreviations and notation systems • uses a large number of illustrations and examples • contains sample problems
Goal 7	7. What factors should you consider when evaluating research sources?	To evaluate research sources, consider the following: • Copyright date • Authority of source • Completeness • Reliability • Bias • Expression of opinion

READING SELECTION 11   BIOLOGY/ALLIED HEALTH

Helping the Body Repair Itself

From Consumer Reports on Health

About the Reading

NEWSPAPER

This reading is taken from Consumer Reports' On Health *newsletter. Consumer Reports is the magazine of the Consumers Union of the United States, a nonprofit organization that seeks to protect consumers from fraud and false advertising. The organization also produces publications on protecting your money and staying healthy.*

Planning Your Reading Strategy*

Directions: *Activate your thinking by previewing the reading (see the Need to Know box on page 64) and answering the following questions.*

____ 1. To which type of information should you pay the most attention when reading the selection?
   a. regenerative therapies and research
   b. liver functions
   c. limb replacement by fish and reptiles
   d. the Web sites mentioned

____ 2. Suppose a particular student previews this reading and decides that she can read it rather quickly. Which course do you think this student has taken and done well in?
   a. sociology
   b. anatomy and physiology
   c. anthropology
   d. political science

3. Based on your preview of the reading, how quickly do you think you should read the selection? (Circle one.)

Very slowly   Slowly   At a moderate pace   Quickly   Very quickly

Regenerative therapies are beginning to bebuild and restore function to injured body parts.

1   When a salamander loses a tail or a leg, it grows another. Starfish also replace injured limbs. And, surprisingly, there have been documented cases in which children under age 7 have naturally regenerated severed fingertips. Scientists now think they're within reach of the therapies that will regrow digits and limbs, cartilage, nerve cells, and even whole organs.

2   "The field of regenerative medicine is accelerating at an extraordinarily rapid pace," says Stephen Badylak, M.D., Ph.D., director of the Center for Pre-Clinical Tissue Engineering at the University of Pittsburgh's McGowan Institute for Regenerative Medicine. He helped pioneer the field with his serendipitous discovery, in the 1980s, that a substance in pig intestines

---

* The Scorecard on p. 296 enables you to compute your reading rate. In order to do so, be sure to record your starting time in the Scorecard box before you begin reading.

can help grow new human tissue. The substance, known as "extracellular matrix," is now being tested in ethical trials to see if it can help regrow fingers and repair wounds.

3   Meanwhile, researchers at Purdue University, where Badylak first did his breakthrough work, are doing clinical trials of electrical field-emitting devices that help severed nerves grow and reconnect in people with spinal-cord injuries.

4   In a preliminary study to assess the safety of implantable stimulators in 10 patients with spinal-cord injuries, investigators observed unexpected levels of sensory recovery. Four of the paralyzed patients showed functional improvement in their arms and two recovered some leg function. "It was absolutely remarkable," says Richard Borgens, Ph.D., a professor of biomedical engineering at Purdue. The experimental treatment will be available to many more patients in multiple centers beginning in 2008 or 2009.

5   Regenerative techniques are being fueled by advances in many fields of research, including stem cells (undifferentiated cells that change into specialized cells) and nanotechnology (the use of microscopic particles to create new materials with astonishing properties).

■ Body Engineering

6   In the next few years, "we'll see regenerative medicine actually making a difference in people's lives," says V. Prasad Shastri, Ph.D., an assistant professor of biomedical engineering at Vanderbilt University. Here's a roundup of the latest and most promising research:

7   **Regenerating digits and limbs.** This summer Badylak will oversee a small government-funded study to determine if the matrix formula can help soldiers who've lost fingers regrow them. The hope is to add enough length to what's left to their fingers to regain some functional use. And a newly created research partnership, the Soldier Treatment and Regeneration Consortium, will focus on growing functional vascular, nerve, and muscle tissue, along with bone and cartilage, to regenerate digits and limbs.

8   **Restoring nerves.** An experimental substance known as 4-AP, now in clinical trials, may help restore damaged nerve cells. If the substance proves safe and effective, it could be a breakthrough treatment—though not a cure—for people with multiple sclerosis, a condition that destroys the protective myelin coating of nerve cells, says Purdue's Borgens.

9   Animal research suggests that an experimental drug called PEG (polyethelene glycol) can help repair damaged nerve cells after a spinal-cord injury, brain trauma, or stroke. PEG forms a seal around damaged cells, which prevents neighboring cells from dying.

10   **Repairing bones and ligaments.** Researchers at Vanderbilt are developing a new procedure for harvesting stem cells from shin bones. Eventually, if tests go well, patients in need of spinal reconstruction will have a renewable source of their own bone and cartilage for transplantation or joint repair.

11   Regenerating knee ligaments is the goal of a research team led by Cato Laurencin, M.D., Ph.D., chairman of the department of orthopedic surgery at the University of Virginia Health System. Researchers have grown new ACLs (anterior cruciate ligament, the major stabilizing ligament of the knee) and successfully transplanted them into

Starfish can regrow injured limbs. Scientists are working to restore human digits and other body parts.

rabbits. "This is an important discovery—the ACL usually does not heal after it is torn during sports or other injuries," he says, noting that there are drawbacks to current treatments.

12   **Regrowing organs.** Attempts at regenerating nearly every type of tissue and organ are under way. Scientists are successfully growing skin and relatively simple structures, such as the esophagus, urethra, and bladder. Others are growing functional heart valves and blood vessels that some day may make it unnecessary to harvest vessels from patients' legs for use in coronary artery bypass surgery.

13   Stem-cell injections have restored some cardiac function in heart-failure patients, and research is in progress to determine if the injections can help rejuvenate damaged heart muscle.

14   Scientists at the McGowan Institute have grown a liver that can filter blood from liver cells and synthetic materials. The institute says 80 percent of patients treated so far with the experimental liver recovered some liver function or hung on until a donor organ was found. To find out more go to *www.clinicaltrials.gov* and *www.centerwatch.com.*

Examining Reading Selection 11*

Checking Your Vocabulary

Directions: *Use context, word parts, or a dictionary, if necessary, to determine the meaning of each word as it is used in the reading.*

____ 1. severed (paragraph 1)
   a. painful
   b. weakened
   c. diseased
   d. cut off

____ 2. serendipitous (paragraph 2)
   a. accidental but fortunate
   b. insignificant or minor
   c. peaceful
   d. disappointing

____ 3. harvesting (paragraph 10)
   a. creating
   b. joining
   c. removing
   d. promoting

____ 4. rejuvenate (paragraph 13)
   a. reject
   b. continue
   c. discover
   d. restore

____ 5. synthetic (paragraph 14)
   a. man-made
   b. damaged
   c. natural
   d. unnecessary

Checking Your Comprehension

Directions: *Select the best answer.*

____ 6. The purpose of this selection is to
   a. discuss the sources of stem cells used in research.
   b. explain legal issues in medical research.
   c. describe research in the field of regenerative medicine.
   d. encourage federal funding for regenerative therapies.

____ 7. The substance in pig intestines that can help grow human tissue is called
   a. 4-AP.
   b. anterior cruciate ligament.
   c. polyethelene glycol, or PEG.
   d. extracellular matrix.

_____

*Writing About the Reading questions appear in the Instructor's Manual.

____ 8. The term *nanotechnology* is defined in this selection as the use of
a. stem cells to regrow organs.
b. synthetic materials to filter blood.
c. microscopic particles to create new materials.
d. injections to restore cardiac function.

____ 9. This selection focuses on all of the following research *except*
a. regenerating digits, limbs, and ligaments.
b. reengineering genetic material.
c. restoring nerves.
d. regrowing organs.

____ 10. According to the selection, electrical field-emitting devices are being tested as a technique for helping people with
a. spinal-cord injuries.
b. liver disease.
c. multiple sclerosis.
d. cancer.

Thinking Critically

____ 11. The types of details used to support the main idea of this selection include
a. descriptions.
b. expert opinions.
c. examples.
d. all of the above.

____ 12. The selection can best be described as
a. a scholarly journal article.
b. a feature article.
c. a personal essay.
d. an abstract.

____ 13. The photograph of the starfish is included to illustrate
a. a potential source of stem cells.
b. an animal capable of repairing itself.
c. the process of evolution.

d. the use of animals in medical research.

____ 14. Of the following statements based on paragraph 11, which one is an opinion?
a. The goal of a research team led by Dr. Cato Laurencin is to regenerate knee ligaments.
b. Researchers have grown new knee ligaments and transplanted them into rabbits.
c. This is an important discovery.
d. After being injured or torn, knee ligaments usually do not heal.

____ 15. The tone of this article could best be described as
a. cynical
b. assertive
c. informative
d. indirect

Questions for Discussion

1. This article first appeared online at http://www.ConsumerReportson-Health.org. Analyze and evaluate the article, and then discuss what differences there might have been if the information in the article had appeared in a medical journal or a blog.

2. Visit the Web sites listed at the end of the article (http://www.clinicaltrials.gov and http://www.centerwatch.com). What information did you find there that might have been included in this selection?

3. What surprised you most about what you read in this selection? If you were to write about one of the techniques or therapies discussed in the selection, which one would you choose and why?

Scorecard

Selection 11:   855 words

Finishing Time: _____ _____ _____
                      HR.   MIN.   SEC.

Starting Time: _____ _____ _____
                      HR.   MIN.   SEC.

Reading Time: _____ _____
                               MIN.   SEC.

WPM Score: _____

Comprehension Score: for Items 6–15
Number Right: _____ × 10 = _____%

Assessing Your Reading Strategy

1. How would you rate your comprehension of the reading? (Circle one.)
   Excellent   Good   Fair   Poor

2. Did you find your reading strategy effective?   Yes   No

3. Suppose you were given an assignment to read another selection from the same source. Based on your experience with this selection, how would you adjust your reading strategy (if at all)?

READING SELECTION 12   BUSINESS

Distracted: The New News World and the Fate of Attention

Maggie Jackson
From *Nieman Reports*

About the Reading

JOURNAL
ARTICLE

This reading was originally published by the Nieman Foundation for Journalism at Harvard University. The foundation's purpose is to "promote and elevate the standards of journalism in the United States and educate persons deemed specially qualified for journalism."

MyReadingLab™ *The exercises following this selection can be completed online at myreadinglab.com*

Planning Your Reading Strategy*

Directions: *Activate your thinking by previewing the reading (see the Need to Know box on page 64) and answering the following questions.*

1. The Need to Know box recommends that you preview the first sentence under each heading, along with the title and the first and last paragraphs. Would this type of preview be adequate for this article? Why or why not? If not, how would you adjust your previewing strategy?

   _____

   _____

2. Based on your preview of the reading, how quickly do you think you should read the selection? (Circle one.) Explain your answer.

   Very slowly   Slowly   At a moderate pace   Quickly   Very quickly

3. Do you multitask while you are watching or reading the news? In general, how do you think multitasking affects how well you pay attention to each task?

As a term, "Multitasking" doesn't quite do justice to all the ways in which we fragment our attention.

1   Last summer, I was a passenger in a car barreling down a Detroit highway when I noticed a driver speeding past us, a magazine propped up beside his steering wheel. Perhaps most amazingly, I was the only person in my group who was surprised by this high-speed feat of multitasking.

2   Today, it's rare to give anything our full attention. Our focus is fragmented and diffused, whether we're conversing, eating, working, minding our kids—or imbibing the news. A new hypermobile, cybercentric and split-focused world has radically changed the context of news consumption—and shifted the environment for

by Maggie Jackson, from Nieman Reports, vol. 62, no. 4.

---

*The Scorecard on p. 302 enables you to compute your reading rate. In order to do so, be sure to record your starting time in the Scorecard box before you begin reading.

newsgathering as well. Attention is the bedrock of deep learning, critical thinking, and creativity—all skills that we need to foster, not undercut, more than ever on both sides of the newsmaking fence. And as we become more culturally attention-deficient, I worry about whether we as a nation can nurture both an informed citizenry—and an informative press.

3   It's easy to point first to rising data floods as a culprit for our distraction. More than 100 million blogs and a like number of Web sites, not to mention 1.8 million books in print, spawn so much information that, as Daniel Boorstin observes, data begin to outstrip the making of meaning. "We are captives of information," writes the cultural historian Walter Ong, "for uninterrupted information can create an information chaos and, indeed, has done so, and quite clearly will always do so."

4   Yet sense-making in today's information-rich world is not just a matter of how much we have to contend with but, more importantly, how we approach the 24/7 newsfeed that is life today. Consider the Detroit driver; where was he consuming media, and how much focus was he allotting to the task?

5   Increasingly, Americans are on the go, whatever they're doing. Just 14 percent of us move each year, yet the average number of miles that we drive annually has risen 80 percent during the past two decades. The car-as-moving-den, the popularity of power bars and other portable cuisine, the rise of injuries related to "textwalking," all of these—and more—attest to our collective hyperactivity. And as we relentlessly hurry through our days toting hand-held foods and portable gadgets, at the same time we keep one ear or eye on multiple streams of news-bytes.

■ Fragmented Attention

6   As a term, "multitasking" doesn't quite do justice to all the ways in which we fragment our attention. Split-focus is sometimes simply the result of living in a highly mediated world. More than half of children ages eight to 18 live in homes where a television is on most of the time, an environment linked to attention difficulties and lowered parent-child interaction. In public spaces from elevators to taxis, screens packed with flickering words and images are increasingly hard to avoid. Despite reconnaissance forays up and down airports, I usually have to succumb to an inescapable TV blare while waiting to fly. Former Microsoft executive Linda Stone deems ours a landscape of "continuous partial attention." Tuning in and out is a way of life.

7   But split focus also occurs when we hopscotch from one task or person to another, as most famously exemplified by the lethal crash of a California commuter train, apparently because the rail engineer at the helm was texting. Our veneration of multitasking can be traced in part to the influential efficiency guru Frederick W. Taylor, who counseled that factory work could be speeded up if broken down into interchangeable parts. As well, we live in an era where we seem to believe that we can shape time at will. We ignore age-old rhythms of sun and season, strain to surpass our biological limitations, and now seek to break the fetters of mechanized time by trying to do two or more things at once. Multitasking is born of a post-clock era.

8   The result on the job is "work fragmentation," according to Gloria Mark, an informatics professor at the University of California, Irvine and a leader in the field of "interruption science." In studies across a range of industries, she and other researchers have found that office workers change tasks on average every three minutes throughout the day. An e-mail, instant message, phone call, colleague's question, or a new thought prompts an interruption. Once interrupted, it takes nearly 25 minutes to return to an original task. Half of the time, people are interrupting themselves.

9   The risks are clear. "If you're continually interrupted and switching thoughts, it's hard to think deeply about anything," Mark once observed to me. "How can you engage with something?"

10   In our rapid-fire, split-focus era, are we able to process, filter and reflect well on the tsunamis of information barraging us daily? Are we hearing, but not listening? If this continues to be the way we work, learn and report, could we be collectively nurturing new forms of ignorance, born not from a dearth of information as in the past, but from an inability or an unwillingness to do the difficult work of forging knowledge from the data flooding our world?

11   I see worrisome signs that our climate of distraction undermines our ability to think deeply. Consider that nearly a third of workers are so busy or interrupted that they often feel they do not have time to reflect on the work that they do, according to the Families and Work institute. David M. Levy, a professor at the University of Washington, has even held a high-level MacArthur Foundation-funded conference tellingly called, "No Time to Think." And for all their tech-fluency, younger generations often have trouble evaluating and assessing information drawn from the Web, studies show. For example, a new national exam of information literacy, the Educational Testing Service's "iSkills" assessment test, found that just half of college students could judge the objectivity of a Web site, and just over a third could correctly narrow an overly broad online search.

■ Multitasking and The News
Related Article

"No Time Left for Reluctant Transformers"

by Jim Kennedy

12   News consumption fares no better, according to a small but in-depth recent study of 18- to

34-year-olds commissioned by The Associated Press. The 18 participants, who were tracked by ethnographers for days, consumed a "steady diet of bite-size pieces of news," almost always while multitasking. Their news consumption was often "shallow and erratic," even as they yearned to go beyond the brief and often repetitive headlines and updates that barraged them daily. Participants "appeared debilitated by information overload and unsatisfying news experiences," researchers observed. Moreover, "when the news wore them down, participants in the study showed a tendency to passively receive versus actively seek news."

13   This is a disturbing portrait: multitasking consumers uneasily "snacking" on headlines, stuck on the surface of the news, unable to turn information into knowledge.

14   Are consumers lazy? Are the media to blame? Or is Google making us stupid, as a recent Atlantic magazine cover story asked? It's far too simplistic to look for a single culprit, a clear-cut driver of such changes. Rather, helped by influential tools that are seedbeds of societal change, we've built a culture over generations that prizes frenetic movement, fragmented work, and instant answers. Just today, my morning paper carried a front-page story about efforts "in a new age of impatience" to create a quick-boot computer. Explained one tech executive "It's ridiculous to ask people to wait a couple of minutes" to start up their computer. The first hand up in the classroom, the hyper-businessman who can't sit still, much less listen—these are markers of success in American society.

15   Of course, the news business has always been quick, fast and fueled by multitasking. Reporters work in one of the most distracting of milieus—and yet draw on reserves of just-in-time focus to meet deadlines. Still, perhaps today we need to consider how much we can shrink editorial attention spans, with our growing emphasis on "4D" newsgathering, Twitter-style reporting, and newsfeeds from citizen bloggers whose influence far outstrips any hardwon knowledge of the difficult craft of journalism. It's not just news consumers who are succumbing to a dangerous dependence on what's first up on Google for making sense of their world.

16   Ultimately, our new world does more than speed life up and pare the news down. Most importantly, our current climate undermines the trio of skills—focus, awareness and planning/judgment—that make up the crucial human faculty of attention. When we split our focus, curb our awareness, and undercut our ability to gain perspective, we diminish our ability to think critically, carry out deep learning, or be creative. Can we afford to create an attention-deficient economy or press, or build a healthy democracy from a culture of distraction? Absolutely not.

Examining Reading Selection 12

[Complete this Exercise at **myreadinglab.com**]

Checking Your Vocabulary

Directions: *Use context, word parts, or a dictionary, if necessary, to determine the meaning of each word as it is used in the reading.*

___ 1. feat (paragraph 1)
   a. purpose
   b. influence
   c. accomplishment
   d. mistake

___ 2. fragmented (paragraph 2)
   a. chosen
   b. broken apart
   c. helpful
   d. directed

___ 3. spawn (paragraph 3)
   a. examine
   b. produce
   c. assist
   d. change

—— 4. allotting (paragraph 4)
   a. giving
   b. commenting
   c. criticizing
   d. distracting

—— 5. veneration (paragraph 7)
   a. disdain
   b. replacement
   c. separation
   d. respect

Checking Your Comprehension

Directions: *Select the best answer.*

—— 6. This selection is concerned primarily
   with how well
   a. technology enables us to
      multitask.
   b. we pay attention to the informa-
      tion we receive.
   c. the media shape our knowledge
      and our opinions.
   d. we adapt to new sources of
      information.

—— 7. According to Jackson, our nation's
   "collective hyperactivity" is demonstrated by
   a. the rise of injuries related to
      texting.
   b. the popularity of portable food
      and gadgets.
   c. our use of the car as a moving
      den.
   d. all of the above.

—— 8. The efficiency expert who said that
   factory work could be sped up if broken down into parts was
   a. Daniel Boorstin.
   b. Walter Ong.
   c. Frederick W. Taylor.
   d. Gloria Mark.

—— 9. The term *split-focus* is used to describe
   the
   a. many ways our attention is
      divided.
   b. use of television screens in public
      places.

   c. difference between printed and
      online information.
   d. conflict between work and play.

——10. The main idea of paragraph 11
   is that
   a. many workers cannot reflect on
      their work because they are too
      busy.
   b. the MacArthur Foundation has
      funded a conference called "No
      Time to Think."
   c. only half of college students are
      able to judge the objectivity of a
      Web site.
   d. too much distraction may be
      hurting our ability to think
      deeply.

Thinking Critically

——11. The authors' main purpose is to
   a. describe ways to improve how
      people multitask.
   b. criticize the media for creating a
      climate of distraction.
   c. discuss the results of workplace
      efficiency studies.
   d. explore the causes and effects of
      multitasking and distraction.

——12. The authors' attitude toward the subject can best be described as
   a. nostalgic.
   b. formal.
   c. concerned.
   d. amused.

——13. The authors support their ideas with
   a. personal experience and
      observations.
   b. statistics and facts.
   c. expert opinions.
   d. all of the above.

——14. This selection can best be described as
   a. a feature article.
   b. a scholarly journal article.
   c. an abstract.
   d. an action story.

___15. The photograph was included as an
example of
a. a reporter facing a deadline.
b. an employee working efficiently.

c. a person in a typical multitasking
situation.
d. a person deciding which device to
use.

Scorecard

Selection 12:   1,505 words

Finishing Time: _____ _____ _____
                    HR.   MIN.   SEC.

Starting Time: _____ _____ _____
                    HR.   MIN.   SEC.

Reading Time: _____ _____
                           MIN.   SEC.

WPM Score: _____

Comprehension Score: for Items 6–15
Number Right: _____ × 10 = _____%

Assessing Your Reading Strategy

1. How would you rate your comprehension
of the reading? (Circle one.)

   Excellent   Good   Fair   Poor

2. Did you find your reading strategy
effective?   Yes   No

3. Suppose you were given an assignment
to read another selection from the same
source (a report from the Nieman Foundation). Based on your experience with
this selection, how would you adjust your
reading strategy (if at all)?

Writing About Reading Selection 12    Complete this Exercise at myreadinglab.com

Checking Your Vocabulary

Directions: *Complete each of the following
items; refer to a dictionary if necessary.*

1. Describe the denotative and connotative
meanings of the word *tsunamis* in paragraph 10.

   _____

   _____

   _____

2. Define the word *foster* (paragraph 2)
and underline the word or phrase
that provides a context clue for its
meaning.

   _____

3. Define the word *undermines* (paragraph
11) and underline the word or phrase that
provides a context clue for its meaning.

   _____

4. Determine the meanings of the following words by using word parts:

   a. *multitasking* (paragraph 1)

      _____

   b. *imbibing* (paragraph 2)

      _____

   c. *portable* (paragraph 5)

      _____

   d. *hyperactivity* (paragraph 5)

      _____

   e. *simplistic* (paragraph 14)

      _____

      _____

Checking Your Comprehension

5. Jackson claims that attention is the "bedrock" of what three important skills?

_____

_____

6. What problems are linked to homes in which television is on most of the time?

_____

_____

7. According to studies, how long does it take for a worker to return to an original task after being interrupted?

_____

8. How do the authors conclude the article?

_____

_____

_____

_____

Thinking Critically

9. Why did Jackson open this selection by describing a person driving by on the highway?

_____

_____

_____

_____

10. Why does Jackson say that the term *multitasking* does not "do justice to all the ways in which we fragment our attention" (paragraph 6)?

_____

_____

11. What would the authors say is more important: our access to vast amounts of information or the way we approach our information-rich world?

_____

_____

12. What other photographs could accompany the reading to effectively illustrate multitasking?

_____

_____

_____

_____

Questions for Discussion

1. Think about the ways you multitask during a typical day. How effective are you at accomplishing each of the tasks you are trying to do at once? Do you think you will multitask more or less often in the future?

2. According to the iSkills assessment test, only half of college students could judge the objectivity of a Web site and only a third could correctly narrow an overly broad online search. Discuss these findings, especially in terms of your own experience and observations.

3. How do you typically "consume" the news? Which news source(s) do you prefer? Explain why.

4. Reread paragraph 10 and respond to the questions posed by the author in that paragraph.

CHAPTER

7

Techniques for Learning Textbook Material

think VISUALLY...

Why is the student in the photograph so obviously overwhelmed? What reading and study strategies could you offer him to help him cope with the heavy reading/study workload of college? This chapter focuses on strategies that can help all college students. You will learn strategies for identifying what to learn and numerous techniques for remembering what you read. These include highlighting textbooks, writing marginal annotations, paraphrasing what you read, outlining to organize your ideas, drawing concept maps, and summarizing ideas.

Learning GOALS

In this chapter, you will learn how to . . .

Goal 1 Use writing as a learning tool

Goal 2 Highlight efficiently

Goal 3 Annotate effectively

Goal 4 Paraphrase accurately

Goal 5 Outline to organize ideas

Goal 6 Use concept maps to show relationships

Goal 7 Summarize concisely

Goal 8 Determine an appropriate level of detail for paraphrases, summaries, and outlines

■ Writing as a Learning Tool

Goal 1
Use writing as a learning tool

As a college student, you are expected to learn large amounts of textbook material. Rereading to learn is *not* an effective strategy. Writing *is* an effective strategy. In fact, writing is an excellent means of improving both your comprehension and your retention.

Writing during and after reading has numerous advantages:

1. **Writing focuses your attention.** If you are writing as well as reading, you are forced to keep your mind on the topic.
2. **Writing forces you to think.** Highlighting or writing forces you to decide what is important and understand relationships and connections.
3. **Writing tests your understanding.** One of the truest measures of understanding is your ability to explain an idea in your own words. When you have understood an idea, you will be able to write about it, but when an idea is unclear or confusing, you will be at a loss for words.
4. **Writing facilitates recall.** Research studies indicate that information is recalled more easily if it is elaborated on. Elaboration involves expanding and thinking about the material by drawing connections and associations, seeing relationships, and applying what you have learned. Writing is a form of elaboration.

> **EFFICIENCY TIP**
> Generally, it will take you longer to complete a reading assignment if you use the writing strategies in this chapter. However, the time is well spent because these techniques are proven to help you improve your comprehension and retention.

This chapter describes six learning strategies that use writing as a learning tool: *highlighting, annotating, paraphrasing, outlining, mapping,* and *summarizing.*

■ Highlighting to Identify Important Information

Goal 2
Highlight efficiently

When reading factual material, the easiest and fastest way to mark important facts and ideas is to highlight them using a pen or marker. Many students are hesitant to mark their texts because they want to sell them at the end of the semester. However, highlighting helps you learn, so try not to let your interest in selling the book prevent you from reading and studying efficiently.

How to Highlight Effectively

Your goal in highlighting is to identify and mark those portions of an assignment that are important to reread when you study that chapter. See the Need to Know box on the following page.

NEED TO KNOW Highlighting Techniques

Here are a few suggestions on how to highlight effectively:

1. **Read a paragraph or section first and then go back and highlight what is important.** If you highlight as you read, you run the risk of highlighting an idea that you think is important, only to find out later in the passage that it is less important than you originally thought.

2. **Use your knowledge of paragraph structure to guide your highlighting.** Try to highlight important portions of the topic sentence and any supporting details that you want to remember. Use transitional words to locate changes or divisions of thought.

3. **Use headings to guide your highlighting.** Turn the headings into questions. Then, as you read, look for the answers to your questions; when you find information that answers the questions, highlight it.

4. **Use a system for highlighting.** You can use a number of systems. They include

   - using two or more colors of ink or highlighters to distinguish between main ideas and details or more and less important information
   - using single underscoring for details and highlighting for main ideas
   - placing brackets around the main idea and using a highlighter to mark important details

   Because no system is the most effective for everyone, develop a system that works well for you. Once you develop that system, use it consistently.

5. **Highlight just enough words to make the meaning clear when rereading.** Avoid highlighting a whole sentence. Usually the core parts of the sentence, along with an additional phrase or two, are sufficient. Notice that you can understand the meaning of the following sentence by reading only the highlighted parts.

   ==Fad diets disregard== the ==necessity for balance== among the various classes of nutrients.

   Now, read only the highlighted parts of the following paragraph. Can you understand what the paragraph is about?

   ### PLEA BARGAINING

   When ==a plea agreement== is made, for whatever reason, ==most states== now require that the agreement be ==in writing== and ==signed by all parties== involved. This ==protects the lawyers,== the ==judge,== and the ==defendant,== and ==ensures== that there is a ==record== that can be ==produced in court== should the ==agreement== be ==denied== or ==contested.== In signing the agreement, the ==defendant== is also ==attesting== to the fact that he or she ==entered== a ==guilty plea voluntarily== and ==knowingly.==

   —Barlow, *Criminal Justice in America,* copyright © 1999 Pearson Education, Inc.

   Most likely you were able to understand the basic message by reading only the highlighted words. You were able to do so because the highlighted words were core parts of each sentence or modifiers that directly explained those parts.

6. **Be sure that your highlighting accurately reflects the content of the passage.** Incomplete or hasty highlighting can mislead you as you review the passage and cause you to miss the main point. As a safeguard against this, occasionally test your accuracy by rereading only what you have highlighted. Does your highlighting tell what the paragraph or passage is about? Does it express the most important idea in the passage?

Highlighting the Right Amount

If you highlight either too little or too much, you will defeat its purpose:

- **If you highlight too little**, you will miss valuable information and your review and study of the material will be incomplete.

- **If you highlight too much**, you are not identifying and highlighting the most important ideas. The more you highlight, the more you will have to reread when studying, and the less of a time-saver the procedure will be.

Here is a passage highlighted in three ways. Read the entire passage and then examine each version of the highlighting. Try to decide which version would be most useful if you were using it for study purposes.

Version 1

THE FUNCTIONS OF EYE MOVEMENTS

With eye movements you can serve a variety of functions. One such function is to seek feedback. In talking with someone, we look at her or him intently, as if to say, "Well, what do you think?" As you might predict, listeners gaze at speakers more than speakers gaze at listeners. In public speaking, you might scan hundreds of people to secure this feedback.

A second function is to inform the other person that the channel of communication is open and that he or she should now speak. You see this regularly in conversation when one person asks a question or finishes a thought and then looks to you for a response.

Eye movements may also signal the nature of a relationship, whether positive (an attentive glance) or negative (eye avoidance). You can also signal your power through "visual dominance behavior." The average speaker, for example, maintains a high level of eye contact while listening and a lower level while speaking. When people want to signal dominance, they may reverse this pattern—maintaining a high level of eye contact while talking but a much lower level while listening.

By making eye contact you psychologically lessen the physical distance between yourself and another person. When you catch someone's eye at a party, for example, you become psychologically close, though physically for apart.

—Devito, Joseph A., *Messages,* 4th Ed., © 1999. Reprinted and electronically reproduced by permission of Pearson Education, Inc., Upper Saddle River, NJ.

Version 2

THE FUNCTIONS OF EYE MOVEMENTS

With eye movements you can serve a variety of functions. One such function is to seek feedback. In talking with someone, we look at her or him intently, as if to say, "Well, what do you think?" As you might predict, listeners gaze at speakers more than speakers gaze at listeners. In public speaking, you might scan hundreds of people to secure this feedback.

A second function is to inform the other person that the channel of communication is open and that he or she should now speak. You see this regularly in conversation when one person asks a question or finishes a thought and then looks to you for a response.

Eye movements may also signal the nature of a relationship, whether positive (an attentive glance) or negative (eye avoidance). You can also signal your power through "visual dominance behavior." The average speaker, for example, maintains a high level of eye contact while listening and a lower level while speaking. When people want to signal dominance, they may reverse this pattern—maintaining a high level of eye contact while talking but a much lower level while listening.

By making eye contact you psychologically lessen the physical distance between yourself and another person. When you catch someone's eye at a party, for example, you become psychologically close, though physically far apart.

Version 3

THE FUNCTIONS OF EYE MOVEMENTS

With eye movements you can serve a variety of functions. One such function is to seek feedback. In talking with someone, we look at her or him intently, as if to say, "Well, what do you think?" As you might predict, listeners gaze at speakers more than speakers gaze at listeners. In public speaking, you might scan hundreds of people to secure this feedback.

A second function is to inform the other person that the channel of communication is open and that he or she should now speak. You see this regularly in conversation when one person asks a question or finishes a thought and then looks to you for a response.

Eye movements may also signal the nature of a relationship, whether positive (an attentive glance) or negative (eye avoidance). You can also signal your power through "visual dominance behavior." The average speaker, for example, maintains a high level of eye contact while listening and a lower level while speaking. When people want to signal dominance, they may reverse this pattern–maintaining a high level of eye contact while talking but a much lower level while listening.

By making eye contact you psychologically lessen the physical distance between yourself and another person. When you catch someone's eye at a party, for example, you become psychologically close, though physically far apart.

This passage on eye movements lists functions of eye movements and briefly explains each. In evaluating the highlighting done in Version 1, you can see that it does not contain enough information. Only four of the five functions are highlighted and practically none of the explanations are highlighted.

Version 2, on the other hand, has too much highlighting. Although all of the important details are highlighted, many less important details are also highlighted. For instance, in the first paragraph, the first function and an explanation are highlighted (though using more text than is necessary), but also additional information about how often speakers and listeners gaze at each other. In fact, nearly every sentence is highlighted, and for review purposes it would be almost as easy to reread the entire passage as it would be to read only the highlighting.

Version 3 is an example of effective highlighting. If you reread only the highlighting, you will see that each of the five functions of eye movements and brief explanations of them have been highlighted.

Try to highlight no more than 20 to 30 percent of the passage. Once you exceed this range, you begin to lose effectiveness. Of course, if a particular section or passage is very factual or detailed it may require more detailed highlighting. However, if you find that an entire assignment or chapter seems to require 60 to 70 percent highlighting, you should consider using one of the other note-taking methods suggested later in this chapter.

> **EFFICIENCY TIP**
> As a rule of thumb, highlight only main ideas, topic sentences, and major details.

EXERCISE 7–1

PRACTICING HIGHLIGHTING

Directions: *Read and highlight the following excerpt from a zoology textbook using the guidelines for highlighting.*

Excerpt

RODS AND CONES OF THE EYE

Among the most complex receptor cells are the photoreceptor cells of vertebrates. These are called rods or cones, depending on their shapes. Rods have cylindrical outer segments that contain approximately 2000 disc-shaped membranes bearing light-absorbing pigments. This pigment is rhodopsin, a yellow substance that absorbs a broad range of wavelengths. Rhodopsin combines a vitamin-A derivative called **retinal** with a protein called **opsin.** Cones are similar, except that their outer segments are cone-shaped, and the opsins differ. Vertebrates typically have several types of cones with different opsins that enable them to perceive different colors. In addition, lungfishes, many reptiles, and birds have colored drops of oil in the cones, which narrow the color sensitivity. Mammals have cones with three different opsins, each of which absorbs light most effectively at a different wavelength from the other two. In humans these three wavelengths are perceived as red, blue, and green. Although we have only three kinds of cones, any color can be perceived from the combination of cones it stimulates. For example, stimulation of both red-sensitive and blue-sensitive cones would indicate the color purple.

Rods and cones also differ in their sensitivity. Rods are so sensitive that they can respond to individual photons, but they become blinded in bright daylight. They are therefore useful mainly at night and in heavy shadow.

Cones are not sensitive enough to work in darkness, but the different color sensitivities enable them to transmit information about color in bright light. Good vision in the dark requires a large number of rods, while color vision in daylight requires numerous cones. The retinas of most mammals, especially nocturnal ones, have primarily rods. The retinas of humans and other primates have a mixture of rods and cones in peripheral areas and have only cones in the center of focus, called the **fovea**. Humans have a total of about 100 million rods and 3 million cones.

—Harris, *Concepts in Zoology,* 2e, HarperCollins Publishers.

EXERCISE 7–2   **USING HIGHLIGHTING**

Directions: *Choose one of the reading selections at the end of this chapter. Assume that you are reading it as part of a class reading assignment on which you will be tested. As you read, highlight the important ideas. Tomorrow, reread what you have highlighted and then answer the multiple-choice questions that follow the selection.*

■ Annotating and Making Marginal Notations

Goal 3
Annotate effectively

FLEXIBILITY TIP
The key to effective annotating is making it work for you. Devise your own system of symbols and abbreviations that you can easily remember.

If you were reading the want ads in a newspaper in search of an apartment to rent, you would probably mark certain ads. As you phoned for more information, you might make notes about each apartment. These notes would help you decide which apartments to visit. Similarly, in many types of academic reading, making notes, or **annotating**, is a useful strategy. Annotating is a means of keeping track of your impressions, ideas, reactions, and questions as you read. Highlighting is a means of identifying important information; annotating is a method of recording *your* thinking about these key ideas.

There are no fixed rules about how or what to annotate. Table 7.1 shows various types of annotations.

 TECH SUPPORT Annotating E-books

Many of the same highlighting tips and strategies discussed in this chapter apply to online versions of college textbooks (e-books). For example, if you are using the e-book version of *Efficient and Flexible Reading* in MyReadingLab, your e-book includes "Highlighter" and "Note" tools in the toolbar. Your annotations and highlighting are saved when you log out of your account and will still be there when you log back in.

TABLE 7.1 | Ways to Annotate

Types of Annotation		Example
Circling unknown words		. . . redressing the apparent (asymmetry) of relationships
Marking definitions	def	To say that the balance of power favors one party over another is to introduce a disequilibrium.
Marking examples	ex	. . . concessions may include negative sanctions, trade agreements . . .
Numbering lists of ideas, causes, reasons, or events		components of power include ① self-range, ② population, ③ natural resources, and geography ④
Placing asterisks next to important passages	*	Power comes from three primary sources . . .
Putting question marks next to confusing passages	? ⟶	war prevention occurs through institutionalization of mediation . . .
Marking notes to yourself	Check def in sec text	power is the ability of an actor on the international stage to . . .
Marking possible test items	T	There are several key features in the relationship . . .
Drawing arrows to show relationships		. . . natural resources . . . , . . . control of industrial manufacture capacity
Writing comments, noting disagreements and similarities	can terrorism be prevented through similar balance?	war prevention through balance of power is . . .
Making summary statements	sum	the greater the degree of conflict, the more Intricate will be . . .

Annotating to Condense Information

Annotating is a helpful technique to use when you work through complicated or lengthy explanations. Often a few marginal notes can be used to summarize an entire paragraph, as shown in the following example.

estimated demand = number of possible buyers × how much each will buy × market share percent

The first step in estimating demand for a particular product is to identify demand for an entire product category in the markets that the company serves. PepsiCo, for example, will estimate the entire demand for soft drinks in domestic and international markets. A small business, such as a start-up premium coffee supplier, will estimate demand only in markets it expects to reach. Marketers predict total demand by first identifying the number of buyers or potential buyers and then multiplying that estimate times the average amount each member of the target market is likely to purchase. For example, the coffee entrepreneur may estimate that there are 10,000 consumer households in his market who would be willing to buy his premium coffee and that each household would purchase approximately 25 pounds of coffee a year. The total annual demand for the product is 250,000 pounds.

Once the marketer estimates total demand, the next step is to predict what the company's market share is likely to be. The company's estimated demand is then its share of the whole (estimated) pie. In our coffee example, the entrepreneur may feel that he can gain 5 percent of this market, or 12,500 pounds or about 1,000 pounds a month—not bad for a new start-up business. Of course, such projections need to take into consideration other factors that might affect demand, such as new competitors entering the market, the state of the economy, and changing consumer tastes.

—Solomon, Michael R.; Stuart, Elnora, *Marketing: Real People, Real Choices,* 2nd Ed., © 2000. Reprinted and electronically reproduced by permission of Pearson Education, Inc., Upper Saddle River, NJ.

You can see that annotations are a useful time-saving device when ideas are complicated and cannot be reviewed quickly by highlighting.

Annotating to Record Reactions

Annotations are particularly useful when reading literature, essays, controversial articles, arguments, or persuasive material. Because each type of work is intended to provoke a reader's response, record your reactions and feelings as you read.

In the following poem by Emily Dickinson, the speaker describes her journey through life to her inevitable death in a way that indicates death is a constant presence throughout all the stages of life.

BECAUSE I COULD NOT STOP FOR DEATH

Emily Dickinson

Because I could not stop for Death,
He kindly stopped for me; — *Death is presented as kind*
The carriage held but just ourselves
And Immortality.

We slowly drove, he knew no haste,
And I had put away
My labor, and my leisure too, — *she gave these up*
For his civility. — *another positive image*

We passed the school, where children strove] *childhood stage*
At recess, in the ring;
We passed the fields of gazing grain, — *reference to maturity*
We passed the setting sun. — *reference to old age*

Or rather, he passed us;
The dews drew quivering and chill,
For only gossamer[1] my gown,   ] clothing offers little
My tippet[2] only tulle[3].   ] protection

We paused before a house that seemed]
A swelling of the ground;
The roof was scarcely visible,   grave
The cornice but a mound.   ]

Since then 'tis centuries, and yet each
Feels shorter than the day   death is eternal
I first surmised the horses' heads
Were toward eternity.

—Emily Dickinson, 1890.

EXERCISE 7–3   **USING ANNOTATION**

Directions: *Refer to the same reading selection used for Exercise 7–2. Review your highlighting and add annotations that clarify or summarize content or record your reactions. Add at least two annotations that reflect your thinking.* ■

LEARNING STYLE TIPS

If you tend to be a . . .	Then strengthen your annotating skills by . . .
Spatial learner	Drawing diagrams in the margin that show the relationships among items of information.
Verbal learner	Writing words and phrases that summarize ideas and show the relationships among items of information.

EXERCISE 7–4   **USING HIGHLIGHTING AND ANNOTATION**

Directions: *Highlight and annotate a section from a current chapter in one of your textbooks using the suggestions for effective highlighting and annotating presented in this chapter.* ■

■ Paraphrasing to Restate Ideas

Goal 4
Paraphrase
accurately

A **paraphrase** restates the ideas of a passage in your own words. You retain the author's meaning, but you use your own wording. In speech we paraphrase frequently. For example, when you relay a message from one person

[1]gossamer—light, delicate
[2]tippet—shoulder cape or scarf
[3]tulle—sheer fabric

FLEXIBILITY TIP
Because a paraphrase requires close attention to the original reading and a full understanding of it, getting the paraphrase right can take some time. Try not to become frustrated if it takes you longer to write the paraphrase than you expected.

to another, you convey the meaning but do not use the person's exact words. A paraphrase makes a passage's meaning clearer and often more concise.

Paraphrasing is a useful technique for

- **recording information from reference sources to use in writing a research paper.**
- **understanding difficult material for which exact, detailed comprehension is required.** For instance, you might paraphrase the steps in solving a math problem or the procedures for a lab setup in chemistry.
- **reading material that is stylistically complex, or with an obvious slant, bias, strong tone, or detailed description.**

Study the following example of a paraphrase of the stylistically difficult preamble of the United States Constitution. Notice that it restates in different words the intent of the preamble.

PREAMBLE

We the people of the United States, in order to form a more perfect union, establish justice, insure domestic tranquillity, provide for the common defense, promote the general welfare, and secure the blessings of liberty to ourselves and our posterity, do ordain and establish this Constitution of the United States of America.

PARAPHRASE

The citizens of the United States established the Constitution to create a better country, to provide rightful treatment, peace, protection, and well-being for themselves and future citizens.

Notice first how synonyms were substituted for words in the original— *citizens* for *people, country* for *union, protection* for *defense,* and so forth. Next, notice that the order of information was rearranged.

Use the suggestions in the box below to paraphrase effectively.

NEED TO KNOW **How to Paraphrase**

1. **Read the entire material before writing anything.** Read slowly and carefully.
2. **As you read, focus on both exact meanings and relationships between ideas.**
3. **Read each sentence and identify its core meaning.** Use synonyms, replacing the author's words with your words. Look away from the original sentence and write in your own words what it means. Then reread the original and add any additional or qualifying information.
4. **Don't try to paraphrase word by word.** Instead, work with clauses and phrases (idea groups). If you are unsure of the meaning of a word or phrase, check a dictionary to locate a more familiar meaning.
5. **You may combine several original sentences into a more concise paraphrase.** It is also acceptable to present ideas in a different order from in the original.
6. **Compare your paraphrase with the original for completeness and accuracy.**

EXERCISE 7–5

Working COLLABORATIVELY

WRITING SYNONYMS

Directions: *Write synonyms in the margin for the highlighted words or phrases in the following excerpt. Compare and discuss your choices with classmates.*

Suppose you and I are debating a moral problem in front of a nonpartisan crowd. You have concluded that a particular course of action is right, while I believe it is wrong. It is only natural for me to ask you, "Why do you think doing such-and-such is right?" If you are unable to give any logical reasons why your position is correct, you are unlikely to persuade anyone. On the other hand, if you can explain the chain of reasoning that led you to your conclusion, you will be more likely to convince the audience that your position is correct. At the very least you will help reveal where there are disputed facts or values. Hence we will reject proposed ethical theories that are not based on reasoning from facts or commonly accepted values.

—Michael J. Quinn, *Ethics for the Information Age,* Second Edition, p. 60
Boston: Pearson/Addison Wesley, 2006. ■

EXERCISE 7–6

WRITING A PARAPHRASE

Directions: *Write a paraphrase of the second paragraph of the following selection from a sociology text.*

_____

_____

_____

_____

_____

_____

_____

_____

THE HOME SCHOOLING MOVEMENT

It is difficult to estimate the number of youngsters involved in home schooling, *where children are not sent to school and receive their formal education from one or both parents.* Legislation and court decisions have made it legally possible in most states for parents to educate their children at home, and each year more people take advantage of that opportunity. Some states require parents or a home tutor to meet teacher certification standards, and many require parents to complete legal forms and affidavits to verify that their children are receiving instruction in state-approved curricula.

Supporters of home education claim that it is less expensive and far more efficient than mass public education. Moreover they cite several advantages: alleviation of school overcrowding, added curricular and pedagogical alternatives not available in the public schools, strengthened family relationships, lower dropout rates, the fact that students are allowed to learn at their own rate, increased motivation, higher standardized test scores, and reduced discipline problems. Proponents of home schooling also believe that it provides the parents with the opportunity to reinforce their moral values through education—something they are not satisfied that the public schools will do.

Critics of the home schooling movement contend that it creates as many problems as it solves. They acknowledge that, in a few cases, home schooling offers educational opportunities superior to those found in most public schools, but few parents can provide such educational advantages. Some parents who withdraw their children from the schools in favor of home schooling have an inadequate educational background and insufficient formal training to provide a satisfactory education for their children. Typically, parents have fewer, not more, technological resources at their disposal than do schools. However, . . . the relatively inexpensive computer technology that is readily available today is causing some to challenge the notion that home schooling is in any way inferior to more highly structured classroom education.

Finally, a sociological concern is the restricted social interaction experienced by children who are educated at home. Patricia Lines, a U. S. Department of Education policy analyst, believes that the possibilities provided by technology and the promise of home schooling are greatly exaggerated and insisted that "technology will never replace the pupil-teacher relationship." Also, while relationships with parents and siblings may be enhanced, children taught at home may develop a distorted view of society. Children who live in fairly homogeneous neighborhoods, comprising people of the same race, socioeconomic status, and religious background, do not experience the diversity that can be provided in the social arena of the schools. They may be ill equipped to function successfully in the larger multicultural world.

—Thompson, William E., *Society in Focus: Introduction Sociology,* 2nd Ed., © 1996. Reprinted and electronically reproduced by permission of Pearson Education, Inc., Upper Saddle River, NJ. ■

EXERCISE 7–7

WRITING A PARAPHRASE

Directions: *Write a paraphrase of the excerpt on page 311–312 ("The first step . . ."). When you have finished, compare your paraphrase with that of another student.*

_____

_____

_____

_____

_____

_____

_____

_____

_____

_____

_____

_____

_____

_____

_____

_____

_____

■ Outlining to Organize Information

Goal 5

Outline to organize ideas

Outlining is an effective way to organize information and discover relationships between ideas. It forces you to select what is important from each paragraph and determine how it is related to key ideas in other paragraphs. Outlining enables you to learn and remember what you read because the process of selecting what is important and expressing it in your own words requires thought and comprehension and provides for repetition and review. Outlining is particularly effective for pragmatic learners who can learn material that is orderly and sequential.

Outlining is particularly useful in the following situations:

- **When reading material that seems difficult or confusing**, outlining forces you to sort ideas, see connections, and express them in your own words.

- **When order or process is important**, an outline is particularly useful. For example, in a data processing course in which various sets of programming commands must be performed in a specified sequence, an outline is a good way to organize the information.

- **In the natural sciences, in which classifications are important**, outlines help you record and sort information. In botany, for example, one important focus is the classification and description of various plant groups. An outline enables you to list subgroups within each category and to keep track of similar characteristics.

Developing an Outline

To be effective, an outline must show the relative importance of ideas and the relationship between ideas. The easiest way to achieve this is to use the following format:

   I. **First Major Topic**

      A. First major idea

         1. First important detail

         2. Second important detail

      B. Second major idea

         1. First important detail

            a. Minor detail or example

            b. Minor detail or example

         2. Second important detail

II. Second Major Topic

      A. First major idea

Notice that the more important ideas are closer to the left margin, and less important details are indented toward the middle of the page. A quick glance at an outline indicates what is most important and how ideas support or explain one another.

Use the suggestions in the box below to write effective outlines.

NEED TO KNOW How to Outline

1. **Read a section completely before writing.**
2. **Be brief and concise; do not write in complete sentences.** Unless the outline is to be submitted to your instructor, use abbreviations, symbols, or shorthand words as you would in lecture note taking.
3. **Use your own words rather than those in the text.**
4. **Be certain that all information beneath a heading supports or explains it.**
5. **Make sure every heading that is aligned vertically is of equal importance.**

To illustrate further the technique for outlining, read the following passage and then study the outline that follows it.

NONBIODEGRADABLE POLLUTANTS

Heavy metals, such as mercury, cadmium, and arsenic, and manufactured chemicals, such as PCBs and some pesticides, are examples of nonbiodegradable pollutants. These chemicals are highly toxic, so that low levels of exposure or low concentrations of these compounds are poisonous. Such chemicals are so foreign to living organisms that they are not metabolized and remain in the ecosystem basically unchanged. Worse than that, if eaten, they may be stored within the body. Each time chemicals such as PCBs, mercury, or dioxin are taken into the body they are added to the existing stock. If this accumulation continues, a toxic level is reached. The Romans were great poisoners, and they knew the toxic value of gradually administering poisons such an antimony or arsenic. Each meal was safe to eat, but the steady diet of a little poison time after time led to the death of the victim. Even though nonbiodegradable pollutants may be relatively rare, they are stored in the bodies of an organism and passed on up the food chain in a process called **biological amplification** (also referred to as biological magnification).

A predator absorbs all the stored pollutants in the hundreds or thousands of prey items that it eats, and each meal provides a dose of the toxin. The chemical is stored in the body of the predator, where the successive doses accumulate and become more concentrated. If the predator then falls prey to a larger carnivore, the entire dose of toxicity is taken to the next step in the food chain. Thus, the concentration of the toxin is amplified at each link in the food chain.

—By permission of Mark Bush, *Ecology of a Changing Planet,* Second Edition, © 1997.

Here is the outline for the above selection:

I. Nonbiodegradable Pollutants
   A. examples
      1. heavy metals
         a. mercury
         b. cadmium
      2. manufactured chemicals
         a. PCBs
         b. pesticides
   B. highly toxic
      1. poisonous at low exposure and concentrations
      2. not metabolized; remain in ecosystem unchanged
   C. stored within body when eaten
      1. added to existing stock in body
      2. can eventually reach toxic level
   D. biological amplification (magnification)
      1. predator eats many prey with stored pollutants
      2. doses accumulate and become more concentrated
      3. carnivore eats predator
      4. toxicity taken up food chain

You can see that it represents, in briefest form, the contents of the passage. Reading an outline is an effective way to reacquaint yourself with the content and organization of a chapter without rereading it.

Other Uses for Outlining in Academic Situations

Outlining can be useful in a variety of other academic situations:

EFFICIENCY TIP
Some textbooks provide a chapter outline at the beginning of each chapter. If an outline isn't provided, use the headings in each chapter to begin your own outline.

• Use outlining to test yourself. Turn each main entry into a question and try to recall the answer without looking at the subentries beneath it.

• Use outlining to plan an essay or organize a speech or presentation. Outlining can help you structure your own ideas and present them in a clear, understandable form.

• Use outlining to organize research. When using a variety of sources, it is often necessary to group and arrange the information in a logical, easy-to-understand manner. An outline will help you see how ideas fit together.

TECH SUPPORT **Outlining Using a Computer**

Use the following tips for outlining using your computer:

- Use the tab key to make indenting easy and systematic.
- Devise a system for using different typefaces or cases to designate the relative importance of ideas (caps for major topics, lowercase for details, for example).
- Use symbols, such as asterisks or brackets, to mark important information and definitions.
- Use the cut and paste function to rearrange information and group together ideas on a specific topic.

EXERCISE 7–8   **WRITING AN OUTLINE**

Directions: *Read the following excerpt from Brian Fagan's* People of the Earth: An Introduction to World Prehistory, *an archaeology textbook, and write a brief outline.*

For hundreds of thousands of years, *Homo erectus* flourished in the tropical and temperate regions of the Old World. Except for an overall increase in brain size, *H. erectus* remained remarkably stable in evolutionary terms for more than a million years, until less than 500,000 years ago. Eventually, *H. erectus* evolved into early *H. sapiens,* but we do not even know when the gradual transition began or how it took place. Some researchers believe it began as early as 400,000 years ago; others, much later, sometime around or after 200,000 years ago.

For hundreds of thousands of years, both *H. erectus* and early *H. sapiens* survived and evolved with the aid of what Steven Mithen calls multiple intelligences separated by walls analogous to those dividing the chapels of a medieval cathedral. As Mithen says (1996), the thoughts in one chapel could barely be heard in another. Archaic humans lacked one vital component of the modern mind: cognitive flexibility, the ability to bridge the walls between their many intelligences. Such flexibility appears to have been the prerogative of modern humans, *Homo sapiens sapiens.*

Homo sapiens sapiens means "wise person," and the controversies surrounding the origins of modern humanity—of ourselves—rank among the most vigorous in archaeology. What is it that separates us from earlier humans, scientists wonder? First and foremost must be our ability to speak fluently and articulately. We communicate, we tell stories, we pass on knowledge and ideas—all through the medium of language. Consciousness, cognition, self-awareness, foresight, and the ability to express oneself and one's emotions—these are direct consequences of fluent speech. They can be linked with another attribute of the fully fledged human psyche: the capacity for symbolic and spiritual thought, concerned not only with subsistence and technology but also with defining the boundaries of existence and the relationship among the individual, the group, and the universe.

WRITING AN OUTLINE

Directions: *On a separate sheet of paper, write an outline of "The Home Schooling Movement" on page 315–316.*

■ Mapping to Show Relationships

Goal 6

Use concept maps to show relationships

Mapping is a process of drawing diagrams to describe how a topic and its related ideas are connected. It is a means of organizing and consolidating information by using a visual format. Maps facilitate learning because they group and consolidate information. Although mapping appeals to visual learners, verbal learners will also find it to be effective in organizing information. This section discusses two types of maps: *concept maps* and *thought pattern maps*.

Concept Maps

Concept maps are visual outlines; they show how ideas within a passage are related. Maps can take different forms. You can draw them in any way that shows the relationships among the ideas. Sketching rather than exact, careful drawing is appropriate. When drawing maps, feel free to abbreviate, add lines to show relationships, add notes, or redraw to make changes. Figure 7.1 shows two sample maps. Each was drawn to show the organization of Chapter 2 of this text. Refer to Chapter 2, pages 52–90, then study each map.

FIGURE 7.1 Two Sample Concept Maps of Chapter 2

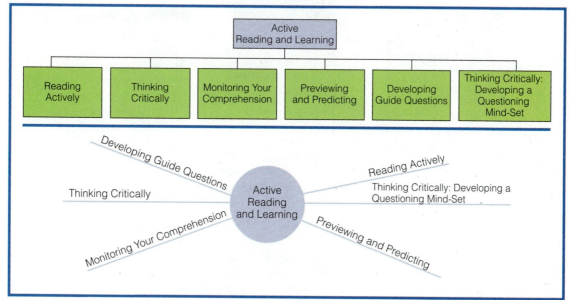

Think of a map as a diagram that shows how ideas are connected. Maps, like outlines, can vary in the amount of detail included, ranging from very general to highly specific. The maps shown in Figure 7.1 only provide an overview of the chapter and reflect its general organization. A more detailed map of one of the topics, previewing, included in Chapter 2 (p. 63) is shown in Figure 7.2 below.

Use the steps shown in the box below to draw a map.

NEED TO KNOW **How to Draw a Concept Map**

1. **Identify the overall subject and write it in the center or at the top of the page.** How you arrange your map will depend on the subject matter and its organization. Circles or boxes are useful but not absolutely necessary.

2. **Identify the major supporting information that relates to the topic.** State each fact or idea on a line connected to the central topic.

3. As you discover details that further explain an idea already mapped, **draw a new line branching from the idea it explains.**

FIGURE 7.2 A Detailed Concept Map

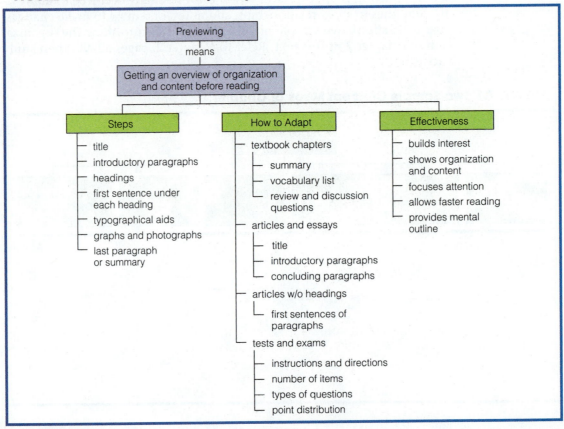

EXERCISE 7–10   **DRAWING A MAP**

Directions: *Draw a map that reflects the overall organization of this chapter.*   ■

EXERCISE 7–11   **DRAWING A MAP**

Directions: *Draw a map that reflects the organization of one of the end-of-chapter readings in this book that you have read this semester.*   ■

EXERCISE 7–12   **DRAWING A CONCEPT MAP**

Directions: *Select a section from one of your textbooks. Draw a concept map that reflects its organization.*   ■

Thought Pattern Maps

When a particular organizational thought pattern is evident throughout a passage, you may wish to draw a map reflecting that pattern. Maps for each common organizational pattern are shown in Chapter 5. Now that you are familiar with the idea of mapping, review Chapter 5, paying particular attention to the diagrams shown for each pattern. When reading a history text, for example, you may find it helpful to draw time lines (see p. 193) to organize events within historical periods. Or, when reading a text that compares two works of philosophy or two key political figures, you may find one of the maps shown on pages 204–205 helpful in distinguishing similarities and differences.

EXERCISE 7–13   **DRAWING A CONCEPT MAP**

Directions: *Draw a concept map showing the overall organization of Chapter 8, "Learning and Retention Strategies."*   ■

EXERCISE 7–14   **EVALUATING OUTLINING AND MAPPING**

Directions: *Conduct an experiment to see whether you prefer outlining or mapping to show relationships between ideas. Choose and read a substantial section from one of your textbooks. Write a brief outline of it, then draw a map of this same section. Which of these two methods was easier for you to do? Which of these will be more useful for you? Why?*   ■

■ Summarizing to Condense Information

Goal 7
Summarize
concisely

A **summary** is a compact restatement of the important points of a passage. You might think of it as a shortened version of a longer message. Unlike a paraphrase, a summary does not include all information presented in the original. Instead, you must select what to include. A summary contains only the gist of the text, with limited background, explanation, or detail. Although summaries vary in length, they are often one-quarter or less of the length of the original.

Summaries are useful in a variety of reading situations in which a condensed overview of the material is needed. You might summarize information in preparation for an essay exam, or key points of news articles required in an economics class. Some class assignments also require summarization. Lab reports for science courses include a summary of results. A literature instructor may ask you to summarize the plot of a short story.

Use the steps in the box below as a guide when writing a summary.

 NEED TO KNOW How to Write a Summary

1. **Read the entire original work first.** Do not write anything until you understand it completely and have a complete picture of the work.

2. **Reread and highlight key points.** Look in particular for topic sentences and essential details.

3. **Review your highlighting.** Cross out all but vital phrases. Eliminate repetitious information.

4. **Write sentences to include all remaining highlighted information.** Condense and combine information wherever possible.

5. **Present ideas in the summary in the same order in which they appeared in the original,** unless you are purposely regrouping ideas.

6. **Revise your summary.** Try to make your summary more concise by eliminating repetition and combining ideas.

Read this selection by Joyce Carey, and study the sample summary.

ART AND EDUCATION

A very large number of people cease when quite young to add anything to a limited stock of judgments. After a certain age, say 25, they consider that their education is finished.

It is perhaps natural that having passed through that painful and boring process, called expressly education, they should suppose it over, and that they are equipped for life to label every event as it occurs and drop it into its given pigeonhole. But one who has a label ready for everything does not bother to observe any more, even such ordinary happenings as he has observed for himself, with attention, before he went to school. He merely acts and reacts.

For people who have stopped noticing, the only possible new or renewed experience, and, therefore, new knowledge, is from a work of art. Because that is the only kind of experience which they are prepared to receive on its own terms, they will come out from their shells and expose themselves to music, to a play, to a book, because it is the accepted method of enjoying such things. True, even to plays and books they may bring artistic prejudices which prevent them from seeing *that* play or comprehending *that* book. Their artistic sensibilities may be as crusted over as their minds.

But it is part of an artist's job to break crusts, or let us say rather that artists who work for the public and not merely for themselves, are interested in breaking crusts because they want to communicate their intuitions.

—Estate of Joyce Carey

Sample Summary

Many people consider their education to be complete at an early age and, at that time, cease to observe and react to the world around them. Art forces people to think and react. For some people, their artistic sensibility may be as stagnant as their minds. It is the artist's responsibility to intervene in order to communicate.

TECH SUPPORT Summarizing Using a Computer

Summarizing on a computer has several advantages over handwriting summaries:

- The cut and paste function allows you to move ideas around within a summary.
- You can group related summaries together into one document, creating a useful study sheet.
- As a course progresses, you can merge several summaries into one, deleting information you no longer need.

EXERCISE 7–15   **WRITING A SUMMARY**

Directions: *Read and summarize the following essay by James M. Henslin.*

THE McDONALDIZATION OF SOCIETY

The McDonald's restaurants that are located across the United States—and, increasingly, the world—have a significance that goes far beyond the convenience of quick hamburgers, milk shakes, and salads. As sociologist George Ritzer says, our everyday lives are being "McDonaldized." Let's see what he means by this.

The McDonaldization of society does not refer just to the robotlike assembly of food. This term refers to the standardization of everyday life, a process that is transforming our lives. Want to do some shopping? Shopping malls offer one-stop shopping in controlled environments. Planning a trip? Travel agencies offer "package" tours. They will transport middle-class Americans to ten European capitals in fourteen days. All visitors experience the same hotels, restaurants, and other scheduled sites—and not one need fear meeting a "real" native. Want to keep up with events? USA Today spews out McNews—short, bland, non-analytical pieces that can be digested between gulps of the McShake or the McBurger.

Efficiency brings dependability. You can expect your burger and fries to taste the same whether you buy them in Los Angeles or Beijing. Although efficiency also lowers prices, it does come at a cost. Predictability washes away spontaneity, changing the quality of our lives. It produces a sameness, a bland version of what used to be unique experiences. In my own travels, for example, had I taken packaged tours I never would have had the eye-opening experiences that have added so much appreciation of human diversity. (Bus trips with chickens in Mexico, hitchhiking in Europe and Africa, sleeping on a granite table in a nunnery in Italy and in a cornfield in Algeria are just not part of tour agendas).

For good or bad, our lives are being McDonaldized, and the predictability of packaged settings seems to be our social destiny. When education is rationalize, no longer will our children have to put up with real professors who insist on discussing ideas endlessly, who never come to decisive answers, and who come saddled with idiosyncrasies. At some point, such an approach to education is going to be a bit of quaint history.

—Henslin, James, M., *Sociology: A Down-to-Earth Approach,* 10th Ed., © 2010. Reprinted and electronically reproduced by permission of Pearson Education, Inc., Upper Saddle River, NJ.

_____

_____

_____

_____

_____

EXERCISE 7–16   **WRITING A SUMMARY**

Directions: *Write a summary of "The Home Schooling Movement" on pages 315–316. Use the outline you constructed in Exercise 7–9 to guide your writing.*

_____

_____

_____

_____

_____

_____

_____

_____

_____

■ Thinking Critically: Deciding How Much Information to Include in Your Paraphrase, Summary, or Outline

Goal 8

Determine an appropriate level of detail for paraphrases, summaries, and outlines

Depending on the length of the reading, a paraphrase, summary, or outline can be very brief or quite long. At one end of the scale, you may choose to cover only major topics. At the other end of the scale, you may choose to provide a very detailed, extensive review of information.

Your purpose should determine how much detail you include. For example, suppose your instructor asks you to be familiar with the author's viewpoint and general approach to a problem. In this case, your summary or outline needs little detail. On the other hand, if you are outlining a chapter of an anatomy and physiology textbook for an upcoming midterm exam, you will benefit from a much more detailed outline. To determine the right amount of detail, ask yourself:

- What do I need to know?
- What is my instructor asking for?
- What exactly is the assignment?
- What type of test situation, if any, am I preparing for?

EXERCISE 7–17   **DECIDING HOW MUCH DETAIL TO INCLUDE**

Directions: *Use the excerpts found in this chapter to answer the following questions.*

1. Refer to "The Home Schooling Movement," pages 315–316. Suppose you are preparing for an examination, and your instructor says that you are responsible for knowing the pros and cons of home schooling. What is your best method of preparing for the exam?

   _____

   _____

2. Refer to the excerpt from *People of the Earth* in Exercise 7–8 on page 320. Your archaeology professor says you will be expected to understand the information in that selection in great detail because it is the foundation for the entire course. She also says that you should be able to provide all the information from that excerpt in your own words. What is your best method of learning this material?

   _____

   _____

3. Refer to "The Functions of Eye Movements" on page 307. Your assignment is to prepare an outline of this passage. How many points would you include under the heading "The Functions of Eye Movements"?

   _____

   _____

   _____

EXERCISE 7–18

WRITING A PARAPHRASE AND SUMMARY

Directions: *Select a section of at least five substantial paragraphs from one of your current textbook chapters. Write a paraphrase of its first paragraph; then write a summary of the entire section.*

EXERCISE 7–19

HIGHLIGHTING, ANNOTATING, AND SUMMARIZING

Directions: *Choose one of the reading selections at the end of this chapter. Read the selection, highlight it, and annotate it. Then write a brief outline and summary of its content. Be sure to show the relationships between ideas as well as record the most important ideas.*

SELF-TEST SUMMARY

Goal 1

1. Why is writing during and after reading an effective learning strategy?

Writing during and after reading enhances both your comprehension and retention. Writing activities such as highlighting, annotating, paraphrasing, outlining, mapping, and summarizing can
- focus your attention
- force you to think
- test your understanding
- aid your recall

Goal 2

2. How can you highlight more effectively?

To make highlighting an efficient means of identifying what is important within each paragraph you should
- read first, then highlight
- use paragraph structure to guide you
- use headings as a guide
- develop your own highlighting system
- highlight as few words as possible
- reread your highlighting to test its accuracy

Goal 3

3. Why should you annotate and make marginal notations in conjunction with your highlighting?

Annotating involves recording ideas, reactions, impressions, and questions as you read. Using symbols and brief phrases as marginal notes is useful in condensing, supplementing, and clarifying passage content because you are adding your own thinking to the highlighted material.

Goal 4

4. Why is paraphrasing a useful study strategy?

Paraphrasing is the restatement of a passage's ideas in your own words. It is a particularly useful strategy for recording the meaning and checking your comprehension of detailed, complex, precise, difficult, or unusually written passages. Using your own words rather than the author's expresses the meaning of the passage more clearly and concisely, thereby making study and review easier.

Goal 5

5. What is an outline and what are its advantages?

Outlining is a form of organizing information that provides you with a structure that indicates the relative importance of ideas and shows the relationships among them. When done well, it helps you sort out ideas, improves your concentration, and aids your recall.

Goal 6

6. What is mapping?

Mapping is a process of drawing diagrams to show the connection between a topic and its related ideas. Both concept maps and thought pattern maps enable you to adjust to both the type of information being recorded and its particular organization. Grouping and consolidating information in this way makes it easier to learn and remember.

Goal 7

7. What is involved in summarizing?

Summarizing involves selecting a passage's most important ideas and recording them in a condensed, abbreviated form. A summary provides a brief overview of a passage that can be useful in completing writing assignments and reports, preparing for class participation, or reviewing for exams.

Goal 8

8. How do you decide how much information to include in a paraphrase, summary, or outline?

Consider the following questions
- What do I need to know?
- What does my instructor expect?
- What exactly is the assignment?
- What type of test am I preparing for?

READING SELECTION 13 PSYCHOLOGY

Liking and Loving: Interpersonal Attraction

Saundra K. Ciccarelli and J. Noland White

About the Reading

TEXTBOOK EXCERPT

This excerpt is taken from the "Social Psychology" chapter of an introductory psychology textbook, Psychology: An Exploration, *by Saundra K. Ciccarelli and J. Noland White. Social psychology is the branch of psychology that deals with social interactions and their effects on individuals and groups.*

Planning Your Reading Strategy*

Directions: *Activate your thinking by previewing the reading (see the Need to Know box on page 64) and answering the following questions.*

_____ 1. Based on your preview of the reading, on which types of information should you focus as you read?
   a. the causes of dislike and the various forms of prejudice
   b. the factors involved in attraction and the three components of love
   c. the definitions of interpersonal attraction and companionate love
   d. the role of compassionate love as the highest form of human emotion

2. Is there any truth to the old cliché "Opposites attract"?

3. Suppose you had to create a classification of the different types of love. What categories would you suggest?

4. Based on your preview of the reading, how quickly do you think you should read the selection? (Circle one.) Explain your answer.

Very slowly   Slowly   At a moderate pace   Quickly   Very quickly

---

1   Prejudice pretty much explains why people don't like each other. What does psychology say about why people like someone else? There are some "rules" for those whom people like and find attractive. Liking or having the desire for a relationship with someone else is called **interpersonal attraction**[†], and there's a great deal of research on the subject. (Who wouldn't want to know the rules?)

■ The Rules of Attraction

What factors govern attraction and love, and what are some different kinds of love?

2   Several factors are involved in the attraction of one person to another, including both superficial physical characteristics, such as physical beauty and proximity, as well as elements of personality.

Ciccarelli, Saundra K.; White, J. Noland, Psychology: An Exploration, 1st Ed., © 2010. Reprinted and electronically reproduced by permission of Pearson Education Inc., Upper Saddle River, NJ.

[†]**interpersonal attraction** liking or having the desire for a relationship with another person

---

*The Scorecard on p. 335 enables you to compute your reading rate. In order to do so, be sure to record your starting time in the Scorecard box before you begin reading.

3 PHYSICAL ATTRACTIVENESS When people think about what attracts them to other people, one of the topics that usually arises is the physical attractiveness of the other person. Some research suggests that physical beauty is one of the main factors that influence people's choices for selecting people they want to know better, although other factors may become more important in the later stages of relationships.

4 PROXIMITY—CLOSE TO YOU The closer together people are physically, such as working in the same office building or living in the same dorm, the more likely they are to form a relationship. **Proximity*** refers to being physically near someone else. People choose friends and lovers from the pool of people available to them, and availability depends heavily on proximity.

5 One theory about why proximity is so important involves the idea of repeated exposure to new stimuli. The more people experience something, whether it is a song, a picture, or a person, the more they tend to like it. The phrase "it grew on me" refers to this reaction. When people are in physical proximity to each other, repeated exposure may increase their attraction to each other.

6 BIRDS OF A FEATHER—SIMILARITY Proximity does not guarantee attraction, just as physical attractiveness does not guarantee a long-term relationship. People tend to like being around others who are *similar* to them in some way. The more people find they have in common with others—such as attitudes, beliefs, and interests—the more they tend to be attracted to those others. Similarity as a factor in relationships makes sense when seen in terms of validation of a person's beliefs and attitudes. When other people hold the same attitudes and beliefs and do the same kinds of actions, it makes a person's own concepts seem more correct or valid.

■ When Opposites Attract

7 *Isn't there a saying that "opposites attract"? Aren't people sometimes attracted to people who are different instead of similar?*

8 There is often a grain of truth in many old sayings, and "opposites attract" is no exception. Some people find that forming a relationship with another person who has *complementary* qualities (characteristics in the one person that fill a need in the other) can be very rewarding. Research does not support this view of attraction, however. It is similarity, not complementarity, that draws people together and helps them stay together.

9 RECIPROCITY OF LIKING Finally, people have a very strong tendency to like people who like them, a simple but powerful concept referred to as **reciprocity of liking**†. The only time that liking someone does not seem to make that person like the other in return is if a person suffers from feelings of low self-worth. In that case, finding out that someone likes you when you don't even like yourself makes you question his or her motives. This mistrust can cause you to act unfriendly to that person, which makes the person more likely to become unfriendly to you in a kind of self-fulfilling prophecy.

■ Love is a Triangle—Robert Sternberg's Triangular Theory of Love

10 Dictionary definitions of love refer to a strong affection for another person due to kinship, personal ties, sexual attraction, admiration, or common interests.

11 *But those aren't all the same kind of relationships. I love my family and I love my friends, but in different ways.*

12 Psychologists generally agree that there are different kinds of love. One psychologist, Robert Sternberg, outlined a theory of what he

---

***proximity** physical or geographical nearness

†**reciprocity of liking** tendency of people to like other people who like them in return

Famed athlete Joe DiMaggio and actress Marilyn Monroe are seen driving away after their 1954 marriage ceremony. While they had in common the fact that they were two of the most famous people in the United States at that time, many people viewed the marriage of the very modest and somewhat shy Joe to the outgoing, vivacious sex symbol that was Marilyn as an example of "opposites attract."

determined were the three main components of love and the different types of love that combinations of these three components can produce.

13 THE THREE COMPONENTS OF LOVE
According to Sternberg, love consists of three basic components: intimacy, passion, and commitment.

14 *Intimacy,* in Sternberg's view, refers to the feelings of closeness that one has for another person or the sense of having close emotional ties to another. Intimacy in this sense is not physical but psychological. Friends have an intimate relationship because they disclose things to each other that most people might not know, they feel strong emotional ties to each other, and they enjoy the presence of the other person.

15 *Passion* is the physical aspect of love. Passion refers to the emotional and sexual arousal a person feels toward the other person. Passion is not simply sex; holding hands, loving looks, and hugs can all be forms of passion.

16 *Commitment* involves the decisions one makes about a relationship. A short-term decision might be, "I think I'm in love." An example of a more long-term decision is, "I want to be with this person for the rest of my life."

17 THE LOVE TRIANGLES   A love relationship between two people can involve one, two, or all three of these components in various combinations. The combinations can produce seven different forms of love, as seen in Figure A.

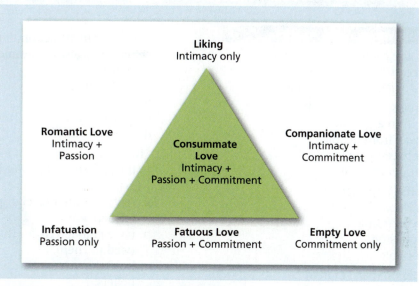

FIGURE A   Sternberg's Triangle of Love

This diagram represents the seven different types of love that can result from combining the components of love: intimacy, passion, and commitment. Notice that some of these types of love are more desirable or positive than others. What is the element missing from the less positive types?

Source: Adapted from Sternberg (1986).

18   Two of the more familiar and more heavily researched forms of love from Sternberg's theory are romantic love and companionate love. When intimacy and passion are combined, the result is the more familiar **romantic love***, which is sometimes called passionate love by other researchers. Romantic love is often the basis for a more lasting relationship. In many Western cultures, the ideal relationship begins with liking, then becomes romantic love as passion is added to the mix, and finally becomes a more enduring form of love as a commitment is made.

19   When intimacy and commitment are the main components of a relationship, it is called **companionate love†**. In companionate love, people who like each other, feel emotionally close to each other, and understand one another's motives have made a commitment to live together, usually in a marriage relationship. Companionate love is often the binding tie that holds a marriage together through the years of parenting, paying bills, and lessening physical passion. In many non-Western cultures, companionate love is seen as more sensible. Choices for a mate on the basis of compatibility are often made by parents or matchmakers rather than the couple themselves.

20   Finally, when all three components of love are present, the couple has achieved *consummate love,* the ideal form of love that many people see as the ultimate goal. This is also the kind of love that may evolve into companionate love when the passion lessens during the middle years of a relationship's commitment.

---

*romantic love type of love consisting of intimacy and passion

†companionate love type of love consisting of intimacy and commitment

Examining Reading Selection 13*

Checking Your Vocabulary

Directions: *Use context, word parts, or a dictionary, if necessary, to determine the meaning of each word as it is used in the reading.*

____ 1. interpersonal (paragraph 1)
    a. within a person
    b. away from people
    c. between people
    d. around people

____ 2. superficial (paragraph 2)
    a. surface
    b. extraordinary
    c. opposing
    d. sociable

____ 3. validation (paragraph 6)
    a. distinction
    b. confirmation
    c. organization
    d. requirement

____ 4. disclose (paragraph 14)
    a. warn
    b. deny
    c. replace
    d. reveal

____ 5. binding (paragraph 19)
    a. restricting
    b. unifying
    c. mending
    d. opening

Checking Your Comprehension

Directions: *Select the best answer.*

____ 6. This reading is primarily concerned with
    a. interpersonal communication.
    b. interpersonal attraction.
    c. social interaction.
    d. the elements of emotion.

____ 7. The factor in attraction that refers to being physically near someone else is known as
    a. complementarity.
    b. similarity.
    c. proximity.
    d. compatibility.

____ 8. The term "reciprocity of liking" refers to the tendency of people to like those who
    a. have a similar level of physical attractiveness.
    b. have characteristics that fill a need in them.
    c. hold the same attitudes and beliefs.
    d. like them in return.

____ 9. According to Robert Sternberg, each of the following is a main component of love *except*
    a. infatuation.
    b. intimacy.
    c. passion.
    d. commitment.

____ 10. In Sternberg's theory, the ideal form of love in which all three components are present is known as
    a. fatuous love.
    b. consummate love.
    c. romantic love.
    d. companionate love.

Thinking Critically

____ 11. The authors' primary purpose is to
    a. describe ways people can improve their relationships.
    b. inform readers about interpersonal attraction and types of love.

---

*Writing About the Reading questions appear in the Instructor's Manual.

c. compare love relationships in Western and non-Western cultures.

d. recommend a set of rules in developing lasting relationships.

___ 12. The authors' attitude toward the subject can best be described as
   a. concerned.
   b. objective.
   c. admiring.
   d. judgmental.

___ 13. The photograph of Joe DiMaggio and Marilyn Monroe is included as an example of
   a. a love triangle.
   b. reciprocity of liking.
   c. birds of a feather.
   d. opposites attract.

___ 14. The authors support their ideas primarily by
   a. recounting their personal experience.
   b. making comparisons and analogies.
   c. describing theories and research.
   d. quoting statistics.

___ 15. In Figure A (p. 333), the key element that is missing from the less positive types of love is
   a. romance.
   b. commitment.
   c. intimacy.
   d. passion.

Questions for Discussion

1. Discuss the different factors involved in interpersonal attraction. How important is each factor to you? Do the "rules of attraction" described in the selection reflect your own experiences?

2. Discuss the idea that opposites attract. Do you find it more rewarding to form a relationship with someone who has similar qualities or complementary qualities?

3. Consider the seven different kinds of love depicted in Figure A. Which types of love sound least desirable or positive? Why is intimacy such an important element in relationships?

4. Discuss the differences between romantic, companionate, and consummate love. Which type of love do you think is the ideal form of love? Why?

Scorecard

Selection 13:   1,413 words

Finishing Time: ___ ___ ___
                HR. MIN. SEC.

Starting Time: ___ ___ ___
                HR. MIN. SEC.

Reading Time: ___ ___
                     MIN. SEC.

WPM Score: _____

Comprehension Score: for items 6–15
Number Right: _____ × 10 = _____%

Assessing Your Reading Strategy

1. How would you rate your comprehension of the reading? (Circle one.)

   Excellent   Good   Fair   Poor

2. Did you find your reading strategy effective?   Yes   No

3. Suppose you were given an assignment to read a similar selection to the one you just read. Based on your experience with this selection, how would you adjust your reading strategy (if at all)?

READING SELECTION 14 PHYSICS

Sound: A Form of Energy

Paul G. Hewitt, John A. Suchocki, and Leslie A. Hewitt

About the Reading

TEXTBOOK EXCERPT

This reading is taken from a physics textbook, Conceptual Physical Science. *Physics is the study of matter and energy.*

MyReadingLab™ *The exercises following this selection can be completed online at myreadinglab.com*

Planning Your Reading Strategy*

Directions: *Activate your thinking by previewing the reading (see the Need to Know box on page 64) and answering the following questions.*

____ 1. Based on your preview, to which type of information should you pay the closest attention as you read?
   a. the design of performance spaces
   b. the senses of dolphins
   c. the properties of sound
   d. the science behind x-rays

____ 2. Which topic will not be discussed in the reading?
   a. echoes
   b. ultrasound
   c. refraction
   d. radar

3. Based on your preview of the reading, how quickly do you think you should read the selection? (Circle one.) Explain your answer.

Very slowly   Slowly   At a moderate pace   Quickly   Very quickly

_____

_____

1   When something moves periodically back and forth, side to side, or up and down, we say it vibrates. When a vibration is carried through space and time it is a **wave**. A wave is a pattern of matter or energy that extends from one place to another. Sound is the movement of vibrations of matter—through solids, liquids, or gases. If there is no matter to vibrate, then no sound is possible. Sound cannot travel in a vacuum.

■ FYI

Many things in nature vibrate—the string on a guitar, the reed in a clarinet, and your vocal cords when you speak or sing. When they vibrate in air they make the air vibrate in the same way. When these vibrations reach your ear they are transmitted as impulses to a part of your brain and you hear sound.

Hewitt, Paul G.; Suchocki, John A., Hewitt, Leslie A., Conceptual Physical Science: Explorations (Nasta Edition) With Practice Book and cd, 2nd Ed., © 2012. Reprinted and electronically reproduced by permission of Pearson Education Inc., Upper Saddle River, NJ.

*The Scorecard on p. 341 enables you to compute your reading rate. In order to do so, be sure to record your starting time in the Scorecard box before you begin reading.

FIGURE A   *Reflecting surfaces above the orchestra nicely reflect sound.*

Sound Can Be Reflected

2   We call the reflection of sound an *echo*. A large fraction of sound energy is reflected from a surface that is rigid and smooth. Less sound is reflected if the surface is soft and irregular. Sound energy that is not reflected is either transmitted or absorbed.

3   Sound reflects from a smooth surface the same way light does—the angle of incidence is equal to the angle of reflection. Reflected sound in a room makes it sound lively and full, as you have probably noticed while singing in the shower. Sometimes when the walls, ceiling, and floor of a room are too reflective, the sound becomes garbled. This is due to multiple reflections called *reverberations.* On the other hand, if the reflective surfaces are too absorbent, the sound level is low and the room may sound dull and lifeless. In the design of an auditorium or concert hall, a balance must be achieved between reverberation and absorption. The study of sound properties is called *acoustics.*

4   In concert halls, good acoustics require highly reflective surfaces behind the stage to direct sound out to an audience. Sometimes, reflecting surfaces are suspended above the stage. In the San Francisco opera hall, the reflective surfaces are large, shiny, plastic plates that also reflect light. A listener can look up at these reflectors and see the reflected images of the members of the orchestra (the plastic reflectors are somewhat curved, which increases the field of view). Both sound and light obey the same law of reflection, so if a reflector is oriented in such a way that you can see a particular musical instrument, you'll also hear it. Sound from the instrument follows the line of sight to the reflector and then to you.

Reading Check

Compared with the way in which light reflects, how does sound reflect?

■ Sound Can Be Refracted

5   Sound waves bend when parts of the waves travel at different speeds. This occurs in uneven winds or when sound is traveling through air of varying temperatures. This bending of sound is called **refraction**. On a warm day, air near the ground may be warmer than air above, and so the speed of sound near the ground is greater. Sound waves therefore tend to bend away from the ground, resulting in sound that does not seem to carry well (Figure B).

6   The refraction of sound occurs under water, too, where the speed of sound varies with temperature. This poses a problem for surface vessels that chart the bottom features of an ocean by bouncing ultrasonic waves off the bottom. This is a blessing for submarines that wish to escape detection. Layers of water at different temperatures (thermal gradients) result in refraction of sound that leaves gaps, or "blind spots," in the water. This is where submarines hide. If it weren't for refraction, submarines would be easier to detect.

7   The multiple reflections and refractions of ultrasonic waves are used by physicians in a technique for harmlessly "seeing" inside the body without the use of X-rays. When high-frequency sound (ultrasound) enters the body, it is reflected more strongly from the outside of organs than from their interior. A picture of the outline of the organs is obtained (Figure C). This ultrasound echo technique has always been used by bats, which emit ultrasonic squeaks and locate objects by their echoes. Dolphins do this and much more.

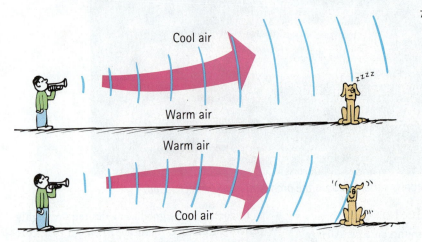

FIGURE B   *Sound waves are bent in air of uneven temperatures.*

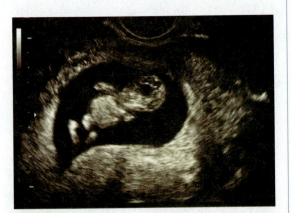

FIGURE C   *Megan Hewitt Abrams when she was a 14-week-old fetus.*

■ Link to Zoology: Dolphins and Acoustical Imaging

8   The primary sense of the dolphin is acoustic, for sight is not a very useful sense in the often murky and dark depths of the ocean. Whereas sound is a passive sense for us, it is an active sense for dolphins when they send out sounds and then perceive their surroundings via echoes. The ultrasonic waves emitted by a dolphin enables it to "see" through the bodies of other animals and people. Because skin, muscle, and fat are almost transparent to dolphins, they "see" only a thin

FIGURE D   *A dolphin emits ultra-high-frequency sound to locate and identify objects in its environment. Distance is sensed by the time delay between sending sound and receiving its echo, and direction is sensed by differences in time for the echo to reach its two ears. A dolphin's main diet is fish and since hearing in fish is limited to fairly low frequencies, they are not alerted to the fact they are being hunted.*

outline of the body, but the bones, teeth, and gas-filled cavities are clearly apparent. Physical evidence of cancers, tumors, and heart attacks can all be "seen" by dolphins—as humans have only recently been able to do with ultrasound.

9   What's more interesting, a dolphin can reproduce the sonic signals that paint the mental image of its surroundings. Thus the dolphin probably communicates its experience to other dolphins by communicating the full acoustic image of what is "seen," placing the image directly in the minds of other dolphins. It needs no word or symbol for "fish," for example, but communicates an image of the real thing. It is quite possible that dolphins highlight portions of the images they send by selective filtering, as we similarly do when communicating a musical concert to others via various means of sound reproduction. Small wonder that the language of the dolphin is very unlike our own!

■ Reading Check

In terms of speed, what occurs when sound bends from a straight-line course?

■ Concept Check

A depth-sounding vessel surveys the ocean bottom with ultrasonic sound that travels an average 1530 m/s in seawater. How deep is the water if the time delay of the echo from the ocean floor is 2 s?

■ Check Your Answer

The 2-s delay means it takes 1s for the sound to reach the bottom (and another 1s to return). Sound traveling at 1530 m/s for 1s tells us the bottom is 1530 m deep.

Examining Reading Selection 14

Complete this Exercise at myreadinglab.com

Checking Your Vocabulary

Directions: *Use context, word parts, or a dictionary, if necessary, to determine the meaning of each word as it is used in the reading.*

____ 1. fraction (paragraph 2)
   a. description
   b. portion
   c. motion
   d. expression

____ 2. garbled (paragraph 3)
   a. distorted
   b. silent
   c. similar
   d. isolated

____ 3. oriented (paragraph 4)
   a. attached
   b. connected
   c. positioned
   d. prevented

____ 4. emit (paragraph 7)
   a. erase
   b. request
   c. include
   d. send

____ 5. selective (paragraph 9)
   a. carefully chosen
   b. irregularly chosen
   c. needlessly chosen
   d. secretively chosen

Checking Your Comprehension

Directions: *Select the best answer.*

____ 6. This reading is primarily concerned with
   a. how animals use sound to communicate.
   b. how humans and animals communicate differently.
   c. how sound can be reflected and refracted.
   d. what humans can learn from dolphins.

____ 7. The authors wrote this selection in order to
   a. compare and contrast different forms of energy.
   b. inform readers about sound as a form of energy.
   c. encourage research into animal behavior.
   d. demonstrate the intelligence of dolphins.

____ 8. According to the selection, more sound is reflected from a surface that is
   a. rigid and smooth.
   b. soft.
   c. irregular.
   d. very absorbent.

____ 9. The main point of paragraph 4 is that
   a. the San Francisco opera hall uses reflective plates above the stage.
   b. sound and light both obey the same law of reflection.
   c. audience members can use reflective surfaces to improve their view.
   d. reflective surfaces are used in concert halls to achieve good acoustics.

____ 10. Dolphins use acoustical imaging in all of the following ways *except*
   a. to perceive their surroundings.
   b. to locate and identify objects in their environment.
   c. to see the skin, muscle, and fat of other animals and people.
   d. to communicate images to other dolphins.

Thinking Critically

____ 11. The intended audience for this selection most likely is
   a. sound researchers.
   b. science students.

c. animal experts.

d. physical scientists.

_____ 12. The authors' attitude toward the subject can best be described as

a. cynical.

b. impatient.

c. objective.

d. optimistic.

_____ 13. The photograph in Figure A illustrates how reflective surfaces are used to

a. direct sound out to an audience.

b. improve lighting in an auditorium.

c. absorb sounds made by the audience.

d. control temperature in an auditorium.

_____ 14. The diagram in Figure B illustrates the concept of

a. echoes.

b. refraction.

c. reverberation.

d. reflection.

_____ 15. The authors support their ideas primarily by

a. quoting opinions.

b. describing research.

c. making analogies.

d. explaining facts.

Scorecard

Selection 14:   1,214 words

Finishing Time: _____ _____ _____
                     HR.   MIN.   SEC.

Starting Time: _____ _____ _____
                     HR.   MIN.   SEC.

Reading Time: _____ _____
                            MIN.   SEC.

WPM Score: _____

Comprehension Score: for Items 6–15

Number Right: _____ × 10 = _____%

Assessing Your Reading Strategy

1. How would you rate your effectiveness on comprehension?

   Excellent   Good   Fair   Poor
   (circle one)

2. Did you find your reading strategy effective?   Yes   No   (circle one)

3. Suppose you are given an assignment to read a similar selection to the one you just read (that is, a chapter in a biology textbook). Based on your experience with this selection, how would you adjust your reading strategy (if at all)?

Writing About Reading Selection 14

Checking Your Vocabulary

Directions: *Complete each of the following items; refer to a dictionary if necessary.*

1. Define the word *wave* (paragraph 1) and identify the type of context clue that provides its meaning.

   _____

   _____

2. Describe the denotative and connotative meanings of the word *lifeless* in paragraph 3.

   _____

   _____

3. Explain the meaning of the word *bless-ing* and how it is used in paragraph 6.

_____

_____

_____

_____

_____

4. Define the word *passive* (paragraph 8) and identify the type of context clue that provides its meaning.

_____

_____

_____

5. Determine the meanings of the following words by using word parts:

a. *extends* (paragraph 1)

_____

b. *transmitted* (paragraph 2)

_____

c. *multiple* (paragraph 3)

_____

d. *auditorium* (paragraph 3)

_____

_____

e. *submarines* (paragraph 6)

_____

_____

f. *reproduce* (paragraph 9)

_____

Checking Your Comprehension

6. What is refraction and why does it occur?

_____

_____

_____

7. How does refraction affect surface vessels and submarines differently?

_____

_____

_____

_____

8. What is the technique used by physicians to "see" inside the human body without X-rays?

_____

9. Why is the dolphin's primary sense acoustic?

_____

_____

Thinking Critically

10. What is the purpose of the "FYI" text box next to the first paragraph?

_____

_____

_____

11. Why do the authors mention singing in the shower?

_____

_____

_____

12. The purpose of the photograph in Figure D is to

_____

_____

13. How do the authors conclude the selection?

_____

_____

_____

Questions for Discussion

1. What buildings or auditoriums have you been in that have good acoustics? Where have you experienced "bad" acoustics? Describe the features in each place that may have contributed to the acoustics.

2. Why do the authors say sound is a passive sense for us? What is our primary sense? Discuss the ways we use our senses to navigate the world.

3. Discuss the last paragraph of the selection. Would you be interested in learning more about how dolphins communicate images to other dolphins? What applications might there be for human communication?

4. Choose a paragraph in the selection and either paraphrase it or summarize it. How helpful do you think your paraphrase or summary would be as a study strategy? What other strategies would work well with this material?

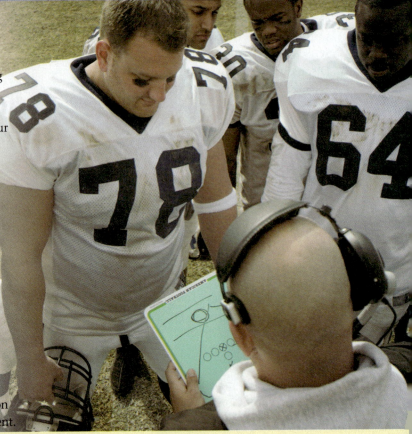

think VISUALLY...

Imagine you have just started learning to play football. Learning to play the game involves learning various plays and game strategies. The first time your coach asks you to practice a play, you may have little idea of how it will work. But once your coach explains it and draws a play diagram, and you practice it several times, you will become comfortable with the play.

Learning a new subject is not so different. Instead of a coach, however, you have a textbook. Each term you will spend hours reading, reviewing, and studying textbooks. Textbooks are very different from any other type of printed material because they are designed to teach. This chapter will show you how to use your textbooks more effectively and how to develop retention and recall strategies to learn their content.

Learning GOALS

In this chapter, you will learn how to . . .

Goal 1 Increase recall using review

Goal 2 Increase recall using other techniques

Goal 3 Increase retention and recall using SQ3R

Goal 4 Adapt SQ3R based on material and learning style

Goal 5 Acquire specialized vocabulary

Goal 6 Understand the difference between memorizing and learning

■ Using Review to Increase Recall

Goal 1
Increase recall
using review

Review refers to the process of going back over something you have already read. There are two types of review: *immediate* and *periodic*. Both types can greatly increase the amount you can remember from a printed page.

Immediate Review

When you finish reading an assignment, your first inclination may be to breathe a sigh of relief, close the book, and go on to another task. Before you do this, however, take a few minutes to go back over the material. Briefly review the overall organization and important ideas presented. In reviewing you should reread the parts of the article or chapter that contain the most important ideas. Concentrate on titles, introductions, summaries, headings, graphic material, and depending on the length of the material, topic sentences. Also review any notes you made and any portions of the text that you highlighted.

Considerable research has been conducted on how individuals learn and remember. These experiments have shown that review immediately following reading greatly improves the amount remembered. However, the review must be *immediate;* it will not produce the same effects if you do it after a ten-minute break or later in the evening.

> **EFFICIENCY TIP**
> Many college textbooks provide a built-in review or summary of key points after each major section. Use these summaries to conduct an immediate review; don't skip them.

Periodic Review

Although immediate review is very effective and will increase your ability to recall information, it is not sufficient for remembering material for long periods. To remember facts and ideas permanently, you need to review them periodically, going back and refreshing your recall on a regular basis. For example, suppose you are reading a chapter on criminal behavior in your sociology text, and a midterm exam is scheduled in four weeks. If you read the chapter, reviewed it immediately, and then did nothing with it until the exam a month later, you would not remember enough to score well on the exam. To achieve a good grade, you need to review the chapter periodically. You might review the chapter once several days after reading it, again a week later, and once again a week before the exam.

Why Review Is Effective

Immediate and periodic reviews are effective for two reasons:

1. **Review provides repetition.** Repetition is one important way that you learn and remember information. Think about how you learned the multiplication tables or why you know the phone numbers of your closest friends. In both cases, frequent use enables you to remember.

2. **Review consolidates, or draws together, information into a unified whole.** As you read a chapter, you are processing the information piece by piece. Review, both immediate and periodic, provides a means of seeing how each piece relates to each other piece and to the material as a whole.

EXERCISE 8–1   **USING IMMEDIATE REVIEW**

Directions: *Read one of the selections at the end of the chapter and review it immediately. Highlight the parts of the selection that you reread as part of your immediate review. Then answer the questions that follow the selection.* ■

EXERCISE 8–2   **PLANNING PERIODIC REVIEW**

Academic
APPLICATION

Directions: *Plan a periodic review schedule for one of your courses. Include both textbook chapters and lecture notes.* ■

TECH SUPPORT Creating Electronic Flash Cards

Flash cards are a quick and easy way to learn anything from new vocabulary words for your Spanish class to the symbols on the periodic table of elements. While flash cards are most effective for learning brief, objective facts, you can also create flash cards to help you with self-testing. The software program PowerPoint, which can be found on most computers, can help you create flash cards that can be edited and expanded as you learn more about a subject. In addition, free online services such as Flash Card Machine allow you to create and share Web-based flash cards with your classmates.

■ Strengthening Your Recall

Goal 2
Increase recall using other techniques

Review and repetition are primary methods of increasing retention. Other aids or methods for increasing your recall include the following:

Building an Intent to Remember

Very few people remember things that they do not intend to remember. Do you remember what color of clothing a friend wore last week? Can you name all the songs you heard on the radio this morning? Can you remember exactly what time you got home last Saturday night? If not, why not? Most likely you cannot remember these facts because at the time you did not see the importance of remembering them. Of course, if you had known that you would be asked these questions, you would most likely have remembered the items. You must intend to remember things to be able to do so effectively. The same principle holds true for reading and retention. To remember what you read, you must have a clear and strong intent to do so. Unless you have defined what you intend to remember before you begin reading, you will find that it is difficult to recall specific content.

In Chapter 2 you saw how guide questions can help you keep your mind on what you are reading. Now you can see that they also establish an intent to remember.

Before you begin to read an assignment, define as clearly as possible what you intend to remember. Use the questions in the box below as a guide. Your definition will depend on the type of material, why you are reading it, and how familiar you are with the topic. For instance, if you are reading an essay assigned in preparation for a class discussion, plan to remember not only key ideas but also points of controversy, application, and opinions with which you disagree. Your intent might be quite different in reviewing a chapter for an essay exam. Here you would be looking for important ideas, trends, guiding or controlling principles, and significance of events.

As you read a text assignment, sort important information from that which is less important. Ask and continually answer questions such as those in the box to help you do this.

NEED TO KNOW How to Build an Intent to Remember

To build an intent to remember, ask yourself the following questions:

1. **How important is this information?**
2. **Will I need to know this for the exam?**
3. **Is this a key idea or is it an explanation of a key idea?**
4. **Why did the writer include this?**

Organizing and Categorizing

Information that is organized, or that has a pattern or structure, is easier to remember than material that is randomly arranged. One effective way to organize information is to *categorize* it, to arrange it in groups according to similar characteristics. Suppose, for example, that you had to remember the following list of items to buy for a picnic: cooler, candy, 7-Up, Pepsi, napkins, potato chips, lemonade, peanuts, paper plates. The easiest way to remember this list would be to divide it into groups. You might arrange it as follows:

Drinks	*Snacks*	*Picnic Supplies*
7-Up	peanuts	cooler
Pepsi	candy	paper plates
lemonade	potato chips	napkins

By grouping the items into categories, you are putting similar items together. Then, rather than learning one long list of unorganized items, you are learning three shorter, organized lists.

Now imagine you are reading an essay on discipline in public high schools. Instead of learning one long list of reasons for disruptive student behavior, you might divide the reasons into groups such as peer conflicts, teacher-student conflicts, and so forth.

Associating Ideas

Association is a useful way to remember new facts and ideas. It involves connecting new information with previously acquired knowledge. For instance, if you are reading about divorce in a sociology class and are trying to remember a list of common causes, you might try to associate each cause with a person you know who exhibits that problem. Suppose one cause of divorce is lack of communication between the partners. You might remember this by thinking of a couple you know whose lack of communication has caused relationship difficulties.

Suppose you are taking an introductory physics course and are studying Newton's Laws of Motion. The Third Law states: To every action there is always opposed an equal reaction. To remember this law you could associate it with a familiar everyday situation such as swimming that illustrates the law. When you swim you push water backward with your feet, arms, and legs, and the water pushes you forward.

Association involves making connections between new information and what you already know. When you find a connection between the known and the unknown, you can retrieve the new information from your memory along with the old.

Using a Variety of Sensory Modes

Your senses of sight, hearing, and touch can all help you remember what you read. Most of the time, most of us use just one sense—sight—as we read. However, if you are able to use more than one sense, you will find that recall is easier. Activities such as highlighting, note taking, and outlining involve your sense of touch and enable you to reinforce your learning. If you are having particular difficulty remembering something, try to use your auditory sense as well. You might try repeating the information out loud or listening to someone else repeat it.

Visualizing

Visualizing, or creating a mental picture of what you have read, often aids recall. In reading descriptive writing that creates a mental picture, visualization is an easy task. In reading about events, people, processes, or

FLEXIBILITY TIP
"Visualizing" need not be limited to the mind. If you like to draw or doodle, sketching out pictures and images (or time lines or any other type of map) can also help cement concepts in your mind.

procedures, visualization is again relatively simple. However, visualization of abstract ideas, theories, philosophies, and concepts may not be possible. Instead, you may be able to create a visual picture of the relationship of ideas in your mind or on paper. For example, suppose you are reading about invasion of privacy and learn that there are arguments for and against the storage of personal data about each citizen in large computer banks. You might create a visual image of two lists of information—advantages and disadvantages.

Using Mnemonic Devices

Memory tricks and devices, often called *mnemonics,* are useful in helping you recall lists of factual information. You might use a rhyme, such as the one used for remembering the number of days in each month: "Thirty days hath September, April, June, and November . . . ." Another device involves making up a word or phrase in which each letter represents an item you are trying to remember. If you remember the name Roy G. Biv, for example, you will be able to recall the colors in the light spectrum: **r**ed, **o**range, **y**ellow, **g**reen, **b**lue, **i**ndigo, **v**iolet.

EXERCISE 8–3

USING RETENTION AIDS

Directions: *Five study learning situations follow. Decide which of the retention aids described in this section—organization/categorization, association, sensory modes, visualization, and mnemonic devices—might be most useful in each situation and write it (them) on the line provided.*

1. In a sociology course, you are assigned to read about and remember the causes of child abuse. How might you remember them more easily?

   _____

2. You are studying astronomy and you have to remember the names of the eight planets: Mercury, Venus, Earth, Mars, Jupiter, Saturn, Uranus, and Neptune. What retention aid(s) could help you remember them?

   _____

3. You are taking a course in anatomy and physiology and must learn the name and location of each bone in the human skull. How could you learn them easily?

   _____

4. You have an entire chapter to review for a history course, and your instructor has told you that your exam will contain 30 true/false questions on Civil War battles. What could you do as you review to help yourself remember the details of various battles?

   _____

5. You are taking a course in twentieth-century history and are studying the causes of the Vietnam War in preparation for an essay exam. You find that there are many causes, some immediate, others long-term. Some have to do with international politics; others, with internal problems in North and South Vietnam. How could you organize your study for this exam?

_____

EXERCISE 8–4

USING RECALL STRATEGIES

Directions: *Find a classmate or group of classmates who are taking one of the same courses you are. (If no one is taking the exact same course, join a group of classmates who are taking a similar course: another social science course, another English course, and so forth.) Discuss how you could use each of the recall strategies described in this section to improve your performance in that course.*

EXERCISE 8-5

USING RETENTION AIDS

Directions: *Read the following excerpt. Then decide which retention aid(s) you might use to learn the three types of groups discussed in the material.*

FRIENDSHIP TYPES

Not all friendships are the same. But how do they differ? One way of answering this question is by distinguishing among the three major types of friendship: friendships of reciprocity, receptivity, and association.

The *friendship of reciprocity* is the ideal type, characterized by loyalty, self-sacrifice, mutual affection, and generosity. A friendship of reciprocity is based on equality: Each individual shares equally in giving and receiving the benefits and rewards of the relationship.

In the *friendship of receptivity*, in contrast, there is an imbalance in giving and receiving; one person is the primary giver and one the primary receiver. This imbalance, however, is a positive factor, because each person gains something from the relationship. The different needs of both the person who receives and the person who gives affection are satisfied. This is the friendship that may develop between a teacher and a student or between a doctor and a patient. In fact, a difference in status is essential for the friendship of receptivity to develop.

The *friendship of association* is a transitory one. It might be described as a friendly relationship rather than a true friendship. Associative friendships are the kind we often have with classmates, neighbors, or coworkers. There is no great loyalty, no great trust, no great giving or receiving. The association is cordial, but not intense.

—Devito, Joseph, A., *Human Communication: The Basic Course,* 12th Ed., © 2012. Reprinted and electronically reproduced by permission of Pearson Education, Inc., Upper Saddle River, NJ.

■ Reading and Learning with the SQ3R System

Goal 3
Increase retention and recall using SQ3R

Throughout this chapter you have become familiar with devices and techniques to improve your ability to remember what you read. You may be wondering how you will be able to use all these techniques and how to combine them most effectively. Many students have asked similar questions. As a result, systems have been developed and tested that combine some of the most useful techniques into a step-by-step procedure for learning as you read.

The SQ3R Reading-Study System

The SQ3R system has been used successfully for many years. Considerable experimentation has been done, and the system has proven effective in increasing students' retention. It is especially useful for studying textbooks and other highly factual, well-organized materials. Basically, SQ3R is a way of learning as you read. The steps in the system are listed below.

NEED TO KNOW How to Use SQ3R

1. **Survey.** Become familiar with the overall content and organization of the material. You have already learned this technique and know it as previewing.

2. **Question.** Formulate questions about the material that you expect to be able to answer as you read. As you read each successive heading, turn it into a question. This step is similar to establishing guide questions as discussed in Chapter 2.

3. **Read.** As you read each section, actively search for the answers to your guide questions. When you find the answers, highlight or mark portions of the text that concisely state the information.

4. **Recite.** Probably the most important part of the system, "recite" means that you should stop after each section or after each major heading, look away from the page, and try to remember the answer to your question. If you are unable to remember, look back at the page and reread the material. Then test yourself again by looking away from the page and "reciting" the answer to your question.

5. **Review.** Immediately after you have finished reading, go back through the material again and read titles, introductions, summaries, headings, and graphic material. As you read each heading, recall your question and test yourself to see if you can still remember the answer. If you cannot, reread that section again.

Now, to give you a clear picture of how the steps in the SQ3R method work together to produce an efficient approach to reading-study, the method will be applied to a textbook excerpt. Suppose you have been assigned to read the following excerpt, "Social Influences on Consumers' Decisions," taken from *Marketing: Real People, Real Choices* by Michael R. Solomon, Greg W. Marshall, and Elnora W. Stuart for a business class that is studying marketing techniques. Follow each of the SQ3R steps in reading the selection.

FLEXIBILITY TIP
Note that the first step in the SQ3R system is Survey, which is a synonym for *preview*. Your preview of the material will help you determine the best reading strategy and rate for the selection.

1. **Survey.** Preview the article, noticing the introduction, headings, first sentences, and the last paragraph. From this preview you should have an overall picture of what this article is about and what factors influence buying decisions.

2. **Question.** Using the headings as a starting point, develop several questions that you might expect the article to answer. You might ask questions such as these:
   - What is culture?
   - How do rituals influence consumers' decisions?
   - How do values influence buying decisions?
   - What is a subculture and how does it influence buying decisions?

3. **Read.** Now read the entire selection, keeping your questions in mind as you read. Stop at the end of each major section and proceed to step 4.

4. **Recite.** After each section, stop reading and check to see if you can recall the answers to your questions.

5. **Review.** When you have finished reading the entire article, take a few minutes to reread the headings and recall your questions. Check to see that you can still recall the answers.

Social Influences on Consumers' Decisions

Although we are all individuals, we are also members of many groups that influence our buying decisions. Families, friends, and classmates often sway us, as do larger groups with which we identify, such as ethnic groups and political parties. Now let's first consider how culture affects the consumer decision-making process.

Culture

Think of culture as a society's personality. It is the values, beliefs, customs, and tastes a group of people produce or practice. Although we often assume that what people in one culture (especially our own) think is desirable or appropriate will be appreciated in other cultures as well, that's far from the truth. Middle Eastern youth may not agree with U.S. politics, but they love Western music and find Arab TV music channels boring. Enter MTV Arabia, a 24-hour free satellite channel. Sure, many U.S. and European videos have to be cleaned up for the Arab audience and many are simply too edgy to air. To meet the values of the Middle Eastern audience, bad language and shots of kissing, revealing outfits, or people in bed are blurred or removed and sometimes replaced by more acceptable copy. Culture matters.

Rituals

Every culture associates specific activities and products with its *rituals*, such as weddings and funerals. Some companies are more than happy to help us link products to cultural events. Consider the popularity of the elaborate weddings Disney stages for couples who want to reenact their own version of a popular fairy tale. At Disney World, the princess bride wears a tiara and rides to the park's lakeside wedding pavilion in a horse-drawn coach, complete with two footmen in gray wigs and gold lamé pants. Disney stages about 2,000 of these extravaganzas each year.

In most countries, rituals are involved in the celebration of holidays. Americans purchase and/or cook turkeys, cranberry sauce, and pumpkin pies to have the perfect Thanksgiving dinner. In Christian cultures, the Christmas ritual is so strongly tied to gifts, Christmas trees, lights, and decorations that it becomes the make-or-break sales season of the year for retailers. In many Muslim countries, the Ramadan season means fasting during the day but consuming gigantic amounts of food after sunset each day. Is it any wonder that marketers of so many companies study consumer rituals?

Values

Cultural values are deeply held beliefs about right and wrong ways to live. Marketers who understand a culture's values can tailor their product offerings accordingly. For example, today we see the economic growth of some *collectivist* cultures (those cultures in which loyalty to a family or tribe overrides personal goals). In collectivist countries such as India, Japan, and China, economic growth is making many consumers more affluent—and individualistic. For marketers, this means growth opportunities for products such as travel, luxury goods, sports activities like tennis and golf, and entertainment.

Subcultures

A **subculture** is a group that coexists with other groups in a larger culture but whose members share a distinctive set of beliefs or characteristics, such as members of a religious organization or an ethnic group. **Microcultures** are groups of consumers who identify with a specific activity or art form. These form around music groups such as the Dave Matthews Band, media creations such as *World of Warcraft*, or leisure activities such as extreme sports. Social media has been a real boon to subcultures and microcultures; it provides an opportunity for like-minded consumers to share their thoughts, photographs, videos, and so on.

For marketers, some of the most important subcultures are racial and ethnic groups because many consumers identify strongly with their heritage, and products that appeal to this aspect of their identities appeal to them. To grow its business, cereal maker General Mills targets Hispanic consumers through its *Qué Vida Rica* marketing program that tells mothers about the benefits of its products and offers nutrition tips and recipe suggestions.

—Solomon, Michael R.; Marshall, Greg W.; Stuart, Elnora W., *Marketing: Real People, Real Choices*, 7th Ed., © 2012. Reprinted and electronically reproduced by permission of Pearson Education, Inc., Upper Saddle River, NJ.

How SQ3R Improves Your Reading Efficiency

The SQ3R system improves your reading efficiency in three ways: it increases your comprehension, increases your recall, and saves you time because you learn as you read. This means you will find that you need much less time to prepare for exams, as you only need to refresh your memory of the material and review difficult portions.

EXERCISE 8–6

Working COLLABORATIVELY

EVALUATING SQ3R

Directions: *Divide the class into two groups. Your instructor will assign a reading selection from the text. One group should read the selection using the SQ3R method. The other group should only read the selection once, without using any parts of the SQ3R system. Neither group should highlight or annotate. When both groups have finished, groups may question one another to determine which group learned and recalled more information or compare their scores on the comprehension test that accompanies the reading.*　■

■ Adapting the SQ3R System

Goal 4
Adapt SQ3R based on material and learning style

To make the best use of SQ3R, be sure to adjust and adapt the system to fit the material you are studying and your learning style.

Adapting SQ3R to Suit the Material

Your texts and other required readings vary greatly from course to course. For example, a mathematics text is structured and written quite differently from a sociology text. A chemistry text contains numerous principles, laws, formulas, and problems, whereas a philosophy text contains mostly reading selections and discussions. To accommodate this wide variation in your textbooks and other assigned readings, use the SQ3R system as a base or model. Add, vary, or rearrange the steps to fit the material:

- **When working with a mathematics text,** you might add a "Study the Sample Problems" step in which you analyze the problem-solving process.
- **When reading an essay, short story, or poem** for a literature class, add a "React" step in which you analyze various features of writing, including the writer's style, tone, purpose, and point of view.
- **For textbooks with a great deal of factual information to learn,** you might add "Highlight," "Take Notes," or "Outline" steps.

EXERCISE 8–7

USING SQ3R

Directions: *Read one of the selections at the end of the chapter using the SQ3R system and follow each of the steps listed here. Add to or revise the system as necessary. After you complete the "Review" step, answer the multiple-choice questions that follow the selection.*

Adapting SQ3R to Suit Your Learning Style

Throughout this text you have probably found that some techniques work better for you than others due in part to your learning style. As part of the process of developing your own reading-study system, consider your learning style. Ask yourself the following questions:

- Is writing and rewriting information a good way for me to learn?
- Does asking challenging questions and answering them help me to learn?
- Does writing summaries or outlines help me to remember information?

✔ LEARNING STYLE TIPS

If you tend to be a(n) . . .	Then build your retention skills by . . .
Visual learner	Using visualization. Draw charts and diagrams to organize information.
Auditory learner	Repeating information aloud to aid your learning.

When you have discovered some features of your own learning style, you can adapt the SQ3R system to suit it. For instance, if writing outlines helps you recall the idea structures, replace the "Recite" step with an "Outline" step and make the "Review" step a "Review of Outline" step. Or, if you have discovered that you learn well by listening, replace the "Recite" and "Review" steps with "Record" and "Listen" steps, in which you dictate and record information to be learned and review it by listening to the recording.

EXERCISE 8–8

ADAPTING SQ3R

Directions: List the courses you are taking this semester. Next to each, indicate what modification(s) in the SQ3R system you would make to suit each course's content and learning requirements. ■

■ How to Learn Specialized Vocabulary

Goal 5

Acquire specialized vocabulary

The volume of new terminology to learn in many college courses can be overwhelming unless you develop strategies for identifying, organizing, and learning it. Use the following suggestions:

1. **Keep a notebook or a notebook section for listing new words in each course.** Add words to the list as they appear in the text.

2. **Use context clues to try to discover the definition of a new term.** (Refer to Chapter 3 for more information.) A definition clue is often provided when the word is introduced for the first time. As each new word is introduced, mark it in your text and later transfer it to your notebook. Organize this portion of your notebook by chapter. Refer to your notebook for review and reference. Use the card system (see Chapter 3) to learn words you are having trouble remembering.

3. **Prefix-root-suffix learning is a particularly useful approach for developing technical vocabulary.** In many fields, the technical words use a particular set of prefixes, roots, and suffixes that are meaningful in that area. For example, health-related fields use a core set of prefixes, roots, and suffixes in many words. Here are several examples using prefixes:

Prefix	Meaning	Example	Definition
cardi-	heart	cardiogram	test that measures contractions of the heart
hem-/hema-	blood	hematology	study of the blood
hypo-	under	hypodermic needle	needle that goes under the skin
osteo-	bone	osteopath	doctor who specializes in treatment of the bones

In most scientific/technical fields you will find a core of commonly used prefixes, roots, and suffixes. Keep a list of common word parts in your notebook. Add to the list as you work through the course. For those word parts you have difficulty remembering, use a variation of the word card system. Write the word part on the front of the card and its meaning, pronunciation, and an example on the back.

4. **Learn to pronounce each new term you come across.** Pronouncing the word is a good way to fix it in your memory and make you feel confident in its use.

5. **Use the glossary in the back of your text.** A glossary is more useful than a dictionary because it gives the meanings of the words as used in the field you are studying; you won't have to waste time sorting through numerous meanings to find the appropriate one.

6. **If you are majoring in a technical field, consider purchasing a subject-area dictionary.** Many academic disciplines have a specialized dictionary that indexes commonly used terminology particular to that field. Nursing students, for example, often buy a copy of Taber's *Cyclopedic Medical Dictionary*.

■ Thinking Critically: Memorizing Versus Learning

Goal 6
Understand the difference between memorizing and learning

Many students prepare for their exams by "cramming" or by trying to memorize long lists of facts, numbers, symbols, or key terms. There is no denying that memorization is a key part of learning. In fact, in some science courses (such as introductory biology or introductory anatomy) you will spend hours trying to memorize all the bones in the body or all the parts of a plant, and certainly the exams you take will require you to understand and define key words and concepts.

Most college exams and writing assignments, however, ask students to go beyond remembering, which is considered the lowest level of thinking. (See the Need to Know Box on page 55, "Levels of Thinking.") Your instructors will be looking for clues that you also understand what you have memorized, and that you can apply, analyze, and evaluate claims, statements, and other sources. So, if you have focused your study solely on memorization, you cannot expect to get a high grade.

In addition, key terms or concepts that are memorized solely for the purpose of passing a test are usually forgotten very quickly. Why? Because in this situation your motivation—your intent to remember—is very short-term. By definition, learning occurs only when the information has found a permanent place in your brain.

So how do you move beyond memorizing into the higher levels of thinking? Use the techniques outlined in this chapter: organize and categorize, associate ideas, visualize, and look for connections to your life and the world around you.

EXERCISE 8–9   **THINKING CRITICALLY ABOUT TEXTBOOK CONTENT**

Directions: *Refer to "Social Influences on Consumers' Decisions" on pages 352–353 to answer the following questions.*

1. Organize and categorize the reading in an outline, as if you were preparing for an exam on the topic.

   _____

   _____

2. What rituals from your own life can you associate with the material under the "Rituals" heading?

   _____

3. When you read the material under the heading "Subcultures," which subcultures do you visualize (in addition to those provided by the author)?

   _____ ■

SELF-TEST SUMMARY

Goal 1	1. Describe the two types of review that you can use to increase retention.	Immediate review is done right after reading while the information is still fresh in your mind. Periodic review is done at a later time to refresh your recall of the material.
Goal 2	2. What other strategies or methods can be used to increase your recall?	Other retention strategies include • intent to remember • organization/categorization • association • use of sensory modes • visualization • mnemonic devices
Goal 3	3. What is the SQ3R system for reading and learning?	The SQ3R system is a method for increasing reading efficiency and flexibility that directly enhances your retention. The steps are • survey • question • read • recite • review
Goal 4	4. What should be considered when adapting the SQ3R system?	To make the best use of the SQ3R method, you should adapt it to suit both the material you are reading and how you learn best. You should consider the reading material's structure and content when adapting SQ3R. Also, you should make adjustments that incorporate the methods of learning that work best for you.
Goal 5	5. How can you learn specialized terminology?	Use the following strategies: • Keep a notebook of new terms. • Use context clues. • Use word parts. • Pronounce each term. • Use the glossary. • Use a subject-area dictionary.
Goal 6	6. What is the difference between memorizing and learning?	Memorizing is the mechanical storage of information, whereas learning involves higher-level thinking skills.

READING SELECTION 15 PSYCHOLOGY

Problem Solving

Josh R. Gerow
From *Essentials of Psychology*

About the Reading

TEXTBOOK
EXCERPT

This reading selection is taken from a chapter in an introductory psychology text-book. The textbook's title, Essentials of Psychology, *implies that the text will cover only the most important (essential) topics in the discipline.*

Planning Your Reading Strategy*

Directions: *Activate your thinking by previewing the reading (see the Need to Know box on page 64) and answering the following questions.*

____ 1. Based on your preview, to which information in the reading should you pay the closest attention?
   a. the process of defining and solving a problem
   b. the definition of anagrams and how they work
   c. the most efficient way to prepare breakfast
   d. the clear setting of goals

2. Will you be able to achieve full understanding of paragraph 16 if you do not know the meaning of the words *anagram* and *heuristic* in the first sentence? How will this affect your reading strategy?

3. Based on your preview of the reading, how quickly do you think you should read the selection? (Circle one.) Explain your answer.

   Very slowly   Slowly   At a moderate pace   Quickly   Very quickly

4. How would you define a problem? What are its characteristics? What steps do you follow in working through a problem?

1   Sometimes our goals are obvious, our present situation is clear, and how to get from where we are to where we want to be is obvious. In these cases, we really don't have a problem, do we? Say you want to have a nice breakfast. You have butter, eggs, bacon, and bread. You also have the implements needed to prepare these foods, and you know how to use them. You know that, for you, a nice breakfast would be two eggs over easy, three strips of fried bacon, and a piece of buttered toast. With little hesitation, you can engage in the appropriate behaviors to reach your goal.

2   A problem exists when there is a discrepancy between one's present state and one's perceived goal, *and* there is no readily apparent way to get from one to the other. In situations where the

* The Scorecard on p. 363 enables you to compute your reading rate. In order to do so, be sure to record your starting time in the Scorecard box before you begin reading.

path to goal attainment is not clear or obvious, you need to engage in problem-solving behaviors.

3   A problem situation has three major components: (1) an *initial state,* which is the situation as it is perceived to exist at the moment; (2) a *goal state,* which is the situation as the problem solver would like it to be; and (3) *routes or strategies* for getting from the initial state to the goal state.

4   In addition, psychologists make a distinction between well-defined and ill-defined problems. Well-defined problems are those in which both the initial state and the goal state are clearly defined. "What English word can be made from the letters *teralbay*?" We recognize this question as presenting a problem. We understand the question, have some ideas about how we might go about answering it, and surely we'll know when we have succeeded. "How do you get home from campus if you discover that your car won't start?" We know our initial state, we'll know when we have reached our goal (when we are at home), but we have to undertake a new or different way to get there.

5   Most of the problems that we face every day, though, are of the ill-defined variety. We don't have a clear idea of what we are starting with, nor are we able to identify a ready solution. "What should my college major be?" Many high school seniors (and some college seniors) do not even know what their options are. They have few ideas about how to find out about possible college majors. And once they have selected a major, they are not at all sure that their choice was the best one—which may be why so many college students change their majors so often.

6   Because ill-defined problems usually involve many variables that are difficult to define, much less control, psychologists tend to study problems that are at least reasonably well-defined.

■ Problem Representation

7   Once we realize that we're faced with a problem, the first thing we need to do is to put it in a form that allows us to think about it in terms that we can work with. We need to come up with a way to *represent* the problem in our own minds, interpreting it so that the initial state and the goal state are clear to us. We also need to note if there are restrictions on how we can go about seeking solutions. In short, we need to understand the nature of the problem. We need to make the problem meaningful, relating it to information we have available in our memories.

8   Finding the best way to represent a problem is not a simple task. Very often, problem representation is *the* stumbling block to finding a solution. Once you realize that you are faced with a problem, your first step should be to represent it in a variety of ways. Eliminate any inessential information. Relate the problem to other problems of a similar type that you have solved before. Having done so, if the solution is still not obvious, you may have to develop some strategy to find a solution. We now turn to how one might go about generating possible solutions.

■ Problem-Solving Strategies

9   Once you have represented the initial state of a problem and have a clear idea of what an acceptable goal might be, you still have to figure out how to get to your goal. Even after you have adequately represented a problem, how to go about solving it may not be readily apparent. You might spend a few minutes guessing wildly at a solution, but soon you'll have to settle on some strategy. In this context, a strategy is a systematic plan for generating possible solutions that can be tested to see if they are correct. The main advantage of cognitive strategies appears to be that they permit the problem solver to exercise some degree of control over the task at hand. They allow individuals to choose the skills and knowledge that they will bring to bear on any particular problem. There are several possible strategies that one might choose. In this section, we'll consider two different types of strategies—algorithms and heuristics.

10   An algorithm is a problem-solving strategy that guarantees that you will arrive at a solution. It will involve systematically exploring and evaluating all possible solutions until the correct one is found. It is sometimes referred to as a *generate-test* strategy because one generates hypotheses about potential solutions and then tests each one in turn. Because of their speed of computation, most computer programs designed to solve problems use algorithmic strategies.

11   Simple anagram problems (letters of a word presented in a scrambled fashion) can be solved using an algorithm. "What English word has been scrambled to make *uleb*?" With sufficient patience, you systematically can rearrange these four letters until you hit on a correct solution: *leub, lueb, elub, uleb, buel, beul, blue!* There it is, *blue*. With only four letters to deal with, finding a solution generally doesn't take long—there are only 24 possible arrangements of four letters ($4 \times 3 \times 2 \times 1 = 24$).

12   On the other hand, consider the anagram composed of eight letters that we mentioned earlier: *teralbay*. There are 40,320 possible combinations of these eight letters—$8 \times 7 \times 6 \times 5 \times 4 \times 3 \times 2 \times 1 = 40,320$. Unless your system for moving letters around just happens to start in a good place, you could spend a lot of time before finding a combination that produces an English word. If we were dealing with a 10-letter word, there would be 3,628,800 possible combinations to check.

13   Imagine that you go to the supermarket to find just one item: a small jar of horseradish. You're sure the store has horseradish, but you have no idea where to find it. One plan would be to systematically go up and down every aisle of the store, checking first the top shelf, then the second, then the third, until you spied the horseradish. This strategy will work *if* the store really does carry horseradish *and if* you search carefully. There must be a better way to solve such problems. We could use some heuristic strategy.

14   A heuristic strategy is an informal, rule-of-thumb method for generating and testing problem solutions. Heuristics are more economical strategies than algorithms. When one uses a heuristic, there is no guarantee of success. On the other hand, heuristics are usually less time-consuming than algorithm strategies and lead toward goals in a logical, sensible way.

15   A heuristic strategy for finding horseradish in a supermarket might take you to different sections in the store in the order you believed to be most reasonable. You might start with spices, and you'd be disappointed. You might look among the fresh vegetables. Then, upon recalling that horseradish needs to be refrigerated, you go to the dairy case, and there you'd find the horseradish. You would not have wasted your time searching the cereal aisle or the frozen food section—which you might have done if you tried an algorithmic search. Another, more reasonable, heuristic would be to ask an employee where the horseradish is kept.

16   If you have tried the *teralbay* anagram problem, you probably used a heuristic strategy.

To do so, you rely on your knowledge of English. You seriously consider only those letter combinations that you know occur frequently. You generate and test the most common combinations first. You just don't worry much about the possibility that the solution may contain a combination like *brty*. Nor do you search for a word with an *aae* string in it. You explore words that end in *able*, because you know these to be fairly common. But that doesn't work. What about *br* words? No, that doesn't work either. How about words with the combination *tray* in them? *Traybeal?* No. *Baletray?* No. "Oh! Now I see it: betrayal."

Examining Reading Selection 15*

Checking Your Vocabulary

Directions: *Use context, word parts, or a dictionary, if necessary, to determine the meaning of each word as it is used in the reading.*

___ 1. discrepancy (paragraph 2)
   a. condition
   b. option
   c. signal
   d. disagreement

___ 2. components (paragraph 3)
   a. difficulties
   b. road blocks
   c. routes
   d. parts

___ 3. variables (paragraph 6)
   a. differences
   b. solutions
   c. factors
   d. restrictions

___ 4. inessential (paragraph 8)
   a. critical
   b. descriptive
   c. unimportant
   d. inaccurate

___ 5. cognitive (paragraph 9)
   a. mental
   b. physical
   c. random
   d. representational

Checking Your Comprehension

Directions: *Select the best answer.*

___ 6. This reading is primarily concerned with
   a. types of problems.
   b. the heuristics of problem solving.
   c. the process of problem solving.
   d. algorithms and heuristics.

___ 7. The main point of this reading is that problem solving
   a. depends largely on intuition.
   b. is a random process.
   c. is a systematic, logical process.
   d. varies according to an individual's cognitive style.

___ 8. According to the reading, a problem can best be defined as
   a. being unable to make reasonable choices.
   b. an unresolved or undefinable issue.
   c. a conflict among strategies.
   d. a discrepancy between present state and goal state.

___ 9. An algorithmic strategy is a process of
   a. brainstorming possible solutions.
   b. generating and testing all possible solutions.
   c. distinguishing initial state from goal state.
   d. devising a systematic plan for problem solving.

*Writing About the Reading questions appear in the Instructor's Manual.

____10. This textbook excerpt focuses primarily on
- a. differences.
- b. processes.
- c. solutions.
- d. causes.

Thinking Critically

____11. A heuristic strategy differs from an algorithmic solution in that
- a. an algorithmic solution does not guarantee a solution.
- b. a heuristic system explores fewer possible solutions.
- c. a heuristic strategy is more systematic.
- d. an algorithmic strategy is less time-consuming.

____12. Searching for your lost car keys by checking places where you usually place them is an example of
- a. problem representation.
- b. an ill-defined problem.
- c. an algorithmic solution.
- d. a heuristic solution.

____13. Which of the following words best describes the author's attitude toward his subject?
- a. casual
- b. respectful
- c. indifferent
- d. serious

____14. The writer relies on which of the following to explain his ideas to the reader?
- a. examples
- b. comparisons
- c. statistics
- d. personal experiences

____15. Assume the woman in the photograph on page 360 is shopping for the most nutritious brand of a particular product. What does the photograph illustrate about problem-solving?
- a. collecting inessential information
- b. using an anagram
- c. using an algorithm
- d. pursing an ill-defined problem

Questions for Discussion

1. Give an example of a well-defined problem faced by the government today. Explain a strategy that could be used to resolve it.

2. Discuss why a heuristic solution to a problem you currently have is more economical than an algorithmic solution.

3. Think about a problem you've had with transportation. How could it have been solved using an algorithmic strategy? How could it have been solved using a heuristic strategy?

Scorecard

Selection 15:   1,510 words

Finishing Time: _____ _____ _____
                   HR.   MIN.   SEC.

Starting Time: _____ _____ _____
                   HR.   MIN.   SEC.

Reading Time: _____ _____
                          MIN.   SEC.

WPM Score: _____

Comprehension Score: for Items 6–15
Number Right: _____ × 10 = _____%

Assessing Your Reading Strategy

1. How would you rate your comprehension of the reading? (Circle one.)

    Excellent   Good   Fair   Poor

2. Did you find your reading strategy effective?   Yes   No

3. Suppose you were given an assignment to read a similar selection to the one you just read. Based on your experience with this selection, how would you adjust your reading strategy (if at all)?

READING SELECTION 16   SOCIOLOGY

May I Take Your Order, Please?

William E. Thompson and Joseph V. Hickey

About the Reading

TEXTBOOK
EXCERPT

This selection is the chapter-opening story from a sociology textbook, Society in Focus. *Many textbooks begin each chapter with an interesting story to introduce the key concepts that will be discussed in that chapter.*

MyReadingLab™ *The exercises following this selection can be completed online at myreadinglab.com*

Planning Your Reading Strategy*

Directions: *Activate your thinking by previewing the reading (see the Need to Know box on page 64) and answering the following questions.*

____ 1. Based on your preview, which two concepts is the reading intended to illustrate?
    a. marketing and public relations
    b. economics and sociocultural evolution
    c. ethnic sensitivity and environmentalism
    d. glocalization and grobalization

____ 2. Which two words or phrases in the first paragraph are clues to the authors' attitude toward their topic?
    a. fast-food restaurant, American culture in general
    b. the world today, global corporation
    c. programmed worker greetings, standardized formula
    d. McDonald's, Starbucks

3. Which word in paragraph 6 is a synonym for "opening story"?

_____

4. Based on your preview of the reading, how quickly do you think you should read the selection? (Circle one.) Explain your answer.

Very slowly   Slowly   At a moderate pace   Quickly   Very quickly

---

"America is the only culture that went from barbarism to decadence without civilization in between."
—Oscar Wilde

1   The request, "May I take your order, please?" is familiar to everyone in the world today. Obviously you are in a McDonald's, Burger King, Starbucks, or some other fast-food restaurant, where global corporations have programmed worker greetings, worker routines, and even worker attitudes to a standardized formula. You can be assured that the menu, the food, and the service will be the same no matter where the particular restaurant is located. Many people believe that McDonald's, for instance, is such a potent source of American fast-food culture and American culture in general that when it transplants itself overseas "American values" are widely adopted.

Thompson, William E.; Hickey, Joseph V., Society In Focus: An Introduction To Sociology, Census Update, *7th Ed., © 2012. Reprinted and electronically reproduced by permission of Pearson Education Inc., Upper Saddle River, NJ.*

*The Scorecard on p. 369 enables you to compute your reading rate. In order to do so, be sure to record your starting time in the Scorecard box before you begin reading.

McDonald is known throughout much of the region as "Uncle McDonald," a wise and understanding figure-not unlike similar figures in traditional Chinese folklore. Another novel twist that reflects a long-standing East Asian value is the nature of staff-customer interactions. In Beijing, for example, each restaurant has between 5 and 10 female "receptionists" who talk to parents and care for their children during their visits. One receptionist in Beijing had over 100 young friends. Moreover, borrowing from traditions that value close and long-term personal interactions in business and elsewhere, the receptionists' care goes well beyond company time. Many visit children's homes and classes after work, send cards on their birthdays and holidays, and otherwise become part of their families. Because of this, they are called "Aunt McDonald" in many parts of East Asia.

3   Even in the United States, McDonald's makes cultural adaptations for local purposes. For example, Jennifer Talwar found that in places like Chinatown and the Little Dominican Republic in New York City. McDonald's combines rigid standardization with remarkable flexibility to market its products. In Chinatown, for example, consumer marketing strategies present McDonald's as an "authentic Chinese" fast-food restaurant. The sign outside is in Chinese, a two-story Chinese arch inside is painted red for good luck, and the "front wall displays four Chinese characters that symbolize long life, happy marriage, lots of children, and lucky money." Mandarin Chinese is spoken in addition to English, and, just as in Beijing, China, the outlet hires "hostesses" to greet families and entertain children. "Cultural managers" represent the neighborhood, and most workers are from China, although a "United Nations staff" (from more than a dozen countries including Malaysia, the Dominican Republic,

2   In effect, this thesis holds that no matter the cultural setting, the arrival of the Golden Arches inevitably leads to cultural homogenization in the American model, a trend that is supposedly sweeping the globe. Once again, however, things may not be what they seem. Although McDonald's relies on standardization and emphasizes that a person always knows what to expect from a McDonald's anywhere in the world, local franchises adapt to local cultural customs, biases, and traditions. Today, virtually all East Asian McDonald's restaurants have added features to accommodate local cultures. Teriyaki burgers are popular from Japan to China, and local owner-operators are the norm. Likewise, Ronald

Honduras, and Togo, Africa) pool their talents to portray McDonald's as an "American and Chinese eatery"—all in one. Likewise, select "Chinese values," including teamwork and loyalty, are emphasized at some restaurants; "United Nations" potluck dinners are held to promote "organizational unity"; and employees—regardless of ethnicity—"are more apt to be dismissed or suspended . . . for having poor school grades than for refusing to work when not scheduled."

4   Restaurants in the Little Dominican Republic demonstrate similar sensitivity to ethnic heritage and community life, and the McDonald's in the very heart of the neighborhood has almost completely reinvented itself as a "Latino-American" experience. Spanish is spoken almost exclusively by workers and customers alike, and, ironically, McDonald's has redefined itself as a place of "leisure" rather than "fast food" where Dominicans and other Latinos can munch on a chicken fajita and chat with friends for long periods. Talwar remarks that she "stood on line at one McDonald's in Little Dominican Republican for 20 minutes . . . and then waited another 10 minutes for a table." Employees have been instructed to say "permisso," not "excuse me," and "honor and respect" have infiltrated worker-customer relations, with some managers instructing employees on how to tactfully "defend themselves" against rude customer behavior and insults.

5   Not to be outdone by its rival, Burger King launched an advertising and marketing campaign in 2009 in which it introduced "Whopper virgins"—people who lived in remote tribes and villages around the world and had never seen or heard of McDonald's or Burger King—to their menu staple, the Whopper. People were asked to sample a Big Mac and a Whopper for the first time and choose which one they preferred. Perhaps one of the most telling responses came from an Inuit tribe member, who indicated that

both were okay, but he much preferred the taste of seal meat.

6   This opening vignette not only illustrates the impact of globalization on society and culture, but also demonstrates an example of **glocalization**, the interdependence of the global and the local, resulting in standardized values producing unique outcomes in different geographic areas and cultural settings. It also reflects what George Ritzer calls **grobalization**, or the imperialistic ambitions of nations, corporations, and organizations and their desire to impose themselves on various societies and cultures.

■ Glocalization
The interdependence of the global and the local, resulting in standardized values producing unique outcomes in different geographic areas and cultural settings.

■ Grobalization
The imperialistic ambitions of nations, corporations, and organizations and their desire to impose themselves on various societies and cultures.

7   Because of the media and globalization, few people are unaware of the extraordinary diversity of societies and cultures in the world today. They can be seen in television shows, movies, and on the Internet on any given day. Or they can be experienced during a walk through almost any large city and many small towns throughout the world. Far-reaching global changes have tremendous local impact, and today few people have much difficulty comprehending how different cultures and societies affect others. However, most of us find it much harder to understand how culture and society affect our thoughts and behaviors. Even seasoned teachers of culture acknowledge

Today, the foods and cultures of the world are so common in cities that few people notice the extraordinary cultural diversity all around them. What type of cultural diversity do you notice in your home community?

that they have learned a great deal about their own values and cultural assumptions by teaching in undergraduate classrooms in diverse cities such as Hong Kong, New York City, London, and others. This is because culture is so pervasive and taken for granted that it rarely enters into our consciousness. However, more is involved: If asked, most people around the world would probably agree that their societies and cultural beliefs and values are either "natural" or the "best."

Examining Reading Selection 16

 **Complete** this **Exercise** at **myreadinglab.com**

Checking Your Vocabulary

Directions: *Use context, word parts, or a dictionary, if necessary, to determine the meaning of each word as it is used in the reading.*

_____ 1. potent (paragraph 1)
  a. pleasant
  b. hesitant
  c. powerful
  d. private

_____ 2. novel (paragraph 2)
  a. unique
  b. public
  c. similar
  d. single

_____ 3. infiltrated (paragraph 4)
  a. escaped
  b. passed into
  c. reversed
  d. regulated

_____ 4. launched (paragraph 5)
  a. left
  b. practiced
  c. lessened
  d. began

_____ 5. staple (paragraph 5)
  a. paper fastener
  b. basic item
  c. resource
  d. display

Checking Your Comprehension

Directions: *Select the best answer.*

___ 6. This reading focuses primarily on
   a. competition between fast-food restaurants.
   b. standardized training for restaurant workers.
   c. cultural adaptations by fast-food restaurants.
   d. American values in fast-food restaurants.

___ 7. The statement that best expresses the main idea of this selection is
   a. "McDonald's . . . is such a potent source of American fast-food culture and American culture in general that when it transplants itself overseas 'American values' are widely adopted."
   b. "No matter the cultural setting, the arrival of the Golden Arches inevitably leads to cultural homogenization in the American model."
   c. "McDonald's relies on standardization and emphasizes that a person always knows what to expect from a McDonald's anywhere in the world."
   d. "Local franchises adapt to local cultural customs, biases, and traditions."

___ 8. The McDonald's restaurants in Beijing feature "receptionists" who
   a. take food orders and deliver them to customers' homes.
   b. promote company loyalty through potluck dinners.
   c. greet parents and care for their children during visits.
   d. instruct employees on how to handle rude customers.

___ 9. The main idea of paragraph 3 is that, in the United States, McDonald's
   a. markets itself in Chinatown as a Chinese restaurant.
   b. may fire its employees for having poor grades in school.
   c. hires people from more than a dozen countries.
   d. adapts to the cultures of local communities.

___ 10. In the Little Dominican Republic, McDonald's reflects the local ethnic community by
   a. not allowing employees to speak English.
   b. emphasizing fast service with no waiting in line.
   c. marketing itself as a place for leisurely Latino-American dining.
   d. using a character named "Uncle McDonald" in its advertisements.

Thinking Critically

___ 11. The authors wrote this selection in order to
   a. inform readers about why American restaurants are successful overseas.
   b. argue that corporations should not impose themselves on other cultures.
   c. promote the use of local cultural customs by American corporations.
   d. describe the cultural adaptations made by global corporations.

___ 12. The authors' attitude toward the subject can best be described as
   a. sympathetic.
   b. objective.
   c. concerned.
   d. disapproving.

___13. The purpose of the photograph of a McDonald's employee (p. 365) is to illustrate
    a. the consistent image of McDonald's in other countries.
    b. the rejection of American values in other countries.
    c. differences between McDonald's and other fast-food restaurants.
    d. ethnic food choices at McDonald's restaurants overseas.

___14. One conclusion that can be made based on information in the reading is that
    a. McDonald's will probably discontinue its overseas restaurants.
    b. Ronald McDonald is not a popular figure in East Asian countries.

    c. McDonald's recognizes the marketing value of being culturally sensitive.
    d. most American fast-food restaurants are not willing to adapt to other cultures.

___15. The authors support their ideas primarily with
    a. facts and statistics.
    b. descriptions and examples.
    c. cause-effect relationships.
    d. their own observations.

Scorecard

Selection 16:   1,203 words

Finishing Time: _____ _____ _____
                  HR.   MIN.   SEC.

Starting Time: _____ _____ _____
                  HR.   MIN.   SEC.

Reading Time: _____ _____
                          MIN.   SEC.

WPM Score: _____

Comprehension Score: for Items 6–15
Number Right: _____ × 10 = _____%

Assessing Your Reading Strategy

1. How would you rate your comprehension of the reading? (Circle one.)
   Excellent   Good   Fair   Poor

2. Did you find your reading strategy effective?   Yes   No

3. Suppose you were given an assignment to read a similar selection to the one you just read. Based on your experience with this selection, how would you adjust your reading strategy (if at all)?

   _____

   _____

Writing About Reading Selection 16

Checking Your Vocabulary

Directions: *Complete each of the following items; refer to a dictionary if necessary.*

1. Define the word *standardized* (paragraph 1) and underline the words or phrases that provide a clue for its meaning.

   _____

2. Define the word *accommodate* (paragraph 2) and underline the words or phrases that provide a clue for its meaning.

   _____

3. Explain the meaning of the phrase "the norm" and how it is used in paragraph 2.

_____

_____

_____

_____

4. Describe the denotative and connotative meanings of the word *rival* in paragraph 5.

_____

_____

_____

5. Define the word *vignette* (paragraph 6) and underline the words or phrases that provide a clue for its meaning.

_____

6. Determine the meanings of the following words by using word parts:
   a. *transplants* (paragraph 1)

   _____

   b. *homogenization* (paragraph 2)

   _____

   _____

   c. *interactions* (paragraph 2)

   _____

   _____

   d. *reinvented* (paragraph 4)

   _____

   e. *interdependence* (paragraph 6)

   _____

   _____

Checking Your Comprehension

7. What is the main idea of this selection?

_____

_____

_____

_____

8. What are three adaptations that McDonald's made to their restaurants in the Little Dominican Republic?

_____

_____

_____

_____

_____

9. Who are "Whopper virgins" and why were they introduced?

_____

_____

_____

_____

_____

10. What is *glocalization*?

_____

_____

_____

_____

Thinking Critically

11. What is the purpose of the title?

_____

_____

12. Why do the authors say cultural homogenization is "a trend that is supposedly sweeping the globe?"

_____

_____

_____

_____

_____

_____

13. What traditional East Asian values are discussed in the selection?

_____

_____

_____

_____

14. What is the purpose of the photograph on page 367 of restaurants and storefronts?

_____

_____

_____

1. Have you ever visited an American fast-food restaurant in another country or in a strongly ethnic community? Describe any similarities and differences you observed during your visit.

2. Discuss the terms *glocalization* and *grobalization*. What positive or negative connotations can you find in the definitions of these terms?

3. Discuss what is meant by "cultural homogenization." What is good or bad about the idea?

4. How culturally diverse is your hometown or the community you are living in now? Do you notice marketing strategies that are directed to local ethnic groups?

think VISUALLY...

This Web site diagram appeared in a college health book in a chapter on nutrition. Why do you think it was included? Is it more effective than a sentence or two advising students to eat more vegetables?

Today's textbooks include plenty of diagrams, as well as other types of visuals—maps, graphs, charts, photographs, and infographics. To read textbooks effectively, be sure to pay attention to and learn from visuals. The purpose of this chapter is to equip you with visual literacy skills that will improve your textbook reading skills and your ability to interpret a wide variety of visual materials.

MyPlate, USDA.

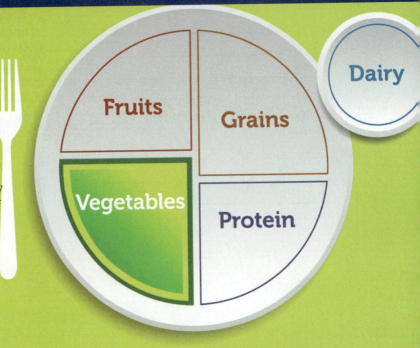

Fruits

Grains

Vegetables

Protein

Dairy

Choose**MyPlate**.gov

Learning GOALS

In this chapter, you will learn how to . . .

Goal 1 Understand the function of visuals

Goal 2 Read and interpret visuals

Goal 3 Integrate text and visuals

Goal 4 Read and interpret different types of visuals

Goal 5 Think critically about visuals

■ Why Visuals Are Used

Goal 1
Understand the function of visuals

Visuals are typically included in textbooks, resource materials, and classroom lectures for two main reasons: (1) to clarify complex information and (2) to help you interpret that information. Visuals serve a number of important functions that enhance your reading and learning efficiency.

Visuals Consolidate Information

Most visuals display information in a condensed, more easily accessible form than written material. Try this experiment. Look at Figure 9.1 and imagine presenting its information in sentence and paragraph form.

FIGURE 9.1   A SAMPLE VISUAL

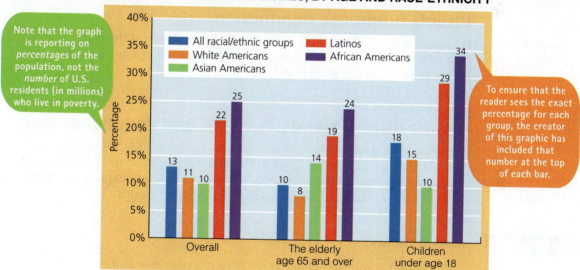

POVERTY IN THE UNITED STATES, BY AGE AND RACE-ETHNICITY

Note that the graph is reporting on *percentages* of the population, not the *number* of U.S. residents (in millions) who live in poverty.

To ensure that the reader sees the exact percentage for each group, the creator of this graphic has included that number at the top of each bar.

Source: Henslin, James M., *Sociology: A Down-To-Earth Approach: Core Concepts,* 3rd Ed., © 2009. Reprinted and electronically reproduced by permission of Pearson Education, Inc., Upper Saddle River, NJ.

The result might begin as follows:

The overall poverty rate for all racial/ethnic groups is 13 percent. For white Americans the rate is 11 percent; for Asian Americans the rate is 10 percent; for Latinos the rate is 22 percent; and for African Americans the rate is 25 percent. For the elderly, age 65 and over, the overall poverty rate is 10 percent. For elderly white Americans the rate is 8 percent; for Asian Americans the rate is 14 percent. For Latinos the rate is 19 percent, while for African Americans the rate is 24 percent.

You probably found the paragraph tedious to read. Certainly reading it is more time-consuming than studying the graph in Figure 9.1. Moreover, the graph presents the same information more concisely and in a form that clearly shows the relationships between the individual pieces of information.

Visuals Explain and Illustrate

In a human anatomy course, imagine trying to understand the digestive system without diagrams to assist you. Some graphics, especially drawings, diagrams, and flowcharts (all covered later in this chapter), explain an unfamiliar and complex object or process by showing the relationships among the various parts.

Visuals Dramatize Information

What could more clearly and dramatically illustrate the differences in levels of poverty faced by Latinos and African Americans as compared to other groups than the graph shown in Figure 9.1?

Visuals Display Trends, Patterns, and Variations

Graphics make it easy to see differences and changes. As a result, trends and patterns become clearer and more noticeable. For example, in Figure 9.1, you can clearly see that Latino and African American children experience higher levels of poverty than children in other racial/ethnic groups.

EXERCISE 9-1   **READING VISUALS**

Directions: *Locate one visual in one of your textbooks or in a newspaper (USA Today frequently includes numerous visuals). Identify which function(s) the visual fulfills.*

■ A Strategy for Reading and Interpreting Visuals

Goal 2
Read and interpret visuals

Because graphics clarify, summarize, or emphasize important facts, concepts, and trends, you need to study them closely. Following are some general suggestions that will help you get the most out of graphic elements in the material you read.

NEED TO KNOW How to Read Visuals

1. **Read the title or caption and legend.** The title tells you what situation or relationship is being described. The legend is the explanatory caption that may accompany the visual. The legend may also function as a key, indicating what particular colors, lines, or pictures mean. For example, in Figure 9.1, the legend shows the color bar associated with each ethnic group (red for Latinos, purple for African Americans, and so on).

2. **Determine how the visual is organized.** If you are working with a table, note the column headings. For a graph, notice the labels on the vertical axis (the top-to-bottom line on the left side of the graph) and the horizontal axis (the left-to-right line at the bottom of the graph). In Figure 9.1, for example, the vertical axis shows percentages from 0 percent to 40 percent.

3. **Determine what variables (quantities or categories) the visual illustrates.** Identify the pieces of information that are being compared or the relationship that is being shown. Note any symbols and abbreviations used.

4. **Determine the scale or unit of measurement.** Note how the variables are measured. For example, does a graph show expenditures in dollars, thousands of dollars, or millions of dollars?

5. **Identify the trend(s), pattern(s), or relationship(s) the visual is intended to show.** The following sections discuss this step in greater detail.

6. **Read any footnotes and identify the source.** Footnotes, printed at the bottom of a graph or chart, indicate how the data were collected, explain what certain numbers or headings mean, and describe the statistical procedures used. Identifying the source is helpful in assessing the reliability of the data.

7. **Make a brief summary note.** In the margin, jot a brief note about the key trend or pattern emphasized by the visual. Writing will crystallize the idea in your mind, and your note will be useful when you review.

FLEXIBILITY TIP
Graphs often contain large amounts of information and many colors. They can be overwhelming. Be sure to read the title and caption first to gain insight into the graph's purpose. Then focus on one element (color, variable, line, or bar) at a time to gain a better understanding of the graph's details.

■ Integrating Text and Visuals

Goal 3
Integrate text and visuals

In both textbooks and reference sources, most visuals do not stand alone; they have corresponding printed text that may introduce, explain, summarize, or analyze the visual. Be sure to consider the text and the visual together to get their complete meaning. Below are some guidelines for integrating text and visuals.

NEED TO KNOW How to Integrate Text and Visuals

1. **Notice the type and number of visuals included in the material as you preview the chapter** (see Chapter 2, p. 64).

2. **Refer to the visual when the author directs you to.** Writers tell you when they want you to look at the visual by saying "See Figure 17.2" or by introducing the visual with a phrase like "Table 12.7 displays. . . ."

3. **Read the visual, using the previously listed steps.**

4. **Move back and forth between the text and visual.** As you study the visual, refer back to the text as needed, following the explanation of the visual provided by the author. This technique is particularly effective with illustrations and diagrams, which often show the meaning or function of particular terms or parts.

5. **Determine why the author included the visual.** Ask these questions:

   • What am I supposed to learn from this visual?
   • Why was it included?
   • What new information does the visual contain?
   • On what topic(s) does the visual provide more detail or further explanation?

LEARNING STYLE TIPS

If you tend to be a . . .	Then study visuals by . . .
Spatial learner	Learning the content of the visual by looking away and visualizing it
Verbal learner	Writing sentences that summarize what the visual shows

■ Types of Visuals

Goal 4
Read and interpret different types of visuals

Many types of visuals are used in textbooks. In addition to describing some type of relationship or illustrating a particular point, each type is intended to achieve a particular purpose. By *reading* the visual, you view the information it contains. By *interpreting* the visual, you look more closely at the information and identify trends, patterns, or key ideas.

EFFICIENCY TIP
In textbooks, photos are used in two ways. Either they contain content that helps you better understand the concepts, or they are used "cosmetically" to make the page look more appealing. When reading and examining photos, determine which photos offer insight into the topic and which ones are purely decorative.

Photographs

Photographs are included in texts for a variety of reasons:

- **To introduce a new idea.**
- **To add interest or to help you visualize an event, concept, or feeling.**
- **To provide an example of a concept.** For example, photographs in a biology textbook may be used to illustrate variation among species.
- **To create emotional responses or provide perspective.** For example, a photograph of a malnourished child may help readers visualize the conditions of poverty and sympathize with its victims.

When studying a photograph, read the caption. It may provide clues to the importance or meaning of the photograph. The purpose of the photograph in Figure 9.2, taken from a psychology textbook, could be unclear without the caption. This caption helps you understand how and why peer groups form and how the members of these groups act.

FIGURE 9.2   A SAMPLE PHOTOGRAPH AND CAPTION

What is the "dress code" for females?

What is the "dress code" for males?

Being a social outcast as an adolescent is often seen as a fate worse than death, resulting in groups of teen clones all anxious to fit in by talking, dressing, and acting like their peers. For many parents, the possibility of negative peer pressure luring their child into a world of alcohol, drugs, and casual sex is a constant source of worry. Research suggests that these fears are well-founded—teenagers of the same friendship group usually indulge in similarly risky behaviors, and teens who start smoking usually do so because one of their friends offered them a cigarette or made it look cool. But peer pressure can also have positive effects. Conforming to a peer group can help adolescents form a sense of identity. And peer groups of ambitious students can meet to do homework together and encourage one another to do well academically.

FIGURE 9.3 A SAMPLE PHOTOGRAPH AND CAPTION

What do you think this in-group's social position is within its school? Are these students likely to be popular?

An *in-group* is a group with which people identify and have a sense of belonging. In contrast, an *out-group* is a group that people do not identify with and consider less worthy and desirable than their own. Sports fans provide excellent examples of in-group and out-group behavior. Do you have a favorite sports team to which you feel allegiance and, hence, a sense of belonging?

EXERCISE 9-2

INTERPRETING A PHOTOGRAPH

Directions: *Study the photograph in Figure 9.3 and answer the following questions.*

1. What is this photograph intended to illustrate?

_____

_____

2. What does it show that a verbal description could not?

_____

_____

Maps

There are two types of maps: locational and thematic. **Locational maps** show the exact positions of physical objects: countries, cities, states, rivers, mountains, and so forth. You will find these maps in history, astronomy, geography, archaeology, and anthropology textbooks. To read these types of maps, concentrate on each item's position in relation to other objects. For instance, when referring to a map of our solar system in an astronomy text, concentrate on the locations of planets relative to one another, of the planets to the sun and to their moons, and so forth.

Thematic maps provide statistical or factual information about a particular area or region. For example, a color-coded map of the United States may be used to show average income levels within each state. A map of Africa may be coded to represent each country's form of government.

When reading thematic maps, look for trends or patterns. For example, when studying a map of the United States showing average income levels, you should look for regional clusters or patterns. Are incomes higher in the North or South? Are they higher in highly populated states such as New York and California or in lower-population states such as Montana or Idaho? When reading a map of Africa showing types of government, you should look for most and least common forms and try to discover regional similarities. Do the northern or eastern African countries, for example, have similar forms of government?

FIGURE 9.4   A SAMPLE MAP

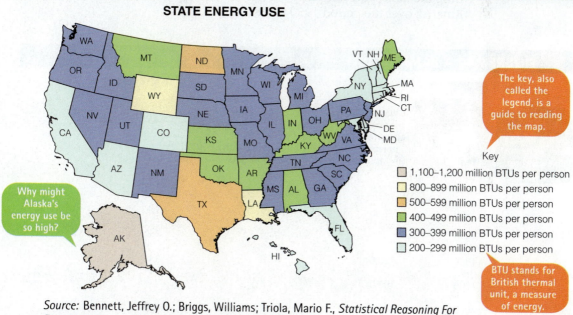

STATE ENERGY USE

The key, also called the legend, is a guide to reading the map.

Why might Alaska's energy use be so high?

Key
- ▢ 1,100–1,200 million BTUs per person
- ▢ 800–899 million BTUs per person
- ▢ 500–599 million BTUs per person
- ▢ 400–499 million BTUs per person
- ▢ 300–399 million BTUs per person
- ▢ 200–299 million BTUs per person

BTU stands for British thermal unit, a measure of energy.

Source: Bennett, Jeffrey O.; Briggs, Williams; Triola, Mario F., *Statistical Reasoning For Everyday Life*, 2nd Ed., © 2003. Reprinted and electronically reproduced by permission of Pearson Education Inc., Upper Saddle River, NJ.

EXERCISE 9-3   **INTERPRETING A MAP**

Directions: *Study the map in Figure 9.4 (p. 379) and answer the following questions.*

1. What is the purpose of this map?

2. What type of map is this?

_____

3. Which state uses the largest amount of energy per person? Which use the least?

_____

_____

Tables

A **table** displays facts, figures, statistics, and other data in a condensed orderly sequence for convenience of reference and clarity. The information in tables is classified or organized in rows and columns so that the data can easily be compared. Figure 9.5, a table taken from a sociology text, displays data about the number of television sets in American households. By scanning the table, you can easily see how ownership of televisions has grown in America over the period 1950–2008.

FIGURE 9.5   A SAMPLE TABLE

TABLE 1.2   Television Sets in American Households

In the early days of TV, which households were most likely to own televisions?

List three possible reasons why 100% of U.S. households do not own at least one TV set.

How is it possible for a household to own 2.8 television sets?

Year	Television Sets in Homes (in Millions)	Percentage of Households with Television Sets	Number of Television Sets per Household
1950	3.9	9.0	1.01
1960	45.8	87.1	1.13
1970	81.0	94.9	1.39
1980	128.0	97.9	1.68
1990	193.0	98.2	2.00
2000	245.0	98.2	2.40
2003	260.0	98.2	2.40
2004	268.0	98.2	2.5
2005	287.0	98.2	2.6
2008	301.0	98.2	2.8

Source: Adapted from Table 1090, U.S. Bureau of the Census Statistical Abstract of the United States 2011.

NEED TO KNOW How to Read Tables

Use the following steps when reading tables:

1. **Determine how the data are classified or divided. Look closely at column headings.**
2. **Make comparisons and look for trends.**
3. **Draw conclusions.**

EXERCISE 9-4   **INTERPRETING A TABLE**

Directions: *Answer the following questions based on the table shown in Figure 9.5.*

1. For what period has the percentage of American households with TV sets remained unchanged?

_____

2. In which year did the number of TV sets in American households exceed 300 million for the first time?

_____

3. The largest increase in the number of TV sets in American households took place between which two years?

_____

4. The percentage of households with television sets has not changed since which year?

_____

5. The number of television sets in an American household hit 2.0 for the first time in which year?

_____

Graphs

A **graph** clarifies the relationship between two or more sets of information. A graph often reveals a trend or pattern that is easily recognizable in visual form but is not as obvious when the data appear in list or paragraph form. Graphs are often divided into four categories: bar graphs, stacked bar graphs, line graphs, and circle graphs.

Bar Graphs

A **bar graph** compares quantities or amounts using bars of different lengths. Bar graphs are especially useful in showing changes that occur over time, and they are often included in textbooks to emphasize differences. The graph shown in Figure 9.6 displays the number of Internet users in various world regions. By glancing at the chart you can quickly determine that the largest number of the world's Internet users are found in Asia. However, you need to read the chart more closely to see that the world region with the largest percentage of Internet users is North America (at 73.9 percent). This means that 73.9 percent of the North American population uses the Internet, while only 18.5 percent of the Asian population uses the Internet.

When reading bar graphs, pay particular attention to differences in the lengths of the bars (which show data for the variables). Notice which variables have the largest and smallest values and try to think of reasons that account for the differences.

FIGURE 9.6   A SAMPLE BAR GRAPH

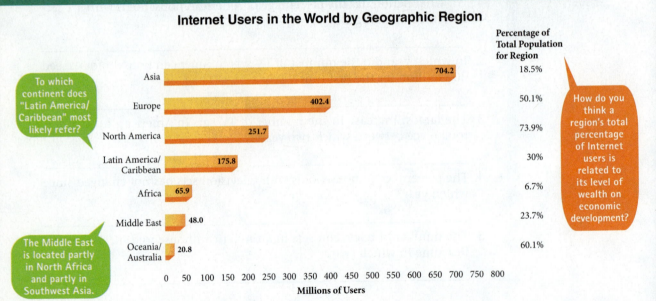

Internet Users in the World by Geographic Region

EXERCISE 9-5   **INTERPRETING A BAR GRAPH**

Directions: *Study the bar graph shown in Figure 9.6 and answer the following questions.*

1. What is the purpose of this graph?

_____

_____

2. Why might Africa have the smallest percentage of residents that use the Internet?

_____

_____

3. In which region is a person most likely to be an Internet user: Asia, the Middle East, or Oceania/Australia?

_____

4. In 2009, approximately how many people in the world were using the Internet?

_____

Stacked Bar Graphs

In a stacked bar graph, as shown in Figure 9.7, bars are placed on top of one another instead of being side by side.

A **stacked bar graph** is often used to emphasize whole/part relationships. That is, it shows the component parts that make up a total. Because stacked bar graphs are intended to make numerous comparisons, study the graph carefully to be sure you "see" all possible relationships. For example, in Figure 9.7 you can see differences in how immigration patterns into the United States have changed between the period 1971–1980 and 2008. From 1971–1980, 30 percent of immigrants to the United States came from Latin

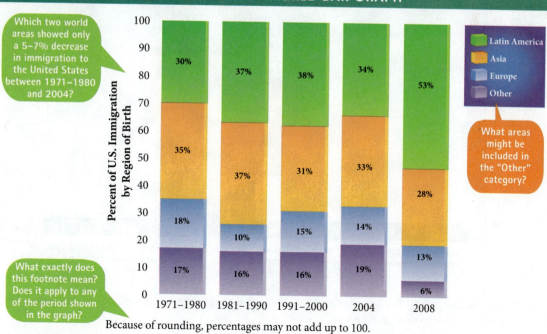

FIGURE 9.7 A SAMPLE STACKED BAR GRAPH

Which two world areas showed only a 5–7% decrease in immigration to the United States between 1971–1980 and 2004?

What areas might be included in the "Other" category?

What exactly does this footnote mean? Does it apply to any of the period shown in the graph?

Percent of U.S. Immigration by Region of Birth

Latin America
Asia
Europe
Other

1971–1980: 30%, 35%, 18%, 17%
1981–1990: 37%, 37%, 10%, 16%
1991–2000: 38%, 31%, 15%, 16%
2004: 34%, 33%, 14%, 19%
2008: 53%, 28%, 13%, 6%

Because of rounding, percentages may not add up to 100.

America, but by 2008 that number had increased to 53 percent. Every other group represented in the stacked bar graph had reduced immigration to the United States between the two periods.

Line Graphs

In **line graphs**, information is plotted along a vertical and a horizontal axis, with one or more variables plotted on each axis. A line graph connects points along these axes. A line graph usually includes more data points than a bar graph. Consequently, it is often used to present detailed and/or large quantities of information. If a line graph compares only two variables, then it consists of a single line. Often, however, line graphs compare two or more variables, in which case multiple lines are used. The line graph in Figure 9.8 shows how marital satisfaction (that is, how happy married people are) varies over the course of a long-term marriage.

Line graphs are often used to display data that occur in a sequence. You can see this in Figure 9.8, which displays a sequence starting with the early days of marriage without children and progressing through "empty nest" and the death of the first spouse.

FIGURE 9.8   A SAMPLE LINE GRAPH

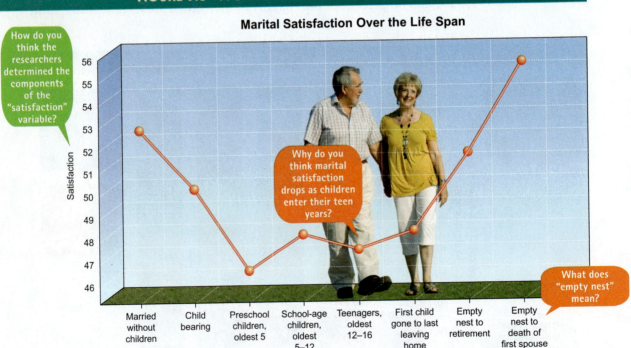

Source: Marital Satisfaction over the Family Life Cycle, by Rollins & Feldman, Vol. 32, No. 1. Copyright © 1970. Reproduced by permission of Wiley.

EXERCISE 9-6	INTERPRETING A LINE GRAPH

Directions: *Study the line graph shown in Figure 9.8 and answer the following questions.*

1. How many stages of married life are used to draw the line graph?

   _____

2. At which stage of life are married people the most satisfied and happy with their marriage?

   _____

3. At which stage of life do married people report the least satisfaction with their marriage?

   _____

4. What trends are illustrated by this graph?

   _____

   _____

   _____

   _____

   _____

Circle Graphs

A **circle graph**, also called a **pie chart**, is used to show whole/part relationships or to show how parts of a unit have been divided or classified. Circle graphs often emphasize proportions or emphasize the relative size or importance of various parts. For example, Figure 9.9 (p. 386) shows how people spend their time each day. Use the steps in the following Need to Know box to read circle graphs.

NEED TO KNOW **How to Read Circle Graphs**

1. **Determine the subject of the circle graph.** What is being divided into parts or slices?
2. **Notice how the subject is divided and how the slices are arranged.** Are they arranged from largest to smallest pieces? What labels or headings are used?
3. **Notice trends and patterns.** What does the circle graph reveal about the subject?

FIGURE 9.9   A SAMPLE CIRCLE GRAPH

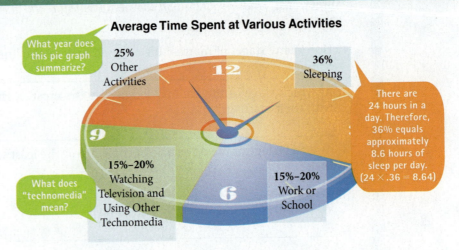

Average Time Spent at Various Activities

What year does this pie graph summarize?

25% Other Activities

36% Sleeping

There are 24 hours in a day. Therefore, 36% equals approximately 8.6 hours of sleep per day. (24 × .36 = 8.64)

What does "technomedia" mean?

15%–20% Watching Television and Using Other Technomedia

15%–20% Work or School

Source: Adapted from Bureau of Labor Statistics, Table 1.

EXERCISE 9-7

INTERPRETING A CIRCLE GRAPH

Directions: *Use the circle graph in Figure 9.9 to answer the following questions.*

1. Which activity do people spend the largest portion of their day doing?

   _____

2. On which two sets of activities do humans spend roughly equal time each day?

   _____

   _____

3. What activities might fall into the "Other Activities" category?

   _____

   _____

Diagrams

A **diagram** is a drawing that explains an object, idea, or process by outlining parts or steps or by showing the object's organization. Use the steps listed in the following box to read diagrams effectively.

NEED TO KNOW How to Read Diagrams

1. **Plan on switching back and forth between the diagram and the text paragraphs that describe it.**

2. **Get an overview.** Study the diagram and read the corresponding text paragraphs once to discover what the diagram is illustrating. Pay particular attention to the heading of the text-book section and the diagram's title.

3. **Read both the diagram and the text several more times, focusing on the details.** Examine each step or part and understand the progression from one step or part to the next.

4. **Try to redraw the diagram without referring to the original, including as much detail as possible.**

5. **Test your understanding and recall by explaining the diagram, step-by-step, using your own words.**

EFFICIENCY TIP

Many textbooks, especially those in the sciences, provide unlabeled diagrams on their Web sites. These can be a valuable study aid. You download the unlabeled diagram and write in the labels yourself. This can save you quite a bit of time because you don't have to redraw the entire diagram.

The diagram from a biology textbook in Figure 9.10 illustrates the structure of two common viruses. This diagram clearly explains their structures while showing their differences.

To read a diagram, focus on its purpose. What is it intended to illustrate? Why did the author include it? To study a diagram, cover the diagram and try to draw it and label its parts without referring to the text. This activity will provide a good test of whether or not you truly understand the process or concept illustrated.

FIGURE 9.10   A SAMPLE DIAGRAM

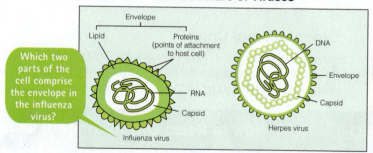

The Structure of Viruses

Viruses are extremely small particles that infect cells and cause many human diseases. Their basic structure includes an outer envelope, composed of lipid and protein, a protein capsid, and genetic material that is enclosed within the capsid.

Source: Mix, Michael C., *Biology: The Network of Life,* 1st Ed., © 1992. Reprinted and electronically reproduced by permission of Pearson Education Inc., Upper Saddle River, NJ.

EXERCISE 9-8   **INTERPRETING DIAGRAMS**

> **Directions:** *Study the diagram shown in Figure 9.10 (p. 387) and answer the following questions.*

1. What are the two viruses shown in the diagram?

   _____

2. Identify two similarities between the virus structures.

   _____

   _____

3. How does the genetic material contained within each virus differ?

   _____

4. Cover the diagram and try to draw each virus structure without referring to the text. Compare your drawing with the diagram. ■

EXERCISE 9-9   **DRAWING A DIAGRAM**

Working COLLABORATIVELY

> **Directions:** *Draw a diagram that illustrates one of the following, and then compare your diagram with those of several classmates.*

a. the registration process at your college

b. a process explained in one of your textbooks

c. the floor plan of one of your college's buildings

d. an object described in one of your textbooks ■

Charts

Two types of charts are commonly used in college textbooks: *organizational charts* and *flowcharts*. Each is intended to display a relationship, either quantitative (that is, based on numbers) or cause-effect.

Organizational Charts

An **organizational chart** divides an organization, such as a corporation, hospital, or university, into its administrative parts, staff positions, or lines of authority. Use the steps below to read organizational charts effectively.

NEED TO KNOW **How to Read Organizational Charts**

1. **Identify the organization being described.**
2. **Study its organization.** What do various boxes and arrows represent?
3. **Identify lines of authority and responsibility.** Determine who is in charge of what.

Figure 9.11 shows the organization of Atlantic College. It depicts how authority flows in this college.

FIGURE 9.11 A SAMPLE ORGANIZATIONAL CHART

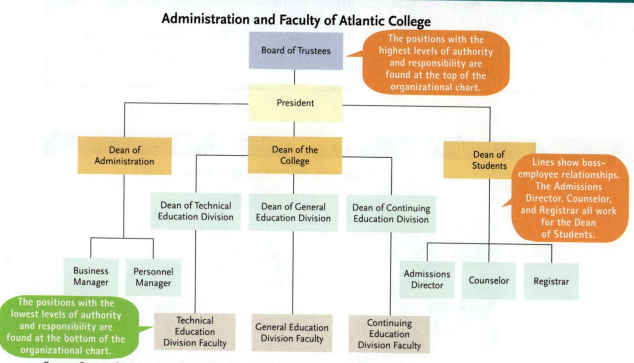

Source: Bovee, Courtland L.; Thill, John V., *Business Communication Today*, 9th Ed., © 2008. Reprinted and electronically reproduced by permission of Pearson Education, Inc., Upper Saddle River, NJ.

Flowcharts

A **flowchart** shows how a process or procedure works. Use the steps in the Need to Know box on the following page to read flowcharts effectively. Lines or arrows are used to indicate the direction (route or routes) through the procedure. Various shapes (boxes, circles, rectangles) enclose what is done at each stage or step. You could draw a flowchart, for example, to describe how to apply for a student loan or how to locate a malfunction in your car's electrical system. The flowchart shown in Figure 9.12 (see p. 390) shows how an invoice is processed by an accounting department.

NEED TO KNOW How to Read Flowcharts

1. **Decide what process the flowchart shows.**
2. **Next, follow the chart, using the arrows and reading each step.** Start at the top or far left of the chart.
3. **When you've finished, describe the process in your own words.** Try to draw the chart from memory without referring to the text. Compare your drawing with the chart and take note of anything you forgot or misplaced.

FIGURE 9.12 A SAMPLE FLOWCHART

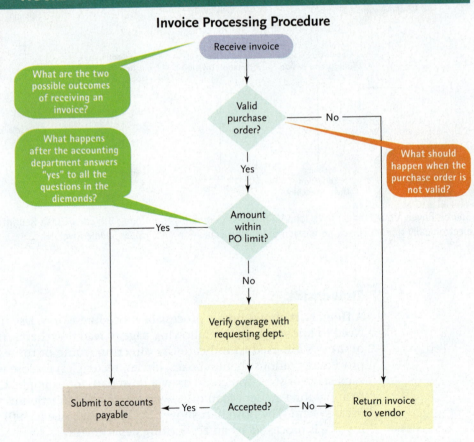

Source: Bovee, Courtland L.; Thill, John V., *Business Communication Today,* 9th Ed., © 2008. Reprinted and electronically reproduced by permission of Pearson Education, Inc., Upper Saddle River, NJ.

Infographics

Graphic designers are always looking for new, visually interesting ways to present information. In recent years, a new type of visual aid called an *infographic* has become popular. While the definition is not precise, **infographics** usually combine several types of visual aids into one, often merging photos with text, diagrams, or tables.

Unlike other graphics, infographics are sometimes designed to stand on their own; they do not necessarily repeat or summarize what is in the text. Consider the following excerpt from a health textbook:

Cigarette smoking adversely affects the health of every person who smokes, as well as the health of everyone nearby. Each day, cigarettes contribute to more than 1,000 deaths from cancer, cardiovascular disease, and respiratory disorders. In addition, tobacco use can negatively impact the health of almost every system in your body. Figure 9.13 summarizes some of the physiological and health effects of smoking.

—Rebecca J. Donatelle, *Health The Basics,* Green Edition, p. 241. Copyright © 2011 Benjamin Cummings, a division of Pearson Education, Inc.

Figure 9.13, on page 392, lists many effects of smoking that are *not* listed in the text. To understand this material, you must carefully read and learn the infographic, because the information cannot be found in the text. Use the suggestions in the following Need to Know box to read infographics effectively.

NEED TO KNOW **How to Read Infographics**

1. **Identify the subject.** What is the purpose of the infographic?
2. **Identify how you should follow the "flow" of the infographic.** Should you read it from top to bottom, left to right, clockwise or counterclockwise? Look for visual clues, such as arrows or headings, to determine where you should start.
3. **Examine how the artist has chosen to present the information.** That is, how is the infographic organized? Does it fit into any particular pattern?
4. **How do the words and pictures work together?** How close is the correspondence between the words and the visual elements?
5. **When you've finished, describe the infographic and its information in your own words.** Try to draw it from memory. Compare your drawing with the infographic and take note of anything you forgot or misplaced.

FIGURE 9.13   A SAMPLE INFOGRAPHIC

Effects of Smoking on Body and Health

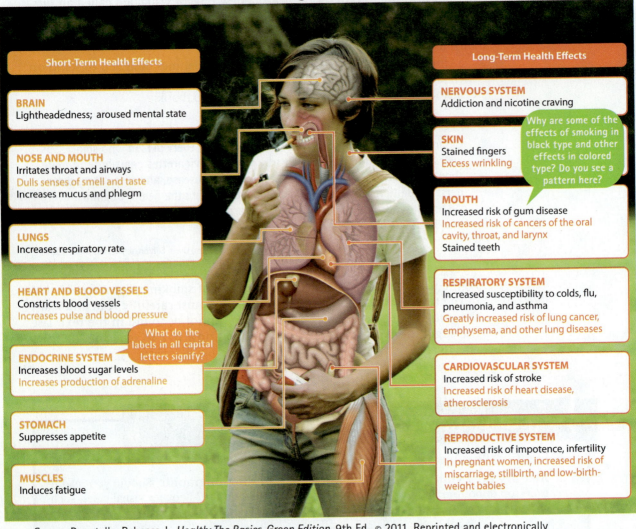

Short-Term Health Effects

BRAIN
Lightheadedness; aroused mental state

NOSE AND MOUTH
Irritates throat and airways
Dulls senses of smell and taste
Increases mucus and phlegm

LUNGS
Increases respiratory rate

HEART AND BLOOD VESSELS
Constricts blood vessels
Increases pulse and blood pressure

What do the labels in all capital letters signify?

ENDOCRINE SYSTEM
Increases blood sugar levels
Increases production of adrenaline

STOMACH
Suppresses appetite

MUSCLES
Induces fatigue

Long-Term Health Effects

NERVOUS SYSTEM
Addiction and nicotine craving

Why are some of the effects of smoking in black type and other effects in colored type? Do you see a pattern here?

SKIN
Stained fingers
Excess wrinkling

MOUTH
Increased risk of gum disease
Increased risk of cancers of the oral cavity, throat, and larynx
Stained teeth

RESPIRATORY SYSTEM
Increased susceptibility to colds, flu, pneumonia, and asthma
Greatly increased risk of lung cancer, emphysema, and other lung diseases

CARDIOVASCULAR SYSTEM
Increased risk of stroke
Increased risk of heart disease, atherosclerosis

REPRODUCTIVE SYSTEM
Increased risk of impotence, infertility
In pregnant women, increased risk of miscarriage, stillbirth, and low-birth-weight babies

Source: Donatelle, Rebecca J., *Health: The Basics, Green Edition,* 9th Ed., © 2011. Reprinted and electronically reproduced by permission of Pearson Education, Inc., Upper Saddle River, NJ.

EXERCISE 9-10   **INTERPRETING AN INFOGRAPHIC**

Directions: *Study Figure 9.13 and answer the following questions.*

1. What two major categories is the infographic exploring? How can you tell?

_____

_____

_____

2. Why do you think the artist has shown the body's interior anatomy superimposed on the photo of the woman?

_____

3. What are the effects of smoking on pregnant women?

_____

4. Are people who smoke more likely to gain weight or lose weight? How can you tell from the infographic?

_____

_____

5. Is smoking more likely to keep you looking young or to make you look older than you are? How can you tell from the infographic?

_____

_____

Cartoons

Cartoons are included in textbooks and other materials to make a point quickly or simply to lighten the text by adding a touch of humor about the topic at hand. Cartoons usually appear without a title or legend and there is usually no reference within the text to the cartoon.

Cartoons can make abstract ideas and concepts concrete and real. Pay close attention to cartoons, especially if you are a visual learner. They may help you remember ideas easily by serving as a recall clue that triggers your memory of related material.

The cartoon shown in Figure 9.14 (see p. 394) appears in a U.S. history textbook chapter titled "A Global Nation for the New Millennium." It appears in a text section that discusses the growth of the Internet. The cartoon effectively makes the point that you cannot always be sure whom you are communicating with on the Internet.

TECH SUPPORT Creating Visuals

Learning to present data in a visual format will help you in many college writing assignments (especially in social science and business courses) and will also be useful in workplace writing. It's easy to create simple bar graphs, line graphs, pie charts, and other basic graphs in most word processing and spreadsheet programs. For details, refer to the software manual or use the "Help" function of the program you are using. If your visual uses color, be sure that you have access to a color printer before printing a final copy of your paper to turn in to your professor.

FIGURE 9.14 A SAMPLE CARTOON

"On the Internet, nobody knows you're a dog."

EXERCISE 9-11   **SELECTING AN APPROPRIATE VISUAL**

Directions: *Indicate what type of visual(s) would be most useful in presenting each of the following sets of information.*

1. the effects of flooding on a Midwestern town

_____

2. the top five soft drink brands by percent of market share

_____

3. changes in yearly income per person from 2005 to 2010 in Germany, France, Japan, and the United States

_____

4. the suicide rates for various age groups

_____

5. the top 20 places to live in the United States and their average income, cost of housing, quality of schools, level of taxes, amount of crime, and availability of cultural and recreational activities

_____

6. government spending in 2010 and 2011 for payments to individuals, defense, interest on debt, grants to state and local governments, and all other spending

_____

7. the basic parts of a solar-powered automobile

_____

8. a description of how acid rain affects the environment

_____

9. the main areas of earthquakes and volcanic activity throughout the world

_____

10. book sales in each of ten categories for the years 2008 through 2010

_____

■ Thinking Critically: Considering Visuals

Goal 5
Think critically about visuals

Because writers choose the visual aids to accompany their text, they can select photos that reflect their opinions or beliefs. Consider the excerpt below and the accompanying photo and caption on page 396.

> **EXCERPT**
>
> Alcohol is the standard recreational drug of Americans. The average adult American drinks 25 gallons of alcoholic beverages per year—about 21 gallons of beer, 2 gallons of wine, and almost 2 gallons of whiskey, vodka, and other distilled spirits. Beer is so popular that Americans drink more of it than they do tea and fruit juices combined.
>
> Is alcohol bad for health? This beverage cuts both ways. One to two drinks a day for men and one drink for women reduces the risk of heart attacks, strokes, gallstones, and diabetes. Beyond these amounts, however, alcohol scars the liver, damages the heart, and increases the risk of breast cancer. It also increases the likelihood of birth defects. One-third of the 43,000 Americans who die each year in vehicle accidents are drunk. Each year, 700,000 Americans seek treatment for alcohol problems.

—Henslin, James, M., *Sociology: A Down-to-Earth Approach*, 10th Ed., © 2010. Reprinted and electronically reproduced by permission of Pearson Education, Inc., Upper Saddle River, NJ.

PHOTOGRAPH AND CAPTION

Everyone knows that drinking and driving don't mix. Here's what's left of a Ferrari in Newport Beach, California. The driver of the other car was arrested for drunk driving and vehicular manslaughter.

Note that the passage is very matter-of-fact. It talks about alcohol consumption in the United States, then summarizes the benefits and drawbacks of alcohol. But also note how intense the photo is. Just looking it at, you know that a horrible accident has occurred and someone has died. Thus the photo has the effect of making the author's message about the drawbacks of alcohol much stronger than his message about the benefits of alcohol. If the author had wanted to emphasize the benefits of alcohol, he would have perhaps included a photo showing friends enjoying a drink together with a caption emphasizing its positive effects when people drink it in moderation.

EXERCISE 9-12

THINKING CRITICALLY ABOUT VISUALS

Directions: *Refer to the visuals in this chapter to answer the following questions.*

1. Figure 9.3 (p. 378) portrays an in-group. Suppose the authors wanted to show a photo of an out-group instead. What type of photo might they have chosen to use?

   _____

   _____

2. How might a politician take advantage of the information found in Figure 9.7 (p. 383)?

   _____

   _____

   _____

3. How could Figure 9.8 (p. 384) be used to argue that married people should not have children?

_____

_____

4. Which part of Figure 9.9 (p. 386) makes it clear that the graph summarizes daily activities for both adults and children?

_____

_____

SELF-TEST SUMMARY

Goal 1	1. Why are visuals included in textbooks, classroom lectures, and other course materials?	Visuals serve a number of different functions in your courses. They are used to • consolidate information • explain and illustrate ideas • dramatize information • display trends, patterns, and variations
Goal 2	2. What steps should you take to read visuals more effectively?	To get the most from all types of visuals, you should begin by reading the title or caption and determining how the visual is organized; what symbols, abbreviations, and variables are presented; and what scale, values, or units of measurement are being used. You should then study the data to identify trends, patterns, and relationships within the visuals. Note any explanatory footnotes and the source of the data. Finally, making marginal summary notes will aid your further reading or review.
Goal 3	3. How can you integrate visuals with their corresponding printed text?	To integrate text and visuals • Be alert to the visuals as you preview chapters. • Refer to each visual when you are directed to. • Read the visual carefully. • Move back and forth between the text and visual frequently. • Figure out why the visual was included.
Goal 4	4. What types of visuals are commonly used in textbooks and academic sources?	Many types of visuals are used in conjunction with print materials. They include photographs, maps, tables, graphs, diagrams, charts, infographics, and cartoons.
Goal 5	5. How can you think critically about visuals?	Be aware of the images and other visuals that the author chooses to include with a piece of writing. They may provide clues regarding the author's attitude or opinion toward the topic.

READING SELECTION 17   HEALTH

Enhancing Your Body Image

Rebecca J. Donatelle

About the Reading

TEXTBOOK EXCERPT

This reading originally appeared in a health textbook, Access to Health. *Today, many experts consider "wellness" (the state of being in good physical and mental condition) to be just as important as "health" (the state of being free from illness or injury).*

Planning Your Reading Strategy*

Directions: *Activate your thinking by previewing the reading (see the Need to Know box on page 64) and answering the following questions.*

___ 1. Based on your preview, which of the following is *not* a factor in determining a person's body image?
   a. the body's ability to regulate neurotransmitters
   b. images in the media, often of celebrities
   c. the people with whom a person interacts
   d. the social class of the person's parents

2. Is it true that most people are born with a set body image?

3. Based on your preview of the reading, how quickly do you think you should read the selection? (Circle one.) Explain your answer.

   Very slowly   Slowly   At a moderate pace   Quickly   Very quickly

4. Do you think males and females are equally concerned about body image? Do you think young people and old people are equally concerned about body image? Why or why not?

---

1   As he began his arm curls, Ali checked his form in the full-length mirror on the weight-room wall. His biceps were bulking up, but after 6 months of regular weight training, he expected more. His pecs, too, still lacked definition, and his abdomen wasn't the washboard he envisioned. So after a 45-minute upper-body workout, he added 200 sit-ups. Then he left the gym to shower back at his apartment: No way was he going to risk any of the gym regulars seeing his flabby torso unclothed. But by the time Ali got home and looked in the mirror, frustration had turned to anger. He was just too fat! To punish himself for his slow progress, instead of taking a shower, he put on his Nikes and went for a 4-mile run.

2   When you look in the mirror, do you like what you see? If you feel disappointed, frustrated, or even angry like Ali, you're not alone. A spate of recent studies is revealing that a majority of adults are dissatisfied with their bodies. For instance, a study of men in the United States, Austria, and France found that the ideal bodies they envisioned for themselves were an average of 28 pounds more muscular than their actual bodies. Most adult women—80 percent in one study—are also dissatisfied with their appearance, but for a different

---

*The Scorecard on p. 404 enables you to compute your reading rate. In order to do so, be sure to record your starting time in the Scorecard box before you begin reading.

reason: Most want to lose weight. Tragically, negative feelings about one's body can contribute to disordered eating, excessive exercise, and other behaviors that can threaten your health—and your life. Having a healthy body image is a key indicator of self-esteem, and can contribute to reduced stress, an increased sense of personal empowerment, and more joyful living.

Dissatisfaction with one's appearance and shape is an all-too-common feeling in today's society that can foster unhealthy attitudes and thought patterns, as well as disordered eating and exercising patterns.

What Is Body Image?

3   Body image is fundamental to our sense of who we are. Consider the fact that mirrors made from polished stone have been found at archaeological sites dating from before 6000 BCE; humans have been viewing themselves for millennia. But the term **body image** refers to more than just what you see when you look in a mirror. The National Eating Disorders Association (NEDA) identifies several additional components of body image:

- How you see yourself in your mind
- What you believe about your own appearance (including your memories, assumptions, and generalizations)
- How you feel about your body, including your height, shape, and weight
- How you sense and control your body as you move

4   NEDA identifies a *negative body image* as either a distorted perception

of your shape, or feelings of discomfort, shame, or anxiety about your body. You may be convinced that only other people are attractive, whereas your own body is a sign of personal failure. Does this attitude remind you of Ali? It should, because he clearly exhibits signs of a negative body image. In contrast, NEDA describes a *positive body image* as a true perception of your appearance: You see yourself as you really are. You understand that everyone is different, and you celebrate your uniqueness—including your "flaws," which you know have nothing to do with your value as a person.

5   Is your body image negative or positive—or is it somewhere in between? Researchers at the University of Arizona have developed a body image continuum that may help you decide (see Figure 1, p. 400). Like a spectrum of light, a continuum represents a series of stages that aren't entirely distinct. Notice that the continuum identifies behaviors associated with particular states, from total dissociation with one's body to body acceptance and body ownership.

Many Factors Influence Body Image

6   You're not born with a body image, but you do begin to develop one at an early age as you compare yourself against images you see in the world around you, and interpret the responses of family members and peers to your appearance. Let's look more closely at the factors that probably played a role in the development of your body image.

80%
of adult American women report dissatisfaction with their appearance.

---

body image   Most fundamentally, how you see yourself when you look in a mirror or picture yourself in your mind and how you feel about your body.

Body hate/ dissociation	Distorted body image	Body preoccupied obsessed	Body acceptance	Body ownership
I often feel separated and distant from my body—as if it belongs to someone else.	I spend a significant amount of time exercising and dieting to change my body.	I spend a significant amount of time viewing my body in the mirror.	I base my body image equally on social norms and my own self-concept.	My body is beautiful to me.
I don't see anything positive or even neutral about my body shape and size.	My body shape and size keep me from dating or finding someone who will treat me the way I want to be treated.	I spend a significant amount of time comparing my body to others.	I pay attention to my body and my appearance because it is important to me, but it only occupies a small part of my day.	My feelings about my body are not influenced by society's concept of an ideal body shape.
I don't believe others when they tell me I look OK.	I have considered changing or have changed my body shape and size through surgical means so I can accept myself.	I have days when I feel fat.	I nourish my body so it has the strength and energy to achieve my physical goals.	I know that the significant others in my life will always find me attractive.
I hate the way I look in the mirror and often isolate myself from others.		I am preoccupied with my body.		
		I accept society's ideal body shape and size as the best body shape and size.		

Figure 1 Body Image Continuum

This is part of a two-part continuum. Individuals whose responses fall to the far left side of the continuum have a highly negative body image, whereas responses to the right indicate a positive body image.

Source: Adapted from Smiley/King/Avery, Campus Health Service. Original continuum, C. Schislak, Preventive medicine and Public Health, © 1997 Arizona Board of Regents. Used with permission.

The Media and Popular Culture

7   Today images of six-pack loaded actors such as Taylor Lautner send young women to the movies in hoards and snapshots of emaciated celebrities such as Lindsay Lohan and Paris Hilton dominate the tabloids and sell magazines. The images and celebrities in the media set the standard for what we find attractive, leading some people to go to dangerous extremes to have the biggest biceps or fit into size 2 jeans. Most of us think of this

obsession with appearance as a recent phenomenon. The truth is, it has long been part of American culture. During the early twentieth century, while men idolized the hearty outdoorsman President Teddy Roosevelt, women pulled their corsets ever tighter to achieve unrealistically tiny waists. In the 1920s and 1930s, men emulated the burly cops and robbers in gangster films, while women dieted and bound their breasts to achieve the boyish "flapper" look. After World War II, both men and women strove for a healthy, wholesome appearance, but by the 1960s, tough-guys like Clint Eastwood and Marlon Brando were the male ideal, whereas rail-thin supermodel Twiggy embodied the nation's standard of female beauty.

8   Today, more than 66 percent of Americans are overweight or obese; thus, a significant disconnect exists between the media's idealized images of male and female bodies and the typical American body. At the same time, the media—in the form of television, the Internet, movies, and print publications—is a more powerful and pervasive presence than ever before. In fact, one study of more than 4,000 television commercials revealed that approximately one out of every four sends some sort of "attractiveness message." Thus, Americans are bombarded daily with messages telling us that we just don't measure up.

Family, Community, and Cultural Groups

9   The members of society with whom we most often interact—our family members, friends, and others—strongly influence the way we see ourselves. Parents are especially influential in body image development. For instance, it's common and natural for fathers of adolescent girls to

Is the media's obsession with appearance a new phenomenon?

Although the exact nature of the "in" look may change from generation to generation, unrealistic images of both male and female celebrities are nothing new. For example, in the 1960s, images of brawny film stars such as Clint Eastwood and ultrathin models such as Twiggy dominated the media.

experience feelings of discomfort related to their daughters' changing bodies. If they are able to navigate these feelings successfully, and validate the acceptability of their daughters' appearance throughout puberty, it's likely that they'll help their daughters maintain a positive body image. In contrast, if they verbalize or indicate even subtle judgments about their daughters' changing bodies, girls may begin to question how members of the opposite sex view their bodies in general. In addition, mothers who model body acceptance or body ownership may be more likely to foster a similar positive body image in their daughters, whereas mothers who are frustrated with or ashamed of their bodies may have a greater chance of fostering these attitudes in their daughters.

10   Interactions with siblings and other relatives, peers, teachers, coworkers, and other community members can also influence body image development. For instance, peer harassment (teasing and bullying) is widely acknowledged to contribute to a negative body image. Moreover, associations within one's cultural group appear to influence body image. For example, studies have found that European American females experience the highest rates of body dissatisfaction, and as a minority group becomes more acculturated into the mainstream, the body dissatisfaction levels of women in that group increase.

11   Body image also reflects the larger culture in which you live. In parts of Africa, for example, obesity has been associated with abundance, erotic desirability, and fertility. Girls in Mauritania traditionally were force-fed to increase their body size in order to signal a family's wealth, although the practice has become much less common in recent years.

Physiological and Psychological Factors

12   Recent neurological research has suggested that people who have been diagnosed with a body image disorder show differences in the brain's ability to regulate chemicals called *neurotransmitters*, which are linked to mood. Poor regulation of neurotransmitters is also involved in depression and in anxiety disorders, including obsessive-compulsive disorder. One study linked distortions in body image to a malfunctioning in the brain's visual processing region that was revealed by MRI scanning.

Examining Reading Selection 17*

Checking Your Vocabulary

Directions: *Use context, word parts, or a dictionary, if necessary, to determine the meaning of each word as it is used in the reading.*

____ 1. envisioned (paragraph 1)
   a. concealed
   b. pictured
   c. defended
   d. examined

____ 2. spate (paragraph 2)
   a. number
   b. delight
   c. remedy
   d. damage

____ 3. continuum (paragraph 5)
   a. contrast
   b. connection
   c. range
   d. copy

*Writing About the Reading questions appear in the Instructor's Manual.

___ 4. emaciated (paragraph 7)
   a. famous
   b. abnormally thin
   c. scared
   d. ordinary

___ 5. emulated (paragraph 7)
   a. performed
   b. profited
   c. requested
   d. copied

Checking Your Comprehension

Directions: *Select the best answer.*

___ 6. The primary focus of this reading is on
   a. managing weight.
   b. building a positive self-image.
   c. understanding body image.
   d. improving eating habits.

___ 7. The author wrote this selection in order to
   a. offer tips for working out and increasing muscle.
   b. expose the media's obsession with appearance.
   c. promote behaviors that lead to a healthy lifestyle.
   d. discuss what body image is and how it develops.

___ 8. According to the National Eating Disorders Association (NEDA), a positive body image is characterized by all of the following *except*
   a. you are convinced that only other people are attractive.
   b. you see yourself as you really are.
   c. you understand that everyone is different.
   d. you know your physical flaws have nothing to do with your value as a person.

___ 9. The main idea of paragraph 7 is that
   a. the obsession with appearance is a recent phenomenon.
   b. celebrities set the standard for what we find attractive.

   c. men and women strove for a healthy appearance after World War II.
   d. men tend to idolize hearty outdoorsmen and burly characters.

___ 10. According to the Body Image Continuum, the response that indicates the most positive body image is
   a. "I don't see anything . . . neutral about my body shape."
   b. "I spend a significant amount of time exercising and dieting to change my body."
   c. "I know that the significant others in my life will always find me attractive."
   d. "I accept society's ideal body shape and size as the best body shape and size."

Thinking Critically

___ 11. The author's attitude toward the subject can best be described as
   a. judgmental.
   b. informative.
   c. anxious.
   d. condescending.

___ 12. The young man in the opening paragraph and photograph is meant to be an example of someone who is
   a. exercising to lose weight.
   b. pleased with how he looks.
   c. dissatisfied with his appearance.
   d. against society's concept of an ideal body.

___ 13. One conclusion that can be made based on the selection is that parents can best influence a daughter's body image development by
   a. validating the acceptability of her appearance throughout puberty.
   b. verbalizing judgments about her changing appearance.

c. showing frustration or shame regarding their own bodies.

d. repeating the media's messages about attractiveness.

___ 14. The purpose of the photographs of Clint Eastwood and Twiggy is to show

a. how the media promotes unrealistic body types.

b. why certain celebrities are considered attractive.

c. which celebrities were most popular in the 1960s.

d. how males and females view themselves differently.

___ 15. The author supports her ideas with all of the following *except*

a. facts and statistics.

b. examples.

c. research.

d. personal experience.

Questions for Discussion

1. Consider your answer to the author's question in paragraph 2: When you look in the mirror, do you like what you see? Where do you typically find yourself on the body image continuum?

2. Discuss the author's reference to a "significant disconnect" between the typical American body and the media's idealized images. Why do you think such a disconnect exists? What trends do you see in advertising messages regarding attractiveness?

3. In your opinion, which celebrities set the current standard for what is attractive? Why?

4. Discuss the influence of family, community, and culture on body image development. What attitudes were fostered in your family? How have interactions with peers, teachers, co-workers, and other community members contributed to your body image?

Scorecard

Selection 17   1,798 words

Finishing Time: _____ _____ _____
                  HR.   MIN.   SEC.

Starting Time: _____ _____ _____
                  HR.   MIN.   SEC.

Reading Time: _____ _____ _____
                  HR.   MIN.   SEC.

WPM Score: _____

Comprehensive Score: for items 6–15
Number Right _____ × 10 = _____%

Assessing Your Reading Strategy

1. How would you rate your comprehension of the reading? (Circle one.)

   Excellent   Good   Fair   Poor

2. Did you find your reading strategy effective?   Yes   No

3. Suppose you were given an assignment to read a similar selection to the one you just read. Based on your experience with this selection, how would you adjust your reading strategy (if at all)?

Schools Go Sustainable: Greening College Food Services

Talia Berman
Reprinted from *WiretapMag.org*

About the Reading

WEB RESOURCE

The following article was originally published on Wiretap, a Web-based magazine that was written by young people from diverse backgrounds. Unfortunately, the magazine lost its funding and stopped updating its content in 2010.

MyReadingLab™ *The exercises following this selection can be completed online at myreadinglab.com*

Planning Your Reading Strategy*

Directions: *Activate your thinking by previewing the reading (see the Need to Know box on page 64) and answering the following questions.*

___ 1. Based on your preview, what is the single most important term you should be able to define in this reading?
   a. platitude
   b. like-minded
   c. sustainability
   d. greenmarkets

___ 2. Which student is most likely to say she can read this selection quickly?
   a. a nursing major
   b. a woman who is raising two children
   c. a man who served in the military
   d. a woman who is active in environmental causes

3. Based on your preview of the reading, how quickly do you think you should read the selection? (Circle one.) Explain your answer.

   Very slowly   Slowly   At a moderate pace   Quickly   Very quickly

4. Does your college have a green food service? If you don't know the answer, how can you go about finding out?

---

1 Young people often turn deaf ears to the adult platitudes hurled at them every day, such as "you are what you eat." As good as that advice may be, youth often make better judgments based on personal experiences. For environmentally conscious youth, that means it's not just *what* you eat but where the food comes from and how it was grown or raised.

Talia Berman, "Schools Go Sustainable: Greening College Food Services," WireTap, May 5, 2008, by permission of the author.

---

*The Scorecard on p. 410 enables you to compute your reading rate. In order to do so, be sure to record your starting time in the Scorecard box before you begin reading.

2   These days, college students around the country are demanding sustainable food practices from their dining services. From supporting local farm stands on campuses to teaching dining service staff how to cook with local and sustainable ingredients to participating in national campaigns to raise awareness about green eating, young learners have become integral to the larger process of change. The term "sustainable" in this case refers to agricultural practices that are environmentally friendly (i.e. organic or with minimal pesticides), support local small farmers and promote healthy, diversified diets.

3   "Students get it," said Anna Lappé, a sustainability food expert, author and the co-founder of the Small Planet Institute who often speaks at campuses around the country to promote sustainable eating. "The most common question I get from students is, 'We know we need to be promoting sustainable food—what can we do?'" She usually responds to the question with examples of what other schools have done, which is no short list.

■ Tracking Food Change

4   Julian Dautremont-Smith, sustainability expert and associate director at the Association for Advancement of Sustainability in Higher Learning, or AASHE, says that one thing his organization does is connect like-minded students at schools across the country so they can compare notes and learn from each other. "We do a lot of information-sharing—there is a lot of reinventing the wheel, and it is helpful for people to hear about what other schools have done." said Dautremont-Smith. The Association also runs a program that allows both students and administrators to track and compare the sustainability of their practices, a large part of which is devoted to sustainable eating. The program, called the "Sustainability Tracking, Assessment and Rating System," or STARS, is a guide and comparison tool, and its existence unites and strengthens the growing community of colleges that care about their environmental footprint.

5   According to Dautremont-Smith, more than 90 colleges are participating in the pilot project for the new system. "It is already catalyzing change," he said. The project gives points for enacting and sustaining various practices, and it includes a substantial dining services section. "Universities get points for using organic and environmentally sound methods," said Dautremont-Smith. "I think the food elements of STARS will be really big in the program."

■ Campus Progression

6   On an individual level, many schools have come especially far in their quest for sustainable dining on campuses. According to Galarneau, pioneer schools like Yale University and UC Santa Cruz are exporting their sustainability models to help other schools get closer to their green goals. Others are also setting the bar high, which has the added benefit of allowing students around the country to see what is possible. Portland State University was the first to include reports on local food purchases for food service in 2005 in their Request for Proposal (or RFP—a document inviting suppliers to solicit business from Portland State), according to sustainable coordinator Noelle Studer at PSU's Facilities and Planning Department.

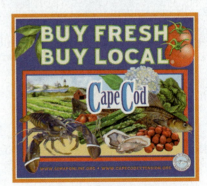

7   Visionaries across the country model a variety of ways to reach sustainability goals. Dautremont-Smith reports that the Maharishi University of Management serves the country's first 100 percent organic and vegetarian menu on their campus in Fairfield, Iowa. As more and more schools join the sustainability movement, they are looking to these innovators

for inspiration and real advice. At Columbia University in New York City, a small army of students led by sophomore Becky Davies is working hard to resurrect the defunct Columbia University Food Sustainability Project. "We are always looking to see what other schools do," said Davies, "because they work with a lot of the same companies and have a lot of the same problems."

Big Food, Big Challenges

8   One challenge that Davies and many of her peers encounter is dealing with long-term contracts with food distributors, like Columbia's with Sysco, North America's largest food service distributor. "It is not easy to make changes when you are working with such a huge company," said Davies, "The hardest part about it is figuring out where the food even comes from," said Davies, who is in communication with Sysco to help change the menus at Columbia. "Sysco will tell you these eggs are local, for example—from New Jersey—but they could still be industrial standard eggs, and those are the ones that come whole, not in a box, which is definitely not what we want," she said, "There is a lot of just trying to figure out where the food comes from before we do anything else." Determining where the supply comes from is usually more difficult when dealing with national food services like Sysco, Aramark, and Sodexo, whose enormous

warehouses and transportation infrastructure make it possible for food to come from, well, anywhere.

9   "The big challenge is finding your supply," Lappé said. Choosing a food supplier that you support—like a local farmer—is one easy way to avoid having to hunt for the source of the food in the bowels of a national warehouse, according to Lappé. Brown University, for example, teamed up with Farm Fresh Rhode Island, a local farmers' organization, to open a market on campus hawking fresh seasonal foods.

10   However, Lappé says that not all campuses have ready access to local farms, and in some states liability issues arise with small farmers that are uninsured. In these cases, Lappé said, it might be more fruitful to negotiate with national food service groups. According to Noelle Studer, Sodexo was "a great partner" in their endeavor to enlarge their local food portfolio, and Davies is part of a growing community that applauds Sysco's commitment to transparency in their food supply.

Climate and Collaboration

11   For Davies, communication with other programs like the Real Food Challenge and the Council on the Environment of New York City, the group that manages the city's outdoor Greenmarkets, is crucial for success. "We really need them for advice and help, and to make sure the school takes us seriously," she said.

12   At some schools, competing philosophies about what sustainability is can make it difficult to make changes. One issue, organic and pesticide-free

food versus local food, comes into play at schools where the climate is fickle. At Columbia in New York City, for example, Sysco Foods offers some organic options but very little in the way of local ingredients. "We would like to focus on local stuff more than organic, but it is really difficult," said Davies. At the California schools, it is much easier to focus on local ingredients, because local agriculture is in large supply. "We really have a wide range of choices," said Galarneau.

13   For Dautremont-Smith, getting bogged down with philosophy is missing the point, "It is too complicated to focus on organic versus local," he said. "I think that issue needs holistic evaluation, taking into account what the students want and the specific circumstances of the school." Often, the specific circumstances of the school are determined by whatever their contract with the big food distributor dictates. Some students would like to see these contracts terminated because of the limitations of the terms. When Galarneau was at UC Santa Cruz in 2002, students and staff teamed up to pressure the administration to end their contract with Sodexo-Marriott. The administration responded, terminated the contract and helped students develop an in-house food service system. They set up a collaborative model that allowed students, staff and community members to work, and the dining service went from zero to 24 percent local and socially responsible food.

14   While this story is inspiring, analysts say that terminating contracts completely might be untenable for many other schools, particularly for schools that are in places where sustainable food might be in short supply. Furthermore, Galarneau says that pressuring major food distributors to operate sustainably might be an effective way to promote change. "Talking to the distributor and buyers can be the most useful [tactic]," Galarneau said. Indeed, Sodexo has recently hired a vice president of sustainability to address students' concerns. "Once you have trust and a relationship with the distributors, you can start to make changes when contracts are up for renewal or reevaluation" he said. Furthermore, Galarneau points out that creating contacts with the food distributors promotes lasting relationships between them and the school. "Student advocates will be gone in a year," he said. "If you build a relationship with distributors you might see lasting change," he said.

Examining Reading Selection 17

Checking Your Vocabulary

Directions: *Use context, word parts, or a dictionary, if necessary, to determine the meaning of each word as it is used in the reading.*

____ 1. integral (paragraph 2)
   a. essential
   b. doubtful
   c. similar
   d. inexpensive

____ 2. pilot (paragraph 5)
   a. personal
   b. model
   c. navigational
   d. former

____ 3. catalyzing (paragraph 5)
   a. interfering
   b. harming
   c. sparking
   d. discarding

____ 4. defunct (paragraph 7)
   a. useful
   b. current
   c. unfortunate
   d. inactive

____ 5. fickle (paragraph 12)
   a. unpredictable
   b. dramatic
   c. supportive
   d. unimportant

Checking Your Comprehension

Directions: *Select the best answer.*

_____ 6. This selection is primarily about
   a. agricultural practices.
   b. organic food markets.
   c. national food services.
   d. sustainable food practices.

_____ 7. The purpose of the STARS program described in the selection is to
   a. allow college students and administrators to track and compare the sustainability of their food practices.
   b. connect national food service companies with a network of local and regional food producers.
   c. teach food service workers how to prepare food using environmentally conscious methods.
   d. promote organic food to consumers, grocery stores, restaurants, and college campuses around the country.

_____ 8. The country's first 100 percent organic and vegetarian menu was served on the campus of
   a. Portland State University.
   b. UC Santa Cruz.
   c. Yale University.
   d. the Maharishi University of Management.

_____ 9. According to the selection, one of the biggest challenges of dealing with large national food service distributors is
   a. determining the source of the distributors' food supply.
   b. persuading distributors to follow fair trade practices.
   c. negotiating new contracts with distributors.
   d. communicating sustainability goals to distributors.

_____ 10. At UC Santa Cruz, pressure from students and staff over the university's food service contract resulted in
   a. the administration terminating the contract.
   b. students developing an in-house food service system.
   c. the dining service using more local and socially responsible food.
   d. all of the above.

Thinking Critically

_____ 11. The author's attitude toward the subject can best be described as
   a. humorous.
   b. formal.
   c. informative.
   d. disapproving.

_____ 12. The author includes the example about Columbia University in paragraph 12 in order to show that
   a. the commitment to local food is stronger at California schools.
   b. efforts to use local food can be hindered by the climate.
   c. focusing on organic food is more important than having local food.
   d. some national food distributors are willing to provide organic food.

_____ 13. In paragraph 10, the author uses the word *transparency* to refer to Sysco's commitment to
   a. describing how its food is prepared.
   b. revealing where its food comes from.
   c. discussing the terms of its contract.
   d. choosing only local, organic suppliers.

___ 14. The type of Web site from which this selection is taken can best be described as
   a. news.
   b. advocacy.
   c. personal.
   d. commercial.

___ 15. What function does the "Buy Fresh/ Buy Local—Cape Cod" image on page 406 serve?

a. It emphasizes sustainability as a program practiced mostly in New England.
b. It summarizes most people's approach to sustainability.
c. It shows that some foods—such as fish and asparagus—are more sustainable than others.
d. It illustrates how to plant a sustainable garden.

Scorecard

Selection 18:   1,494 words

Finishing Time: _____ _____ _____
                 HR.   MIN.   SEC.

Starting Time: _____ _____ _____
                HR.   MIN.   SEC.

Reading Time: _____ _____
                     MIN.   SEC.

WPM Score: _____

Comprehension Score: for Items 6–15

Number Right: _____ × 10 = _____%

Assessing Your Reading Strategy

1. How would you rate your comprehension of the reading? (Circle one.)

   Excellent   Good   Fair   Poor

2. Did you find your reading strategy effective?   Yes   No

3. Suppose you were given an assignment to read a similar selection to the one you just read. Based on your experience with this selection, how would you adjust your reading strategy (if at all)?

Writing About Reading Selection 18

Checking Your Vocabulary

Directions: *Complete each of the following items; refer to a dictionary if necessary.*

1. Describe the denotative and connotative meanings of the word *quest* in paragraph 6.

   _____

   _____

   _____

2. Define each of the following words:
   a. *diversified* (paragraph 2)

   _____

   b. *resurrect* (paragraph 7)

   _____

   c. *infrastructure* (paragraph 8)

   _____

   _____

   d. *holistic* (paragraph 13)

   _____

   _____

   e. *collaborative* (paragraph 13)

   _____

3. Define the word *platitudes* (paragraph 1) and underline the word or phrase that provides a clue for its meaning.

_____

_____

_____

4. Define the word *innovators* (paragraph 7) and underline the word or phrase that provides a clue for its meaning.

_____

_____

5. Determine the meanings of the following words by using word parts:

a. *reinventing* (paragraph 4)

_____

b. *exporting* (paragraph 6)

_____

c. *portfolio* (paragraph 10)

_____

d. *untenable* (paragraph 14)

_____

_____

e. *advocates* (paragraph 14)

_____

_____

Checking Your Comprehension

6. How is the term *sustainable* defined in this selection?

_____

_____

_____

_____

7. How does the STARS project award points to participants?

_____

_____

_____

_____

8. Identify at least four of the colleges that were cited in the selection as part of the sustainability movement.

_____

_____

_____

_____

9. Aside from terminating food service contracts, what other tactics are suggested for improving a school's sustainability?

_____

_____

_____

_____

Thinking Critically

10. What is the author's purpose?

_____

_____

_____

11. What types of evidence does the author provide to support her thesis?

_____

_____

_____

12. Why might a college choose to negotiate with national food service groups rather than use a local farmer as a food source?

_____

_____

_____

_____

_____

_____

13. What does the photograph on page 407, illustrate?

_____

_____

1. Describe your own experience with sustainable food practices. For example, does your school practice sustainability? Do you try to include sustainable food in your own diet? Why or why not?

2. Compare some of the programs described in the selection, such as STARS (paragraph 4) and the in-house food service at UC Santa Cruz (paragraph 13), or look up others that are mentioned (Small Planet Institute, Real Food Challenge, Farm Fresh Rhode Island). Which programs do you think have the most potential for success? Why?

3. Which issue do you think is more important: organic and pesticide-free food or locally produced food? Explain your answer.

4. Evaluate the visuals included with this selection. What other types of visuals might have been useful with this selection?

CHAPTER 10

Critical Analysis and Evaluating Online Sources

think VISUALLY...

Study the cartoon to the right. Write a sentence explaining what point the cartoonist is making. How did you know what to write? What thinking processes did you use to figure out the cartoonist's message? You had to study the details in the cartoon and consider them along with its caption to figure out that the cartoonist is commenting on the rapidly changing forms of communication.

The thinking processes you used involved critical reasoning. You had to go beyond the information presented in the cartoon and reason about it. Through choice of words, descriptions, facts, arrangement of ideas, and suggestions, an author often means more than he or she says. The purpose of this chapter is to present skills that will enable you to interpret and evaluate what you read. These processes require critical reading and thinking skills—the careful and deliberate evaluation of ideas for the purpose of making a judgment about their worth or value. This chapter presents numerous strategies to help you respond to academic reading assignments that demand critical reading.

" I DON'T KNOW WHAT IT IS . I THINK IT'S SOME KIND OF OLD-FASHIONED CEL PHONE . "

Learning GOALS

In this chapter, you will learn how to . . .

Goal 1 Make inferences

Goal 2 Distinguish facts from opinions

Goal 3 Recognize generalizations

Goal 4 Identify tone

Goal 5 Identify an author's purpose

Goal 6 Recognize bias

Goal 7 Understand figurative language

Goal 8 Evaluate online sources

413

■ Making Inferences

Goal 1
Make inferences

Suppose you are ten minutes late for your psychology class, and you find the classroom empty. After a moment of puzzlement and confusion you might remember that your instructor has been ill and decide that your class has been canceled. Or you might recall that your instructor changed classrooms last week and, therefore, you decide that she has done so again. In this situation you used what you did know to make a reasonable guess about what you did not know. This reasoning process is called an **inference**. An inference is a logical connection that you draw between what you observe or know and what you do not know. All of us make numerous inferences in daily living without consciously thinking about them. When you wave at a friend and he or she does not wave back, you assume that he or she didn't see you. When you are driving down the highway and see a police car with its lights flashing behind you, you usually infer that the police officer wants you to pull over and stop.

Although inferences are reasonable guesses made on the basis of available information, they are not always correct. For instance, though you inferred that the friend who did not wave did not see you, it may be that he or she did see you, but is angry with you and decided to ignore you. An inference is the best guess you can make given the available information and circumstances.

If you are a pragmatic or applied learner, you may tend to concentrate on the facts at hand and may overlook their implications. Be sure to question, challenge, and analyze the facts; look for what further ideas the facts, when considered together, suggest.

EXERCISE 10–1 **MAKING INFERENCES**

Directions: *For each of the following items, make an inference about the situation that is described.*

1. A woman seated alone at a bar offers to buy a drink for a man sitting several seats away.

   _____

2. A dog growls as a teenager walks toward the house.

   _____

3. Your seven-year-old brother will not eat his dinner. A package of cookies is missing from the kitchen cupboard.

   _____

4. A woman seated alone in a restaurant nervously glances at everyone who enters. Every few minutes she checks her watch.

   _____

5. A close friend invites you to go out for pizza and beer on Tuesday. When you meet her at her home on Tuesday, she tells you that you must have confused the days and that she will see you tomorrow evening.

Making Inferences as You Read

An inference is a reasonable guess about what the author does *not* say based on what he or she *does* say. You are required to make inferences when an author suggests an idea but does not directly state it. For instance, suppose a writer describes a character as follows:

> In the mirror John Bell noticed that his hair was graying at the temples. As he picked up the morning paper, he realized that he could no longer see well without his glasses. Looking at the hands holding the paper he saw that they were wrinkled.

From the information the author provides, you may infer that the character is realizing that he is aging. However, notice that the author does not mention aging at all. By the facts he or she provides, however, the writer leads you to infer that the character is thinking about aging.

Now, read the following description of an event:

> Their actions, on this sunny afternoon, have been carefully organized and rehearsed. Their work began weeks ago with a leisurely drive through a quiet residential area. While driving, they noticed particular homes that seemed isolated and free of activity. Over the next week, similar drives were taken at different times of day. Finally, a house was chosen and their work began in earnest. Through careful observation and several phone calls, they learned where the occupants worked. They studied the house, noting entrances and windows and anticipating the floor plan. Finally, they were ready to act. Phone calls made that morning confirmed that the occupants were at work.

What is about to happen in this description? From the facts presented, you probably realized that a daytime home burglary was about to occur. Notice, however, that this burglary is not mentioned anywhere in the paragraph. Instead, using the information provided, you made the logical connection between the known and the unknown facts regarding what was about to occur.

How to Make Inferences

Below are a few general guidelines for making inferences about what you read.

NEED TO KNOW How to Make Inferences

1. **Be sure you understand the literal meaning first.** For each paragraph, you should identify the topic, main idea, supporting details, and organizational pattern.

2. **Ask yourself a question.** To be sure that you are making necessary inferences to get the fullest meaning from a passage, ask yourself questions such as:

   > What is the author trying to suggest from the stated information?
   >
   > What do all the facts and ideas point toward or seem to add up to?
   >
   > For what purpose did the author include these facts and details?

   In answering any of these questions, you must add together the individual pieces of information to arrive at an inference. Making an inference is somewhat like putting together a complicated picture puzzle, in which you try to make each piece fit with all the rest of the pieces to form something recognizable.

3. **Use clues provided by the writer.** A writer's choice of words often suggests his or her attitude toward a subject. Try to notice descriptive words, emotionally charged words, and words with strong positive or negative connotations. Here is an example of how the choice of words can lead you to an inference:

   > Grandmother had been an unusually attractive young woman, and she carried herself with the graceful confidence of a natural charmer to her last day.

   The highlighted phrases "unusually attractive," "graceful confidence," and "natural charmer" suggest that the writer feels positive about her grandmother. However, in the following example, notice how the highlighted words and phrases create a negative image of the person.

   > The withdrawn child eyed her teacher with a hostile disdain. When directly spoken to, the child responded in a cold but carefully respectful way.

   In this sentence, the highlighted words suggest that the child is unfriendly and that he or she dislikes the teacher.

4. **Consider the author's purpose.** An awareness of the author's purpose for writing is often helpful in making inferences. If an author's purpose is to convince you to purchase a particular product, such as in an advertisement, you already have a clear idea of the types of inferences the writer hopes you will make. For instance, a magazine ad for a stereo system reads:

   > If you're in the market for true surround sound, a prematched system is a good way to get it. The components in our system are built for each other by our audio engineers. You can be assured of high performance and sound quality.

   You can guess that the writer's purpose is to encourage you to buy his particular prematched stereo system.

5. **Verify your inference.** Once you have made an inference, check to be sure that it is accurate. Look back at the stated facts to see that you have sufficient evidence to support the inference. Also, be sure that you have not overlooked other equally plausible or more plausible inferences that could be drawn from the same set of facts.

EXERCISE 10–2   **IDENTIFYING REASONABLE INFERENCES**

Directions: *Read each main statement. Put a check mark in front of all the substatements that are reasonable inferences.*

1. The students in the nursing program work harder than any other students at our school.

   _____ Nursing students are highly motivated.

   _____ The nursing program requires a great deal of work.

   _____ Students not in the nursing program are lazy.

   _____ Only the best students can become nurses.

2. The moose population on the island was no longer overcrowded once a wolf pack was brought over from the mainland.

   _____ Hunting is not the best way to reduce moose herd populations.

   _____ The wolves are an enemy to the moose.

   _____ Humans introduced the wolf pack to the island.

   _____ A moose cannot kill a wolf in a fight.

3. Many pioneers died on their journey along the Oregon Trail because of illness, diseases, and accidents.

   _____ The Oregon Trail crossed dangerous terrain.

   _____ One in five women was pregnant at some part in their journey along the trail.

   _____ There are many pioneer graves along the Oregon Trail.

   _____ The pioneers could not get the medical attention they needed.

4. Most Americans have tried an alternative health-care product or service without telling their regular primary care physician.

   _____ More and more insurance companies are covering alternative medicine.

   _____ Patients are afraid their regular doctors would not approve of an alternative therapy.

   _____ Everyone likes to try new things.

   _____ Doctors are out of touch with popular attitudes toward the medical field.

5. Small businesses and large corporations are now requiring that their network administrators have a college education, specialized computer training, and even certification.

_____ Network administrators earn a relatively high wage.

_____ Companies have had difficulties with young computer wizards who lack specialized training or college degrees.

_____ Employers want highly skilled employees running their computer systems.

_____ The best network administrators have Ph.D.s in computer science.

6. Super strong megathrust earthquakes occur in the Pacific Northwest on average about once every 500 years. The last such earthquake was around 300 years ago.

_____ Residents of the Pacific Northwest need not prepare for earthquakes.

_____ There is no chance of a megathrust earthquake in the Pacific Northwest for at least 200 more years.

_____ The Pacific Northwest is a very dangerous place to live.

_____ Within the next 200 years a megathrust earthquake may occur in the Pacific Northwest.

7. Attendance at women's professional basketball games is not as high as attendance at men's professional basketball games even though ticket prices are lower.

_____ Men's basketball is more popular than women's basketball.

_____ The female teams play in smaller arenas.

_____ People do not mind paying higher prices to see men's basketball.

_____ More families attend women's basketball games.

8. Library users oftentimes do not know if they are speaking to a professional librarian, circulation clerk, volunteer, or student worker when they ask a library employee a question.

_____ Library users should avoid asking student workers questions.

_____ All library personnel should know enough to answer all questions.

_____ Only librarians should answer questions.

_____ It would be helpful if library personnel wore name tags with job titles.

9. Many motivated high school graduates have decided to attend trade or technical school instead of a traditional four-year college or university. Many of these students are training to be auto mechanics, construction workers, plumbers, or electricians.

_____ The students who attend technical schools are probably skilled at working with their hands.

_____ Students at four-year colleges are less likely to know what they want to study than students in technical schools.

_____ Students who obtain a four-year degree will probably owe more money than students who graduate with a technical degree.

_____ The students who attend technical schools will be learning specific on-the-job skills that they will use in their careers.

10. Young children learn by experiencing and doing. Passive teaching tools such as television and battery-operated toys should be avoided.

_____ Battery-operated toys limit a child's opportunity to experience the real world.

_____ Planting seeds in the garden will teach a child more than watching a video of someone planting seeds.

_____ Children are active learners.

_____ Children are not learning in the best way by watching television.

EXERCISE 10–3   **MAKING INFERENCES**

Directions: *Read each paragraph and then answer the questions that follow.*

A.   Our parents and grandparents worked hard during their lives, in many cases for decades at one company. Upon retirement they were rewarded with a nice pension and a monthly government check—some well-deserved security in their old age. Today's workers cannot rely on that same retirement scenario. Corporate pension funds are gambled away on bad investments, and Social Security is running out of cash. As executives retire early with obscene bonuses, people who have worked hard on the front lines of America's companies are left to struggle during the years when they should be relaxing and treating themselves and their families. When did corporate America forget about the people who keep it going?

1. What can you infer about the author's attitude toward large corporations and the Social Security Administration?

_____

_____

_____

2. What inference can you make about the author's feelings toward the older generation?

_____

_____

3. What would the author think about a corporation that shared profits with all its workers?

_____

B.   Modern building techniques and materials have helped make Americans more comfortable and more healthy. We no longer have to live in drafty old houses or work in unpleasant buildings. Today's windows, doors, and insulation keep the cold air out of our homes. Meanwhile, climate-controlled work environments ensure a constant comfortable temperature all year round. Airtight construction keeps us healthy and happy, which in turn makes living and working more enjoyable and productive.

1. What inference does the author make about our health and being warm or cold?

_____

2. How concerned is the author likely to be about "sick building syndrome," an illness that workers get from indoor air pollution?

_____

_____

3. How would the author react to someone who believes a window should always be open, even just a crack in winter?

_____

C.   Documentary films and films based on true stories do so much more than purely fictional movies to enlighten and educate us. Stories of real life adventures, drama, and successes bring with them hope and inspiration. Through such tales brought to life on the big screen, we can learn and plan and strive for our dreams. These types of films also give our young people the introduction to real accessible heroes whom they can learn more about and perhaps even emulate. With so many great true stories in the world and in history, why watch fiction?

1. What inference can you make about the author's attitude toward fiction?

_____

2. How would the author respond to someone who said he or she was inspired by a film such as *Star Wars?*

_____

_____

D.   Standardized tests measure whether students have learned the basics. Children whose scores are less than the national average should receive special instruction until their scores increase. Through this process teachers will be able to identify children with learning difficulties and put them into the appropriate special education programs. Likewise, students who excel on standardized tests can be grouped together for more challenging lessons and work. Everyone can be measured and assessed through the use of standardized tests.

1. What inferences can you make about the author's attitude toward standardized testing?

   _____

2. How would the author respond to a school district's plan to mix high- and low-ability students in each classroom?

   _____

3. What would this author say to someone who worries about teachers "teaching to the test"?

   _____

   _____

   _____

E.   People who live in densely populated areas are not as friendly as people living in rural areas. Since most of the world's population now lives in urban centers, that makes the vast majority of the inhabitants of Earth rude and pushy. Living so close to each other makes us edgy and irritable. We need more space to feel comfortable with others and ourselves.

1. What can you infer about the author's feelings toward people who live in the country?

   _____

2. What would the author say to someone who believes densely populated areas build community and develop positive human relationships?

   _____

   _____

EXERCISE 10–4   **MAKING INFERENCES**

Directions: *Read the following passage and then answer the questions. The answers are not directly stated in the passage; you will have to make inferences in order to answer them.*

One morning I put two poached eggs in front of Charlie, who looked up briefly from his newspaper.

"You've really shaped up, Cassie," he smiled. "A dreadful lady went to the hospital and a very nice Cassie came back. I think you've learned a lesson and, honey, I'm proud of you."

He went to work and I started the dishes, trying to feel thrilled at having shaped up for Charlie. *He sounds as though the hospital performed some sort of exorcism,* I mused, scraping egg off the dish with my fingernail. *Evil is banished, goodness restored. Then why don't I feel transformed?*

The dish slipped out of my hand and smashed into the sink, spraying chips over the counter. I looked down at the mess, then at the cluttered kitchen table, and beyond that to the dust on the television set in the den. I pictured the four unmade beds and the three clothes-strewn bedrooms and the toys in the living room and last night's newspaper on the floor next to Charlie's reclining chair and I yelled at the cat who was licking milk out of a cereal bowl, "What lesson? What goddamn lesson was I supposed to learn?"

I grabbed my coat and the grocery money and was waiting at the liquor store when it opened.

"You find a place where they give it away for free?" the man behind the counter leered. "We haven't seen you for weeks. Where you been?"

"Nowhere," I answered. "I've been nowhere." He gave me my bottle and I walked out thinking that I'd have to start trading at another store where the creeps weren't so free with their remarks.

—Rebeta-Burditt, *The Cracker Factory*, Macmillan.

1. What problem is Cassie experiencing?

   _____

2. For what purpose was Cassie hospitalized?

   _____

3. How does Cassie feel about household chores?

   _____

4. What is Cassie's husband's attitude toward her problem? Is he part of her problem? If so, how?

   _____

   _____

   _____

✓ LEARNING STYLE TIPS

If you tend to be a(n) . . .	Then build your critical reading skills by . . .
Applied learner	Asking these questions: How can I use this information? Of what value is this information?
Conceptual learner	Studying to see how the ideas fit together, looking for connections and relationships, as well as inconsistencies

■ Distinguishing Between Fact and Opinion

Goal 2
Distinguish facts from opinions

The ability to distinguish fact from opinion is an essential critical reading skill. **Facts** are statements that can be verified—that is, proven to be true. **Opinions** are statements that express feelings, attitudes, or beliefs and are neither true nor false. Here are a few examples of each:

FACTS

1. The average American adult spends 25 hours per week on housework.
2. U.S. military spending has increased over the past ten years.

OPINIONS

1. By the year 2030, tobacco will be illegal, just as various other drugs are currently illegal.
2. If John F. Kennedy had lived, the United States would be a different country today.

Facts, once verified or taken from a reputable source, can be accepted and regarded as reliable information. Opinions, however, are not reliable sources of information and should be questioned and carefully evaluated. Look for evidence that supports the opinion and indicates that it is reasonable.

Some authors are careful to signal the reader when they are presenting an opinion. Watch for words and phrases such as

it is believed	one explanation is	in my opinion
in my view	apparently	this suggests
it is likely that	presumably	possibly
seemingly		

In the following excerpt from a psychology textbook, notice how the author carefully distinguishes factual statements from opinion by using qualifying words and phrases (highlighted).

Some research has suggested that day care can have problematic effects on children's development. For example, studies indicate that children who begin day care as infants are more aggressive, more easily distracted, less considerate of their peers, less popular, and less obedient to adults than children who have never attended day care or haven't attended for as long.

Other studies have found that day care is associated with adaptive behaviors. For example, researchers have reported that children who attend day care develop social and language skills more quickly than children who stay at home, although the children who don't attend day care catch up in their social development in a few years. Poor children who go to day care are likely to develop better reading and math skills than poor children who stay at home.

EFFICIENCY TIP
In general, you can assume that most of what you read in introductory college textbooks is fact, though authors' opinions can sometimes creep in. Often, textbook authors will discuss both sides of a controversial issue without taking either side. To do this, they cite research studies by various scholars.

Further complicating this picture of day care's developmental effects are additional studies finding no differences between children who attended day care and those who didn't. What can we conclude about the reasons for these different—and in some cases, contradictory—findings?

—From Laura Uba and Karen Huang, *Psychology,* p. 323. New York: Longman, copyright © 1999 Pearson Education, Inc.

Other authors, however, mix fact and opinion without making clear distinctions. This is particularly true in the case of *informed opinion,* which is the opinion of an expert or authority. Ralph Nader represents expert opinion on consumer rights, for example. Textbook authors, too, often offer informed opinion, as in the following statement from an American government text.

In the early days of voting research, the evidence was clear: voters rarely engaged in policy voting, preferring to rely on party identification or candidate evaluation to make up their minds.

—Robert A. Lineberry and George C. Edwards, *Government in America,* Fourth Edition, p. 309. Glenview, IL: Scott, Foresman, copyright © 1989 Pearson Education, Inc.

The author of this statement has reviewed the available evidence and is providing his expert opinion as to what the evidence indicates.

EXERCISE 10–5

DISTINGUISHING FACT AND OPINION

Directions: *Read each of the following statements and decide whether it is fact or opinion. Write "Fact" or "Opinion" in the space provided.*

1. The sexual division of labor in middle-class homes will change in the next 50 years.

2. An infection is an illness produced by the action of microorganisms in the human body.

3. When measured by earning power, the American standard of living has increased steadily since the early 1970s.

4. Work, or the lack of it, is the primary influence on lifestyle.

5. Increased job opportunities for women and other minorities depends primarily on the future of the economy.

6. Parents now spend less time with their children than they did 30 years ago.

7. Librarians should take rare, valuable books out of circulation in order to preserve them.

8. Art and music classes are being cut from high school curricula in several states.

9. Most people believe that Meriwether Lewis (of Lewis and Clark fame) committed suicide.

10. Being courageous is more important than being clever.

EXERCISE 10–6   **DISTINGUISHING FACT AND OPINION**

Directions: *Read each topic sentence. Mark the statements that follow as fact (F), opinion (O), or informed opinion (IO).*

1. **Topic sentence:** Cotton farmers use large amounts of fertilizers and pesticides.

   _____ a. Chemical use should be avoided in cotton farming.

   _____ b. Researchers who have studied chemically sensitive individuals state that organically grown cotton is better for them.

   _____ c. Cotton seeds are treated with fungicide.

   _____ d. In some countries, farmers use DDT on cotton fields.

2. **Topic sentence:** Many universities now offer courses in popular culture.

   _____ a. Students watch films and television shows as homework assignments.

   _____ b. It is wonderful that our young people have the opportunity to study their own culture!

   _____ c. Popular culture studies are vital to sustaining interest in the history department.

   _____ d. Learning specialists acknowledge that students learn better when they are interested in the material; therefore, our students are expected to do very well in these courses.

3. **Topic sentence:** Noise pollution is becoming a major health issue.

   _____ a. Most of us experience exposure to high levels of noise on a daily basis.

   _____ b. Contractors recommend thick walls and floors to reduce noise from neighbors in apartment buildings.

   _____ c. Traffic, construction, and airplanes can contribute to noise pollution.

   _____ d. Neighborhood children produce the most annoying type of noise pollution.

4. **Topic sentence:** Exercise is an important part of maintaining a healthy lifestyle.

   _____ a. Regular exercise can improve your grades in school.

   _____ b. People who do not exercise are lazy.

   _____ c. Aerobic exercise stimulates blood circulation.

   _____ d. Doctors suggest stretching and relaxing every time you exercise.

5. **Topic sentence:** Water is fundamental to life.

_____ a. Health organizations around the world have studied the availability of fresh water and believe that reforms are necessary to provide equal access to clean drinking water.

_____ b. Most of the Earth's water is sea water or ice.

_____ c. Fountains and ponds provide relaxing decorations in city gardens.

_____ d. Water can be used to produce electricity.

6. **Topic sentence:** Many groups disagree internally on the issue of drilling for oil in the Arctic National Wildlife Refuge.

_____ a. Some native peoples are worried about endangering vital caribou populations.

_____ b. It is not surprising that the politicians do not agree on the drilling issue.

_____ c. Although scientists disagree as to the extent of damage, they all acknowledge there will be an impact upon the region.

_____ d. Some environmentalists have stated that they are not sure whether no development is the best solution.

7. **Topic sentence:** Thailand's first settlements, made up of farmers, potters, and weavers, were located on hillsides.

_____ a. The very first inhabitants of Thailand were wandering hunter-gatherers.

_____ b. The Ban Chiang settlement was founded about 3500 B.C.

_____ c. Scientists have found Ban Chiang artifacts buried with the dead, so they believe these items must have been quite valuable.

_____ d. The craftsmen of Ban Chiang produced their best work from 300 B.C. to 200 A.D.

8. **Topic sentence:** In America, attitudes toward family have changed over the past one hundred years.

_____ a. Several well-known sociologists report that the immediate family has become more important than the extended family.

_____ b. Divorce is more common now than it was in 1903.

_____ c. Many fathers now stay home with the children while the mothers work full-time.

_____ d. The collapse of the family structure has caused widespread societal chaos.

9. **Topic sentence:** Mercury, the planet nearest to the sun, has no atmosphere.

_____ a. We know all we need to know about the planet Mercury.

_____ b. Mercury's year equals 88 Earth days.

_____ c. Scientists believe that Mercury is uninhabitable.

_____ d. In 2011, an unmanned spacecraft entered orbit around Mercury.

10. **Topic sentence:** Many communities now have recycling programs as part of their waste management services.

_____ a. Recycling alone is not enough; people must reuse and reduce as well.

_____ b. People do not like rinsing out bottles and cans and sorting them into different bins.

_____ c. You can avoid extra packaging by buying in bulk.

_____ d. Some environmental scientists believe the process of recycling paper is as harmful as making new paper.

EXERCISE 10–7

Working
COLLABORATIVELY

IDENTIFYING FACT AND OPINION

Directions: _Read each of the following passages and underline factual statements in each. Place brackets around clear statements of opinion. In class, discuss the statements about which you are unsure._

PASSAGE 1

Opponents of day care still call for women to return to home and hearth, but the battle is really over. Now the question is: will day care continue to be inadequately funded and poorly regulated, or will public policy begin to put into place a system that rightly treats children as our most valuable national resource?

More than 50% of the mothers of young children are in the work force before their child's first birthday. An estimated 9.5 million preschoolers have mothers who work outside the home. Most women, like most men, are working to put food on the table. Many are the sole support of their families. They are economically unable to stay at home, although many would prefer to do so.

—Maxine Phillips, Dissent Magazine

PASSAGE 2

Elvis Presley is the king of rock and roll, the best and most famous performer to ever hit the top ten charts. Due to his fame, fans line up outside his former home, Graceland. Fans include teenagers, parents, and the elderly, and they are all waiting to tour his residence. Cash registers are very busy. People with credit card in hand pay outrageous amounts of money for worthless souvenirs and other useless memorabilia. Music plays as people wait.

Of course it is songs such as: "Hound Dog" or "Can't Help Falling in Love." The music sets a nostalgic mood and makes people even more willing to waste their hard earned dollars.

—"Forever Elvis," by Jim Miller Newsweek, Aug. 3rd, 1987.

PASSAGE 3

Americans consume far too many refined carbohydrates which have few health benefits and are a major factor in our growing epidemic of overweight and obesity. Many of these simple sugars come from added sugars, sweeteners that are put in during processing to flavor foods, make sodas taste good, and ease our cravings for sweets. A classic example is the amount of added sugar in one can of soda: over two teaspoons per can! All that refined sugar can cause tooth decay and put on pounds; however, the greater threat may come from the sudden spike in blood glucose that comes from eating it. In response to an overload of blood glucose, insulin levels also may surge in order to drive blood glucose levels down. Through a typical day, these surges of sugar, insulin, and resultant dips in blood glucose may cause a cascade of ill health effects. Clearly, government action is required to regulate the amount of added sugars that companies are allowed to put into the products they sell and market, especially to children.

—Donatelle, Rebecca J., *Health: The Basics, Green Edition,* 9th Ed., © 2011. Reprinted and electronically reproduced by permission of Pearson Education, Inc., Upper Saddle River, NJ.

EXERCISE 10–8   **WRITING FACT AND OPINION**

Directions: *For each topic, write a statement of fact and an opinion.*

1. racial and ethnic diversity on college campuses

    Fact: _____

    _____

    Opinion: _____

    _____

2. substance abuse

    Fact: _____

    _____

    Opinion: _____

    _____

3. airport security

    Fact: _____

    _____

    Opinion: _____

    _____

4. reality TV

Fact: _____

_____

Opinion: _____

_____

5. space exploration

Fact: _____

_____

Opinion: _____

_____

EXERCISE 10–9

Academic **APPLICATION**

IDENTIFYING INFORMED OPINION

Directions: *From a chapter in one of your textbooks, identify two statements that represent an author's informed opinion.* ■

EXERCISE 10–10

Electronic **APPLICATION**

IDENTIFYING OPINION AND INFORMED OPINION

Directions: *Visit a Web site or newsgroup, or choose a print magazine advertisement or newspaper editorial. Identify statements of opinion and/or informed opinion.* ■

■ Recognizing Generalizations

Goal 3

Recognize generalizations

A **generalization** is a statement that is made about a large group or a class of items based on observation of or experience with a part of that group or class. Suppose you interviewed a number of students on campus. You asked each why he or she was attending college, and each indicated that he or she was preparing for a career. From your interview you could make the generalization "Students attend college to prepare for a career." Of course, you could not be absolutely certain that this statement is true until you asked *every* college student. Here are a few more generalizations. Some may seem very reasonable; you may disagree with others.

- All college freshmen are confused and disoriented during their first week on campus.
- Most parents are concerned for the happiness of their children.
- Psychology instructors are interested in the psychology of learning.
- College students are more interested in social life than scholarship.

As you evaluate the evidence a writer uses to support his or her ideas, be alert for generalizations that are used as facts. Remember that a generalization is not a fact and represents the writer's judgment only about a particular set of facts. In the following paragraph, generalizations, not facts, are used to support the main idea:

The wedding is a tradition that most young adults still value. Most engaged couples carefully plan their wedding and regard it as an important occasion in their life. Couples also are very concerned that their ceremony follow rules of etiquette and that everything be done "just so." Most give a great deal of attention to personalizing their ceremony, including their own vows, songs, and symbols.

Notice that the writer does not use concrete, specific information to develop the paragraph. Instead, the author provides generalizations about how young adults feel about their weddings. If the writer is a sociologist who has studied the attitudes toward and customs of marriage, the generalizations may be accurate. However, if the paragraph was written by a parent and based on experience with his or her children and their friends, then you have little reason to accept the generalizations as facts because they are based on limited experience. Both the expertise of the writer and the method by which he or she arrived at the generalizations should influence how readily you should accept them.

When reading material that contains generalizations, approach the writer's conclusion with a critical, questioning attitude. When a generalization is unsubstantiated by facts, regard it as an opinion. Generalizations presented as facts are dangerous and misleading; they may be completely false.

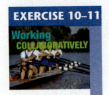

EXERCISE 10–11

Working COLLABORATIVELY

EVALUATING GENERALIZATIONS

Directions: *Indicate which of the following statements are generalizations. Then discuss what type(s) of information or documentation would be necessary for you to evaluate their worth or accuracy.*

1. Worker productivity in the United States is rapidly declining.

   _____

2. Government spending on social programs is detrimental to national economic growth.

   _____

3. In 1964 the federal government officially declared a War on Poverty.

   _____

4. Male computer scientists earn more than female computer scientists with similar job responsibilities.

   _____

5. Illegal aliens residing within the United States are displacing American workers and increasing the unemployment rate.

   _____

EXERCISE 10–12   IDENTIFYING GENERALIZATIONS

Directions: *Visit a Web site sponsored by a company that is advertising its product, or choose an advertisement from a print magazine. Search and make note of any generalizations made about the product advertised.* ■

■ Identifying Tone

Goal 4
Identify tone

A speaker's tone of voice often reveals his or her attitude and contributes to the overall message. Tone is also evident in writing and also contributes to its meaning. Considering an author's tone may help you identify feelings, attitudes, or viewpoints not directly stated by the author.

Tone, then, reveals feelings. Many human emotions can be communicated through tone—disapproval, hate, admiration, disgust, gratitude, forcefulness. Table 10.1 lists words commonly used to describe tone.

TABLE 10.1   Words Frequently Used to Describe Tone

abstract	condemning	forgiving	joyful	playful
absurd	condescending	formal	loving	reverent
amused	cynical	frustrated	malicious	righteous
angry	depressing	gentle	melancholic	sarcastic
apathetic	detached	grim	mocking	satiric
arrogant	disapproving	hateful	nostalgic	sensational
assertive	disrespectful	humorous	objective	serious
awestruck	distressed	impassioned	obsequious	solemn
bitter	docile	incredulous	optimistic	sympathetic
caustic	earnest	indignant	outraged	tragic
celebratory	excited	indirect	pathetic	uncomfortable
cheerful	fanciful	intimate	persuasive	vindictive
comic	farcical	ironic	pessimistic	worried
compassionate	flippant	irreverent		

Read the following passage, paying particular attention to the feeling it creates.

> Among the worst bores in the Western world are religious converts and reformed drunks. . . . I did give up drinking more than a dozen years ago. This didn't make me feel morally superior to anyone. If asked, I would talk about going dry but, from the first, I was determined to preach no sermons and stand in judgment of no human being who took pleasure in the sauce.

But I must confess that lately my feelings have begun to change. Drinking and drunks now fill me with loathing. Increasingly, I see close friends—human beings of intelligence, wit and style—reduced to slobbering fools by liquor. I've seen other friends ruin their marriages, brutalize their children, destroy their careers. I've also reached the age when I've had to help bury a few people who allowed booze to take them into eternity.

—*"The Wet Drug"* by Pete Hamill.

Here the author's disapproval of the use of alcohol is apparent. Through choice of words—*slobbering, loathing*—as well as choice of detail, he makes the tone obvious.

Tone can also establish a distance or formality between the writer and reader, or can establish a sense of shared communication and draw them together. In the excerpts that follow, notice how in the first passage, a formality or distance is established, and in the second, how a familiarity and friendliness are created.

PASSAGE 1

It's not entirely clear whether party voting differences are caused directly by party affiliation or indirectly by the character of constituencies. Some scholars have found strong independent party effects. Others argue that the tendency of people in the same party to vote together is a reflection of the fact that Democratic lawmakers come from districts and states that are similar to each other and that Republican lawmakers come from ones that are different from those of Democrats. Republicans generally come from higher-income districts than Democrats. Democratic districts, in turn, tend to have more union members and racial minorities in them. The strongest tie, in this line of argument, is between the member of Congress and the constituency and not between the member and the party.

—Greenberg and Page, *The Struggle for Democracy,* copyright © 2011 Pearson Education, Inc.

PASSAGE 2

Each time I visit my man in prison, I relive the joy of reunion—and the anguish of separation.

We meet at the big glass door at the entrance to the small visitors' hall at Lompoc Federal Correctional Institution. We look at each other silently, then turn and walk into a room jammed with hundreds of molded fiberglass chairs lined up side by side. Finding a place in the crowded hall, we sit down, appalled that we're actually in a prison. Even now, after four months of such clocked, supervised, regulated visits, we still can't get used to the frustrations.

Yet, as John presses me gently to his heart, I feel warm and tender, and tears well up inside me, as they do each weekend. I have seven hours to spend with the man I love—all too brief a time for sharing a lifetime of emotion: love and longing, sympathy and tenderness, resentment and anger.

—King, *"Love in the Afternoon—In a Crowded Prison Hall,"* Los Angeles Times.

Use the suggestions below to help you identify tone.

NEED TO KNOW How to Identify Tone

1. Consider how the material makes you feel. What emotions surface as you read?
2. Study the author's word choice. Does he or she use words that provoke strong feelings? Which words and phrases have positive or negative associations or connotations (see p. 119 for information about connotative language)?
3. Study how the author writes. Is the material straightforward and factual, or does the writer play with language, use sarcasm or humor, or use figurative language?

EXERCISE 10–13   IDENTIFYING TONE

Directions: *Using Table 10.1 as a reference, choose at least one word that describes the tone of each of the following pieces of writing.*

1. an essay that treats a serious subject lightly and casually

   _____

2. a magazine article that idolizes a motion picture celebrity, describing her amazing talent and beauty while remaining deferential

   _____

3. a comic strip that makes fun of or ridicules the American expression, "Have a good day!"

   _____

4. a section of a criminal justice textbook titled "The Consequences of Unlawful Searches"

   _____

5. a newspaper editorial that attacks a local mayoral candidate with the intent to injure his reputation and that of his family

   _____

EXERCISE 10–14   IDENTIFYING TONE

Directions: *For each item, choose a word from the box that expresses the tone of the sentence.*

awestruck	cynical	depressing	comic	disapproving
compassionate	forgiving	nostalgic	indirect	cheerful
optimistic	sympathetic	outraged	persuasive	serious

_____ 1. Mark Twain has stated that "Man is the only animal that blushes. Or needs to."

_____ 2. The U.S. economy is bound to turn around sooner than later. It can really only get better at this point!

_____ 3. Road construction is the best way to alleviate traffic. Since people are not going to give up their automobiles, they need the new and bigger highways that can accommodate everyone.

_____ 4. So many nations are scarred by war. Our community sends out support to the innocent people caught in unfortunate circumstances.

_____ 5. Station programmers choose such objectionable programming for children. Our household takes a very dim view of the offerings on any commercial channel.

_____ 6. Back in the good old days, scientists could perform any kind of experiments they wanted. Now there is too much government supervision and regulation.

_____ 7. Our history is full of instances in which people acted in ways that we now consider to be abhorrent. However, these early societies did not understand human rights and democracy the way we do now.

_____ 8. The nursing shortage in our country is reaching a critical stage. We must fill our hospitals with fully qualified and educated nurses to avert a health disaster.

_____ 9. How can people let their homes and neighborhoods fall apart and rot away? It is not acceptable to allow such degradation.

_____ 10. Spring is the absolute perfect time for graduations. As Nature herself is bursting forth with newness, so are the hardworking students blossoming with the flowers of their education.

EXERCISE 10–15   **IDENTIFYING TONE**

Directions: *Describe the tone of each of the following passages.*

PASSAGE 1   _____

Rude or indifferent waiters and waitresses should be fired. Nothing can ruin a pleasant meal in a restaurant like a snippy waitress or a superior-acting waiter. Part of the cost of any restaurant meal is the service, and it should be at least as good as the food.

Passage 2 _____

Over the past 20 years I have been involved in working with special education students who have been placed in a classroom for students with serious emotional disturbances and behavioral disorders. During this time, I have been amazed by the "miracle" that special education programs can achieve with students. The miracle is that students go from a *failure identity* to a *success identity*. When they come into the program, they have a failure identity. They hate school because they have never been successful at it. Many are a step away from dropping out.

With these special education programs, these students begin to gain a success identity. They learn to follow the rules and get their work done. Gradually, they begin to feel pride in accomplishment, which plants the seed for intrinsic motivation. In addition, they become aware of choices regarding their behavior and learn to assume responsibility for what they have done. Becoming responsible leads to self-respect, which in turn earns the respect of others.

—Michael S. Nystul, *Introduction to Counseling: An Art and Science Perspective,*
4e, Boston: Pearson, © 2011, pp. 315-316.

Passage 3 _____

Incidence of Schizophrenia

Schizophrenia was originally thought to be confined to North America and Western Europe. We now understand that the disorder (or varieties of the disorder) can be found around the world at the same rate: about 1 percent of the population. People in developing countries tend to have a more acute (intense, but short-lived) course—and a better outcome—of the disorder than do people in industrialized nations. In the United States, schizophrenia accounts for 75 percent of all mental health expenditures. Schizophrenia occurs at the same rate for both sexes, but symptoms are likely to show up earlier in males, and males are more likely to be disabled by the disorder.

—Elliott Currie and Jerome H. Skolnick, *America's Problems,* Second Edition,
p. 217. Glenview, IL: Scott Foresman, 1988.

Passage 4 _____

The most important predictor of student success in school is readiness to learn to read. Unfortunately, many children from high-poverty homes enter school with limited readiness skills. Until we do a more successful job in educating children who have been placed at risk of failure, their communities, and our society in general, will fail to cultivate a substantial reservoir of human talent that will be greatly needed in the years ahead.

—CRESPAR, www.csos.jhu.edu/crespar/

Passage 5 _____

Alcoholism hurts everyone who is involved with the person afflicted with the disease. Alcoholics may be ill and can get treatment for that, but the damage they do while sick is unforgivable and cannot be fixed. People who abuse alcohol to such a degree that they neglect the basic needs of their own children can never reverse the negative effects upon those innocent, developing personas. Children of alcoholics grow up much faster than they should have to—learning early how to fend for themselves at mealtime, keep secrets from their friends, neighbors, teachers and relatives, make excuses, stay out of the way. Twelve steps will never be enough steps for any alcoholic to cure the pain and injury to a child.

PASSAGE 6 _____

As the former gold-medal-winning Olympic athletes entered the arena, the crowd quieted down into a silence and respect worthy of a great cathedral. While each athlete came forward to receive his or her special honor we listened in awe to their inspiring tales of courage and dedication. Such deep emotion was stirred within us by these remarkable individuals!

PASSAGE 7 _____

I am 33 years old and I just called in sick. I'm not really sick. In fact, I'm not the least bit sick. I am totally faking it. And as I dance around my living room singing, "Sick day, sick day!" I think, "Ah, it's good to be nine!" The call was award-winning. A slightly raspy voice with a hint of fatigue combined with a slow, deliberate delivery. "I started throwing up around 3 A.M.," I told my boss. "I'm exhausted and I can't even keep water down. I must have caught that bug that's going around the office." I was told to stay home, rest, and feel better. Exactly what I had in mind.

—McKinnon, *"The Magic of a 'Sick Day': Feigning Illness Can Be Good for You— Especially When Mom's a Co-Conspirator."* Maclean's.

PASSAGE 8 _____

Let's call him "Joe Six Pack." Every Saturday night, he drinks way too much, cranks up the rock 'n roll way too loud, and smacks his girlfriend for acting just a bit too lippy. Or let's call him "Mr. Pillar of the Community." He's got the perfect wife, the perfect kids. But he's also got one little problem: every time he argues with his wife, he loses control. In the past year, she's been sent to the emergency ward twice. Or let's say they're the Tenants from Hell. They're always yelling at each other. Finally a neighbor calls the police. Here is the question. Are the men in these scenarios: (a) in need of help; (b) in need of being locked up; or (c) upholders of the patriarchy?

—"Domestic Violence Laws Are Anti-Male" by Satel.

PASSAGE 9 _____

Crime victims who survive the ordeals to which they were involuntarily subjected must be treated with the utmost kindness and helpfulness. No amount of love and caring is too much to gently guide these poor, broken spirits back to healthy, full lives. We must not blame or condemn them for their suffering, but patiently help them through the cloud of pain back to the sunshine of life.

PASSAGE 10 _____

America has entered a great struggle that tests our strength, and even more our resolve. Our nation is patient and steadfast. We continue to pursue the terrorists in cities and camps and caves across the earth. We are joined by a great coalition of nations to rid the world of terror. And we will not allow any terrorist or tyrant to threaten civilization with weapons of mass murder. Now and in the future, Americans will live as free people, not in fear, and never at the mercy of any foreign plot or power.

—Bush, *"Remarks to the Nation, September 11, 2002,"*
http://www.whitehouse.gov/news/releases/2002/09/20020911-3.html ∎

EXERCISE 10–16   **EXPRESSING TONE**

Directions: *For each topic, write a sentence or two that expresses the given tone.*

1. **Topic:** adoption **Tone:** excited

_____

_____

2. **Topic:** human rights **Tone:** tragic

_____

_____

3. **Topic:** sex education **Tone:** worried

_____

_____

_____

4. **Topic:** endangered species **Tone:** apathetic

_____

5. **Topic:** poverty **Tone:** impassioned

_____

_____

_____ ∎

EXERCISE 10–17   **IDENTIFYING TONE**

Directions: *Choose two of the following end-of-chapter reading selections that appear earlier in the book. Identify the tone of the two that you choose.*

1. "Latino Heritage Month: Who We Are . . . and Why We Celebrate" (Selection 1, p. 41)

_____

2. "Talking a Stranger Through the Night" (Selection 2, p. 46)

_____

3. "Just Walk On By: A Black Man Ponders His Power to Alter Public Space" (Selection 4, p. 84)

_____

4. "Cutting-Edge Word-of-Mouth Advertising Strategies" (Selection 8, p. 183)

_____

5. "New Ways of Administering Justice and Punishment"(Selection 9, p. 234)

_____

■ Identifying the Author's Purpose

Goal 5

Identify an author's purpose

Authors write for a variety of purposes: to inform or instruct the reader, to amuse or entertain, to arouse sympathy, or to persuade the reader to take a particular action or to accept a certain point of view. To be an effective reader you must be aware of the author's purpose. Sometimes the writer's purpose will be obvious, as in the following advertisements:

- At Hair Design Salons we'll make you look better than you can imagine. Six professional stylists to meet your every need. Stop in for a free consultation today.
- Puerto Rican white rum can do anything better than gin or vodka.

The first ad is written to encourage the readers to have their hair styled at Hair Design Salons. The second is intended to encourage readers to use rum instead of gin or vodka in their mixed drinks. In both ads the writer is clearly trying to persuade you to buy a certain product. However, in many other types of reading material, even other advertisements, the writer's purpose is not so obvious.

For instance, in an ad for a particular brand of cigarettes, a stylishly dressed woman is pictured holding a cigarette. The caption reads, "You've come a long way, baby." In this case, although you know that all ads are intended to sell a product or service, the ad does not even mention cigarettes. It is left up to you, the reader, to infer that stylish women smoke Virginia Slims.

EFFICIENCY TIP
Tone is often tied to an author's purpose for writing. When you correctly identify the tone, it is often easy to determine why an author has written a specific piece.

You will often be able to predict the author's purpose from the title of the article or by your familiarity with the writer. For instance, if you noticed a book titled _The Audacity of Hope: Thoughts on Reclaiming the American Dream_ written by Barack Obama, you could predict that the author's purpose is to explain beliefs and policies. An article titled "The President Flexes His Muscles but Nobody Is Watching," written by the CEO of a major corporation, suggests that the author's purpose is to describe how the president is attempting to exert power but having little success.

To identify the author's purpose when it is not apparent, first determine the subject and thesis of the material and notice how the writer supports the thesis.

Ask the questions shown in the box below to identify the author's purpose.

NEED TO KNOW   How to Identify the Author's Purpose

What to Consider	Questions to Ask	Example
Consider the source of the material.	• Is the source specific and detailed? • To whom do the examples appeal? • Are the ideas complex and sophisticated or obvious and straightforward? • Is the language simple or difficult?	A review of a rock concert that appeared in the magazine *Rolling Stone* would be quite different in style, content, and purpose from an article that appeared in *Popular Music and Society.*
Consider the intended audience.	• To what interest level, age, sex, or occupational or ethnic groups would this material appeal?	An article about a musical rock group appearing in *Teen Vogue* may be written to encourage concert attendance or increase its popularity.
Consider the point of view (the perspective from which the material is written).	• Is the point of view objective (factual) or subjective (showing emotion and feeling)? • Are both sides of an issue shown, or does the writer present or favor only one side?	A rock concert may be described quite differently by a music critic, a teenager, and a classical music fan, each expressing different attitudes and opinions.
Consider what the writer may be trying to prove.	• Is the material written to persuade you to accept a particular viewpoint or take a particular action?	A rock concert promoter may write to encourage concert attendance; a music critic may argue that the group has copied the style of another group.

To test the use of the questions in the Need to Know box, read the following passage and apply the critical thinking questions to it.

When you wonder what the land, sky, or ocean is made of, you are thinking about chemistry. When you wonder how a rain puddle dries up, how a car acquires energy from gasoline, or how your body finds energy from the food you eat, you are again thinking about chemistry. By definition, *chemistry* is the study of matter and the transformations it can undergo. Matter is anything that has mass and occupies space. It is the stuff that makes up all material things—anything you can touch, taste, smell, see, or hear is matter.

Chemistry is often described as a central science, because it touches all the other sciences. It springs from the principles of physics, and it serves as the foundation for the most complex science of all—biology. Indeed, many of the great advances in the life sciences today, such as genetic engineering, are applications of some very exotic chemistry. Chemistry is also an important part of space science. Just as we learned about the origin of the moon from the chemical analysis of moon rocks in the early 1970s, we are now learning about the history of Mars and other planets from the chemical information gathered by space probes.

Over the course of the past century, we became very good at manipulating atoms and molecules to create materials to match our needs. At the same time, however, mistakes were made when it came to caring for the environment. Waste products were dumped into rivers, buried in the ground, or vented into the air without regard for possible long-term consequences. Many people believed that Earth was so large that its resources were virtually unlimited and that it could absorb wastes without being significantly harmed.

Most nations now recognize this as a dangerous attitude. As a result, government agencies, industries, and concerned citizens are involved in extensive efforts to take care of the environment. For example, members of the American Chemistry Council, who, as a group, produce 90 percent of the chemicals manufactured in the United States, have adopted a program called Responsible Care. Through this program, members of this organization have pledged to manufacture their products without causing environmental damage. By using chemistry wisely, most waste products can be minimized, recycled, engineered into useful products, or rendered environmentally safe.

The subject of this excerpt is chemistry as a science. The passage seems to be written for people who have limited knowledge of the subject. The point of view is somewhat personal; the author feels excited about his subject and wants his readers to feel the same way. At the same time, he does not want to mislead readers into thinking that chemistry is a magical discipline that solves all problems. He acknowledges that chemistry is partially responsible for environmental problems and talks about the ways chemists are addressing these problems.

EXERCISE 10–18   **IDENTIFYING THE AUTHOR'S PURPOSE**

Directions: *Identify the author's purpose for two of the reading selections listed in Exercise 10–17.*

1. _____

2. _____

   _____

3. _____

_____

4. _____

5. _____

_____ ■

EXERCISE 10–19   **EVALUATING THE AUTHOR'S PURPOSE**

Directions: *Visit a Web site in an area of interest. Browse through the site, evaluate its purpose, and write a brief statement that summarizes its purpose.* ■

EXERCISE 10–20   **DESCRIBING THE AUTHOR'S PURPOSE**

Directions: *Read each of the excerpts in Exercise 10–15. For each, write a statement describing the author's purpose.*

1. _____

2. _____

3. _____

4. _____

5. _____

6. _____

7. _____

8. _____

9. _____

10. _____ ■

■ Recognizing Bias

Goal 6

Recognize bias

Bias refers to an author's partiality, inclination toward a particular viewpoint, or prejudice. A writer is biased if he or she takes one side of a controversial issue and does not recognize opposing viewpoints. Perhaps the best example of bias is in advertising. A magazine advertisement for a new car model, for instance, describes only positive, marketable features—the ad does not recognize the car's limitations or faults. In some material the writer is direct and outright in expressing his or her bias; other times the bias is hidden and left for the reader to discover through careful analysis.

Read the following description of the environmental protection group Greenpeace. The author expresses a favorable attitude toward the organization and a negative one toward whale hunters. Notice, in particular, the highlighted words and phrases.

Greenpeace is an organization dedicated to the preservation of the sea and its great mammals, notably whales, dolphins, and seals. Its ethic is nonviolent but its aggressiveness in protecting our oceans and the life in them is becoming legendary. In their roving ship, the *Rainbow Warrior*, Greenpeace volunteers have relentlessly hounded the profiteering ships of any nation harming the resources Greenpeace deems to be the property of the world community. Whales, they believe, belong to us all and have a right to exist no matter what the demand for shoe-horns, cosmetics, and machine oil.

—Wallace, Robert A., *Biology: The World of Life,* 7th Ed., © 1997. Reprinted and electronically reproduced by permission of Pearson Education, Inc., Upper Saddle River, NJ.

NEED TO KNOW How to Recognize Bias

To identify bias, do the following:

1. **Analyze connotative meanings.** Do you encounter a large number of positive or negative terms used to describe the subject?
2. **Notice descriptive language.** What impression is created?
3. **Analyze the tone.** The author's tone often provides important clues.
4. **Look for opposing viewpoints.**

Recognizing Your Own Bias

Did you know that research studies suggest you will more easily comprehend and recall a message you agree with than one with which you disagree? Suppose you are reading a section in your biology book about the need for tighter controls on industrial pollution. Suppose you once lived next to a factory and feel strongly that tighter controls are needed. You are more likely to understand and recall the information than another student who is opposed to tighter controls. In fact, readers who disagree with an idea tend to miss or overlook ideas that do not support their beliefs.

Be sure to take extra care when reading ideas with which you think you disagree. Try the following suggestions:

1. Keep an open mind until you've read what the author has said and have evaluated the evidence provided.
2. Work harder than usual to follow the writer's development and reasoning process.
3. Outline the writer's main points so you don't overlook anything.

Then, once you've grasped the writer's ideas, feel free to evaluate these ideas and disagree with them.

EXERCISE 10–21   **RECOGNIZING BIAS**

Directions: *Read the following passage and underline words and phrases that reveal the author's bias.*

Not unlike drugs or alcohol, the television experience allows the participant to blot out the real world and enter into a pleasurable and passive mental state. The worries and anxieties of reality are as effectively deferred by becoming absorbed in a television program as by going on a "trip" induced by drugs or alcohol. And just as alcoholics are only inchoately aware of their addiction, feeling that they control their drinking more than they really do ("I can cut it out any time I want—I just like to have three or four drinks before dinner"), people similarly overestimate their control over television watching. Even as they put off other activities to spend hour after hour watching television, they feel they could easily resume living in a different, less passive style. But somehow or other while the television set is present in their homes, the click doesn't sound. With television pleasures available, those other experiences seem less attractive, more difficult somehow.

—*The Plug-In Drug* by Winn, Viking Press, a division of Penguin Books. ■

EXERCISE 10–22   **EVALUATING A READING SELECTION**

Directions: *Choose one of the selections at the end of the chapter and write a one-page paper evaluating the reading. You might focus on one of the following:*

1. Identify what inferences can be made about the subject.

2. Evaluate statements of opinion.

3. Identify several generalizations.

4. Describe the tone of the article.

5. Summarize the author's purpose.

6. Discuss the author's bias and describe how it is revealed. ■

EXERCISE 10–23   **IDENTIFYING BIAS**

Electronic
APPLICATION

Directions: *Visit a Web site or join a newsgroup that addresses a controversial issue. As you browse through the site, look for and make brief notes about any bias you detect.* ■

■ Understanding Figurative Language

Figurative language is a way of describing something that makes sense on an imaginative level but not on a literal or factual level. Notice in each of the following sentences that the highlighted expression cannot be literally true but that each is understandable and is effective in conveying the author's message.

An overly ambitious employee may find the door to advancement closed.
(There is no actual door that may close.)

The federal government is draining taxpayers of any accumulated wealth.
(Nothing is literally being drained or removed from the insides of taxpayers.)

The judge decided to get to the heart of the matter.
(Matters do not really have hearts.)

In each of these expressions, one distinct thing is compared with another for some quality that they have in common.

Using figurative language is an effective way to describe and limit relationships. By your choice of figurative expressions you can create either a positive or a negative impression. For instance, this first statement is somewhat negative:

The blush spread across her face like spilled paint.
(Spilled paint is usually thought of as messy and problematic.)

This second statement, however, creates a more positive image.

The blush spread across her face like wine being poured into a glass.
(Wine filling a glass is commonly thought of as a pleasing image.)

Because figurative language involves impressions and judgments, you should regard them as interpretations, as expressions of opinion and judgment rather than as factual statements.

There are two common types of figurative expressions—similes and metaphors. **Similes** make an explicit comparison by using the words *like* or *as*. **Metaphors** directly equate the two objects. Here are several examples of each:

SIMILES

1. My belly is as cold as if I had swallowed snowballs for pills to cool the views. (Shakespeare)
2. He says the waves in the ship's wake are like stones rolling away.

—By Levertov, from *Poems 1960–1967*, New Directions Publishing Corp.

METAPHORS

1. I will speak daggers but use none. (Shakespeare, *Hamlet*)
2. Hope is the thing with feathers—
   That perches in the soul—

—Emily Dickinson

| EXERCISE 10–24 | **UNDERSTANDING FIGURATIVE LANGUAGE** |

Directions: *Explain the meaning of each of the following metaphors or similes.*

1. The scarlet of the maples can shake me like the cry of bugles going by. (Bliss Carman)

   _____

   _____

   _____

2. Every thread of summer is at last unwoven. (Wallace Stevens)

   _____

   _____

   _____

3. What happens to a dream deferred?
   Does it dry up
   like a raisin in the sun?
   or fester like a sore—
   and then run?
   (Langston Hughes)

   _____

   _____

4. An aged man is but a paltry thing,
   a tattered coat upon a stick, . . .
   (W. B. Yeats)

   _____

■ Thinking Critically: Evaluating Online Sources

Goal 8

Evaluate online sources

The Internet is an impressive and comprehensive resource that requires unique reading and critical analysis skills. Because the Internet is open to all, it is home not only to excellent information but also a good deal of misinformation, as well as rumor and gossip that is mistakenly reported as factual. People can post anything they want on the Internet, regardless of whether it is true or false, objective or subjective, biased, opinionated, or even offensive. And, while certain organizations verify all the information that appears on their Web sites, many do not.

Use the following tips to help you conduct Internet research and evaluate whether you have uncovered reliable, factual information.

1. **While the Internet is vast, not all information on a topic is available on the Web**. Due to copyright restrictions, costs, author preferences, and so on, some information is available only in print form. In addition, many materials written prior to the 1980s are not available on the Web.

2. **Sometimes print sources are better and more convenient.** If you are searching for specific statistics and basic facts (such as population statistics, biographical or historical information, or background information), it may be more efficient to use standard print reference books such as an encyclopedia, world almanac, or *The Statistical Abstract of the United States.*

   Suppose you want to learn more about ear infections. If you type "ear infection" into Google, you will receive an overwhelming amount of information. Instead, start with a subject-area dictionary or encyclopedia to gain a basic understanding of the topic. Print sources can also be very useful when conducting in-depth research. Books often represent years of study by the author. You will find hundreds of pages devoted to all aspects of one topic collected in one place and interpreted by an authority on the subject.

3. **Recognize that articles posted on the Web (which originally appeared in print) lack many of the usual reliability clues.** When you read an article in a magazine, you have a full set of surrounding clues that suggest its reliability or unreliability. In print sources, the table of contents, design, layout, cover content, surrounding articles and essays, and types of advertising all provide clues to the article's trustworthiness. When you read the same article on the Web, many of these clues may be absent. Close scrutiny or further research may be needed to determine reliability.

4. **Do not assume that every source contains accurate and reliable information**. Many hoaxes and scams appear on the Internet. Online as in life, something that is too good to be true usually cannot be trusted.

Evaluating the Content of a Web Site

Use the following suggestions to evaluate the content of a Web site.

Evaluate the Source

An important step in evaluating a Web site is to determine its source. Ask yourself "Who is the sponsor?" and "Why was this site put up on the Web?" The sponsor of a Web site is the person or organization who paid for it to be created and placed on the Web. Knowing the sponsor will often help you determine the purpose of a Web site. For example, a Web site sponsored by Nike is designed to promote its products, while a site sponsored by a university library is designed to help students learn to use its resources more effectively.

If you are uncertain who sponsors a particular Web site, check its URL, its copyright, and the links it offers. The copyright should indicate the owner of the site. If you cannot determine the owner from the copyright, links may reveal the sponsor. Some links may lead to commercial advertising by the sponsor; others may lead to sites sponsored by nonprofit groups, for example.

Another way to check the ownership of a Web site is to try to locate the site's home page. You can do this by using just the first part of its URL—up to the first slash (/) mark. For example, suppose while researching Amy Tan's book *The Joy Luck Club* you find the following Web site: http://www.msu.edu/~shoopsar/joyluck.htm. You can trace this Web site by shortening it to http://www.msu.edu/~shoopsar/. This URL takes you to the Web site author's personal Web site. If you take this a step further and shorten the URL to http://www.msu.edu/, and then search the Michigan State University Web site for "Joy Luck Club," you will discover the home page for ATL 140 with a link to the student writers.

Evaluate Level of Technical Detail

A Web site should contain a level of technical detail that is suited to your purpose. Some sites may provide information that is too sketchy; others may assume a level of background knowledge or technical sophistication that you lack. For example, if you are writing a short, introductory-level paper on threats to the survival of marine animals, information on the Web site of the Scripps Institution of Oceanography (http://www-sio.ucsd.edu) may be too technical and contain more information than you need, unless you have some previous knowledge in that field.

Evaluate the Presentation

Information on a Web site should be presented clearly; it should be well written. If you find a site that is not clear and well written, you should be suspicious of it. If the author did not take time to present ideas clearly and correctly, he or she may not have taken time to collect accurate information either.

Evaluate Completeness

Determine whether the site provides complete information on its topic. Does it address all aspects of the topic that you feel it should? For example, if a Web site titled "Important Twentieth-Century American Poets" does not mention Robert Frost, then the site is incomplete. If you discover that a site is incomplete, search for sites that provide a more thorough treatment of the topic.

Evaluate the Links

Many reputable sites supply links to other related sites. Make sure that the links work and are current, and check to see if the sites to which you were sent are reliable sources of information. If the links do not work or the sources appear unreliable, you should question the reliability of the site itself. Also determine whether the links provided are comprehensive or only present a representative sample. Either is acceptable, but the site should make clear the nature of the links it is providing.

EXERCISE 10–25   **EVALUATING CONTENT**

> **Directions:** *Visit the following Web sites and evaluate their content. Explain why you would either trust or distrust each site for reliable content.*

1. http://www.carboncapturereport.org/

   _____

   _____

   _____

   _____

   _____

2. http://www.rxlaughter.org/   ■

Evaluating the Accuracy of a Web Site

One way to determine the accuracy of a Web site is to compare it with print sources (periodicals and books) on the same topic. If you find a wide discrepancy between the Web site and the printed sources, do not trust the Web site. Another way to determine the accuracy of a site's information is to compare it with other Web sites that address the same topic. If discrepancies exist, further research is needed to determine which site is more accurate.

The site itself will also provide clues about the accuracy of its information. Ask yourself the following questions:

- **Are the author's name and credentials provided?** A well-known writer with established credentials is likely to author only reliable, accurate information. If no author is given, you should question whether the information is accurate.

- **Is contact information for the author included on the site?** Often, sites provide an e-mail address where the author may be contacted.

- **Is the information complete or in summary form?** If it is a summary, use the site to find the original source. Original information has less chance of error and is usually preferred in academic papers.

- **If opinions are offered, are they presented clearly as opinions?** Authors who disguise their opinions as facts are not trustworthy. (See p. 423.)

- **Does the writer make unsubstantiated assumptions or base his or her ideas on misconceptions?** (See "Identifying Assumptions," Chapter 11, p. 477.) If so, the information presented may not be accurate.

- **Does the site provide a list of works cited?** As with any form of research, sources used to put information up on a Web site must be documented. If sources are not credited, you should question the accuracy of the Web site.

EXERCISE 10–26   **EVALUATING ACCURACY**

> **Directions:** *Go to your search engine and type in a key word (or words) related to a topic you are interested in. Choose three sites that come up close to the top of the search list. Using the guidelines on page 448, evaluate each site for accuracy.*

Evaluating the Timeliness of a Web Site

Although the Web is well known for providing up-to-the-minute information, not all Web sites are current. Evaluate the timeliness of a site by checking

- the date on which the Web site was mounted (put on the Web)
- the date on which the document you are using was added
- the date on which the site was last revised
- the date on which the links were last checked

This information is usually provided at the end of the site's home page or at the end of the document you are using.

EXERCISE 10–27   **EVALUATING TIMELINESS**

> **Directions:** *Visit two of the following Web sites and evaluate their timeliness. Follow the directions given below for each site.*

1. http://www.state.gov/r/pa/ei/bgn/ Choose a geographic region, such as Africa, and evaluate whether information is up-to-date.

2. http://www.nytimes.com/2005/08/28/fashion/sundaystyles/ 28MYSPACE.html?pagewanted=all. Evaluate the timeliness of this paper as a whole and the references within it.

   _____

   _____

   _____

   _____

3. http://www.hwg.org/resources/?cid=30 Notice the date when these links were last checked. Follow several of the links. What happens?

Evaluating the Purpose of a Web Site

There are five basic types of Web sites: *informational*, *news*, *advocacy*, *personal*, and *commercial*. Each has a different purpose, and you should approach each differently. These differences are summarized in Table 10.2.

TABLE 10.2 Types of Web Sites	
Type	**Purpose and Description**
Informational	To present facts, information, and research data. May contain reports, statistical data, results of research studies, and reference materials.
News	To provide current information on local, national, and international news. Often supplement print newspapers, periodicals, and television news programs.
Advocacy	To promote a particular cause or point of view. Usually concerned with a controversial issue; often sponsored by nonprofit groups.
Personal	To provide information about an individual and his or her interests and accomplishments. May list publications or include the individual's résumé.
Commercial	To promote goods or services. May provide news and information related to products.

EXERCISE 10–28   **IDENTIFYING PURPOSE**

Directions: *Using the information in Table 10.2, determine the purpose(s) of five of the following Web sites. Be sure to investigate the whole site carefully and explain your choices.*

1. http://bioguide.congress.gov/

2. Washington Post Online, http://www.washingtonpost.com

3. http://www.sustainablecommunities.gov/

4. http://explore.georgetown.edu/people/tannend/?PageTemplateID=129

5. http://www.psychology.org/

6. http://www.computers4africa.org/

7. www.astronomy.ua.edu/4000WS

8. http://scorecard.org

9. http://www.amnestyusa.org/

EXERCISE 10–29   **EVALUATING WEB SITES**

Directions: *Visit the following two combination sites.*

1. http://www.arborday.org/
2. http://www.ivu.org/recipes/

Evaluating the Structure of a Web Site

A Web site should be easy to use. You should be able to navigate among pages and links easily, and you should be able to find the information you need quickly, usually within two or three clicks. A complex site should have a site map or directory that visually displays the organization and content of the site. The graphics and art should serve specific functions; they should be more than simply decoration. Graphics, sound, color, and animation should not detract from the usability of the site.

EXERCISE 10-30   **EVALUATING WEB SITES**

Directions: *Evaluate how easy it is to navigate within one of the following Web sites. Consider, for example, whether it has a site map or search capabilities. Does it use graphics, sound, and color?*

1. http://www.census.gov/prod/www/abs/statab1995_2000.html
2. http://jobstar.org/
3. http://www.recipesource.com/special-diets/vegetarian/

EXERCISE 10–31   **EVALUATING USEFULNESS AND RELIABILITY**

Directions: *Suppose you are writing a research paper on the effects of video games on children. You use the search engine Google.com and enter the terms "video games effect children." Among others, you will find the following two Web sites. Visit each site and evaluate its overall usefulness and reliability. Compare your answers with those of a classmate.*

1. http://en.wikipedia.org/wiki/video_game_controversy
2. http://www.msnbc.msn.com/id/16099971/

NEED TO KNOW A Checklist for Evaluating Web Sources

Use the following questions to evaluate Web sites:

1. What is the purpose of the site?
2. Is the site appropriate for your research purpose?
3. Who is the site's sponsor and who is the author?
4. Does the site have an appropriate level of detail?
5. Is the information presented clearly?
6. Is the information complete?
7. Are sources documented?
8. Are opinions distinguished from facts?
9. Is the information available in print form?
10. When was the site last revised?
11. Are the links useful and up-to-date?
12. What role, if any, does advertising play?

SELF-TEST SUMMARY

Goal 1	1. What is involved in making an inference?	An inference is a reasonable guess made on the basis of available information. To make an inference as you read, • be sure you understand the literal meaning first • ask questions about the stated information • use clues provided by the writer • consider the writer's purpose • verify your information
Goal 2	2. How can facts be distinguished from opinions?	Facts can be shown to be true; they can be verified and regarded as reliable information. Because opinions express attitudes, beliefs, or feelings, they are not reliable and should be carefully questioned and evaluated.
Goal 3	3. What are generalizations?	Generalizations are statements made about a large group or class of items based on experience with only a part of the group or class. When generalizations are stated as facts, carefully evaluate them before you accept them as true.
Goal 4	4. How can you detect a writer's tone?	The tone of a piece of writing often reveals an author's attitude, feelings, and viewpoints about a subject. Paying attention to the choice of words and the style of writing can reveal a writer's tone.
Goal 5	5. How can you identify an author's purpose?	An awareness of the author's purpose—or reason for writing—is important in evaluating a work. To identify an author's purpose you should ask four questions: • What is the source of the material? • Who is the intended audience? • What is the point of view? • What is the writer trying to prove about the subject?
Goal 6	6. How can you detect bias in a piece of writing?	Bias refers to an author's favoring a particular viewpoint on an issue. To detect bias, • analyze connotative meanings • notice descriptive language • analyze the tone • look for opposing viewpoints
Goal 7	7. What is figurative language?	Figurative language involves the use of expressions that make sense on an imaginative level but not on a literal level.
Goal 8	8. How can you evaluate an online source?	Consider all of the following: • content • accuracy • timeliness • purpose • structure

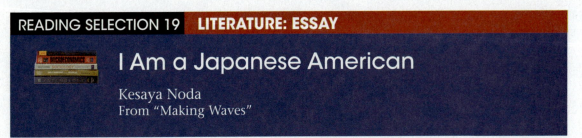

READING SELECTION 19   LITERATURE: ESSAY

I Am a Japanese American

Kesaya Noda
From "Making Waves"

About the Reading

EXCERPT FROM ESSAY

The piece that follows is an excerpt from a longer essay that focuses on the author's experiences as a person of color growing up in the United States. In the full essay, the author confronts stereotypes by reflecting on the many aspects of her identity—racial (Japanese), historical/cultural (Japanese-American), gender based (Japanese-American woman), and finally, human (for her, a spiritual perspective). The essay describes two experiences of identity: the painful experience of having identity imposed from the outside through stereotypes, and the freeing, empowering experience of defining identity oneself from within a rich context of culture, family, and community.

Planning Your Reading Strategy*

Directions: *Activate your thinking by previewing the reading (see the Need to Know box on page 64) and answering the following questions.*

____ 1. To which information should you pay closest attention while reading the essay?
   a. the Japanese experience during the war
   b. the challenges of being a woman in a man's world
   c. the complexities of identity
   d. the Japanese-born population of California

____ 2. Suppose a particular student decides that he or she can read this essay fairly quickly. What course is the student likely to have taken and done well in?
   a. art history
   b. biology
   c. economics
   d. sociology

3. Based on your preview of the reading, how quickly do you think you should read the selection? (Circle one.) Explain your answer.

   Very slowly   Slowly   At a moderate pace   Quickly   Very quickly

4. To which minority groups do you belong, if any? How does membership in these groups affect your self-perception and your identity?

Reprinted by permission of the author; Kesaya Noda, from *Making Waves*, by Asian Woman United, 1989.

---

* The Scorecard on p. 458 enables you to compute your reading rate. In order to do so, be sure to record your starting time in the Scorecard box before you begin reading.

1   Sometimes when I was growing up, my identity seemed to hurtle toward me and paste itself right to my face. I felt that way, encountering the stereotypes of my race perpetuated by non-Japanese people (primarily white) who may or may not have had contact with other Japanese in America. "You don't like cheese, do you?" someone would ask. "I know your people don't like cheese." Sometimes questions came making allusions to history. That was another aspect of the identity. Events that had happened quite apart from the me who stood silent in that moment connected my face with an incomprehensible past. "Your parents were in California? Were they in those camps during the war?" And sometimes there were phrases or nicknames: "Lotus Blossom." I was sometimes addressed or referred to as racially Japanese, sometimes as Japanese American, and sometimes as an Asian woman. Confusions and distortions abounded.

2   How is one to know and define oneself? From the inside—within a context that is self defined, from a grounding in community and a connection with culture and history that are comfortably accepted? Or from the outside—in terms of messages received from the media and people who are often ignorant? Even as an adult I can still see two sides of my face and past. I can see from the inside out, in freedom. And I can

see from the outside in, driven by the old voices of childhood and lost in anger and fear.

3   "Weak." I hear the voice from my childhood years. "Passive," I hear. Our parents and grandparents were the ones who were put into those camps.[1] They went without resistance; they offered cooperation as proof of loyalty to America. "Victim," I hear. And, "Silent."

4   Our parents are painted as hard workers who were socially uncomfortable and had difficulty expressing even the smallest opinion. Clean, quiet, motivated, and determined to match the American way; that is us, and that is the story of our time here.

5   "Why did you go into those camps," I raged at my parents, frightened by my own inner silence and timidity. "Why didn't you do anything to resist? Why didn't you name it the injustice it was?" Couldn't our parents even think? Couldn't they? Why were we so passive?

6   I shift my vision and my stance. I am in California. My uncle is in the midst of the sweet potato harvest. He is pressed, trying to get the harvesting crews onto the field as quickly as possible, worried about the flow of equipment and people. His big pickup is pulled off to the side, motor running, door ajar. I see two tractors in the yard in front of an old shed; the flat bed harvesting platform on which the workers will stand has already been brought over from the other field. It's early morning. The workers stand loosely grouped and at ease, but my uncle looks as harried and tense as a police officer trying to unsnarl a New York City traffic jam. Driving toward the shed, I pull my car off the road to make way for an approaching tractor. The front wheels of the car sink luxuriously into the soft, white sand by the roadside and the car slides to a dreamy halt, tail still on the road. I try to move forward. I try to move back. The front bites contentedly into the sand, the back lifts at a jaunty angle. My uncle sees me and storms

---

[1]During World War II, many Japanese in the United States were placed in camps.

down the road, running. He is shouting before he is even near me.

7   "What's the matter with you," he screams. "What the hell are you doing?" In his frenzy, he grabs his hat off his head and slashes it through the air across his knee. He is beside himself. "Don't you know how to drive in sand? What's the matter with you? You've blocked the whole roadway. How am I supposed to get my tractors out of here? Can't you use your head? You've cut off the whole roadway, and we've got to get out of here."

8   I stand on the road before him helplessly thinking, "No, I don't know how to drive in sand. I've never driven in sand."

9   "I'm sorry, uncle," I say, burying a smile beneath a look of sincere apology. I notice my deep amusement and my affection for him with great curiosity. I am usually devastated by anger. Not this time.

10   During the several years that follow I learn about the people and the place, and much more about what has happened in this California village where my parents grew up. The issei, our grandparents, made this settlement in the desert. Their first crops were eaten by rabbits and ravaged by insects. The land was so barren that men walking from house to house sometimes got lost. Women came here too. They bore children in 114 degree heat, then carried the babies with them into the fields to nurse when they reached the end of each row of grapes or other truck farm crops.

11   I had had no idea what it meant to buy this kind of land and make it grow green. Or how, when the war came, there was no space at all for the subtlety of being who we were—Japanese Americans. Either/or was the way. I hadn't understood that people were literally afraid for their lives then, that their money had been frozen in banks; that there was a five-mile travel limit; that when the early evening curfew came and they were inside their houses, some of them watched helplessly as people they knew went into their barns to steal their belongings. The police were patrolling the road, interested only in violators of curfew. There was no help for them in the face of thievery. I had not been able to imagine before what it must have felt like to be an American—to know absolutely that one is an American—and yet to have almost everyone else deny it. Not only deny it, but challenge that identity with machine guns and troops of white American soldiers. In those circumstances it was difficult to say, "I'm a Japanese American." "American" had to do.

12   But now I can say that I am a Japanese American. It means I have a place here in this country, too. I have a place on the East Coast, where our neighbor is so much a part of our family that my mother never passes her house at night without glancing at the lights to see if she is home and safe; where my parents have hauled hundreds of pounds of rocks from fields and arduously planted Christmas trees and blueberries, lilacs, asparagus, and crab apples; where my father still dreams of angling a stream to a new bed so that he can dig a pond in the field and fill it with water and fish. "The neighbors already came for their Christmas tree?" he asks in December. "Did they like it? Did they like it?"

13   I have a place on the West Coast where my relatives still farm, where I heard the stories of feuds and backbiting, and where I saw that people survived and flourished because fundamentally they trusted and relied upon one another. A death in the family is not just a death in a family; it is a death in the community. I saw people help each other with money, materials, labor, attention, and time. I saw men gather once a year, without fail, to clean the grounds of a ninety-year-old woman who had helped the community before, during, and after the war. I saw her remembering them with birthday cards sent to each of their children.

14   I come from a people with a long memory and a distinctive grace. We live our thanks. And we are Americans. Japanese Americans.

Examining Reading Selection 19*

Checking Your Vocabulary

Directions: *Use context, word parts, or a dictionary, if necessary, to determine the meaning of each word as it is used in the reading.*

____ 1. stereotypes (paragraph 1)
   a. unchanging images or attitudes
   b. discriminatory acts
   c. insulting comments
   d. racial slurs

____ 2. incomprehensible (paragraph 1)
   a. uneventful
   b. embarrassing
   c. futile
   d. not understandable

____ 3. passive (paragraphs 3 and 5)
   a. angry
   b. resentful
   c. inactive
   d. frightened

____ 4. harried (paragraph 6)
   a. awkward
   b. rushed
   c. disciplined
   d. commonplace

____ 5. arduously (paragraph 12)
   a. with great effort
   b. in a haphazard, lazy fashion
   c. in a disinterested manner
   d. with little skill

Checking Your Comprehension

Directions: *Select the best answer.*

____ 6. This reading is primarily about Noda's
   a. racial background.
   b. ancestors.
   c. racial identity.
   d. experiences in America.

____ 7. The author's main point is that she
   a. is unsure if she belongs in America.
   b. views herself in two ways.

   c. feels she has rejected her Japanese heritage.
   d. has disappointed her family.

____ 8. During her childhood, Noda thought of her grandparents as
   a. weak.
   b. important.
   c. influential.
   d. stupid.

____ 9. As described in the reading, death in the Japanese community is regarded as
   a. a private family matter.
   b. a religious experience.
   c. a completion of the life cycle.
   d. a community concern.

____ 10. The author organizes her ideas using
   a. chronology.
   b. classification.
   c. comparisons.
   d. order of importance.

Thinking Critically

____ 11. Which of the following best describes Noda's attitude toward being a Japanese American?
   a. embarrassed
   b. dismayed
   c. angry
   d. proud

____ 12. The author would probably agree with which one of the following statements?
   a. Attitudes are fixed and unchanging.
   b. Ancestors make unfortunate errors in judgment.
   c. Many Americans express stereotyped perceptions of Japanese Americans.
   d. A person's identity is related to his or her ethnic heritage.

---

*Writing About the Reading questions appear in the Instructor's Manual.

___ 13. The author explains her ideas by
   a. analyzing them.
   b. recounting events that illustrate them.
   c. comparing them with those of her parents.
   d. giving reasons.

___ 14. The form of this reading suggests it may have been part of
   a. an argumentative essay.
   b. a newspaper article.
   c. an autobiography.
   d. a novel.

___ 15. The author likely included the photo on page 455 in order to
   a. emphasize that Japanese Americans do not like to mix with other cultural groups in the United States.
   b. show that Japanese Americans, once known for having small families, now have much larger families than they used to.
   c. provide a rare example of a Japanese American family that did not return to Japan after World War II.
   d. hint at the ways in which a person's identity is tied to the experiences of previous generations.

Questions for Discussion

1. Have you ever been stereotyped because of your ethnic background?

2. How is death regarded in your ethnic community? How is this different from the way it is regarded in the Japanese community?

3. What factors other than ethnic origin do you think constitute or define identity?

Scorecard

Selection 19:   1,359 words

Finishing Time: _____ _____ _____
                 HR.   MIN.   SEC.

Starting Time: _____ _____ _____
                HR.   MIN.   SEC.

Reading Time: _____ _____
                      MIN.   SEC.

WPM Score: _____

COmprehension Score: for Items 6–15
Number Right: _____ × 10 = _____%

Assessing Your Reading Strategy

1. How would you rate your comprehension of the reading? (Circle one.)
   Excellent   Good   Fair   Poor

2. Did you find your reading strategy effective?
   Yes   No

3. Suppose you were given an assignment to read another selection from the same source (a popular news magazine). Based on your experience with this selection, how would you adjust your reading strategy (if at all)?

READING SELECTION 20 **MUSIC**

Experiencing Music

Steven Cornelius and Mary Natvig

About the Reading

TEXTBOOK
EXCERPT

"Experiencing Music" is an excerpt from the first chapter of an introductory music textbook titled Music: A Social Experience, *by Steven Cornelius and Mary Natvig.*

MyReadingLab™ *The exercises following this selection can be completed online at myreadinglab.com*

Planning Your Reading Strategy*

Directions: *Activate your thinking by previewing the reading (see the Need to Know box on page 64) and answering the following questions.*

____ 1. Based on your preview, the material to which you should pay closest attention in this reading is
   a. the medical problems experienced by Veva Campbell.
   b. the role of music in ancient Rome.
   c. music's effects on the brain and on human culture.
   d. the differences between classical and modern music.

____ 2. Knowing the source of the reading and its location in the book's first chapter, the authors' primary purpose for writing "Experiencing Music" is most likely to
   a. motivate students to see music in different and perhaps unexpected ways.
   b. teach students how to read the notes on the musical scale.
   c. encourage music as a form of therapy for invalids and recovering patients.
   d. insist that readers learn to play a musical instrument of their choice.

3. The "Did You Know?" feature states, "Listeners really do 'get high' from music." What type(s) of music have this effect on you?

"Music produces a kind of pleasure which human nature cannot do without."

—Confucius (ca. 551 BCE to 479 BCE)

■ Introduction

1 Ninety-three-year-old Veva Campbell slumps wordlessly in her wheelchair. A victim of Alzheimer's disease, she has not spoken, walked, fed herself, or recognized friends and family for over two years. This afternoon, her granddaughter, an out-of-town musician, comes to visit. There is nothing to say or do, so she pulls out her violin and begins to play. Miraculously, Mrs. Campbell sits up and begins singing along to the traditional hymns and old-time songs she recognizes from her youth. When the music stops, Mrs. Campbell retreats back into silence.

2 Our story is not apocryphal. Mrs. Campbell was the coauthor's grandmother. And this demonstration of music's power, remarkable as

Cornelius, Steven; Natvig, Mary, Music: A Social Experience, *1st Ed., © 2012. Reprinted and electronically reproduced by permission of Pearson Education Inc., Upper Saddle River, NJ.*

---

* The Scorecard on p. 463 enables you to compute your reading rate. In order to do so, be sure to record your starting time in the Scorecard box before you begin reading.

it may be, is not an isolated example. All over the world music unites and heals, transforms and inspires. This appears to have been the case since the beginning of civilization.

■ Music and the Brain

3   The foundation of musical experience resides deep within the mind. Medical science is just beginning to document these complexities. We know, for example, that severe stutterers, even those unable to get out single spoken words, can sometimes perfectly sing entire sentences. We know that by setting instructions to song, sufferers of autism can learn to execute sequential tasks otherwise far beyond their reach. And we know that when medication fails, those with the neuropsychiatric disorder Tourette syndrome can successfully use drum circles to calm their tics.

4   There is much to learn. Scientists cannot explain the case of Tony Cicoria, a middle-aged physician who, after being struck by lightning, suddenly developed a passion and gift for playing the piano and composing. Nor can they explain the case of Clive Wearing, a British amnesia victim who, despite being able to remember just a few seconds into the past, can still play the piano, read music, and even direct choral rehearsals.

5   The human brain seems to be programmed for song. So fundamental is the human capacity for music that it may have evolved even before speech. Physiologists have shown that a mother's lullaby does double duty by lowering a child's arousal levels while simultaneously increasing the child's ability to focus attention. Music therapists have found that listening to music induces the release of pleasure-producing endorphins that both lower blood pressure and ease the sensation of physical pain. Social scientists believe that music, by bringing people together to perform and listen, may have provided an early model for social cooperation, cohesion, and even reproductive success. If this is correct, then music would seem to be a fundamental building block in the development of culture.

6   Attentive listening is good for the brain. It helps us organize our thinking, give shape to our consciousness, and focus our ideas. These phenomena seem to happen for a variety of reasons and in a number of ways. Our involuntary nervous system—including heart rate, brain waves, and other basic bodily functions—automatically entrains to the sounds we hear. We also respond to music's emotional qualities. Lovely melodies softly played relax us, whereas beating drums and searing trumpets excite us. A favorite song recalls times gone by, whereas the sounds of a national anthem invite us to reflect upon our identity.

7   Music helps structure the analytical mind. Psychological studies suggest that musical training improves one's organizational skills and can even have a positive effect on IQ. Indeed, scientists hypothesize that while performing, musicians are actually engaged in high-powered brain calisthenics. These skills transfer to other areas of life.

DID YOU KNOW?

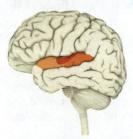

The auditory cortex, which grows with musical training, can be up to 130 percent larger in musicians than in nonmusicians. Brains grow when challenged with physical tasks as well. The part of the brain that governs a violinist's left-hand fingers will be larger than the part that governs the right-hand fingers. Presumably, Jimi Hendrix, who played the guitar "backwards," would have shown more brain growth for the right-hand fingers.

The human brain, highlighting the auditory cortex.

8   Clearly, active musical experience affects consciousness in profound ways. But what does this mean for you? What if you do not play music, sing, or dance? Research shows that one need not perform to reap music's benefits. Simply engaging in *active* listening is enough to set the brain in high gear. And the best part of all this is that the effects of listening skills are cumulative. The better you learn to listen today, the more listening techniques you will have available tomorrow.

■ Music and Culture

9   Societies, both ancient and modern, have recognized music's transformative agency. Indeed, Greek mythology tells us that music had power over death itself. When Orpheus's beloved wife Eurydice died and passed into the underworld, he followed. Empowered by the irresistible strains of his lyre, Orpheus swayed the will of the gods; Eurydice was thus allowed to return to the land of the living. The idea of music's regenerative power remains relevant today. As was witnessed worldwide in the remarkable concerts following the tragedy of 9/11, music making often signifies a return to life.

10   Cultures around the world have stories about the power of music. For the Temiar people of Malaysia in Southeast Asia, shamans heal with songs received from spirit guides. In the American Southwest, Hopi mythology tells of the primordial beings Tawa and Spider Woman, who sat together and sang humanity into existence. The rhythmic dance of the Hindu deity Shiva is said to animate the universe.

11   There are micro cultures as well. Consider, for example, a large corporation such as Sony BMG Music Entertainment. Top executives live in a very different world from the company's general desk-bound workforce and from the company's contracted musicians, such as Alicia Keys or the band AC/DC.

12   What might constitute a musical culture? Perhaps it is a group of people who share particular values that are reflected in the way they make, hear, and use music. In North America, for example, the music industry divides itself for marketing purposes into specific **genres**—Top Forty, bluegrass, jazz, world music, classical, blues, zydeco, country and western, hip-hop, and many more. These designations offer commercial boundaries. Do they also represent distinct musical cultures?

13   Cultural identities are flexible and constantly negotiated. In today's society, people often move from one cultural circle to another as they pass through adolescence, go to college, learn new languages, enter the workforce, travel, or get married. Some people will use music to reinforce their identities or to form stronger links to their cultural heritage. Teenagers, however, often use music to break free of cultural expectations. For

Orpheus depicted on a Roman mosaic, playing his lyre to tame wild animals.

teens, listening habits often represent an expression of individuality and independence.

14   Think about the ideas presented here. Which musical compositions are used to wield power? To persuade? To soothe? How do these works fit into the artists' cultural milieux? And finally, how might considering music from the composers' or performers' social perspectives enhance your understanding of the world and your own listening choices?

DID YOU KNOW?

MUSIC AND THE MIND

Some cultures fear music's power; others dress it in mysticism. There's good reason for this. Music activates the same chemical reactions in the brain as food, sex, and addictive drugs. Listeners really do "get high" from music. Thousands of scientific studies have been undertaken in an attempt to understand music's remarkable impact on human consciousness.

Examining Reading Selection 20

Complete this Exercise at myreadinglab.com

Checking Your Vocabulary

Directions: *Use context, word parts, or a dictionary, if necessary, to determine the meaning of each word as it is used in the reading.*

___ 1. isolated (paragraph 2)
   a. single
   b. lonely
   c. remote
   d. desolate

___ 2. sequential (paragraph 3)
   a. unusual
   b. in order
   c. partial
   d. uncertain

___ 3. induces (paragraph 5)
   a. alters
   b. causes
   c. prevents
   d. limits

___ 4. profound (paragraph 8)
   a. casual
   b. negative
   c. common
   d. deep

___ 5. wield (paragraph 14)
   a. harm
   b. want
   c. exert
   d. conceal

Checking Your Comprehension

Directions: *Select the best answer.*

___ 6. This reading is primarily concerned with
   a. types of music.
   b. the history of music.
   c. the power of music.
   d. musical traditions.

___ 7. The central idea of this selection is that
   a. music therapy is an effective way to treat a variety of disorders.
   b. music has a powerful impact on the human brain and on culture.
   c. music was an important element of ancient societies.
   d. musicians are able to develop their brains in unique ways.

___ 8. According to the selection, listening to music produces all of the following physiological effects *except*
   a. lowering a child's arousal levels.
   b. increasing a child's ability to focus attention.
   c. preventing the release of endorphins.
   d. easing the sensation of physical pain.

___ 9. The power of music is illustrated in Hopi mythology by the story of
   a. a rhythmic dance which animated the universe.
   b. primordial beings who sang humanity into existence.

c. shamans healing with songs from spirit guides.

d. lyre music played to bring a loved one back to life.

_____ 10. All of the following statements about the benefits of music are true *except*

a. musical training improves one's organizational skills.

b. musical training can have a positive effect on intelligence.

c. learning music causes the auditory cortex in the brain to grow.

d. performing is the only way to gain the benefits of music.

Thinking Critically

_____ 11. The best guide question based on this reading is:

a. What is music?

b. In what ways can music be classified?

c. How do people learn to play music?

d. What impact does music have on the human brain?

_____ 12. The authors' tone can best be described as

a. informative and engaging.

b. formal and detached.

c. critical and disapproving.

d. serious and concerned.

_____ 13. The diagram of the human brain was included to show

a. how the brain is affected by Alzheimer's disease.

b. which part of the brain grows with musical training.

c. how music creates a "high" in the brain.

d. how part of the brain is programmed for song.

_____ 14. The authors' primary purpose in writing this selection is to

a. persuade researchers to study the powerful effects of music.

b. generate sympathy for people with disorders treated by musical therapy.

c. compare and contrast the different perceptions of music throughout history.

d. inform readers about the physical, mental, and cultural effects of music.

_____ 15. The authors support their ideas by doing all of the following *except*

a. giving examples.

b. describing research.

c. citing statistics.

d. discussing reasons.

Scorecard

Selection 20:   1,283 words

Finishing Time: _____ _____ _____
                  HR.   MIN.   SEC.

Starting Time: _____ _____ _____
                  HR.   MIN.   SEC.

Reading Time: _____ _____
                          MIN.   SEC.

WPM Score: _____

Comprehensive Score: for items 6–15

Number Right: _____ × 10 = _____%

Assessing Your Reading Strategy

1. How would you rate your comprehension of the reading? (Circle one.)
Excellent   Good   Fair   Poor

2. Did you find your reading strategy effective?   Yes   No

3. Suppose you were given an assignment to read a similar selection to the one you just read. Based on your experience with this selection, how would you adjust your reading strategy (if at all)?

Writing About Reading Selection 20

Checking Your Vocabulary

Directions: *Complete each of the following items; refer to a dictionary if necessary.*

1. Describe the denotative and connotative meanings of the word *miraculously* in paragraph 1.

   _____

   _____

   _____

2. Describe the denotative and connotative meanings of the word *searing* in paragraph 6.

   _____

   _____

3. Explain the meaning of the word *apocryphal* and how it is used in paragraph 2.

   _____

   _____

   _____

4. Define the word *cumulative* (paragraph 8) and underline the words or phrases that provide clues to its meaning.

   _____

5. Define the word *genres* (paragraph 12) and underline the words or phrases that provide a clue for its meaning.

   _____

6. Determine the meanings of the following words by using word parts:
   a. *transforms* (paragraph 2)

   _____

b. *physiologists* (paragraph 5)

   _____

   _____

c. *irresistible* (paragraph 9)

   _____

d. *regenerative* (paragraph 9)

   _____

e. *perspectives* (paragraph 14)

   _____

Checking Your Comprehension

7. What four conditions or disorders do the authors use to illustrate the positive effects of music?

   _____

   _____

8. Who are Tony Cicoria and Clive Wearing and why are they included in the selection?

   _____

   _____

   _____

   _____

   _____

   _____

9. In what three ways do the authors say attentive listening is good for our brains?

   _____

   _____

   _____

10. What is the difference between the auditory cortex in musicians and nonmusicians?

_____

_____

Thinking Critically

11. Why did the authors open this selection by describing a person with Alzheimer's disease?

_____

_____

_____

12. What is meant by the term "brain calisthenics" (paragraph 7)?

_____

_____

_____

13. Why do the authors compare top executives at Sony BMG Music Entertainment with the company's contracted musicians?

_____

_____

14. What do the authors mean when they say "cultural identities are flexible" (paragraph 13)?

_____

_____

_____

_____

15. Why do you think the authors included the photograph on page 461?

_____

_____

_____

Questions for Discussion

1. Think about how you listen to music. What is your favorite music for different activities, such as studying, going out, or relaxing at home? How many purposes can you name for music in your own life?

2. Discuss the authors' question in paragraph 12: What might constitute a musical culture? To what musical cultures do you belong?

3. Discuss the idea that listeners can "get high" from music. Can you think of a song or musical composition that has had an extraordinary impact on your consciousness?

4. Discuss the use of music as a form of therapy. In addition to the examples in the selection, what other applications can you think of for music therapy?

think VISUALLY...

Study the photograph. What issue is at stake? What position are the demonstrators taking on the issue? What evidence would you need to evaluate their position and, then, either agree or disagree with it?

The photograph presents two essential ingredients of an argument; an *issue*, in this case sending manufacturing work overseas, and a *position* on the issue—that companies should retain manufacturing jobs in America.

In this chapter you will learn how to read arguments and other forms of persuasive writing, evaluate source and authority, recognize the structure of arguments, and identify reasoning errors.

Learning GOALS

In this chapter, you will learn how to . . .

Goal 1 Evaluate sources and author qualifications

Goal 2 Understand the elements of an argument

Goal 3 Evaluate the soundness of an argument

Goal 4 Identify reasoning errors

Goal 5 Recognize emotional appeals

■ Evaluating Source and Authority

Goal 1
Evaluate sources and author qualifications

Two very important considerations in evaluating any written material are the source in which it was printed and the authority, or qualifications, of the author.

Considering the Source

Your reaction to and evaluation of printed or online material should take into account its source. Be sure to assess whether or not the writer has carefully researched and accurately reported the subject. Although many writers are careful and accurate, some are not. Often the source of a piece of writing can indicate how accurate, detailed, and well documented the article is.

Let's consider an example. Suppose you are in the library trying to find information on sleepwalking for a term paper. You locate the following sources, each of which contains an article on sleepwalking. Which would you expect to be the most factual, detailed, and scientific?

- an online encyclopedia entry on sleepwalking
- an article titled "Strange Things Happen While You Are Sleeping," in *Woman's Day*
- an article titled "An Examination of Research on Sleepwalking" in *Psychological Review*

From the source alone you can make predictions about the content and approach used. You would expect the online encyclopedia entry to provide only a general overview of the topic. You might expect the article in *Woman's Day* to discuss various abnormalities that occur during sleep; sleepwalking might be only one of several topics discussed. Also, you might expect the article to relate several unusual or extreme cases of sleepwalking, rather than to present a factual analysis of the topic. The article in *Psychological Review,* a journal that reports research in psychology, is the one that would contain a factual, authoritative discussion of sleepwalking.

EFFICIENCY TIP
A fast way to evaluate written material is to look for footnotes or endnotes. These are usually a sign that the material is a compilation of accepted research. Sometimes footnotes appear directly in the text in parentheses. For example, (Simon 1980) refers to a research study published in 1980 by a person with the last name Simon. You can get more information about this study by looking at the Works Cited or References list at the end of the reading.

NEED TO KNOW How to Evaluate a Source

In evaluating a source you might ask the following questions:

1. **What reputation does the source have?**
2. **What is the audience for whom the source is intended?**
3. **Are documentation or references provided?**

Considering the Authority of the Author

To evaluate printed or online material, you must also consider the competency of the author. Use the following guidelines:

- **In textbooks, the author's credentials may be described in one of two places.** The author's college or university affiliation, and possibly his or her title, may appear on the title page beneath the author's name.
- **In nonfiction books and general market paperbacks, a synopsis of the author's credentials and experiences may be included on the book jacket or the back cover.**
- **In newspapers, magazines, and reference books, you are given little or no information about the writer.** You are forced to rely on the judgment of the editors or publishers to assess an author's authority.

EXERCISE 11–1

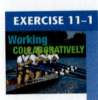
Working COLLABORATIVELY

EVALUATING SOURCES

Directions: *Predict and discuss how useful and appropriate each of the following sources would be for the situation described.*

1. using an article from *Working Women* on family aggression for a term paper for your sociology class

   _____

   _____

2. quoting an article in *The New York Times* on recent events in China for a speech titled "Innovation and Change in China"

   _____

3. reading an article titled "Bilingual Education in the Twenty-First Century" printed in the *Educational Research Quarterly* for a paper arguing for increased federal aid for bilingual education

   _____

4. using an article from *People* magazine to write a paper examining the effects of reality TV on the current generation of teenagers and young adults

   _____

   _____

5. using information from an autobiography written by former First Lady Laura Bush in a class discussion on use and abuse of presidential power

   _____

   _____

   _____

■ Reading Arguments

Goal 2
Understand the elements of an argument

Argument is used to establish and evaluate positions on controversial issues. In a philosophy course you might read arguments on individual rights, the rights of the majority, or the existence of God. For a literature class you may read a piece of literary criticism that argues for or against the value of a particular work, debates its significance, or rejects an interpretation.

Here are a few examples of arguments:

- Many students have part-time jobs that require them to work late afternoons and evenings during the week. These students are unable to use the library during the week. Therefore, library hours should be extended to weekends.
- Because parents have the right to determine their children's sexual attitudes, sex education should take place in the home, not at school.
- No one should be forced to inhale unpleasant or harmful substances. That's why the ban on cigarette smoking in public places was put into effect in our state. Why shouldn't there be a law to prevent people from wearing strong colognes or perfumes, especially in restaurants, since sense of smell is important to taste?

An argument has three essential parts:

- issue
- claim
- support

First, an argument must address an **issue**—a problem or controversy about which people disagree. Abortion, gun control, animal rights, capital punishment, and drug legalization are all examples of issues. Second, an argument must take a position on an issue. This position is called a **claim.** An argument may claim that capital punishment should be outlawed or that medical use of marijuana should be legalized. Finally, an argument offers **support** for the claim. Support consists of reasons and evidence that the claim is reasonable and should be accepted. An argument may also include a fourth part—a **refutation.** A refutation considers opposing viewpoints and attempts to disprove or discredit them.

Here is an example: baseball players' use of steroids is an issue. A claim could be made that baseball players' use of steroids is unhealthy and unfair and that owners and players need to take the issue seriously. Support for the claim could include reasons why steroid use is unhealthy and unfair. An opposing viewpoint to the author's argument may be that steroid use creates enhanced performance, which makes the game more fun and competitive for fans. This argument could be refuted by providing evidence that fans dislike extraordinary feats of performance and would prefer to see the game played without the use of performance-enhancing drugs.

When reading arguments, use the steps shown in the box below.

NEED TO KNOW How to Read an Argument

1. **Identify the issue and the assertion—what is being argued for.** Determine what position, idea, or action the writer is trying to convince you to accept.

2. **Read the entire article or essay.** Underline important parts of the argument.

3. **Watch for conclusions.** Words and phrases like *since, thus, therefore, accordingly, it can be concluded, it is clear that,* and *it follows that* are signals that a conclusion is about to be given.

4. **Notice the types of evidence the author provides.**

5. **Identify the specific action or position the writer is arguing for.**

6. **Reread the argument and examine its content and structure.** What is stated? What is implied or suggested? What assertions are made?

7. **Write a brief outline of the argument and list its key points.** Pragmatic learners may find this step especially helpful.

8. **Discuss the argument with a friend or classmate.** Especially if you are a social or auditory learner, you may "hear" yourself summarizing the assertion or evaluating the evidence supplied.

Now, read the following brief article and apply the previous steps.

MISSTEP ON VIDEO VIOLENCE

In the booming world of video games, there are more than a few dark corners: Murder and mayhem. Blood and gore. Explicit sex and abuse of women. In one of the best-selling series, Grand Theft Auto, car stealing is accompanied by drug use, shootouts that kill police and bystanders, and simulated sex with comely prostitutes who are beaten with baseball bats afterward.

Small wonder some parents are concerned over what game-crazed teens may be up to. And small wonder, too, that legislators in several states are playing to these concerns by trying to outlaw the sale of violent and sexually explicit games to minors. A bill banning the sale of such games to anyone younger than 18 is awaiting the governor's signature in Illinois. A similar proposal is moving in the Michigan Legislature. The issue has been raised this year in at least nine other states and the District of Columbia. But to what useful end?

This is the latest chapter in a very old story. When teenage entertainment offends adult sensibilities—think Elvis Presley's pulsating hips or the arrival on newsstands of Hugh Hefner's *Playboy*—the first response is to see the new phenomenon as a threat to social order. The second is to attempt to ban it.

Parents—former teenagers all—seem to forget history's lesson: The bans never work. And they're probably not constitutional, anyway. Courts have ruled that today's sophisticated video games are protected as creative expression. If communities want to limit access, they must show overriding evidence that the games pose a public threat. That evidence does not exist.

Lawmakers and activist groups assert that the thrill of engaging in virtual criminal activity will spur teens to try the real thing. But the violent crime rate has gone down nearly 30% since the first bloody shoot-'em-up games debuted in the early 1990s. Youth crime rates have dropped even more. And a Federal Trade Commission survey found parents already involved in 83% of video-game purchases and rentals for minors.

Judges have repeatedly rejected as flawed the studies that advocates say show a link between fantasy violence and anti-social behavior. To the extent there is a threat, it is mainly to the individual, vulnerable teenager, and it can be addressed only by parents.

Unknown to many parents, they're getting some help. The game industry's rating system classifies games in six categories from "early childhood" to "adults only" and requires detailed content descriptions. Also, newer models of popular games include parental controls that can block their use for age-inappropriate games. Manufacturers have announced an expanded ratings-education program, and major retailers are tightening their restrictions on sales to minors.

There will always be a market for the dark, tasteless, even the outrageous, and parents ought to keep kids away from it. But even with the best intentions of legislators, the problem is beyond their reach. New laws are likely to give parents only the false impression that someone else is solving that problem for them.

The issue discussed in the argument is legislation banning video violence. The author takes the position that legislation is not effective in controlling video violence.

The author offers the following reasons:

- The bans never work. The author cites the examples of Elvis Presley and *Playboy* magazine.
- The games do not pose a public threat. The author offers statistics that violent crime has dropped since video games came on the market.
- Many parents already monitor video game use.
- The game industry already classifies the games, gives detailed descriptions of content, and plans a ratings education program.
- Retailers are tightening restrictions to minors.

The action called for by the author is for parents to keep their children away from undesirable video games.

| EXERCISE 11–2 | READING AN ARGUMENT |

Directions: *Read the following argument and answer the questions that follow.*

"The life of each man should be sacred to each other man," the ancients tell us. They unflinchingly executed murderers. They realized it is not enough to proclaim the sacredness and inviolability of human life. It must be secured as well, by threatening with the loss of their own life those who violate what has been proclaimed as inviolable—the right of innocents to live. Else the inviolability of human life is neither credibly proclaimed nor actually protected. No society can profess that the lives of its members are secure if those who did not allow innocent others to continue living are themselves allowed to continue living—at the expense of the community. To punish a murderer by incarcerating him as one does a pickpocket cannot but cheapen human life. Murder differs in quality from other crimes and deserves, therefore, a punishment that differs in quality from other punishments. There is a discontinuity. It should be underlined, not blurred.

—Van den Haag, *"The Collapse of the Case Against Capital Punishment,"*
National Review.

1. What is the author's position on the death penalty?

_____

2. Summarize the argument.

_____

_____

_____

_____

_____

■ Evaluating Arguments

Goal 3
Evaluate the soundness of an argument

You can evaluate the soundness, correctness, and worth of an argument by examining the evidence. Consider the type and relevancy, definition of terms, cause-effect relationships, value systems, counterarguments, and assumptions.

Types of Evidence

An **inductive** argument reaches a general conclusion from observed specifics. The validity of an inductive argument rests, in part, on the soundness and correctness of the evidence provided to draw the conclusion. The validity of a **deductive** argument, on the other hand, rests on the accuracy and correctness of the premises on which the argument is based. A deductive argument begins with a general conclusion and moves to specifics. Evaluating each type of argument involves assessing the accuracy and correctness of statements on which the argument is based. Writers often provide evidence to substantiate their observations or premises. As a critical reader, your task is to assess whether or not the evidence is sufficient to support the claim. Here are a few types of evidence often used:

Personal Experience

Writers often substantiate their ideas through experience and observation. Although a writer's personal account of a situation may provide an interesting perspective on an issue, personal experience should not be accepted as proof. The observer may be biased or may have exaggerated or incorrectly perceived a situation.

Examples

Examples are descriptions of particular situations that are used to illustrate or explain a principle, concept, or idea. To explain what aggressive behavior is, your psychology instructor may offer several examples: fighting, punching, and kicking. Examples should *not* be used by themselves to prove the concept or idea they illustrate, as is done in the following sample:

> The American judicial system treats those who are called for jury duty unfairly. It is clear from my sister's experience that the system has little regard for the needs of those called as jurors. My sister was required to report for jury duty the week she was on vacation. She spent the entire week in a crowded, stuffy room waiting to be called to sit on a jury and never was called.

Statistics

Many people are impressed by statistics—the reporting of figures, percentages, averages, and so forth—and assume they are irrefutable proof. Actually, statistics can be misused, misinterpreted, or used selectively to give other than the most objective, accurate picture of a situation.

Comparisons and Analogies

Comparisons or analogies (extended comparisons) serve as illustrations and are often used in argument. Their reliability depends on how closely the comparison corresponds or how similar it is to the situation to which it is being compared. For example, Martin Luther King Jr., in his famous letter from the Birmingham jail, compared nonviolent protesters to a robbed man. To evaluate this comparison you would need to consider how the two are similar and how they are different.

| EXERCISE 11–3 | **EVALUATING EVIDENCE** |

Directions: *For the article "Misstep on Video Violence" on pages 470–471, evaluate whether the author uses adequate evidence to support the claim.* ■

Relevancy and Sufficiency of Evidence

Once you have identified the evidence used to support an argument, the next step is to decide whether there is enough of the right kind of evidence to lead you to accept the writer's claim. This is always a matter of judgment; there are no easy rules to follow. You must determine whether the evidence provided directly supports the statement, and whether sufficient evidence has been provided.

Suppose you are reading an article in your campus newspaper that states that Composition 101 should not be required of all students at your college. As evidence, the writer provides the following:

Composition does not prepare us for the job market. Besides, the reading assignments have no relevancy to modern times.

This argument provides neither adequate nor sufficient evidence. The writer does nothing to substantiate his claims of irrelevancy of the course to the job market or modern times. For the argument to be regarded seriously, the writer needs to provide facts, statistics, expert opinion, or other forms of documentation.

| EXERCISE 11–4 | **EVALUATING EVIDENCE** |

Directions: *Read the following argument, and pay particular attention to the type(s) of evidence used. Then answer the questions that follow.*

It is predictable. At Halloween, thousands of children trick-or-treat in Indian costumes. At Thanksgiving, thousands of children parade in school pageants wearing plastic headdresses and pseudo-buckskin clothing. Thousands of card shops stock Thanksgiving greeting cards with images of cartoon animals wearing feathered headbands. Thousands of teachers and librarians trim bulletin boards with Anglo-featured, feathered Indian boys and girls. Thousands of gift shops load their shelves with Indian figurines and jewelry.

Fall and winter are also the seasons when hundreds of thousands of sports fans root for professional, college and public school teams with names that summon up Indians—"Braves," "Redskins," "Chiefs." (In New York State, one out of eight junior and senior high school teams call themselves "Indians," "Tomahawks" and the like.) War-whooping team mascots are imprinted on school uniforms, postcards, notebooks, tote bags and car floor mats.

All of this seems innocuous; why make a fuss about it? Because these trappings and holiday symbols offend tens of thousands of other Americans—the

Native American people. Because these invented images prevent millions of us from understanding the authentic Indian America, both long ago and today. Because this image-making prevents Indians from being a relevant part of the nation's social fabric.

—Hirschfelder, *"It's Time to Stop Playing Indians,"* Los Angeles Times.

1. What types of evidence are used?

   _____

2. Is the evidence convincing?

   _____

   _____

3. Is there sufficient evidence?

   _____

4. What other types of evidence could have been used to strengthen the argument?

   _____

Definition of Terms

A clear and effective argument carefully defines key terms and uses them consistently. For example, an essay arguing for or against animal rights should state what is meant by the term, describe or define those rights, and use that definition through the entire argument.

The following two paragraphs are taken from two different argumentative essays on pornography. Notice how in the first paragraph the author carefully defines what he means by pornography before proceeding with his argument, while in the second the term is not clearly defined.

PARAGRAPH 1: CAREFUL DEFINITION

There is unquestionably more pornography available today than 15 years ago. However, is it legitimate to assume that more is worse? Pornography is speech, words, and pictures about sexuality. No one would consider an increase in the level of speech about religion or politics to be a completely negative development. What makes speech about sexuality different?

—Lynn, *"Pornography's Many Forms: Not All Bad."* Los Angeles Times.

PARAGRAPH 2: VAGUE DEFINITION

If we are not talking about writing laws, defining pornography doesn't pose as serious a problem. We do have different tastes. Maybe some of mine come from my middle-class background (my mother wouldn't think so!). I don't like bodies presented without heads, particularly female bodies. The motive may sometimes be the protection of the individual, but the impression is decapitation, and I also happen to be someone who is attracted to people's faces. This is a matter of taste.

—Jane Rule, *"Pornography is a Social Disease."* The Body Politic.

Cause-Effect Relationships

Arguments are often built around the assumption of a cause-effect relationship. For example, an argument supporting gun control legislation may claim that ready availability of guns contributes to an increased number of shootings. This argument implies that availability of guns causes increased use. If the writer provides no evidence that this cause-effect relationship exists, you should question the accuracy of the statement.

Implied or Stated Value System

An argument often implies or rests on a value system (a structure of what the writer feels is right, wrong, worthwhile, and important). However, everyone possesses a personal value system, and although our culture promotes many major points of agreement (murder is wrong, human life is worthwhile, and so forth), it also allows points of departure. One person may think that telling lies is always wrong; another person may say it depends on the circumstance. Some people have a value system based on religious beliefs; others may not share those beliefs.

In evaluating an argument, look for value judgments and then decide whether the judgments are consistent with and acceptable to your personal value system. Here are a few examples of value judgment statements:

- Abortion is wrong.
- Financial aid for college should be available to everyone regardless of income.
- Capital punishment violates human rights.

Recognition of Counterarguments

An effective argument often includes a refutation of **counterarguments**—a line of reasoning that can be used to deny or refute what the writer is arguing for. For example, if a writer is arguing against gun control, he or she may recognize the counterargument that availability of guns causes shootings and refute it by saying "Guns don't kill people: people kill people."

Notice how in this excerpt from an essay advocating capital punishment, the author recognizes the counterargument that everyone has a right to live and argues against it.

Abolitionists [of the death penalty] insist that we all have an imprescriptible right to live to our natural term: if the innocent victim had a right to live, so does the murderer. That takes egalitarianism too far for my taste. The crime sets victim and murderer apart; if the victim died, the murderer does not deserve to live. If innocents are to be secure in their lives murderers cannot be. The thought that murderers are to be given as much right to live as their victims oppresses me. So does the thought that a Stalin, Hitler, an Idi Amin should have as much right to live as their victims did.

—Van den Haag, *"The Collapse of the Case Against Capital Punishment,"* National Review.

TECH SUPPORT **Researching Opposing Viewpoints Online**

When searching for opposing viewpoints, try several approaches. Online, there are several Web sites intended for debate that provide basic positions plus sources for further research. Some of these are:

- **The International Debaters Education Association** (http://www.idebate.org/)
- **Debate Central from the National Center for Policy Analysis** (http://debate-central.ncpa.org/)
- **Public Agenda** (http://www.publicagenda.org/citizen).

Be sure to check the sources of information that these sites present for accuracy.

There are other online tools that your school's library might subscribe to. One of these is CQ Researcher. You can view a sample of one of their reports here: http://www.cqpress.com/docs/ CQ_Researcher_V18-27_Internet_Accuracy.pdf. This is a high-quality, reputable source. Check your library's Web site or with a librarian to find out if you have access.

Also at your library, there might be books in the series called *Opposing Viewpoints*. Each book covers both sides of one particular issue. The books are updated regularly and new editions are published. Check in the library catalog or ask a librarian to obtain these.

EFFICIENCY TIP
Certain key words or phrases often signal an underlying assumption: *let us assume, given that, everyone knows, it is commonly accepted, everybody agrees,* and *society believes.*

Identifying Assumptions

Many writers begin an argument assuming that a particular set of facts or principles is true. Then they develop their argument based on that assumption. Of course, if the assumption is not correct or if it cannot be proven, the arguments that depend on that assumption may be incorrect. For instance, the following passage begins with an assumption (*highlighted*) that the writer makes no attempt to prove or justify. Rather, he uses it as a starting point to develop his ideas on the function of cities.

> Given that the older central cities have lost their capacity to serve as effective staging areas for newcomers, the question inevitably poses itself: What is the function of these cities? Permit me to suggest that it has become essentially that of a sandbox.
>
> A sandbox is a place where adults park their children in order to converse, play, or work with a minimum of interference. The adults, having found a distraction for the children, can get on with the serious things of life. There is some reward for the children in all this. The sandbox is given to them as their turf. . . .

— *City Scenes: Problems and Prospects,* by J John Palen, Little, Brown and Company.

The author offers no reasons or evidence in support of the opening statement: it is assumed to be true. This assumption is the base on which the author builds his argument that the city is a sandbox.

As you read arguments, always begin by examining the author's initial assumptions. Decide whether you agree or disagree with them and check to see whether the author provides any evidence that his or her assumptions are accurate. Once you have identified an assumption, consider this question: If the assumption were untrue, how would it affect the argument?

EXERCISE 11-5

EVALUATING AN ARGUMENT

Directions: *Read the following arguments and discuss the questions that follow.*

REGULATION OF COAL PLANTS: PRO/CON
Are new EPA standards for coal plants beneficial?

PRO

Michael E. Kraft, EPA Rules Will Create Jobs, Clean the Air

GREEN BAY, Wis.—There is great deal of confusion about new EPA regulations affecting coal-fired power plants, and also opposition to regulations that could lead to plant closings or loss of jobs. Yet, as the business community has argued for years, the merits of regulatory proposals must be judged by comparing their overall benefits and costs to society and by focusing on only some economic effects they might have.

Let's consider some facts: First, the Obama administration is not advocating the closure of all coal-fired power plants. It has proposed new public health standards in response to court mandates, and, yes, some could lead to closure of older, inefficient plants.

One of these standards addresses how much toxic air pollutants, such as mercury, can be released from coal-burning plants. Another sets limits on "cross-state pollution," such as fine particles, nitrogen oxides and sulfur dioxide, generated by these plants that also affect public health. Actions to lower these emissions have been debated since 1990 when Congress authorized the EPA to regulate them. The Obama rules, issued in 2011 under court order, require more extensive reductions than comparable rules under the George W. Bush administration that federal courts in 2008 found to be unacceptably weak.

Second, these new regulations take effect this year, and they clarify what is expected of electric utilities after years of uncertainty. This is a positive development for the industry.

Third, the EPA anticipates that most plants can meet the standards using available technology, and that these changes are likely to create tens of thousands of jobs in the construction and pollution-control industries. The rules also will improve labor productivity throughout the economy because fewer days will be lost to respiratory illnesses.

Let's put some numbers on these benefits. EPA reports that each year these two regulations together would prevent as many as 18,000 to 46,000 premature deaths, 540,000 asthma attacks, 20,000 heart attacks, 25,000 hospital and emergency room visits, and 2 million missed work or school days, while providing important health protection for children and older Americans. Using standard economic analysis, the agency values these benefits at between $150 billion and $380 billion a year; they clearly exceed the estimated $10 billion annual costs of compliance for the industry. Even if one quarrels with the accuracy of these estimates, it is apparent that the health benefits are much greater than the costs to utilities.

In a separate and more controversial proposal, the EPA seeks to set the first limits on greenhouse gas emissions from new power plants, an action required under a 2007 Supreme Court decision. The high court ruled that under the Clean Air Act the agency must regulate the release of greenhouse gases if they endanger the public welfare, which they do.

The Obama administration has long preferred a legislative solution, such as a cap-and-trade policy, over regulation, but Congress could not agree on such a policy. Now the administration is forced to use regulation. The proposed New Source Performance Standards are indeed likely to end new construction of conventional coal-fired power plants as utilities will choose natural gas over coal or eventually adopt carbon capture technology. However, this new rule does not affect existing facilities, and new plants will have years to comply.

Some utilities do plan to shut down coal-fueled boilers at existing plants. This makes economic sense given the abundance and low cost today of cleaner natural gas.

Critics in Congress and elsewhere have demanded that the EPA back off, but they exaggerate the costs and ignore the enormous benefits for public health. It's time for the electrical generating industry to modernize its plants and give us the clean energy we deserve in the 21st century. It should not continue to use outmoded and dirty technologies to produce electricity.

Writer Michael E. Kraft is professor emeritus of environmental studies at the University of Wisconsin-Green Bay. His email address is kraftm@uwgb.edu. Distributed by MCT Information Services.

Con

Andrew P. Morriss, EPA Foolishly Seeks to Destroy Nation's Coal Industry

TUSCALOOSA, Ala.—The U.S. Energy Information Administration estimates the share of U.S. electricity generated from coal will fall from 42 percent in 2011 to 36.8 percent in 2013. Some of that decline is due to advances in fracking making cheaper natural gas available. That's bad news for coal miners but no different than problems all industries face from competition.

Cheaper natural gas cannot explain all coal's decline, however. A federal study found that coal use in electricity declined just 1.4 percent for every 10 percent change in relative prices between the coal and natural gas. This is not surprising because electric plants cannot change from coal to natural gas by just throwing a switch.

An important reason for coal's decline is the administration's war on coal.

Vice President Joe Biden made that clear during the 2008 campaign when he said the Obama policy was "No coal plants here in America." Similarly, candidate Obama told the San Francisco Chronicle that he would ensure that building a coal plant would "bankrupt" the operator because of the cost of complying with new carbon-dioxide emission regulations.

Deliberate government efforts to end an industry are not part of normal competitive market pressures and bad for the U.S. economy for three reasons.

First, virtually all our coal production goes directly to generate electricity. Changing that is costly: our electric grid was designed based on generation patterns dominated by multiple coal plants. Eliminating coal requires both costly new generation facilities and expensive grid modifications. Moreover, while the rapid development of domestic natural gas is cutting generation costs today, it is not guaranteed to continue indefinitely. If anti-fracking activists—who are also often anti-coal activists—succeed in their campaign to restrict natural gas production and pipeline construction, natural gas costs will rise.

Second, diversity in sources enhances our energy security by minimizing the chance that politics or wars in unstable and unfriendly countries will disrupt our energy supplies. America is called the "Saudi Arabia of coal" because it has more than a quarter of world coal reserves. Energy security is vital because energy is embedded in most goods and services. Almost half of our energy use is indirect and so invisible to consumers. Among the most energy intensive sectors of our economy are health care and food; we risk much more than higher utility bills if we remain vulnerable to unfriendly and unstable energy suppliers.

Third, the coal industry is a significant source of jobs. The typical coal miner earns $73,000 a year, says the National Mining Association, which represents the mining industry in Washington. An estimated 60,000 Americans work in coal-fired power plants. These are high-productivity jobs because the employees work with large amounts of capital. Electricity generated by coal takes just 0.18 employees per megawatt of plant capacity. Coal-fired power plant jobs pay high wages because their employees are skilled. Yet new EPA regulations are estimated to cut total coal employment by 1.4 million job-years between 2011 and 2020.

Besides destroying jobs, the new regulations imposed by the administration will lead to the closing of 40 gigawatts of electric generation capacity. A staggering 12 percent of America's current coal capacity will be shut down. There could be many long, hot summers if we lose these reliable sources of power.

Coal plays a key role in electricity generation. The power produced from coal-fired plants is embedded in everything from our prescription medications to the food we eat. Tens of thousands of Americans earn good livings in coal-related industries. Domestically produced coal reduces our dependence on unstable and unfriendly suppliers. Those facts make it obvious that market forces—not Washington bureaucrats—should determine the role coal plays in our economy.

Contact Morriss, a law professor at the University of Alabama, at amorriss@ law.ua.edu

—By permission of Andrew P. Morriss, D. Paul Jones, *Jr. & Charlene Angelich Jones Chairholder of Law,* University of Alabama.

1. Summarize the claim of each author makes about the issue.

2. What assertions are made?

3. What types of evidence does each author offer?

4. Do you feel the evidence each offers is adequate? Which is more convincing? Why?

5. What values does each author hold?

6. What assumptions do the authors make?

7. Does either or both authors recognize or refute the counterargument? If not, how could they do so?

LEARNING STYLE TIPS

If you tend to be a(n) . . .	Then evaluate arguments by . . .
Social learner	Discussing the argument with classmates. Identify strengths, weaknesses, opposing viewpoints, and errors in reasoning.
Independent learner	Rereading the argument several times. Highlight the assertion and the evidence that supports it. Use annotations to record your evaluation of the argument.

■ Errors in Logical Reasoning

Goal 4
Identify reasoning errors

Errors in reasoning, often called *logical fallacies,* are common in arguments. These errors invalidate the argument or render it flawed. Several common errors in logic are described below.

Circular Reasoning

Also known as begging the question, this error involves using part of the conclusion as evidence to support it. Here are a few examples:

> Cruel medical experimentation on defenseless animals is inhumane.
>
> Female soldiers should not be placed in battle situations because combat is a man's job.

In circular reasoning, because no evidence is given to support the claim, there is no reason to accept the conclusion.

Hasty Generalization

This fallacy means that the conclusion has been derived from insufficient evidence. Here is one example: You taste three tangerines and each is sour, so you conclude that all tangerines are sour. Here is another: By observing one performance of a musical group, you conclude that the group is unfit to perform.

Non Sequitur ("It Does Not Follow")

The false establishment of cause-effect is known as a *non sequitur.* To say, for example, that "Because my instructor is young, I'm sure she'll be a good teacher" is a non sequitur because youth does not cause good teaching. Here is another example: "Sam Goodwin is the best choice for state senator because he understands the people." Understanding the people will not necessarily make someone an effective state senator.

False Cause

The false cause fallacy is the incorrect assumption that two events that follow each other in time are causally related. Suppose you walked under a ladder and then tripped on an uneven sidewalk. If you said you tripped because you walked under the ladder, you would be assuming false cause.

Either-Or Fallacy

This fallacy assumes that an issue is only two sided, or that there are only two choices or alternatives for a particular situation. In other words, there is no middle ground. Consider the issue of censorship of violence on television. An either-or fallacy is to assume that violence on TV must either be allowed or banned. This fallacy does not recognize other alternatives such as limiting access through viewing hours, restricting the showing of certain types of violence, and so forth.

False Analogy

An analogy is an extended comparison between two otherwise unlike things. A sound analogy assumes that two things are alike in some ways. A false analogy compares two things that do not share a likeness. A writer arguing against gun control may say, "Guns are not a major problem in this country. Fatal accidents on the road, in the workplace, and at home kill many more people than do guns." Here the writer is suggesting that death by guns is similar to fatal accidents in the car, on the job, or at home. Yet, accidents and murder are not similar.

Bandwagon Appeal

The bandwagon appeal suggests that readers should accept an idea or take a particular action because everyone else believes or does it. In arguing that an idea or action is popular, and therefore, right or just, the writer evades discussing the issue itself and avoids presenting evidence to support the claim. Here is an example of a bandwagon appeal. "Eighty-five percent of women say they prefer gas ovens and stovetops. Women in the know use gas—so should you."

Ad Hominem

An *ad hominem* (against the man) is an attack on a person rather than on the issue or argument at hand. An *ad hominem* argument may attack the speaker or author of a statement, rather than the statement itself. For example, a bulimic teenager may reject the medical advice of her physician by arguing that her physician knows nothing about bulimia since the physician has never experienced it. Or a politician may attack an opponent's personal characteristics or lifestyle rather than his or her political platform.

Abstract Concepts as Reality

Writers occasionally treat abstract concepts as real truths with a single position. For example, a writer may say, "Research proves that divorce is harmful to children." Actually, there are hundreds of pieces of research on the effects of divorce and they offer diverse findings and conclusions. Some but not all research reports harmful effects. Here is another example: "Criminology shows us that prisons are seldom effective in controlling crime." Writers tend to use this device to make it seem as if all authorities are in agreement with their positions. This device also allows writers to ignore contrary or contradictory opinions.

Red Herring

A red herring is something that is added to an argument to divert attention from the issue at hand. It is introduced into an argument to throw readers off track. Think of a red herring as an argumentative tactic, rather than an error in reasoning. Suppose you are reading an essay that argues for the death penalty. If the author suddenly starts reporting facts about high rates of suicides by inmates in prisons, the writer is introducing a red herring. Facts about suicides in prisons are not directly relevant to whether the death penalty is just.

EXERCISE 11–6   **IDENTIFYING LOGICAL FALLACIES**

Directions: *Identify the logical fallacy in each of the following statements; write your answer in the space provided.*

1. All Native American students in my accounting class earned A grades, so Native Americans must excel with numerical tasks.

   _____

2. If you are not in favor of nuclear arms control, then you're against protecting our future.

   _____

3. Linguistics proves that the immersion approach is the only way to learn a second language.

   _____

4. My sister cannot compose business letters or memos because she has writer's block.

   _____

5. People who smoke have a higher mortality rate than nonsmokers. Urban dwellers have a higher mortality rate than suburban dwellers. Now, since we do not urge urban dwellers to move to the suburbs, why should we urge smokers to quit smoking?

   _____

6. A well-known senator, noting a decline in the crime rate in the four largest cities in his state, quickly announced that his new "get-tough on criminals" publicity campaign was successful and took credit for the decline.

   _____

7. I always order cheesecake for dessert because I am allergic to chocolate.

   _____

8. Stricter driving while intoxicated laws are needed in this country. It is a real shame that some adults allow preschool age children to drink sips of wine and to taste beer long before they reach the age of reason. If stricter driving laws were in place, many lives would be saved.

   _____

9. Did you know that Dr. Smith is single? How could she possibly be a good marriage counselor?

_____

10. Two million pet owners feed their pets VitaBrite Tabs to keep their dogs healthy and increase longevity. Buy some today for your best friend.

_____

EXERCISE 11–7

EVALUATING ARGUMENTS

Directions: *The following two essays were written in response to the question "Should animals be used in research?" Read each essay and answer the questions that follow. Then compare your answers with those of a classmate.*

ARGUMENT 1: SHOULD ANIMALS BE USED in RESEARCH?

The use of animals in research has become an extremely emotional as well as legal issue. Very strict federal regulations on the care, maintenance, and use of animals in research now exist. But even though research using animals is closely monitored to identify and eliminate any potential source of pain or abuse of experimental animals, activists still object to the use of animal species, particularly the vertebrates, for research.

Those who oppose the use of animals have become caught up in the developments of the "high tech" world and frequently propose the use of simulators and computer modeling to replace biological research with live animals. Unfortunately, simulators and computer modeling cannot generate valid biological data on their own. Scientific data obtained from experiments using live animals must first provide base data before modelers can extrapolate results under similar conditions.

Simulators and computer modeling do have their place in teaching and research, but they will not and cannot replace the use of animals in many kinds of critical medical research. For example, consider modern surgical procedures in human organ repair and transplanting. The techniques in use today were developed and perfected through the use of laboratory animals. Would you want a delicate operation to be performed by a physician trained only on simulators?

Laboratory animal research is fundamental to medical progress in many other areas as well. Vaccines for devastating human diseases like polio and smallpox and equally serious animal diseases like rabies, feline leukemia, and distemper were all developed through the use of research animals.

The discovery, development, and refinement of drugs that could arrest, control, or eliminate such human diseases as AIDS, cancer, and heart disease all require the use of laboratory animals whose physiological mechanisms are similar to humans.

I have only noted above a few of the many examples where animals have been used in human and veterinary medical research. It's also important to note that studies in behavior, ecology, physiology, and genetics all require the use of animals, in some capacity, to produce valid and meaningful knowledge about life on this planet.

—Tuff, *"Animals and Research,"* NEA Higher Education Advocate, National Education Assoc.

ARGUMENT 2: SHOULD ANIMALS BE USED in RESEARCH?

I cannot accept the argument that research on animals is necessary to discover "cures" for humans. Many diseases and medications react very differently in animals than they do in humans. Aspirin, for example, is toxic to cats, and there are few diseases directly transmittable from cats to humans.

I particularly abhor the "research" conducted for cosmetic purposes. The Draise test—where substances are introduced into the eyes of rabbits which are then examined to see if ulcers, lesions or other observable reactions take place—is archaic and inefficient. Other alternatives exist that are more accurate and do not cause unnecessary suffering to our fellow creatures.

Household products are also tested needlessly on animals using the LD-50 test. Animals, in many cases puppies, are force-fed these toxic chemicals to determine the dosage at which exactly 50 percent of them die. These tests are not necessary and do not give very useful information.

Many top medical schools no longer use animals for teaching purposes, but have their medical students practice on models, computer simulations, and then observe techniques on human patients. A medical doctor is expected to honor and revere life, and this approach emphasizes that idea.

If medical students are deliberately taught that animal life is not important, then the next step to devaluing human life is made that much easier. Anatomy and biology classes do not need to use cats for all their students, either. A video of a dissection that is shown to the entire class or a model or computer simulation would be just as effective.

If an experiment using animals is deemed absolutely necessary, then that claim should be fully documented and all previous research should be examined thoroughly to avoid needless replication. In addition, the facility should not be exempt from cruelty laws and should be open to inspection by animal rights advocates not affiliated with the research institution.

Humans have a duty to take care of the earth and to respect all life, for if we poison the earth and annihilate other life on the planet, we are poisoning and annihilating ourselves. We were put on this earth to take care of our earth and the creatures upon it.

—Tuff, *"Animals and Research,"* NEA Higher Education Advocate, National Education Assoc.

ARGUMENT 1

1. Summarize Tuff's position on the use of laboratory animals.

   _____

   _____

2. Outline the main points of his argument.

   _____

   _____

_____

_____

3. What types of evidence does he offer?

_____

_____

_____

4. Evaluate the adequacy and sufficiency of the evidence provided.

_____

5. Does the author recognize or refute counterarguments?

_____

_____

ARGUMENT 2

1. Summarize Molina's position.

_____

2. Outline the main points of her argument.

_____

_____

_____

_____

_____

3. What types of evidence does she offer?

_____

_____

4. Evaluate the adequacy and sufficiency of the evidence provided.

_____

_____

_____

5. Does the author recognize or refute counterarguments?

_____

BOTH ARGUMENTS

1. Which argument do you feel is stronger? Why?

_____

2. Compare the types of evidence each uses.

_____

_____ ■

EXERCISE 11-8

Academic APPLICATION

EVALUATING AN ARGUMENT

Directions: *From among the reading assignments you have completed this semester, choose one that involved persuasive or argumentative writing. Review this piece of writing and then complete the following.*

1. Summarize what is being argued for.
2. List the key points of the argument.
3. Indicate what type of evidence the writer uses.
4. Determine whether the evidence is adequate and sufficient to support the author's point.
5. Identify any counterarguments the author recognizes or refutes.   ■

■ Thinking Critically: Evaluating Emotional Appeals

Goal 5
Recognize emotional appeals

Emotional appeals attempt to involve or excite readers by appealing to their emotions, thereby influencing the reader's attitude toward the subject. As you read, look for the following types of emotional appeals and examine their effects on you.

1. **Emotionally charged or biased language**. By using words with connotations that create an emotional response, writers establish positive or negative feelings. For example, an advertisement for a new line of fragrances may promise to "indulge," "refresh," "nourish," and "pamper" the user. An ad for an automobile may use phrases such as "limousine comfort," "European styling," and "animal sleekness" to interest and excite readers.

2. **Testimonials**. A testimonial uses the opinion or image of a famous person. We have all seen athletes endorsing underwear and movie stars selling shampoo. Testimonials work on the notion that people admire celebrities and strive to be like them, respect their opinions, and trust their good taste.

3. **Association**. An emotional appeal can be made by associating a product, idea, or position with others that are already accepted or highly regarded. Patriotism is already valued, so to call a product "all-American" is an appeal to the emotions. Other examples of associations are a car being named a Cougar to remind you of a fast, sleek animal; a cigarette ad picturing a scenic waterfall; and a speaker standing in front of a country's flag.

4. **Appeal to "common folk."** Some people distrust those who are well educated, wealthy, artistic, or distinctly different from the average person in other ways. Advertisers sell a product or idea to this group by indicating that it is originated from or is purchased by ordinary citizens. For example, a politician may describe her background and education to suggest that she is like everyone else; a salesperson may dress in styles similar to his or her clients.

EXERCISE 11–9   **IDENTIFYING TYPES OF EMOTIONAL APPEAL**

Directions: *Determine which type of emotional appeal is being used in each of the following situations.*

1. Vote for Jane Rodriguez for Congress. As the daughter of immigrants, she knows what it's like to struggle to feed her family and pay the bills.

_____

2. Angelina Jolie and Brad Pitt have donated money to help feed the poor children of Africa. So should you.

_____

3. Only egotistical madmen would support the concealed carry laws that allow them to tote their handguns anywhere.

_____

4. Grab one of Mrs. Smith's frozen apple pies, and you'll feel like you're at the county fair on a cool autumn day, bobbing for Granny Smith apples picked freshly from the trees.

_____

5. If we don't pass this new education law, tomorrow's children will be wandering the streets, homeless, hungry, and filled with despair.

_____

6. Milk provides essential nutrients to our athletes and helps them bring home the gold.

_____

7. I'm just your regular soccer mom who cares about my kids' future. Reelect me to the Greenfield school board.

_____

EXERCISE 11–10   **EVALUATING TECHNIQUES AND EMOTIONAL APPEALS**

Electronic APPLICATION

Directions: *Visit a newsgroup that focuses on a controversial issue and either follow or participate in the discussion. What persuasive techniques or emotional appeals did you observe?*

SELF-TEST SUMMARY

Goal 1	1. Why should you consider the source of the material and the author's authority when reading arguments and persuasive writing?	Evaluating both the source in which material was printed and the competency of its author is essential in evaluating any argument or piece of persuasive writing. Where a piece of writing came from can be an indication of the type of information that will be presented as well as its accuracy and value. The author's qualifications and level of expertise with the subject provide a further indication of the reliability of this information.
Goal 2	2. How can you read arguments more effectively?	Since both inductive and deductive arguments make assertions and give evidence to support them, when reading them it is important to • identify what is being argued for • read very closely and carefully • watch for conclusions • be alert to the types of evidence given • reread to examine both content and structure • underline or outline the key parts
Goal 3	3. How should you evaluate an argument?	Critical readers evaluate the soundness, correctness, and worth of an argument. To do so, • determine the type of evidence used • decide whether there is enough evidence and whether it is the right kind • notice whether key terms are defined and used properly • be alert to value judgments, assumptions, or cause-effect connections • look for counterarguments and whether they are adequately refuted
Goal 4	4. What are the common errors in logical reasoning?	Eleven common logical fallacies that can weaken or destroy an argument are: • circular reasoning • hasty generalization • non sequitur • false cause • either-or fallacy • false analogy • bandwagon appeal • *ad hominem* • abstract concepts as reality • red herring
Goal 5	5. What are emotional appeals and what types do authors use?	Emotional appeals are efforts to execute or engage readers by appealing to their feelings. Types include • emotionally charged language • testimonials • association • appeal to "common folk"

READING SELECTION 21   ARGUMENTATIVE ESSAY

From a Vegetarian: Looking at Hunting from Both Sides Now

Timothy Denesha
From *The Buffalo News*

About the Reading

NEWSPAPER ARTICLE

This article was originally published in The Buffalo News *as an editorial—that is, an opinion piece written by the newspaper's editor. Activate your critical reading skills and evaluate the author's statements as you read.*

Planning Your Reading Strategy*

Directions: *Activate your thinking by previewing the reading (see the Need to Know box on page 64) and answering the following questions.*

1. The Need to Know box on page 64 recommends that you preview the first sentence under each heading, along with the title and the first and last paragraphs. Would this type of preview be adequate for this article? Why or why not? If not, how would you adjust your previewing strategy?

   _____

   _____

2. Based on your preview of the reading, how quickly do you think you should read the selection? (Circle one.) Explain your answer.

   Very slowly   Slowly   At a moderate pace   Quickly   Very quickly

   _____

3. How do you feel about hunting? Is it always acceptable, sometimes acceptable, or never acceptable? Why?

4. Based on your reading of the first paragraph only, what do you expect the article's tone to be? Do you think the author will be highly biased in favor of one side of the debate? Do you expect him to be fair? How does the first paragraph affect your attitude as you begin reading the full selection?

1   Deer hunting season opened Nov. 18, and as the gunfire resumes in our woodlands and fields so will the perennial sniping between hunters and animal rights supporters. I always feel caught in the cross-fire on this matter, because I have been a vegetarian and animal rights advocate for over 25 years, but I also have friends I respect who are hunters. I've learned the issue is not as black-and-white as I once believed.

by Timothy Denesha, from The Buffalo News.

2   Growing up with many beloved pets and no hunters in my life, I assumed these people were bloodthirsty animal haters. When, in my 20s, I read the great humanitarian Albert Schweitzer's writings on reverence for life, I became a vegetarian and even more contemptuous of hunters.

3   But I had to revise my opinion after seeing the classic 1981 African film, "The Gods Must Be Crazy." The hero, a good-hearted bushman, slays a small gazelle, then tenderly strokes her, apologizing for taking her life. He explains his family is hungry and thanks her for providing food. I was stunned: a hunter practicing reverence for life! Later, I learned that Native American tradition has the same compassionate awareness about life lost so another life may be sustained.

4   My position softened further several years ago when Alex Pacheco, a leading animals-rights activist, spoke here. Detailing inhumane practices at meat-packing plants and factory farms, he said the most important thing anyone could do to lessen animal suffering was to stop eating meat. I decided to work toward being vegan (eating no animal products) and reluctantly admitted that hunters were not the animal kingdom's worst enemies. However, I still disliked them.

5   What really changed my perspective was getting to know some hunters personally, through my job at a Red Cross blood-donation center. Some of my co-workers and a number of our donors are civic-minded people who donate blood (which most people don't) but also shed animal blood with their guns and arrows. Confronting this paradox brought me some realizations.

6   First, hunters are like any group that differs from me: lacking personal experience of them made it easier to demonize them. They aren't monsters. I don't know if any of them apologizes to or thanks his kill as the hungry bushman did, but I do know they aren't cruel, sadistic or bloodthirsty—quite the opposite, as I later discovered.

7   Second, these people aren't just amusing themselves by ending a life; they are acquiring food. This death that sustains another life has a meaning that, for example, fox hunting does not. To the animal, this distinction may mean little. But it is significant when considering a person's intentions.

8   Also, I was informed that hunters don't "like to kill." They enjoy the outdoors, the camaraderie and the various skills involved. (One of these skills, the "clean kill," is prized precisely because it minimizes suffering.) Like vegetable gardeners, they enjoy providing food [for] themselves and their families with their own hands. Like those who fish, they enjoy a process of food acquisition that involves an animal's death, but not because it does. Again, this may seem a small point (especially to the prey), but I feel it is meaningful from the standpoint of the hunter's humanity.

9   In addition, I've come to see a certain integrity in hunters as meat-eaters who "do their own dirty work." Packaged cold-cuts and fast-food burgers mask the fact of lives bled out on the killing floor. Hunters never forget this, for they accept personal responsibility for it.

10   Furthermore, were I an animal that had to die to feed a human, I'd rather it happen one-on-one, at the hands of that person in the woods that were my home, than amidst the impersonal mass-production machinery of a meat factory. Either way is death, but one way has more dignity, less fear and less suffering.

11   There are bad hunters who trespass, shoot domestic animals, hunt intoxicated or disregard that cardinal rule of hunting's unwritten code of ethics: wounded prey must not be allowed to suffer. Last Thanksgiving morning in Chestnut Ridge Park, I found a fresh trail of deer tracks in the snow, heavily splashed with blood. It was horrible.

12   One of my hunter co-workers was also upset when I told him about it, and had this story. He himself was able to hunt only one day last season and sighted a small, wounded doe. As a student on a tight budget with a family, he hunts for food and would have preferred to ignore the doe's plight and meet his license limit with a large buck. Instead, he devoted a long, difficult day to trailing her until he was close enough to end her suffering. This was an act of mercy and even self-sacrifice, not the action of a heartless person insensitive to animals. It was reverence for life. He claims many hunters would do and have done the same.

13   And I realized that compassion has many faces, some of the truest the most unexpected.

Examining Reading Selection 21*

Checking Your Vocabulary

Directions: *Use context, word parts, or a dictionary, if necessary, to determine the meaning of each word as it is used in the reading.*

___ 1. contemptuous (paragraph 2)
    a. scornful
    b. suspicious
    c. disrespectful
    d. patronizing

___ 2. reverence (paragraph 3)
    a. tenderness
    b. disbelief
    c. respect
    d. honesty

___ 3. inhumane (paragraph 4)
    a. lacking pity or compassion
    b. not respectful
    c. not purposeful
    d. lacking self-awareness

___ 4. paradox (paragraph 5)
    a. evidence
    b. variation
    c. behavior
    d. contradiction

___ 5. camaraderie (paragraph 8)
    a. risk
    b. thrill
    c. companionship
    d. self-sufficiency

Checking Your Comprehension

Directions: *Select the best answer.*

___ 6. This reading is primarily concerned with
    a. the barbarism of hunting.
    b. the reverence hunters have for human life.
    c. the defensibility of hunting.
    d. why people become vegetarians.

___ 7. The main point in this reading is
    a. it is unethical to hunt.
    b. animals suffer as a result of hunting.
    c. hunters have as much integrity and compassion as nonhunters.
    d. most hunters are only interested in killing helpless creatures for sport.

___ 8. It is clear from the article that the author is *not*
    a. a vegetarian.
    b. a health care worker.
    c. a hunter.
    d. an animal rights advocate.

*Writing About the Reading questions appear in the Instructor's Manual.

___ 9. Initially, what made the author begin
to change his mind about hunters?
a. a speech by Alex Pacheco.
b. the African film *The Gods Must Be Crazy.*
c. the Red Cross blood donation center.
d. the writings of Albert Schweitzer.

___ 10. The author discusses the issue of
sports hunting primarily by
a. comparing hunters and nonhunters.
b. classifying types of hunters.
c. examining his own changing beliefs.
d. defining sports hunting.

Thinking Critically

___ 11. As used in the first paragraph, a synonym for *sniping* is
a. shooting.
b. cutting.
c. killing.
d. arguing.

___ 12. Which of the following statements
best describes the author's attitude
about hunting?
a. Hunters are aggressive and bloodthirsty.
b. Hunters often take animals' lives with respect and compassion.
c. Hunting should not be allowed under any circumstances.
d. Hunting is just a sport like any other sport.

___ 13. From this reading, we can infer that
deer hunters' licenses allow them to
a. kill as many deer as they choose.
b. hunt on any property where deer can be found.
c. hunt only one day per season.
d. kill only a limited number of deer.

___ 14. Which of the following is an example
of a deer hunter abiding by hunting's
unwritten code of ethics?
a. He hunts with a bow and arrow instead of a rifle.
b. He kills a deer that is already wounded.
c. He brings a wounded deer to the vet for treatment.
d. He kills only to supply his family with food.

___ 15. What does the photo on page 491
contribute to the reading?
a. It shows that some hunters prize animals as trophies and suggests that this is the reason why some hunters engage in the sport.
b. It is somewhat inconclusive and shows both sides of the argument.
c. It demonstrates that hunters are focused on tracking and killing animals purely for the sport of it.
d. It illustrates the fact that true hunters enjoy hunting to acquire food, not as an opportunity to kill animals.

Questions for Discussion

1. Do you think hunting is moral or immoral? Justify your position.

2. Discuss the ways in which hunters prevent animals from suffering.

3. What lessons can be learned from the author's statement that "Hunters are like any group that differs from me: lacking personal experience of them made it easier to demonize them"?

4. When the author refers to hunting he states that "compassion has many faces." What does he mean? Give an example to support your point.

Scorecard

Selection 21:   862 words

Finishing Time: _____ _____ _____
                     HR.   MIN.   SEC.

Starting Time: _____ _____ _____
                     HR.   MIN.   SEC.

Reading Time: _____ _____
                            MIN.   SEC.

WPM Score: _____

Comprehension Score: for items 6–15
Number Right: _____ × 10 = _____%

Assessing Your Reading Strategy

1. How would you rate your comprehension of the reading? (Circle one.)
   Excellent   Good   Fair   Poor
2. Did you find your reading strategy effective?
   Yes   No
3. Suppose you were given an assignment to read another selection from the same source (a popular news magazine). Based on your experience with this selection, how would you adjust your reading strategy (if at all)?

READING SELECTION 22   SOCIOLOGY

Native Americans: An American Holocaust

Mona Scott

About the Reading

TEXTBOOK EXCERPT

This article is a case study published in a sociology textbook titled Think Race and Ethnicity, *by Mona Scott. Case studies usually focus on exploring one key topic in detail.*

 MyReadingLab™ *The exercises following this selection can be completed online at myreadinglab.com*

Planning Your Reading Strategy*

Directions: *Activate your thinking by previewing the reading (see the Need to Know box on page 64) and answering the following questions.*

_____ 1. By previewing only the first and last paragraphs of this reading, what can you reasonably expect it to cover in detail?
  a. the extermination of Jews in Hitler's Germany
  b. modern problems like genocide in Kosovo and Darfur, Sudan
  c. the systematic destruction of the Native American population
  d. the racial superiority of those who conquered the "New World"

_____ 2. Based on the first and last paragraphs of the reading, what do you expect regarding the author's attitude toward her topic and the tone of the selection?
  a. It is likely to be a balanced look at both sides of the story (European conquest versus Native American resistance).
  b. It is likely very sympathetic toward Native Americans and very critical of Europeans.
  c. It is likely to be presented with completely factual language and very little slanted language.
  d. It is likely to be very opinionated and not factually based.

3. Do you think any groups of people in the modern United States are systematically discriminated against? If so, describe those groups and the discrimination they often encounter.

4. Based on your preview of the reading, how quickly do you think you should read the selection? (Circle one.) Explain your answer.

Very slowly   Slowly   At a moderate pace   Quickly   Very quickly

Scott, Mona, Think Race and Ethnicity, *1st Ed., © 2011. Reprinted and electronically reproduced by permission of Pearson Education Inc., Upper Saddle River, NJ.*

*The Scorecard on p. 499 enables you to compute your reading rate. In order to do so, be sure to record your starting time in the Scorecard box before you begin reading.

1   When you think of the word *holocaust*—the systematic, bureaucratic elimination of a culture or people—you often think of Adolf Hitler's persecution of the Jewish people. However, the United States has its own holocaust. What's more, most people would like to believe the **American holocaust** never happened. Nevertheless, it's very real. Over hundreds of years, White Americans have taken part in the destruction of the Native Americans. The ideologies of whiteness and white supremacy made it possible to exterminate Indigenous people in the Americas.

2   It started when the Puritans arrived, bringing with them diseases, especially smallpox. However, the Puritans saw the devastation of Native Americans as a divine measure. Those who survived were demonized in spite of their benign attitude toward the Puritans, who insisted the Native Americans posed a threat to their pious way of life.

3   Over time, demonizing Native Americans became sport, eventually leading the colonists to one of two choices: annihilation or enslavement. Many chose annihilation and delighted in the murder of the Native Americans. Some of them slaughtered people and then used their bodies to make skin products like leggings and reins. Others simply burned Native Americans alive. William Bradford wrote, "It was a fearful sight to see them, thus frying in the fire and the streams of blood quenching the same, and horrible was the stink and scent thereof; but the victory seemed a sweet sacrifice."

4   Others chose slavery, which had actually begun in the early 1500s. Spanish ships were coming to ports to befriend and capture the Native Americans before bringing them to the Caribbean islands. There, they forced the Native Americans to work on plantations, where most of them died. Between 1526 and 1576, French and English ships followed suit.

5   However, some colonists found the treatment and genocide of the Native Americans too much to take. They admired the Native American way of life, which involved being peaceful, generous, and trustworthy, even after seeing their friends and family murdered. As a result, some colonists ran away to live with the natives, who welcomed, them. Of course, the remaining colonists considered this a threat and only furthered their genocidal attitudes toward the Indigenous people.

6   The Indian Wars began and continued through the centuries as a series of **pogroms,** or organized massacres. One of the worst was the Sand Creek Massacre. In 1864, a group of 700 soldiers from the Colorado Territory decimated a village of friendly Cheyenne and Arapaho Indians. These men slaughtered more than 160 natives, most of whom were women and children.

7   Following the attack, congressmen confronted the Colorado governor. One person asked what should be done in the future to handle issues with Indigenous peoples. The crowd reportedly shouted, "Exterminate them!" Later, President Theodore Roosevelt said the Sand Creek Massacre was "as righteous and beneficial a deed as ever took place on the frontier."

8   Roosevelt wasn't the only president who held this belief. In 1779, George Washington, then the commander of the Continental Army, told Major General John Sullivan to destroy Iroquois villages, instructing him not to "listen to any overture of peace before the total ruin of their settlements is effected." Thomas Jefferson, too, was an anti-Indian activist, who wrote that any Native American who resisted American expansion be killed. Andrew Jackson acted similarly, calling for the extermination of the Cherokee people.

9   Jackson's desire to eliminate the Cherokee Nation resulted in years of mistreatment. He oversaw states taking land from the Cherokees through shady legal means, causing the Native Americans to take their case to the Supreme Court. Even when Justice John Marshall sided with them, little could be done because Jackson wouldn't enforce the ruling.

10   This inevitably resulted in more coerced land treaties in which Native Americans were forced to give up their land for food and smaller

amounts of territory. The Indian Removal Act of 1830 allowed the U.S. militia to move thousands of Native Americans to the western United States, an event now known as the Trail of Tears. Hundreds died along the way.

11   This treatment continued long after Jackson's presidential term ended. At Wounded Knee, in 1890, troops were going to South Dakota to arrest Chief Sitting Bull, the leader of the Lakota Sioux. White settlers had been frightened of the Sioux, calling for Sitting Bull's removal. Instead, fighting ensued. More than 100 Sioux were slaughtered, and their bodies were left in the snow.

12   One of the only survivors was a baby, who was adopted by General William Colby and named Lost Bird. Colby didn't take the baby in to raise her as his family, but rather use her as a symbol of extermination. The child was eventually put on display in Buffalo Bill's Wild West Show. Upon her death at age 29, the Lakota had Lost Bird's body brought back home to South Dakota, where she was buried with her family in the mass grave.

13   These examples of devastation are painful to read, but so are the overall statistics. Between the late 18th and 19th centuries, the number of Illinois Indians decreased by 96 percent. In Baja California, Mexico, only 60,000 Indigenous people had survived by the end of the 17th century. Two-thirds of the Huron were killed. By 1862, only 1 percent of the 20,000 Quapaw living in the lower Mississippi and Arkansas valleys were left.

14   Mistreatment of Native Americans has by no means disappeared. In 1996, Native Americans brought their case to the secretary of the interior, stating that the U.S. government had breached its agreement to build their trust, resulting in the loss of several billion dollars. After lengthy trials, the federal government agreed to create new trusts totaling more than $3 billion.

15   Despite all this evidence, American society largely denies this holocaust took place. People often say that what happened to the Native Americans was exaggerated, which likely helps them feel better. A big part of that denial is that they can't imagine their Founding Fathers, nor the subsequent settlers, whom they were socialized to view as patriots and respected forefathers dedicated to independence, attempting to wipe out an entire race of people.

Gen. Custer's surprise attack on a camp of over two thousand Native Americans.

Examining Reading Selection 22

⚙️ Complete this Exercise at myreadinglab.com

Checking Your Vocabulary

Directions: *Use context, word parts, or a dictionary, if necessary, to determine the meaning of each word as it is used in the reading.*

___ 1. devastation (paragraph 2)
   a. frustration
   b. destruction
   c. protection
   d. demonstration

___ 2. benign (paragraph 2)
   a. strange
   b. frequent
   c. kindly
   d. unfriendly

___ 3. pious (paragraph 2)
   a. religious/devout
   b. healthy
   c. cheerful
   d. respected

___ 4. decimated (paragraph 6)
   a. allowed
   b. handled
   c. helped
   d. destroyed

___ 5. coerced (paragraph 10)
   a. benefited
   b. forced
   c. wanted
   d. reserved

Checking Your Comprehension

Directions: *Select the best answer.*

___ 6. This reading is primarily concerned with the
   a. colonization of America.
   b. settlement of the American West.
   c. history of North American tribes.
   d. treatment of Native Americans.

___ 7. The statement that best expresses the main point of this reading is
   a. "When you think of the word *holocaust*, you often think of Adolf Hitler's persecution of the Jewish people."
   b. "Over hundreds of years, White Americans have taken part in the destruction of the Native Americans."
   c. "Some colonists found the treatment and genocide of the Native Americans too much to take."
   d. "People often say that what happened to the Native Americans was exaggerated."

___ 8. Of the following people mentioned in the selection, the only one who sided with the Native Americans was
   a. Theodore Roosevelt.
   b. George Washington.
   c. Justice John Marshall.
   d. Andrew Jackson.

___ 9. The disease brought by Puritans that was especially devastating to Native Americans was
   a. influenza.
   b. smallpox.
   c. scarlet fever.
   d. tuberculosis.

___ 10. The Indian Removal Act of 1830 resulted in an event known as
   a. the Sand Creek Massacre.
   b. Custer's Last Stand.
   c. the Trail of Tears.
   d. the Massacre at Wounded Knee.

Thinking Critically

___ 11. The author supports her ideas by doing all of the following *except*
   a. describing historical events.
   b. quoting historical figures.
   c. citing relevant statistics.
   d. recounting her own experiences.

____12. The author's feelings toward Native Americans can best be described as
   a. sympathetic.
   b. indifferent.
   c. critical.
   d. objective.

____13. The illustration is included as an example of
   a. a massacre of Native Americans.
   b. early Native American artwork.
   c. a typical Native American village.
   d. an attempt to enslave Native Americans.

____14. All of the following words are emotionally charged *except*
   a. *holocaust.*
   b. *enslavement.*
   c. *treatment.*
   d. *genocide.*

____15. The author ends the reading by claiming that
   a. the forefathers of America were patriots dedicated to independence.
   b. most Americans are ashamed of how Native Americans have been treated.
   c. significant progress has been made in the treatment of Native Americans.
   d. American society continues to deny the Native American holocaust.

Scorecard

Selection 22:   1,072 words

Finishing Time: ____ ____ ____
                     HR.   MIN. SEC.

Starting Time: ____ ____ ____
                     HR.   MIN. SEC.

Reading Time: ____ ____
                          MIN. SEC.

WPM Score: _____

Comprehensive Score: for items 6–15
Number Right _____ × 10 = _____ %

Assessing Your Reading Strategy

1. How would you rate your comprehension of the reading? (Circle one.)
   Excellent   Good   Fair   Poor

2. Did you find your reading strategy effective?   Yes   No

3. Suppose you were given an assignment to read a similar selection to the one you just read. Based on your experience with this selection, how would you adjust your reading strategy (if at all)?

Writing About Reading Selection 22

Checking Your Vocabulary

Directions: *Complete each of the following items; refer to a dictionary if necessary.*

1. Describe the denotative and connotative meanings of the word *exterminate* in paragraph 1.

   _____

   _____

   _____

   _____

2. Describe the denotative and connotative meanings of the word *shady* in paragraph 9.

   _____

   _____

   _____

3. Explain the meaning of the phrase "divine measure" and how it is used in paragraph 2.

   _____

   _____

   _____

   _____

4. Define the word *annihilation* (paragraph 3) and underline the word or phrase that provides a clue for its meaning.

   _____

5. Define the word *pogroms* (paragraph 6) and identify the type of context clue that provides its meaning.

   _____

   _____

6. Determine the meanings of the following words by using word parts:
   a. *ideologies* (paragraph 1)

   _____

   _____

   b. *beneficial* (paragraph 7)

   _____

   c. *mistreatment* (paragraph 9)

   _____

   d. *inevitably* (paragraph 10)

   _____

   e. *territory* (paragraph 10)

   _____

Checking Your Comprehension

7. To what does the author compare the treatment of Native Americans?

   _____

   _____

8. According to the reading, what did some colonists admire about the Native American way of life?

   _____

   _____

9. Who was Lost Bird and what happened to her?

   _____

   _____

   _____

   _____

   _____

   _____

10. What did Native Americans claim in bringing their case to the secretary of the interior in 1996 and what was the result?

_____

_____

_____

_____

_____

Thinking Critically

11. What is meant in paragraph 2 when the author says that Native Americans were *demonized*?

_____

_____

12. What is the author's attitude toward the subject and how is it revealed?

_____

_____

_____

_____

_____

13. What claim does the author make at the beginning and end of the selection?

_____

_____

_____

_____

_____

14. What aspects of the selection are depicted in the illustration?

_____

_____

_____

_____

_____

Questions for Discussion

1. Discuss the words *holocaust* and *pogrom*. Do you know of other "systematic, bureaucratic eliminations of a culture or people" or "organized massacres" besides the ones discussed in this selection?

2. Do you agree with the author's claim that most people want to believe the American holocaust never happened? Why or why not? Did this selection change your point of view about the subject?

3. Discuss the crowd's response described in paragraph 7: "Exterminate them!" Do you think this is an example of "mob mentality" or a reflection of the general sentiments at the time?

4. Discuss the idea of a person or group being "demonized." Have you ever witnessed this personally or seen an example in the news? What was your response?

CHAPTER

12

Skimming and Scanning

think VISUALLY...

Suppose you are in a rush to catch a flight and need to locate the departure gate for your flight quickly. What is the best and fastest way to locate the information you need?

First you would look at the departures screens and determine how they are organized—alphabetically by city, chronologically by time, or grouped by airline? Once you determined how the screens were organized, you could quickly find your flight.

This situation is a good example of the use of scanning—a method of quickly searching for a specific piece of information. In this chapter you will learn techniques for scanning as well as for skimming—a method of selectively reading some parts and skipping others in order to get the gist of a text.

Learning GOALS

In this chapter, you will learn how to . . .

Goal 1 Skim to get an overview of an article

Goal 2 Scan to locate specific information quickly

◼ Skimming

Goal 1

Skim to get an overview

Suppose that you are browsing through Web sites on the Internet, and just before it is time to leave for your next class, you follow a link and find a two- or three-page article that you are interested in reading. You do not want to bother bookmarking the site and returning to it later, and you do not have time to read it before class. What do you do?

One alternative is to forget about the article and go to class. A second alternative is to *skim* the article, reading some parts and skipping others, to find the most important ideas. You would read the parts of the article that are most likely to provide the main ideas and skip those that contain less important facts and details. **Skimming** means reading selectively to get a general idea of what an article is about.

This chapter discusses the purposes and types of skimming, presents a step-by-step procedure for skimming, and shows how to adapt the technique to various types of reading material.

Purposes for Skimming

It is not always necessary to read everything completely. In fact, in some circumstances thorough reading may be an inefficient use of your time. Let's take a moment to consider a few examples of material for which skimming would be the most effective technique to use:

- **A section of a text chapter that reviews the metric system.** If you have already learned and used the metric system, you can afford to skip over much of the material.

- **A Web site that you are using to complete a research paper.** If you have already collected most of your basic information, you might skim through the list of links, looking only for new sites that you had not previously visited.

- **A newspaper report of a current political event.** If you are reading the article only to learn the basic information, skimming is appropriate. You can skip sections of the article that give details.

- **A movie review.** If you are reading the review to decide whether you want to see the movie, you are probably looking for the writer's overall reaction to the movie: Was it exciting? Was it boring? Was it humorous? You can skip in-depth descriptions of characters, particular scenes, and particular actors' or actresses' performances.

Now try to think of some other situations or types of material that might be appropriate for you to skim. List them in the spaces provided.

1. _____

2. _____

3. _____

Skimming is appropriate when complete information is *not* required. Use skimming when you need *only* the most important ideas or the "gist" of the article.

How to Skim

In skimming, your overall purpose should be to read only those parts of an article or selection that contain the most important information. Skip what is not important. The type of material you are reading will, in part, determine how you should adapt your reading techniques.

To acquaint you with the process of skimming, a basic, step-by-step procedure is presented below and applied to a sample article. Then adaptations of this general technique to specific types of reading materials are discussed.

 NEED TO KNOW **How to Skim**

1. **The title.** The title often announces the subject and provides clues about the author's approach or attitude toward the subject.

2. **The subtitle or introductory byline.** Some types of material include a statement underneath the title that further explains the title or is written to catch the reader's interest.

3. **The introductory paragraph.** The introductory paragraph often provides important background information and introduces the subject. It may also provide a brief overview of how the subject is treated.

4. **The headings.** A heading announces the topic that will be discussed in the paragraphs that follow. Together, the headings form an outline of topics covered.

5. **The first sentence of each paragraph.** It often states the main idea of the paragraph. If you read a first sentence that clearly *is not* the topic sentence, you might jump to the end of the paragraph and read the last sentence. (See Chapter 4.)

6. **Keywords.** Quickly glance through the remainder of the paragraph. Try to pick out keywords that answer *who, what, when, where,* or *how much* about the main idea of the paragraph. Try to notice names, numbers, dates, places, and capitalized or italicized words and phrases. Also notice any numbered sequences. This quick glance will add to your overall impression of the paragraph and will confirm that you have identified the main idea of the paragraph.

7. **The title or legend of any maps, graphs, charts, or diagrams.** The title or legend will state concisely what the graphic depicts and suggest what important event, idea, or relationship it is intended to emphasize.

8. **The last paragraph.** The last paragraph often provides a conclusion or summary for the article. It might state concisely the main points of the article or suggest new directions for considering the topic. If it is lengthy, read only the last few lines.

Your reading rate should generally be 800 wpm or above for skimming, or about three or four times as fast as you would normally read.

As a general rule of thumb, you should skip more than you read. Although the amount to skip varies according to the type of material, a safe estimate might be that you should skip about 70 to 80 percent of the material. Because you are skipping large portions of the material, your comprehension will be limited. An acceptable level of comprehension for skimming is often 50 percent, although it may vary according to your purpose.

To give you a better idea of what the technique of skimming is like, the following article has been highlighted to indicate the portions of the article that you might read when skimming.

ELEMENTS OF RELIGION

Most religions contain four common elements: sacred objects or places, rituals, a system of beliefs, and an organization of believers.

The Sacred

According to Durkheim, the **profane** consists of all the elements of everyday life that are considered part of the ordinary physical (natural) world. The **sacred**, on the other hand, is anything set apart from everyday life that is capable of evoking deep respect and awe. This sense of awe in the presence of the sacred is the underlying and most basic religious impulse whether one regards the ultimate source of awe as the supernatural or transcendent itself or whether one agrees with Durkheim's theory that it is the subconscious recognition of the power of society over the individual that is the best explanation for the awe experienced by the believer. In any event, when confronted by the sacred, people generally feel in touch with the eternal source of life and believe that they are experiencing a special power that cannot be understood by reason alone. Because the sacred is so supremely desirable, it arouses feelings of great attraction. Because of its power, the sacred also can provoke feelings of dread.

The experience of the sacred is frequently linked with material objects, such as an altar, a statue, or a cross. Almost anything can be considered sacred: certain locations, such as a grove of trees, a spring, or a cave; particular times, such as sunrise or Easter; or animals or plants, such as cows, rattlesnakes, or trees. Sometimes, the sacred is connected with unusual events, such as erupting volcanoes or overflowing rivers. People with rare abilities and the dates of unusual occurrences may also be regarded as sacred.

Ritual

A religious **ritual** is an established pattern of behavior closely associated with the experience of the sacred. It is typically performed to express or revive powerful experiences of the sacred or to ask the sacred power for some favor.

By holding certain ceremonies along the banks of the Nile, for example, the ancient Egyptians felt that they could bring on, or symbolically participate in, the annual flooding that brought needed water and silt to the fields. Ritual is also a way of protecting the sacred from contamination by the profane. A sacred chalice or cup is not routinely used for drinking water. It may be used only in special ceremonies, when it is filled with special wine and passed from one person to another.

Ritual is a means of organizing the believers of a religion; it brings them together in a group. The repetition of a ritual, psychologists believe, helps to restore people's feeling of integration, identity, and security. By worshiping the crocodile in formal ceremonies, for example, certain African tribes felt that they were protecting themselves from attack by these frightening beasts.

Ritual itself can become sacred through its connection with the sacred. The objects used in ritual—the herbs or potions consumed, the clothes worn by the participants, the place where the ritual is conducted—can all come to be revered. For this reason, a house of worship, the location of religious ritual, is generally considered to be sacred.

A System of Beliefs

The system of religious beliefs is the element of religion that has undergone more development than any other. In traditional religions, the main function of the belief system was to relate sacred objects to religious rituals and to define and protect the sacred. In the Old Testament, for example, God is portrayed as a superhuman figure who nevertheless can be understood in human terms. The abstract concept of God is transformed into a symbol that people can identify with and relate to.

Belief systems also explain the meaning and purpose of ritual. Muslims, for instance, learn that they must wash before evening prayers because physical cleanliness is a sign of moral cleanliness, and one must always appear morally clean before God. In light of this knowledge, the ritual of washing becomes a meaningful event.

Most modern systems of religious belief go far beyond merely supporting the other elements of religion. They often include moral propositions (such as the equality of all people) that are considered important truths. Although not necessarily considered "holy" by the faithful, these beliefs have a sacred quality. Because they are frequently translated into constitutions, political ideology, and education doctrine, these beliefs are important not only to the religions themselves but also in the nonreligious affairs of a society.

An Organization of Believers

An organization of believers is needed to ensure the continuity and effectiveness of the religious experience. Conducting rituals, building places of worship, and choosing specialists such as priests, monks, and ministers to cultivate and safeguard the sacred all call for some kind of organization. For example, the Second Methodist Church of Great Falls, Montana, builds the church building, selects and pays the minister, buys the hymnals and the organ, and recruits the choir. The culmination of these activities is that the believers can go to church on Sunday morning and share their experience of the sacred.

—Popenoe, David, *Sociology,* 11th Ed., © 2000. Reprinted and electronically reproduced by permission of Pearson Education, Inc., Upper Saddle River, NJ.

EXERCISE 12–1   EVALUATING SKIMMING

Directions: *After you have skimmed the article "Elements of Religion," answer the following questions. For each item, indicate whether the statement is true or false by marking "T" or "F" in the space provided.*

___ 1. The same basic elements are found in most religions.

___ 2. The term *profane* in this passage refers to life experiences that are vulgar or unpleasant.

___ 3. The element of religion that has developed the most is ritual.

___ 4. A system of beliefs explains the meaning and purpose of various rituals.

___ 5. Some type of organization is essential to the religious experience. ■

EXERCISE 12–2   PRACTICING SKIMMING

Directions: *Skim the following article by Susan Gilbert, from* Science Digest, *on noise pollution. Your purpose for reading is to learn about the causes, effects, and control of noise pollution. Answer the questions following the article when you have finished skimming.*

NOISE POLLUTION

The Volume Continues to Rise, Yet the Research Money Dwindles

Loud noise is the most pervasive kind of pollution. Scientific studies have shown that it not only harms the ears, it alters moods, reduces learning ability and may increase blood pressure. It doesn't take the earsplitting clatter of a jackhammer for a city dweller to experience, daily, enough noise to cause permanent hearing loss. The screeching of traffic, the din in a crowded restaurant, the roar of airplanes overhead—even music from blaring radios—are enough to exceed the maximum noise the federal government permits in workplaces for an eight-hour day.

The Environmental Protection Agency, once committed to reducing the insidious problem of noise, has been stifled in its attempts to do anything. Its $14-million program to curb noise pollution was eliminated four years ago. Some government agencies, however, have been successful. The Federal Aviation Administration has forced airplanes to cut noise levels by half within two miles of taking off and landing at major airports. New York City adopted the nation's first antinoise code in 1972 and imposes $25 fines for violations, although a majority of cab drivers still lean more on their horns than on their brakes. Chicago, San Francisco and a host of other cities have taken similar measures. In fact, it was such legislation that rallied the forces opposed to the Chicago Cubs playing night baseball at Wrigley Field.

Hazardous Headphones

Many of the most damaging noises, however, are within the power of all of us to control, simply by using a little common sense. Consider the use of stereo headphones—devices that mask uncomfortable noise with entertaining sound. A study by otolaryngologist Phillip Lee, of the University Hospital in Iowa City, disclosed that teenagers who used stereo headphones for three hours suffered temporary hearing loss. These devices proved to be exceptionally damaging when played at 100 decibels or more, the intensity of a chain saw. "People should not turn them up above a normal, conversational level," says Lee.

While stunning and sudden explosions can cause deafness by rupturing an eardrum, hearing can be at least partially restored by surgery. Not so with sustained environmental noises; the damage they cause is often irreversible. As sounds enter the inner ear, they wave hair cells back and forth, causing them to release a chemical transmitter to the nerve fibers that carry auditory messages to the brain. This is how we hear. But too much noise can exhaust—even kill—some hair cells. The effect may be a slight temporary hearing loss or a ringing in the ears.

"A few missing hair cells won't damage hearing permanently," says neurobiologist Barbara Bohne, of the Washington University School of Medicine in St. Louis. "But a few lost each weekend will gradually lead to noticeable hearing problems. Once this happens, it's too late to do anything." But some precautions can be taken. Earplugs and muffs, which reduce noise by as much as 25 decibels, can make the difference between hazardous and safe exposure. And, adds Bohne, "If you have to cut wood with a chain saw, do it for an hour one Saturday and another hour the following week, rather than for two hours at once." Separating periods of intense noise with at least a day of relative quiet can allow stunned hair cells time to recover.

Noise certainly makes us angry, but does it increase our blood pressure? Studies have been contradictory. Otolaryngologist Ernest Peterson, of the University of Miami, found that noise makes monkeys' blood pressure rise. But in a letter published in *The Lancet* last fall, a Swedish doctor reported no such effect on shipyard workers after studying them for eight years.

Noise's impact on the brain has been measured with more certainty. Children in schools located on loud streets score well below their socioeconomic counterparts in quiet schools, according to the California Department of Health Services.

Two British psychologists, reporting last year in the *Journal of the Acoustical Society of America,* found that suburban traffic of about 46 decibels (comparable to the hum of a refrigerator) impairs sleep. When the amount of noise entering subjects' bedrooms was reduced by five decibels (to the level of soft speech), their brains showed an increase in low-frequency, high-amplitude delta waves—a sign of deep sleep.

Audiologist John Mills, of the Medical College of South Carolina, believes that the brain is "the most significant area in need of further study." He reports that in several animal experiments, 65 decibels of sound sustained for 24 hours (the same level as that produced by an air conditioner) were found somehow to damage the brain stem.

This, says Mills, is reason enough to investigate whether the same damage occurs in humans. "When does injury to the brain begin?" he asks. "Is it independent of injury to the ear? These are the things we must learn."

Susan Gilbert is a journalist and author in New York.

1. How does noise pollution affect humans?

_____

_____

2. Give several examples of noise pollution.

_____

3. Has the Environmental Protection Agency been successful in controlling noise pollution?

_____

4. What questions remain unanswered about the effects of noise pollution on humans?

_____

✔ LEARNING STYLE TIPS

If you tend to be a . . .	Then improve your skimming skills by . . .
Pragmatic learner	Defining your purpose and assessing the material's organization before you begin skimming.
Creative learner	Discovering what interests you about the article you will skim. Create questions you hope to be able to answer as you skim.

Using Skimming Effectively

Now that you are familiar with the steps involved in skimming, you may realize that it is very similar to a technique you learned earlier in this book—previewing. Actually, previewing may be considered one form of skimming. Generally, there are three types of skimming:

1. **Preview skimming.** To become generally familiar with the organization and content of material *before* reading it. This is the type of skimming that is equivalent to previewing. (See Chapter 2.)

2. **Overview skimming.** To get an *overview* of the content and organization without reading the material completely. Often referred to as *skim-reading*, this form of skimming is used when you do not intend to

return to reading the material for another more thorough reading and when skimming alone meets your needs.

3. **Review skimming.** To go back over material you have already read to *review* the main points. Your purpose is to become reacquainted with the basic content and organization of the material. (Chapter 8 discusses review in detail.)

Limitations of Skimming

Because skimming involves skipping large portions of the material, you should not expect to retain the less important facts and details. As mentioned previously, you can expect a comprehension level of about 50 percent when skimming. Use skimming *only* when your purpose for reading allows you to read for general concepts rather than specific information.

Alternating Skimming and Reading

Many effective readers alternate between skimming and more careful reading. In a given article, for example, you may skim several sections until you come to a section that is of particular interest or that fulfills your purpose for reading. At that point, you may read completely rather than skim, and then continue skimming later sections. At other times, it may be necessary to read completely when you feel confused or when you encounter difficult or unfamiliar ideas.

 TECH SUPPORT Skimming Online Sources

Skimming online sources is easily done by scrolling through the document by using the down arrow or the page down key. Soon you'll develop a rhythm that allows you to quickly glance at each screen before moving on to the next.

When you skim an online source, you do not have the benefit of the full text in front of you at one time. By paging through a print source, you can pick up initial clues about length, organization, placement of graphics, and relative importance of ideas. To obtain these initial clues, consider scrolling through the entire document very quickly, noticing only major headings, graphics, and length. Then skim the document using the suggestions given in the Need to Know box on page 504.

Skimming Various Types of Material

Effective skimming hinges on the reader's ability to recognize the organization and structure of the material and to locate the main ideas of the selection. The procedure for skimming outlined in the earlier section "How to Skim" is a general guide that must be adapted to the material. Table 12.1 lists suggestions for skimming textbooks, reference sources, newspaper and magazine articles, and nonfiction books.

TABLE 12.1 Adapting Your Skimming Strategy

Type of Material	Focus On
Textbook chapters	• Chapter objectives and introductions • Headings and typographical aids • Graphic and visual aids • Review and discussion questions
Reference sources	• Date • Organization of the source • Topical index
Newspaper articles	• Title • Opening paragraphs • First sentences of remaining paragraphs
Magazine articles	• Title/subtitle/byline • Opening paragraphs • Photograph/captions • Headings/first sentences • Last several paragraphs
Nonfiction books	• Front and back cover of book jacket • Author's credentials • Table of contents • Preface • First and last chapters

EXERCISE 12–3   PRACTICING SKIMMING

Directions: *Suppose your communications instructor mentions in class that different cultures have different concepts of time. You decide you want to learn more about these cultural differences. In your research, you locate the following article on the topic. Skim this article and then answer the questions that follow it.*

TIME AND CULTURAL DIFFERENCES

Time is another communication channel with great cultural differences. Two types of cultural time are especially important in nonverbal communication: formal and informal. In American culture, **formal time** is divided into seconds, minutes, hours, days, weeks, months, and years. Other cultures may use phases of the moon or the seasons to delineate time periods. In some colleges courses are divided into 50- or 75-minute periods that meet two or three times a week for 14-week periods called semesters. Eight semesters of fifteen or sixteen 50-minute periods per week equal a college education. Other colleges use quarters or trimesters. As these examples illustrate, formal time units are arbitrary. The culture establishes them for convenience.

Informal time refers to the use of general time terms—for example, "forever," "immediately," "soon," "right away," "as soon as possible." This area of time creates the most communication problems because the terms have different meanings for different people.

Another interesting distinction is that between **monochronic** and **polychronic time** orientations. Monochronic people or cultures (the United States, Germany, Scandinavia, and Switzerland are good examples) schedule one thing at a time. Time is compartmentalized; there is a time for everything, and everything has its own time. Polychronic people or cultures (Latin Americans, Mediterranean people, and Arabs are good examples), on the other hand, schedule a number of things at the same time. Eating, conducting business with several different people, and taking care of family matters may all be conducted at the same time. No culture is entirely monochronic or polychronic; rather these are general tendencies that are found across a large part of the culture. Some cultures combine both time orientations; Japanese and parts of American culture are examples where both orientations are found.

Attitudes toward time vary from one culture to another. In one study, for example, the accuracy of clocks was measured in six cultures—Japan, Indonesia, Italy, England, Taiwan, and the United States. Japan had the most accurate and Indonesia had the least accurate clocks. A measure of the speed at which people in these six cultures walked found that the Japanese walked the fastest, the Indonesians the slowest.

Another interesting aspect of cultural time is your "social clock." Your culture and your more specific society maintain a time schedule for the right time to do a variety of important things—for example, the right time to start dating, to finish college, to buy your own home, to have a child. And you no doubt learned about this clock as you were growing up . . . On the basis of this social clock, you then evaluate your own social and professional development. If you're on time with the rest of your peers—for example, you all started dating at around the same age or you're all finishing college at around the same age—then you will feel well adjusted, competent, and a part of the group. If you're late, you will probably experience feelings of dissatisfaction. Recent research, however, shows that this social clock is becoming more flexible; people are becoming more willing to tolerate deviations from the established, socially acceptable timetable for accomplishing many of life's transitional events.

—Devito, Joseph A., *Messages,* 4th Ed., © 1999. Reprinted and electronically reproduced by permission of Pearson Education, Inc., Upper Saddle River, NJ.

1. Explain the differences between informal and formal time.

   _____

   _____

2. Explain monochronic time and indicate at least one country in which it is used.

   _____

   _____

3. Explain polychronic time and indicate at least one country in which it is used.

_____

_____

4. Define the term "social clock."

_____

_____

EXERCISE 12–4

PRACTICING SKIMMING

Directions: _Locate an article on a topic of interest on the Internet. Skim it and then answer the questions that follow._

1. What is the main point of the article?

_____

2. How does the author support or explain this point?

_____

3. How is skimming an online source different from skimming a print source?

_____

EXERCISE 12–5

Academic
APPLICATION

PRACTICING SKIMMING

Directions: _Select a chapter from one of your textbooks, skim-read the first five pages of it, and answer the following questions._

1. What general subject is discussed in the chapter?

_____

2. How is the chapter organized?

_____

3. Write a brief list of ideas or topics that are discussed in the pages you skimmed.

_____

_____

EXERCISE 12–6

PRACTICING SKIMMING

Directions: _Skim-read the reading selection at the end of the chapter and answer the questions that follow the selection. Do not be concerned if you are unable to answer all the questions correctly; you should expect your reading rate to be higher but your comprehension lower than on most other readings you have completed up to this point._

■ Scanning

Goal 2
Scan to locate
specific information
quickly

Have you ever searched through a crowd of people for a particular person or looked through a rack of clothing for an item of a particular size, color, or price? Have you checked a bus schedule or located a particular book on a library shelf? If so, you used a technique called **scanning**. Scanning is searching for a specific piece of information; your only purpose is to locate that information. In fact, when you scan you are not at all interested in anything else on the page; you have no reason to notice or remember any other information.

Scanning Techniques

Many people do not scan as efficiently as possible because they randomly search through material, hoping to stumble on the information they are seeking. Scanning in this way is time-consuming and frustrating, and it often forces the reader to "give up" and read the entire selection. The key to effective scanning is a systematic approach, described in the following steps:

NEED TO KNOW **How to Scan**

1. **Check the organization.** Before you begin to scan, check to see how the article or material is organized.
   - For a *graphic,* check its title and other labels, keys, and legends. They state what the graphic is intended to describe and tell you how it is presented.
   - For *prose selections,* notice the overall structure of the article so that you will be able to predict where in the article you can expect to find your information.
   - For an *online* source, scroll through the entire document to discover its overall organization or check the site map.

2. **Form specific questions.** Fix in your mind what you are looking for by forming specific questions about the topic. For example, when scanning for information about heart transplants in New York State, ask questions such as these:
   - How many transplants were performed in a certain year?
   - What rules and guidelines apply to heart transplants?
   - What is the success rate of heart transplants?

3. **Anticipate word clues.** Anticipate clues that may help you locate the answer more rapidly. For example, if you were trying to locate the population of New York City in an article on the populations of cities, you might expect the answer to appear in digits such as 8,310,212, or in words such as "eight million" or "nine million." If you were looking for the name of a political figure in a newspaper article, you should expect to find two words, both capitalized. Try to fix the image of your clue words or phrases in your mind as accurately as possible before you begin to scan.

4. **Identify likely answer locations.** Try to identify likely places where the information you are looking for might appear. You might be able to identify a column or section that contains the needed information. You might be able to eliminate certain sections, or you might be able to predict that the information will appear in a certain portion of the article.

5. **Use a systematic pattern.** Do not randomly skip around, searching for information. Instead, rhythmically sweep your eyes through the material. For material printed in narrow six- or seven-word columns, such as newspaper articles, you might move your eyes straight down the middle, catching the phrases on each half of the line. For wider lines of print, a zigzag or Z pattern might be more effective. Using this pattern, you would move your eyes back and forth, catching several lines in each movement. When you do come to the information you are looking for, clue words may seem to "pop out" at you.

6. **Confirm your answer.** Once you think you have located your information, check to be sure you are correct. Read the sentence that contains the answer to confirm that it is the information you need.

Now let us try out this procedure. Assume that you are writing a paper on competitive pricing among large retail stores. You are searching for information on the pricing policies of large discount stores, specifically Wal-Mart. You have located a section of a business textbook titled "Wal-Mart: Competitive Pricing". Use each of the steps listed in the Need to Know box to find information you need.

WAL-MART: COMPETITIVE PRICING

It probably comes as no surprise to hear that Wal-Mart is the biggest retailer in the world. But did you know that it is the biggest company in the world? With over 7,000 stores worldwide, Wal-Mart's 2006 revenue of $351 billion was more than 2.5 times larger than the combined revenue of its closest competitors, Target, JCPenny, and Kmart/Sears. What's more, the annual revenue of this behemoth is bigger than the combined revenues of IBM, Dell, Microsoft, and Cisco, some of the largest companies in the world.

Each year, over 80% of Americans make at least one purchase at Wal-Mart. The stores sell over 30% of all household staples American consumers buy, and this percentage is growing. And, this dominance is not exclusive to the United States. Wal-Mart operates over 2,800 stores in 13 countries outside the United States and is also the largest retailer in Canada and Mexico. How has this company, with humble roots in Arkansas, achieved success of such proportions?

Some might say Wal-Mart succeeds because it gives customers what they want. "Low price" is more than just a slogan at Wal-Mart. One study shows that on average, Wal-Mart offers products at prices 14% below its rivals. In addition, Wal-Mart is constantly adding more and more products as it tries to be the ultimate one-stop shop. And finally, it offers the convenience of numerous stores and extended (often 24-hour) operations. Ninety percent of Americans live within range of at least one Wal-Mart store. That number will only increase as the company plans to continue opening one new U.S. store every day for at least the next five years.

First, when you assess the organization of this material, you see that it is divided into three paragraphs, with only one heading provided. Next, you fix in your mind what you are looking for by forming a question such as "How do Wal-Mart's prices compare to its competitors'?" Then you anticipate the form of the answer, expecting phrases such as *prices, higher* or *lower, competitors* or *rivals,* and a number or percentage. As you begin scanning you see that the first paragraph is about size and number of stores. The second paragraph is about the percentage of household staples the chain sells in the United States and abroad. The third paragraph is about customers and you notice the phrase "low price," see the percentage sign, and the word *rivals,* so you know this is the most likely place to find the answer. You read the third sentence to confirm the answer that Wal-Mart's prices are 14 percent lower than its competitors'.

Scanning Lists

Much information is presented in list format including print dictionaries, TV listings, and plane schedules. Use the following steps to scan lists.

NEED TO KNOW How to Scan Lists

1. **Check to determine the overall organization and then see if it is divided in any particular way.** Notice whether column titles, headings, or any other clues are provided about the material's organization. For instance, you would note that a TV program schedule is organized by day of the week, but that it is also arranged by time. In scanning a zip code directory, you would see that it is arranged alphabetically but that there is a separate alphabetical list for each state.

2. **Scan for a specific word, phrase, name, date, or place name.** For example, in checking the meaning of a term in *Taber's Cyclopedic Medical Dictionary,* you are looking for a specific word. Similarly, in looking up a metric equivalent in the glossary of your physics textbook, your purpose is quite specific.

3. **Use the arrow scanning pattern; it is a straight-down-the-column pattern.**

4. **For alphabetical lists, focus on the first letter of each line until you reach the letter that begins the word you are looking for.** Then focus on the first two letters until you reach the two-letter combination you are searching for. Successively widen your focus until you are looking for whole words.

EXERCISE 12–7   **PRACTICING SCANNING**

Directions: *Scan the table shown in Figure 12.1 and answer each of the following questions.*

1. How is this table organized?

_____

_____

_____

2. How do the numbers shown under "Adult literacy rate" differ from those shown under the heading "Number of adults unable to read and write"?

_____

_____

3. Which world region has the greatest number of illiterate men?

_____

4. In the entire world, what percentage of men are literate? What percentage of women are literate?

_____

5. Which world region has the lowest total literacy rate?

_____

FIGURE 12.1 Material in List Format

TABLE A

Adult literacy rate by World Region, 2008

World Region	Adult literacy rate (%)				Number of adults unable to read and write (000s)			
	Total	Male	Female	GPI	Total	Male	Female	% F
Developed regions	99.0	99.2	98.9	1.00	8,358	3,438	4,921	58.9
Commonwealth of Independent States (CIS)	99.5	99.7	99.4	1.00	1,061	311	750	70.7
Northern Africa	67.3	76.7	58.1	0.76	36,290	12,882	23,408	64.5
Sub-Saharan Africa	62.5	71.6	53.6	0.75	175,871	65,748	110,123	62.6
Latin America and the Caribbean	91.0	91.9	90.3	0.98	36,056	15,945	20,111	55.8
Eastern Asia	93.8	96.8	90.7	0.94	70,233	18,656	51,577	73.4
Southern Asia	61.9	73.2	50.9	0.70	412,432	150,668	261,764	63.5
South-Eastern Asia	91.9	94.5	89.5	0.95	32,782	11,097	21,685	66.1
Western Asia	84.5	91.5	76.9	0.84	21,332	6,061	15,271	71.6
Oceania	66.4	70.2	62.6	0.89	1,750	783	967	55.3
World	83.4	88.2	78.9	0.90	796,165	285,588	510,577	64.1

Source: UNESCO Institute for Statistics, Data Centre, stats.uis.unesco.org

GPI = gender parity index, or the rate of female to male literacy rates
% F = percentage female
UNESCO Institute for Statistics, Data Centre, stats.uis.unesco.org

EXERCISE 12–8   **SCANNING AN INDEX**

> **Directions:** *Using the portion of a book's index shown in Figure 12.2, scan to locate the answer to each of the following questions.*

1. On what page(s) would you find information on the housing of slaves?

_____

2. What page contains information on the 1932 election of Herbert Hoover?

_____

3. On what page can you find information on Hispanic Americans in the Great Depression?

_____

FIGURE 12.2 Reference Book Index

Hemingway, Ernest, 462
Henry, Andrew, 205
Henry, O., 347
Henry, Patrick, 80, 86, 88
Henry VII, King of England,
    10–11, 18
Henry VIII, King of
    England, 11, 18
Henry of Portugal, Prince, 12
Hepburn Act of 1906, 404, 413
Hessian mercenaries, 97, 99, 100
Hidatsa Indians, 204
Higher Education Act of 1965,
    540
Highway Act of 1916, 415
Hill, Anita, 586
Himmelfarb, Gertrude, 294
Hippies, 545
Hiroshima, 505
Hispanic Americans:
    barrios, 460
    Brown Power movement, 548
    in Great Depression, 473
    New Deal and, 483–84
Hispaniola, 16
Hiss, Alger, 522
Hitler, Adolf, 489, 490, 493, 501
Ho Chi Minh, 532
Ho Chi Minh Trail, 543
Hohokam Indians, 3

Holly, Buddy, 528
Hollywood, Red Scare and,
    520–21
Hollywood Ten, 521
Holocaust, 501
Holy Roman Empire, 11
Home mission societies, 330
Home Owners Loan Act of
    1933, 471
Home Owners Loan
    Corporation (HOLC), 476
Homestead Act of 1862,
    292, 375
Homestead strike, 350–51
Homosexuals, 569, 571
Honduras, U.S. intervention
    in, 467
Hood, John Bell, 299, 300
Hooker, Joseph, 283, 284, 287
Hooper, William, 115
Hoover, Herbert, 442, 456,
    457, 466–67
    election of 1928, 467–68
    election of 1932, 475
    Great Depression and, 473–75
Hoover, J. Edgar, 450, 528
Hoover Dam, 485
Hoovervilles, 472
Hope, Lugenia Burns, 337
Hopi Indians, 4, 43, 211, 365

Hopkins, Harry, 476, 479, 482
Horizontal integration, 345
Horseshoe Bend, battle of, 155
Horton, Willie, 582
House, Edward, 437
House Committee on
    Un-American Activities
    (HUAC), 520–21
House of Burgesses, 25
House of Commons, 66, 81
House of Lords, 66
House of Seven Gables, The
    (Hawthorne), 242
Housing:
    African-Americans
        and, 357–58, 510
    colonial era, 28, 60
    post-World War II, 509–10
    settlement house
        movement, 403
    slave, 223
    slums, 186–87, 349
    sod houses, 376
    tenements, 349
    urban, 187–88, 527
    in World War II, 496–97
Housing Act of 1949, 512
Houston, Charles Hamilton,
    536
Houston, Sam, 209

Source: Goldfield, David; Abbott, Carl E.; Anderson, Virginia Dejohn; Argersinger, Jo Ann E.; Argersinger, Peter H.; Barney, William M.; Weir, Robert M., *The American Journey: A History of the United States, Combined Volume,* 2nd Ed., © 2001. Reprinted and electronically reproduced by permission of Pearson Education, Inc., Upper Saddle River, NJ.

Scanning Prose Materials

Prose materials are more difficult to scan than material in list format. Their organization is less apparent, and the information is not as concisely or obviously stated. For prose materials, you must rely heavily on identifying clue words and predicting the form of your answer. Think of scanning prose materials as a floating process in which your eyes drift quickly through a passage searching for clue words and phrases. Your eyes should move across sentences and entire paragraphs, noticing only clue words that indicate that you may be close to locating the answer.

EXERCISE 12–9   **PRACTICING SCANNING**

> **Directions:** *Scan each of the following prose selections to locate the answer to the question indicated. Write your answer in the space provided.*

1. What two factors determine how a shopper will react to a store environment?

_____

It's no secret that people's moods and behaviors are strongly influenced by their physical surroundings. Despite all their efforts to presell consumers through advertising, marketers know that the store environment influences many purchases. For example, consumers decide on about two out of every three of their supermarket product purchases in the aisles. Therefore, the messages they receive at the time and their feelings about being in the store are important influences on their decisions.

Two dimensions, *arousal* and *pleasure*, determine if a shopper will react positively or negatively to a store environment. In other words, the person's surroundings can be either dull or exciting (arousing), and either pleasant or not. Just because the environment is arousing doesn't necessarily mean it will be pleasant—we've all been in crowded, hot stores that are anything but! Maintaining an upbeat feeling in a pleasant context is one factor behind the success of theme parks such as Disney World, which try to provide consistent doses of carefully calculated stimulation to patrons.

The importance of these surroundings explains why many retailers are combining two favorite consumer activities, shopping and eating, into elaborate *themed environments*. According to a recent Roper Starch survey, eating out is the top form of out-of-home entertainment, and innovative firms are scrambling to offer customers a chance to eat, buy, and be entertained all at once. Planet Hollywood, for example, is crammed full of costumes and props, and the chain now grosses over $200 million a year around the world.

—Solomon, Michael R., *Marketing: Real People Real Choices,* 1st Ed., © 1998. Reprinted and electronically reproduced by permission of Pearson Education, Inc., Upper Saddle River, NJ.

2. Where does gas exchange occur in the lungs?

_____

Among mammals, external respiration takes place by means of special pouches called lungs. External respiration is accomplished as oxygen-laden air is brought into the lungs by **ventilation,** or **breathing.** Air passes from the large **trachea** into the branched **bronchi** (singular, *bronchus*) and on into increasingly smaller **bronchioles** that terminate in the many saclike **alveoli,** which is where gas exchange occurs. The alveoli are so numerous that they give a spongelike quality to the lung. The total area of the alveoli in human lungs, by the way, is about equal to the area of a tennis court—a large exchange surface, indeed.

The surface of the lungs is moist, as is the respiratory surface of any animal. The moistness is necessary because oxygen must dissolve before it can cross these delicate membranes of the alveoli and enter the bloodstream. The blood transports the oxygen to the body's tissue, where it diffuses into the cells. In the cells, the oxygen has the humble but critical role of picking up spent electrons from the electron-transport chain, thereby producing metabolic water.

—Wallace, Robert A., *Biology: The World of Life,* 7th Ed., © 1997. Reprinted and electronically reproduced by permission of Pearson Education, Inc., Upper Saddle River, NJ.

3. What causes both Dutch elm disease and chestnut blight?

_____

For the last 30 years, the composition of European and American deciduous forests has been dramatically changed by disease. Two diseases—Dutch elm disease and chestnut blight—have virtually eliminated large elms and American chestnut trees from the North American landscape. The diseases are caused by fungi that infect and kill mature trees or young trees that are just old enough to reproduce. Very few trees survive infestation, so disease-tolerant strains among the native species of elms or chestnuts have yet to be identified. Consequently, there has been a precipitous decline in the populations of these trees in the forests of the eastern United States. These species were once major components of the forest canopy. As they have died, their replacement by other species has led to continued shifts in forest composition.

—By permission of Mark Bush, *Ecology of a Changing Planet,* Second Edition, © 1997.

4. Which of these four distances is appropriate for conducting business?

_____

Edward Hall distinguishes four distances that define the type of relationship between people and the type of communication in which they're likely to engage. In **intimate distance,** ranging from actual touching to 18 inches, the presence of the other individual is unmistakable. Each person experiences the sound, smell, and feel of the other's breath. You use intimate distance for love-making, comforting, and protecting. This distance is so short that most people do not consider it proper in public.

Personal distance refers to the protective "bubble" that defines your personal distance, ranging from 18 inches to 4 feet. This imaginary bubble keeps you protected and untouched by others. You can still hold or grasp another person at this distance but only by extending your arms, allowing you to take certain individuals such as loved ones into your protective bubble. At the outer limit of personal distance, you can touch another person only if both of you extend your arms. At this distance you conduct much of your interpersonal interactions, for example, talking with friends and family.

In **social distance**, ranging from 4 to 12 feet, you lose the visual detail you have at personal distance. You conduct impersonal business and interact at a social gathering at this social distance. The more distance you maintain in your interactions, the more formal they appear. In offices of high officials, the desks are positioned so the official is assured of at least this distance from clients.

Public distance, from 12 to more than 25 feet, protects you. At this distance you could take defensive action if threatened. On a public bus or train, for example, you might keep at least this distance from a drunkard. Although at this distance you lose the fine details of the face and eyes, you're still close enough to see what is happening.

—Devito, Joseph A., *Messages,* 4th Ed., © 1999. Reprinted and electronically reproduced by permission of Pearson Education, Inc., Upper Saddle River, NJ.

5. What is the distinction between open and closed societies?

_____

_____

Stratification systems differ in the ease with which people within them can move from one social status to another. A completely *open* society has never existed. But if it did, people could achieve whatever status their natural talents, abilities, and desires allowed them to attain. An open society would not be a society of equals; unequal social positions would still exist, but these positions would be filled solely on the basis of merit. Therefore, such a system could be described as a perfect *meritocracy.*

In a completely *closed* society everyone would be assigned a status at birth or at a certain age. That status could never be changed. No society has ever been completely closed, although some have been fairly close to this extreme.

The chief distinction between relatively open and relatively closed societies concerns the mix of statuses each contains. Open societies are characterized by greater reliance on *achieved* status than are closed societies; closed societies rely more on *ascribed* status. Many studies have shown that industrial, technologically advanced societies such as the United States tend to be relatively open. In contrast, preindustrial societies with economies based on agriculture tend to be relatively closed.

—Popenoe, David, *Sociology,* 11th Ed., © 2000. Reprinted and electronically reproduced by permission of Pearson Education, Inc., Upper Saddle River, NJ. ■

EXERCISE 12–10

Academic **APPLICATION**

USING SKIMMING AND SCANNING

Directions: *Make a list of your academic reading tasks for the past week. Indicate which of these tasks involved overview or review skimming and which involved scanning.* ■

SELF-TEST SUMMARY

Goal 1

1. What is skimming? What steps should you follow to skim effectively? What are the three types of skimming?

Skimming is a selective reading technique used to obtain important ideas. It is used when complete detailed information is *not* required.

Skimming involves reading only those parts of articles or selections containing key ideas, such as

- the title and subtitle
- headings
- the introductory paragraph
- the first sentence of other paragraphs
- keywords
- graphic elements
- the last paragraph

There are three general types of skimming depending upon your purpose:

- **Preview:** for becoming familiar with the material before reading it thoroughly
- **Overview:** for getting just the main ideas when you won't read the material completely
- **Review:** for refreshing your memory about material you have already read

Goal 2

2. What is scanning? What steps are involved in the process of scanning?

Scanning is a process of rapidly locating information in printed material. It differs from skimming in that scanning involves looking only for a specific piece of information—a word, fact, or statistic—and ignoring the rest of the material.

Effective scanning involves the following steps:

- checking the organization
- forming specific questions
- anticipating clue words
- identifying likely answer locations
- using a systematic pattern
- confirming your answer

READING SELECTION 23 HEALTH

Improving Your Sleep

Rebecca J. Donatelle

About the Reading

TEXTBOOK EXCERPT

This selection is an excerpt from a health textbook, Access to Health, *by Rebecca J. Donatelle. In an effort to make textbooks engaging and interesting, many authors include material that is relevant to the student's everyday life. As you read, think about how you can use the author's suggestions in your own life.*

Planning Your Reading Strategy*

Directions: *Activate your thinking by previewing the reading (see the Need to Know box on page 64) and answering the following questions.*

_____ 1. All of the following questions will be answered in the reading *except*:
   a. Do naps help you catch up on your sleep?
   b. How do men's sleeping habits differ from women's?
   c. How much sleep do you need each night?
   d. Which techniques can you use to get a good night's sleep?

_____ 2. Which of the following suggestions is not made for promoting restful sleep?
   a. Drink milk before bed.
   b. Stay active.
   c. Don't toss and turn.
   d. Create a sleep cave.

3. Based on your preview of the reading, how quickly do you think you should read the selection? (Circle one.) Explain your answer.

Very slowly   Slowly   At a moderate pace   Quickly   Very quickly

_____

4. How many hours of sleep do you get on a typical night? Do you believe you can make up for lost sleep?

▪ How Much Sleep Do You Need?

1   Given the importance of adequate sleep, especially REM sleep, you're probably asking yourself how much you really need. Unfortunately, there's no magic number. Let's find out why.

Sleep Need Includes Baseline Plus Debt

2   The short answer to how much sleep you need is about 7 to 8 hours. This recommendation is used by researchers as the standard for "average" sleep time, and is supported by a variety of studies over many years. For instance, research has shown

Donatelle, Rebecca J.; Ketcham, Patricia, Access to Health, *12th Ed., © 2012. Reprinted and electronically reproduced by permission of Pearson Education Inc., Upper Saddle River, NJ.*

* The Scorecard on p. 527 enables you to compute your reading rate. In order to do so, be sure to record your starting time in the Scorecard box before you begin reading.

REM sleep (paragraph 1)   a deep sleep characterized by rapid eye movement or REM

that adults who sleep 7 to 8 hours a night have a lower risk of mortality than those who get fewer than 7 or more than 8 hours of sleep.

3   But what if you're absolutely certain that you get by just fine on 5 or 6 hours a night? Then you might be interested in the results of another study in which young people who claimed they needed less sleep were found to need the average 7 to 8 hours when monitored in a sleep lab!

4   Still, sleep is not a "one size fits all" proposition. Individual variations do occur according to age (kids need more sleep), gender (women need more sleep), and many other factors. In addition, when trying to figure out your sleep needs, you have to consider two aspects: your body's physiological need plus your current **sleep debt.*** That's the total number of hours of missed sleep you're carrying around with you, either because you got up before your body was fully rested, or because your sleep was interrupted. Let's say that last week you managed just 5 hours of sleep a night Monday through

Every night you don't get 8 hours of sleep creates a "sleep debt." What with a busy schedule and late-night studying and socializing, the average college student gets 5 hours of sleep a night. In just one semester, that's a sleep debt of 336 hours, or 14 days!

Thursday. Even if you get 7 to 8 hours a night Friday through Sunday, that unresolved sleep debt of 8 to 12 hours will still leave you feeling tired and groggy when you start the week again. That means you need *more than* 8 hours a night for the next several nights to "catch up."

5   The good news is that you *can* catch up if you go about it sensibly. Getting 5 hours of sleep a night all semester long, then sleeping 48 hours the first weekend you're home on break won't restore your functioning, and it's likely to disrupt your circadian rhythm. Instead, whittle away at that sleep debt by sleeping 9 hours a night throughout your break—then start the new term resolved to sleep 7 to 8 hours a night.

What do you think?

Do you find it difficult to get 7 or 8 hours of sleep each night? • Do you think you are able to catch up on sleep you miss? • Have you noticed any negative consequences in your own life when you get too little sleep?

Do Naps Count?

6   Speaking of catching up, do naps count? Although naps can't entirely cancel out a significant sleep debt, they can help to improve your mood, alertness, and performance. It's best to nap in the early to mid-afternoon, when the pineal body in your brain releases a small amount of melatonin and your body experiences a natural dip in its circadian rhythm. Never nap in the late afternoon, as it could interfere with your ability to fall asleep that night. Keep your naps short, because a nap of more than 30 minutes can leave you in a state of **sleep inertia**, which is characterized by cognitive impairment, grogginess, and a disoriented feeling.

---

sleep debt (paragraph 4)   The difference between the number of hours of sleep an individual needed in a given time period and the number of hours he or she actually slept.

circadian rhythm (paragraph 5)   A daily cycle of biological activity influenced by regular variations in the environment, such as the alternation of night and day.

sleep inertia (paragraph 6)   A state characterized by cognitive impairment, grogginess, and disorientation that is experienced upon rising from short sleep or an overly long nap.

■ How Can You Get a Good Night's Sleep?

7 Do you need a jolt of caffeine to get you jump-started in the morning? Do you find it hard to stay awake in class? Have you ever nodded off behind the wheel? These are all signs of inadequate or poor quality sleep.

To Promote Restful Sleep, Try These Tips

8 The following tips can help you get a longer and more restful night's steep.

9 • **Let there be light.** Throughout the day, stay in sync with your circadian rhythm by spending time in the sunlight. If you live in an area where the sun seldom shines for weeks at a time, invest in special light-emitting diode (LED) lighting designed to mimic the sun's rays. Exposure to natural light outdoors is most beneficial, but opening the shades indoors and, on overcast days, turning on room lights can also help keep you alert.

What should I do if I can't fall asleep?

If you have difficulty falling asleep, it may be that noises, lights, interruptions, or persistent worries are keeping you awake. Use ear plugs or a white noise machine to block out noise, wear an eye shade to block out light, and turn off your phone and computer to prevent interruptions. If a worry keeps you awake, jot it down in a journal. You'll be better prepared to handle it in the morning after you've had a good night's sleep.

10 • **Stay active.** It's hard to feel sleepy if you've been sedentary all day, so make sure you get plenty of physical activity during the day. Resist the temptation to postpone exercise until you're sleeping better. Start gently, but start now, because regular exercise may help you maintain regular sleep habits.

11 • **Sleep tight.** Don't let a pancake pillow, scratchy of pilled sheets, or a threadbare blanket keep you from sleeping soundly, If your mattress is uncomfortable and you can't replace it, try putting a foam mattress overlay on top of it.

12 • **Create a sleep "cave."** Take a lesson from bats, bears, and burrowing animals! As bedtime approaches, keep your bedroom quiet, cool, and dark. Start by turning off your computer and cell phone. If you live in an apartment or dorm where there's noise outside or in the halls, wear ear plugs or get an electronic device that produces "white noise" such as the sound of gentle rain. Turn down the thermostat or, on hot nights, run a quiet electric fan. Install room-darkening shades or curtains or wear an eye mask if necessary to block out any light from the street.

13 • **Condition yourself into better sleep.** Go to bed and get up at the same time each day. Establish a bedtime ritual that signals to your body that it's time for sleep. For instance, sit by your bed and listen to a quiet song, meditate, write in a journal, take a warm bath or shower, or read something that lets you quietly wind down.

14 • **Breathe.** Do it deeply, as soon as your head hits the pillow. Inhale through your nose slowly, filling your lungs completely, then exhale slowly through slightly pursed lips. Repeat several times. Giving your body the oxygen it needs, deep breathing can also decrease anxiety and tension that sometimes make it difficult to fall asleep.

15 • **Don't toss and turn.** If you're not asleep after 20 minutes, get up. Turn on a low light, and read something relaxing, not stimulating, or listen to some gentle music. Once you feel sleepy, go back to bed.

Examining Reading Selection 23

Checking Your Vocabulary

Directions: *Use context, word parts, or a dictionary, if necessary, to determine the meaning of each word as it is used in the reading.*

___ 1. adequate (paragraph 1)
   a. difficult
   b. enough
   c. harmless
   d. inferior

___ 2. monitored (paragraph 3)
   a. traded
   b. carried
   c. observed
   d. received

___ 3. sync (paragraph 9)
   a. harmony
   b. mistake
   c. upset
   d. trap

___ 4. mimic (paragraph 9)
   a. avoid
   b. expose
   c. copy
   d. allow

___ 5. ritual (paragraph 13)
   a. achievement
   b. prediction
   c. service
   d. routine

Checking Your Comprehension

Directions: *Select the best answer.*

___ 6. This reading addresses all of the following questions *except*:
   a. How much sleep do you need?
   b. What is sleep debt?
   c. What causes sleep disorders?
   d. How can you get a better night's sleep?

___ 7. The author wrote this selection in order to
   a. describe substances and behaviors that interfere with sleep.
   b. inform readers about the importance of adequate sleep.
   c. promote exercise and rest as part of a healthy lifestyle.
   d. discuss ways to identify and address sleep disorders.

___ 8. The recommendation used by researchers as the standard for "average" sleep time is
   a. five to six hours.
   b. seven to eight hours.
   c. ten hours.
   d. eight to twelve hours.

___ 9. All of the following statements about sleep needs are true *except*
   a. children need more sleep than adults.
   b. women need more sleep than men.
   c. the average college student needs only five hours of sleep a night.
   d. resolving a sleep debt involves catching up on sleep gradually.

___ 10. According to the selection, a good way to promote a restful night's sleep is by
   a. keeping your room dark throughout the day.
   b. getting plenty of physical activity during the day.
   c. varying the time you go to bed each night.
   d. napping in the late afternoon or evening.

Thinking Critically

___11. The author supports her ideas primarily with
   a. research and reasons.
   b. personal experience.
   c. comparisons and analogies.
   d. examples and descriptions.

___12. The author's attitude toward the subject can best be described as
   a. detached and formal.
   b. solemn and pessimistic.
   c. informative and helpful.
   d. playful and amused.

___13. The purpose of the photograph of a woman at her desk (p. 524) is to illustrate the concept of
   a. sleep inertia.
   b. sleep debt.
   c. circadian rhythm.
   d. a sleep cave.

___14. The photograph with the caption "What should I do if I can't fall asleep?" (p. 525) corresponds to the idea of promoting restful sleep by
   a. reading in bed.
   b. recording dreams in a journal.
   c. writing persistent worries in a journal.
   d. working on homework in bed.

___15. One conclusion that can be made based on information in the reading is that
   a. sleep is important to good overall health.
   b. young people need less sleep than they typically get.
   c. age and gender are the most important factors in determining sleep needs.
   d. using a computer or cell phone at bedtime will not interfere with sleep.

Scorecard

Selection 23:   1,337 words

Finishing Time: _____ _____ _____
                  HR.   MIN.   SEC.

Starting Time: _____ _____ _____
                 HR.   MIN.   SEC.

Reading Time: _____ _____
                          MIN.   SEC.

WPM Score: _____

Comprehensive Score: for items 6–15
Number Right: _____ × 10 = _____%

Assessing Your Reading Strategy

1. How would you rate your comprehension of the reading? (Circle one.)

   Excellent   Good   Fair   Poor

2. Did you find your reading strategy effective?   Yes   No

3. Suppose you were given an assignment to read a similar selection to the one you just read. Based on your experience with this selection, how would you adjust your reading strategy (if at all)?

Writing About Reading Selection 23

Checking Your Vocabulary

Directions: *Complete each of the following items; refer to a dictionary if necessary.*

1. Define the phrase "one size fits all" (paragraph 4) and underline the word or phrase that provides a clue for its meaning.

   _____

   _____

   _____

2. Define the phrase "sleep inertia" (paragraph 6) and identify the type of context clue that provides its meaning.

   _____

   _____

3. Describe the denotative and connotative meanings of the word *cave* in paragraph 12.

   _____

   _____

   _____

4. Determine the meanings of the following words by using word parts:
   a. *mortality* (paragraph 2)

   _____

   b. *physiological* (paragraph 4)

   _____

   _____

   c. *exhale* (paragraph 14)

   _____

Checking Your Comprehension

5. What factors impact the amount of sleep a person needs?

   _____

   _____

6. What is the best way to reduce sleep debt?

   _____

   _____

7. When is the best time to nap and why?

   _____

   _____

   _____

   _____

8. How can you condition yourself to sleep better?

   _____

   _____

Thinking Critically

9. What claim does the author make in paragraph 1? Contrast the author's claim with the studies and rules she lays out. Do they agree or contradict each other?

   _____

   _____

   _____

   _____

_____

_____

_____

10. How would you describe the author's tone?

_____

_____

_____

_____

11. What does the author assume about college students?

_____

_____

1. Do you agree with the author's claim that sleep debt has to be made up gradually? Have you ever slept a long time after not getting a lot of sleep? How did you feel afterwards?

2. How much sleep do you feel you need? Do you feel the author's estimates are correct? Do you know anyone who needs a lot more or a lot less sleep than the author recommends?

3. How do you feel about sleep after having read this selection? Was the information useful and helpful or did it make you feel even more pressured?

13

Techniques for Reading Faster

think VISUALLY...

What does the photograph suggest about our culture's regard for time? It suggests that time is important to us. You probably feel as if you do not have enough time to do everything you want to do and find yourself juggling school, work, and family responsibilities.

One way to create more time for yourself is to improve your reading rate. If a student improves her reading rate by only 25 words per minute (and her current average reading rate is 250 words per minute), for example, she can save approximately 6 minutes per hour! Over the course of a week of 20 hours of reading, that amounts to two hours!

In this chapter you will learn various techniques for reading faster. You will learn about the physical aspects of reading, learn to cluster read, and practice five other methods for improving your rate—keyword reading, using transitional words, rapid reading drills, pacing, and rereading.

Learning GOALS

In this chapter, you will learn how to . . .

Goal 1 Control your eye-movement patterns

Goal 2 Read in meaning clusters

Goal 3 Read using keywords

Goal 4 Use transitions as speed cues

Goal 5 Practice rapid reading

Goal 6 Use pacing techniques

Goal 7 Reread to increase reading rate

■ Eye-Movement Patterns

Goal 1
Control your eye-movement patterns

Reading is primarily a thinking process. However, it has physical aspects: your eyes recognize words and transmit them in the form of signals to the brain. These physical aspects of reading are far less important than the cognitive processes. Still, the following brief overview of the physical aspects will help you recognize habits that interfere with rate and comprehension.

What Happens When You Read

Your eyes are highly specialized and complicated instruments. They have the capacity to recognize words rapidly and to transmit them in the form of signals to the brain. Mental processes become involved as your brain attaches meaning to the signals it receives. As these two processes occur, you comprehend what you are reading. To explain what occurs as your eyes move across a line of print, let us look at some physical features of the eye-movement process.

Left-to-Right Progression

Your eyes are already well trained to move in a left-to-right pattern across the page. The speed of this progression, however, is variable and can be significantly increased with practice and training.

Fixation

As your eyes move across a line of print, they move and stop, move and stop. When your eyes are in motion, they do not see anything. When your eyes stop, or focus, this is called a *fixation*. As your eyes move across a line of print, they make a number of stops, or fixations, and the number of fixations you make per line is directly related to your reading efficiency.

Eye Span

As your eyes stop, or fixate, while progressing from left to right across the line, they see a certain number of words or letters. The amount you see during each fixation is called your *eye span*. Some readers see only a part of a word in each fixation; others are able to see a whole word in one fixation. Still others may see several words in each fixation.

You may find that your eye span varies greatly according to the type of material you are reading. For example, if you are reading a children's book to a child, you may be able to see several words at a time. On the other hand, when you read a chemistry textbook, you may need to focus on single words. Occasionally, when identifying an unfamiliar word, you may look at one part of a word and then another part.

Return Sweep

When your eyes reach the end of a line of print, they return to the beginning of the next line. This return motion is called the *return sweep*. Although your eyes are already trained to return automatically, the speed with which they make this return is variable.

Regression

Your eyes normally progress in a left-to-right direction, seeing each word in the order in which it was written. Occasionally, your eyes will move backward, or *regress,* to a word already read instead of moving to the next word. This word may be on the same line or on a previous line. In the following line, each fixation is numbered consecutively to show a sample reader's regression pattern.

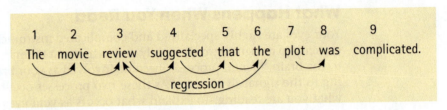

Notice that this reader moved from left to right through the sixth fixation. Then, instead of progressing to the next word, the reader regressed to the word "review" before proceeding with the sentence.

Regression is often unnecessary and slows you down. In fact, regressing may scramble the sentence order. As a result, you may have difficulty comprehending what you are reading.

Observing Eye-Movement Patterns

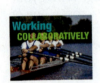

Most of the processes described so far can be readily observed by watching another person read. To get a better understanding of eye-movement patterns, choose another person to work with and try the following experiments. Be sure to sit so that the other person is facing you, and select sample pages from a book or text neither of you has already read.

EXPERIMENT 1: OBSERVING EYE MOVEMENT

Ask the other person to hold up the book so that you can see his or her eyes as he or she reads. Then direct the person to start reading a paragraph. As he or she reads, notice how the eyes move and stop, move and stop. Also notice the return sweep to the beginning of the next line.

EXPERIMENT 2: COUNTING FIXATIONS

As the person reads, count the number of eye stops or fixations made on each line. By counting the average number of words on the line and dividing it by the average number of fixations per line, you will be able to compute the person's eye span.

EXPERIMENT 3: REGRESSION

When observing the other person reading, ask him or her to deliberately regress to a word on a previous line. Notice the eye movement that occurs. Then have the person continue reading, and notice if he or she unknowingly makes any regressions.

Now allow the other person to try each of these three experiments while you read.

Reducing Regressions

Although even very good readers occasionally regress, you will find that frequent regression interferes with your comprehension and slows you down. Various mechanical devices can reduce regression, but you can easily get the same results by using one or more of the following techniques:

1. **Be conscious of your tendency to regress, and force yourself to move your eyes only from left to right.** Do not regress in the middle of a sentence. Instead, if the meaning of a sentence is unclear after you have finished reading it, reread the entire sentence.

2. **Use a 4" × 6" index card to prevent regression to previous lines.** As you read, slide the index card down the page so that it covers what you have already read. This technique will help you eliminate regressions, because when you look back to a previous line it will be covered up. If you look back and find the line is not visible often enough, eventually you will stop looking back.

3. **Use a pen, pencil, or finger to guide your eyes in a left-to-right direction across each line as you read.** Move the object or your finger at the speed at which you normally read. You will find that the forward motion of your finger or the pen will force you to continue reading toward the right and will discourage you from regressing.

Vocalization and Excessive Subvocalization

Some ineffective readers actually vocalize or sound out each word on a page by moving their lips and pronouncing each word. Others "hear" each word mentally as they read silently. This process is known as *subvocalization*. Research indicates that while subvocalization may be necessary and, at times, may enhance comprehension, it should not occur continuously as one reads. Mentally hearing each word may help clarify a confusing passage, but when done continuously, subvocalization usually limits the reader to word-by-word reading. Some students vocalize or subvocalize as a habit even though it is unnecessary.

If you find that you vocalize or subvocalize frequently, practice pushing yourself to read so rapidly that it is impossible. Also, if you discover that you move your lips as you read, place your hand or fingers near your lips as you read. You will feel your lips moving and can work to eliminate the habit.

✔ LEARNING STYLE TIPS

If you tend to be a . . .	Then improve your reading rate by . . .
Spatial learner	Paying attention to page layout, headings, diagrams, charts, and photos. These provide meaning clues that will enable you to read faster.
Verbal learner	Focusing on ideas, not single words. You can move through text faster if your focus is on concepts rather than facts.

■ Reading in Meaning Clusters

Goal 2
Read in meaning clusters

Most adult readers concentrate on a single word at a time. Although most are capable of grouping words together, they have not developed the skill of doing so. Word-by-word reading is time-consuming and, in many cases, actually detracts from understanding the meaning of a sentence.

To understand how slow word-by-word reading can be, read the following paragraph. It is written so that you will have to read it from *right to left,* forcing you to read each word separately.

> spirits neutral of combination a is Vodka
> bring to added is water The .water and
> neutral Since .proof final its to vodka
> ,neutral equally much pretty are spirits
> but subtle for makes that water the is it
> .differences appreciable

Clustering is the technique of grouping words together. Your eyes move and stop, move and stop, as they proceed across a line of print. Clustering involves widening your eye span so that you see several words in one fixation.

How to Cluster Read

Clustering involves widening your eye span or point of concentration to encompass two or three words. To cluster most effectively, group words together that naturally fit or go together. In both written and spoken language, words fall into natural groupings. Our language contains many words that carry little meaning alone but, when combined with others, express a thought or idea. For example, the words *in* and *the* have meaning mainly when combined with other words: for example, "in the house." The word grouping "in the house" is a meaningful cluster and could be read as a unit. When you group words together in meaning units, you will find that it is easier to understand what you read. To illustrate this point, read both versions of the following sample paragraph. One version divides the paragraph into meaningful clusters; the other does not. Decide which version is easier to read.

VERSION 1

(Public libraries) (provide access) (to a world) (of information.) (But they also) (contribute to) (the preservation) (of our valuable forests.) (Each library) (saves a forest) (of trees) (by making) (individual purchase) (of books and periodicals) (unnecessary.)

VERSION 2

(Public libraries provide) (access to a) (world of) (information. But they) (also contribute to the) (preservation of our) (valuable forests. Each) (library saves a) (forest of) (trees by) (making individual) (purchase of books) (and periodicals unnecessary.)

You probably decided that the first version is easier to read because the words that are grouped together belong together.

Cluster reading can have a dramatic effect on your reading efficiency. By grouping words together into meaningful clusters, you make sentences easier to understand. Also, by widening your eye span, and thereby reducing the number of fixations per line, you are reducing the time it takes to read a line and are increasing your reading rate.

Learning to Cluster Read

For most students, learning to read in clusters requires considerable practice. It is not a skill that you can develop after a few trial reading sessions. Instead, you may find that it takes several weeks of continued practice to develop the habit. To develop the skill, try to read as many things as possible in clusters. Begin by reading easy material, such as newspaper and magazine articles, in phrases. Later, as you feel more confident about the skill, progress to more difficult types of material.

As you begin cluster reading, you may find that you frequently lapse back into word-by-word reading. This is a natural happening since your attention focuses on the content of the material rather than the technique of reading.

EXERCISE 13–1

PRACTICING CLUSTER READING

Directions: *Read the following passages that have been divided into clusters. They are designed to give you an idea of how it feels to cluster read. As you read, you should feel your eyes moving from cluster to cluster in a rhythmical motion.*

1. When you   cluster read   it should feel   like this.
   Your eye should   move and stop,   move and stop.
   Each time   your eye stops   or fixates   it should see
   a meaningful phrase.   Cluster reading   will improve
   your comprehension   and help you   read faster.

2. As a   used car shopper,   your first task is
   to decide   what kind   of car   is going   to fill
   your needs.   Then   shop around   until you
   have a   good feel   for the market value   of that car.
   This way   you'll know   a bargain   when you   see one.
   You can   also check   the National   Automobile Dealers
   Association Used Car Guide   and the   Kelly Blue Book
   for prices   of used cars.   They'll give   you prices
   to work with,   *but they're   only guides.*
   Condition and mileage   will adjust   the price up
   or down.

3. Anytime   you're told   that you   need surgery
   and it's   not an emergency,   it's a good idea
   to get   a second   opinion from   a qualified specialist
   in the appropriate   field.   To find   this specialist,
   ask your   primary care physician   for a recommendation,
   or call   the nearest   teaching hospital   or an accredited
   hospital for   a recommendation.   You can   also consult
   the *Directory   of Medical Specialists.*

4. Actually,   the common cold   is not   as simple
   as it seems.   It can   be caused   by any
   of 200 different   viruses,   and it can   bring misery
   eight ways: sore throat,   sneezing,   runny nose,
   watery eyes,   aches and pains,   mild fever,
   nasal congestion,   and coughing.   Thus
   the thinking behind   "combination"   products: they
   supposedly contain   a little something   for each
   different symptom.   One pill   or capsule,
   the advertisers say,   handles the   whole malady.
   A little like   one-stop shopping.

—Items 2–4 from Richard George, *The New Consumer Survival Kit,* p. 69. Little, Brown & Co.

5. Psychological principles   can be applied   by everyone.
   You can learn   to use   scientific psychology
   to help solve   your own problems.   There are
   a number   of important advantages   of do-it-yourself
   psychology.   One factor   is manpower.   For most people
   the major problem   a few   generations ago
   was physical   survival: now it is psychological   survival.
   We seem to be tense,   alienated, confused.
   Suicide, addiction,   violence, apathy,   neurosis—

are all   problems of   the modern world.
Psychological problems   are accelerating
and there   are not enough   professional psychologists
to go around.   Non-psychologists *must*   practice psychology
if psychology   is to be applied   to our problems.

—Morris K. Holland and Gerald Tarlow, *Using Psychology,* Second Edition,
pp. 8–9. Boston: Little, Brown and Company, 1980. ■

EXERCISE 13–2   **PRACTICING CLUSTER READING**

Directions: *The following material has already been clustered. Practice reading each cluster with only one eye fixation. Move your eyes down each column, making only one fixation per line.*

1. There is
   no better way
   to test
   fishing boats
   than under
   actual fishing
   conditions.
   Actual conditions
   provide the
   opportunity to
   try out
   the fishing boat
   under the most
   adverse weather
   conditions and
   the most rapid
   and unexpected
   passenger movements.

2. The purpose of
   life insurance
   is to prevent
   financial difficulty
   for someone else
   in the event
   of your death.
   With that in mind,
   you can determine
   if you need
   life insurance
   by simply
   asking yourself
   if your death
   would put someone

else in a tough
financial position.
If the answer
is yes,
you need insurance.

3. The job interview
   is your best chance
   to sell yourself,
   so it pays
   to be well prepared.
   First, rehearse
   in your mind
   the qualifications
   that would make
   you an asset
   to the organization.
   Second, learn
   something about it.
   Most employers
   will be impressed
   if you can
   ask intelligent questions
   about their company,
   questions that show
   you've done
   your homework.
   Your local librarian
   can direct you
   to a number
   of reference books
   that "profile"
   business organizations.

—From Richard George, *The New Consumer Survival Kit,* p. 69. Copyright © 1978 by the Maryland
Center for Public Broadcasting. By permission of Little, Brown and Company. ■

EXERCISE 13–3   **PRACTICING CLUSTER READING**

Directions: *Read the first five paragraphs of the reading selection at the end of this chapter and, as you read, divide each sentence into meaningful clusters. Separate each cluster by using a slash mark (/) as has been done in the following example.*

Studying economics/is difficult/because it requires/careful attention/to facts and figures.

Then, reread the five paragraphs, trying to see each cluster rather than each single word.

■ Keyword Reading

Goal 3
Read using keywords

Read each of the following versions of a paragraph.

VERSION 1

Keyword reading new technique. Faster than careful reading. Decrease factual comprehension. Worth loss, depending purpose type material. (17 words)

VERSION 2

Keyword reading is a new technique. Although it is faster than most of the careful reading techniques, the reader must expect a decrease in factual comprehension skill. In some situations, it is worth the loss, depending on the reader's purpose and the type of material being read. (47 words)

Were you able to understand the passage conveyed in Version 1? If so, then you are already on your way to mastering the technique of keyword reading. You have already read in a manner similar to keyword reading. Compare the number of words in each version. Notice what is deleted in the first version that is included in the second. Did you gain much additional information about keyword reading from the complete version that you had not acquired in the first?

What Is Keyword Reading?

From our example, you can see that keyword reading involves skipping nonessential words and reading only those words and phrases that carry the primary or core meaning of each sentence.

Now read the following paragraph in which the keywords have been highlighted. Read the paragraph two ways. First, read only the highlighted keywords in the paragraph. Can you understand the message the paragraph conveys? Second, read the entire passage. How much additional information did you acquire?

America's only nonelected president, Gerald Ford, became chief executive at a time when the nation desperately craved an end to distrust and uncertainty. Ford seemed the right man to initiate the healing process. A stolid legislator who had served in the House for many years without great distinction, he was an open, decent, and generous person, and most Americans seemed to like him.

—Unger, *These United States,* Little, Brown and Company.

By reading only the keywords, you were probably able to understand the basic message of the paragraph. Then, when you read the complete paragraph, you only learned a few additional details about Ford.

In developing skill in keyword reading, it sometimes helps to think of the process as similar to that of reading a headline in a newspaper or a news caption that is run across the bottom of a television screen.

TV News Caption: AIRLINE HIJACKING LOS ANGELES. 52 HOSTAGES. FOUR HIJACKERS. IDENTITY AND PURPOSE UNKNOWN.

This message contains only the words that carry the basic meaning. Most frequently, these meaning-carrying words are nouns, action verbs, and important descriptive adjectives and adverbs. They are the words that tell the "who, what, when, and where" and frequently include names, dates, places, numbers, capitalized words, and italicized words.

When to Use Keyword Reading

When keyword reading, you should expect your comprehension to be 70 percent or lower, usually in the 50–70 percent range. But, as a tradeoff for lower comprehension, you can expect an increase in rate. You actually gain more than you lose because, although you read less than half the material, normally you can expect to get more than 50 percent of the message. You might expect to achieve reading rates of between 600 and 700 words per minute when using keyword reading.

Keyword reading cannot be used on all types of material. In many situations a comprehension level below 80 percent is not acceptable. Especially when reading textbooks or highly technical material, keyword reading is inappropriate. However, in many other situations, a level of comprehension in the 60–70 percent range is adequate. Here are a few situations in which keyword reading might be an appropriate technique:

- when you are visiting a Web site to determine whether the site contains any information you do not already have for a research paper
- when you are reading newspaper articles to find the key ideas and primary details about a recent local event
- when you are using reference books to gain a general idea of an author's approach and treatment of an event, idea, concept, or theory
- when you are reading correspondence to determine the writer's purpose and the level and nature of response required

Aids to Keyword Reading

Your knowledge and familiarity with the structure of the English language, which you have acquired naturally throughout your lifetime, helps you locate keywords. Although you may not be aware of them, you have learned many rules and patterns of the structure of English.

Using Sentence Structure

Sentences contain core parts that tell you what the sentence is about (the subject), what action occurred (the predicate), and who or what received the action (the object). These parts carry the basic meaning of the sentence. Look at the following paragraph in which these key parts have been highlighted. Read only the highlighted words and phrases; you will notice that you get the basic meaning of each sentence and the paragraph as a whole.

And so, by 1968 or 1969, the country found itself caught in a giant whirlpool of anger and change. Nothing from the past, apparently, was sacred any longer. Patriotism was in bad repute: students burned their draft cards and desecrated the American flag. Chastity had become a thing of the past: college students lived in open "sin," and skirts had crawled two-thirds the way up the female thigh. Civility in public life had almost disappeared: every group was demanding "liberation" and would take to the streets, occupy public buildings, attack the police, riot, or even throw bombs to get it. Worst of all, the family was disintegrating: despite parental protest, children dressed the way they wanted, smoked "pot," and abandoned promising careers and futures to become political activists.

—Unger, *These United States,* Little, Brown and Company.

Now read the complete paragraph. Notice that it fills you in on the details you missed when you read only keywords, but also notice that you did not miss any of the key ideas.

EXERCISE 13–4

IDENTIFYING KEYWORDS

Directions: *In each of the following sentences, draw a line through the words that do not carry the essential meaning of the sentence. Only keywords should remain.*

EXAMPLE

Work should be arranged so there are specific stopping points where you can feel something has been accomplished.

1. In some large businesses, employees are practically strangers to each other and often do not discuss problems or ideas.

2. Criminal law as we know it today is a product of centuries of change.

—Barlow, *Introduction to Criminology,* 2e, Little, Brown and Company.

3. From the standpoint of criminal law, a criminal is an individual who is legally capable of conduct that violates the law and who can be shown to have actually and intentionally engaged in that conduct.

—Barlow, *Introduction to Criminology,* 2e, Little, Brown and Company.

4. By the time Congress assembled on December 4, 1865, the Republican majority—Radicals as well as most moderates—were seething with anger at the Johnson government.

—Unger, *These United States,* Little, Brown and Company.

5. During the 1960s the United States attained a level of material well-being beyond anything dreamed of in the past.

—Unger, *These United States,* Little, Brown and Company. ■

Using Punctuation

Punctuation can serve as an aid in locating keywords. For example, the use of a colon or semicolon indicates that important information is to follow. When you see a colon, you may anticipate a list of items. Often, you can expect to find a separate but closely related idea when a semicolon is used. In both cases you are alerted to look for keywords ahead.

Commas, depending on their use, provide several types of clues for the location of keywords. When used to separate an introductory phrase from the main sentence, the comma tells you to pay more attention to the main sentence as you look for keywords.

When used to separate items in a series, the comma indicates that all items are important and should be read as keywords. When a comma is accompanied by a conjunction and is used to join two complete thoughts, expect to find keywords on both sides of the comma. The parenthetical use of the comma tells you that the information enclosed within the commas is nonessential to the basic meaning of the sentence and may be skipped when you read keywords.

Using Typographical Aids

Typographical aids include boldfaced print, colored print, italics, capitalization, underlining, enumeration, or lists of information. Most typographical aids emphasize important information; others help the reader organize the information. Italics, underlining, and boldfaced print are all used to make important information more noticeable.

Using Grammatical Structure

Your knowledge of grammar can also help you read keywords effectively. You have learned that certain words modify or explain others. You know that adjectives explain or describe nouns and that adverbs give further information about verbs. Adjectives and adverbs that modify the key parts of the sentence, then, are also important in keyword reading.

For example, in the following sentence you see that the adjectives and adverbs (single underlining) make the meaning of the key parts (double underlining) more complete.

The <u>psychology</u> <u><u>instructor</u></u> <u>hastily</u> <u><u>summarized</u></u> his <u><u>lecture</u></u>.

You also know that many words in the English language work very much like glue—they stick other, more important, words together. If classified by parts of speech, these "glue words" are usually prepositions, conjunctions, or pronouns.

In the following sentence, all the glue words have been deleted.

> . . . summary, it seems safe . . . say . . . society, . . . whole, believes . . . individuals can control . . . destiny.

Can you still understand the sentence? Most likely you can guess the words that were deleted. Try it. Now, compare the words you supplied with the complete sentence.

> In summary, it seems safe to say that society, on the whole, believes that individuals can control their destiny.

EXERCISE 13–5   **PRACTICING KEYWORD READING**

Directions: *Assume you are working on a research paper on the psychological effects of color. You located the following article by Kelly Costigan in* Science Digest, *and you want to see if it presents any new information on the psychology of color that you do not already have. Read the article using the keyword reading technique. To help you get started, the first few lines have been shaded so that the keywords are emphasized. After reading the article, answer the questions that follow.*

HOW COLOR GOES TO YOUR HEAD
ORANGE MAKES YOU HUNGRY; BEIGE MAKES YOU NEAT AND EFFICIENT

Can simply looking at a color affect your behavior or alter your mood? Although some researchers are skeptical, others suggest that color may have a profound influence on human behavior and physiology.

A report in the *International Journal of Biosocial Research* revealed that after a change in the color and lighting scheme at a school in Wetaskiwin, Canada, the IQ scores of some students jumped and absenteeism and disciplinary problems decreased. The study, conducted by visual-arts professor Harry Wohlfarth of the University of Alberta, involved substituting yellow and blue for orange, white, beige and brown and replacing fluorescent lights with full-spectrum ones.

Clinical psychologist Alexander Schauss, director of the American Institute for Biosocial Research in Tacoma, Washington, spearheaded the now widespread use of bubblegum-pink rooms to calm delinquents and criminals in correctional facilities across the country. Schauss evaluated the effect on subjects as they looked at this pink shade on a piece of cardboard. He reported later in the *Bulletin of the Psychonomic Society* that the color relaxed the subjects so much that they did not perform simple strength tests as well as they did when viewing other hues. A U.S. Navy brig in Seattle took notice of Schauss's work and permitted him to test his calming-color hypothesis on its inmates. Now hundreds of institutions place individuals in pink rooms when tempers flare.

"We used to have to give them drugs, even use handcuffs," says Paul Boccumini, director of clinical services at California's San Bernardino County Probation Department. "But this works."

Schauss and Wohlfarth are not certain how color can have an impact on biology or behavior. But Schauss conjectures that response to color is determined in the brain's reticular formation, a relay station for millions of the body's nerve impulses. And there have been studies indicating that when subjects look at warm hues, such as red, orange or yellow, their blood pressure rises, brain-wave activity increases, respiration is faster and perspiration greater. A UCLA study showed that blue had the opposite effect. Given these data, researchers speculate that the perception of color by the eye ultimately spurs the release of important biochemicals in the body.

The human eye is sensitive to millions of colors. Each is a distinctive wavelength of light that strikes color-sensitive cones on the back of the eye in a unique way. These cells then fire, sending nerve signals to the brain. Wohlfarth and others contend that the release of hormones or neurotransmitters may be triggered during this process, and they in turn influence moods and activities such as heart rate and breathing.

COLORED LIGHT AIDS HEALTH

There is also some evidence that colored light affects health. Baths of light emitting a high concentration of blue wavelengths are now used in many hospitals to cure infants of neonatal jaundice. The light penetrates the skin and breaks down the chemical bilirubin, which causes the condition.

Psychologists and commercial color consultants are already prescribing the use of a variety of hues to elicit certain behaviors. Gradations of blue are used on the walls of a Canadian dental clinic to ease patients' fears; rooms painted in peach, yellow and blue are said to relax residents at Aid for the Retarded in Stamford, Connecticut; and orange, which stimulates the appetite, adorns the walls of fast-food chains. Even machinery is painted light blue or beige instead of battleship gray to inspire neatness and efficiency in workers at a gas-turbine plant in the northeastern United States.

But the idea that color is a legitimate tool for modifying behavior is still being debated. "We need to speak from hard data," says Norman Rosenthal, a psychiatrist at the National Institute for Mental Health. "And how do you get by the cultural bias that might be built into a response, that red is stimulating and blue is connected to depression?"

—Costigan, "How Color Goes to Your Head," *Science Digest*

1. The article mentions numerous effects of color. List as many as you can recall.

_____

_____

2. Summarize one theory that explains how color affects behavior.

_____

_____

3. What references or sources does the article provide for further research?

_____

_____

EXERCISE 13-6   **PRACTICING KEYWORD READING**

Directions: *Select a magazine or newspaper article or two or three pages from a nonfiction book you are reading. Before beginning to read, underline the keywords in the first paragraph and in five to six sentences randomly selected from the remainder of the passage. Use keyword reading on the article and record your results in the space provided.*

Source of material: _____

Estimated level of comprehension: _____ ■

■ Using Transitional Words

Goal 4
Use transitions as speed cues

Not every sentence, paragraph, or section within a work must be read in the same way. When reading an essay or textbook chapter, for instance, your speed may vary, depending on the content and its relative importance. Fortunately, many materials contain cue words and phrases that indicate when to speed up, when to maintain your pace, and when to slow down. These words and phrases often function as transitions, connecting and leading from one idea to another.

For example, readers often find it necessary to slow down when a new or different idea is presented. One word that signals a change in thought is *however*, as in the following statement.

Selecting a career to match your interests, skills, and abilities is critically important. *However,* few students are able to find a perfect match. Instead, most students must settle for . . .

In this statement the author is switching from discussing a perfect match to other alternatives.

A decrease in reading speed may also be necessary when the author is presenting key points, emphasizing important information, or concluding or summarizing. Transitional words and phrases for these conditions are listed in Table 13.1.

EXERCISE 13–7   **IDENTIFYING TRANSITIONAL WORDS**

Academic APPLICATION

Directions: *Choose a section of a chapter from one of your textbooks and circle the transitional words contained in it. Determine whether each cue is a speed-up, slow-down, or maintain-speed cue.* ■

TABLE 13.1	Reading Rate Transitional Words	
Speed-Up Cues		
Repetitious information	again, in other words, that is	
Examples	to illustrate, for example, suppose, for instance, such as	
Slow-Down Cues		
Change in thought	however, nevertheless, instead of, despite	
Summary	in summary, for these reasons, to sum up, in brief	
Conclusion	in conclusion, thus, therefore	
Emphasis	most important, it is essential, above all, indeed	
Maintain-Speed Cues		
Continuation	likewise, similarly, also, furthermore, and added to, in addition	
Enumeration (listing)	first, second . . . , next, then, (1) . . . , (2) . . .	

■ Rapid Reading Drills

Goal 5
Practice rapid reading

Many students read more slowly than is necessary. In fact, some students read so slowly that it interferes with their comprehension. A gap sometimes occurs between rate of intake of information and speed of thought. If information is taken in too slowly, the mind has time to drift or wander, resulting in loss of concentration or weak comprehension.

One effective way to build reading rate is to practice reading various materials at an uncomfortably high rate. Do not be too concerned if at first your comprehension is incomplete. Your first goal is to gain speed—to cover material faster than ever before. Then, as you become more skilled at faster reading, you will find that your comprehension will improve.

You might think of this strategy as similar to stretching a rubber band. A new rubber band is very tight and narrow in length. However, as it is stretched, it loosens and becomes longer and more flexible. A similar change occurs with reading rate: it loosens, stretches, and becomes more flexible.

The following rapid reading drills are intended to stretch your reading rate. Complete each drill as rapidly as possible.

EXERCISE 13–8   **READING RAPIDLY**

Directions: *For each item, read the word in column A. Find a word in column B that means the same, and underline it. Sweep your eye rapidly across each line. Do not reread if you are unable to find a match; go to the next item.*

Set I

Begin timing.

Column A	Column B				
1. secure	secret	output	luckiness	improve	possess
2. imprint	bearable	engrave	treaty	flutter	improper
3. fabricate	extra	eyeless	make	façade	tremor
4. disturb	question	review	tremble	interrupt	dilute
5. blush	redden	submit	treasure	social	dim
6. backing	shaken	support	register	grate	obstacle
7. desert	observer	goodness	quarter	typical	abandon
8. authentic	twisting	resign	genuine	stimulate	reasonable
9. dateless	ageless	serving	qualm	permit	perjury
10. cunning	perish	clever	rejoice	grateful	graphic

Time: _____ seconds

Set II

Begin timing.

Column A	Column B				
1. author	query	tread	writer	grave	miracle
2. defect	ministry	grapple	misbehavior	murky	flaw
3. posterior	back	haven	façade	frontal	haul
4. sentiment	shadow	extort	feeling	mirage	extreme
5. equivalent	cheeky	decompose	opposite	equal	declare
6. decrease	historical	flog	bombard	cheat	diminish
7. defer	reign	together	dual	token	delay
8. extract	remove	quarter	hoard	snap	tipple
9. squeal	tread	object	yelp	pester	soar
10. hint	profane	sensual	suggest	taint	uprising

Time: _____ seconds

EXERCISE 13–9   INCREASING YOUR READING SPEED

Directions: *Read as rapidly as possible each of the following passages from* Discovering Mass Communication *by Samuel L. Becker. Time yourself, circle the speed closest to yours, and answer the questions that follow each passage. Do not hesitate to take risks: read faster than you think you are able to.*

PASSAGE A

The Mall of America

The Mall of America outside Minneapolis, Minnesota, is the largest enclosed mall in the United States. It is also the nation's most popular tourist destination, visited by 100,000 people every day. This mall, like many others, was also once a popular hangout for young people. On Friday and Saturday nights, as many as 10,000 teenagers would gather there. But this practice ended in 1996, when the Mall of America instituted a 6:00 P.M. weekend curfew on teenagers under 16 unless accompanied by an adult. Since then, hundreds of malls have adopted similar curfews.

Teenagers, who on the average spend 3.5 hours a week in malls, howled in protest. "We just want to be able to hang out at the mall," complained Kimberly Flanagan, 16, of Charlotte, North Carolina. Kary Ross, an attorney for the American Civil Liberties Union, sided with the teenagers: "We're opposed to curfews that treat all minors as if they're criminals."

Malls insist that as privately owned enterprises, they are exempt from First Amendment protections, such as freedom of speech and the right to assemble. Malls are not public property. Yet recent malls have been designed to evoke the public spaces of the nineteenth-century city. The Mall of America includes an exhibition gallery, amusement park, wedding chapel, assembly hall, school, medical clinic, and a central "Rotunda" for staging "public events" ranging from gardening shows to Hulk Hogan wrestling matches.

—Carnes, Mark C.; Garraty, John A., *American Destiny: Narrative of a Nation,* Concise Edition, Combined Volume (Second Printing), 3rd Ed., © 2008. Reprinted and electronically reproduced by permission of Pearson Education, Inc., Upper Saddle River, NJ.

Words: 232
Timing:

Seconds	WPM
20	696
30	464
40	348
50	278
60	232
70	199
80	174
90	155

Questions

1. The Mall of America instituted a _____ for teenagers.

2. In addition to stores, the Mall of America includes _____

_____

(List at least one item.)

PASSAGE B

The History of Baseball

Three major team games—baseball, football, and basketball—developed in something approaching their modern form during the last quarter of the nineteenth century. Various forms of what became baseball were played long before that time. Organized teams, in most cases made up of upper-class amateurs, first emerged in the 1840s, but the game only became truly popular during the Civil War, when it was a major form of camp recreation for the troops.

After the war professional teams began to appear (the first, the Cincinnati Red Stockings, paid players between $800 and $1,400 for the season), and in 1876 teams in eight cities formed the National League. The American League followed in 1901. After a brief period of rivalry, the two leagues made peace in 1903, the year of the first World Series.

Organized play led to codification of the rules and improvements in technique and strategy, for example, the development of "minor" leagues; impartial umpires calling balls and strikes and ruling on close plays; the use of catcher's masks and padded gloves; the invention of various kinds of curves and other erratic pitches (often enhanced by "doctoring" the ball). As early as the 1870s, baseball was being called "the national game" and losing all upper-class connotations. Important games attracted crowds in the tens of thousands; betting became a problem. Despite its urban origins, its broad green fields and dusty base paths gave the game a rural character that only recently has begun to fade away.

—Carnes, Mark C.; Garraty, John A., *American Destiny: Narrative of a Nation, Concise Edition, Combined Volume (Second Printing)*, 3rd Ed., © 2008. Reprinted and electronically reproduced by permission of Pearson Education, Inc., Upper Saddle River, NJ.

Words: 246

Timing:

Seconds	WPM
20	738
30	492
40	369
50	295
60	246
70	211
80	185

Questions

Indicate whether each statement is true or false by writing "T" or "F" in the space provided.

___ 1. Baseball became popular during the Civil War.

___ 2. Baseball did not became known as "the national game" until the 1920s.

■ Pacing Techniques

Goal 6
Use pacing techniques

An established method of improving reading rate is called **pacing**. Pacing involves forcing yourself to read slightly faster than you normally would and trying to keep up with a preestablished pace. To better understand the concept of pacing, imagine that you are in a crowd of people and suddenly everyone starts walking forward quickly. You are forced along at the pace at which the crowd is moving, regardless of how fast you want to move. Similarly, in reading you can read more rapidly if you are "forced along" by some external means. Pacing is a way of forcing yourself to read faster than your normal speed while maintaining your level of comprehension.

Pacing Methods

There are two easy ways to pace yourself for speed increase.

1. **Use an index card.** Slide a 3" × 5" card down the page, moving it so that it covers up lines as you read them. This technique will force you along and keep you moving rapidly.

2. **Use a timer or alarm clock.** Start by measuring what portion of a page you can read in a minute. Then set a goal for yourself: Determine how many pages you will attempt to read in a given period of time. Set your goal slightly above what you measured as your current rate.

As you begin to use one of these pacing methods, here are several suggestions to keep in mind:

- **Keep a record of your time, the amount you read, and your words per minute.**

- **Be sure to maintain an adequate level of comprehension.** To test your comprehension, try to summarize what you read. If you are unable to remember enough ideas to summarize what you read, you have probably read too fast.

- **Push yourself gradually, across several weeks of practice.**

EXERCISE 13–10   **USING PACING**

Directions: *Select an article from a periodical or use material that you have been assigned to read for one of your courses. Using one of the pacing techniques described in this section, try to increase your current reading speed by approximately 50 wpm. Record your results in the space provided.*

Source of material: _____

Estimated level of comprehension: _____ ■

■ Rereading for Rate Increase

Goal 7
Reread to increase
reading rate

Rereading is an effective method to build your reading rate. It involves building your rate gradually in small increments. To reread for speed increase, use the steps below.

NEED TO KNOW **How to Use Rereading**

1. Select an article or passage and read it as you normally would for careful or leisure reading.
2. Time yourself and compute your speed in words per minute after you finish reading.
3. Take a break (five minutes or so). Then reread the same selection. Push yourself to read faster than you read the first time.
4. Time yourself and compute your speed once again. You should be able to reread the selection at a faster rate than you read it initially.
5. Read a new selection, pushing yourself to read almost as fast as you reread the first selection.

Rereading serves as a preparation for reading new material faster. Rereading establishes the mechanical process of more rapid eye movements and gives you preliminary practice, or a "trial run," with reading at a higher reading rate. It helps you learn things about reading faster while keeping your comprehension in balance. Because you already have a basic understanding of the selection from your first reading, you are free to focus and concentrate on improving your rate.

TECH SUPPORT **Improving Your Reading Rate**

Your computer is an ideal tool for building your reading speed. By controlling the speed at which you scroll down the screen, you can push yourself to read faster. Locate some easy-to-read, factual Web site that contains large amounts of text. Use the scroll down button to force yourself to read at a slightly uncomfortable pace.

EXERCISE 13–11

Working
COLLABORATIVELY

COMPARING CLUSTER AND KEYWORD READING

Directions: *Using one of the end-of-chapter reading selections in this book, apply the technique of keyword reading. For another end-of-chapter reading selection of similar difficulty, use the cluster reading technique. When you have completed both selections, compare your performance by reviewing your rate and comprehension scores with those of a classmate. Discuss what can you conclude about the relative effectiveness of the two techniques.*

SELF-TEST SUMMARY

Goal	Question	Answer
Goal 1	1. What are five aspects of eye movement that can directly affect your reading rate? What two reading habits, when taken to excess, can decrease your reading efficiency?	Reading rate is directly affected by the following physical aspects of eye movement: • speed of left-to-right progression • number of fixations or "eye stops" • size of eye span, or amount of print seen in each fixation • speed of return sweep from the end of one line to the start of the next • number of regressions or backward eye movements Unnecessary regressions and vocalization/subvocalization can reduce your reading efficiency. Frequent regressions can increase your reading time and interfere with your comprehension. Likewise, your speed and comprehension are decreased by vocalizing (saying every word) and subvocalizing (mentally hearing every word) because they limit you to word-by-word reading.
Goal 2	2. How do you cluster read?	Widen your eye span to read words in meaningful groupings
Goal 3	3. How do you keyword read?	Read only the words and phrases that carry the core meaning of a sentence and skip nonessential words.
Goal 4	4. How can transitions help you read?	Transitional words and phrases are cues that indicate when to speed up, maintain, or decrease your pace.
Goal 5	5. How can you practice rapid reading?	Read at an uncomfortably fast pace, pushing yourself to gain speed.
Goal 6	6. How does pacing work?	Pacing is a way of forcing yourself to read faster than your normal speed while maintaining your level of comprehension.
Goal 7	7. How does rereading work?	Reread previously read material at a higher speed, and then attempt to read new material at the higher speed.

READING SELECTION 24 **TECHNOLOGY**

Ten Things for Ten Days That Will Make the World a Better Place

Meghan H.

About the Reading

BLOG ENTRY

This article was originally published in the blog section of the Life 360 *Web site (http://www.life360.com/blog). The Web site is devoted to family safety through the use of technology, particularly cell and smart phones that can use GPS (global positioning systems) to locate a person's position anywhere on Earth.*

Planning Your Reading Strategy*

Directions: *Activate your thinking by previewing the reading (see the Need to Know box on page 64) and answering the following questions.*

____ 1. Based on your preview of the reading, into what general category would you place the 10 tips listed by the author?
   a. tips for helping bring about social change from your own home
   b. ways to recycle outdated technology in an environmentally conscious way
   c. suggestions for moving away from oil and toward solar or wind energy
   d. ideas for using social media, such as Facebook, to expand your friendship network

2. Based on your preview of the reading, how quickly do you think you should read the selection? (Circle one.) Explain your answer.

Very slowly   Slowly   At a moderate pace   Quickly   Very quickly

_____

3. What do you use your smart phone for? List some ways you might use your smart phone for the good of the community. _____

_____

By Meghan Hardy, courtesy of Life360.

_____

* The Scorecard on p. 556 enables you to compute your reading rate. In order to do so, be sure to record your starting time in the Scorecard box before you begin reading.

1 These days, thanks to the internet and smart phones, helping bring about social change from the comfort of your own home is getting easier every single day. While getting out there and volunteering in and around your community is still needed, you can also accomplish a great deal while sitting at your computer or perusing the apps on your phone.

2 Here are a few actions you and your kids can take every day from home to help bring about social change around the world.

1. Write a Letter

3 This is actually one of the oldest tools for taking action that we have. But with the World Wide Web, writing letters (or emails) has taken on another level of impact. You can email organizations, politicians, and companies about every issue under the sun. If you really want to make a difference or express your concern about an issue, sit down and write a letter or email and make your voice heard. There are many websites out there that will even give you the template and all you have to do is sign your name and click send.

2. Freecycle

4 Every year we throw 175 million tons of waste into landfills. Instead use Freecycle.org and give away your old stuff (and look for stuff you may need). It's another way to Reduce, Re-use, and Recycle.

3. Walk

5 Not only is walking good for you, it's spectacular for the environment and helps the entire nation by lessening our dependence on foreign oil. If everybody could give up one drive a day and instead walk, could you imagine how much money and energy we would save as well as how much healthier the world would be?

4. Make a Birthday Wish on Facebook

6 Many people are on Facebook (let's face it, there's a good chance you saw this post on Facebook) and have been lucky enough to celebrate a "Facebook birthday." This is when the barrage of Facebook friends you've made fills your profile with warm Birthday greetings. Why not try and use those birthday wishes for the greater good? Through Causes.com (http://wishes.causes.com/?bws=causes_header) you can make a "Birthday Wish" then share that wish with Facebook friends by asking them instead of birthday wishes or gifts to please donate to the cause of your choice. Even if you have 100 Facebook friends who all only donated $1 that's $100 to go to the cause that means the most to you. Whether it's $10 or $1,000 you raise, it's still going towards a good cause.

▸ 5. Subscribe to 20/20 Action

7   The goal of the 20/20 Action organization is that for only $20 a year and 20 minutes a
month you can help change the world. When you subscribe to 20/20 you receive a
monthly postcard with a simple action you can do to help save the world. Each postcard
will contain everything you need to send an effective, short personal message—by letter,
email, fax, or phone—to a policymaker facing a critical decision on an important
environment or peace issue.

▸ 6. Buy Local

8   There are many ways that buying things locally helps make the world a better place.
It puts your taxes to good use, ensures a better economy and encourages local
prosperity. But don't forget that by buying local you're also helping reduce your carbon
footprint!

▸ 7. Surf the Web

9   That's right, something as easy and simple as searching the internet can help you
raise money for your favorite charity or cause. Visit GoodSearch.com (http://www.
goodsearch.com/), fill in your favorite charity, and start surfing! They'll donate to your
cause for every search you do.

▸ 8. Support Your Local School

10   You don't have to have kids attending your local school to help support it and the
neighborhood. When the school in your neighborhood is having a bake sale, carnival,
book sale, mini-mall or any other fundraising event head on over and do some off-season
Christmas shopping. Supporting the local school is always beneficial to the entire community, not just the school you're helping.

▸ 9. Donate Your Voice

11   At LibriVox (http://librivox.org/volunteer-for-librivox/) volunteers record chapters of
books that are listed in the public domain as digital audio (e.g., MP3), and then make
the audio files available to the world, for free. You can volunteer to read and record
chapters of books. This is something you can do from the comfort of your home at your
computer.

▸ 10. Teach Your Kids to Care

12   Of all the things you can do in your daily life to help make the world a better place, nothing compares to the impact of teaching the children in your life to care about the world.
Visit the library and get books on conservation, watch documentaries about different
issues around the world, and whenever you can teach your children by example. When
they see you doing little things in your every day life because you care about making a
difference, they will simply follow suit.

13   Will you choose one thing above to do today? Maybe 2 . . . 3? What other ways do YOU
help promote positive social change?

Examining Reading Selection 24

[Complete this **Exercise** at **myreadinglab.com**

Checking Your Vocabulary

Directions: *Use context, word parts, or a diction-ary, if necessary, to determine the meaning of each word as it is used in the reading.*

___ 1. perusing (paragraph 1)
   a. offering
   b. copying
   c. looking at
   d. interfering

___ 2. template (paragraph 3)
   a. consent
   b. pattern
   c. benefit
   d. characteristic

___ 3. spectacular (paragraph 5)
   a. fantastic
   b. alarming
   c. fundamental
   d. preventable

___ 4. barrage (paragraph 6)
   a. location
   b. outpouring
   c. value
   d. sympathy

___ 5. prosperity (paragraph 8)
   a. assistance
   b. adjustment
   c. success
   d. position

Checking Your Comprehension

Directions: *Select the best answer.*

___ 6. This selection is primarily concerned with how to
   a. raise money on the Internet.
   b. improve the environment.
   c. promote positive social change.
   d. donate through social networking sites.

___ 7. The author wrote this selection in order to
   a. generate support for her local community.
   b. encourage adults to become volunteers.
   c. promote environmentally con-scious living.
   d. suggest ways to make the world better.

___ 8. The organization that helps people avoid adding waste to landfills by giv-ing away their stuff is called
   a. Causes.com.
   b. Freecycle.org.
   c. LibriVox.
   d. GoodSearch.com.

___ 9. According to the author, buying local does all of the following *except*
   a. puts your taxes to good use.
   b. ensures a better economy.
   c. increases your carbon footprint.
   d. encourages local prosperity.

___ 10. The goal of 20/20 Action is to offer subscribers a way to
   a. send a monthly message to poli-cymakers on important issues.
   b. donate to the cause of their choice through Facebook.
   c. record chapters of books and make the audio files available for free.
   d. support their favorite charity while searching the Internet.

Thinking Critically

___ 11. The best guide question based on this reading is:
   a. How has the Internet changed the world for the better?
   b. What actions can we take to bring about social change?

c. How can we lessen our dependence on foreign oil?

d. How can we improve the
environment?

___ 12. The author's attitude toward the subject can best be described as
a. enthusiastic and optimistic.
b. indignant and concerned.
c. mocking and cynical.
d. objective and detached.

___ 13. The photograph on page 553 was included as an example of
a. reducing your carbon footprint.
b. supporting your local school.
c. buying locally produced food.
d. teaching kids to care about others.

___ 14. The author develops her thesis primarily by
a. recounting personal experiences.
b. making comparisons and
analogies.
c. listing actions and reasons.
d. citing expert opinions.

___ 15. One inference you can make based on
the selection is that the
a. selection first appeared in a
textbook.
b. author works for 20/20 Action.
c. author does not have children.
d. author is hoping to inspire
change.

Scorecard

Selection 24:   899 words

Finishing Time: _____ _____ _____
                      HR.   MIN.   SEC.

Starting Time: _____ _____ _____
                      HR.   MIN.   SEC.

Reading Time: _____ _____
                             MIN.   SEC.

WPM Score: _____

Comprehensive Score: for items 6–15
Number Right: _____ × 10 = _____ %

Assessing Your Reading Strategy

1. How would you rate your comprehension
of the reading? (Circle one.)

   Excellent   Good   Fair   Poor

2. Did you find your reading strategy
effective?   Yes   No

3. Suppose you were given an assignment
to read a similar selection to the one you
just read. Based on your experience with
this selection, how would you adjust your
reading strategy (if at all)?

Writing About Reading Selection 24

Checking Your Vocabulary

Directions: *Complete each of the following items; refer to a dictionary if necessary.*

1. Describe the denotative and connotative meanings of the word *accomplish* in paragraph 1.

   _____

   _____

   _____

2. Describe the denotative and connotative meanings of the word *surf* in paragraph 9.

   _____

   _____

   _____

3. Explain the meaning of the word *domain* and how it is used in paragraph 11.

   _____

   _____

   _____

   _____

4. Define the word *impact* (paragraph 3) and underline the words or phrases that provide clues to its meaning.

   _____

   _____

5. Define the word *critical* (paragraph 7) and underline the words or phrases that provide a clue for its meaning.

   _____

6. Determine the meanings of the following words by using word parts:
   a. *recycle* (paragraph 4)

   _____

b. *dependence* (paragraph 5)

   _____

c. *subscribe* (paragraph 7)

   _____

d. *beneficial* (paragraph 10)

   _____

d. *audio* (paragraph 11)

   _____

Checking Your Comprehension

7. What do volunteers for LibriVox do?

   _____

   _____

   _____

8. How does the author suggest people use Causes.com to raise money?

   _____

   _____

   _____

9. According to the author, what are the three benefits of walking?

   _____

   _____

   _____

10. What do you receive when you subscribe to 20/20 Action?

   _____

   _____

   _____

   _____

   _____

Thinking Critically

11. Who is the intended audience for this selection?

_____

_____

_____

_____

12. What does the author mean when she says "with the World Wide Web, writing letters (or emails) has taken on another level of impact" (paragraph 3)?

_____

_____

_____

13. What two areas seem to be the focus of 20/20 Action?

_____

_____

14. What does the author say has the most impact in making the world a better place?

_____

_____

Questions for Discussion

1. Think about the author's suggestions. Which one(s) are you most likely to try? Why? What might you add to her list?

2. Discuss the tone of the selection. How is the author's tone appropriate for her subject? Would the selection be as effective if it were written in a more objective voice?

3. Discuss the idea of using birthday wishes or Facebook contacts for "the greater good." Would you feel comfortable asking friends to donate to a cause on your behalf? Why or why not?

4. Discuss what it means to teach by example. What little things do you do in your everyday life that show others you care about making a difference?

CHAPTER 14

Sample Sociology Textbook Chapter: Application of Skills

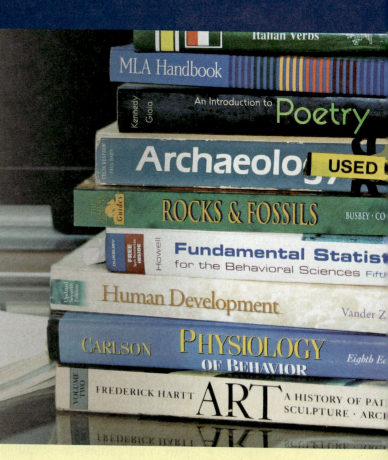

think VISUALLY…

Textbooks are one of your most important learning tools. While your instructor guides you through the textbook, the book itself is your primary source of information. In class, your instructor may expand upon, interpret, explain, or supplement what is in your textbook, but the textbook is the foundation of most college courses.

This chapter contains a section of a sociology textbook chapter on socialization. It is representative of most college textbooks and contains features that commonly appear in most introductory-level texts. You can use this chapter to practice skills taught in Parts 1–5 of this book. Following the sociology chapter you will find activities that help you pull together and apply the skills you learned in each section (see pp. 573–576).

■ Sociology Textbook Chapter

This textbook chapter excerpt is taken from *Sociology: A Brief Introduction,* a text widely used nationally in sociology courses. Like most textbooks, it was written by a college professor. Because the author Alex Thio is an expert in the field of sociology and an experienced teacher, he knows how students learn. He is careful to include a variety of learning aids to help his readers be successful in their sociology courses.

This chapter is representative of most freshman-level college textbooks, and it features many of the same learning aids as many other textbooks. Here is a quick overview of the learning aids this chapter offers and how they can help you learn. For each textbook that you purchase, spend some time acquainting yourself with its features and decide how to use them to help you study. (Hint: Check the book's preface; often, learning aids are described there.)

- **Boxed Chapter Preview.** This chapter opener is intended to motivate you to read the chapter by previewing some of the interesting topics you will learn about.
- **Chapter Outline.** This outline provides a list of important topics the chapter covers. When you finish the chapter, test your understanding of each of these items.
- **Myth/Reality Boxes.** Here, Thio challenges you to think by listing several common myths about social behavior, followed by a brief explanation of the facts about them. These boxes appear on pages where the topics they address are discussed, and they are designed to help you develop a critical, questioning mind-set.
- **Opening Scenario.** This thought-provoking situation is intended to focus your attention on the chapter's main points. Reread it after reading the chapter. Identify the key points it emphasizes.
- **Photos.** These make the chapter interesting, but they also serve to emphasize important ideas and concepts. Don't skip over photos; instead, ask yourself "Why did the author include these?" and "What important ideas do they illustrate?"
- **Figures and Tables.** These call your attention to important concepts in the chapter. Be sure to read the caption that accompanies each.
- **Sociological Frontier.** This feature takes a topic of current interest and explores its sociological implications. These make good class discussion topics.
- **Chapter Review.** This feature functions as a summary. Test yourself using these questions.
- **Key Terms.** Make sure you know the definition of each of these key terms introduced in the chapter.
- **Questions for Discussion and Review.** This is a list of what is important in the chapter. Use this list to test yourself.

Socialization

■ **The New World of Teen Sex**

Intelligence is either inherited or learned. (p. 564)

Infants will not die as long as they are well fed. (p. 564)

To be a genius, you must be born one. (p. 565)

Born with the ability to have feelings, children do not have to learn how to be happy, fearful, or anxious. (p. 567)

Men and women know what morality is because they both have learned how to be moral in the same way. (p. 570)

Soon after *3-year-old Rebecca* and her family moved to another town, her mother wanted to find a good pediatrician. She talked to many new neighbors and friends, and they all recommended the same doctor. After five minutes of watching Rebecca undergo a checkup, the mother was extremely pleased at how well her little girl was responding to the doctor. He was very friendly, talking gently to her and explaining everything he was doing. When it was time to test her reflexes, he said, "Rebecca, I'm going to hit your knee very lightly with a hammer." Immediately, Rebecca let out a bloodcurdling scream. Shaken and puzzled, the doctor turned to her mother and asked, "What did I do wrong?"

"Her father," said the mother, "is a carpenter" (Espinosa, 1992).

Actually, Rebecca is just like all of us. To a significant degree, she is a product of **socialization**, the process by which a society transmits its cultural values to its members. Socialization is carried out through society's agents, such as parents and teachers. Without socialization, Rebecca could not have become a truly human being, a person who could take part in society and its culture, like most children her age.

Simultaneously, though, Rebecca has developed through socialization a **personality**—a fairly stable configuration of feelings, attitudes, ideas, and behaviors that characterizes an individual—that is different from those of most of her peers. As we have seen, unlike other children, Rebecca reacts fearfully to the word *hammer*. She obviously associates the physician's harmless little hammer with the carpenter's powerful hammer, a result of being socialized by a carpenter father.

In this chapter, we will explore how personality develops and how socialization transmits society's values to its young members.

THE SIGNIFICANCE OF HEREDITY

Are children like clay, waiting to be shaped in one way or another? The roles of *nature* (heredity or what we inherit) and *nurture* (environment or what we learn) in making us what we are have long been argued. To the seventeenth-century philosopher John Locke, the mind of a child was a *tabula rasa* (blank slate). People became what they were taught to be. By the second half of the nineteenth century, however, a quite different view was popular. Instead of looking to nurture—what people are taught—to explain human behavior, many social scientists looked to nature—what people inherit. The pendulum of opinion has swung back and forth ever since.

Obviously, we do inherit some of what makes us who we are. But what? Physical traits such as skin color and facial features are inherited, but how they affect human behavior and personality depends to a great extent on what society makes of them.

People also appear to inherit *temperament*—an inclination to react in a certain way. Some people are inclined to be active, nervous, or irritable. Others, even when brought up in a similar environment, tend to be passive, calm, or placid. Psychologists have found that even infants show consistent temperaments. For instance, some are active most of the time, whereas others move rather little. Some cry and fuss a lot, and others rarely do. These differences may influence personality development. Very active infants, for example, are more likely than passive ones to become aggressive and competitive adults (Pinker, 2002; W. Gallagher, 1996).

The role of heredity in determining intelligence and aptitude is more controversial. **Intelligence** is the capacity for mental or intellectual achievement, such as the ability to think logically and solve problems. **Aptitude** is the capacity for developing physical or social skills, such as athletic prowess. The *extent* to which intelligence, in particular, is inherited has been the subject of some of the most bitter, emotional debates in all of social science. Richard Herrnstein and Charles Murray (1994) assume that more than half of our intelligence comes from genes. But most social scientists consider intelligence to be largely learned from the social environment. The debate is far from settled, as can be seen in Judith Harris's (1999) and Steven Pinker's (2002) controversial books attacking the nurture assumption.

myth	Intelligence is either inherited or learned.
reality	Intelligence is both inherited and learned. Nature sets limits on what we *can* achieve, and socialization plays a very large role in determining what we *do* achieve.

For our purposes, what is significant is that although nature sets limits on what we *can* achieve, socialization plays a very large role in determining what we *do* achieve. Whatever potential is inherited may be *enhanced or stunted* through socialization. Suppose certain infants are born with overly aggressive tendencies. They will likely grow up violent if raised by abusive parents but less aggressive if raised by affectionate parents. Similarly, an intellectual parenting style, which includes frequent reading to children, can boost children's inherited intelligence while nonintellectual parenting can keep their IQs low. Thus, heredity offers only a probability that a given trait will emerge, not a guarantee, and what is inherited can be changed—either encouraged or suppressed—by socialization (Guo, 2005; Ridley, 2003; Reiss, 2000).

THE SIGNIFICANCE OF SOCIALIZATION

What makes socialization both necessary and possible for human beings is their lack of *instincts*, biologically inherited capacities for performing relatively complex tasks. Whatever temperament and potential abilities human infants may be born with, they are also born helpless, depending on adults for survival. What may be more surprising is the extent to which traits that seem very basic and essential to human nature also appear to depend on socialization. Evidence of the far-reaching significance of socialization comes both from case studies of children deprived of socialization and from instances in which children are socialized into geniuses.

■ Impairing Development

Since the fourteenth century, there have been more than 50 recorded cases of *feral children*—children supposedly raised by animals. One of the most famous is the "wild boy of Aveyron," who was captured in the woods by hunters in southern France in 1797. He was about 11 years old and completely naked. The "wild boy" ran on all fours, had no speech, preferred uncooked food, and could not do most of the simple things done by younger children (Lane, 1976; Malson, 1972). The French boy had obviously been deprived of socialization.

In the United States, there have been three similar well-known cases. The first, Anna, was born in Pennsylvania in 1932 to a young unwed mother, a fact that outraged the mother's father. After trying unsuccessfully to give Anna away, the mother hid Anna in her attic and fed her just enough to keep her alive. Anna was neither touched nor talked to, neither washed nor bathed. She simply lay still in her own filth. When she was found in 1938 at the age of 6, Anna could not talk or walk. She could do nothing but lie quietly on the floor, her eyes vacant and her face expressionless (Davis, 1947).

Like Anna, Isabella was born to an unwed mother in Ohio. Her grandfather kept her and her deaf-mute mother secluded in a dark room. When Isabella was discovered in 1938, she, too, was 6 years old. She showed great fear and hostility toward people. Unable to talk, she could only make a strange croaking sound (Davis, 1947).

Genie, who was found in California in 1970, had been deprived of normal socialization for nearly 13 years—twice as long as Anna and Isabella. Since birth, Genie had been isolated in a small, quiet room. During the day, she was tied to her potty seat, able only to flutter her hands and feet. At night, her father straitjacketed and caged her in a crib with an overhead cover. He beat her if she made any noise. He never spoke to her except occasionally to bark or growl like a dog at her. Her terrified mother, forbidden to speak to Genie, fed her in silence and haste. Discovered at age 13, Genie could not stand straight, was unable to speak except to whimper, and had the intelligence and social maturity of a 1-year-old (Rymer, 1993; Pines, 1981).

myth	Infants will not die as long as they are well fed.
reality	Despite being well fed, infants can become physically and psychologically impaired and even die if deprived of human contact.

NATURE NEEDS NURTURE We inherit most of our physical makeup, including eye, hair, and skin color. But much debate revolves around whether we inherit nonphysical characteristics, such as intelligence, aptitude, and personality. Sociologists maintain that although nature sets limits on what we *can* achieve, socialization plays a large role in determining what we *do* achieve.

These four cases are, to say the least, unusual. But even less severe forms of deprivation can be harmful. In 1945, researcher René Spitz reported that children who received little attention in institutions suffered very noticeable effects. In one orphanage, Spitz found infants who were about 18 months old that were left fed but lying on their backs in small cubicles most of the day without any human contact. Within a year, all had become physically, mentally, emotionally, and socially impaired. Two years later, more than a third of the children had died. Those who survived could not speak, walk, dress themselves, or use a spoon.

■ Creating Geniuses

While the lack of normal socialization can destroy minds, specialized socialization can create geniuses. A young woman named Edith finished grammar school in four years, skipped high school, and went straight to college. She graduated from college at age 15 and obtained her doctorate before she was 18. Was she born a genius? Not at all. Ever since she had stopped playing with dolls, her father had seen to it that her days were filled with reading, mathematics, classical music, intellectual discussions and debates, and whatever learning he could derive from the world's literature. When she felt like playing, her father told her to play chess with someone like himself, who would be a challenge to her (Hoult, 1979).

myth	To be a genius, you must be born one.
reality	Geniuses such as Einstein and Picasso are not only born but also made. From childhood, these men worked intensely to develop their potential abilities under the guidance of parents who valued learning and achievement.

Like Edith, many geniuses have been deliberately subjected to a very stimulating environment. A well-known example is Norbert Wiener, a prime mover in the development of computers and cybernetics. He entered college at age 11 and received his Ph.D. from Harvard at 18. According to his father, Norbert was "essentially an average boy who had had the advantage of superlative training." Another example is Adragon Eastwood DeMello, who graduated with a degree in mathematics from the University of California at age 11. When he was a few months old, his father gave up his career as a science writer to educate Adragon (Radford, 1990). In his study of Einstein, Picasso, Gandhi, and other world-renowned geniuses in various fields, Howard Gardner (1993) found that they were all born into families that valued learning and achievement and that had at least one loving and supportive adult.

These people may have been born with a *potential* for becoming geniuses, but that potential was transformed into reality only through extraordinary socialization. Without socialization, no infant can naturally grow into a genius. Consider ace test pilot Chuck Yeager. He may have been born fearless. But if his parents had been overprotective and kept him from jumping off barns, he might never have grown up to be the first flier to break the sound barrier.

PROCESSES OF SOCIALIZATION

Children go through various processes of socialization that help them become who they are. The most important processes involve learning how to think, how to feel, how to be normal, how to be moral, and how to be a man or woman. We can learn much about these socialization processes from traditional and modern theories and research data.

Learning How to Think

From close observation, Swiss psychologist Jean Piaget (1896–1980) concluded that children learn how to think by passing through certain stages of *cognitive* (mental or intellectual) development:

1. *Sensorimotor stage (birth to age 2):* Infants lack language and cannot think in order to make sense of their environment. In their view, something exists only if they can see or touch it. Thus, to the infant, a parent no longer exists after leaving the child's field of vision. Unlike older children, who interact with the world by using their brains, infants use their senses and bodily movements to interact with the environment. Infants, for example, use their hands to touch, move, or pick up objects, and they put things in their mouths or suck on some objects.
2. *Preoperational stage (ages 2 to 7):* Children are not yet capable of performing simple intellectual operations. Precausal, they cannot understand cause and effect. When Piaget asked 4-year-olds what makes a bicycle move, they replied that the street makes it go. When he asked 6-year-olds why the sun and moon move, the youngsters said that the heavenly bodies follow us in order to see us. These children are also *animistic*: They attribute human-like thoughts and wishes to the sun and moon. Moreover, they are *egocentric*, seeing things only from their own perspective. If we ask a young boy how many brothers he has, he may correctly say "One." But if we ask him "How many brothers does your brother have?" he would say "None." He has difficulty seeing himself from his brother's perspective.

SHOW AND NOT TELL Jean Piaget described four stages of cognitive development that each child goes through. At the third, concrete operational stage (ages 7–12), children can perform simple intellectual tasks, but their mental abilities are restricted to dealing with concrete objects, such as lining up blocks in order of size. However, children cannot solve a similar problem stated verbally in abstract terms.

3. *Concrete operational stage (ages 7 to 12):* By now, children can perform simple intellectual tasks, but their mental abilities are restricted to dealing with concrete objects. If children between ages 8 and 10 are asked to line up a series of dolls from the tallest to the shortest, they can easily do so. But they cannot solve a similar problem stated verbally—in abstract terms—such as "John is taller than Bill; Bill is taller than Harry; who is the tallest of the three?" The children can correctly answer this question only if they actually see John, Bill, and Harry in person.
4. *Formal operational stage (ages 12 to 15):* Adolescents can think and reason formally (abstractly). They can follow the form of an argument while ignoring its concrete content. They know, for example, that if A is greater than B and B is greater than C, then A is greater than C—without having to know

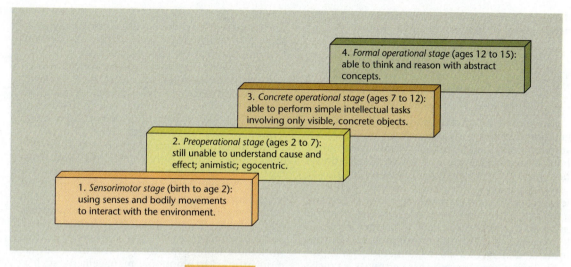

1. *Sensorimotor stage* (birth to age 2): using senses and bodily movements to interact with the environment.

2. *Preoperational stage* (ages 2 to 7): still unable to understand cause and effect; animistic; egocentric.

3. *Concrete operational stage* (ages 7 to 12): able to perform simple intellectual tasks involving only visible, concrete objects.

4. *Formal operational stage* (ages 12 to 15): able to think and reason with abstract concepts.

FIGURE 3.1

Piaget's Stages of Cognitive Development

Piaget suggested that virtually all children go through the same sequence of mental development. For instance, they think concretely (stage 3) before thinking abstractly (stage 4), rather than the other way around.

Critical Thinking: *As a child, how did you learn to think concretely and then abstractly? Give examples of the things that you learned.*

in advance whether the concrete contents of A, B, and C are vegetables, fruits, animals, or other items that can be seen or touched.

Today's sociologists find Piaget's stages of cognitive development, summarized in Figure 3.1, useful for understanding how children learn new cognitive skills—such as perception, reasoning, and calculation—as they grow up. Piaget has been criticized, however, for treating cognitive development as if it occurred in a social vacuum. Obviously, children cannot learn any cognitive skill by themselves, without some help from parents, teachers, and other important people in their lives. Piaget did not necessarily ignore the influence of these people on a child's cognitive development. He simply chose to focus on what new intellectual skills children develop at each stage of their lives. Moreover, research has proved Piaget right in suggesting that virtually all children go through the sequence of mental development he laid out. All children, for example, think concretely before thinking abstractly, rather than the reverse.

■ Learning How to Feel

While developing their cognitive abilities, children also learn to understand their own emotions. This knowledge contributes significantly to how well they will function as adult members of society. Emotional socialization involves two tasks: how to identify feelings and how to manage them.

myth	Born with the ability to have feelings, children do not have to learn how to be happy, fearful, or anxious.
reality	Emotions are not innate; they must be learned. Through parents and other caretakers, children learn to feel happy when receiving a compliment, fearful when being threatened, or anxious when facing uncertainty.

Human emotions abound, ranging from such basic feelings as fear, anger, and happiness to more refined emotions such as frustration, love, and jealousy. Children are taught how to *identify* these feelings because by themselves, they cannot know what they are. Suppose a little boy at a day-care center engages in such expressive behaviors as fidgeting, sulking, biting, and kicking while waiting for his mother to pick him up. He may learn from an adult that what he feels is anger. Here is how such a scenario may occur (Pollak and Thoits, 1989):

Boy [restless]: My mom is late.
Staff member: Does that make you *mad?*
Boy: Yes.
Staff member: Sometimes kids get *mad* when their moms are late to pick them up.

The adult, in effect, teaches the child to identify an emotion by making a causal connection between a stimulus event (mother being late) and an emotional outcome (boy being angry). Through socialization—not only by parents and other caretakers but also by television, movies, and other mass media—children learn that a compliment is expected to give pleasure, a threat is expected to arouse fear, and uncertainty is expected to give rise to anxiety. While they learn that it is logical to feel resentful toward someone who has mistreated them, they also learn that it is not logical to feel affectionate toward that person. It is crucial for children to acquire this emotional logic. Failure to do so is popularly considered a symptom of mental disorder. If a 10-year-old boy tells you with a big smile that his mother has just died, you may suspect him of having abnormal psychological development (Smith-Lovin, 1995; Rosenberg, 1990).

Children also learn how to *manage* their emotions in at least three ways. First, they learn how they *should* feel. For example, they should love their parents and they should feel guilty for displeasing their parents.

Second, children learn how to *display* or *conceal* emotions. They should look happy at a wedding, seem sad at a funeral, and appear reverent at a religious service. Sometimes children learn to display an emotion that they do not have in them or to conceal a feeling that they do have. If a grandparent gives them a present they do not like, they are taught to show how much they like it. If they dislike their teachers, they learn to conceal the negative feeling.

Finally, while they learn to display or conceal certain emotions, children also learn how to *change* some feelings in themselves. When children are feeling sad, they may learn to manipulate that feeling by, for example, telephoning or visiting a friend (Smith-Lovin, 1995; Rosenberg, 1990).

Not all children learn to feel in the same way. Social forces, particularly gender roles and social classes, exert a strong influence on emotional socialization. Compared with boys, girls are taught to be more empathetic, more loving, less able to feel and express anger, but more able to feel and express fear and sadness (Thoits, 1989; Hochschild, 1983). Because middle-class and upper-class people tend to work more with people than with things, they are more attuned to emotional management, such as smiling at customers even when they do not feel like smiling. Therefore, in teaching emotional management to their children, they are more likely than people of the lower classes to show respect for the youngsters' feelings by using reasoning and persuasion. Suppose a child says "I don't want to kiss Grandpa—why must I kiss him all the time?" Parents of the higher social classes would respond, "I know you don't like kissing Grandpa, but he's unwell and he's very fond of you." By contrast, lower-class and working-class parents, who tend to be less sensitive to their offspring's feelings, would answer, "Children should kiss their Grandpa" or "He's not well—I don't want any of your nonsense." In effect, they order the child to kiss his or her grandfather (Hochschild, 1983).

WHEN NOT TO BE A COLD FISH Children learn how to manage their emotions in at least three ways. First, they learn how they *should feel,* such as feeling guilty for displeasing their parents. Second, they learn how to *display emotions,* such as looking happy at a wedding or sad at a funeral. Third, they learn how to *change their feelings,* such as seeking consolation from a friend when sad.

TABLE 3.1

Freud's Stages of Personality Development

Stage	Characteristics	Normal and Abnormal Personalities
Oral stage (birth to age 1)	The infant is at the mercy of the id (because the ego and superego have not emerged) and seeks pleasure through oral activities such as sucking.	If the drive for oral pleasure is adequately met, the child may grow up to engage in oral activities, such as eating and talking, in moderation, but if the drive is overindulged or frustrated, the pursuit of oral pleasure may become extreme, such as overeating or talkativeness.
Anal stage (ages 1 to 3)	The infant seeks pleasure from holding in and pushing out feces. The ego emerges, aided by toilet training, through which the child learns self-control and self-dependence.	If toilet training and other self-control lessons are satisfactory, the child may grow up to be self-composed and autonomous, but if the lessons are too lax or strict, the child may turn out to be extremely messy and wasteful or too concerned with order, cleanliness, and possessions.
Phallic stage (ages 3 to 6)	The child feels sexual love for the opposite-sex parent and learns that this desire must be suppressed. Through learning restrictions, the child internalizes society's norms and values, and thus the superego develops.	If the superego develops adequately, the child may grow up to be moralistic or law abiding, but if the superego fails to develop adequately, as an adult, the person may be inclined to engage in unconventional or antisocial activities.
Latency stage (ages 6 to 11)	The id quiets down, and the child focuses on developing intellectual and social skills. The ego and superego become stronger.	If there are adequate opportunities for learning and socializing, the child may grow up to be self-assured and sociable; if not, the child may turn out to be withdrawn or extremely individualistic.
Genital stage (adolescence)	The id resurges, and interest in sex develops, with which the habits of modesty and sympathy give way to pleasure in exhibitionism and aggressiveness; but gradually the adolescent learns to cope with these problems.	If frustrations are few or often successfully dealt with, the youth will get along well sexually with others as an adult and, if married, may have few or no serious problems. If frustrations repeatedly occur without resolution, the adult may have many sexual and marital problems.

■ Learning How to Be Normal

One of the most influential theories of how children develop their personalities is that of Sigmund Freud (1856–1939). In his view, personality consists of three parts: the id, ego, and superego. The **id** is the part of personality that is irrational, concerned only with seeking pleasure. The id is our inborn desire to live, enjoy ourselves, make love, or celebrate life in one way or another. But such desires cannot be successfully fulfilled unless we have learned *how* to fulfill them. Thus we have learned innumerable ways to live as best we can.

The knowledge that results from this learning becomes the **ego**, the part of personality that is rational, dealing with the world logically and realistically. In trying to help us enjoy ourselves, our ego tells us that there is a limit to the satisfaction of our id. If we want to satisfy our sexual desire, we cannot simply make love anywhere, such as on a street corner. This limit to our self-enjoyment is imposed by society in the form of rules and injunctions—"You should not do this. You should not do that."

Our acceptance of society's rules and injunctions becomes the cornerstone of the **superego**, the part of personality that is moral; it is popularly known as *conscience*. The ego, in effect, advises the id to obey the superego so that we will enjoy life in a normal, socially acceptable way.

Freud proposed that these three parts of personality develop through a series of five stages in childhood. Influenced primarily by interaction with parents, these early experiences will have a significant impact on adult personalities. Table 3.1 shows how children may grow up to be normal or abnormal, depending on whether their experiences are mostly positive or negative (Kahn, 2002).

Sociologists have often criticized Freud for explaining human behavior in terms of inborn or unconscious motivations, particularly the id. Feminists have further criticized Freud for devaluing women with his concept of *penis envy*—the unconscious desire to be men. Nevertheless, Freud's work is sociologically significant in at least three ways: (1) the emphasis on the role played by parents in children's development; (2) the view that childhood experiences have a great impact on adult personality; and (3) the assumption that the superego, which has a great influence on human personality, reflects society's norms and values.

■ Learning How to Be Moral

According to U.S. psychologist Lawrence Kohlberg (1981), children go through three levels of moral development. This idea came from his research on how youngsters of different ages deal with moral dilemmas. The children were presented with a hypothetical situation: A man did not have the money to buy a drug that might save his dying wife. He became desperate and broke into a store to steal the drug. Should he have done that?

Some children answered yes; others said no. But Kohlberg was more interested in the responses to a crucial question: *Why* did they answer as they had? He found three distinct patterns of response, each reflecting a certain level of moral development.

At the first level, generally under the age of 10, children have a **preconventional morality**, the practice of defining right and wrong according to the *consequence* of the action being judged. The consequence involves reward or punishment. Thus, some of these children said that it was all right to steal the drug because it could save the wife (reward), while others regarded the stealing as wrong because the offender could be arrested (punishment).

At the second level, between ages 10 and 16, children have a **conventional morality**, the practice of defining right and wrong according to the *motive* of the action being judged. Thus, most of these children said that they could not blame the man for stealing the drug because of his love for his wife.

At the third level, over age 16, most young adults have a **postconventional morality**, the practice of judging actions by taking into account the importance of *conflicting norms*. Some of these young adults supported the stealing but still believed in the general principle that stealing is wrong. They felt that the man was justified in stealing the drug for his wife, but they also believed that the stealing was not right. Other young adults opposed the drug theft but were nevertheless sympathetic to the thief. To such young adults, the ends do not justify the means, but the caring husband cannot be completely blamed for stealing the drug. In sum, adults are more likely than

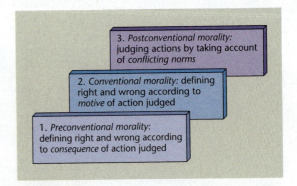

1. *Preconventional morality:* defining right and wrong according to *consequence* of action judged

2. *Conventional morality:* defining right and wrong according to *motive* of action judged

3. *Postconventional morality:* judging actions by taking account of *conflicting norms*

FIGURE 3.2

Kohlberg's Levels of Moral Development

According to Gilligan, in growing up, men may have gone through these levels of moral development, but most women may not have. Instead of being concerned with the impersonal issue of justice, women tend to develop morally by progressing from an interest in their own survival to a concern for others' welfare.

Critical Thinking: *Which type of moral maturity would you consider more beneficial to society: that of women or that of men? Why?*

youngsters to appreciate the conflict between norms in a moral dilemma.

myth	Men and women know what morality is because they both have learned how to be moral in the same way.
reality	There is a gender difference in moral development: While men have learned to be more concerned with *justice*, women have learned to be more concerned with *relationships and the welfare of others*.

This view of moral development, outlined in Figure 3.2, has been criticized for being applicable to males more than females because it was based on research on males alone. According to Carol Gilligan (1989; 1982), Kohlberg focuses on men's interest in *justice*, which is impersonal in nature, and neglects women's lifelong concern with *relationships*, which are personal. In Gilligan's view, the moral development of most women differs from that of men. It involves progressing from an interest in one's own survival to a concern for others. Thus, women are said to have achieved a great deal of moral maturity if they have developed a compassionate concern for others.

■ Learning How to Be Masculine or Feminine

From feminist theory, we can see how boys and girls learn to be masculine and feminine by developing **gender identities**, images of who they are expected to be on the basis of their sex. Under the influence of a patriarchal society, gender development involves socializing males to be dominant over females.

A major source of gender development is the family. In a patriarchal society, child care is assigned primarily to the mother, and children consequently spend much time with her. During the first 2 years or so after birth, children of both sexes lack self-awareness and see themselves as a part of their mothers. But beginning at about age 3, when children begin to see themselves as separate individuals, girls and boys start to develop different gender identities.

As gender identity develops, girls continue to identify with their mothers because they are of the same sex. Girls consequently develop the traditionally feminine appreciation for relationships and nurturance. By contrast, boys begin to differentiate themselves from their mothers because of the sexual difference. Further influenced by their fathers' primarily dominant role in the family, boys try to suppress the feminine traits they have acquired from their mothers, learn to devalue anything they consider feminine, and identify with their fathers by being independent and aggressive (Small, 2001).

Another important source of gender development is the school. Also influenced by patriarchal society, teachers tend to socialize girls to see themselves as less important than boys and boys to see themselves as more important than girls. Thus, teachers praise boys' contributions more lavishly and call on boys more frequently. Teachers also tend to socialize girls to be quiet and polite and boys to be assertive and aggressive. This involves, among other things, accepting answers that boys shout out but reprimanding girls for speaking out of turn (Corsaro and Eder, 1995; Wood, 1994).

The mass media also help socialize girls to be submissive and boys to be dominant. Analyzing some 80 television series and more than 500 characters, the National Commission on Working Women found a preponderance of women working as secretaries and homemakers and a world of young, beautiful, scantily dressed women. Even in advertisements that portray women as being in charge of their own lives, the women are shown "literally being carried by men, leaning on men, being helped down from a height of two feet, or figuratively being carried away by emotion" (Sidel, 1990). There is, though, a growing trend toward presenting successful and assertive women in the media (Baehr and Gray, 1996; Sengupta, 1995).

sociological frontier

The New World of Teen Sex

When it comes to sex among teenagers, the mass media is a powerful socializing agent but the school is not. According to recent research, teenagers, ages 12 to 17, who watch a lot of TV programs with sexual content are more likely to initiate sexual intercourse and other erotic activities such as oral sex. It does not matter whether sex on TV is merely talked about or explicitly depicted. Both have the same impact on teen viewers (Conlon, 2004). Similar sexual content in other media—movies, music, and magazines—also encourages teenagers to engage in sexual intercourse (Brown et al., 2006).

In recent years the school has been trying to persuade adolescents to abstain from sex before marriage in order to protect them against pregnancy and sexually transmitted diseases (STD). But a study ordered by U.S. Congress found that students who attended abstinence classes were just as likely to have sex and have similar numbers of sexual partners as students who did not (Freking, 2007). In another study, students who have taken a virginity pledge are just as likely to get STD as others who have not taken a pledge. But the pledgers are more likely to engage in oral and anal sex. Apparently they do not consider this kind of sex as sex without realizing that it is as risky as intercourse (Bruckner and Bearman, 2005).

Whether they have taken a virginity pledge or not, oral sex is relatively popular among teenagers as a whole, with 55 percent having engaged in it. While vaginal intercourse is more common than oral sex among adults above the age of 20, oral sex is more prevalent than intercourse among young people under 20. This may be due to the fear of becoming pregnant and the false assumption that oral sex cannot cause STD. It has further been found that relatively large numbers of teenage girls (about 11 percent) have had same-sex partners. The reasons may include the fear of getting pregnant, the feeling that it is a cool thing to do, and the belief that boys their age can be so crude, as one girl said: "At least another girl isn't always trying to push her penis into you" (Mosher, 2005; Lemonick, 2005).

▌CHAPTER REVIEW
- -

1. *What is socialization?* It is the process by which a society transmits its cultural values to its members.

2. *Can either nature or nurture alone explain human behavior?* No. Both heredity and environment make us what we are. The importance of heredity can be demonstrated by how our temperament, intelligence, and aptitude influence the development of our personality. The significance of socialization can be seen in the case studies of children who are feral, isolated, institutionalized, or gifted.

3. *How do children learn to think?* They develop increasingly advanced forms of mental ability as they grow from birth through adolescence.

4. *How do they learn to feel?* Largely through their parents, they learn to identify and manage their emotions.

5. *How do they learn to be normal?* With their parents' help, they learn to be normal by resolving the conflicts among their id, ego, and superego.

6. *How do they learn to be moral?* They develop morally from a low, preconventional level of judging right and wrong to higher levels.

7. *How do they learn to be masculine or feminine?* They develop their sex-based identities through the influence of patriarchal society via its parents, schools, and media.

8. *What is teen sex like today?* Frequent exposure to the media encourages teenagers to have sex; attending abstinence classes and pledging abstinence fail to deter teens from premarital sex; and oral sex and same-sex activities are relatively prevalent among young people.

KEY TERMS

Aptitude The capacity for developing physical or social skills (p. 563).

Conventional morality Kohlberg's term for the practice of defining right and wrong according to the *motive* of the action being judged (p. 570).

Ego Freud's term for the part of personality that is rational, dealing with the world logically and realistically (p. 569).

Gender identity People's images of what they are socially expected to be and do on the basis of their sex (p. 571).

Id Freud's term for the part of personality that is irrational, concerned only with seeking pleasure (p. 569).

Intelligence The capacity for mental or intellectual achievement (p. 563).

Personality A fairly stable configuration of feelings, attitudes, ideas, and behaviors that characterizes an individual (p. 563).

Postconventional morality Kohlberg's term for the practice of judging actions by taking into account the importance of *conflicting norms* (p. 570).

Preconventional morality Kohlberg's term for the practice of defining right and wrong according to the *consequence* of the action being judged (p. 570).

Socialization The process by which a society transmits its cultural values to its members (p. 563).

Superego Freud's term for the part of personality that is moral; popularly known as *conscience* (p. 569).

QUESTIONS FOR DISCUSSION AND REVIEW

THE SIGNIFICANCE OF HEREDITY

1. How does heredity influence personality?

THE SIGNIFICANCE OF SOCIALIZATION

1. What happens to children deprived of socialization?
2. How can children become geniuses?

PROCESSES OF SOCIALIZATION

1. According to Piaget, what mental abilities develop from birth through adolescence?
2. How do children learn to identify and manage their emotions?
3. In Freud's view, what does personality consist of, and how does it develop?
4. How does moral development differ between males and females?
5. How does feminist theory explain the development of gender identity?
6. How do teenagers behave sexually today?

Applying Your Skills to a Textbook Chapter

To locate a paragraph by number as referred to in an exercise, start counting with the first paragraph on the page, regardless of whether it is an incomplete paragraph continuing from the preceding page or a new full paragraph. Part numbers shown below refer to parts of Efficient and Flexible Reading.

Part 1: Developing a Basis for Reading and Learning

Directions: *Preview the entire textbook chapter excerpt, "Socialization," and answer questions 1 and 2.*

1. What is the overall topic of this chapter?

   _____

2. According to this chapter, what are the five processes of socialization?

   a. _____

   b. _____

   c. _____

   d. _____

   e. _____

   _____

Directions: *Read pages 563–566, beginning with the introduction and ending before the heading "Processes of Socialization," and complete items 3–6.*

____ 3. In this chapter, the term *socialization* is defined as the process by which
   a. social skills are passed on from generation to generation.
   b. a society transmits its cultural values to its members.
   c. parents transmit their genetic traits to their children.
   d. environmental factors determine how well individuals socialize.

____ 4. The capacity for mental or intellectual achievement is known as
   a. personality.
   b. intelligence.
   c. aptitude.
   d. temperament.

____ 5. According to the author, the significance of socialization has to do with the role it plays in
   a. encouraging or impairing development.
   b. guaranteeing that given traits will emerge.
   c. establishing biologically inherited capacities.
   d. providing the instincts for completing complex tasks.

____ 6. In this section, all of the following girls were described to illustrate the effects of social deprivation *except*
   a. Anna.
   b. Isabella.
   c. Edith.
   d. Genie.

Directions: *Use context, word parts, or a dictionary, if necessary, to determine the meaning of each word as it is used in the selection.*

____ 7. placid (page 563, paragraph 8)
   a. aggressive
   b. mild-mannered
   c. intelligent
   d. competitive

____ 8. prowess (page 563, paragraph 9)
   a. ability
   b. fear
   c. attitude
   d. area

____ 9. suppressed (page 564, paragraph 2)
   a. enhanced
   b. promoted
   c. inhibited
   d. responded

____ 10. superlative (page 565, paragraph 3)
   a. average
   b. emotional
   c. harmful
   d. exceptional

Part 2: Improving Your Comprehension

Directions: *Items 1–5 are based on the section "Learning How to Think" (pp. 566–567). Complete each item by selecting the best answer.*

____ 1. The primary pattern used to organize the information under the heading "Learning How to Think" is
   a. comparison-contrast.
   b. definition.
   c. cause-effect.
   d. chronological order/process.

____ 2. Context clues in this section indicate that the term *cognitive* means
   a. normal.
   b. emotional.
   c. mental.
   d. process.

____ 3. Children at the preoperational stage are described as *animistic,* which means they
   a. believe something exists only if they can see or touch it.
   b. cannot understand cause and effect.
   c. attribute humanlike thoughts and wishes to nonhuman things.
   d. see things only from their own perspective.

____ 4. The main idea of paragraph 2 on page 567 is that Piaget's stages of cognitive development are
   a. outdated.
   b. useful.
   c. criticized.
   d. misunderstood.

____ 5. To support the ideas in this section of the chapter, the author relies primarily on

a. illustrations and examples.
b. facts and statistics.
c. analogies.
d. personal experience.

Directions: *Items 6–10 are based on the section "Learning How to Feel" (pp. 567–568). Complete each item by filling in the blanks with the correct word or phrase.*

6. Emotional socialization involves two tasks: how to _____ feelings and how to _____ feelings.

7. On page 568, the author uses the _____ organizational pattern to describe how adults teach children to identify emotions.

8. Children learn how to manage their emotions by first learning how they _____, then learning how to _____ their feelings, and finally, learning how to change their feelings.

9. In the last paragraph on page 568, the author uses the _____ pattern to show differences in emotional socialization according to both _____ and _____.

10. In the last paragraph on page 568, two transitional phrases that indicate the pattern are _____ and _____.

Part 3: Reading Critically

Directions: *Items 1–5 are based on the section "Learning How to Be Normal" (pp. 569–570), including Table 3.1. Complete each item by selecting the best answer.*

____ 1. The author's purpose in writing this section is to
   a. entertain.
   b. inform.
   c. persuade.
   d. criticize.

____ 2. The author's attitude toward the information in this part of the chapter can best be described as
a. playful.
b. skeptical.
c. serious.
d. objective.

____ 3. According to Table 3.1, the ego emerges during the
a. oral stage.
b. anal stage.
c. phallic stage.
d. latency stage.

____ 4. In Freud's view, the superego is the part of personality that is
a. irrational.
b. concerned only with pleasure.
c. logical and realistic.
d. moral.

____ 5. Of the following statements based on this section, the one that is an opinion is
a. Sigmund Freud formulated a three-part theory of personality development.
b. Freud's theory emphasized the role played by parents in children's development.
c. Freud proposed that personality development takes place through a series of five stages.
d. According to feminists, Freud devalued women by theorizing that they have an unconscious desire to be men.

Directions: *Items 6–10 are based on the section "Learning How to Be Masculine or Feminine" (p. 571). Complete each item by selecting the best answer.*

____ 6. All of the following questions are answered in this section *except*
a. How do boys and girls develop gender identities?
b. How does family influence gender development?
c. How does society help to promote gender equality?
d. How does the mass media portray women?

____ 7. In comparison to boys, girls are socialized at school to
a. be more aggressive.
b. see themselves as more important.
c. be more polite.
d. speak out more in class.

____ 8. Of the following word pairs from this section, the one that has a mostly positive connotation is
a. *dominant* and *aggressive.*
b. *successful* and *assertive.*
c. *quiet* and *submissive.*
d. *suppress* and *devalue.*

____ 9. One inference that can be made from this section is that
a. gender identities develop the same way in matriarchal and patriarchal societies.
b. the media's portrayal of women may be changing to better reflect modern society.
c. only children in two-parent families are able to develop gender identities.
d. girls learn to be more assertive as a result of their socialization at school.

____ 10. To support the ideas in this section, the author uses all of the following types of evidence *except*
a. personal experience.
b. facts and statistics.
c. comparisons.
d. reasons.

Part 4: Reading and Learning from College Texts

Directions: *This section is based on material found throughout the chapter. Complete items 1–7 by selecting the best answer.*

____ 1. The author begins the chapter with the story about 3-year-old Rebecca in order to
    a. introduce readers to an example of a feral child.
    b. illustrate the concepts of socialization and personality.
    c. compare and contrast normal and abnormal behavior.
    d. show the importance of gender identities.

____ 2. Based on the myth/reality features found on different pages throughout the chapter, all of the following statements are true *except*
    a. Intelligence is both inherited and learned.
    b. Moral development is different in men and women.
    c. Emotions must be learned.
    d. To be a genius, you must be born one.

____ 3. The photograph on page 566 shows a child at the stage of cognitive development known as the
    a. formal operational stage.
    b. concrete operational stage.
    c. preoperational stage.
    d. sensorimotor stage.

____ 4. According to Figure 3.1 on page 567, children in the formal operational stage are
    a. egocentric.
    b. able to perform tasks involving only visible, concrete objects.
    c. unable to understand cause and effect.
    d. able to think and reason with abstract concepts.

____ 5. The photograph on page 568 corresponds to the text discussion of
    a. how children learn to manage their emotions.
    b. the different stages of cognitive development.
    c. the different levels of moral development.
    d. how children learn to be masculine or feminine.

____ 6. Table 3.1 on page 569 illustrates Freud's view of how children
    a. develop personalities through a series of five stages.
    b. grow up to be normal or abnormal depending on their experiences.
    c. learn to accept society's rules and restrictions.
    d. all of the above.

____ 7. The feature called "Sociological Frontier" (page 571) is included to help readers understand
    a. why schools use abstinence programs.
    b. how people develop gender identities.
    c. when teens develop moral awareness.
    d. how socializing agents influence teen sex.

Directions: *Fill in the blanks to complete the following summary of the first five paragraphs of the section titled "Learning How to Be Moral" (p. 570).*

8. Psychologist Lawrence Kohlberg found that children go through _____ levels of moral development. Under age 10, children have a _____ morality, defining right and wrong according to the _____ (reward or punishment) of the action being judged. Between ages _____, children have a conventional morality, defining right and wrong according to the _____. Over age 16, young adults have a postconventional morality, judging actions by considering the importance of _____.

Appendix A

Words-per-Minute Conversion Chart

Reading Time (minutes)	Reading Selection 1	2	3	4	5	6	7	8	9	10	11	12	13	14
1:00	1166	889	938	1670	926	1075	991	1569	1190	1260	855	1505	1413	1214
1:15	933	711	750	1336	741	860	793	1255	952	1008	684	1204	1130	971
1:30	777	593	625	1113	617	717	661	1046	793	840	570	1003	942	809
1:45	666	508	536	954	529	614	566	897	680	720	489	860	807	694
2:00	583	445	469	835	463	538	496	785	595	630	428	753	707	607
2:15	518	395	417	742	412	478	440	697	529	560	380	669	628	540
2:30	466	356	375	668	370	430	396	628	476	504	342	602	565	486
2:45	424	323	341	607	337	391	360	571	433	458	311	547	514	441
3:00	389	296	313	557	309	358	330	523	397	420	285	502	471	405
3:15	359	274	289	514	285	331	305	483	366	388	263	463	435	374
3:30	333	254	268	477	265	307	283	448	340	360	244	430	404	347
3:45	311	237	250	445	247	287	264	418	317	336	228	401	377	324
4:00	292	222	235	418	232	269	248	392	298	315	214	376	353	304
4:15	274	209	221	393	218	253	233	369	280	296	201	354	332	286
4:30	259	198	208	371	206	239	220	349	264	280	190	334	314	270
4:45	245	187	197	352	195	226	209	330	251	265	180	317	297	256
5:00	233	178	188	334	185	215	198	314	238	252	171	301	283	243
5:15	222	169	179	318	176	205	189	299	227	240	163	287	269	231
5:30	212	162	171	304	168	195	180	285	216	229	155	274	257	221
5:45	203	155	163	290	161	187	172	273	207	219	149	262	246	211
6:00	194	148	156	278	154	179	165	262	198	210	143	251	236	202
6:15	187	142	150	267	148	172	159	251	190	202	137	241	226	194
6:30	179	137	144	257	142	165	152	241	183	194	132	232	217	187
6:45	173	132	139	247	137	159	147	232	176	187	127	223	209	180
7:00	167	127	134	239	132	154	142	224	170	180	122	215	202	173
7:15	161	123	129	230	128	148	137	216	164	174	118	208	195	167
7:30	155	119	125	223	123	143	132	209	159	168	114	201	188	162
7:45	150	115	121	215	119	139	128	202	154	163	110	194	182	157
8:00	146	111	117	209	116	134	124	196	149	158	107	188	177	152

(continued)

						Reading Selection								
Reading	1	2	3	4	5	6	7	8	9	10	11	12	13	14
Time (minutes)														
8:15	141	108	114	202	112	130	120	190	144	153	104	182	171	147
8:30	137	105	110	196	109	126	117	185	140	148	101	177	166	143
8:45	133	102	107	191	106	123	113	179	136	144	98	172	161	139
9:00	130	99	104	186	103	119	110	174	132	140	95	167	157	135
9:15	126	96	101	181	100	116	107	170	129	136	92	163	153	131
9:30	123	94	99	176	97	113	104	165	125	133	90	158	149	128
9:45	120	91	96	171	95	110	102	161	122	129	88	154	145	125
10:00	117	89	94	167	93	108	99	157	119	126	86	151	141	121
10:15	114	87	92	163	90	105	97	153	116	123	83	147	138	118
10:30	111	85	89	159	88	102	94	149	113	120	81	143	135	116
10:45	108	83	87	155	86	100	92	146	111	117	80	140	131	113
11:00	106	81	85	152	84	98	90	143	108	115	78	137	128	110
11:15	104	79	83	148	82	96	88	139	106	112	76	134	126	108
11:30	101	77	82	145	81	93	86	136	103	110	74	131	123	106
11:45	99	76	80	142	79	91	84	134	101	107	73	128	120	103
12:00	97	74	78	139	77	90	83	131	99	105	71	125	118	101
12:15	95	73	77	136	76	88	81	128	97	103	70	123	115	99
12:30	93	71	75	134	74	86	79	126	95	101	68	120	113	97
12:45	91	70	74	131	73	84	78	123	93	99	67	118	111	95
13:00	90	68	72	128	71	83	76	121	92	97	66	116	109	93
13:15	88	67	71	126	70	81	75	118	90	95	65	114	107	92
13:30	86	66	69	124	69	80	73	116	88	93	63	111	105	90
13:45	85	65	68	121	67	78	72	114	87	92	62	109	103	88
14:00	83	64	67	119	66	77	71	112	85	90	61	108	101	87
14:15	82	62	66	117	65	75	70	110	84	88	60	106	99	85
14:30	80	61	65	115	64	74	68	108	82	87	59	104	97	84
14:45	79	60	64	113	63	73	67	106	81	85	58	102	96	82
15:00	78	59	63	111	62	72	66	105	79	84	57	100	94	81

				Reading Selection						
Reading	*15*	*16*	*17*	*18*	*19*	*20*	*21*	*22*	*23*	*24*
Time (minutes)										
1:00	1510	1203	1798	1494	1359	1283	862	1072	1337	899
1:15	1208	962	1438	1195	1087	1026	690	858	1070	719
1:30	1007	802	1199	996	906	855	575	715	891	599
1:45	863	687	1027	854	777	733	493	613	764	514
2:00	755	602	899	747	680	642	431	536	669	450
2:15	671	535	799	664	604	570	383	476	594	400
2:30	604	481	719	598	544	513	345	429	535	360
2:45	549	437	654	543	494	467	313	390	486	327
3:00	503	401	599	498	453	428	287	357	446	300
3:15	465	370	553	460	418	395	265	330	411	277
3:30	431	344	514	427	388	367	246	306	382	257
3:45	403	321	479	398	362	342	230	286	357	240
4:00	378	301	450	374	340	321	216	268	334	225
4:15	355	283	423	352	320	302	203	252	315	212
4:30	336	267	400	332	302	285	192	238	297	200
4:45	318	253	379	315	286	270	181	226	281	189
5:00	302	241	360	299	272	257	172	214	267	180
5:15	288	229	342	285	259	244	164	204	255	171
5:30	275	219	327	272	247	233	157	195	243	163
5:45	263	209	313	260	236	223	150	186	233	156
6:00	252	201	300	249	227	214	144	179	223	150
6:15	242	192	288	239	217	205	138	172	214	144
6:30	232	185	277	230	209	197	133	165	206	138
6:45	224	178	266	221	201	190	128	159	198	133
7:00	216	172	257	213	194	183	123	153	191	128
7:15	208	166	248	206	187	177	119	148	184	124
7:30	201	160	240	199	181	171	115	143	178	120
7:45	195	155	232	193	175	166	111	138	173	116
8:00	189	150	225	187	170	160	108	134	167	112
8:15	183	146	218	181	165	156	104	130	162	109
8:30	178	142	212	176	160	151	101	126	157	106
8:45	173	137	205	171	155	147	99	123	153	103
9:00	168	134	200	166	151	143	96	119	149	100

(*continued*)

					Reading Selection					
Reading	15	16	17	18	19	20	21	22	23	24
Time (minutes)										
9:15	163	130	194	162	147	139	93	116	145	97
9:30	159	127	189	157	143	135	91	113	141	95
9:45	155	123	184	153	139	132	88	110	137	92
10:00	151	120	180	149	136	128	86	107	134	90
10:15	147	117	175	146	133	125	84	105	130	88
10:30	144	115	171	142	129	122	82	102	127	86
10:45	140	112	167	139	126	119	80	100	124	84
11:00	137	109	163	136	124	117	78	97	122	82
11:15	134	107	160	133	121	114	77	95	119	80
11:30	131	105	156	130	118	112	75	93	116	78
11:45	129	102	153	127	116	109	73	91	114	77
12:00	126	100	150	125	113	107	72	89	111	75
12:15	123	98	147	122	111	105	70	88	109	73
12:30	121	96	144	120	109	103	69	86	107	72
12:45	118	94	141	117	107	101	68	84	105	71
13:00	116	93	138	115	105	99	66	82	103	69
13:15	114	91	136	113	103	97	65	81	101	68
13:30	112	89	133	111	101	95	64	79	99	67
13:45	110	87	131	109	99	93	63	78	97	65
14:00	108	86	128	107	97	92	62	77	96	64
14:15	106	84	126	105	95	90	60	75	94	63
14:30	104	83	124	103	94	88	59	74	92	62
14:45	102	82	122	101	92	87	58	73	91	61
15:00	101	80	120	100	91	86	57	71	89	60

Credits

Index